SOCIAL PROBLEMS IN CANADA

Conditions, Constructions, and Challenges

Third Edition

Augie Fleras

University of Waterloo

Prentice Hall

Toronto

To Jocelyn

Canadian Cataloguing in Publication Data

Fleras, Augie, 1947–
    Social problems in Canada : conditions, constructions, and challenges

3rd ed.
Previous eds. written by Adie Nelson, Augie Fleras.
Includes index.
ISBN 0-13-025870-9

1. Social problems — Canada. 2. Canada — Social conditions — 1991– . I. Nelson, Adie, 1958– . Social problems in Canada. II. Title.

HN103.5.N45 2001   361.1'0971   C00-930517-3

ISBN 0-13-025870-9

Vice President, Editorial Director: Michael Young
Acquisitions Editor: Jessica Mosher
Marketing Manager: Tim Collins
Developmental Editor: Lise Creurer
Production Editor: Joe Zingrone
Copy Editor: Jim Zimmerman
Production Coordinator: Peggy Brown
Page Layout: Janette Thompson (Jansom)
Permissions Research: Susan Wallace-Cox
Art Director: Mary Opper
Interior Design: Sarah Battersby
Cover Design: Sputnik
Cover Image: Tony Stone

1 2 3 4 5   05 04 03 02 01

Printed and bound in Canada.

Contents

CHAPTER 8 Media   197

CHAPTER 9 Schooling and Education   229

CHAPTER 10 Work and Workplace   255

CHAPTER 11 Aboriginal Peoples and the Canada Problem   284

CHAPTER 12 The Quebec Question   310

Preface

SOCIAL PROBLEMS AT THE MILLENIUM

It was a century that entered on horseback and exited behind the wheel of an SUV. Buggies, outhouses, and slate chalkboards were discarded in exchange for atomic power, modern sewer systems, and laptop computers, each of which bolstered both technology and consumerism as 20th century icons (Labadie, 1999). Yet for all its bravado and inventiveness, the 20th century has proven something of a paradox; advances in some areas have been tempered by reversals in others. The same century that witnessed the deaths of tens of millions from war, "cleansing," and forced starvation also saw the invention of miracle crops, antibiotics, and the birth control pill. Solutions for some have proven problems for others, and vice versa—a not surprising admission in light of the enormity of challenges pertaining to globalization and global capitalism, de-colonialism, ethnic cleansing, the environment, status of women, rights of minorities, indigenous nationalism, the politics of poverty, political correctness, and human rights. The profusion of countries, proliferation of concerns and conflicts, and explosion of sheer numbers has transformed this century into something considerably more complicated than previous eras. For better or worse, the 20th century has yielded an astonishing array of "posts" and "isms," from fascism and communism to capitalism and globalism, with multiculturalism and postmodernism sandwiched in between. Predictably, reactions are varied: Many are trumpeting the 20th century as the triumph of freedom, consolidation of democracy and capitalism, and ascendancy of the American way over the dark forces of totalitarianism and command economies (*Economist,* 1999). A few prefer to dwell on the darker side as its definitive characteristic and, sadly, the mix of greed with hate continues to exact a staggering cost in human and environmental life. Fewer still are heralding the emergence of resistance movements such as feminism, labour, peace, anti-colonialism, and environment, most of which aspire to those goals of value to humanity, namely, greater control over lives, decent standards of living, full and equal participation, and improved social justice and civil rights (Brazier, 1999).

Developments and advances notwithstanding, the world remains a site of stunning contradictions. Unparalleled global prosperity stands astride the poles of poverty and powerlessness; a commitment to equity clashes with the reality of escalating inequalities; and a growing recognition of human rights is betrayed by spasms of butchery so stunningly barbaric as to question the nature of human nature. An emergent respect for diversity is compromised by the demands of universal commercialism and a global monoculture, both of which subscribe to the adage "one size fits all." The status and aspirations of certain groups have soared on the wings of civil rights statutes and multicultural initiatives; the less fortunate remain locked in cycles of deprivation or despair. Nationalist movements have empowered some, destroyed others. Technological innovations come with costs: They have compromised the environment, redefined patterns of communication and interaction, redesigned the nature of work and workplaces, entrenched consumerism as an acceptable lifestyle, and alienated people from themselves and others. Of particular worry is the environment. In the space of a century, perceptions of nature have evolved from a foe to be vanquished, to a friend in need of protection, including the preservation of some 5000 endangered species of plants and animals (Allen, 1999). The list could go on, but the point should be evident: The interplay of the progressive with the regressive has created a century of maddening paradoxes, and the consequences of this interpenetration of opposites must not be underestimated in securing human survival. So ensnared are people by the crosswinds of competing dynamics and baffling contradictions that many are reeling from the magnitude of change, while others are rebelling at reforms that expose our vulnerabilities or magnify the consequences of any mistakes.

This interpenetration of good with the bad and the confusing has complicated the process of assessing the end of the millennium. This same lack of clarity makes it doubly difficult to predict a package of problems and solutions for the 21st century. Perhaps a kind of paranoid optimism is in order. On one side is an unshakable optimism that human ingenuity will solve all problems. On the other is the paranoia that things that can go wrong will go astray. The fact that solutions to these problems remain as elusive as ever ensures even more madness in the new millennium—no more so than in Canada where plenty coexists with paucity in ways that are contradictory yet mutually reinforcing. Canada at the millennium exudes an astonishing array of physical resources and social riches. Yet for all its munificence, this "adventure called Canada," as Vincent Massey, a former governor general of Canada, once proclaimed, is racked with a raft of social problems that imperil or provoke. In an age of relative abundance and affluence, Canadians are experiencing insecurity and bewilderment in coming to terms with new realities. Many are consumed by fears that our very material wealth could subvert the search for what many so desperately seek: namely, contentment, security, and peace of mind. Canada's paradox at the threshold of the new millennium is expressed in another way. While Canada appears to be tottering on the brink of disintegration, it remains the envy of many, given its knack for forging unity from the strands of diversity without denying either the legitimacy of the parts or the integrity of the whole (Ward, 1999). Perhaps Laurier was right after all: In many ways, the 20th century did belong to Canada, with its success, recognition, and prosperity. And its precedent-breaking work in proposing that people can live together with their differences may prove that century's single most important legacy.

Predictions of 20th century greatness notwithstanding, Canadian society is undergoing a period of transition in adapting to such trends as globalization, technology, trade liberalization, and information-based economy. In some ways, Canada appears to have faltered in its evolutionary development, inasmuch as it is leaving the century in the same way as it began: that is, as a colony—first under Britain, and now as an economic colony of the United States (Urquhart, 1999). Canada's national identity has long been defined and debated by its relationship to the United States, most recently with the free trade agreements in 1988 and 1993, with believers in closer economic union clashing with those who fear that continentalization will Americanize Canada, both literally and figuratively (Hoberg, 1999). Only a brief interlude of economic and cultural nationalism under the Trudeau government provided a respite from ongoing colonialization. Compounding this dependency relationship are potentially divisive national unity problems. In their quest for autonomy and self-determination, both aboriginal peoples and the Québecois are challenging the very notion of Canada as a society, prompting the columnist Ian Urquhart to question whether Canada will even survive the 21st century if pulled apart internally by ethnic strife or absorbed externally by the forces of globalization. Mixed messages underscore the fragility of Canada.

One arm of the UN has designated Canada as the best place to live, while another has lambasted Canadians for their human rights record. A host of problems has been centred out for censure, ranging from the deplorable state of aboriginal reserves and violation of indigenous peoples' rights, to the dilemmas of homelessness and the feminization of poverty (Philp, 1998). Canadians may be benefiting from significant advances in medicine, technology, and science; nevertheless, many are perplexed by the often unanticipated yet negative consequences of these leaps. Inasmuch as prevailing ideologies appear incapable of accommodating these apparent contradictions in an intellectually satisfying way, the overall effect is to fan public fears and frustration over who we are or where we are going.

Canada's institutional structures continue to be a fecund source of social problems. Canada's much maligned economy is currently firing on all cylinders, according to the Conference Board of Canada in its quarterly Canadian Outlook report (*National Post,* 28 April 1999), with unemployment rates dropping below 7 percent, massive job creation in the private sector, escalating consumer spending, real wage gains after years of stagnation, and a national deficit that appears to be under control. Yet consider the downside: The economy may be improving by conventional accounts, but much of this boom is levered by an unhealthy dependence on the American economy. Moreover, not everyone is benefiting from an improved economy. The net result? Canada is bifurcating into two: the rich and the poor. To the extent that the gap broadens and "bullies" as market forces take a bigger bite of national resources and commitment, the future for the have-nots appears bleak. Elsewhere, inequities continue to mount. Increasing numbers of Canadians are condemned to poverty status; the escalating costs of crime and control are worrying; gender relations remain as contested as ever, as women and men grapple with the re-scripting of rules, roles, and relationships; and racism continues to demean the lives and life chances of immigrants and people of colour, despite seemingly progressive initiatives. Also on the critical list of social problems are key institutions: The family, once revered as the social bedrock of society, is itself evolving in ways that elicit stinging rebukes or evoke unstinting praise; education and schooling from primary to tertiary levels are reeling from an identity crisis of confidence of such proportions that grave concerns are mounting over who they are or what they are supposed to do; and the media have become so demonized for conveying images and messages at odds with Canada that calls for censorship are routinely invoked without acknowledging the repercussions of such restrictions. Finally, fears are escalating that Canada is losing its way because of the demands of a freewheeling, globalizing world order. Global issues related to poverty and global apartheid are generating problems that cannot be casually dismissed without imperilling our collective existence. Yet Canada's efforts to address these global problems by way of quick fix, foreign aid solutions have proven inadequate and self-serving.

Which interpretation of Canada—problem-free or problem-plagued—is more accurate? If Canada is as progressive and egalitarian as is often contended, why do Canadians continue to tolerate glaring extremes of poverty and affluence, mistreatment of aboriginal peoples, gender inequities, and ambivalence toward immigrants? Alternatively, if Canada is the "mother of all evils," as some make it out to be, why does it remain a magnet for worldwide migration? Does the "correct" answer depend on where we stand in relation to ethnicity, class, gender, region, sexual preference, ability, or age? To what extent does each interpretation possess a kernel of truth that accentuates one dimension of Canadian society while glossing over others? Perhaps the question itself is inappropriate. After all, social problems may be a "normal" and necessary component of human social existence in a society both diverse and changing. Social problems are intrinsic to the social arrangements and cultural values of a liberal democratic capitalism. The same values and structures that generate normal behaviour can also foster anti-social behaviour, depending on context or consequence. A sense of perspective is critical: Compared to its past or in relation to the human rights records of other countries, Canada is indeed a paragon of virtue. But in comparison with the ideals that Canadians have established for themselves, there is still a long way to go in matching principles with practice. Canada may not be a perfect society; nevertheless, it may well be one of the least imperfect societies because of its commitment to equality (in principle if not always in practice); endorsement of diversity as virtue rather than vice; a relatively high threshold for negotiation and a preference for compromise as a way of muddling through problems, and a commitment to unity and identity despite mounting costs. The conclusion may appear counterintuitive: Canada has actually set itself up for "failure." The ideals that Canadians have defined for themselves ensure the proliferation of social problems that other jurisdictions might dismiss as "normal" or suppress as "inevitable." A sense of perspective is badly needed: To the extent that Canada is a society of social problems because of its decision to establish higher standards of justice, equality, and fairness while aspiring to lofty ideals that may be impossibly difficult to attain, these problems should be seen as a credit to rather than a condemnation of its people.

In light of such effusive praise—some of it earned, some not—Canadians have much to be grateful for, and the very idea of fixating on Canada's social problems may strike the reader as morbidly cynical or nitpicking to the extreme. Yet Canada at the millennium is perched at a crossroads. It must make choices that will bolster its reputation as a pacesetter in "society-building" or, alternatively, unravel the social fabric of Canadian society. Canadians must also engage with the challenges of diversity and change at a time when global capitalism is threatening to impose a cultural gridlock. In seeking a society that is safe for diversity and change, yet safe from these same forces, time will tell whether Canada is large enough to solve the big problems of a globalizing world, yet sufficiently small to cope with the smaller problems of a fragmented society. The 3rd edition of *Social Problems in Canada* addresses this interplay of opposites by exploring those social problems that continue to perplex or provoke Canadians at the millennium. A sociological perspective is employed to explore a host of social problems with respect to prevailing conditions, evolving constructions, and challenges to Canadian society at interpersonal, institutional, national, and global levels. An emphasis on social problems as conditions examines the antecedent causes of social problems, proposed cures, anticipated outcomes, and inadvertent consequences of problem-solving initiatives. Social problems are also analyzed as social constructions. The focus is on public reaction to problematic conditions and political responses to the claims-making activities of aggrieved groups. Accorded prominence is the role of government policy in defining, controlling, and solving social problems. So too is an emphasis on how interest groups seek to challenge and transform those values, institutions, and structures that create and sustain problematic conditions.

Two themes undergird this edition of *Social Problems in Canada*. In doing so, a coherent framework is imposed for organizing the material, while conferring a rationale for what might otherwise look like a random collection of social issues and conditions. First and foremost is the commitment to improve our understanding of Canadian society by looking at Canada through the prism of social problems. Focusing on the social dimensions of social problems and their relationship to society at large promises a distinctive and rewarding grasp of recurrent issues in Canadian society. Second, but no less important, is the commitment to better understand the concept of social problems by refracting conceptual concerns through the prism of Canadian society. The goal is not simply to propose solutions to a series of popular social problems on the basis of wrong or right, but to look behind and beneath these social problems from a sociological point of view. The challenge rests in "problematizing" the process by which some conditions get to be defined as social problems (how, why, and by whom), debated in the public sphere, and subjected to proposed solutions by way of policies and politics. As a critical approach for making transparent those issues ("problems") that are taken for granted, the point of this exercise is not to tell the readers what to think or to dismiss their opinions. One objective is learning to go "against the grain," to be counter-intuitive, by questioning what is taken for granted as a natural way of looking at the world. The other objective is looking at the broader context in which issues appear, while acknowledging that appearances can be deceiving when interpreting social phenomena. This two-pronged approach may equip each student with the critical skills for addressing contemporary problems, the contours of which were skilfully articulated by a Rabbi Hillel in Babylon thousands of years ago when he posed his now famous three questions (cited in Rae, 1999:9): "If I am not for myself, who is for me? But if I am only for myself, what am I? And if not now, when?"

The 3rd edition of *Social Problems in Canada* subscribes to the well-worn adage of "continuity in change." In terms of continuity, the book continues to explore the conditions and constructions that challenge Canadian society at the millennium. The social dimensions of objective conditions are examined around "causes," characteristics, consequences, and "cures." Attention is also devoted to the socially constructive ways in which both interest groups and the political sector act upon conditions that are defined as socially problematic. The challenges these conditions and contructions pose to Canadian society are central themes through the text. Core questions provide a coherent framework for analysis and organization. What are "social problems"? Who says so, why, and on what grounds? How are they manifest? What are the impacts and implications for society? What has been done to solve these problems? What, if anything, is "doable" as solutions? How do inappropriate solutions complicate the situation? Responses tend to emphasize the structural roots of social problems, without losing sight of human agency in shaping definitions, responses, and outcomes. And the new edition subscribes to the axiom that quick-fix solutions do not exist when social problems are woven into the very social fabric of society. Only politicians or pundits appear bold enough to dispense glib solutions and magical formulas for solving social problems that may ultimately prove unsolvable.

With respect to changes, the book has been thoroughly revised to incorporate unforeseen circumstances both personal and professional. The text is organized around four levels of analysis; that is, social problems at the mutually interrelated but analytically separate levels of: (a) interpersonal, (b) institutions, (c) society, and (d) globality. The introduction of a new section on "Canada as a Contested Society" provides a framework for discussing the concept of national unity. Two new chapters for framing Canada as a social problem have been added, including a chapter on Canada at the millennium, and another on immigration and multiculturalism. Two chapters have been deleted (addiction and sexuality), fours chapters have been rewritten in their entirety—introduction, gender, deviance, and family, and six chapters have been added by subdividing the original chapters into more manageable units of analysis. The original chapter on inequality is now partitioned into stand-alone chapters on education and another on poverty; the original globalization chapter has expanded into chapters on global problems, globalism and Canada, and a new chapter on Canada at the millennium; finally, the chapter on race, ethnic, and aboriginal relations has been re-constituted into four new chapters, including a chapter on racism and discrimination, in addition to three expanded chapters in the new national unity section. The remaining chapters on media, work and workplaces, and inequality have been revised and updated.

Changes are also evident at the level of organization. The first section of *Social Problems in Canada* explores the concept of social problems by utilizing the insights and perspectives of sociology. In recent years, the way in which social problems are framed has shifted because of social, cultural, political, and economic changes. The first chapter attempts to draw attention to how sociologists problematize the concept of social problems. Particular attention is centred on deconstructing both the "problem" in social problems as well as the "social" in social problems. The second section begins with the notion that social structures remain a key cause of Canada's social problems. Patterns of inequality are analyzed with respect to class, race and ethnicity, gender, and crime. Analyzed as well are proposals for solutions that entail a rethinking of equality. Racism and discrimination are examined as social problems that have proven difficult to define and even more difficult to eradicate. Gender is problematized not only as a site of social problems, but also as an increasingly contested script for defining femininity and masculinity, and relationships between men and women. Following this is a look at the costs associated with deviance, crime, and control from a social problem perspective. The third section explores the concept of institutions in crisis. Portrayal of the media (including newscasting, TV programming, advertising, movie-making, and the Internet) as a social problem should come as no surprise, given the oft-stated relationship between media consumption and anti-social behaviour, especially among young males. The so-called disarray in family structures is shown to elicit a wide range of responses, from those who lament the decline of traditional families as the bedrock of society, to those who endorse the creative and liberating possibilities of a post-patriarchal era. A crisis in confidence that currently engulfs the education system in Canada—especially tertiary education—is also addressed. Changes to the workplace and concept of work are interpreted as problems in their own right as well as creating social problems in need of solutions. The fourth section delves into Canadian society as a social problem. The national unity debate is shown to be animated by Canada's perpetual quest for independence, against the backdrop of demands for autonomy by aboriginal peoples and the Quebecois. Insofar as the most critical, long-term problem confronting Canada is along the aboriginal front, yet nobody appears to be addressing it properly, according to Tom Kierans, president of the CD Howe Institute (cited in *The Globe and Mail*, Dec. 30, 1999), a chapter on the "Indian problem" will attempt the impossible. The fifth and final section deals with the problems of globalism and Canada's evolving relationship to a new global order. The forces of globalism are explained in terms of their impact and implications for Canadian society, most notably concerning the role of markets versus states as competing perspectives for governance. Global problems pertaining to the environment, population, ethnic nationalism, global monoculture, and poverty and urbanism are also discussed, with particular attention to Canada's complicity in solidifying problems by contributing to a global division of labour that segregrates the rich from the poor.

Of the many changes to the 3rd edition, the most obvious and significant is that I have taken on the role of sole revising author. For this endeavour, I have been fortunate in having such a strong foundation as the previous edition to build upon. As such, I wish to thank Adie Nelson for her collaboration on the 2nd edition of this text; her formidable intellect and razor sharp wit has helped shape this current edition.

PROBLEMATIZING SOCIAL PROBLEMS

FRAMING THE PROBLEM

Both Canada and the United States have been rocked by a spate of incidents that have triggered what media experts call a "moral panic" (Mitchell, 1997). Moral panics arise when a crime is so shocking and sensational that it becomes the starting point for soul-searing debates over a complex web of painful social problems. The dragging death of a Black male in Texas, the torture killing of a gay college student in Wyoming, and the mass school murders in Colorado have confirmed the obvious: People consumed by hate continue to kill others because of appearance or lifestyle. Canada too has been wracked by a demoralizing turn of events: The brutal slaying of 14-year-old Reena Virk in Victoria drew widespread dismay because the violence seemed counterintuitive in a society where things like this just don't happen. The fact that young women were involved in the rampage only intensified the disillusionment. The beating death of a young Toronto teenager in late 1999 also prompted Canadians to ask what kind of society they wanted, one in which all decisions are filtered through a materialistic lens, that emphasizes "having" as more important than being, that treats other people as commodities for instant gratification, and that reinforces a myth of personal happiness without social responsibility? And the entire country was convulsed by shock waves following the shooting death of a young male student in Taber, Alberta. The perception of a society in disarray was poignantly articulated by the father of Jason Lang, who told a news conferrence: "May God have mercy on this broken society and all the hurting people in it. ...that a lot of things have to change in our society, lots of things need to be healed" (cited in the *National Post*, 30th April, 1999: A–10).

Reaction to each of these events has stimulated an intense flurry of collective self-examination about the health of contemporary society. Fears are mounting that the rules, roles, and relationships of society are becoming increasingly irrelevant or contested, particularly among young Canadians, with the result that a new order is evolving and doing so without mainstream ("adult") approval. That Canadians are perplexed and provoked by the enormity of these transformations is beyond debate. So too are sociologists who must live with the rather awkward realization that the worse things get, the more appealing their discipline becomes. Central to sociological debates is the question, "What are social problems?" To what extent can intensely personal incidents that involve individuals as victims or perpetrators be defined as social problems? Or are such seemingly personal troubles the manifestation of more fundamental problems associated with the challenges of change, diversity, and uncertainty? Does a social problem imply the primacy of human agency, or should the focus be on values, structures, and institutional arrangements? Does anything that happens in society automatically qualify as a social problem? Or should only events that elicit a public response be included as social problems? Should the enormity of any event and scale of its impact be the criteria for defining a social problem? Media reaction is not much help in gauging whether the scope of an incident is a key indicator in defining a social problem. Why does the tragic shooting death of one Canadian student garner enormous coverage, however horrifying this may be to family and friends; yet the same depth of coverage is not extended to thousands of Canadians who are killed each year on highways, about half (1700) involving alcohol. Only horrific pile-ups with multiple fatalities seem to get much publicity. To the extent that media prefer a different approach to each of these conditions, despite the lack of justifiable criteria for making such a distinction, the problem with social problems deserves closer scrutiny.

Additional questions help to frame the problem for analysis. In what way does sociology offer a different spin to the topic of social problems? Are there common denominators or shared attributes that distinguish social problems from other types of problems? Are social problems a thing "out there," or a thing "in here," or something that interacts "in between" the "out there" and the "in here"? Do social problems exist in their own right, or are they an attribute or label that is applied to something after the fact because of context or consequences? Do solutions exist for every social problem? What is it about problems that preclude solutions? What is it about the nature of solutions that render them seemingly incapable of solving social problems? This chapter explores many of the issues that confront a sociological analysis of social problems. The concept of social problems is problematized; that is, the assertion of something as a social problem is neither self-evident nor does it reflect common sense. There is nothing natural or normal about social problems in the sense of inevitability; rather as social constructions, social problems reflect definitions of the world by those with the power to impose such definitions. In problematizing what others take for granted, social problems are subject to debate over who says so, why, and on what grounds, and with what impact and implications for society and its members. At the core of problematizing are the questions: What is meant by the "problem" in social problems? And what is the "social" in social problems? The socially constructed nature of social problems invites us to deconstruct these conventions as a way of going "behind" and "beneath."

How then do sociologists cope with the paradox of social problems that are deeply embedded in contemporary society and seemingly resistant to solutions? Other than a collective belief that the personal is social and that all behaviour is contextual, sociologists tend to be a remarkably diverse lot of scholars. In fact, one of the few things that sociologists have in common is a willingness to agree to disagree. Of particular note is disagreement over the parameters of their discipline with respect to subject matter, underlying assumptions, key concepts, major perspectives, levels of proof, methods and methodologies, and findings and conclusions. Such diversity comes with a cost: A lack of consensus or conviction may be off-putting to those who seek definitive answers; alternatively, this rejection of conformity may prove a pillar of strength in expanding and exploring disciplinary horizons. The sub-field of sociology known as social problems is no less prone to dissent. Sociologists who specialize in this area prefer to disagree over the most basic of issues, including: (a) what constitutes a social problem, who says so, and why; (b) the magnitude and scale of social problems; (c) preferred methods of analysis; (d) proposed solutions; and (e) what (if any) solutions are doable. Nevertheless, there is some consensus over the general contours of a sociological study of social problems. Instead of relying on personal, biological, or psychological variables to explain a problem, both social structures and institutional arrangements are invoked as sources and solutions (Scarpitti and Cylke Jr., 1995). Sociologists prefer to dwell on the social dimensions of human problems: That is, priority is assigned to the often enigmatic and evolving relationship between social problems and society in terms of impact and implications. Additional commonalities can be discerned. Social problems are thought to involve conditions that are socially constructed and contested, yet reflect objective reality; vary over time and place; frequently exhibit a life-cycle from birth to demise to rebirth; are inseparable from the broader context in which they are located; and respond differently to treatment. Inasmuch as attempted solutions are as likely to intensify existing problems or create new ones, few sociologists ever need worry about a shortage of subject matter.

The chapter begins by examining the prospect of defining social problems. This is followed by a look at the contested notion of "social" and "problem," in each case asking what is so "social" about social problems, and what is meant by the "problem" in social problems. Particularly relevent is the distinction between constructionists and "conditionists" (including both objectivists and subjectivists) in defining the subject matter for analysis. The next section looks at how sociologists approach the concept of social problems. The major perspectives of functionalism, conflict, and interactionism are offered as alternative vantage points for analysis and assessment. A case study on suicide delves into how sociologists transform an ostensibly personal trouble into a fundamentally social problem. The chapter concludes by discussing how proposed solutions to social problems have proven a problem in their own right, thus complicating the attainment of consensus for doing what is workable, necessary, and fair (see also Scarpitti and Cylke Jr., 1995).

DEFINING SOCIAL PROBLEMS

Defining social problems is not as simple as it seems. Definitions of social problems are as varied and numerous as they are confusing and contradictory. Much of this definitional disarray reflects the nature of the definition process: That is, things or events can be defined in terms of what they look like; what they are supposed to do; and what they actually do. For example, Canada's official multiculturalism can be defined: (a) in descriptive terms that reflect Canadians' ethno-cultural diversity; (b) prescriptively with respect to goals and objectives; (c) proscriptively with regards to underlying ideas and ideals; and (d) as a pragmatic government device for securing consensus and control. None of these definitions is more correct; nor is there such a thing as a right or wrong definition, since each casts light on one aspect of multiculturalism instead of another. Rather than reflecting an accurate appraisal of reality, definitions are best evaluated in terms of their usefulness as explanatory tools for advancing our understanding of social reality. It stands to reason that a comprehensive understanding of multiculturalism would capitalize on different aspects for illumination.

A similar line of reasoning applies to social problems where the proliferation of definitions is matched only by a corresponding disarray in this area. A sample of definitions provides some sense of the profusion; nevertheless, definitions seem to be sorted into two major streams, condition(ist)s (both subjectivists and objectivists), and constructionists. The earliest definitions emphasized social problems as conditions that posed a threat to (a) society, (b) the prevailing social order, and (c) existing institutional structures. Both deviant activities or defective (poorly socialized) individuals were seen as largely responsible for disrupting an inherently sound arrangement. Problem-inducing disruptions also arose because of slippages in the system; for example, Robert Merton (1976) defined social problems as a gap in the fit between ideals and reality, between goals and actual achievements. The notion of social problems as conditions continues in the present. But, whereas social problems were once framed as pathologies to the social order by deviant persons, the current focus is on those structures, institutional frameworks, and value configurations that foster inequality or deny human rights (Bolaria, 2000).

Definitions of social problems as conditions may emphasize a subjective or objective component. For subjectivists, social problems come into existence only when a condition is defined as problematic by a critical mass of people. Awareness is key: One of the earliest definitions by Fuller and Myers (1941) explained social problems as a condition perceived by a significant number of people as a harmful departure from some cherished norm (see also Coleman and Cressey, 1987; Mooney et al., 1997). Other definitions focus on the objective dimensions of social problems. Objective definitions approach conditions as external realities that inflict harmful effects ("problems"), irrespective of public awareness of what is going on (Green, 1994). For example, capitalist exploitation is a social problem, whether the exploited are aware of it or not. In fact, one might argue that the whole point of exploitation is to construct ideas and ideals that deflect, distract, or deny the inequities. Richard Henshel (1990) also defines social problems as a set of conditions and structures that adversely affect a significant number of people in a similar way. Eitzen and Zinn (1992) concur: Social problems can be described as conditions that cause harm to segments of society, regardless of public awareness. While both subjectivists and objectivists differ in emphasis, they share a common commitment to focus on conditions as the primary field of study. These problematized conditions are then analyzed in terms of causes, characteristics, consequences, and cures.

Other definitions reflect a constructionist orientation by dwelling on the interactionist and dynamic component of social problems, rather than harmful conditions per se. The primary focus is not on conditions per se, but on how interest groups act upon these conditions, together with the political reaction to these claims-making activities as part of the never-ending spiral of applying solutions to problems that never seem to be solved. As noted by Blumer (1971) and others (Julian, 1973; Ritzer, 1986; Mooney et al., 1997), certain conditions become problematic only when perceived or defined as such by some sector of society, and are acted upon accordingly by way of response, resistance, or reaction. More recently, Gusfield (1996) has defined social problems as a way of framing certain conditions in a way that stimulates the call for change through collective action or public policy. Central to constructionist definitions is the notion of social problems as socially constructed (Spector and Kitsuse, 1977; 1987). Problematic conditions are neither normal nor inevitable, despite pressures to make them seem so, but are socially constructed by individuals making choices in contexts that are not necessarily of their making. Even more crucial to constructionists is the notion of claims-making. Social problems encompass those claims-making activities by aggrieved groups who collectively challenge perceived flaws in society through activism and reform. In other words, problems are not social problems in the sociological sense without the interactive component of people taking situations into their own hands by way of collective action.

Is there a common denominator that underpins each of these definitions? All definitions of social problems point to certain conditions as being problematic because of their ability to cause harm to all or part of society. For some, these harmful conditions are objectively real and analyzed as such by sociologists, regardless of public or political awareness. Objectivist definitions prefer to study social problems in terms of their causes, characteristics, and consequences, with an eye to proposing cures as solutions to problems "out there." For others, people's perceptions of and responses to conditions are critical to any definition. For, no matter how contemptible or destructive a particular situation, few conditions are inherently problematic until defined as such by some interest group. As a result, what is defined as problematic will vary from one time period to another, and is relative to particular cultural contexts. To be sure, the difference between objectivists and subjectivists is more apparent than real, since both focus on the condition per se, together with the attendant causes, consequences, characteristics, and cures. Others prefer to define social problems around people's responses to perceived conditions. In defining social problems as socially constructed by way of claims-making actions, "constructionists" are concerned with what becomes defined as a social problem; who says, why, and on what grounds; and what is being done about the situation, by whom, with what tactics, and with what kind of outcomes? Constructionist approaches tend to focus on the processes by which some conditions rather than others are acted upon; how power is exercised in shaping agendas; what measures are invoked to draw public and political attention; to what extent official responses prove satisfactory; and what is involved in repriming the process if political responses prove inadequate? Constructionists perceive conditions as little more than background for the true focus of study: that is, the claims-making activities of groups who articulate grievances and make claims with respect to some perceived conditions, whether real or imagined (Kitsuse and Spector, 1987). This notion of conditions as problematic only when acted upon by claims-making individuals imparts a distinctively sociological spin to the study of social problems.

Which definition "works" for this edition of *Social Problems*? Is it best to select a definition that endorses one perspective rather than another, and to defend this choice to the hilt? Or is it better to select aspects of different definitions, thus creating a more comprehensive definition without sacrificing consistency and compatibility in the process? In preferring to side with the latter approach rather than former, this book defines a social problem as those conditions that are defined by a critical mass of people to be harmful to society or its members, together with the process by which these "problematized" conditions are collectively challenged and acted upon by way of claims-making activity. This definition is not without flaws; for example, what is meant by "critical mass," and how can this term be specified with respect to specific numbers? References to "harmful" are equally vague, given the difficulties of operationalizing this term for the benefit of those reference groups making the judgment. To further complicate matters, the salience of power in defining social problems reminds us that perhaps the key issue is not numbers per se. More to the point is the number of *significant* people who have the power to impose definitions, and who propose one line of action rather than another. Despite these shortcomings, the definition has proven of benefit for study. First, it acknowledges that social problems reflect objective conditions in society, but only acquire sociological status when these conditions are defined by those with the resources and resourcefulness to do something about them. Second, the definition also concedes the importance of process; that is, conditions called social problems do not simply exist for analysis or assessment; rather, they are defined, debated, and subject to transformation by way of protest, collective action, or government policy.

What Is Meant by the "Problem" in Social Problems?

What kind of problems are sociologists attracted to? Under what circumstances are conditions defined as problematic? By whom? What for? On what grounds? And why? Answers to these questions are more elusive than many might imagine. Part of the difficulty arises from the fact that most problems are not self-evident. For example, in what way is inequality a social problem? Who says so, and why? And on what criteria can such an assessment be made? Nor do social problems exist as discrete and readily labelled categories for analysis or assessment. Cross-cultural studies confirm the near lack of universally defined conditions as problematic, in effect reinforcing the socially constructed nature of social problems. To be sure, some conditions are readily acknowledged as problematic; a few that come to mind include murder, random violence, racism and discrimination, and child pornography. Self-report surveys may offer assistance: In response to the question, "What is the most important problem facing Canada?," the following concerns were highlighted by Macleans in its15th annual year-end poll involving 1400 adult Canadians between November 13th and 22nd, 1998: unemployment (15%); deficit/government spending (14%); economy (13%); health care (13%); national unity (8%); education (4%); crime/violence (3%); environment (2%); and other/don't know (18%). In another survey, by the Angus Reid Group (cited in the *Globe and Mail*, 7 Feb., 2000), the most pressing issues confronting Canada included health care (55%), education (23%), taxes (19%), unemployment (15%), and poverty (15%). Yet self-report categories are problematic in their own right; after all, one person's problem may be another individual's solution. For example, crime may be widely condemned as a problem except among those whose livelihood is dependent on proceeds from criminal activity or who have jobs in the criminal justice system. For the most part, actions forbidden by law are generally defined as problems. Nevertheless, those who are "criminalized" by authorities may not see their condition as problematic, but point their finger at those who enforce these laws. The tendency to confuse laws with problems must be tempered by the relativities of a specific context. Chewing gum, spitting on sidewalks, or driving around with less than half a tank of gas may be viewed as problems in some Malaysian countries, and defined by authorities as crimes punishable by fines. Such actions would not be regarded as criminal or even problematic in many North American jurisdictions. Similarly, acts of deviance involving widely accepted norms may or may not be a problem depending on the context. For example, speeding on a highway is illegal, yet many act as if such actions were normal and acceptable rather than a problem. By contrast, any excessive speed in a school zone may be harshly deplored.

For the most part, then, problems are difficult to define or defend, thanks to the abandonment of absolute standards of right or good. In the postmodernist world of the millennium, everything appears to be up for grabs. The rules, roles, and relationships that once secured the moorings of a predictable society have been cut adrift because of defiance toward convention or authority, with the result that some virtues are now seen as vices, and vice versa. As a result, what are social problems for some are normal and desirable conditions for others, depending on one's preferred vision of society. Of particular note is the perception that problems themselves are relative to time and place, with the result that what once was defined as a problem may lose its sting over time. For example, comic books and pool halls were demonized as problems because of their potential for misleading impressionable youth. Few would bother to label either of these activities as problems at present. Both videos and video arcades, in addition to internet-access, constitute the social problems of choice at the millennium. As well, one-time problem situations are increasingly endorsed as acceptable or positive. Consider divorce: Except perhaps within certain religious circles, divorce rarely elicits the moral indignation or social stigma that it once did. Rather than being defined as a personal failure or problem, divorce is increasingly tolerated as an unfortunate but inevitable component of a "me first" society that is becoming more egalitarian, tolerant, and accommodative. Paradoxically, divorce may now be endorsed as a hallmark of personal growth and maturity rather than a regressive or pathological action, notwithstanding the possibility of negative outcomes such as the feminization of poverty or the adverse emotional impact on children. Conversely, historic verities may be re-evaluated as problems. For example, the spanking of children by parents or guardians once was regarded as obligatory and good ("spare the rod, spoil the child"). Today it is increasingly defined as a problem in its own right, and a recipe for problems in later life. Domestic abuse was rarely conceived of as a social problem when an openly patriarchal society endorsed the primacy of a man as "king of his castle" and his dependents as his "property." Changes in society have shattered this sexism to the point where domestic abuse is increasingly perceived as a social problem and is dealt with accordingly by law. Similarly, a raft of new social problems have entered into public awareness in recent years, including smoking, drinking and driving, suntanning, fur-wearing, meat-eating, homelessness, and the emergent troika of "road rage," "air rage," and "work rage." In short, problems come and go because of changes in the social environment rather than deterioration or improvement in individuals. The catalyst is a change in people's perceptions, definitions, and assessment of certain situations in relation to an evolving society. Power is the key variable, as we shall see, in establishing which problems appear on the public agenda and whose definitions will prevail within political circles (Feagin and Feagin, 1994).

Even the word "problem" is problematic. For most, the term "problem" conjures up something that is devalued or disruptive, a departure from the norm or the usual or natural. However, there is nothing unusual or unnatural about social problems. Social problems are a recurrent feature of social reality in a complex, changing, and diversity society. The normalcy of social problems may be attributed to certain structures in society; for example, some conflict theorists view capitalist society as a site involving unequal and opposing groups in competitive struggle for scarce resources. Confrontation, conflict, and contradiction are inevitable under these circumstances, given the existence of diverse publics with divergent agendas over who gets what. Social problems are also known to arise from normal decision-making processes, or from well-meaning actions that are rooted in miscalculation or incorrect assumptions, but have the effect of creating new problems or intensifying existing ones. The same values that induce pro-social behaviour (for example, competitive individualism) can also elicit anti-social activity, depending on the context, or when they are taken to extremes. In short, social problems are a normal and inevitable component of society, and the frequency of social problems is no less a departure from the norm than appeals to consensus or regulation. No one should be surprised by this admission. In a postmodern world of diversity and change, with its defiance of authority or convention, a problem-free society is no more possible than a perfectly integrated person.

The debate over the "problem" in social problems is critical for sociology. At the heart of sociological interest are debates over the objective status of problems. Put simply: Do problems really exist as objective conditions that fall outside public or political awareness? Or do social problems, by definition, reflect objective conditions that are perceived and defined as problems by a significant number of people? Or are problems properly viewed not as conditions—real or perceived—but as constructions involving people doing something about the conditions around them. This conflict between the conditionists (both "objectivist" and "subjectivists") and "constructionists" over problem-definition is reminiscent of the famous philosophical conundrum about whether a tree makes a sound when it falls in the forest, but no one is around to hear it fall (the best answer is "no": the tree makes energy waves that may be converted into sound but only "ears" can transform this energy into sound). Three scenarios are possible when applied to the domain of social problems. First, social problems entail objective conditions that harm individuals regardless of their awareness. Second, conditions exist that are perceived as harmful by sectors of society, and sociologists are suitably placed by their training to study the causes, conditions, characteristics, consequences, and cures. Third, social problems do not exist until a critical mass of people define a situation as problematic, and then act upon this socially constructed condition by way of protest, pressure, reform, and resolution (Green, 1994). For example, an objectivist may approach the problem of homelessness as a condition to be studied in terms of what, why, how, where, when, and who. Studies might focus on measuring the size of the homeless population, exploring why some become homeless, examining the adequacy of programs to deal with this condition, and proposing solutions based on a reading of homelessness as a real problem created by structural arrangements. A constructionist would look at homelessness by asking whose claims catapulted this condition into public attention, the manner in which both the public and politicians responded to these claims-making activities, and how the homeless perceive their plight in relationship to those around them. In other words, objectivists/subjectivists and constructionists have radically different views of the "problem" in social problems (Best, 1989). For objectivists, the problem is the condition; for subjectivists, problems are perceived conditions; for constructionists, the problem is properly situated in the of claims-making process surrounding conditions.

What's So "Social" about Social Problems?

Problems exist everywhere. They vary in scale from the trivial to the cataclysmic, in experience from the intensely personal to the remote and abstract, and in impact from the petty to the profound. The content can extend to the economic and political realms as well as the cultural and legal, and range from the personal to the global. Such an array raises the question, What is distinctive about social problems? Is there a subject matter that can be labelled "social problems," or does the study of social problems simply refer to a distinctive way of looking at the world around us? What distinguishes social problems from other problems in society? How do personal problems differ from social problems? Put bluntly, what do we mean by the "social" in social problems? A closer look at the "social" of social problems casts light on what is distinctive about sociology and distinguishes it from other approaches. The resulting insights also provide clues about how to correctly read "social problems," in applying workable solutions.

A useful point of contrast begins with the concept of personal problems. A problem is defined as personal when the individual serves as the centre of analysis, assessment, reform, and outcome. Both the source of and solution to the problem are thought to reside within the person. Two variants of a personal problem are evident. First, personal problems are the result of biology or inherited characteristics. Problems are attributed to flaws in the bio-genetic hard-wiring of a person, thus contributing to anti-social behaviour for which the person must take responsibility. In some cases, the problem is seen as a pathology ("sickness"), or is defined as a disease. Second, problems are "individualized" as a result of flaws in the maturational process. By emphasizing unresolved conflicts in early childhood, these psychological explanations tend to focus on the individual as primarily but passively responsible for behavioural outcomes. Faulty early socialization is also seen as a contributing factor. Each of these individualistic types of explanations shares a common attribute: They tend to blame the individual for social problems. They also tend to emphasize the precipitating or immediate causes of problems, thus failing to see the wider social context in which problems germinate. Not surprisingly, solutions not only focus on changing the person, but also address symptoms rather than root or fundamental causes.

The classic distinction between private troubles and public issues is relevant (Mills, 1967). If one person is unemployed because of sloppy work habits, according to C. Wright Mills, this personal problem is of marginal interest to sociologists. If, however, thousands are unemployed because of corporate decisions or government policy, the situation qualifies as a public issue, since the problem lies within the system rather than with the person. Sociologists are rarely interested in the suicide of one person, but do take an interest in the 4000 suicides that occur in Canada and that vary along the lines of gender, age, location, and ethnicity. This is not to suggest a lack of sociological interest in the problems of individuals. On the contrary, sociologists may be interested in studying the social reasons why problems tend to be personalized and are attributed to the individual, rather than seen within the broader context in which individuals think and act. For example, in mid-May of 1999, the British press pilloried Julia Roberts for going out in public without shaving the hair under her armpits. An accompanying article on the front page of a major Canadian daily indicated that women who did not shave leg or armpit hair tended to have higher levels of self-confidence and self-esteem. The social dimensions of this seeming "tempest in a teapot" over unwanted hair (unwanted by whom?) is reflective not only of broader gender issues, but also of how problems are socially constructed. Most would agree that Ms. Roberts' hairy armpits should not qualify as a social problem per se, although the accompanying media frenzy might prompt questions about the magnitude of coverage given this essentially private (and trivial?) matter. But the concept of social problem comes into play over the somewhat rigid definition of femininity that compels many women to conform or to pay the price. In that sense, all human and personal problems are potentially social problems because of the social dimension inherent in all human actions. In a world in which the personal is often seen to be political, all human actions are inseparable from the social, contextual, and patterned. This willingness to tackle problems as part of the "big picture" imparts a distinctive spin to the study of social problems.

What, then, is meant by the "social" in social problems? Social problems are not the result of random events by maligned individuals. Rather, the "social" in social problems refers to conditions that: (a) originate in society at large, including values, institutions, or structures; (b) reflect slippage between society and culture (i.e., behaviour patterns at odds with prevailing norms, values, or visions of society); (c) acknowledge that certain actions or issues have the intent or effect of negatively impacting on society or its members; (d) emerge from competitive interaction as individuals or groups struggle to define situations, secure resources, and manipulate agendas; and (e) violate human rights and endorse gaping inequities. Framing the problem socially is critical for a sociological analysis. Instead of asking why people are poor or live in poverty, sociologists might well ask, What is it about society that creates poor people and tolerates their presence? Why is it that the poor rather than the affluent are defined as a social problem? Why are individuals rather than institutions and government policies blamed for being poor? According to many sociologists, a problem is social and amenable to sociological analysis if it meets three criteria: (a) origin, (b) definition, and (c) treatment. A fourth criterion, impact, may be included.

First, a problem is seen as social in origin when it is perceived to originate in a social context (including values, institutions, and structures) rather than in the individual by way of biology or psychology. Of course, no one is dismissing biology as irrelevant to a study of human problems. The interplay between genes and society may foster the grounds for social problems. A mismatch may be discerned between our collective genetic makeup and modern society because of an increasingly asocial world where detachment and withdrawal from others require people to live under conditions that are radically different from those under which the human species evolved (Wright, 1995). While a genetic inheritance may be in play, social factors are equally if not more compelling in accounting for actions at odds with social norms.

Second, a problem is social in definition when it is defined as a social problem by a "critical mass" of society. This sector is prone to define something as a social problem when they find their interests compromised, privileges challenged, and values and visions in conflict with others. This raises the question of why some inequities are defined as problems, and others not. For example, in 1999, women in Canada had an average life span of 81 years, while men on average lived to 76. Why is this discrepancy not defined as a problem? Or, how do we account for the fact that some conditions are not defined as problems even though they exact an enormous toll in human suffering and social costs? For example, even though thousands are killed each year on Canadian highways, few would define road accidents as a social problem, preferring instead to see it in terms of factors beyond human control (from bad luck to an acceptable risk). Interestingly, drinking and driving has come to be defined as a social problem, and considerable effort is put into curbing this increasingly "problematized" behaviour. Social problems may be explained by blaming the victims for their predicament; blaming the enemy, such as minorities or immigrants, for creating problems; blaming the institution by pointing to discriminatory barriers to full and equal involvement; and blaming the system—from values to capitalist structures—for the existence of harmful conditions (Elias, 1986).

Third, a problem is social in treatment when the proposed solution to the problem falls within the framework of human agency. On the assumption that problems created by human action can be undone by social activity, a problem qualifying as social must have the potential to be corrected or controlled by way of collective action or institutional reform. Yet solutions may be as problematic as the problems, as demonstrated in the last section of this chapter.

I would be inclined to add a fourth dimension to the "social" in social problems. A problem is social when it exerts a negative impact on society or on segments thereof. Social problems are those actions or omissions that have the intent or effect of undermining the social fabric of society to the detriment of those concerned, in the main by eroding the trust and predictability inherent in all forms of social existence. Social problems arise when certain groups in society (from women to people of colour to gays) are singled out adversely and denied full and equal treatment in society. The emergence of human rights as an important social problem will be examined at the end of the book.

youth, a growing crisis in youth suicide, and concern over copy-cat suicides.

The Legacy of Durkheim: Rethinking the Personal

Emile Durkheim, a pioneering figure in early sociology, advocated a social dimension to understanding suicide. Durkheim was one of the first scholars to call himself a sociologist, and an understanding of his work cannot ignore a lifelong devotion to establishing sociology as a distinct and respectable discipline. In 1897, Durkheim proposed the then provocative idea that suicides are, fundamentally, social (rather than personal) facts. Durkheim's contemporaries had linked suicide with mental illness, inherited tendencies, and general unhappiness. But Durkheim rejected this reductionism because of its excessive reliance on the individual in isolation from the group or social structure (Teevan, 1989). He explored rates that could account for relatively predictable patterns of behaviour within certain populations. His conclusions were anchored in precisely that observation. Suicide rates were both constant and high among some groups, but not among others. Men committed suicide more frequently than women, the elderly more than the young, Protestants more than Catholics, Catholics more than Jews, and the single more than the married. Durkheim also observed a certain constancy in these rates over time, thus ruling out the effect of periodic fluctuations and historical accidents.

Durkheim argued that group differences as expressed in constant rates were best explained by reference to social factors. Particularly important to his brand of sociology were variations in the degree of social solidarity, the salience of cultural norms, level of individual incorporation, and the intensity of interaction.

Patterns of suicides varied with degrees of structural integration and normative guidance. Suicide rates varied proportionately with those groups characterized by supportive social ties in contexts of close interaction. The four types of suicide were not mutually exclusive; nor were they doled out on the basis of one per society. Conditions in complex societies were such that several could operate at the same time. Suicides were less likely to be committed by individuals who were insulated from disconnected contexts, such as a stable marriage, involvement in cohesive groups and community life, high levels of religious devotion, and identification with normative value systems. Conversely, individuals who committed suicide had fewer social ties to others. They were also less integrated and acted more independently. From this Durkheim surmised that suicide prevailed within contexts of too much attachment (altruistic/fatalistic), too little (egoistic), or not enough (anomic). Suicides also occurred in contexts of disruptive change in the social order. Explaining rates of suicides, in other words, was inseparable from understanding the social ("integration") and cultural ("normative") dimensions of social behaviour.

Contemporary Trends in Suicide

How valid are Durkheim's assertions regarding suicide and its relation to society? Do his observations stand the test of time, or are they culturally bound by the intellectual constraints of that era in the same way many see Freud as culturally circumscribed? Is the growing rate of suicide in Canada and the United States an accurate reflection of what is really going on? Or is the increase indicative of a greater willingness to report deaths as suicide, in addition to changing definitions and burdens of proof? How does the rate of 3941 suicides in Canada in 1997 compare with other societies?

Suicide as the "act of deliberately killing oneself" is a global phenomenon. It is sanctioned in some societies as a face-saving device, but reviled in others because of cultural values and social costs (Edgerton, 1976). Worldwide rates of teen suicide are increasing. For New Zealand teens between the ages of 15 and 19, the rate of suicide per 100 000 in 1991 stood at 15.7, up from 5.8 in 1970, according to the World Health Organization (cited in *Maclean's*, Jan. 29, 1996). Norway's rate of 13.4 per 100 000 was up dramatically from 1.3 in 1970. Canada is no exception to this trend. The number of teen suicides in this country has increased dramatically: from 7 per 100 000 in 1970, the rate leapt to 13.5 per 100 000 in 1991. In some countries, the rates decrease. For example, the rates for the former Czechoslovakia dropped from 18.3 per 100 000 in 1970 to 7.7 in 1991, while Japan's rate declined to 3.8 per 100 000 in 1991 from 7.8 in 1970. Canada's alarming rate of teenage suicide is highlighted in a 1994 report by the federal health department's national task force on suicide (cited in *Maclean's*, Jan. 29, 1996). According to the report, while the overall suicide rate increased by 78 percent between 1952 and 1992, the rate for 15 to 19-year-olds increased by over 600 percent. (This increase may be attributed in part to the decriminalization of suicide in 1972, followed by a possible decline in social stigma or public scorn.) In Quebec the rate multiplied 14 times in those forty years, while suicide rates among teenage males in Saskatchewan stood at 42.4 per 100 000. Yet nobody knows why! Groups at high risk include older White males (men over 80 had a rate of over 40 per 100 000 in 1997), young men,

gays, individuals with mental disabilities, inner-city minorities, the unemployed, divorced, and widowed. Teens constitute a high-risk group; so too are middle-aged people between 45 to 55, who now have one of the highest rates of suicide for any age group, exceeding adolescent rates by 28 percent (Goar, 1999). The combination of work pressures, family problems, financial difficulties, spiralling complications, and dashed expectations may account for this rate. The suicide rate for men in Quebec was more than twice that of Ontario in 1997—30.2 compared to 12.8 per 100 000—partly because of the separatist upheaval, and in part because of social disconnectedness created by high levels of common-law relations, divorce rates, and unwed mothers (Stonehouse, 1999). Elderly males are prone to suicide because of disconnection from social routines and meaningful interaction in a society where worth is equated with youth, strength, beauty, productivity, and the ability to work (Stewart, 1995). It is interesting to note that senior citizens in other cultures may have relatively low suicide rates because of greater acceptance of elders as much-valued repositories of traditional wisdom.

Young men are also at risk. Those between 15 and 19 committed suicide at a rate of just over 19.9 per 100 000 population in 1997, nearly double the rate in 1971 (Statistics Canada, Suicide Information and Education Centre, cited in the *Toronto Star*, Oct. 10, 1999). Men between the ages of 20 and 24 years are the most likely to kill themselves. Suicides are now second only to accidents as the leading cause of death for those under 35, and the rate is growing. How do we account for this upsurge, especially among men? Sociologically speaking, quadrupling of rates for men since the 1950s may be contingent on cultural norms and social disruptions. Males are conditioned to be strong, silent types without gratuitous displays of inner emotions and dependency. The continued circulation of masculine images and macho expectations serves as a breeding ground for failure because of continual testing (and teasing) over symbols and standards of masculinity that few can hope to achieve. Efforts to escape from this rigid stereotyping because of culture changes are greeted as a sign of weakness rather than a show of strength. The loss of control is also a contributing factor. Suicide is likely to occur following the breakup of relations, an inability to take control of a situation, or a lack of perspective about personal failure. Taking one's life becomes a viable option when one is confronted by disappointment or excessive pressure for conformity within mainstream norms. Young men believe they have little recourse except to self-destruct by resorting to one final act of defiance in defence of (or rejection of) male norms and masculinity. The fact that few may appreciate the finality or consequences of their act may increase the risk factor.

Gender differences are apparent. Women and men rarely approach suicide in the same way, as might be expected in light of varied life experiences and the different worlds they inhabit. Men commit suicide more frequently than women (in 1997, the rate for men was 19.6 per 100 000, versus for women at 5.1 per 100 000); women, however, are more likely to attempt suicide (possibly up to 10 times the rate for men). Aboriginal women are an exception to this rule. Unlike males, who commit suicide when young or extremely old, the highest rates for women are between the ages of 45 to 49, with a ratio of just over 10 per 100 000 (cited in the *Toronto Star*, Oct. 10,

1999). Even the reasons behind suicide may be gendered. Suicide may provide an escape from an impossible situation for men, whereas women may resort to suicide as a belated call for assistance. No less gender-related are the instruments of choice. Men tend to rely on guns (38%) and hanging (27%), whereas women prefer to employ non-disfiguring techniques such as pills or drugs (37%). Firearms were used in only 12 percent of the cases, and hanging/strangulation constituted 19 percent. The choice of instrument may explain the preponderance of successful male suicides compared with women.

Suicide rates also vary by region in Canada. Historically, rates of suicide have been higher in the west and north, as Table 1–1 reveals.

International comparisons are equally revealing, with England and Wales near the bottom of rates in industrialized countries, and Scandinavian countries near the top (Beneteau, 1990). Between 1970 and 1993, Hungary topped the list with 36 suicides per 100 000 (as recorded by the World Health Organization) having relinquished this title only recently to Russia and the Baltics (*Kitchener-Waterloo Record*, 11 March, 1995). Cross-national comparisons are difficult, however, since each country defines and enumerates suicides differently.

Minority groups also reflect a variable pattern. Of the various groups in Canada, few have experienced as much distress as the First Nations, whose suicide rates outpace the national norm by a considerable margin. Aboriginal men commit suicide at the rate of 56.3 per 100 000, quadruple the national rate for males in general; while the rates for young men between 15 and 19 years-of-age on certain reserves stands at 6 to 8 times the national average, with the highest rate

TABLE 1-1	National Suicide Rates	
	1997 Suicides	**1997 Suicide Rates per 100 000**
Canada	3681	12.0
Newfoundland	46	8.2
Prince Edward Island	14	10.4
Nova Scotia	92	9.5
New Brunswick	89	11.7
Quebec	1370	18.1
Ontario	925	8.0
Manitoba	144	13.0
Saskatchewan	140	14.0
Alberta	403	14.3
British Columbia	425	10.4
Yukon	5	23.6
North-West Territories	28	46.0

Statistics Canada. Cited in the *National Post*, December 21, 1999.

among Inuit, followed by Dene.That figure makes this age group one of the most suicide-prone in the entire world. A lethal combination of risk factors that are systemic to the life experiences of aboriginal communities may account for the alarmingly high rates; namely, rapid social change, identity confusion, rising expectations (versus stalled reality), alcohol and drug abuse, family violence, poverty, and lack of opportunity (up to 95 percent unemployment in some areas). Personal factors appear equally important, spanning the range from alienation and boredom to frustration, poor self-image, self-hatred, and hopelessness at being caught between two cultures (Shkilnyk, 1985; Windspeaker, 1995).

Many of the problems that confront First Nations' communities stem from colonialist efforts to transform aboriginal peoples into European clones. Refusal of governments to deal squarely with the problem has contributed to difficulties, according to the Royal Commission on Aboriginal Peoples (*Globe and Mail*,

"Must Act on Native Suicides, Report Says." Feb. 2, 1995). In addition, some aboriginal leaders have been reluctant to press for solutions, partly from shame and embarrassment, and partly for fear of distracting from their political agenda related to land claims settlement or inherent self-government. Aboriginal initiatives to establish institutional structures for expressing inherent rights to land, identity, and political voice offer the best opportunity for healing and renewal (Mercredi and Turpel, 1993).

Caution must be exercised when interpreting the available data. As Mark Twain once quipped, "There are lies, damned lies, and statistics." Statistics are never as objective and reliable a source of information as many believe. Selectivity and bias are inherent in all aspects of research, from data collection to interpretation. The field of suicide is no exception. Both data collection and cross-national comparisons lack consistency, reflect subjectivity, are subject to second-guessing, and resist verification. The validity of any data-based information must remain open to scrutiny, since increased rates may reflect changes in the way suicide is defined, catalogued, and reported. Even Canadian data are suspect. A death is certified as a suicide by medical or legal authorities only when a victim's intent is known, although only about one-quarter of all successful suicides bother with such legal niceties (Beneteau, 1990). Without a suicide note or other corroborating evidence, it is a coroner who ultimately determines whether death resulted from an accident or unnatural causes, or stemmed from a self-inflicted injury with intent to cause death (Douglas, 1967; Windspeaker, 1995). Evidence to date suggests a conservative bias in suicide rates: an underreporting of suicide remains a perennial concern because of the stigma associated with self-killing. Coroners are pressured to mislabel suicides as "accidents" to ease the trauma and stigma for family and relatives, to comply with religious observances that define suicide as self-murder, and to circumvent insurance companies that withhold payment for what, prior to 1972, was defined as an illegal act. (At present, it is illegal only to aid and abet someone in committing the act). Whatever the causes, the costs of suicide are exorbitant. A 1996 study in New Brunswick estimated the average cost of each suicide in the province at $849 878, which includes direct costs for police investigations, etc., as well as the indirect costs of lost productivity and earnings. Even more costly are unsuccessful suicides, many of which end up in expensive intensive-care units (Canadian Press, 7 Sept., 1999).

Putting the Social Back into the Personal

Sociology begins with the Durkheimian assumption that the personal is social and that all behaviour is contextual. It continues by acknowledging how individual behaviour is socially constructed within the framework of society. Sociologists prefer to deal with probabilities and patterns as subject matter, rather than the isolated and random. Instead of precipitating triggers, the focus is on root causes within the structures, values, and institutions of society. A distinction is required between root and precipitating causes. Precipitating causes point to immediate factors that may inspire a suicidal impulse, such as alcohol and drug abuse, coupled with anxiety and depression. Sociologists are more interested in the underlying ("root") causes that give rise to recurrent patterns. They concentrate on the social conditions that may lead to dependency or alienation. Patterns are more important than personalities: The suicide of musician Kurt Cobain of the Seattle grunge group Nirvana may be less interesting to sociologists than explaining the propensity for celebrity suicides. A sociological perspective offers valuable insights into the "big picture" surrounding suicide rates. Suicides are not a random occurrence based on personal whims or rash decisions. Fluctuations and evolving trends cannot disguise the fact that suicide rates are relatively constant, that suicide is endemic to certain groups or areas rather than others, and that suicides are more likely to occur during periods of rapid social change and cultural upheaval.

A sociological approach does not deny the existence of free will; few would be bold enough to reject the possibility of individual choice or personal responsibility. Nor does it posit a direct causal relationship between suicide and society. Society does not "determine" behaviour; nor does it "cause" suicides. Rather, it provides the context in which certain choices and chances are more probable than others. The importance of the inter-subjective should dismiss popular misconceptions of sociology as a discipline which studies why people don't have any choices to make. Nor can we confidently predict who will commit suicide. Sociological or statistical data can only yield estimates ("probabilities") that apply to groups or categories of persons. But specific cases may elude the power of statistics to predict with accuracy. The relationship is indirect: Society creates the conditions and responses that may enhance the tendency to suicidal behaviour for members of certain groups. Individuals make choices freely, must be accountable for their actions, and must take responsibility for what they do. Nevertheless, alternatives are socially defined and choices are made within a social context. Choices are never made in a moral vacuum, but in a social context in which alternatives and options are socially defined and constrained by the demands of the situation. Individuals bring their own unique characteristics to each situation. However, individuals also live out their lives within a shared framework of social institutions and cultural conventions that constitute the basis of society. In short, individual behaviour may involve high levels of human agency or indeterminancy. Yet much of our behaviour is constrained by social circumstances and cultural conditions. The constancy in suicide rates from one year to the next attests to the staying power of society as a social force.

Also evolving over time are differences in conceptualizing social problems. Sociologists themselves have experienced a shift in how problems are discussed, the type of questions asked, the manner in which responses are framed, and the kind of answers that are permissible. Once sociologists were preoccupied with social stability as the norm, and defined social problems as patterns of deviance created by social misfits and defective individuals that challenged this harmony (Coleman and Cressey, 1984). At present, there is growing emphasis on the structures, values, and institutions that create inequality and human rights violations as social problems (Bolaria, 2000). Each of these narratives about social problems corresponds with sociological perspectives on society. Diverse perspectives within sociology—namely, functionalism, conflict, and interactionism—also ensure different ways of talking about social problems.

Functionalists interpret society as a complex system of interrelated parts, with each part contributing to the stability, order, and consensus of the whole. Society is envisaged as fundamentally sound, and anything that detracts from this fundamental goodness is defined as a social problem. Put bluntly, then, social problems are seen as aberrations in a normally functioning society. Social problems arise from rapid social change and corresponding culture lag; they reflect the fact that different groups have different values, agendas, and demands, and that institutions do not necessarily do what they were intended to do. Such a functionalism characterized the study of social problems from the onset. Sociology as a discipline originated to study the social problems associated with the decline of the traditional order and its replacement by a modern social order. Early sociologists were preoccupied with the concept of social harmony and the social glue that bonded society. Any behaviour at odds with conventional rules, roles, and relationships was deemed pathological (dysfunctional), and in need of solution if a functioning society was to survive. Emphasis was on how deviant lifestyles or pathological individuals eroded the normative basis of society (Henshal, 1990; Bolaria, 2000).

Conflict theorists also interpret society as an integrated whole of interrelated parts, although most assign a priority to the economy as a basis for organization. Conflict theorists argue that the interrelated functions of values, institutions, and structures exist to maintain systems of exploitation. According to conflict theorists, society is essentially "exploitative"; therefore, anything that contributes to this inequality is a social problem, while practices and developments that challenge the system are perceived as solutions. For conflict theorists, then, social problems are not an aberration in society, but are intrinsic to its structure and process. In other words, social problems are inherent in those societies organized around the capitalist principles of profit, competitive individualism, and class conflict. Their view of society is one in which contradiction, confrontation, and conflict are integral to the very functioning of a system devoted to exploitation and oppression, even though considerable effort is expended to convey the impression of social order and inter-group harmony. Current studies tend to emphasize social inequality as a key to understanding social problems. Society is defined as a set of competing forces involving conflict, exploitation, and domination, and culminating in patterns of inequality that are unjust and unfair. The social problems discourse is geared toward analyzing those structural arrangements, institutional frameworks, and ideological assumptions. Particular attention is devoted to the idea that social relations are ultimately unequal relations, and that this makes it imperative to study how these predominantly unequal relations are created, expressed, sustained, challenged, and transformed.

Interactionist perspectives on society tend to avoid debates over the inevitability of social problems, preferring instead to see human social reality as constructed and contested. Society is neither good nor bad; it just is, and it is up to the sociologists to discover how people go about defining situations as a problem. Rather than focusing on objective conditions as the source of problems, the emphasis is on people's perceptions, definitions, and reactions to these conditions. For interactionists, especially symbolic interactionists, there is no such thing as external human reality (or conditions) that are independent of human experience or logically prior to everyday existence. Social reality is a human accomplishment, constructed by human actors who symbolically define conditions, assign meanings, and act accordingly. Similarly, social problems are constructed through meaningful interaction, insofar as people define situations as problematic and act upon their decisions in search of a solution. Questions posed by interactionists embrace an interactional and inter-subjective dimension: Why are some conditions rather than others defined as social problems? How are individuals mobilized to resist and challenge these socially defined conditions? In what ways are problems publicized and drawn to the attention of central authorities? To what extent will authorities devote attention or expend resources to ignore, deflect, modify, or respond to the claims-making activities of aggrieved groups? What happens when social problems are perceived to be addressed inadequately? Table 1–2 provides a quick reference.

In short, functionalists tend to define society as fundamentally good. Anything that challenges this goodness is seen as a social problem. Solutions are proposed that restore order by eliminating the source of disruption. For conflict theorists, society is "compromised" because of pervasive differences in power, wealth, and privilege. Whatever contributes to this inequality is perceived as a social problem. Only major transformation of societal structures can possibly qualify as solutions. For interactionists, society just is. It constitutes a socially constructed human accomplishment. As a result, social problems are whatever the interactants define as social problems. Solutions, in turn, come about when people and authorities decide to do something about a perceived problem. Finally, both functionalist and conflict theorists posit social structures as external realities that have a powerful effect on

TABLE 1–2	Sociological Perspectives: Society and Social Problems		
	Functionalism	**Conflict**	**Interactionism**
Nature of society	Society = an integrated whole with parts that contribute to stability, coherence, and order	Society = a complex and unstable site of inequality and competition	Society = an active and ongoing human accomplishment through meaningful interaction
Normal state of society	equilibrium, consensus	confrontation, contradiction, change	dynamic, emergent, evolving
Source of social problems	disruptions to stability and order through faulty socialization, urbanism, social change	class exploitation and domination	through the social construction of reality
Nature of the social problem	normlessness, competing value systems, violation of norms	inequality alienation oppression unhealthy competition	as per definition of the situation
Solutions to social problems	restore order by removing disruption	transform values, structures, institutions of society	mobilization of people into claims-making groups; political reaction via policy/programs

defining conditions as problems, with corresponding solutions. For interactionists, people define and react to structures and conditions that are subjectively defined and constructed as though they were social problems.

SOLVING SOCIAL PROBLEMS

> The chief cause of problems are solutions.
>
> — Eric Severeid

Sociology as a discipline originated around a commitment to explore the nature and causes of social problems in rapidly changing societies. Exploring solutions to these problems remains an important component of the sociology of social problems. Yet the link between problems and solutions is extremely tenuous. Over time, solutions have been designed to address problems as they were defined and understood at the time. As the problem definition changed, so too did the proposed solutions, at least in theory, if not always in practice (Walker, 1999). For too long, people have been asking the wrong questions, and finding inappropriate answers, suggesting that if we don't have the answers ("solutions"), perhaps we've been asking the wrong questions all along. Moreover, with growing awareness of the complexity of social problems, the possibility of solutions has grown increasingly remote. In many cases, just recognizing a problem as a social problem is a major step toward solution. Not surprisingly, the optimism associated with sociology's ameliorist tradition has gradually diminished. The contemporary sociology of social problems has tended to be characterized instead by an "almost paralyzing pessimism" (Scarpitti and Cylke Jr., 1995:x). Sadly, perhaps, this pessimism about solving social problems is well-founded, given the growing proliferation of problems in search of solutions.

Defining a social problem is critical in influencing how the issue is to be framed for analysis or solution. The importance of definition is reflected in the abortion debate. Does abortion reflect an objective but problematic condition, despite the fact that it involves terminating a fetal life? (Is it possible to talk about abortion as a social problem without relying on loaded terms that prejudge the issue?) Or do we define abortion as a perceived social problem that is acted upon accordingly by special interest groups? It is interesting that few in this ongoing controversy want to align themselves as either pro-abortion or anti-abortion. Rather, the debate is organized around the conflict between pro-life (those who see abortion as a problem in terminating a human life) versus pro-choice (those who see abortion as an individual's choice of solution to the problem of an unwanted pregnancy). Both sides choose to define the debate in terms that resonate with cultural meaning; for example, is there anyone out there who is not in favour of choosing life? Conversely, most are in favour of protecting an individual's right to choose in a liberal democracy. But in rephrasing their position to reflect a more politically astute reading of the situation, the protagonists tend to talk past one another, thus eliminating any chance of consensus or compromise. Even the fact that both sides are "pro" something rather than "anti" something demonstrates the difficulty of establishing a common frame of reference for debate, much less the basis for a workable compromise.

Solving a social problem is also contingent on who or what is defined as responsible for creating the problem in the first place. Historically, the causes of social problems and the preferred way of explaining them have been conceived of in four ways: blaming the victim; blaming the enemy; blaming the institution; and blaming the system (Elias, 1986).

Blaming the Victim

With "blaming the victim" explanations, those who constitute the problem are seen as responsible for their condition because of attributes that contribute to their marginalization or oppression. For example, the poor are seen as responsible for their poverty because of psychological dispositions, cultural deprivation, faulty socialization, or circumstances of their own making. But as Parenti (1978) shrewdly observed, "blaming the poor for being poor while ignoring the system of power, privilege, and wealth that creates poverty, is a little bit like blaming the corpse for its murder." Solutions to problems that blame the victim are anchored in changing the person rather than in addressing the broader context. It is important to note that this line of thinking has grown in popularity. The Keynesian mentality that for half a century encouraged a government-driven sense of community, caring, and cooperation by way of social spending, has gradually given way to an outlook which sees government spending as the enemy, and poverty as the fault of the poor, and believes that the poor had best look out for themselves (Bruning, 1995).

Blaming the Enemy

This category of explanation attributes culpability to some non-mainstream group. Immigrants, for example, may be perceived as taking jobs from "real" Canadians, thus adding to this country's unemployment woes. By pitting one group of Canadians against another, the demonizing of particular groups as the cause of social problems distracts from the possibility of looking at the broader picture of power, profit, and privilege as a primary source of the problem (Davis, 1998). The scapegoating of certain groups as the cause of Canada's social problems (for example, youth) also simplifies an often complex situation. Solutions to problems created by the enemy are based on transforming or removing the offending group.

Blaming the Institution

Blaming institutions acknowledges that social problems are located in the processes that organize institutional arrangements with respect to access, treatment, rewards, and external relations. Institutions are criticized for discriminatory barriers that either have the intent or the effect of denying, excluding, or exploiting others on the basis of race, ethnicity, gender, class, sexual preference, ability, or age. As we shall see, institutions such as media or policing are often targeted as sites that wilfully or inadvertently deny or exclude both workers and customers who do not fit a mainstream profile (Henry et al., 1999). Solutions to institutional failures range from the minimal, such as improved training or removal of discriminatory barriers, to transformative strategies for removing those systemic structures that favour one group at the expense of others.

Blaming the System

Blaming the system looks at society as the source of social problems. Social problems stem from cultural values and the political ideals of capitalist structures. The problems are often seen as systemic; that is, the rules, roles, and relationships that constitute society are not openly discriminatory or exploitative, but their very arrangement is likely to have that effect on vulnerable groups. For example, in a patriarchal society, sexism and misogyny are perceived as the logical outcome of androcentrism; that is, the idea of interpreting reality from a male point of view as normal and necessary, and assuming that others will or want to do so. Marxists also like to blame the capitalist system as the ultimate cause of oppression or exploitation. In a capitalist system, everything is reduced to a commodity for exchange in the market, including labour power. The underlying motive is to make a profit through the accumulation of private productive property (Teeple, 1994). Solutions to such systemic problems must go beyond the control of problematic populations or modifications to institutional flaws; only comprehensive, structural changes have much chance of success.

The Politics of Solutions

Once a situation has been (mis)diagnosed, a whole slew of solutions may be implemented, many of which have little hope of solving the problem. The following vignettes provide a glimpse into why the proliferation of solutions has done little to diminish the number of social problems. They also provide a rather sad overview of why the relationship between solutions and problems is tenuous at best and contradictory at worst.

Solutions That Backfire

The introduction of even well-intentioned solutions may boomerang because of unforeseen impacts. In surely one of the more counterintuitive examples of solutions that have gone astray, an American study has found that women's shelters tend to save more male lives than female lives (Masters, 1999). How so? A national campaign against domestic violence in the United States since the 1970s has resulted in growing public awareness of the problem, together with a network of legal resources and safe shelters for abused women. A study of 29 cities suggests these initiatives have saved thousands of lives, both male and female.

In 1976, 1357 men and 1437 women nationwide were killed by their partners, according to an analysis of FBI statistics. In 1997, male deaths fell by two-thirds, to 430; yet 1174 women were killed in domestic violence cases. This disparity is puzzling. Perhaps the solution was misplaced, since resources were aimed at getting women to change their behaviour by leaving an abusive relationship before resorting to deadly force to protect themselves. But men, who often kill out of rage or to exert control, may resort to revenge on the assumption that "if I can't have her, no one can." In other words, solutions that encourage women to leave their partners may trigger the very rage in men that culminates in their partners' deaths.

Solutions: A Problem-Generating Machine

Solutions may be introduced that inadvertently create new and largely unanticipated problems. Many would agree that the popularization of relativism has proven one of 20th century's crowning intellectual achievements. With its commitment to the principle that all cultures and practices as equally good and valid expressions of the human condition, progressive thinkers endorsed relativism as a way to secure racial equality by rejecting classic notions of White superiority (D'Souza, 1995). But this solution to an old problem has become the source of a new one. According to Dinesh D'Souza, a commitment to relativism has imprisoned liberals and progressive thinkers by forcing them to condone actions that threaten the normative fabric of society. Such a commitment has also endorsed the position of exonerating victims of any personal responsibility for their plight or misdeeds. Instead of holding individuals personally responsible for actions or inaction, the pendulum has swung to the point where the system is routinely blamed. This shifting of the blame from victim to system also makes it difficult for liberals to support programs for assisting minorities that uphold any standard of personal responsibility, while encouraging minorities to blame every problem on systemic discrimination, White racism, and its institutional legacy.

Consider the inception of employment equity/affirmative action programs. Many Canadians balk at the idea of singling out a category of people for preferential treatment on the basis of supposedly irrelevant characteristics such as gender or race. According to the tenets of a liberal-pluralist society, what we have in common is more important than what separates us; what we do and accomplish as individuals is more important than entitlement because of membership in a group; and the content of each individual's character is more important than the colour of one's skin. True equality arises from treating all people the same regardless of who they are. The prospect of establishing preferences on the basis of race or gender is just as racist as old-fashioned racism, and just as unlikely to create equality. Such an outlook is in contrast to those who argue that differences and disadvantage must be taken into account if true equality is to be achieved. Treating everyone the same in an unequal situation is likely to preserve the prevailing distribution of power, privilege, and resources rather than bringing about substantive equality. Not surprisingly, employment equity programs tend to encounter fierce resistance in liberal-democratic societies such as Canada, since the value of fairness (treating everyone the same) clashes with the value of justice (treating others differently by taking disadvantage into account).

Quick-Fix Solutions/Sure-Fire Problems

Solutions may be proposed that are not really intended to get at the root of the problem. Some, failing to correctly conceptualize the situation (Staggers and Gray, 1998), attribute problems to individuals or cultures, ignoring the social, political, economic, and structural.

Symptoms are addressed, but not root causes. In recent years, injuries and deaths associated with bicycling have come to be defined as a social problem rather than an unavoidable risk. A combination of publicity, petitions, collective protest, and a backbencher's bill in the Ontario Parliament resulted in a water-downed law that made bicycle helmets mandatory for youth under 16 years of age. While there is no doubt that helmets diminish head injuries and loss of life (provided helmets are worn properly), the solution really does very little to address the more fundamental problem: How can cyclists and motorists share the road? By putting the onus on cyclists to change their behaviour, the solution is misplaced. After all, when a cyclist meets two tons of metal, solutions arguably should rest with the more intimidating of the two. Moreover, rather than addressing the problem in structural terms such as road improvements, driver education, and bicycle safety, the solution has created a law-enforcement nightmare for understaffed police departments. Only politicians who have little stomach for a costly and intrusive infringement appear satisfied with the solution. This notion of a technological fix to problems was again put to the test when the government proposed "road" solutions to alleviate the carnage on a 66-km strip of Highway 401 between London and Chatham. To be sure, there is much to commend in the decision to pave the right-hand shoulder, add rumble strips to the shoulder, and cats-eyes to curves. But do these cosmetic reforms begin to get at the underlying triggers behind the carnage, from unsafe trucks to aggressive drivers?

Faulty Definitions: Solutions That Cannot Possibly Work.

It is commonly known that attempted solutions do not solve problems that are improperly defined. Attempts at solution are also known to intensify and aggravate certain conditions, in effect setting in motion a series of actions that may create new problems. The decision by NATO in mid-1999 to bomb Yugoslavia for mistreatment of its minorities in Kosovo is a prime example of an attempted solution that backfired for a variety of reasons. These reasons include an all-too frequent tendency to: (a) rely on quick-fix solutions to complex problems; (b) think that the use of force will intimidate people into submission or retreat; and (c) think that solutions that worked in one context (the Persian Gulf War) will be equally effective in another. Rather than solving the problem, the bombing solution appeared to strengthen Serbian resolve to exercise their sovereignty, to consolidate the grip of Yugoslavian leaders, and to silence any opposition to the forcible removal of Kosovars. Moreover, the decision of Canada to participate in the NATO bombing may have the effect of discrediting Canada's reputation in brokering future compromises to messy international entanglements. Similarly, consider the case of zero tolerance towards violence in schools. Punishing and expelling children and adolescent troublemakers from schools may provide a short-term solution. But the long-term effects of such a punitive approach can be extremely deadly, as demonstrated by the recent spate of high school shootings, since marginalizing youth by expelling them can breed violence (Crane, 1999). The onus is on schools to create a place for all youth in the system, at a time of dwindling resources and overworked teachers.

Solutions That Misread the Problem

Too much of what passes for solutions is not really intended to solve anything, except to convey the impression that something is being done about the problem. The point of the solution is to appease the public or interests, rather than to initiate progressive change. Racism and racial discrimination are widely defined as social problems. To eliminate racism and remove discriminatory barriers, anti-racist measures have been implemented at individual and institutional levels, with little appreciable effect, judging by the tenacity of racism and discrimination in Canada (Satzewich, 1998; Henry et al., 1999). Can we attribute this failure to flaws in the anti-racism program? Or should we consider the possibility that not all Canadians regard racism and discrimination as a problem, despite lip service to the contrary? For many White Canadians, racism may be a regrettable but necessary means of preserving power and privilege in society. A dislike of others may also be critical in fostering an identity on the basis of attributes that distinguish Whites from non-Whites. In other words, anti-racist solutions can only begin to be effective when people are convinced that racism is a serious problem and worthy of sustained efforts at eradication. Moreover, anti-racist solutions will continue to be simply lip service so long as the structural basis of a profit-driven system is left unchallenged. Finally, it must be acknowledged that the face of racism continues to express itself in different ways, making it extremely difficult to find a solution to a problem that masks itself in various ways.

Solutions for Some/Problems for Others

Certain solutions are destined for failure because irreconcilable differences complicate the possibility of compromise. Consider the recent onset of whale-hunting among some aboriginal nations along the Pacific coast (Martiniuk, 1999). The confict of interest between animal rights activists and aboriginal peoples is one that may be impossible to resolve. At the core of this conflict are competing values over the hunting of whales and other endangered species. For animal rights activists, animals have rights, and it is immoral to use or exploit them as a means to an end except to hunt for subsistence or survival. Aboriginal peoples contend that animals rights discourses are inapplicable to them. Aboriginal peoples are fundamentally autonomous political communities with an inherent right to indigenous models of self-determination over jurisdictions pertaining to land, identity, and political voice as a basis for engagement or entitlement. Whale-hunting is endorsed as a traditional cultural practice that needs to be resuscitated in order to regain threatened aboriginal identities. Besides, aboriginal leaders argue, hunting whales is an aboriginal right reaffirmed in treaties, and outsiders have no right to dictate what aboriginal peoples can or cannot do. A similar conflict of interest is revealed in the recent decision by the Supreme Court of Canada to allow aboriginal peoples in Atlantic Canada to fish and hunt without a license all year round for subsistence or moderate livelihood. For some, this right will consolidate aboriginal rights in Canada; for others, aboriginal peoples now have another advantage and a right over and above those of other Canadians. Finally, passage of Canada's Species at Risk Act is condemned by aboriginal groups as a barrier to local economic development and an infringement of aboriginal sovereignty rights.

Solutions in Search of a Problem

Common sense dictates that solutions are more effective when the problem is properly defined. Yet situations arise in which the problem is deliberately distorted by vested interests, in hopes of eliciting a solution that caters to hidden agendas. There are mounting concerns that Canadian professionals are flocking to the United States. Various reasons are cited, including the lure of booming opportunities; higher salaries and standards of living (at $36 634 income per person in 1997, American salaries are 30 percent higher); leading edge technology;

generous research venues; and lower taxes. For example, a Canadian will pay 35.8 percent of his/her $100 000 (Canadian) income on taxes, while an American earning $100 000 (US) pays only 30.1 percent tax. At $250 000 (Canadian), a Canadian is taxed at 41.2 percent; by contrast, an American pays only 29.7 percent on $250 000 income (McCarthy, 1999). With such favourable tax breaks, about 98 000 Canadians are thought to have emigrated to the United States in 1997, up from 16 000 in 1986, according to the business-supported Conference Board of Canada (cited in the *Globe and Mail*, 17 Aug, 1999:B-3). This depletion of Canada's skilled labour pool (from physicians and nurses to computer analysts and engineers) can only erode Canada's quality of life. This exodus of experts and expertise constitutes a waste in terms of potential productivity, Tom Ford concludes, as well as a waste in educational investment. Still, the figures are somewhat misleading. Most Canadians leave on temporary work permits. By contrast, the annual figure for permanent departures has remained about the same since 1986, with the result that about 9770 Canadians emigrated permanently to the U.S. in 1996, while 3835 Americans came to Canada. A sense of perspective would be useful. According to Statistics Canada (cited in David Crane), Canada is attracting more skilled people than it's losing. For example, between 1990 and 1996, the average annual outflow of Canadian university graduates was 8512, a minuscule proportion of managerial and professional workers, while the average annual inflow from the United States and abroad was 32 829, for an average net annual gain of 24 317. Could the call for lower taxes to curb this southerly brain drain reflect the interests of the freewheeling market sector?

Solutions Stuck in a Time Warp

Solutions are designed to solve problems as the problems are defined and understood at a particular point in time. Ideally, as the definition of the problem changes, so too will the corresponding solutions. Yet solutions are known to outlive their usefulness and need to be reassessed in light of evolving circumstances. This is not the case, however. Solutions are known to persist over time even if they are increasingly incommensurate with the reality of the situation. Consider, for example, Canada's federalist system as a 19th century Victorian solution to problems that Canadians confronted when society was agriculture-based and unitary. The jury is out as to whether the federalist system remains a viable means of organizing a society in the 21st century. Many believe this political framework is inappropriate. English-speaking Canadians remain convinced that this system is still the best for the world's third-oldest federal system.

Problems That Are Better Left Unsolved

Is it possible that some social problems are better left unresolved? Take the case of Quebec and the question of national unity. It has always been assumed that there is a problem here, and that rational efforts must be directed to fixing Quebec's threat to separate. However, as suggested by David Cameron, a University of Toronto political scientist, it is also possible that this problem cannot be fixed, despite costly and sometimes risky ventures to do so, and that Quebec will not separate (Gwyn, June 10, 1998). Rather than a problem to be solved, according to Cameron, the relationship between Quebec and Canada is "a tension to be accommodated, an arrangement to be lived with, a practical situation which is not perfect but eminently tolerable." Moreover, Cameron observes, efforts to solve the national unity problem over the past thirty years may well have kept the problem in the foreground. In other words, perhaps doing nothing is more likely to solve the problem by taking pressure off finding a solution to a solutionless dilemma.

Problems That Have No Solution

The idea that some problems cannot be solved to everyone's satisfaction in a liberal-democratic society is off-putting to those who believe that all problems can be solved given sufficient data, resources, and resourcefulness. Yet not every social problem can be solved. In cases where problems are part of a society's structure, history, and identity, solutions may have the opposite effect of producing new and more damaging imbalances. For example, crime is usually perceived as a social problem; the criminal justice system is endorsed as one solution to this problem. Will prisons ever solve the problem of crime? Will more police? Harsher sentences? It is hard to imagine a society that could eliminate all crime without trampling on basic democratic and human rights principles. A certain degree of criminal activity is inevitable given the imbalances of power, privilege, and profit in contemporary society. In a competitive society in which demand is meant to exceed supply, the gap between expectations and achievements encourages people to rely on shortcuts to achieve the culturally prescribed "good life." Mix in youthful defiance and rebelliousness toward authority, convention, and tradition, and the prospect of a crime-free society begins to fade. Or consider how one driver in Ontario was nabbed five times in four days for moving traffic violations, despite police crackdowns and massive publicity in the aftermath of the eight-death pile-up outside of Windsor. To be sure, this notion of unsolvable problems runs counter to the world view of Canadian and American society, with its belief that everything is solvable through know-how, commitment, and technology. Time will tell whether Canadians can acquire the degree of ambiguity and uncertainty needed to put things in perspective.

What can we infer from this discussion on the politics of solution? First, quick-fix solutions tend to ignore the complexity of problems, both in terms of history and culture. Second, solutions tend to emphasize either agency (blaming individuals for misfortune by focusing on immediate causes and ignoring structures) or structure (blaming the system and absolving individuals of responsibility for actions and reforms), thus failing to acknowledge the interplay between agency and structure in creating problems and proposing solutions. Third, many solutions fail to take into account how problems in one area are related to other problem areas, with the result that most solutions are at best piecemeal or at worst trigger unintended repercussions. Elements exist only in relation to others, with the result that changes in one area may ripple out to others because of this interconnection. The complexity of these interrelations makes it difficult to predict events or control outcomes (Jackson, 1992). Fourth, solutions may be implemented for the best of intentions, but may trigger unintended effects that either intensify the original condition or create a host of new problems. Fifth, a "one-size-fits-all" mentality to problem solving may be inappropriate in a changing and diverse world; and sixth, solutions to problems may never get going because the problem is inappropriately defined. Or the solutions may never get off the starting block, given a lack of consensus regarding how to approach the problem, or the absence of the political will to implement any reforms except, perhaps, as exercises in public relations.

SOCIAL INEQUALITY

FRAMING THE PROBLEM

Canadians possess a reputation at home and abroad as a "kind and compassionate" people. Rather than jarring extremes of conspicuous wealth and abject poverty, such as in the United States where some are prospering while others work more and get paid less, Canada is perceived as a remarkably egalitarian society, with only moderate differences in wealth, status, or power. Canada cherishes its image as an egalitarian and largely middle-class society that is intolerant of extremes in poverty or wealth. This portrayal of Canada is arguably true in a relative sense, given the magnitude of inequities and racial oppression elsewhere. Canada indeed represents a remarkably open and pluralist society with a powerful commitment to equality before the law, regardless of a person's background or beliefs. In theory, all parts of Canada's much ballyhooed national "mosaic" are envisaged as contributing equally to the whole. Each of these diverse components is also viewed as deserving of a fair share of the entitlements of wealth or power. Enlightened government intervention has ensured that few Canadians are denied the basic physical necessities of food, clothing, and shelter, even though a few may lack some of the creature comforts that others take for granted. Even Canadian seniors are healthier, wealthier, and living longer, according to the Statistics Canada report, *A Portrait of Seniors in Canada* (cited in Carey, 1999), with incomes rising 18 percent over 17 years to $20 451, largely because of improvements in pension plans (especially for women) and Old Age Security payments. Evidence of Canada's seemingly enviable status is bolstered by UN quality of life surveys that consistently rank Canada near the top of the global heap. In 1999 Canada was again declared the best country in the world to live in for the sixth consecutive year, according to UN development panel, with the highest standard of living in terms of income, education, and life expectancy. Such an exalted status complicates the challenge of discussing inequality as a social problem in Canada.

However, not everyone is convinced by this benign portrayal of Canada. On closer inspection, Canada's reputation as egalitarian and tolerant is tarnished by gaping levels of inequality that expose glaring inequities between the "haves" and "the have-nots." Economic gaps have broadened in recent years, with the result that Canadian society partitions into three layers. One is growing more prosperous and powerful, the second is being squeezed by stagnant incomes, and the third appears to be drifting into increased poverty and powerlessness (see also Fischer et al., 1998). Women and men who stray outside the script for success routinely experience prejudice and discrimination by way of economic dislocation, powerlessness, inadequate levels of service delivery, and threats to a cherished identity. Employment equity initiatives notwithstanding, women in full-time employment—with the possible exception of single, university-educated women—continue to earn less than men. The presence of women in the workplace is now routinely accepted, although this was not the case in the past. Nevertheless, most women continue to bump into glass ceilings when scaling the corporate ladder of success. With respect to minority women and men, income and opportunity inequalities have reflected, reinforced, and reformulated the pattern of inequalities initially exposed by the eminent Canadian scholar John Porter in his groundbreaking book, *The Vertical Mosaic* (1965). The introduction of official multiculturalism and employment equity initiatives have not appreciably altered this arrangement. Indeed, some measures have had the perverse effect of perpetuating inequality, especially since short-term gains from social assistance may induce long-term dependencies. Racial, aboriginal, and ethno-cultural groups continue to be sorted out unequally against a "mosaic" of raised (dominant) and lowered (subordinate) tiles (Tepper, 1988). Pyramids of privilege exist that elevate Whites, males, the middle-class, middle-aged, and the able-bodied to the top of scale (Pendakur and Pendakur, 1995). People of colour, such as African-Canadians and Chinese-Canadians, earn considerably less than the mainstream average, and this applies equally to women and men. The fact that aboriginal incomes hover well below half of the national average, with a standard of living comparable to that of many developing world countries, is surely a scathing indictment of Canada's priorities and self-delusions (Royal Commission, 1996). Insofar as those of Northern European origin seem to have more options and opportunities, as reflected by their control of the economy, the vertical mosaic appears firmly entrenched in Canadian society.

In short, all the deeply ingrained myths in the country cannot disguise the fact that Canada remains a stratified society where people are denied, excluded, or exploited—often through little fault of their own. Socially defined yet devalued differences in background or skin colour continue to make a difference and do so in persistent and predictable ways. Patterns of inequality are neither temporary nor randomly distributed across society. To the contrary, these patterns tend to coalesce around the poles of race, ethnicity, gender, class, and region. Those on the bottom layer are more likely to suffer from poor health or to be denied access to proper medical attention; to endure lower educational levels and revolving cycles of poverty; to reside in substandard housing; to relinquish prospects for career advancement; and to be punished more harshly by the justice system. Neither public ignorance nor political excuses can diminish the reality or magnitude of social inequality in Canada. Yet most Canadians are only superficially acquainted with these gaping realities, despite constant reminders that not all is well in our "kinder, gentler, society," even in comparison with the ruthless competitiveness of the United States. Inequality is not only about economic privilege or material distribution between different categories of people (Grabb, 1999). Peoples' lives are affected by economic insecurity; so too is their state of emotional and physical health, a personal sense of well-being and involvement, and their relationship to others and society at large (Kendall et al., 1999). The life chances of many Canadians are adversely affected by the centralization of power and resources in the hands of a power elite, many of whom benefit from the very dynamics that relegate others to the margins (Clement,1998; Curtis et al., 1999). Wealth begets wealth in a spiralling process that consolidates the privileges of the few at the expense of the masses. But a society that condones instant millionaires, yet tolerates grinding poverty, at some point must confront its contradictions and inconsistencies. How do we reconcile the seemingly inflated salaries of pampered sports stars and CEOs with the fact that hundreds of thousands of Canada's children live in poverty? What will happen to Canada's social fabric and social cohesion if inequities further polarize those at the top from those at the bottom (Crane, 1999)? Can we deplore the poverty on many aboriginal reserves in Canada, then turn around and condemn other countries for violation of human rights?

Put candidly, Canada is a land of contradiction. It may be one of the luckiest countries in the world, yet it is hardly immune to the harsh realities of inequality in a society that overvalues the affluent few while undervaluing the marginal many (Frizzell and Pammett,1996). At local levels, even Canadians who consciously oppose inequality are known to replicate inequities in everyday encounters (Henry et al., 1999); at national and international levels, inequities are exacerbated by recourse to market principles and a reliance on wealth as a barometer of success. The emergence of a capitalist global economy has sharpened disparities between those at the top of the hierarchy and those at its bottom (including the aged, the young, single parents, and minorities), many of whom are losing out because of an inability to take advantage of new opportunities. While a few have prospered, many have suffered from the deficit-cutting obsession of many governments, together with the punishing cost-cutting measures of the corporate-driven global economy. Consider the paradox of corporate executives who receive preposterous raises compared with increasingly beleaguered workers who must confront wage freezes and pink slips (Report, "The Growing Gap," cited by Philp, 1998). Although the economy has recovered robustly from the recession of the early 1990s, average family after-tax incomes have yet to reach the peak of $48 300 in 1989, and continue to stagnate into the 21st century, according to a new study for the Vanier Institute for the Family (cited in Carey, 2000). Inequality in Canada is not simply the result of market imperfections amenable to resolution through cosmetic reform. Individuals are not necessarily at fault, nor are they the architects of their misfortune, for which they alone must accept blame. Nor can the problem be attributed entirely to earlier solutions that either addressed the wrong issue or incorrectly assessed the situation. Inequities in wealth and power appear to be chronic and persistent over time, firmly embedded within the structures of a capitalist society, and resistant to even carefully considered solutions. To be sure, few would go so far as to downgrade Canada to the level of an entrenched oligarchy or a rigid caste-like system. Nevertheless, inequality is deeply entrenched in Canada, and its pervasiveness and persistence in a land of plenty is unconscionable. Paradoxically, however, the ideal of equality is also elusive in both principle and practice. And it is precisely this enigma between the ideals of equality and the reality of inequality that prods sociologists into delving more deeply into this most baffling of social problems.

This chapter addresses the concept of inequality as an evolving yet contested social problem in Canada. Attention is devoted to the social dimensions of inequality with respect to causes, cures, characteristics, and consequences to society. Particular attention is focused on the process by which patterns of inequality are created and maintained by human agency, in addition to being challenged and transformed by way of collective movements and government policy. Likewise, interest is directed at patterns of stratification because of race, class, gender, ethnicity, and location, each of which may be analyzed separately even though inextricably linked to overlapping and intersecting patterns of inequality. Proposed solutions to the inequality problem are shown to vary with differing notions of equality. The chapter revolves around four key premises: (1) patterns of inequality are socially constructed rather than anything inherent or inevitable in society; (2) inequality is amenable to sociological analysis when reflected in measurable rates that persist over time; (3) patterns of inequality are not random, but tend to cluster around the correlates of race, ethnicity, gender, class, and location; and (4) equality is preferable and attainable even if few can concur on "means" or "outcomes." It is predicated on the notion that unequal relations are best understood in terms of social power, as sites of domination and subordination that are not static, but contested, and that attempts by vested interests to "naturalize" these inequities as normal or commonsense are resisted by subordinate classes who offer interpretations that reflect their own interests (Storey, 1996). In rejecting any notion of "naturalness" or "normality," inequality is shown to be the result of public policies, social structure, and human behaviour, rather than of culture, psychology, or human nature. It is in the self-interest of all Canadians to ensure that inequality is reduced to the point where everyone shares in the social and economic largesse that Canada has to offer. Failure to do so will sharpen the likelihood of conflict between the haves and the have-nots, to the detriment of all Canadians. It may also erode the carefully constructed reputation of Canada as one of the world's least imperfect places to live.

DEFINING INEQUALITY

What exactly is meant by inequality? Defining a problem is more than an analytical exercise. Definitions are critical in shaping responses; after all, people are known to act on the basis of how a problem is defined, how public issues are framed, and how solutions are identified (Spector and Kitsuse, 1979). In general, inequality is about entitlements: that is, who gets what, how, and why? It reflects a condition and a process in which preferential access to the good things in life is not randomly distributed, but patterned around those human differences that are defined as socially significant for purposes of entitlement (Grabb, 1999). Debates over social inequality are largely questions about human differences that have consequences, especially those that become a structured and recurrent feature of society. For various reasons related to race, class, sexuality, or gender, certain individuals are ranked lower than others in terms of wealth, power, and status. Other individuals, by virtue of their skills, expertise, or inheritance, are thought of as deserving more rather than less. These inequities are socially constructed insofar as there is nothing natural or normal about them—despite concerted efforts by vested interests to make them appear so—but reflect conventions by individuals who make choices in social contexts. These inequities are also socially constructed in the sense that access to social rewards is patterned and reflects the recurrent ways in which people interact with one another. Those who are advantaged because of birth or achievement tend to be rewarded in a cyclical process that "structures and reproduces" the pattern of inequality in time and space (Grab, 1993, xi).

Defining social inequality as a social problem encompasses three dimensions: objective conditions, ideological supports, and social reforms (Curtis et al., 1993). First, an emphasis on the objective conditions invariably leads to questions about the scope of inequality in society, its manifestations, and the reasons behind its existence. Stratification is but one manifestation of inequality that is virtually universal and widely acknowledged. Social scientists have argued that perfect equality is a contradiction in terms. No human society is "equal" in the sense that everyone has identical access to valued resources. Certain individuals dominate by virtue of achieved skills or ascribed status; by contrast, others are dominated because of who they aren't and what they don't do. Both simple and complex societies are stratified by the universals of age or gender; however, only agricultural-industrial societies can tolerate extremes of structured inequality in which individuals and groups are ranked in different layers according to occupation, income, wealth, class, and race or ethnicity. In acknowledging that all human societies are unequal and stratified to some extent, stratification can be conceptualized in two ways. It can refer to the unequal allocation of scarce resources among different groups or households; it can refer also to the unequal distribution of people in relation to scarce resources such as income or educational levels. This division of society into unequal horizontal layers is known as strata (Lundy and Warme, 1990). A society is said to be stratified when a category of individuals who differ because of their race, ethnicity, gender, class, or location is ranked along a hierarchy of ascending and descending order with respect to varying amounts of power, privilege, and wealth (Barrett, 1994). Each category of individuals occupies a similar status (position) within this stratum, based on shared characteristics. The combination of these hierarchically ranked strata constitutes the pattern of inequality in society (Boughey, 1978). Power is critical in securing inequality, power being the ability to command resources for controlling situations and shaping outcomes. Power as a relational dynamic and set of hierarchical relations is not simply an abstract force, but human accomplishment, situated in and subjected to negotiation in everyday interaction, and instrumental to the construction of social reality (Prus, 1998).

Second, attention to ideological supports focuses on the ideas that justify and prop up the realities of inequality, regardless of how it is measured or conceived. The expression of ideology in formal laws, public policies, and dominant values secures the justification for objective patterns of inequality (Curtis et al., 1999). A host of self-serving clichés continue to distort people's perception of inequality, thus camouflaging its most pernicious effects, with the most common being:

- Canada is a classless society with everyone bunched into the middle.
- Hard work will produce success.
- People who are poor or unsuccessful have only themselves to blame.
- Individuals are judged and rewarded on the basis of merit only.
- As a land of equal opportunity, Canada is an open and socially mobile society.
- Inequality is natural and normal, and there isn't much we can—or should—do about it.

Third, social reforms consist of both formal and informal strategies for challenging inequality, including state-inspired policies such as employment equity. Also evident is the proliferation of organized resistance and protest groups among the historically disadvantaged—women, racial minorities, homosexuals, people with disabilities, and the poor and the homeless.

CAUSES OF INEQUALITY

That inequality exists is an established fact of life. Inequities reflect patterns of social stratification by which society is divided into unequal "strata" along the lines of class, race and ethnicity, gender, age, sexual orientation, or disability (Gillespie, 1996). Less well established are the reasons behind its origins and persistence. What causes inequality? Should blame be pinned on individuals or on the institutional structures of the system at large? Should persons be held responsible for their predicament or are they victims of forces beyond their control? Do we look to genes or developmental schedules as probable causes or to the social and the cultural? Numerous answers exist, yet most responses can be sorted into four explanatory streams: biological, psychological, cultural, and social/structural.

Biology

Some prefer to blame individual poverty on inherited genetic characteristics. Those who subscribe to the theory of biological determinism portray certain racial and ethnic minorities as genetically and intellectually inferior. By invoking evolutionary principles, it is argued that certain individuals are better suited for success than others in the competitive struggle for survival (Herrnstein and Murray, 1994). Individuals of "superior stock" will prevail and succeed, in keeping with the Darwinian doctrine of "survival of the fittest." Conversely, those without the "right stuff" will be banished to the edges. In his most provocative work, *Race, Evolution, and Behavior: A Life History Perspective* (New York: Transaction, 1994), Philippe Rushton of the University of Western Ontario posits a theory of evolution to account for racial differences across a broad spectrum of physical, social, mental, and moral domains. Rushton argues that separate races, namely "Oriental," "Caucasoid," and "Negroid" (Rushton's terminology), evolved distinctive packages of physical, social, and mental characteristics because of different reproductive strategies in diverse environments. A racial pecking order can be observed, according to Professor Rushton, because of this evolutionary adaptation. "Orientals" are superior to "Caucasoids" on a range of sociobiological factors, who in turn are superior to "Negroids" on the grounds of measurements involving skull size, intelligence, strength of sex drive and genital size, industriousness, sociability, and rule following. "Orientals" as a group have proven more intelligent, more family-focused, more law-abiding, but less sexually promiscuous than "Negroids." "Caucasoids" happily occupy the terrain in between these extremes. Although a theory of genetic inferiority appeals to some people because of simplicity and self-interest, there is little scientific evidence to support these racist explanations.

Psychology

Others believe that the origin of inequality rests with the psychological attributes people acquire as they mature. For various reasons, some individuals do not develop normally, but internalize a host of attitudes contrary to commonly accepted definitions of success. This line of thinking holds that victims of poverty and discrimination are responsible for their plight. Under a victim-blame approach, victims are blamed for their predicament because of poor "moral fibre," or personality flaws for which they alone are responsible. The proposed solution is consistent with this assessment: With hard work and application to the task at hand, anyone can succeed in a society organized around the virtues of merit, equal opportunity, and open competition. Alternatively, inequality arises because of prejudice towards "others," once again demonstrating the relevance of psychological attitudes in fostering inequality.

Culture

Another perspective focuses on the primacy of culture (and socialization to a lesser extent) as an explanatory variable. Inequalities continue to arise and are resistant to solutions because the cultural lifestyles of the poor and marginal are self-perpetuating. Oscar Lewis' (1964) work on the culture of poverty is an example of this school of thought. For Lewis, living in poverty creates a cultural response to marginal conditions. This response is characterized by low levels of organization, resentment towards authority, hostility to mainstream institutions, and feelings of hopelessness and despair. Once immersed in this culture, a self-fulfilling prophecy is set in motion (a belief leads to behaviour that confirms the original belief), which futher amplifies those very behaviours and beliefs that inhibit mobility and advancement. To be sure, the emphasis on kinship, sharing, and generosity that one finds in families of the poor or the different may be commendable; nevertheless, such lifestyles may be an anachronism, at odds with a competitive and consumerist present, and contrary to the blueprint for success in the future. The interplay of welfare dependency with female-headed households and lack of ambition and resourcefulness reinforces the perpetuation of poverty from generation to generation.

Not everyone concedes the validity of a cultural interpretation. Recourse to culture as an explanation is perceived as yet another version of the victim-blame approach (Eitzen and Zinn, 1992). Social problems are "individualized" by locating their causes within the culture of the victims themselves (Satzewich, 1991). Ignored in this type of explanation is the external environment, with its structural constraints and social barriers. Even the very status of a culture of poverty is challenged. What passes for a "poverty culture" may be less a coherent lifestyle in the anthropological sense than a strategic response to destitute conditions (Bolaria, 1991). Nor is cultural deprivation per se the problem. Cultures themselves are not inferior or deprived in the absolute sense of the word; more accurately, certain cultures are defined as inferior or irrelevant by the powerful, and are deemed unworthy of equitable treatment.

Social/Structural

There is yet another set of explanations at our disposal. For many sociologists, inequality is not necessarily the fault of individuals, much less the result of cultural deprivation. Rather, the inequities of power, wealth, and status are embedded in the structures of society itself (Agocs and Boyd, 1993). Social structures refer to those aspects of society that involve a discernible and patterned set of relations. These regularities are seen as structures in themselves or reflect manifestations of deeper structures that produce or regulate behaviour (Gillespie, 1996). Structures may include the following: institutional arrangements, economic opportunities, class entitlements, racist/sexist ideologies, discriminatory practices, core cultural values, and imperatives of the prevailing economic system. Their expression in roles, institutions, classes, and regions provides social structures with the power to shape people's lives and life chances. Inequality and barriers to advancement are contingent on structural constraints, many of which are largely systemic and reflective of a job market constructed around "male stream" interests. As a case in point, studies have shown that educational credentials and hard work are not always the best predictors of employment success. Structures such as parental class may be just as important as individual initiative in making a difference (Groves et al., 1996). In other words, the explanations of inequality are anchored in underlying, or root causes, rather than in precipitating or immediate factors. Inequality, then, is framed within the context of structure or system, not individual differences or defective genes.

Structural explanations of inequality often include the broader contexts of domination, exploitation, and exclusion. In the opinion of conflict sociologists, for instance, the root cause of all social problems is the capitalist commitment to the systematic pursuit of profit (Bolaria,

1991). In capitalist societies such as Canada, the ownership of property and the right of dispossession over economic processes in general are possibly the key defining criteria in sorting out patterns of material inequality. A capitalist system by its nature is riddled with social contradictions and conflict. The owners of the means of production (the ruling class) are constantly on guard to reduce labour costs and protect private property. Predictably, the working class is locked in a struggle to contest this inequity and to carve up wealth more equitably. The clash of these competing interests can only encourage intergroup conflicts over scarce resources. Under capitalism, moreover, repressive structures may include those cultural practices that seek domination and control over individuals on the basis of race (racism) and gender (sexism). In contrast to neoconservatives who put their trust in an open economy, the unfettered market is dismissed as a solution to the problem of inequality. It is identified instead as contributing to inequality through such entrenched barriers as segmented labour fields, racial division of labour, dual labour markets, and systemic structures of discrimination.

Tapping into the Roots of Inequality

How can the merits of the respective approaches be analyzed and assessed? Do biopsychological explanations meet the test, or should sociological validity entail only social and cultural explanations? Sociologists tend to have difficulty condoning biologically based arguments, in part because of a reluctance to accept reductionist explanations of social differences and human similarities; in part because most sociologists are unqualified to judge the quality of research in this area. Nor is there much enthusiasm for individualistic explanations that magnify a person's predicament as personal responsibility. According to most sociologists, people are deprived because of their social circumstances rather than depraved because of their moral blemishes. There is much to commend in the work of Durkheim, who said a century ago that only a social fact can explain another social fact. Similarly, social problems are best explained by structural factors. It is not that individuals as social actors are irrelevant for understanding social problems; on the contrary, individual people are ultimately responsible for their actions. But, human behaviour does not evolve in a vacuum. It is embedded within specific social contexts that are limiting and constraining without being coercive or deterministic. Individuals are free to choose, yet must make selections on the basis of culturally prescribed options. The institutional structures surrounding individual people are powerful forces that can play havoc by opening or closing the doors of opportunity and achievement. For these reasons, most sociologists prefer to couch human behaviour in social terms and to look for causal explanations within a social framework. Such an interactive approach recognizes the constraining influence of social structure without necessarily denying individual agency.

EXPLAINING INEQUALITY

> Man is born free, and he is everywhere in chains.
>
> — Jean-Jacques Rousseau.

In a prophetic way, this eighteenth century indictment of society strikes at the core of sociology as a discipline (Himmelfarb and Richardson, 1991). Despite its glaring lack of gender inclusiveness, Rousseau's assessment captures the ambiguity inherent in society as a moral community. For Rousseau, society had betrayed "man's" natural liberty, equality, and "fraternity." The forces of domination and exploitation had subverted "his" innate goodness by transforming "him" into something sordid and squalid. The legacy of Rousseau continues to persist in Marxist interpretations of inequality as a departure from human "nature." Not everyone concurred with Rousseau's observations. The English philosopher, Thomas Hobbes, concluded that social restrictions were unfortunate but necessary in neutralizing our acquisitive and destructive impulses. Society represented a collective agreement (social contract) to protect individuals from the predations of others. Unfettered individualism had to be sacrificed for the safety and survival of the collective whole. This society-as-prior line of thinking eventually culminated in a functionalist perspective. For functionalists, society is most productive when it exists in a state of equilibrium and harmony, with parts both interrelated and collectively contributing to consensus and regulation. Inequality was inevitable in forging a workable and productive society.

The significance of this proto-sociological observation should be clear by now. If Rousseau was right, then inequality is an artifice perpetuated by vested interests for self-serving reasons. If the functionalists are correct, then inequality and stratification are integral to society. Any attempt to tamper with these functional imperatives can only hinder productivity or deter progress. These competing views of social inequality furnish the starting point for sociological analysis. Both functionalists and conflict perspectives agree on the universality of inequality, since all but the simplest hunting and gathering societies are stratified according to age, gender, race, religion, and family affiliation. Disagreement, however, arises over the nature of the chains that historically have shackled women and men. For Rousseau and conflict theorists, these bonds enslaved the human species by crushing natural creativity and inherent freedom. For functionalists from Durkheim onwards, these restrictions are necessary and morally defensible in any complex system. By unleashing pent up energy and rewarding skills in short supply, functionalists contend, such inequality was pivotal in generating wealth and spurring evolutionary progress. In this section, we shall emphasize the explanations of two major perspectives—the functionalist and the conflict. Comparing these contrasting points of view furnishes additional insights into inequality as a social problem for some, but not for others.

The Functionalist Approach

Functionalist theories portray society as the metaphorical equivalent of a biological organism. That is, both society and non-human organisms can be interpreted as integrated systems composed of interrelated and interdependent parts, each of which contributes to the "needs" of the organism, even if superficially they do not appear to do so. In the case of society, all of these components (such as institutions, values, and practices) are properly understood in terms of their contributions to survival and stability.

For functionalists, then, inequality is integral to a complex society, and even necessary to maintain a productive and cohesive social order. All societies must devise some method for motivating the best individuals to occupy the most important and difficult positions. A sophisticated division of labour in an urban, post-industrial society demands a high level of skill and training. A hierarchy of rewards entices skilled individuals to compete for positions in short supply. Differences in the rates of reward are thus rationalized as the answer to this societal dilemma. For skilled personnel to occupy key positions, functionalists claim, adequate levels of motivation provide an incentive for recruitment. Failure to do so would dilute the pool of talent, with disastrous consequences for society as a whole. Reward structures under this model are supported by the "law" of supply and demand. Premier hockey players such as Patrick Roy or Eric Lindros are reimbursed more generously than unskilled labourers, not because hockey is more important to society, but because topnotch pucksters—unlike manual labourers—are in short supply compared with the demand. Their value is further enhanced because of a talent to generate more income for team owners—either by putting more spectators in seats or by inflating the figures for advertising revenues. A similar line of reasoning applies between different occupations. Physicians are compensated more for their services than childcare workers even though, arguably, both are crucial to our well-being (Davis and Moore, 1945).

A functionalist perspective interprets inequality as normal and necessary: necessary, because of the need to fill critical positions in society with skilled, but scarce, personnel; normal, because a sorting-out process is inevitable in a complex division of labour. Inequality is condoned when the rules of the game are applied fairly and according to market principles. In an open and democratic society, people have a "right" to distribute themselves unequally, provided the competition is based on merit and skills rather than irrelevant factors such as race or ethnicity. To be sure, a minimum degree of government intervention may be required to ensure everyone has a "fair go." "Imperfections" in the system, such as unfair trading practices or monopolies, may interfere with the proper functioning of the system, making it incumbent on the government to curb these market impediments. But such intervention should be kept to a minimum in order to maximize free market expression. Excessive interference also runs the risk of fostering dullness and uniformity, while stifling the creativity and initiative necessary for progress and prosperity. That some individuals suffer more than others in an open competition is unfortunate, even regrettable, but necessary as part of the cost of doing business in a free enterprise system.

The Conflict Approach

A radical conflict perspective is opposed to functionalist interpretations of inequality. In contrast with functionalists who see society as fundamentally sound and dismiss as dysfunctional anything that tampers with its coherence and stability, conflict theorists tend to view complex contemporary societies as fundamentally unsound because of their tilt toward the rich and powerful to the detriment of "ordinary" people. Endorsed first by Karl Marx in the nineteenth century, and subsequently reformulated by legions of followers, inequality for radical conflict theorists is embedded in the capitalist emphasis on the rational and systematic pursuit of profit through private property and commodity production. Inequality is generated and sustained by the contradiction of property relations, with those who own productive property on one side, and those who possess only labour power on the other (see Watkins, 1997). In this cutthroat game of winners and losers, individuals are sorted out in a way that polarizes the affluent from the poor. Inequality would seem to be inevitable in this sorting process: According to radical conflict theorists, no capitalist society could expect to flourish without the exploitation of the working classes.

Is capitalism inevitable in complex societies? Are capitalist societies "naturally" inclined towards inequality? To what extent is inequality inherent in human nature, or does it reflect social imperatives relative to a mode of production? The inevitability of inequality—a basic tenet of capitalism and functionalism—is anathema to Marxist conflict theory. Inequality is not inevitable for Marxists because capitalism is not inevitable, despite ongoing efforts by the ruling classes to naturalize free enterprise as normal. Marked inequities occur only in those societies that pit one class against another. For Marx and Engels, primitive societies lived in a "natural" state of equality and cooperation. With few exceptions, formidable economic disparities rarely intruded into primitive cultures, given the absence of material conditions to secure and solidify patterns of stratification. Blatant forms of exploitation could hardly hope to exist in contexts where everyone had relatively equal access to the basic necessities. Such an egalitarian state of affairs will be reinstituted with the end of capitalism and its replacement by a socialist utopia. Marx predicted proletarian control over the instruments of production, thereby putting an end to alienated labour and the inequality it perpetuated. Once the "dictatorship of the proletariat" was established, all stratification and inequality would cease. It must be emphasized, though, that Marx was speaking of the inequality of social classes rather than its expression in race, age, or gender. Needless to say, no society in the industrialized world has established anything remotely resembling a classless utopia. Moreover, so-called "socialist" experiments to date indicate the persistence of inequalities based on gender or race even under carefully controlled conditions (Spiro, 1975). To the dismay of many, these inequities tend to be reconstituted in more subtle ways.

Competing Perspectives

Conflict and functionalist theorists differ in their approach to inequality. Functionalists explain it on the basis of differences between individuals with different skills and abilities. Class position and social mobility, they say, are predominantly related to personal achievement. Conflict theorists analyze inequality by looking at group competition involving power and capital. Conflicts are inevitable as each group struggles to preserve its privilege or rearrange these inequities. For functionalists, society exists as an integrated entity, inasmuch as value consensus binds social actors into a coherent whole. Inequality is healthy in properly functioning and complex societies, especially if it encourages competition and is based on achieved status, although extremes in wealth may imperil long-term stability and survival. Inequality per se is not a problem. Inequality becomes a problem when this inequity is relatively enduring and permanent; based on irrelevant criteria such as skin colour rather than on merit; rooted in the exploitation of others; entrenched in the institutional structures of society; and seemingly impervious to solutions. For conflict theorists, extremes in inequality are not natural or necessary, but relative to a particular type of economy. Massive inequities are endemic and entrenched only in those societies organized around the pillars of private property, class relations, and profit-making. Efforts to justify these gaps as natural and necessary are dismissed as ideological ploys to shore up societal inequities, in part by cushioning the blows of exploitation. Even the ideals of equal opportunity and merit as routes to success are denounced as excuses for perpetuating privilege and inequality. In the final analysis, neither functionalism nor radical conflict theory is more correct. Each appears to be "trapped within the framework of its own truths," in the process casting illumination on different aspects of social inequality.

DIMENSIONS OF INEQUALITY

Imagine a society of perfect equality! Picture a social setting in which individuals are exempt from extremes of privilege, wealth, or power. Scarce resources and unearned privileges would be distributed in relatively equal fashion. From each according to her/his ability, and to each according to her/his need, as Karl Marx once explained. Individuals, of course, would not be clones of one another; rather, differences would be accepted and valued. This egalitarian ethos would apply as well to groups within society. Intergroup conflict would diminish gradually over time with the removal of unnecessary competition and discriminatory barriers.

Does this scenario sound too good to be true? It probably is—at least outside of some utopian fantasy world. There is no historical evidence of a society that maintained perfect equality among its members. Every society is unequal in that all individuals and groups are stratified according to differences in power (privilege), status (prestige), and wealth (resources). Even the simplest hunting and foraging communities exhibit some degree of stratification. A commitment to egalitarian principles may have ensured relatively open access to the basic necessities for individual survival, but it did little to diminish male privilege. Contemporary attempts to create equal societies—such as the kibbutz in Israel or the Hutterite communities in North America—have also fallen short of their utopian ideals, despite being more egalitarian in material terms than surrounding communities. Nor is there any evidence that most of us would want to live in a perfectly equal society. For many, it is not the principle of inequality that rankles or rubs. Rather, objections arise from the magnitude of the extremes between rich and poor, the use of illegal short cuts for attainment of success at all costs, the inability of certain groups to escape the tyranny of perpetual poverty, and the futility of applying seemingly unfair solutions that challenge conventional patterns of inequality.

Different criteria are employed in the placement of individuals along a stratified system. These intersecting lines of stratification combine to establish patterns of inequality that are durable and enduring. Problems arise when this inequality becomes institutionalized (that is, supported by norms about what ought to be), embedded within the structure of society, rendered permanent and persistent, and resistant to solutions. Insofar as unequal access to these scarce resources is not randomly distributed, as far as sociologists are concerned, but tends to cluster around certain groups of people on the basis of achieved and ascribed characteristics, we can talk about dimensions of inequality with respect to: (a) social class, with its basis in material wealth; (b) race (inequality due to visibility); (c) ethnicity (inequality because of culture); (d) gender (inequality based on perceived sex differences); and (e) region (inequality reflecting physical location).

Social Class

Debates over inequality initially revolved around the concept of social class, even though there was little agreement among sociologists as to its nature and characteristics (Gillespie, 1996). Yet there remains a taboo against talking about the concept of class among both politicians and the public. References to class are dismissed as feudalistic remnants, an outdated concept whose only relevance is in relation to countries such as Britain with its inherited aristocracy. The very prospect of distinct social classes is dismissed by many Canadians; even more contested is the notion that classes might have an impact on people's lives and life chances. In contrast to Britain, where class has long served as a social category for assessing social distinctions, positioning people in relation to others, and evaluating the worth of social practices, Canadians tend to reject the notion of Canada as a graded hierarchy of people in classes (see Cannandine, 1998). To be sure, several exceptions to this studied reluctance exist. For instance, class may be understandable when phrased in terms of material rewards that reflect layered rankings of people who are separated by prestigious occupations or high incomes. Class may also make sense when used to indicate lifestyle differences as they relate to wealth or poverty. But for most people the class concept is rarely applied to an economic framework pertaining to ownership and control of productive property (Grab, 1993).

Many sociologists disagree with this dismissal of class or its depoliticization into lifestyle statements (Grab, 1999). They take exception to the notion of individuals as atomistic actors, preferring, instead, to situate people within a broader context in which they share common interests (Cannandine, 1998). Canada can be stratified into classes that are highly complex and internally diverse (Grab, 1999). For structural functionalists such as Talcott Parsons, classes are defined as sets of occupations that share a similar level of prestige because of common value to society. For Marxists, by contrast, classes are inseparable from the ownership of the means of productive property. This class structure tends to constitute three core elements. The first is a group of individuals who own productive property, the second consists of workers who survive through the sale of their labour power, and a third incorporates a residual class of professionals, small business owners, administrators, and wage-earners with some certifiable credentials, training, or skills. Likewise, classes in Canada are real in terms of their impact. They are a key determinant of work, wealth, income, and education; they also "count" as key variables for explaining inequality, whether people are aware or not; and they help shape individual outcomes over a broad range of lifestyle factors. Nevertheless, the field remains hotly debated because of questions that rarely yield agreed-upon answers. For example:

- How many classes are there? One, two, three...nine?
- What criteria should serve as the basis for class divisions?
- Should criteria be based on subjective elements such as self-definition, or should they reflect objective elements such as income?
- Are classes best restricted to economic grounds, or should they take into account productive control over material resources, in addition to political and ideological control?
- Are classes universal or are they intrinsic only to complex, capitalist societies?
- Should classes be thought of as aggregates of individuals (categories) who happen to occupy a similar set of positions in society? Or do we conceive of classes as groups of persons who embrace a common membership with a shared set of interests?

Others have begun to challenge the primacy of class as a key explanatory variable. They argue that rapid changes in society and the class structure have rendered the term almost meaningless as a basis for studying inequality; that divisions based on race or gender are not reducible to class even if closely related; and that the diversity of social experiences cannot be explained by references to foundational concepts such as class (Gillespie, 1996). In a classless society such as the USA, moreover, vast income disparities do not automatically translate into self-conscious classes with corresponding inequalities.

Despite criticism, not all sociologists are willing to jettison class as a key explanatory variable in analyzing inequality. In general, classes are defined as groups of individuals who can be categorized by their relationship to scarce and valued resources such as wealth, power, or status. More specifically, a class can be defined as a category of persons who occupy a similar rank with respect to their standing in the economy. A popular approach is to divide the population into quintiles. Those Canadians who earn more than $40 000, or the top one-fifth of income-earners, have increased their share of Canada's wealth to 47.3 percent in 1996 from 46.4 percent in 1990 (Janigan, 1999). The bottom three-fifths have dropped, while middle-income earners slipped to 15.6 percent from 16 percent, thus eroding the basis of a large and prosperous middle class. Nevertheless, this emphasis on income may be misleading, since the possession of wealth or assets is a more reliable measurement of who gets what (Oliver and Shapiro, 1995). Income refers to a flow of money over time; wealth is a stock of assets owned at a particular time. Income is what people earn from work or receive as government transfers; wealth is what people own (from stocks and bonds to home ownership), and signifies command over financial resources that a household has inherited or accumulated over a lifetime with which to create opportunities, secure a desired status, or pass status on to children. Command over wealth is more encompassing than income in determining access to life chances. For example, most university students living away from home may be income-poor and fall far short of the federally regulated poverty (low income cut-off) line. Nonetheless, they are asset-rich because of the marketability of their pending degree. Focusing on wealth rather than income also casts a new light on inequality and ethnic stratification. Minority women and men may possess approximately similar levels of income compared with the mainstream. Yet many are asset-poor, thus foreclosing equal access to opportunity structures. For example, middle-class American Blacks earn about 70 percent of White middle-class incomes, but only own about 15 percent of the wealth held by middle-class Whites (Oliver and Shapiro, 1995). This lack of wealth undermines the creation of a sound economic foundation to provide stability and security.

To what extent are social classes a problem? For many, the central issue is not the existence of class inequities per se. Problems arise when the gap between rich and poor creates potential for social instability. For example, it is widely acknowledged that the rich are getting richer, the poor poorer. Those who can cope with workplace changes or with the technical skills in global demand are prospering; others are falling behind or falling away. Being rich or poor can also affect who gets what, and why. For example, heart attack victims who live in wealthy Ontario communities have a better chance of living longer than the poor because of access to state-of-the-art health care, according to a recent issue of New England Journal of Medicine (cited in Picard, 1999). Problems may also stem from failure to secure open and equal opportunities for those qualified to move from one class to another. This ability to change one's position in the social hierarchy is called social mobility. Four kinds of social mobility can be discerned. Vertical mobility is movement up or down the social hierarchy, with a subsequent change in wealth, status, or power. Horizontal mobility is lateral movement with no appreciable difference in income or prestige. Intra-generational mobility refers to movements within a person's lifetime; conversely, intergenerational mobility consists of household movement over a period of generations. How much social mobility exists in Canada? Canada is often perceived to be a relatively open society, a perception honed by constant references to Canada as a land of limitless opportunity. But social mobility is not nearly as extensive as was once believed (Hiller, 1990; Goyder, 1990). As might be expected, rates of mobility can increase during periods of economic expansion and technological growth (Tepperman and Rosenberg, 1991). Yet a rags-to-riches type of mobility is rare; nevertheless, the fact that it happens even occasionally seems sufficient to substantiate people's faith in the virtues of an open system (Lundy and Warme, 1990). The reality of social mobility is often overstated. Few societies—Canada included—can afford unrestricted movement up and down the socio-economic ladder without destabilizing the social order. In other words, Canadians live in a society where social mobility is highly valued in principle, if not always implemented in practice.

Race

From afar Canada is seen as a paragon of virtue in the harmonious management of race and ethnic relations. A closer inspection suggests a slightly different picture. The Canada we know is characterized by a high degree of inequality that rewards certain groups and penalizes others because of who they are. Racial and ethnic minorities do not share equally in the creation or distribution of wealth, power, or social status (Breton, 1998). Canada is characterized by layers of inequality between aboriginal, racial, and ethnic groups. Access to the "good things" in life is not distributed evenly or randomly; it is concentrated among certain minority groups who tend to cluster around certain nodes on the socio-economic continuum—reflecting what is known popularly as ethnic or racial stratification. Instead of an equitable arrangement, racial and ethnic groups are sorted out unequally around a "mosaic" of raised (dominant) and lowered (subordinate) tiles (Tepper, 1988). So-called "White" ethnics tend to perform better in terms of income and education than certain visible minorities (Breton et al., 1990; Pendakur and Pendakur, 1995). By contrast, ethnic inequalities stem from the inferior entry status of ethnic groups, combined with the diminishment of status aspirations and achievement motivation because of ethnic affiliation (Porter, 1965; Hou and Balakrishnan, 1996). The fact that many minorities occupy the lower rungs of the socio-economic ladder is not only unfair, but also costly to society as a whole.

Even a cursory inspection of Canada's race relations record is an exercise in inequality (Henry et al., 1999; Stasiulis, 1997). In the past, immigrants were frequently imported as a source of cheap menial labour, either to assist in the process of society-building (for example, Chinese for the construction of the railway) or to provide manual skills in labour-starved industries such as the garment trade (Bolaria and Li, 1988). Once in Canada, many became convenient targets for abuse or exploitation. Immigrants could be fired with impunity, especially during periods of economic stagnation. Promotions, of course, were entirely out of the question. Political or civil rights were routinely trampled on without many channels for redress. Both native-born and foreign-born minorities continue to be shunted into marginal employment ghettos with few possibilities for escape or advancement. A study for the Human Rights Commission indicated that only 4.1 percent of federal public servants in 1995 were visible minorities, compared to 12 percent in the private sector, despite a federally mandated employment equity program since 1986 (Foster, 1997). Immigrant labourers from the Caribbean are brought to Canada on a temporary basis for seasonal employment, primarily in agricultural fields. Domestic workers (nannies) from the Philippines are taken advantage of by middle-class families who should know better. Working conditions are reported to be among the worst of any occupation, and many domestic workers are denied fundamental worker's rights by discriminatory laws (Stasiulis and Bakan, 1997). African-Canadians are routinely denied equal access to housing and employment (Henry and Ginzberg, 1993; Henry, 1994). For Black youth, relations with the police border on the criminal in certain urban areas (Cryderman, O'Toole, and Fleras, 1998). Indo-Pakistani Canadians continue to experience widespread dislike and resentment, if national attitude surveys are to be trusted (Berry, 1993). In these ways, various ethnic and racial groups are earmarked for the bottom of Canadian society without much hope for escape or redress.

The situation has improved somewhat, thanks to the passage of human rights and multicultural legislation. Income differentials continue to reveal marked disparities, with significant earning differences between (a) Whites and visible minorities; (b) native-born and foreign-born; (c) women and men; and (d) aboriginal and non-aboriginal populations

TABLE 2–1	Mean Earnings by Visible Minority Status, 1995			
Sex	**Immigrant Status**	**Visible Status**	**Earnings (mean)**	**Earnings (% difference)**
Male	Canadian-born	white	$36 563	n/a
		visible	$31 653	−13.4%
		aboriginal	$28 725	−21.4%
	Foreign-born	white	$38 456	+5.2%
		visible	$28 285	−22.6%
Female	Canadian-born	white	$23 173	n/a
		visible	$23 149	−0.1%
		aboriginal	$19 887	−14.2%
	Foreign-born	white	$22 498	−2.9%
		visible	$20 132	−13.1%

Note: Adopted from Pendakur and Pendakur (1995). Based on Census Public Use Microdata, Individual File, three percent sample of the Canadian population. Population includes permanent residents age 20–64 not in school full-time, living in Montreal, Toronto, Hamilton, Edmonton, Calgary, and Vancouver. Does not include persons not reporting an education level, a household type, occupation, or industry, or immigrants arriving after 1989.

(Pendakur and Pendakur, 1995). These differences remain in effect, albeit to a lesser degree, even when controlling for individual characteristics such as age, education level, language knowledge, full-time status, household type, and occupation.

Canadian-born visible minority males earn somewhat less than Canadian-born White males, even when educated and socialized in Canada (Pendakur and Pendakur, 1995). Variation exists within the categories themselves: Canadian-born men of Greek, Portuguese, Black, and Chinese background earned between 12 and 16 percent less than males of British origin. Foreign-born visible minorities, in turn, earned around 15 percent less than Canadian-born visible minorities. Regional variations are noticeable: The wage gap for Canadian-born visible minority men in Toronto was 9 percent, 17 percent in Montreal, but only 4 percent in Vancouver (see also Turner, 1996). Foreign-born males of colour fared worst, with those in Toronto earning 16 percent less, in Montreal 20 percent less, and Vancouver 13 percent less. Aboriginal peoples confront negative earning differentials of between 15 to 19 percent. Earning differentials between men and women proved significant; nevertheless, different earning patterns were observed across the genders. Compared with men, income differences between Canadian-born White females and visible minority females proved minimal. The same applied to foreign-born White females and Canadian-born White and visible minority women. By contrast, aboriginal women earned less than any group of foreign-born and Canadian-born women. Also evident were regional variations. Foreign-born visible minority women earned 20 percent less than White Canadian-born women in Montreal, 6 percent less in Toronto, and virtually the same wage in Vancouver. These earning gaps for women and men, the authors of the report (Pendakur and Pendakur, 1995) conclude, cannot be dismissed because of cultural differences, education quality, price of initial adjustment, or language skills. Rather, these disparities are suggestive of labour market discrimination. Insofar as inequities that stem from racial features or ethnically diverse lifestyles are in many cases now firmly implanted as a major social problem in Canada, and one that shows no sign of diminishing, some degree of intervention may be necessary.

Gender

It is widely acknowledged that women and men suffer discrimination and drawbacks because of class and socio-economic status (Satzewich, 1998). But women are doubly disadvantaged as a result of their membership in a historically devalued category: gender. Unlike men, women face sexist barriers that arise from their gender status in a predominantly patriarchical society. Patriarchy is characterized by the institutionally enforced authority of males over females and children that permeates the entire organization of society, from politics to culture, from the private to the public (Castells, 1997). Nevertheless, the past decade has been a period of remarkable gains for women in the job market, as Madelaine Drohan writes in her weekly *Globe and Mail* column (2 October, 1999). More women than ever are working, average earnings are up, jobs are held onto longer, and the jobs tend to be more senior and skilled. While men have seen their earnings stagnate between 1990 and 1997 (currently at $33 042), the average earnings for women have jumped from $19 773 to $21 167 in the same period—closing the gap to 63.8 percent from 59.8 percent in 1990. The gap closes further if restricted only to full-time workers, and nearly vanishes if only unmarried women with university credentials are included.

Other studies are painting a more complex picture. For example, in a study by Statistics Canada, entitled "The Persistant Gap: New Evidence on Canada's Gender Wage Gap (cited in Chwialkowska, 1999), flaws were pointed out in traditional studies on gender gaps. Measuring annual earnings of full-time workers ignored the fact that men worked on average four more hours per week than women. Studies based on actual wage rates rather than annual earnings could prove more revealing. Overall, in 1997, women earned about 80 percent of male hourly wages ($15.10 per hour versus $18.80 per hour). After controlling for factors such as rank and years of work experience, the average hourly rate rose to between 84 and 89 percent. Women who never married earned 96 percent of what unmarried men earned. Married women earned 77 percent of what married men earned. Women with a university degree earned 85 percent of male hourly wages, but those with less than high school earned only 69 percent. The study concluded that much but not all of the wage disparity between men and women can be attributed to greater male work experience, seniority, and added responsibility. Family commitments also continued to exert a significant impact on women's wages. So too is the fact that women continue to be under-represented on corporate boards and in executive suites, owning just 12 percent of the top jobs at Canada's largest companies (Flavelle, 2000).

Minority women also experience gender differently from White women because of racism and ethnicity (Ng, 2000). Women of colour, immigrant women, and aboriginal women are positioned in a particular and distinctive relationship to White patriarchy, and each expression of subordination is shaped by this relational position (Hurtado, 1996). Women as a group may be united in a common experience of male dominance, yet their experience varies because of differing situations for different groups of women (Gillespie, 1996). For women of colour, but especially Black women, their experiences related to exploitation and discrimination are socially and institutionally structured in ways that are different from mainstream women and men (Elabor-Idemudia, 2000). The allegiance of White women to White men through familial ties around centres of power means that they cannot be dominated in the same way as women of colour. As Hurtado (1996) observes in acknowledging how gender subordination is experienced differently, while women of colour are rejected from the corridors of power, White women are seduced into the inner sanctum. White women are largely concerned with projecting private sphere issues into the public realm (such as unequal division of household labour, media double standards, daycare at places of employment, and childhood identity formation). Women of colour focus on public issues related to female job ghettos (sex, child rearing, and domestic labour), racism, and healthy children. Women of colour also confront discrimination because of race and racism, a situation compounded by the marginality of class status (Macklin, 2000). After all, to be poor in a society that values wealth is to live with shame. To be poor and different—and a woman—is triply demonizing. Even strategies for change differ. In contrast with White women, women of colour are not in a position to distance themselves from the men of their group, since neither can exist without the other in the struggle against oppression (Jahnke, 1997). For aboriginal women, the situation is more complex. Few are in a position to compartmentalize their concerns as women from broader struggles for land, identity, or political voice. In the words of Donna Awatere (1984: 43–44) when chiding White feminists for ignoring the double colonization of indigenous women:

> For Maori women, all our concerns as women centre around the fact that we and our people have no say in the shaping of our destiny as a people... The Maori language is a feminist issue, the land is a feminist issue, separate development is a feminist issue, the venomous hatred of the Maori by the Pakeha is a feminist issue.

Ethnicity

Ethnicity is also a key variable in shaping unequal outcomes. Ethnicity-based inequities are generated in two ways. First, ethnic groups may be singled out as inferior or irrelevant, and dismissed or disparaged accordingly. For some ethnic minorities, ethnicity is thought to interfere with the attainment of equality in Canada by precluding individuals from full and equal participation. Second, ethnic groups may possess cultural values at odds with those of the dominant stream. Endorsement of these values, such as obligations to kin or obedience to tradition, may prove a barrier in the competition for scarce resources. However, under certain conditions involving middle positions or niches in the economy, according to Robert M. Jiobu, in his article "Explaining the Ethnic Effect," ethnicity may prove an economic good that confers advantage to minorities that the majority group cannot readily access; for example, taking advantage of pre-existing networks and common values.

The ethnicity factor may be experienced differently by the different genders. Minority women are subtly, yet profoundly undermined by ethnicity. Women in many ethnic communities are expected to know their place and do as they are told. Actions by women that do not conform to tradition or male values may be criticized as a betrayal of the cause or the community. For the sake of appearances, many women of colour are expected to defer to the authority of tradition and community. Such passivity and submissiveness may foster the facade of unity and cohesion; they also inhibit the expression of skills necessary for women to excel in society at large. Assertiveness or freedom can lead to conflict when it challenges deference to tradition-bound males. Minority women remain the "hushed-over" victims of violence. This violence results from cultural traditions that (a) normalize male abuse of women; (b) naturalize battery as a male right and a rite of passage for both women and men; (c) discourage public disclosure of abusive patterns because of family honour or community pride; and (d) foreclose access to help or escape. The family may be widely regarded as a bastion of privacy that shuns or punishes those who refuse to shield unpleasant issues from the public (Buckley, 1996). This indictment is not to suggest that domestic violence is more prevalent in minority or immigrant communities. Its effects on women may exert a different impact because of ethnicity. Patterns of domestic abuse may intersect with difficulties related to loneliness, dependency, homesickness, lack of knowledge of English, or access to services, and the threat of social ostracism, to provide few options for escape or recourse (Leckie, 1995; Easteal, 1996).

Regions

Some people have remarked that Canada is a country in search of a reason, while others have declared the absurdity of this country's very existence as a society. These musings can be interpreted in different ways. What each emphasizes, however, is the salience of regional differences to any definition of Canadian society (Economic Council of Canada, 1977; Matthews, 1983). The existence of regions gives rise to the problem of regionalism in part because of the federal commitment to extend the principles of justice and equality to all parts of Canada (Wein, 1993). According to this line of thought, unchecked market forces create regional deficiencies; only a major redistribution of resources by the government can correct these market failures (but see Corcoran, 1996). The different regions of Canada are especially vulnerable to the vicissitudes of global market forces and multinational greed. The reality of regionalism is further encouraged by the logic of a federal system in which provincial governments compete with each other in advancing sectoral interests. Rather than disappearing, the forces of regionalism appear to be gathering momentum in response to Québecois demands and federal attempts to placate pleas for decentralization (Brodie, 1997). A series of natural and social "cleavages" has evolved that not only furnishes a basis for Canada's regions (Wein, 1993), but also exposes the dilemmas of building this country along an east-west axis when the natural pull is north-south, with eventual absorption into the United States (Hiller, 1990).

Even consensus over basic concepts such as regions or regionalism seems to elude our grasp (Wein, 1993). By a region we mean a geographical space occupied by a group of people with (a) similar economic conditions and opportunities; (b) a unique political arrangement vis-à-vis the "centre" of the country; and (c) a relatively distinct subculture that fosters a sense of identity and meaning. For our purposes, regions can be divided into Atlantic Canada, southern Ontario (from Windsor to the Quebec border along the MacDonald-Cartier corridor), Quebec (the southern half), the Prairie provinces, the Pacific Rim in British Columbia, the North (or the rest of Canada outside the Arctic), and the Arctic (the part of Canada beyond the tree line). Regionalism, by contrast, is a political concept, and it represents the politicized counterpart of regions as a social or geographical entity. Regionalism is inherently political, Janine Brodie (1997) writes, since economic, social, and cultural interests are defined in territorial terms and articulated around spatial inequalities. In seeking to redefine its relationship with the centre, regionalism begins with the politicization of regional identity over perceived injustices. This politicizing of regions is followed by a mobilization of concerned citizens into a protest movement (Hiller, 1990). Regional parties such as Reform or Bloc Québecois are likely to have an unsettling effect on Canada's political landscape for years to come. How then do we explain regional differences in a federalist system and how should regionalism be addressed?

Canada's regional differences are not merely geographic or demographic curiosities. Regions are also characterized by inequities pertaining to housing, health, education, and the resources available to their respective criminal justice systems (Swan and Serjak, 1993).

Periods of high unemployment and debilitating levels of dependency on government assistance in the poorer provinces are two additional dimensions. Yet regional inequalities have shown a remarkable tenacity despite federal efforts to standardize access to services and goods (Economic Council of Canada, 1977). Government intervention has proven a bane rather than a boom (Gherson, 1997). Federal government policies, from John A. MacDonald's East-West trade policy, and C. D. Howe's manufacturing strategy, have failed Atlantic Canada by privileging the economic interests of Central Canada (Savoie, 1999). According to Fred McMahon (1997), senior policy analyst at the Atlantic Institute of Market Studies, federal transfers to Atlantic Canada—which peaked at about $5000 (in today's dollars) per person in 1980—have failed to elevate the region out of its "have-not" status. The transfers may have contributed unwittingly to local economic decline and deterred private sector growth while reinforcing patterns of dependency (see Corcoran, 1996). Thus, income support without more comprehensive measures pertaining to harvesting, conservation, and professionalization of a diminishing fishing industry has proven inadequate, and a waste of public money (Millen, 1998). The intractable nature of this inequality has given rise to regionally based social protests, regional alienation, and separatist movements (Sinclair, 1991).

Regional inequalities are a chronic and complex social problem rarely amenable to solution by rote formula. The challenge for federal government policy is the creation of sustainable regional development. But how does one go about neutralizing the deleterious effects of poor location and resource depletion, the flight of foreign capital, imbalances in free trade created by continentalism, and continued federal cutbacks across the board? The fact that regional inequities remain as entrenched as ever is deplorable given the volume of energy and resources expended. The lack of results confirms the inadequacy of reforms that concentrate on internal changes rather than external forces. Nor is there much hope for substantial change unless the social and structural aspects are incorporated into comprehensive renewal (Sinclair, 1991). Failure to confer ownership and control on local communities has hindered the problem-solving process. In contrast with the past when the government sought to buffer regional economies from disruptive international forces, central authorities are now under pressure to curtail spending as a costly luxury, while encouraging regional and local economies to compete internationally (Brodie, 1997). Not surprisingly, the federal government has hacked away at transfer payments, regional freight subsidies, regional developmental funds, and retraining programs (such as the $1.9 billion Atlantic groundfish package, which attempted to wean the Atlantic provinces from their dependency on fishing) (Gherson, 1997). Political considerations loom large as government initiatives emphasize voter appeal rather than dealing with the problem at hand. As Wein (1993) notes, proposed initiatives are as likely to reflect political expediency as economic need. The prognosis for regional equality is even more daunting as governments lose interest in rectifying the spatial distributions of inequality (Cohen, 1993). Nevertheless, changes can occur: According to a *Globe and Mail* survey of provinces (cited in Little, 1999), Newfoundland was judged to have the "hottest" provincial economy and fastest economic growth, based on seven economic indicators.

All known societies are characterized by inequalities, with the most privileged enjoying a disproportionate share of the total wealth, power, and prestige (Grusk,1997). Sociologists are interested in describing the contours and distribution of this inequality; they also are interested in explaining its persistence despite the emergence of egalitarian values and programs. Recognizing the multi-faceted nature of social inequality helps to account for the dynamic interaction between different forms of subordination and the different ways in which each is experienced through the other (Bottomley et al., 1991). Race, gender, ethnicity, location, and class may be treated as analytically distinct dimensions of inequality; nevertheless, each is thought to combine with other dimensions to generate overlapping hierarchies of subordination that intersect with one another in ways that are mutually reinforcing yet contradictory in the struggle for equality (Bottomley et al., 1991; Hurtado, 1996). Minority women and men who are socially devalued in two or more hierarchies are suseptible to discrimination. Inclusion in several devalued but interlocking categories of subordination inflates the chances of being left out of the loop.

TOWARDS EQUALITY

That most Canadians aspire to social and economic equality is widely accepted. Many Canadians would also agree that equality is to be preferred over inequality. But the concept of equality is subject to diverse interpretations. Mutually opposed definitions may be endorsed by different groups or individuals, depending on their location on the social spectrum. The situation is further complicated by the possibility of concurrent versions at a given point in time in response to changing circumstances. This proliferation of definitions has culminated in confusion and misunderstanding over the politics of entitlement with respect to who gets what and why. This element of uncertainty has also complicated the process of solving problems. Without new solutions to the old problem of inequality, the goal of equality will remain lofty but elusive.

Competing Equalities

The concept of equality is employed in three different ways. First, equality is used as equivalent to sameness. All are treated the same regardless of their background or circumstances. No one is accorded special privileges in a system designed around equal opportunity and universal merit. This type of "formal" equality focuses on due process and legal equivalents. Second, equality is used in the sense of numerical or "proportional" equivalence. Under systems of preferential hiring and promotion, each group is allocated positions according to its numbers in society or the workforce. Third, the concept of equality is directed towards the principle of "different but equal." With its emphasis on equal outcomes or conditions rather than opportunities, this position takes into account the unique circumstances of a person or group as a basis for entitlement. People cannot be treated alike because some groups have special needs or unique experiences. They need to be treated differently by making substantive adjustments to the social and cultural components of society.

Consider for example the "special" treatment that extends to individuals with disabilities. Wheelchair ramps, closed-caption TV, and designated parking spots are common enough. Yet these concessions can hardly be thought of as special or preferential, but rather as removing barriers to ensure equality of opportunity. Likewise, historically disadvantaged minority women and men encounter barriers that are every bit as real as physical impediments and equally in need of removal for levelling the playing field. In other words, those with social disabilities also require different treatment if only to ensure their right to compete with others on an equal basis.

Each of these perspectives on equality differs from the others in terms of objectives and scope. Formal equality is concerned with mathematical equivalence and a market-driven means for establishing who gets what. It tends to treat individuals as asexual, de-racialized, classless, and lacking a history or context (McIntyre, 1994). Any measure that rewards individuals on grounds other than merit or competition is criticized as contrary to the natural sorting-out process. With its emphasis on formal equality, equality of opportunity and treatment, and individual attitudes, this perspective is at odds with more substantive versions of equality known as equity. Under substantive equity, differences are taken into account; after all, identical treatment may entrench inequality and perpetuate group-based inequities when everyone is treated the same without regard to histories of exclusion or restricted opportunities. This makes it doubly important for social policies to consider inequities based on the realities of the real world rather than derived from formal considerations of gender, race, and class (McIntyre, 1994) Such a claim also raises a host of questions about which version of equality should prevail. Is one more important than the other, or is it a case of one serving as a necessary precondition for the other?

The distinction between equal opportunity (competition) and equal outcomes (conditions) is critical. Equal opportunity focuses on the rights of individuals to be free from discrimination when competing for the good things in life. It operates on the principle that true equality can only come about when everyone is treated equally regardless of gender or race. By contrast, equal outcomes concentrates on the rights of individuals to a fair and equitable share of the goods and services in society. True equality arises when differences and disadvantage are taken into account as a basis for divvying up the goods. A commitment to equal opportunity openly advocates competition, inequality, and hierarchy as natural and inevitable. An equal-outcomes perspective is concerned with controlled distribution and egalitarian conditions for members of a disadvantaged group. This perspective recognizes the need for collective over individual rights when the situation demands it. It also endorses the principle of social intervention for true equality, since equal outcomes are unlikely to arise from competitive market forces.

By themselves, equal opportunity structures are insufficient to overcome the debilitating effects of systemic discrimination and institutional racism. Additional treatment is required over and above that available to the general population, since the application of equal standards to unequal situations has the controlling effect of freezing the status quo. Context and consequences are as important as abstract principles of equal opportunity in righting wrongs. Taking context into account may mean that in some cases differential treatment will be required to achieve an equality of outcome. Taking consequences into account suggests that intent or awareness is less important than effects. The unintended consequences of seemingly neutral practices may lead to the unintentional exclusion of qualified personnel, regardless of motive or consciousness. To be sure, outcome-oriented equity is not opposed to equal opportunities in defining equality. On the contrary, a commitment to the principle of equal opportunity constitutes a necessary first step in overcoming entrenched racism and discrimination. But ultimately such a commitment cannot achieve a fair and just equality in an unequal competition, given that fairness is concerned with treating everyone the same, while justice acknowledges the necessity of taking differences into account when the situation demands, if true ("substantive") equality is to be attained. Only a dual commitment to equitable outcomes and equal opportunities can free up the playing field for open competition. The complexity of this line of thinking is illustrated by way of recent controversy involving gender politics in a post-secondary setting.

Issues to Consider:

- Should an applicant's gender be taken into account in a hiring process?
- Is the university responsible for achieving a gender balance by providing positive female role models?
- Are employment equity programs the best way of rectifying problems?
- Can discriminatory actions ever be justified?

The wording on most university postings has become familiar enough to qualify as a near cliché: The University of "X" is an equal opportunity/employment equity/affirmative action employer committed to diversifying the faculty. No person shall be subjected to discrimination on the basis of age, ethnicity, gender, sexual orientation, or creed. Women, minorities, and people with disabilities are especially encouraged to apply. Qualified individuals with a disability may request a reasonable accommodation to participate in the application process. That few openly object to this type of advertisement, since the principle of merit appears to prevail in the selection process, is a sign of a more inclusive society.

But a small southwestern Ontario institution, Wilfrid Laurier University, broke with this protocol by announcing that only women need apply for a tenure-track position in the psychology department. The chair of the department defended the decision on the grounds of addressing a departmental gender imbalance. Women constituted only 4 of the 22 full-time positions, in effect robbing the overwhelming number of undergraduate female students of positive

role models, while overworking the existing female psychologists because of mandated quotas for women in university committees. WLU was under pressure to rectify a situation that the psychology department defined as unjust and pedagogically unsound, argued the Dean of Social Work, given that women constitute 64 percent of the PhDs and 64 percent of the accessible hiring pool. Moreover, the action was consistent with Section 14 of the Ontario Human Rights Code that prohibits discrimination without a good reason, but which allows positive "discriminatory" measures toward members of a historically disadvantaged group, as long as designed to alleviate economic hardship without violating the fundamental rights of others. In its defence, the department had actively pursued female candidates in the past, but with little success, as larger, more prestigious universities had lured the brightest and best. With such a serious problem of under-representation of women, the university was under mounting pressure from administrators and federal/provincial authorities to comply with federal employment equity initiatives by making all reasonable efforts to redress the gender imbalance. In all fairness to the psychology department, the actions at WLU were not unprecedented. The federal government has allocated $1.3 million for salaries and grants up to 5 years, in addition to an earlier $2.4 million in 1991, to assist universities in hiring 19 more women in science and engineering (Bailey, 1999).

Reaction to this move ranged from support to dismay to outrage. For many, this decision flew in the face of normal hiring procedures based on the principles of hiring on the basis of merit, and that only the best person should get the job. The actions at WLU, though legal and even well-intentioned, were little more than a blatant form of (reverse) discrimination insofar as men were victimized solely on the basis of a condition that they had no control over. Such a discriminatory action had the effect of further distorting the playing field—a situation deemed unnecessary by some since the proportion of women hired across universities has been consistently greater than the proportion of women in the applicant pool. According to statistics submitted to the Senate at University of Western Ontario, women constituted 20.5 percent of all applicants across all fields in 1998, but 42.9 percent of those hired were women (Curtis, 1999). In other words, equity programs are no longer required at Canadian universities, it is argued, especially when infringing on the human rights of men to assist a category of women who are anything but disadvantaged.

For others, the actions at WLU were intellectually repugnant and a violation of natural justice, given that fairness and the pursuit of academic excellence proved secondary to the "politically correct" goal of gender balance. In claiming to reverse gender discrimination against women, the university managed to master the Orwellian doublethink of holding two contradictory beliefs and simultaneously accepting both of them as mutually valid (Loney, 1999). To its credit, the department displayed the honesty, courage, and the courtesy of being out in the open, unlike other departments that routinely discarded male resumes behind closed doors. Nevertheless, the blind commitment to equality as a virtue has distorted the purpose of education,

according to Alan Borovoy in his book, *The New Anti-Liberals*, (Canadian Scholars Press). Ian Hunter of the University of Western Ontario writes:

> "A university should be the cornerstone of a free society, the one sanctuary where free thought and inquiry and speech are not only respected but encouraged...[rather than] islands of repression in a sea of freedom. In their desire to placate the equality lobby, in their postmodern rejection of truth and falsity, in their desire to attract public money and to entice students, universities have sold their intellectual birthright."

Still others endorsed the action at W.L.U. as long overdue, in light of gender imbalances. Something had to be done since universities and departments tended to hire those most like themselves. Positive female role models were desperately needed; so too were women for alleviating the workload of overworked female faculty. Merit is a valid principle, to be sure, but the rightness or wrongness of merit as a basis for making abstract decisions had to reflect existing realities. In balancing the principle of merit as the sole basis for hiring with the claim that gender is a relevant educational qualification, the university was plying the area between the pursuit of fairness or academic excellence (as measured by performance-related criteria, such as knowledge of a discipline and ability to teach and conduct research) and the social goals of an inclusive institution.

Do women in academia need employment equity? Evidence suggests that women are outperforming men at all levels of education. Young women are more likely than men to complete a university education, and are less likely to drop out of school. According to the 1996 census,

16.2 percent of men in their 20s had a university degree, compared with 20.7 percent of women in their 20s, and only 11 percent of women in 1981. Of total enrolments, 55.2 percent of students were women, compared to only 46 percent in 1981. To be sure, proportions are notably smaller in some fields such as engineering, mathematics, and the physical sciences, but noticeably higher in others such as health and education (Little, 1999). Women in engineering account for 19 percent of all undergrads, up from less than 8 percent in 1981, whereas women predominate in nursing at 90 percent, down from 97 percent in 1981. In only one category—computer science— have women fallen back, from 28 percent in 1981 to 18 percent in 1997. Enrolments for women were highest in social sciences, followed by general arts, education, humanities, biology, and agriculture. For men, the highest enrolments were in the social sciences, followed by engineering and applied science, general arts, physical sciences, and humanities. At faculty levels, the picture is slightly more complex. For example, women hold about 6 percent of the engineering and 12 percent of the natural science faculty jobs, up from 2 percent and 7 percent respectively in 1991. The situation in Canada is comparable to the situation elsewhere. Nor has there been much change in the percentage of female faculty, with the 20 percent in tact from 1931. In late 1990s Britain, women occupied 718 professorships, an increase of 250 professors since 1995, but a minuscule number compared to the 1792 males who were hired. Women occupied 8.1 percent of the chairs, but only one in chemistry and one in dentistry, reinforcing the notion that reaching the top may be extremely difficult for women in fields

that are not traditionally female at the highest level (Gold, 1998).

The ideals of equal opportunity and a diverse and inclusive workplace as important goals are widely endorsed. Disagreement seems to reside in how to achieve these goals. At the core of this issue is whether equality is best achieved by treating everyone the same (having one law for all, in which all are equal before the law) or by taking differences into account. To what extent is gender a relevant educational qualification, or should all decisions be based on credentials of research or teaching? Is it right to openly discriminate against individuals who, through no fault of their own, belong to one group, especially at a time when job openings are scarce and qualified candidates in abundance? Can all "affirmative actions" be considered discriminatory, given that the logic of discrimination is to exclude rather than to create a more inclusive environment? After all, discrimination is tolerated in other aspects of contemporary life where distinctions are made to justify differential treatment. Insurance companies charge different rates to men and women for life insurance, and courts treat offenders differently according to age. For example, a recent court ruling concluded that it was reasonable for a religious college to demand that both faculty and staff be of a particular faith and that this action was not a violation of human rights or the ban against religious discrimination (Canadian Press, 1999). Are the actions at WLU a case of reverse discrimination? Or are these equity actions justified in an attempt to reverse the inherent, historic, and systemically embedded discrimination against women (Nelson. 1999) in a predominantly male-centred institution which was created for men and still strongly exudes their perspectives, experiences, and outcomes as the norm (Paul, 1999; also Stalker and Prentice, 1998)?

This controversy at WLU is far too complex for the kind of moral grandstanding that has buoyed the debate. Universities and departments face difficult choices among conflicting goals in a context of dwindling resources and government underspending in education as a public good. The chair of the psychology department captures it nicely when conceding: "I can understand people would be upset with the way we're approaching this. But you can't have it both ways. What do people want us to do here? Be duplicitous? It's a tough situation: We're damned if we do and damned if we don't." (Cited in the WLU student paper, *The Cord Weekly*, Sept. 13, 1999). Much depends on how issues are framed. At one level, the debate represents a classic case of people talking past each other—in the same way the abortion (pro-life vs pro-choice) tends to miscommunicate. On one side are those who see the issue as primarily that of discrimination against men because of unfair hiring practices, resulting in the erosion of academic excellence in an institution devoted to the pursuit and dissemination of knowledge. On the other side, the issue is not about fair hiring practices but about the gender imbalances in an institution that purports to be egalitarian and inclusive. To a degree both positions are valid, and any effort to sort out two competing "rights" is bound to generate misunderstanding or hostility. This debate over "just" versus "fair" is unlikely to subside, as other predominantly White male workplaces such as firehalls have come under pressure to alter their longstanding policy of hiring

with a blind eye to ethnicity or gender (James, 1999). Perhaps the true villains in this episode are the federal and provincial governments whose corporatist views of market efficiency have resulted in an under-investment in post-secondary education as a public good, Thomas Heuglin writes, thus propelling an entire generation of future academics through years of costly public training without much chance of employment, despite an impending explosion of students. (The crisis of confidence pertaining to post-secondary identity will be explored in Chapter 9.)

The controversy at WLU is a microcosm of broader social trends in Canada. Historically, as Professor Murray Miles points out, core Canadian values revolved about the primacy of personal merit rather than group membership as basis for entitlement, the principle of non-discrimination (such as fair hiring principles), rather than gender/colour-conscious programs as a basis for institutional inclusiveness, and a commitment to equality of opportunity rather than equality of outcomes as the definition of a level playing field. The extent to which these core values are being contested and challenged is an indication that Canadians will be living in interesting times in the new millenium. Also raised is the issue of whether employment equity as a strategy of inclusion is little more than a quick-fix solution for public relations purposes, as Jo-Anne Lee and Linda Cardinal point out in their article on "Hegemonic Nationalism." It remains to be seen if the administrative strategy of "quotaism" and "categoricalism" can address historical wrongs and structured inequities, or, simply will serve to buy off troublesome constituents without disrupting existing arrangements.

Sources:

Chilton, S. 1999 "Let's Hire and Promote on Merit." *Kitchener-Waterloo Record,* July 26.

Curtis, J. 1999 "All's Fair for the Fair Sex." The *Globe and Mail,* Aug. 14.

Heuglin, T. 1999 "Honest Condemned." *Kitchener-Waterloo Record,* Aug. 10.

Hunter, I. 1999 "Islands of Repression." *National Post,* Aug. 12.

Kimura, D. 1999 "Affirmative Action Is Junk Science." *National Post,* July 26.

Mather, J. 1999 "Second Opinion." *Kitchener-Waterloo Record,* Aug. 3.

Miles, M. 1999 "The Laurier Affair" *Kitchener-Waterloo Record,* Aug. 17.

Murray, M. 1999 "The Laurier Affair." *Kitchener-Waterloo Record,* Aug. 18.

Nelson, M. 1999 "Hiring Under-Represented Groups to Faculty Is Only Fair." *Kitchener- Waterloo Record,* July 26.

Paul, L. 1999 "Illusions of Inclusion." *SWC Supplement,* 12.

Royson, J. 1999 "Wanted: New-Look Firefighters." *Toronto Star,* July 30.

Stalker, J., and S. Prentice 1998 "Illusion of Inclusion. Women in Post-Secondary Education."

Wente, M. 1999 "Bias Against Men Is Unacceptable Too." *Kitchener-Waterloo Record,* July 24.

3

POVERTY AND HOMELESSNESS

FRAMING THE PROBLEM

> Canada in the late 1990s is a strange place. We pride ourselves on being a society committed to equality and compassion, yet we're living through a period of unparalleled inequality and bitterness.
>
> —Buzz Hargrove and Wayne Skene (1998:13)

The world at the millenium is beset with a raft of paradoxes whose proposed resolutions resonate with either opportunity or destruction. In 1989, many welcomed the dismantling of the Berlin wall because it symbolized the collapse of a system with a commitment to equality at the expense of freedom (Mayor, 1999). Ten years later, with the millenium upon us, the world is witnessing the entrenchment of a freewheeling global market economy that promulgates freedom—particularly the freedom of capital to move across national borders—but disregards much reference to equality, while eschewing social responsibility toward the victims of this global cataclysm. On one side, there is a world that is replete with an affluence beyond people's wildest imaginations. The constituent societies of this affluent world are freer and more dynamic than ever, with limitless potential for everyone to live better and longer. On the other side, however, is a world of poverty, underdevelopment, and disempowerment. The net result? A new global order that is polarized into extremes of wealth and poverty, not just between the north and south, but also between social groups within the affluent countries. This persistence of poverty and impoverishment is not simply a temporary blip. Nor is poverty reducible to an analytical level as if it had no other context or implications for those at the margins (Mayor, 1999). Rather, social divisions caused by deepening poverty pose a threat to civil order within societies and peace between countries. Moreover, argues Frederico Mayor, contributing editor to the March 1999 issue of the *UNESCO Courier*, the cult of competitiveness is ruthlessly eroding social arrangements that once were thought stable and supportive, with the result that few can cavalierly dismiss poverty as a distant prospect. To the extent that destitution may be only one paycheck removed, the gap between poverty and affluence is precarious at best.

In 1989, another event occurred of somewhat less international significance, but one that has perplexed and provoked Canadians since then. In that year, an all-party parliamentary resolution vowed to eliminate poverty among Canadian children by the year 2000. **Resolved** that this House express its concern for the more than one million Canadian children living in poverty and seek to achieve the goal of eliminating poverty among Canadian children by the year 2000. House of Commons, November 24th, 1989. But rhetoric is one thing, reality has proven yet another. With nearly 21 percent of all children (or about 1.5 million) living below the low-income cut-off ("poverty") line—a 58 percent jump, representing some 400 000 children since 1989—Canada appears to be moving in the opposite direction. While the number of millionaires has tripled since 1989 to 220 000 Canadians, and is expected to triple again by 2005, poverty is literally killing Innu children in Labrador and northern Quebec. The child poverty rate in Toronto is a staggering 38 percent; and close to 1000 children sleep in shelters, while another 40 000 are on waiting lists for affordable housing (Editorial, Nov 20th, 1999). In contrast with a well-established system to provide income and assistance for the elderly, Canada appears to have abandoned those in early childhood without realizing the detrimental effects on both individuals and society at large. To the surprise of many, Canada attained the dubious distinction of having the second highest rate of child poverty in the developed world in 1997, second only to the United States. Good intentions notwithstanding, the report card on Canada's war against poverty is nothing short of embarrassing, especially with the economy firing on all cylinders. But rather than redoubling efforts to close the gap between expectation and reality, between the haves and the have-nots, the government appears more anxious than ever to redefine (away) the problem by playing politics with "being poor."

The year 1989 saw yet another event that deserves comment. By the late 1980s, the United States had entered an era of economic prosperity that has proven both unprecedented in scope and astonishing in duration. Yet here, too, the benefits from this prosperity have not been equally shared, with a growing number of BMWs competing for space with a spiralling demand for food stamps. Such a glaring gap has prompted people to make sweeping indictments about poverty and affluence: How does the richest country in the industrialized world condone a poverty level that stood at 16.5 percent in 1997, while nearly 40 percent of the 830 major league ball players on the opening day rosters were millionaires? How can the head of Microsoft, Bill Gates, amass a personal fortune that is greater than the GDP of Iceland and Portugal and is expected to surpass the U.S.A. by 2010, while the problem of homelessness continues to escalate? How to explain the discrepancy? Is it the combined and cumulative effect of rugged individualism, an ethic of self-improvement and hard work, and a distrust of munificent big government that allows an affluent society to tolerate punishing levels of poverty? The fact that the rich are getting richer, the poor poorer, despite a booming economy, is especially acute in the nation's capital, within distance of the White House. While the richest 20 percent in the United States earn 8.9 times more than the poorest 20 percent, according to a UN Developmental Agency, the average income of the poorest 20 percent in Washington, D.C. has fallen by $2 000 in 20 years, and now stands at $5920, the lowest in the country. By contrast, the richest 20 percent of families with children enjoy average incomes of $149 510, according to the Centre on Budget and Policy Priorities, also the highest in the country. For people living in poverty, the real problem is not just about money, although money in a dollar-driven society is the measure of all things. Poverty is also about a lack of power to improve life chances and take control of their lives. Not surprisingly, to be poor in Canada and the United States is tantamount to living in sin, a *stigma that has the effect of robbing each person of their dignity and self-worth (UNESCO Courier*, March 1999).

Everyone agrees that poverty is detrimental to many Canadians. As expressed by the author of a major report on poverty and homelessness, Ann Golden: "A healthy society is one where everyone feels included. Poverty shuts people out. And if large numbers of people don't feel they are part of the mainstream, social cohesion begins to break down." Disagreements over poverty tend to vary over its magnitude and scope. What precisely do we mean by poverty? Is poverty about being poor in the absolute sense, or is it about unequal distribution of income relative to others? How much poverty is there in Canada: Is the figure closer to five percent of the population or to 41 percent in some cities (*Globe and Mail*, Apr. 17, 2000)? What does it mean to be poor in a relatively affluent society? Does being poor mean not having enough to eat or not possessing cable TV? Does poverty mean the same in sub-Saharan Africa as it does in Canada? Where exactly do we draw the line between poverty and discomfort? Is the low-income cut-off point the same as poverty? Who is to blame for being poor? What should be done? Is poverty the result of social injustice, or should the finger be pointed at personal deficiencies such as laziness or parental neglect? Is it best to focus on root causes or to continue to blame the victim by emphasizing moral flaws? How is poverty expressed? Is homelessness an expression or cause of poverty? Answers to these questions are important because policy considerations are contingent on framing the problem appropriately (Greenspon, 1997). Yet a fixation on definitions can be double-edged: Not only are the politics of definition a form of social control in their own right, a "paralysis by analysis" can detract from the spirit of activism to challenge structures, decision-makers, and political wills. Energy is dissipated in endless debate over the parameters of the problems rather than practical solutions. Worse still, relief may be denied to the truly destitute who for one reason or another become lost in the definitional shuffle.

Many Canadians are perplexed by the pervasiveness and tenacity of poverty in such an affluent society. They also are puzzled by how the poor and marginal (from homeless single parents to squeegee kids) are being scapegoated or criminalized, even as wealth is being increasingly concentrated in the hands of the few to the exclusion of the many. How is it, asks Mel Hurtig (1999), that yearly increases in the gross domestic product have not reduced the growing legion of poor men, women, and children in Canada? How is it that somehow Canadians seem prepared to tolerate so much hunger, homelessness, and suffering at a time of soaring business profits and the accumulation of wealth in the hands of the few? How is it that the income gap between the rich and poor has widened despite economic boom times? And how is it that, notwithstanding government mantras about Canada's economic performance, growing numbers of families and individuals are increasingly insecure about their future? In seeking to respond to such awkward questions, this chapter explores the concepts of poverty and affluence as social problems of mounting concern to Canadians. Poverty is examined as a condition that can be analyzed at the level of causes, characteristics, consequences, and cures.

The concept of poverty is also shown to be a socially constructed and contested issue: What is meant by poverty? Who says so, and why? On what grounds? How much of it is there? Should definitions focus on subsistence only or is inclusiveness a key component of poverty? What are its impacts on individuals and implications for society? And what if anything can be done about it? Central to this chapter are ongoing debates over the nature of poverty: Is it based on absolute need or does it reflect relative equality? Responses to this question are crucial in measuring the scope of poverty and proposing solutions on the basis of its magnitude.

Several assumptions underpin this chapter: First, references to poverty are essentially a social construct rather than anything objective about reality. Poverty is real, to be sure, but its magnitude and scope are subject to endless controversy, depending on context or criteria. To the extent that those with power can enforce their definitions by controlling the terms of the debate and proposed solutions, the politics of poverty will become even more intense. Second, technically speaking, it is affluence rather than poverty that should be the problem under consideration. After all, the poor are not the problem per se, but the structures of society that are organized to enrich some while impoverishing many. Also responsible are the actions of the rich who create conditions and constraints that foster poverty. Poverty is the symptom of the affluence and greed that increasingly dominate public debate in Canada, thus reinforcing the marginalization and impoverishment of the poor and powerless. Third, too heavy a reliance on the economic dimensions of poverty overlooks a key factor: For many, poverty is not only about money but also about power. Without power, the poor are robbed of taking control of their lives and are often unable to participate fully in contemporary society. Fourth, while people disagree on specifics, all Canadians concur that poverty is a social problem, especially when young children are involved. As a social problem, it is social in origins, subject to correction by way of resources and political will, and its impact on individuals and society at large cannot be casually brushed aside.

The Scope of Poverty

By almost any measure, Canada has embarked on an era of stunning prosperity (Olive, 1999). After a decade of dismal economic performances, indicators are pointing to often dramatic improvements in virtually every aspect of Canada's economic well-being. Over 800 000 new jobs, more than 90 percent of which are full-time positions, have been created in the past two years. Corporate profits are at all-time highs while business investments are booming, from construction of new plants to installation of equipment, both of which are indicative of business confidence in a robust economy. Real incomes for ordinary Canadians are rising following years of stagnation. The torrid pace of housing starts and new car sales reflects how pent-up consumer demand is finally responding to Canada's economic comeback. To be sure, Canada's miracle economy is riding the American coattails, as David Olive reminds us, while lower productivity and punishing levels of taxation are making this boom more fragile than optimists would believe. References to a "brain drain" to the United States are also worrying. Nonetheless, the continuation of dynamic growth in output with little or no inflation is widely anticipated.

Yet not all Canadians are benefiting from these bullish good times. And those being left behind are the poor and marginal, with the result that poverty is now firmly entrenched as a major social problem in Canada. The concept of poverty can be approached in diverse ways. For some, extremes of inequality reflect market imperfections and lackadaisical work habits. Outside of a utopia, they would say, the best we can hope for is a safety net under the deserving poor. For others, intense levels of poverty and alienation are worrisome in a society that aspires to be the best, yet condones being poor within the context of prosperity. Poverty in Canada is not randomly distributed: Poverty is increasingly concentrated among five high risk groups, including female-headed, lone-parent households, families headed by a person with a disability, young adults between 18 and 24 years of age, unattached individuals, and elderly women on their own (Fawcett, 1999; Policy Research Initiative,1999). Children are particularly vulnerable: Upwards of 25 percent of children in Canada are defined as living in "dire straits." Chronic levels of poverty among aboriginal peoples and people of colour are no less problematic and equally resistant to quick-fix solutions. Poverty is also higher among recent immigrants and the younger generation of immigrants (Kazemipur and Halli, 2000). Regardless of its distribution, in other words, poverty is an embarrassing blot on Canadian society, and nothing short of a fundamental rethink and institutional reform can possibly bring it under control.

Still others believe that living standards have improved for all Canadians. Compared with the past, according to Christopher Sarlo, an economist at Nipissing University in North Bay, rates of poverty have sharply declined, from one in three Canadians in 1951 to only one in twenty by the late 1970s, a figure that has remained constant to the present. The International Labour Organization appears to agree, and concludes that only six percent of Canadians are living in poverty (see Kerstetter, 1999). Compared to international standards, Canada has virtually no poverty if measured by the presence of a destitute underclass living in sprawling ghettos or sordid slums. Those defined as poor in Canada are appreciably better off than even the affluent in some developing world countries. Nobody in Canada needs to starve to death on the streets. Only a handful are forced by circumstances to live out in the open. Few are denied access to health care and welfare services, although some individuals may fall in between bureaucratic cracks. The poor, it is proclaimed, are better off than before because of the "trickle down" of wealth from an expanding economy. The UN Human Development Program seems to agree. In conferring on Canada its sixth title this decade as the world's best place to live, with the highest quality of life based on income, education, and life expectancies, the UN conceded that poverty was decreasing in Canada but increasing in the United States. So, what is the problem? The fact that sociologists continue to harp on the negative and unflattering, despite Canada's lofty standing, is puzzling at times. Much of the criticism is not for criticism's sake, however, but in hopes of improving an already enviable state of affairs.

Unfortunately, there is another side to the story. Compared to its utopian ideals, Canada falls short of its self-appointed benchmark as a trailblazer in social reform. Judging from the evidence, the poor are poorer and the rich are getting richer at the expense of the poor. Canada may bask in the limelight as the best place to live, but too much self-congratulation glosses over how the disproportion of poor has climbed to include: (a) nearly one-fifth of the population; (b) about nine out of ten single women with children under 25 years of age; and (c) virtually all on reserve aboriginal communities. Provincial variations are evident, with Quebec having the lowest rate, compared to exceptionally high rates in B.C. and the Atlantic provinces. The disparity may be partly attributable to different cut-off lines; in Quebec the poverty line is $14 524 for a family of four (reflecting the lower cost of housing), whereas Ontario's cut-off line is $17 230 and B.C.'s is $18 296 (Watson, 1996). Variation by cities is also considerable: 22 percent of people living in Montreal are defined as poor by the Canadian Council of Social Development, with Trois Rivières, Winnipeg, and Sherbrooke right behind at 20 percent. Oshawa has the least number of poor with 9 percent, followed by Kitchener and Thunder

Bay at 12 percent (*Globe and Mail*, June 26, 1996). Intracity variations can be discerned as well: While 33 percent of those who live in inner Montreal fall below the poverty line, the rate falls to only 5 percent in the eastern suburb of Varennes. Increasingly, poverty, hunger, and homelessness are interconnected, since people using food banks can be seen as the "pre-homeless," according to the executive director of the Canadian Association of Food Banks (Levy, 1999). Box 3–1 provides a snapshot look at the scope of poverty in Canada.

BOX 3.1	Poverty Facts and Figures

- The Poverty Profile of 1996 provided a window into the world of poverty in Canada (Fraser, 1998). The poverty rate for all people was 17.6 percent, or 5.19 million people—up from the 14.5 percent in 1989, or 3.7 million people. Provincial variations are noticeable: Newfoundland has the highest rate at 22.8 percent, while P.E.I. is the lowest at 14.9 percent. Ontario stands at 19.9 percent, according to a poverty report card by Campaign 2000. The child poverty rate jumped to 20.9 percent, or 1.49 million children. The poverty rate for the elderly (above 65 years of age) rose to 18.9 percent. 91.3 percent of families headed by single mothers under 25 years of age were poor.
- Canada may be widely regarded as the world's best place to live, at least according to a UN Development Survey. But a new poverty index by the UN (combining income, literacy, and long-term unemployment rates) has placed Canada 10th out of 17 rich nations, ahead of the United States (17th), but behind Italy (5th) and Sweden (1st).
- What is poverty? In the mid-1950s, the average Canadian family of four survived on $4000 per year, equivalent to about $26 000 in 1996 dollars. That middle class family of four today would be classified as poor by some and extremely destitute by others. Still others, including the Fraser Institute, would peg this amount as excessively generous. Who is right, and what is going on here?
- Statistics Canada regards a family to be in "straitened circumstances" or "substantially worse off than the average" (the words "poor" or "poverty" are never used by central authorities) if more than 55 percent of its income is spent on food, shelter, and clothing, compared to the 35 percent by the average Canadian family. In a city the size of Toronto, this low income cut-off threshold in 1998 was drawn at $32 759 for family of four. The figure for Kitchener-Waterloo was $28 379. The Fraser Institute, a right-wing thinktank, argues that a family of four in Toronto only needs about $16 000; a federal market basket approach falls somewhere in between.
- The income gap between the haves and have-nots continues to widen. The average income of the bottom fifth of all Canadians has fallen 32 percent since 1989 (the bottom tenth saw a decline of 61.6 percent between 1986 and 1996!), the number of poor children has escalated by nearly 50 percent, and the number of Canadians living on social assistance has expanded by 68 percent (Hargrove and Skene, 1999). Yet federal spending on social programs as a percentage of GDP has fallen to its lowest levels since the Second World War. While corporate profits are booming and executive salaries scale unprecedented heights (including a 112 percent increase), the

average worker earned 9 percent less after-tax income in1997 than in 1990, an amount effectively less than in 1975. Corporations on average pay less tax than a decade ago; the average worker is paying 22 percent more tax than 10 years ago.

- As recently as 1980, food banks did not exist in Canada; by March of 1999, there were 698 food banks and some 2000 agencies operating an emergency food distribution program for nearly 800 000 Canadians, up 10 percent over the previous year. Are food banks the answer, or are they becoming part of the institutional response they were set up to challenge, even as they respond to immediate needs? As a percentage of the provincial population, Newfoundland had the highest rate of food bank use at 6.6 percent of the population, compared to a Canada-wide average of 2.8 percent. Twenty-eight Canadian universities and colleges have food banks, including thirteen post-secondary institutions in Ontario. While thousands of Canadians rely on food banks for basic subsistence, Canada's six major banks grossed a combined profit of $9.1 billion in 1999.

- Who can collect? In 1990, 87 percent of the jobless were entitled to unemployment benefits. Now only 36 percent of the unemployed can collect "employment" (as it is called now) insurance. The employment insurance fund has accumulated a surplus of $20 billion by cutting back access and refusing to spend money on training.

- Are most welfare recipients too lazy to work, or does this mean-spirited myth disguise factors related to social injustice? Most welfare recipients who re-enter the labour market must accept low wages. As a result, they may earn less than on welfare, once expenses such as childcare or transportation are factored in. Without a strong childcare system, many families cannot participate in the workforce. Thus the classic welfare trap: Those who prefer to work often face a financial penalty, while the government pays people not to work (Lee, 1999). Does this explain the Ontario government's decision to slash welfare payments by up to 21 percent in 1995? A single parent with a child received a maximum of $1221 in 1995, but only $957 in 1999.

- In the United States, poverty is officially defined strictly as economic deprivation, based on specific income thresholds for families of different sizes. In 1997, the threshold for a family of three (one adult and two children) was set at $12 931. The average poor family of this size may also receive up to $6329 in government transfers and welfare payments, according to the March 1999 issue of *UNESCO Courier*.

- Poverty is not a random occurrence. Americans are more likely to be poor if they are Black (26.5 percent), Hispanic (27 percent), a woman (15 percent), or under 18 years of age (23 percent).

- A quarter of the world continues to live in severe poverty, including 1.3 billion who must live on less than a dollar a day, according to a 1997 UN Development Programme Report. South Asia and sub-Saharan Africa fared worst, with 40 percent of their population defined as poor. Despite these disparities, the amount of foreign aid given to poor countries dropped from $55.43 billion in 1996 to $47.58 billion in 1997, according to the March 1999 issue of the *UNESCO Courier*, further compromising any chance of alleviating poverty in the less-developed countries.

- Children living in poverty reflect worldwide variations. According to a UNICEF annual survey that defines a household as poor if its disposable income is less than half that country's overall median income, 16 percent of Canada's children are

poor. Compare this with 26.6 percent of children in the Russian Federation, 26.3 percent in the United States, 21.3 percent in the UK, and 17.1 percent in Australia.
- The poorest 20 percent of the world's population consume only 1.3 percent of the global goods, down from 2.3 percent in 1960; by contrast the wealthiest 20 percent consume 86 percent of the world's goods. The world's richest three people have assets that exceed the combined gross domestic product of the 48 least-developed countries.

Defining Poverty: Subsistence or Inclusiveness?

It has been said that problems can't be solved unless people understand what the problem is about (Editorial, 8 Nov., 1998). Certain problems do not receive the kind of attention they deserve because they lack the glamour or visuals to catch public attention or political commitment. Other problems tend to falter because people are unsure of what if anything to do. The issues are too complex for quick analysis and impervious to easy assessment. Poverty is one of those unsolved problems about which people cannot even agree on a workable definition, let alone take steps on a clear solution. Arguments for and against seem to prove every position simultaneously, with the result that problem definition and solution vary with the context or criteria.

Many acknowledge that women, aboriginal people, persons of colour, Atlantic Canadians, and individuals with disabilities lag far behind "mainstream" Canadians in terms of power, wealth, and prestige. The expression the "feminization of poverty" acknowledges what data support: Single women with young children are especially vulnerable to being poor. Child poverty is perceived as especially debilitating because of its long-term effects, culminating in costly adult problems and expensive social services. Since children are rarely responsible for being poor, yet may be its main victims, public sympathy is slanted toward them rather than toward adults who may be criticized as architects of their misfortune. Moreover, the situation does not appear to be improving despite a doubling of dual-income families since 1967. With minimum wage barely covering the essentials, even a two-income household in a large urban centre may have trouble making ends meet and qualify under the low-income cut-off threshold. The plight of the poor is underlined by the proliferation of soup kitchens and food banks, each of which were once seen as stop-gap solutions, but now are firmly entrenched as part of the Canadian social landscape. Yet the impact of poverty cannot be dismissed: How long can people be deprived without inflicting long-term damage to their self-worth and ability to cope? Poverty wears people down and makes it painfully difficult to be productive under the circumstances (Carey, 1999). That poverty exists—and hurts—is certainly beyond doubt. Still, it is one thing to ponder the magnitude and scope of the problem. It may be quite another to define and implement solutions that are doable and just.

Consider the concept of poverty as a social category. What precisely do we mean by the term "poverty"? How do we separate those who are truly destitute from those who have fewer creature comforts without being insensitive to the poor or trivializing the magnitude of their suffering? Is poverty about being poor in the absolute sense of being deprived of income in relation to the population at large? Is the dividing line an absolute measure or is it relative and constantly adjusting according to time and place? Answers to these questions are contingent on how we define poverty: Is it based on absolute need or relative equality; on subsistence factors alone or on the basis of inclusiveness? To date, the debate over the poverty line has tended to reflect essentially an academic exercise. There are no objective measures for quantifying the number of poor, largely because Canada refuses to officially acknowledge that poverty exists. Each approach contains its own bias, subjective assumptions, and emotional language. Depending on which measure is employed, the results can lead to high or low measures of poverty. Yet poverty is more than a statistical "bean counting" exercise. As Richard Shillington (1997) writes, the way in which we define and measure poverty reflects who we are as a society. It conveys an obligation to our children to grow and participate rather than an admonition about sustenance and basic survival.

Most definitions of poverty fall into one of two categories: (a) absolute versus relative; and (b) restrictive or inclusive. One side of the debate defines poverty as absolute privation/needs, a chronic absence of the fundamental necessities of live pertaining to food, shelter, and clothing. Absolute measures look at what it takes to survive in Canada by examining a basket of goods for physical survival—a position endorsed by the Fraser Institute. The "Basic Needs Measure" excludes non-essentials such as books, toys, haircuts, dental services, and school supplies. The food budget is restricted to basic subsistence; for example, no tea or coffee are included, with a total restricted to $25 per week for an elderly woman (Shillington, 1999). Health items are not included in the basket on the grounds that the poor should use emergency facilities, charity dentists in the community, and eyeglasses from the local Lions Clubs (see Chwialkowska, 1999). Stung by public criticism of this mean-spirited approach, the government is casting about for a less tight-fisted definition. It has proposed the notion of a "Market Basket Measure" for limiting the government's obligation to children to a particular basket of goods. Broader than subsistence, but narrower than full inclusiveness in definition, this measure acknowledges that children should not feel excluded from society by being denied the things that many kids take for granted, including vacations and school trips. The government admits that this litmus test does not provide low-income individuals with a share of Canada's wealth. But, compared to the more relative measures such as LICO (see below), Richard Shillington (1999) argues, estimates of the extent of poverty are reduced by about a third, without any appreciable improvement in the standard of living.

To the other side, poverty is defined in relative terms. In a society in which virtually everyone has access to the necessities of life, poverty is not about subsistence or survival. Poverty is measured in terms of what people have or don't have with respect to commonly accepted standards of living. Rather than a checklist of items, the focus is on how people fare in relationship to the rest of society, particularly in terms of their ability to participate and be involved. For example, the Canadian Council of Social Development defines any family that makes less than half the median income of Canadian households as poor. With the poverty line pegged at $40 560 in 1994, its figure for poverty in Canada stood at 22.9 percent (Watson, 1996). Included in this figure is an annual one-week vacation, a recreation budget, a tobacco and alcohol allowance, and a VCR. Statistics Canada uses a "low-income cut-off point" by comparing the spending on necessities by low-income families with typical families. These lines are relative and increase over time with overall increases in income (Shillington, 1999). Low income ("poverty") is defined as being present in any household that spends more than 55 percent of its income on food, shelter, or clothing. This figure is based on what an average family in 1986 spent on the basic necessities of food, shelter, and clothing (36.2%), plus an additional (and largely arbitrary) 20 percent (Watson, 1996). The low-income cut-off line also takes into account the size of the family, and distinguishes between rural and urban families. With shelter costs rapidly rising in major centres, the emergence of the working poor (those whose minimum wage cannot possibly cover the bare essentials) is increasingly a distinctive feature of Canada's poverty landscape.

Absolute and relative indices of poverty differ in terms of their restrictiveness or inclusiveness. Restrictive definitions of poverty often convey a sense of destitution (DeGroot-Maggetti, 1999). It is what we normally think of as the poor—those who are bedraggled in appearance, perpetually hungry, and homeless. According to this "basic level of subsistence" scenario, poverty-stricken individuals should be given sufficient necessities to ensure they do not sicken and die, become a public nuisance, or impose an unnecessary burden on society. Inclusiveness definitions tend to be associated with more progressive welfare systems. The emphasis is not simply on staving off disease or starvation, but on being able to participate equally and fully in society. Reaction is replaced by a proactive commitment to prevention, development, and problem-solving. Energies are increasingly channelled into encouraging poor families to invest in themselves as first steps in taking control of their destiny. Inclusiveness definitions also recognize the implicit value of child development as the key to breaking the poverty cycle. Poverty for children is more than basic survival: What is at stake is the capacity to participate fully as equals in community life, with enough money to go on school trips or to register for organized sports. As Steve Kerstetter, director of the National Council of Welfare writes (1999:A-19) in denying that poverty lines are about being one calorie away from starvation: "...If they were, we could provide every poor person with a giant bag of oatmeal, a gunny sack, and a cot in the flophouses, and feel we had done our job as a compassionate and fairminded people. In reality, poverty lines are about a minimum standard of living in one of the richest countries of the world. They should mark a standard that allows a person to participate in society, not merely to go on breathing." In other words, references to poverty reflect values about a specific vision of society (DeGroot-Maggetti, 1999): Are we comfortable with huge gaps between the rich and poor in society? Do we believe in a society where everyone has the resources to participate fully in the community? Is there a place for food banks in a society that is the envy of most?

The politics of poverty extend to international levels. According to a UN Study, only six percent of Canadians are living in poverty, less than half the proportion in the United States, and about one-third the rate claimed by some indicators in Canada (cited in Beauchesne, 1999). This gives Canada the second lowest poverty level among major industrial countries, just behind Norway (3%) and Finland, Japan, and Luxemborg at 4 percent, but ahead of United States (14%) and Britain (13%). Ireland, at 37 percent, and Spain, at 21 percent, were the highest. The ILO study employed the American method of measuring poverty: the proportion of people who have to live on less than the equivalent of $14.40 (US) per day, adjusted to reflect the purchasing power in each country. In Canada this works out to about $20 dollars per day or about $8000 per year per person, a figure that is dismissed by some as unconscionable in a rich country like Canada, and well beneath the most recent cut-off for a single person in a large city at $16 061.

International trends also reflect a rethinking of poverty. To be sure, the dollar-a-day poverty line remains a widely used measure of poverty. The poor are those whose income is less than a dollar a day per person, an amount that will purchase a bundle of goods sufficient for survival, adjusted for differences in local costs. As well, poverty initiatives are increasingly focused on children, on the assumption that what may be a temporary condition for adults could well become a permanent condition for children with long-term negative repercussions. (see Coyne, 1999). But poverty is no longer restricted to shortage of income. According to the March 1999 issue of *UNESCO Courier*, poverty increasingly entails a process of denial of basic opportunity and choices for human development. The multi-dimensionality of poverty has been emphasized by the UN Development Programme (see Box 3–2). The Human Development Report of 1997 lists three key variables as part of a human poverty index: the percentage of people who die before forty, the number of illiterate adults, and access to health services and clean water.

It is worth noting that out of 130 countries, 90 have developed operational definitions of extreme poverty. Of these, 86 have definitions of overall poverty which go beyond mere subsistence. Interestingly, Canada does not have an official definition of poverty, preferring instead to depoliticize the issue by relying on a low-income cut-off line to describe those in straitened circumstances.

The Art of Defining Problems Away

The way we define the poor is a reflection of the kind of society we live in.

Zygmunt Bauman (1999: 20)

It is accurate to say that the combination of hunger, homelessness, and hardship is transforming Canada into a land of poverty amid plenty (Goar, 1998). Those who prefer to dwell on the plenty point out that average family incomes have risen, most houses have flush toilets and running water, and no one is denied basic health care. Those who dote on the downside point to rising rates of poverty, a UN committee rebuke of Canada for tolerating poverty, and a dramatic increase in food banks. Not unexpectedly, there has been some backlash in sorting through this confusion. In his controversial publication, *Poverty in Canada*, Christopher Sarlo disagreed that all those living below the poverty line are actually poor. Poverty lines are arbitrarily constructed and the income cut-offs provide more than what is needed to survive. Much of what passes for official poverty, Sarlo contended, confuses being poor with inequality and lack of access to middle-class amenities. It simply indicates that some are doing less well than others, rather than being in straitened circumstances or deprived of necessities. For Sarlo, true poverty is rare when measured in terms of "stomach stretching" starvation and lack of fundamental necessities. To claim that three to five million Canadians are living in poverty is dismissed as a fabrication by welfare advocacy and lobby groups for self-serving purposes. Moreover, measures such as the low-income cut-off point were designed in such a way that even major improvements would not necessarily lead to any discernible drop in numbers. Endorsing this relative position casts doubt on whether poverty can ever be completely eliminated; after all, even an overall doubling of incomes would not disturb the ratio of poor to rich. The pie may be getting bigger, but the poor continue to receive a disproportionately smaller slice because of across-the-board increases. In other words, no matter how rich everyone is, the proportion of those who are poor will always remain the same. Such a relativistic standard not only makes it difficult to measure progress on the poverty front, it also reinforces the counter-intuitive notion that Canada has more poor people now than in the past or in some Third World countries (Coyne, 1999). Still others dispute how the figures for poverty are tabulated. Raw figures are based on pre-tax incomes, and ignore the income-allocating aspects of tax law. Also overlooked is the contribution of income-in-kind, such as free dental care or subsidized housing, that welfare recipients receive. Factoring in parent-supported university students and investment-rich seniors also distorts the picture on poverty.

The political nature of these number games should be self-evident. Those whose livelihood depends on the presence of the poor have a vested interest in inflating poverty figures. Other interests would like nothing better than to reduce the number of official poor in Canada

---

| BOX 3.2 | **Different Dimensions of Poverty** |

In 1998, the UNDP published a report entitled "Overcoming Human Poverty," in which different dimensions of poverty were defined (cited in *UNESCO Courier*, March, 1999):

- Human poverty
    the lack of essential human capabilities such as literacy or nourishment

- Income poverty
    the lack of minimally adequate income

- Extreme poverty
    destitution from an ability to satisfy minimum food needs

- Overall poverty
    inability to satisfy both food and non-food requirements

- Relative poverty
    standards of poverty that vary over time or place

- Absolute poverty
    a fixed standard of poverty such as the dollar-a-day poverty line

It should be obvious that a rethinking of poverty is in store. Poverty now includes more than income deprivation, but reflects discourses about quality of life and participation in society. Poverty also includes those working poor who earn an income but not enough to defray the costs of full and equal involvement in the community. And finally, being poor is not simply having less of something than others have. Poverty may have a debilitating impact on a person's life chances.

---

for self-serving reasons. The current figures are so grossly inflated, they contend, that the government invariably looks derelict in meeting its responsibilities, to the detriment of its international reputation. Conversely, a reduction in absolute numbers can be seen as part of a wider government strategy for reducing the deficit through the elimination of social programs. Put candidly, the government has been accused of trying to define the poor out of existence. The net result is a hardening of public attitudes towards poor people as a social problem, accompanied by cut-backs in government welfare spending and a gradual demonization of the poor as lazy freeloaders and a burden on Canadian taxpayers (Mitchell, 1997).

Still, the reality of poverty cannot be brushed off, no matter how it is defined. People who lack the necessities of life suffer in obscurity while scholars fiddle with the statistics, with little appreciable impact on producing positive outcomes. But the poor are people, not just a problem. Up to one child in five faces a higher than average risk of poor physical and mental health, higher infant mortality rates, and higher rates of delinquency and school drop-out. Children's ability to learn is affected by poverty-related hunger, violence, illness, domestic problems, and deprivation (Galt and Cernetig, 1997). According to the National Longititudinal Survey of Children and Youth by Statistics Canada and Human Resources (cited in the *Globe and Mail*, Nov. 24, 1999), children who live in poverty are less ready to learn when they enter school, are more likely to live in dysfunctional families, exhibit behavioural problems pertaining to aggression or depression, and reflect academic lapses such as failing a grade or becoming easily distracted. They also are subject to substance abuse. In short, debates about who really qualifies as poor merely divert attention from real needs and the reality of the problem. The effects of failing to "walk the talk" may magnify the situation through neglect and default rather than through misdeed and expediency.

HOMELESSNESS: POVERTY IN THE STREETS

Poverty as a social problem is expressed in different ways. Chapter 2 on social inequality demonstrated how certain categories of Canadians are more likely than others to dwell on the margins of society. Of those marginalized, the most common were people of colour, working class Canadians, women, those with ethnic backgrounds at odds with the determinants of success, and Canadians in regions that clearly are destined to occupy the political and economic sidelines. In recent years, the profile of the homeless in Canada has grown rapidly, in the process revealing certain difficulties in defining the problem and proposing solutions. Doing nothing is not an option: The prospect of the homeless creating shanty towns under bridges and viaducts that resemble overseas slums seems strangely incongruous in a society that has so much going for it. Small wonder, then, that to some, homelessness is an indictment of Canadian society; to others its existence is an affront to hardworking Canadians everywhere (Ibbitson, 1999).

Many Canadians were startled to learn that homelessness was a far more pervasive social problem than they had imagined. Homelessness was not restricted simply to those "nutters" or "wackos" who gulped down bottles of aftershave lotion. It went beyond a bunch of hot-headed teens who preferred a life on the streets to the comfortable, if confining, structures of home. Homelessness now included the "deserving poor"—people who, through little fault of their own, found themselves in conditions that denied or excluded. It also included those with jobs who aspired to middle-class status, but did not earn enough for adequate shelter (Picard, 2000). Even more shocking was the realization that homelessness was not always a lifestyle choice; for some, it was an option born of necessity or by default. A moment's consideration suggests that Canadians should have seen the onset of this crisis. The number of poor has increased during the 1990s; yet access to reliable housing has shrivelled up to the point where children are now forced to live in hostels or in substandard private dwellings. The federal government stopped building social housing in 1992; the provincial government got out of funding subsidized housing in 1994. The Ontario government's decision to cut welfare rates, including the shelter allowance, by 21.6 percent compounded the problem. And in 1999, the government lifted the lid on rents by suspending rent control on vacant apartments (Carey, 1999). The combination of fewer subsidized apartments and escalating rents on private rentals has created a situation where waiting lists for public housing are seen as a joke.

Homelessness is a social problem in the same way poverty is a social problem. Both poverty and homelessness are seen as social in origin, definition, impact, and treatment. Moreover, neither poverty nor homelessness can be regarded as good for individual health. The fastest growing group of homeless people are those under 18 years of age and families (usually single mother) with young children (Valpy, 1999). Children who are homeless tend to display behaviour that is consistent with failure to integrate into society. Life is lonely on the streets: Two-thirds of homeless people have less than four people in their social circle, including family, and often their only friends are other homeless people (Picard, 2000). This collapse of a social network or failure to foster a positive self-esteem can only result in major social problems later in life. And young homeless men between the ages of

18 and 24 in Toronto are 8 times more likely to die as a result of accidents, poisonings, or overdoses than men in the general population (Tobin, 1999). According to an in-depth interview survey conducted in Ottawa, most of the homeless reported physical and mental health problems, with 60 percent having a diagnosable mental illness, mainly depression (cited in Picard, 2000). To be sure, there is no consensus among experts as to the causes of homelessness. The usual factors are often cited, including both root and immediate causes: poverty; inadequate affordable housing; greedy landlords; a not-in-my-backyard-mentality which makes it difficult to establish shelters for the needy; declining incomes; soaring rents; slashed social spending; mental illness; substance abuse; lifestyle statement; or domestic abuse. In other words, homelessness is largely a structural problem caused by distortions in the distribution of power, opportunities, and privilege. Even defining who qualifies as homeless is not without its problems. The term itself may include runaways, aboriginal peoples in the streets, psychiatric patients, families on waiting lists for shelters, drug addicts, and panhandlers and squeegee kids (Bulla, 1999). How many? It's widely cited that about 3000 people sleep in Toronto hostels on any given night (Ibbitson, 1999). But nobody can guess the number in parks or derelict buildings, in doorways or on heating grates. It is also believed that about two-thirds of the homeless are male and one-third are mentally ill. This lack of consensus for defining the scope of the problem complicates the search for solutions.

To some, the homeless are largely victims of circumstances beyond their control. To many, homeless Canadians are seen as responsible for their lack of coping skills (i.e., refusal to take medication or to comply with sometimes rigid house rules for overnight shelters) or refusal to lead a normal life (Smith, 1999). Such a blaming the victim mentality makes it difficult to generate empathy for the homeless or to commit resources to improve their welfare. Efforts to improve the plight of the homeless run against the grain of many Canadians who believe that making life too comfortable can only make the homeless more dependent and lazy (see Ibbitson, 1999). That kind of Victorian mentality of the "deserving poor" diffuses the political will and financial investment to do something about the problem. The different needs of the homeless—from addiction treatment and job training to housing or mental health support—can also complicate the possibility of common solutions: Some homeless require access to simple and basic shelter, even if this accommodation comes with a set of rules. Others need to find jobs, while still others incapable of working require information about how to stay off the streets and collect the welfare or disability cheques they are entitled to (Bulla, 1999). Those with mental health problems require a caring community agency. It should be noted that federal authorities have ear-marked nearly $750 million to address the homelessness problem. In short, there is no simple solution to the complex problem of homelessness. Only dozens of initiatives along a broad front can possibly address such a pervasive problem. Failure to act decisively will squander the international reputation of Canadians as a compassionate and caring people.

DOING SOMETHING ABOUT POVERTY

Initiatives to reduce poverty are thwarted by popular misconceptions. The poor are poor, it is argued, because they are idle and prefer hand-outs. The poor are responsible for their own plight, according to this line of thinking, since individuals are in control of their destiny. This mentality of assigning primacy to personal responsibility is consistent with a conservative and market-oriented mindset. Government interventions such as pay equity or employment equity are decried for lowering standards while interfering with the free play of market forces. Welfare, in turn, is accused of both undercutting Canada's international competitiveness and perpetuating the very conditions—including dependency and addiction—that it is supposed to eradicate.

Others disagree with this assessment. In her *Dispatches from the Poverty Line*, Pat Capponi reminds us that poverty is a complex problem that cannot be reduced to simple slogans or quick-fix solutions. Poverty, she observes, is hardly a lifestyle choice, but a by-product of generations of neglect, hunger, and domestic abuse. It may be inadvertently perpetuated by social service agencies that inflict humiliation and foster powerlessness among the poor. Governments are responsible too, but not everything can be laid to government cutbacks. The complexity of poverty as a problem makes the possibility of solutions that much more elusive. Ontario's controversial workfare program (welfare to work) is being touted by the government as a success story. Nearly 425 000 have been taken off the welfare rolls and put to work since 1995 (cited in Orwen, 1999). Yet this program is also creating personal hardship and is seen by others as a social disaster, since getting mothers off welfare into work requires childcare that is subsidized and flexible.

Since poverty is usually defined in terms of income shortage, most solutions tend to revolve around money. Money may be the root of all evil, but without it problems are likely to arise, while solutions are unlikely to materialize. In an interesting study for the Canadian Council on Social Development, David Ross and Paul Roberts found that, across a wide range of developmental factors from health and schooling to behaviour and sports participation, children in poor families consistently displayed poorer outcomes. Even more consistent was the income dividing line: Positive outcomes rose sharply as family incomes rise toward the $30 000 to $40 000 range for a family of four. At this level, a rough equality of life chances begins to kick in, prompting Allan Coyne (1999) to point out that when it comes to poverty, equality of outcomes (or conditions) *is* equality of opportunity (also Carey, 1999). The concept of "throwing money at a problem" may provide only a superficial and temporary solution, but it promises to alleviate the suffering of those at the margins.

How does a sociological perspective assist in defining the problem? How does a sociological approach to poverty lead to certain types of solutions? Functionalists and conflict perspectives disagree over the causes and cures of poverty. Functionalists approach society as a fundamentally sound system of interrelated and functioning structures from roles to institution. Dysfunctionalities within the system are usually attributed to individuals who for various reasons cannot cope, especially during times of rapid social change. Individuals may lack the requisite skills and resources because of improper socialization. Or they may be immersed in a culture at odds with mainstream values. Is poverty a cultural response to circumstances in which individuals are located? Proponents of the culture of poverty thesis contend that the poor are poor because of their socialization into a marginalizing lifestyle. A corresponding set of beliefs and attitudes are internalized, often at odds with mainstream definitions of success and achievement. Those immersed in a culture of poverty are not only hindered because of a so-called "poverty of culture," but are stung by low levels of self-confidence that are conducive to resignation and fatalism. The failure of poor families to resemble their middle-class counterparts is also perceived as a contributing factor. As the culture of poverty takes root, moreover, many relinquish any ability to ever escape its restrictions and constraints. A vicious cycle of deprivation is entrenched instead, consolidating what once may have been a temporary adjustment to dire circumstances.

The relevance of poverty cultures as an explanation continues to be hotly debated. Not everyone agrees with the concept because to do so would imply a victim-blame approach.

To suggest that cultures are responsible for being poor is tantamount to pinning the blame on the bearers of culture, in the process ignoring the wider system that creates discriminatory barriers that preclude full and equal involvement. There is disagreement on the ontological basis of a culture of poverty. Debate on this issue has focused on the culture of poverty either as a permanent lifestyle or as a situational adjustment to exceptional circumstances. Are poverty values fundamentally at odds with the dominant culture, or are they simply variations on the mainstream, but incompletely expressed because of diminished confidence or skills to put them into practice? Is a culture of poverty inferior, or is it simply defined as inferior by those with the power to demonize those who veer outside the orbit of middle-class normalcy? To the extent that sociologists accept a culture of poverty argument, the emphasis is on culture as a socially constructed adaptive device within a broader context, rather than a pathology that hobbles and hinders.

Conflict theorists, by contrast, tend to see society as fundamentally unstable and exploitative. Inequality and poverty are inevitable in a system that is based on the rational pursuit of profit, productive property, and class conflict. For conflict theorists, then, poverty stems from social structures. It is a chronic feature of a society in which differences in wealth, power, and status are not only institutionalized and enforced, but also devalued as a means of worth and acceptance. The interplay of racism and discriminatory barriers, including systemic bias and pervasive double standards, continues to impoverish members of society. The logic of capitalism, with its creation of winners and losers, also serves as an inhibiting factor. Without skills or resources, people are pushed into roles and status not of their own making, and often beyond their control. In other words, the loss of jobs and the absence of opportunities are not always the fault of individuals, but implicit in capitalist economies and global market forces. Not unexpectedly, perhaps, the poor are turning their backs on traditional paths towards upward mobility. In part this is because many blue-collar industries are vanishing, and in part it is because of a growing disdain for jobs defined as demeaning (Wrong, 1992).

The conclusion is disheartening but inescapable. In a country with such promise and wealth, the growing condemnation of Canada for its singular lack of progress in battling poverty should come as no surprise. The persistence of poverty is not an inevitability as suggested by the book of John where it is said the poor will always be with us. Nor is it the result of market forces beyond people's control. Punishing rates of poverty are the result of decisions and choices that people make, especially by political authorities who withhold resources or lack the political will to do something about the structures underlying poverty. Policy changes in the past decade have further eroded Canada's safety net for the poor. A political commitment to pare away a comprehensive social security system has dulled the political will to improve the position of low-income earners. No less troubling is the obsession with deficit reduction in the name of global competitiveness, even at the expense of long-cherished social programs. At a time when downsizing and deficit reduction are more the rule than the exception, it becomes increasingly unrealistic to blame the poor for their predicament (Hurtig, 1999). Perhaps it is time to hold the affluent and powerful accountable for actions that render Canadians expendable and keep them mired in poverty.

PREJUDICE, DISCRIMINATION, AND RACISM

FRAMING THE PROBLEM

From afar, Canada strikes many as a paragon of racial tranquility. Racism may loom as the single most explosive and divisive force in many societies, including the United States, but surely not in Canada where racism is publicly scorned and officially repudiated. In contrast with the United States, where race continues to deny or exclude, racism in Canada is thought to be relatively muted, confined to fringe circles, or relegated to the dustbins of history. Laws are in place that not only prohibit racism and discrimination, but also severely punish those in contravention of Canada's multicultural ideals. Brazen racists such as White supremacists are routinely charged and convicted for disseminating hate propaganda. Race riots are virtually unheard of, while blatant forms of racial discrimination have been driven underground. To their credit, Canadians have learned to "walk their talk": Establishment of multiculturalism and employment equity initiatives have catapulted Canada onto the global map as a beacon of sanity for living together with our differences. The demographic revolution that has transformed stodgy provincial cities such as Vancouver and Toronto into vibrant, racially tolerant cosmopolitan centres is yet another positive indicator (Grayson, 1996). The fact that the UN has repeatedly ranked Canada as the best place in the world to live must surely say something about its peoples and their commitments.

Up close, the picture blurs. We could be smug about our enlightened status if racism were a mere blip on Canada's social and historical landscape. This, sadly, is far from the truth. Minority women and men have experienced varying degrees of intolerance and discrimination because of racial and national origins. Racism in Canada was chronic and historically embedded in its ideology and institutions (Satzewich, 1998; Henry et al., 1999). It secured the ideological life-support for capitalism at large, in part by creating a cheap and docile labour force (Bolaria and Li, 1988; McKague, 1992; Satzewich, 1999), in part by rationalizing the exploitation of certain labour segments. Chinese immigrants in particular bore the brunt of mainstream xenophobia toward anything that remotely rankled the privilege, identity, values, and power of this British dominion (Baureiss, 1985; also Ip, 1997). Hate and fear compelled authorities to intern thousands of ethnic minorities, including Ukrainians during World War I and Italians during World War II, at great personal cost to themselves and their families. An internment even more spiteful was inflicted on Japanese-Canadians in British Columbia. Most were rounded up like the Jews in Nazi Germany, their property confiscated and civil rights suspended, before being placed in labour internment camps which were viewed as a prelude to deportation (Samuels, 1997). An apology and modest reparations did not materialize until 1988.

The present may be equally racist, in consequence or by default if not always in intent. Critics charge that racism is alive and well in Canada; only its worst effects are camouflaged by a teflon veneer of politeness and self-delusion (Henry and Tator, 1997). Instead of seeing racism in terms of egregious actions by bigoted persons, the systemic components of institutional bias are increasingly acknowledged. Institutional structures or operational procedures are no longer regarded as neutral or innocent of intent and consequence; rather, they embody the values, needs, perspectives, and experiences of those in charge, to the detriment of those on the margins. Canadians are less likely to express hatred of others because of sanctions; they are more likely to camouflage dislike toward others by way of coded terms. Canada's relations with aboriginal peoples in the 1990s have been marred by racial violence, from the 78-day standoff at Oka in 1990, to the arson and destruction at Burnt Church in 1999, with violent encounters at Gustafsen Lake and Ipperwash in between. Hate crimes in Toronto rose by 28 percent in 1999, to 292 reported incidents, up from 228 in 1998, and just below the high of 302 in 1995, according to the Toronto Police, with the majority of offences being the distribution of hate literature, public mischief (graffiti) and assault. Of the most victimized groups, involving 1296 criminal incidents against a person or property based on race between 1993 and 1998, Blacks were targeted 372 times and Jews 225 times. According to the annual report of the League for Human Rights of B'nai B'rith Canada, 267 anti-semitic incidents were reported in 1999, an increase of 11% over 1998 (cited in *Canadian Press*, Feb. 9, 2000). Racism may be less blatant or pervasive than in the United States, to be sure, but people of colour continue to suffer indignities while confronting barriers that complicate access to housing, employment, and social services (see Reitz and Breton, 1994). Mainstream institutions such as the police or the media are routinely condemned as discriminatory as are their oft-criticized counterparts in the United States. Even Canada's much-lauded initiatives to accommodate diversity through equity-based policies are denounced by critics on both the left and right as thinly-veiled racism that inflicts more harm than good (Thobani,1995; Loney, 1998). Nor can Canadians take much solace from Canada's relatively peaceful race relations record. Incidents of racial conflict may confirm the presence of racism; their absence, however, does not disprove the pervasiveness of dormant hostility toward outgroups (Brown and Brown, 1995). That Canada has managed to escape the debilitating race riots that periodically engulf the United States is commendable in its own right. Yet such a fortuitous state of affairs may reflect exceptional good fortune and a powerful myth-making machine rather than enlightened policies. Refusal to acknowledge the persistence and pervasiveness of racism may have the effect of redoubling its impact on society.

Which picture is more accurate? On one side, there is talk of the "end of racism," and solutions to the race relations problem, thanks to decreases in discrimination, elimination of overtly racial laws, progressive government policy and sanctions, and general improvement in the tenor of minority relations. On the other, there is growing evidence that racism is alive and well: Consider only the persistence of hate crimes; the proliferation of racial hatred over the internet; incidents of police brutality; patterns of systemic institutional bias; and rampages of ethnic cleansing (see also Feagin and Feagin, 1997). So what is going on? Is there a problem, and how do we define its nature, scope, and impact? Is Canada as racist as critics say, or is it essentially an open and tolerant society, with only isolated and random incidents of racism? For some, racism continues to be a fundamental principle of organization and allocation; for others, racism is seen as more situational and muted in its forms and consequences. For still others, concerns are mounting over its manipulation as a political slogan to: (a) silence individuals; (b) close off public debate over complex or controversial ideas; and (c) demonize those with different philosophical assumptions about the nature of society (Satzewich, 1998). Is Canada properly described as a society where individuals are rewarded on the basis of merit, where no group is singled out for negative treatment, and where racial attributes are irrelevant in determining a person's status? Or is there a different slant on reality (Henry et al., 1999)? Perhaps the answer to each of these questions hovers somewhere in between the poles of naive optimism and cynical pessimism. A sense of perspective is badly needed, given the awkward and conflicting blend of hard-core racists and resolute anti-racists coexisting in Canada, with the vast majority of individuals wavering somewhere along this continuum. Canada's best-documented race riot, in 1931 at Christie Pits in Toronto, involving a scuffle between Jews and non-Jews, claimed a dozen injuries but no fatalities. Many immigrants have experienced discrimination and racism, but rarely death or imprisonment; and people of colour continue to encounter mainstream cultural ethnocentrism, but not ethnic cleansing (Thompson and Weinfeld, 1995; Levitt, 1997). Put bluntly, it is just as wrong to exaggerate the notion of Canada as irrevocably racist, with countless hate groups resorting to violence to achieve supremacist goals, as it is to underestimate the tenacity of racism in conferring privilege on some and disadvantage on others.

The somewhat contested allegation that Canada is racist raises a host of troubling questions. Responses to these questions not only sharpen our understanding of racism, they also impart a conceptual framework for analyzing racism as a social problem in Canada. Of those questions for debate and discussion, the following secure the framework for analysis:

1. Is racism a social problem? How and why? What is its impact?

2. Is racism increasing across Canada, or are Canadians becoming more aware of racism, with a growing willingness to report violations to proper authorities? Do Whites tend to underestimate racism to protect themselves from guilt or charges of racism, while minorities overstate it to keep the pressure on or not be out of step with peers (Holmes, 1999)?

3. Is racism of recent vintage in Canada, or is racism deeply embedded in Canadian history and institutional structures? Is racism a departure from the norm in Canada, or does it constitute an expression and embodiment of Canadian society?

4. To what extent is racism about attitudes or structures? Is racism a case of cultural ignorance, intense dislike, or individual fear? Should racism be defined as a structural feature of Canadian society in which access to power and privilege is systematically controlled? Is there hope for initiatives that focus on influencing attitudes (from diversity training to minority role models) rather than changing discriminatory behaviour?

5. Is racism a "thing" out there, or does racism have nothing to do with the intrinsic quality of the act, but, rather, an attribute that is applied after the fact in light of the context or consequence? To what extent should racism be defined in the "eye of the beholder"; that is, is a racist incident one that is perceived as such by the victim?

6. Is it possible to be colour-blind, yet racist? Can colour-consciousness be regarded as progressive and non-racist? Is racism any kind of differential treatment based of race, regardless of intent or benefit, or does such a label depend on the intent or the context? Is it racist to treat everyone the same irrespective of difference or disadvantage, or is it racist to determine a person's worth by race or ethnicity? Is the term "reverse racial discrimination" a contradiction in terms?

7. How valid are all references to racism? Is any criticism of minorities an expression of racism, by definition? Is there a danger of overuse by seeing racism in everything while ignoring other dimensions or denying valid concerns? If racism is expanded to mean everything, is there a risk of its meaning nothing? When are references to racism a kind of censorship for silencing opponents or suppressing information? Can constant repetition diminish or trivialize the impact of racism on those who routinely endure its presence?

8. Does Canada have a race relations problem implying distinct "races" of people in interaction with others? Or is it more accurate to say that group relations in Canada are racialized in a way that is likely to foster social problems (Satzewich, 1999; Leodakis and Satzewich, 1998)?

9. What would a non-racist society look like? Is such an utopian state of affairs possible in a complex and competitive society, given the question of whether any institution can ever do enough to bridge racially divided perceptions or whether racist attitudes are so deeply embedded that nothing can root them out (Holmes, 1999)?

By using these questions and concerns as a framework for analysis, this chapter will explore racism as a social problem in Canada. Racism is examined as a concept for analysis as well as a reality for many Canadians. Both conditions (including "causes, consequences, characteristics, and cures") and constructions ("acting upon these conditions") are taken into consideration, in hopes of improving our understanding of the so-called "race relations problem." The social and structural conditions that give rise to various forms of racism are explored; so too is the manner by which racism (a) defines who gets what in society; (b) pervades institutional practices and everyday encounters; and (c) resists eradication, but is amenable to challenge at individual and collective levels. Different dimensions of racism are analyzed and assessed in casting about for a definition, including racism as (a) race, (b) culture, and (c) power. The magnitude and scope of racism will be assessed by dissecting its constituent elements, including prejudice (from ethnocentrism to stereotyping) and discrimination (including harassment). The different dimensions of racism are also compared. Those involving the personal and the deliberate are contrasted with the impersonal and systemic. Racism is also expressed at different levels, from the interpersonal (including red-necked and polite) to the institutional (including the systematic and systemic) to the societal (including everyday and cultural). An understanding of the many masks of racism provides a platform for exploring the concept of anti-racism. Anti-racist strategies are classified as personal or institutional, then examined with respect to differences in objectives, means, and outcomes. Also included is a discussion of why racism continues to persist, despite the fact that "we should know better" in these enlightened times. The chapter begins by looking at the constituent components of racism, namely, prejudice and discrimination.

PREJUDICE AND DISCRIMINATION

Racism does not exist as a monolithic reality. Nor is it a kind of thing out there that everyone can agree on. Racism ultimately touches on a variety of social processes, from the immediate and everyday to the remote and systemic. Each of the components that constitutes racism contributes to its totality as an ideology and practice. For purposes of analysis, the building blocks of racism consist of prejudice (including ethnocentrism and stereotypes) and discrimination (including harassment). New ways of looking at discrimination confirm the challenges of solving this problem. They also reinforce the deep embeddedness of racism within Canada's institutional structures.

Prejudice

The concept of prejudice refers to negative, often unconscious, and preconceived notions about others. Prejudice arises because of our tendency to prejudge persons or situations as a way of imposing definition and order on the world around us. Prejudicial thinking is normal and necessary. It is fundamental to the way that individuals process information with respect to ingroup-outgroup relations (Thomas, 1998). It consists of prejudgments that are irrational and not founded on the basis of existing or compelling evidence. Many regard prejudice as a psychological phenomenon with a corresponding set of authoritarian personality traits (Adorno, 1950; Allport, 1954). Others link these prejudgments with a visceral and deep-seated fear of those whose appearance or practices threaten a cherished and comfortable status quo, or a fear of those who are different or who challenge our certitudes and values. Still others equate prejudice with (a) feelings of superiority; (b) a perception of subordinate groups as inferior; (c) a belief in the propriety of White privilege and power; and (d) reluctance to share scarce resources (Blumer, 1958). In that prejudice may involve a projection of "us" on "them," such beliefs may say more about "us" and our need to protect our ego from "them" (Curtis, 1997). For sociologists, prejudice is inseparable from the nature of group dynamics in society. Prejudices do not materialize out of nowhere; nor are they the by-product of unhealthy personal development. The nature and content of prejudice is situated within the social and historical circumstances in which it is generated. In short, prejudice refers to a set of generalized attitudes and beliefs that encourages the perception of others at odds with objective facts (Holdaway, 1996). Unlike ignorance, prejudice is characterized by an inflexible refusal to modify beliefs when presented with contrary evidence.

National surveys confirm what many probably suspect (Henry and Tator, 1985): Many Canadians are inclined to negatively prejudge others because of ignorance or visceral dislike. Tests, such as the Implicit Association Test, suggest that the vast majority of people have unconscious prejudices because of exposure to cultural values and social dynamics (Large, 1998). Prejudicial attitudes are perceived as particularly hard on certain visible minority communities such as Blacks and Chinese, according to the *Toronto Star's* Beyond 2000: Home to the World study project, with 68 percent of Blacks, and 64 percent of Chinese acknowledging prejudice against their community (Carey, 1999). The nature of prejudice may be changing (Pincus and Ehrlich, 1994): The strongly held sense of biological inferiority and hateful stereotypes have given way to rejection and denial on the basis of cultural differences and unacceptable lifestyles. This cultural prejudice is reflected in and reinforced by stereotyping—unwarranted generalizations about others; it also is expressed by ethnocentrism, with its belief in the self-proclaimed superiority of one culture over others. It is quite possible that many references to racism are confused with stereotyping or ethnocentrism.

Nevertheless, the consequences of such cultural rejection may be racist and controlling, given the potential to perpetuate a racialized social pecking order.

Ethnocentrism

Every society socializes its members to accept the normalcy and naturalness of their way of life. People grow up believing that what they think and how they act are universally applicable, and that others tend to think or act along these same lines. Ethnocentrism is the term to describe this prejudgment about ourselves and the world out there. It can be defined in two ways. First, it consists of a process whereby individuals tend to be "trapped within their truths," and interpret reality from their cultural point of view as normal and necessary, while assuming that others will do so also if given a chance. Other realities are dismissed as inferior or irrelevant. Second, ethnocentrism refers to a set of beliefs in the superiority of one's own culture compared to others. It represents an uncompromising loyalty to, and belief in, one's own cultural values and practices as the norm against which all others are judged. Others are dismissed as inferior by virtue of taking cultural practices out of context for comparison, and judging these practices by one's own standards.

There is nothing intrinsically wrong with thinking one's cultural lifestyle is self-evident and preferable. Difficulties arise when these standards are used as a frame of reference for negatively evaluating others as backward, immoral, or irrational in contexts where power differences prevail. Further problems appear when these ethnocentric judgments are used to condone the mistreatment of others. In other words, ethnocentrism is a two-edged social phenomenon: Favouritism towards one's group may forge the bonds of cohesion and morale; it can also foster inter-group tension and hostility.

Stereotyping

Ethnocentrism often leads to a proliferation of stereotypes about outgroup members. Stereotypes are essentially generalizations about others, often reflecting first impressions, and are thought to be unfounded on the basis of available evidence. Stereotyping reflects a universal tendency to reduce a complex phenomenon to simple(istic) explanations that are generalized to a whole category without acknowledging individual differences (Isajiw, 1999). In an information-rich environment, stereotypes allow people to cope with an economy of effort. Others argue that stereotypes are generalizations, but in the sense of statistical approximations that may reflect some measure of reality rather than a literal description of every member in a group (Seligman, 1999). The dangers of exaggeration may result in oversimplified generalizations.

Like ethnocentrism, this stereotypical notion of defining before seeing is harmless on its own. Problems arise when these preconceived mental images give way to discriminatory practices. The dispossession of aboriginal peoples from their lands was facilitated by circulation of negative images of First Nations as savages, cannibals, or brutes (Ponting, 1998). A pervasive anti-Asianism in British Columbia fostered hatred against Asian populations, thereby simplifying the task of expelling 22 000 Japanese-Canadians from the West Coast in 1942. And hostility toward Arab/Muslim Canadians continues to fester in light of demeaning stereotypes that portray Arab Canadians as (a) a Third World visible minority; (b) colonized peoples without democratic traditions; and (c) pro-terrorist religious fanatics who are resolutely anti-Western (Siddiqui, 1998). Finally, stereotypes continue to drive a wedge between young people and the police, each of whom appear willing to believe the worst of the other. According to one youth, in confirming that young people won't respect police because police don't respect them:

> [T]he police perceive me as being a bad person...they judge me by how I look. Just because I am Black, wear baggy jeans, have a gold tooth, and wear a cap or toque, they won't even talk to me properly. (Cited in Moss, 1998:D-1)

All negative stereotypes are hurtful. Failure of minority women and men to perform well in society may have less to do with ability than with the circulation of stereotypes that tend to deny, demean, or distort (Steele, 1999). Nor can people appreciate how insulting it is to be stereotyped by race or ethnicity instead of being judged as individuals on the basis of achievements and personality. Nevertheless, not all stereotypes are equal in impact (Stamm, 1993). Context and consequence are crucial, especially for vulnerable minorities. For example, members of a dominant group may diffuse negative stereotyping about themselves since they as a group have control over a wide range of representations that flatter or empower. Even a constant barrage of negative images can be absorbed without harm or damage. Stereotypes might make White men uncomfortable, yet many possess the resources to resist or neutralize them. Power and privilege provide a protective layer. For minorities, however, stereotyping is a problem. Each negative image or unflattering representation reinforces their peripheral position within an unequal society. The media are a major source of stereotyping; so too are ethnic jokes. Ethnic jokes often portray minorities in a demeaning way, not out of malice, but because such humour by definition is simplistic and prone to exaggeration. The consequences, while unintended, are damaging in unequal contexts: Minorities are portrayed in unidimensional terms such as "comics," "athletes," "victims," "vixens," or "violent." These images, in turn, can be employed to justify daily violence or structural oppression through the negative effects of a "chilly climate" (Ford, 1994). In short, stereotypes are not an error in perception, at least no more so than prejudice reflects psychological flaws. In terms of its social dimension, stereotyping is yet another instrument of social control in preserving the prevailing distribution of power and resources (Stamm, 1993).

Discrimination

Prejudice refers to attitudes and beliefs; by contrast, discrimination consists of the process by which these prejudgments are put into practice. The term "discrimination" can be employed in different ways. Non-evaluative meanings indicate a capacity to distinguish (for example, a colour-blind person may not distinguish between blue and green). Evaluative meanings of discrimination can be used positively ("a discriminating palate") or negatively ("a differential treatment") depending on whether the distinction is appropriate or legitimate. Section 15 of the Charter prohibits discrimination on the basis of race, ethnicity, or origins; it also concedes the necessity for "discriminatory" measures, such as employment equity, to assist historically disadvantaged minorities to compete on a level playing field. D'Sousa (1995) refers to positive discrmination that is based on taking evasive action or making a sound judgment on the strength of perceived or statistical patterns of behaviour, even if these group generalizations are unfair and reflect badly on targeted group members. The noted Black leader, Jesse Jackson, spoke to this effect in 1994:

> There is nothing more painful for me at this stage in my life than to walk down the street and to hear footsteps and to start to think about robbery and then to look around and see its someone White and feel relieved.

Other uses of non-discriminatory distinctions can be applied to private clubs or insurance companies taking into account age or gender in determining levels of benefits or payouts (Schnauer, 1997). In short, some forms of discrimination are inevitable and acceptable—even essential—to the functioning of society (MacQueen, 1995).

Discrimination in the context of unequal relations involves the differential treatment of minority groups not because of their ability or merit, but because of irrelevant characteristics such as skin colour or lifestyle preference. Individuals are lumped together as members of a devalued group rather than valued as individuals with skills and talents. Intrinsic to all types of discrimination are the realities of power. Those with access to institutional power possess the capacity to put prejudice into practice in a way that denies, excludes, or controls. This discrimination may be open and blatant, or it may be covert, thus prompting companies to see whether anything in their hiring or promotional procedures may unintentionally result in the exclusion of otherwise qualified applicants. In some cases indirect discrimination happens when the outcomes of rules or procedures that apply equally to everybody have the unintended effect of undermining some groups' access to benefits or opportunities. Combining these dimensions produces a workable definition: Discrimination can be defined as any act, whether deliberate or not, that has the intent or the effect of adversely affecting ("denying" or "excluding") others on grounds other than merit or ability.

CASE STUDY 4-1	Discrimination by Default

Neither institutions nor workplaces can be regarded as neutral sites that are devoid of intent or consequences. Rather, workplace institutions and practices are loaded with ideological assumptions that inadvertently favour some at the expense of others. Rules and procedures that define how "things are done around here" with respect to "who gets what" tend to reflect the values, perspectives, and expectations of those in charge. These biases in defence of dominant interests are particularly evident in the institutional rules that govern the pursuit of equity in the workplace, even though certain patterns of discrimination may be difficult to discern or to eliminate. Contrary to popular perception, employers have the right to discriminate when distinctions are pertinent to job-related specifications (Levitt, 1999). Discrimination is also permitted

when directed at improving the lot of those historically disadvantaged. Only those grounds prohibited by human rights legislation, such as gender or ethnicity, are defined as discriminatory. Such distinctions raise awkward questions about equality: Should differences be taken into account if true equality is to be attained? Or is true equality based on treating everyone the same regardless of colour or gender?

A recent B.C. Superior Court decision intensified debate over the politics of discrimination. A mandatory fitness test for firefighters was criticized as discriminatory rather than a bona fide occupational requirement for the safe and efficient discharge of work-related duties. The case revolved around a female firefighter who had lost her job for failing a new test of aerobic fitness that was introduced as a precondition of employment for front-line forest firefighters. The running standard of 2.5 kms in 11 minutes or less was established in 1991 when a coroner's inquest recommended that for safety reasons, only physical fit people be assigned to front line firefighting. However, the Court ruled that the standard was discriminatory since it: (a) was based on the physiology of male firefighters; (b) failed to take into account the different physiologies of men and women; (c) evaluated women by male standards; and (d) invoked a level of aerobic capacity that was irrelevant to performing firefighter duties (Lawton, 1999).

The implications of this finding are far-reaching. According to the Court, employers must guard against establishing stringent standards that can have the effect, rather than just the intent, of excluding or denying minorities. If employers propose a certain test for workers that directly or indirectly discriminates by gender, race, or ethnicity, they must demonstrate: (a) its necessity in meeting requirements related to the job; (b) that the exclusionary rule is implemented in good faith, rather than being a cover for discrimination; and (c) that the capabilities and abilities of groups of individuals are taken into account and reasonably accommodated (Mawhinney, 1999). In other words, the Court concluded that it is discriminatory to hold women to a male standard that is not necessarily job-related. It also is discriminatory to make rules that assume everyone is a male, or White, or able-bodied, or Christian, and to be judged accordingly.

This court decision has hardly proven the final word on employing difference as a basis of entitlement. In another case, the LSAT test as a way of assessing student applicants to law school has been deemed discriminatory by the Canadian Bar Association, on the grounds that the test systemically discriminates against racial minorities because of its basis on the academic background of the White middle class (Humphreys, 1999). As for those concerned about a diminuation of the skills of firefighters, thus compromising safety in the name of political correctness when incorporating factors other than merit, such as gender or race, such fears are misplaced. Candidates for the Toronto firefighting service must pass the following physical exam before entry into the fire academy (see Wente, 1999):

- carry a 9.1 kilogram cylinder on one's back
- climb a 12.2 meter ladder
- crawl around blindfolded in a small space to find an object
- lift a ladder weighing 25 kilograms
- drag a dummy the weight of a downed firefighter through an obstacle course
- pass a hose test and rope pull test
- run a short distance wearing 20 kilograms of clothing

These criteria are regarded as bona fide occupational requirements, unlike the situation in B.C. in which the ability to run 2.5 kms in 11 minutes has proven irrelevant and discriminatory in consequence if not necessarily in intent. With each institution under pressure to be inclusive without compromising standards, the politics of difference will continue to transform the workplace into a contested site in which the rightness or wrongness of such tests or requirements must be judged by their actual effect on society or the workplace, rather than by their adherence to abstract legal principles (Cohen, 1999).

Although discrimination is often paired as the behavioural counterpart of prejudice, such a distinction or relationship is not as clear-cut as appearances might suggest. Discrimination can exist without prejudice; conversely, prejudice may flourish without its expression in discrimination. Prejudice and discrimination are analytically distinct concepts that can vary independently under certain conditions. That is, an individual can be prejudiced, yet may not act in a discriminatory manner for a variety of reasons (see LaPiere, 1934). Fear, threats, sanctions, company policy, or good sense may encourage individuals to compartmentalize their prejudice from everyday action. By way of contrast, discrimination can prevail in many domains where wilful malice is absent. What is critical in defining discrimination is the context in which the actions occur, together with the consequences of these actions in unequal situations. This is especially true in situations involving institutional or organizational settings. Here, negative treatment toward outgroups is deeply embedded within formal structures and rules, often beyond the consciousness or personalities of those who occupy organizational offices. Thus institutions can operate on racist principles even though the individuals themselves are free of prejudice. This notion of systemic bias will be explored shortly.

Harassment

Harassment is commonly appraised as a type of discrimination. Racial harassment consists of persistent and unwelcome actions of a racially oriented nature by those who ought reasonably to know that such attention is unwanted (U.W.O, 1993). In the words of Monique Shebbeare (McGill, 1994:6), harassment involves:

> [t]he abusive, unfair, or demeaning treatment of a person or group of persons that has the effect or purpose of unreasonably interfering with a person's or group's status or performance or creating a hostile or intimidating working or educational environment...

As is the case with discrimination, harassment constitutes an abuse of power that need not be explicitly directed at a specific target. Seemingly minor and isolated incidents may amount to harassment when viewed over time or in context. The creation of a chilly climate, or "poisoned environment," because of harassment can also have an adverse effect on work, study, involvement, or well-being (Waterloo, 1994). Others disagree. A distinction is posited between harassment and causing offence. Harassment should be restricted to speech or behaviour that targets a particular individual or group in a way that inhibits that person(s) from full and equal participation within the institution. Merely offending someone because of random ethnic jokes or thoughtless racist remarks should not be considered harassing (Stockholder, 1997). In both cases, harassment is ultimately defined from the perspective of the victim in determining acceptable boundaries, and what distinguishes annoyance from harassment, and consensual conduct from an abuse of power.

To sum up: Many have equated racism as a combination of: Prejudice + Discrimination = Racism. In theory, racism entails a complex interplay of ideas and actions, with its admixture of prejudice (stereotyping and ethnocentrism) and discrimination (harassment). It also encompasses an ideology with a patterned set of responses. These responses combine to explain, justify, rationalize, and legitimize the unequal treatment of minorities through political exclusion, economic exploitation, or social segregation. The key element in this equation is power. When combined with power, the interplay of prejudice and discrimination create fertile grounds for racism to thrive.

Problematizing Racism

Awareness is mounting that racism is an everyday reality for many Canadians, that racist practices affect individuals in very real ways, and that racism is not some anachronistic survivor, but is dynamically active and socially intrusive (Satzewich, 1998). Rather than sitting still or staying pat, racism more closely resembles a moving target that is difficult to pin down or control. The concept of racism is increasingly defined not as a thing with definitive attributes, but as an attribute that is applied to something because of context or consequence. Racism can span the spectrum from the openly defamatory to the systemic, in selectively conferring institutional advantage, with the subtle and discreet in between (Henry, 1997). Certain types of racist behaviour are unplanned and unpremeditated; they are expressed in isolated acts at irregular intervals because of individual impulse or insensitivity. Other expressions of racism are less spontaneous or sporadic; they are systemic and manifest instead through discriminatory patterns that may be unintentional but no less real. Expressions of racism can be wilful, intentional, or conscious; alternatively, they can be involuntary, inadvertent, or unconscious. Racism may be expressed by individuals or entrenched within institutional systems. Some see racism as something individuals do or don't do, while others define it as structural arrangements that exclude and deny. Racism may reflect an exaggeration of differences or, alternatively, a denial of difference. For some, racism consists of any actions that single out a minority for positive or negative treatment. For others, racism is the refusal to recognize people's disadvantages and differences as a basis for recognition or reward. In other words, racism means whatever people want it to mean, and such subjectivity may be helpful, but may also confuse or provoke.

Part of the problem in securing a definition stems from reality itself. Racism is so expansive, with such an array of meanings from context to context, that most despair of a common meaning in the conventional sense of a shared definition. Definitional difficulties are compounded by an indiscriminate use of the term itself. While references may imply a singular type of racism or a population that is divisible into racist and non-racist, in reality, racism represents an omnibus concept with an remarkable capacity to bend, elude, twist, conceal, and shape, depending on context and consequences. Negative comments involving racially different persons are assumed to be racist; nevertheless, the remarks may more accurately reflect ignorance, bad manners, greed, fear, or laziness on the part of the speaker (Wieseltier, 1989). For example, resentment toward employment equity or immigration policy may involve a complex array of attitudes and concerns about society-building, government involvement, or core values, in which race or racism is but one dimension (Satzewich, 1998). Conversely, seemingly neutral or complimentary comments may be interpreted by others as patronizing at best or racist at worst. Repeated references to racism as the precipitating cause of behaviour may gloss over the complexity of motives in shaping actions (Palmer, 1996). Blaming racism for everything when race is irrelevant may be racist in its own right. Doing so may draw attention to racial rather than social causes of minority problems, in effect contributing to perceptions of minorities as victims or villains. Constant and repetitive use of the term also runs the risk of reducing racism to a harmless cliché, thus trivializing its consequences for victims at large. Finally, racism is vulnerable to manipulation by various interests along the political spectrum. Racism as a smokescreen may divert attention from the issues at hand; likewise, it may cower people into silence for fear of being branded a racist. Such labelling raises the question of what it is about racism that makes it so intimidating.

In short, there is no timeless essence or absolute standard for racism (Winant, 1998). The possibility of consensus is complicated by a combination of demographic changes, shifts in intellectual fashion, and global developments. Conceptualizing racism has varied over time and place, has undergone shifts in emphasis and scope, reflects variations in context and consequences, and upholds the cliché of the "eye of the beholder" (see also Salomos and Back, 1996). To further complicate the matter, a take on racism may depend on where we stand in society. Discrepancies in perception can be expected, given the widely divergent experiences and life chances in society. Whites may not deny the existence of racism, preferring instead to see it as an irrational aberration from the normal functioning of society that can be isolated and eradicated. Racism is perceived as a small bunch of "bad apples" in an essentially sound social "barrel." Minority women and men, by contrast, tend to view this barrel as fundamentally "rotten to the core," with the "bad apples" being simply the most obvious manifestation of the rot that has set in. For minorities, racism is a central and recurrent aspect of a racialized society, in which patterns of power and privilege are reproduced in overt and covert ways. The racism that is experienced by minorities is not of the "in-your-face" variety. It is conveyed by power imbalances that "other-izes" people of colour as inferior or irrelevant, and inappropriate. In other words, White refusal to endorse power-sharing in pursuit of equality of group outcomes may be perceived as self-serving and racist, inasmuch as such a stance may have the effect of perpetuating a racialized status quo. This perceptual gap between Whites and people of colour makes it difficult to get a handle on a definition of racism that meets with everyone's approval.

Dimensions of Racism

Conceptual uncertainty over racism is a surprising admission, in light of its profile and pervasiveness. As many definitions exist as specialists in this area. Certain actions are unmistakably racist; others are defined as such because of context or consequence. Generally speaking, reference to racism is multi-dimensional (Winant, 1998). The multi-dimensionality of racism appears to sort itself out into three interwoven streams: racism as biology, as culture, and as power. Racism is expressed in terms of who people are (biology or race), what they do (culture), and where they stand in the broader scheme of things (power). These distinctions are analytically useful for conceptual purposes; in reality, however, they are interrelated.

Racism as Biology ("Racism as Race")

This dimension of racism is derived from the root, "race," with its attendant notion that biology is destiny. Racism as biology (or race) can be used in three ways. First, it entails a belief that people's behaviour is determined by genes or biology. For example, assuming that Blacks are naturally born athletes, while the Japanese are naturally gifted scientists may be regarded as racist. Second, related to this is the use of racism as a basis for any kind of entitlement or evaluation of others. For example, to include visible minorities as an employment equity target is racist regardless of the intent or outcome, since it assigns privilege or preference on the basis of appearance rather than actions. Paradoxically, others would argue that using race to create equality by way of employment equity is the antithesis of racism, even if the rhetoric sounds the same. Third, racism as biology refers to the process of attaching an evaluative and moral quality to perceived biological differences. This racism transforms these differences into an ideology of hierarchy to justify the dominance of one group over another

(Jakubowicz et al., 1994). A relatively cohesive set of beliefs ("ideology") and practices is imposed that labels, classifies, evaluates, and ranks members of a group along a hierarchy by virtue of their inclusion in a predefined category. This racism as race begins with the ideological belief that people can be divided into "races" and assessed or treated accordingly. The human world is partitioned into a set of fixed and discrete categories of population. Each of these racial categories contains a distinctive and inherited assemblage of social and biological characteristics that can be arranged in ascending/descending orders of importance. Unequal treatment of others is then justified on the grounds of innate differences between races. Racial doctrines not only define certain types of behaviour (such as intelligence) as bio-genetically programmed. A moral value of inferiority or superiority is also assigned to human differences. Certain races are judged inherently unequal because of social or mental deficiencies, and subsequently denied rights and opportunities for full participation because of these imputed differences. In some cases, hatred toward others is reflected in and reinforced by this rationale of innate differences as a basis for justifying unequal treatment.

Racism as Culture ("Racism without Race")

The biological focus of racism has shifted in recent years to take into an account assumptions about cultural inferiority rather than a preoccupation with pigment-focused inferiority. Racism is no longer perceived as a universalist discourse on biological dominance, as was the case with colonialism. The objective then was to destroy the "other," to exploit them on the grounds of their biological inferiority, or to subordinate and assimilate them to the colonizer's concept of progress (Wieviorka, 1998). The new racism is rooted in a dislike toward the "other," not only because of who they are ("biology") but also because of what they do ("culture"). Minorities are denied or excluded by racializing cultural differences as a basis for denial or dislike. Instead of assertions about the differing endowments of different races, this discourse on racism is conducted without reference to "race." A cultural framework is invoked for framing debates about inclusion and exclusion as well as about belonging and acceptance.

Under cultural racism, ethnic minorities are no longer dismissed as racially inferior. Dominant sectors are not defined as racially superior, but as culturally normal. This cultural racism prevails when people of one culture assume their way of doing things is normal and necessary, and they possess the power to impose these beliefs and practices on others. The appeal is no longer to biological dominance, but to cultural uniformity in the guise of citizenship, patriotism, and heritage (Wieviorka, 1998). This newer racism is rooted in a coded language that links social cohesion with national identity by way of culture (Jayasuriya, 1998). Racism as culture is predicated on the principle that the cultural "other" poses a danger or threat to the mainstream. Culturally different migrants are defined as the source of a society's social problems, Wieviorka (1998) writes, with dominant groups drawing on racial definitions that combine biology with culture to demonize or scapegoat the "other" on the grounds that they are too aggressive, too "uppity," too demanding, too successful, or not successful enough. Contemporary racist discourses are aimed at isolating or segregating the "other" when differences are seen as beyond the pale of integration. Cultural differences are racialized or vilified to marginalize a group as inferior or irrelevant. Conversely, these differences are subject to intense assimilationist pressure in hopes of preserving a preferred way of living (Madood and Berthoud, 1997). In more extreme cases, those who do not belong to the cultural nation are expelled or eliminated.

Racism as Power ("Racialization as Racism")

Another dimension focuses on the notion of racism as power. This broader definition goes beyond racism as a set of ideas or individual actions. It also acknowledges that racism is not a static or fixed entity. Racism is approached as virtually any type of exploitation or process of exclusion by which the dominant group institutionalizes its privilege and power at the expense of others (Bonilla-Silva, 1996). The idea of racialization is crucial to this domination. Racialization begins with the notion that there is no such thing as race relations involving discrete biological races in relationship to one another (Holdaway, 1997). What prevails instead are relations that have been racialized through a process by which some groups have the power to attach social signficance to, draw boundaries around, and take advantage of each other on the basis of imputed racial ("physical") differences. With racialization, meanings associated with race are negatively assigned to particular practices or objects (Henry et al., 1999). For example, consider how urban crime in Canada is "racialized" around the image of Black criminals. The routine, recurrent, and organized features of society become infused with racial undertones by virtue of the distribution of valuable resources along racist lines. The following conditions are thought to produce a racialized social order: (a) different social rewards or economic penalties are allocated to groups along racial lines; (b) a set of social relations and practices based on racial distinctions are established and entrenched at all societal levels; (c) once this structure is constructed, a racial ideology evolves that not only reflects racialized inequities, but also provides an organizational map to guide the actions of all racial actors; and (d) racial struggles and contestation over scarce resources emerge as part of this racialized hierarchical structure (Bonilla-Silva, 1996). Finally, racism as power also entails the capacity for some to establish agendas regarding what is normal, necessary, desirable, or acceptable, thus reinforcing the superiority of one group over another. Intent and motive may be less important than the context or the consequences of an action on those without the resources to deflect or defuse them. bell hooks (1995:154–155) reinforces the notion that racism is not about prejudice, but about power. She writes:

> Why is it so difficult for many White folks to understand that racism is oppressive not because White folks have prejudicial feelings about Blacks...but because it is a system that promotes domination and subjugation? The prejudicial feelings some Blacks may express about Whites are in no way linked to a system of domination that affords us any power to coercively control the lives and well-being of White folks.

If racism is about power, reverse racism may be a contradiction in terms, since those without access to institutionalized power or resources cannot racialize the other in a way that demeans, controls, or exploits. Racism is not a two-way street, in other words, but an expressway with controlled-access points for those privileged enough to hog the centre lane.

Racism, then, is about power, not pigmentation (Khayatt, 1994). It represents the power held by one group of individuals that has a controlling effect over another on the basis of appearance, intelligence, or moral worth (University of Guelph, 1994). Racism is not only about individual prejudice or cultural space. It is about a refusal to share power (Dei, 1996; Satzewich, 1998). Nor is it about differences per se, although racism challenges a people's humanity and their right to exist as different human beings. It is about how these differences are racialized by those in power to create social hierarchies that deny or exclude because of race. In contrast with perception of race as prejudicial ideas, racism as power points to the primacy of structures, values, and institutions in racializing a society that allocates resources and rewards according to race (Bonilla-Silva, 1996). To be sure, power is not used in the sense of a static resource, with White people holding all the power in some kind of zero-sum game. Power is perceived as a component in social relations that is subject to competition, negotiation, and compromise (Holdaway, 1996). Minorities are not powerless; people of colour may tap into pockets of power to resist, remove, redefine, or renew. Still, only White power is institutionalized within the structures, values, and institutions of society, and it these institutionalized power relations that empower some groups to formulate ideologies that reproduce relationships of inequality (Guibernau, 1996). This power is: (a) expressed at the level of dominant-subordinate interaction; (b) embedded within the institutional framework of society; (c) buttressed by a coherent system of ideas and ideals; and (d) perpetuated by vested interests. In short, power must be situated at the centre of any analysis of racism, with particular attention to how historically constituted relations of domination and subordination are embedded within the institutional structures of society.

A Working Definition

Acknowledging the different dimensions of racism is a blessing and curse. For some, racism is defined as a predisposition to "biologize" the intellectual, moral, and social characteristics of a person or group. A racially based ideology of "who gets what" is created, involving a so-called hierarchy of superior and inferior races that unjustly diminishes others and justifies this discrimination by reference to biological reductionism. Others are leaning toward cultural definitions of racism. Boundaries between groups are drawn by racializing culturally different groups and signifying them as different and a threat to conventions ("racism without race") (Malik, 1996). Others prefer to define racism as any act of denial or exclusion against any identifiable group perceived as inferior. Racism has the intent or effect of reproducing a racially unequal social structure by essentializing racial identities or naturalizing perceived differences (Winant, 1998). For that reason, racism should be interpreted as a system of power relations in defence of the status quo, with a complex array of practices and discourses that are historically defined, embedded within institutional structures, woven into the ideological fabric of society, and acted out through daily actions (Stamm, 1993).

The comprehensive definition of racism should incorporate as many dimensions as possible without losing all sense of internal integrity. For our purposes, then, racism is defined as those ideas and ideals ("ideology") that assert the normalcy or superiority of one social group over another, together with the institutionalized power to put these beliefs into practice in a way that has the intent or effect of demeaning those in a devalued category. Racism is ultimately based on patterns of power involving relations of dominance, control, and exploitation. Those in positions of power are able to invoke a doctrine of race or cultural difference to enforce social control over those deemed inferior in the competitive struggle for scarce resources. In that racism is about power, and all evidence points to a general unwillingness to share power with those perceived as inferior, the pervasiveness of racism is unlikely to diminish in the foreseeable future.

THE MANY MASKS OF RACISM

Racism is not a uniform concept that reflects a singular experience or common reality. On the contrary, different modes of racism can be discerned which embody variations in intent, levels of awareness, magnitude and scope, styles of expression, depth of intensity, and

TABLE 4-1	Types of Racism	
Interpersonal	Institutional	Societal
red-necked	systematic	everyday
polite	systemic	cultural

consequences. These variations have culminated in the recognition of diverse types of racism, including: (a) interpersonal (including red-necked and polite); (b) institutional (including systematic and systemic); and (c) societal (including everyday and cultural). Comparing and contrasting these admittedly ideal types exposes the complex and multi-dimensional nature of racism as principle and practice. The awareness of different types of racism should also assist in devising diverse solutions for purging racism from society.

1. Interpersonal Racism

Interpersonal racism entails a pattern of interaction that occurs primarily between individuals. It reflects a degree of dislike that is directed at another because of who they are or what they stand for. Two types of interpersonal racism can be discerned: red-necked and polite.

1a. Red-Necked Racism

Red-necked racism is the kind of racism that most associate with racism. It refers to the kind of old-fashioned racism that prevailed in the past and continues to exist in the present among a handful of the reactionary or defiant. Intrinsic to red-necked racism is the explicit and highly personalized character of its expression. Whether through physical or verbal abuse, red-necked racism consists of highly personal attacks on others perceived as culturally or biologically inferior. These personalized attacks often consist of derogatory slurs and minority name-calling. Red-necked racists are not intimidated by labels of racism. Unlike many Canadians, who cringe at the prospect of being labelled racist, they take boastful pride in such a label.

Even a cursory glance at Canada's past will reveal the tenacity of red-necked racism (Walker, 1998; Backhouse, 2000). This may come as a shock to many readers. References to the United States as a hotbed of red-necked racism come as no surprise to most (King, 1994). A country with historic claims to slavery and convulsive urban riots is easy to single out as a bastion of racism. But surely not Canada, with its espousal of multiculturalism and human rights? Certain myths are deeply entrenched in our collective memories, especially those that extol Canada's progressive outlooks. Foremost is the absence of American-style race riots, the lack of racist symbols, the omission of prolonged slavery, and the entrenchment of multicultural philosophies within Canadian society. How accurate are these perceptions? Are Canadians really superior to Americans when it comes to the treatment of racial minorities? Close scrutiny suggests not. Racism was a blatant and obvious component of Canadian society until the 1960s in terms of shaping attitudes, state policies, and institutional arrangements—particularly in the fields of immigration and aboriginal peoples-state relations. Minority women and men were regularly exposed to: (a) economic incorporation as basic labour; (b) social and physical segregation; (c) separate cultural development; (d) enforcement of a colour bar through public policy and private acts; and (e) legislation to exclude or deny equality (Walker, 1998). These initiatives created a vicious circle by moulding public perception of minorities as unacceptable, thus intensifying the demand for more restrictive legislation. Institutions in Canada routinely operated and allocated resources to people on the basis of race or ethnicity (Satzewich, 1998). Only with the sensitivities of a war against Nazi racism and decolonization of salt-water colonies did minorities enlist sufficient support from mainstream Canadians to dismantle openly racist policy and structures that segregrated Whites from non-Whites. The American Civil Rights movement also influenced official response to minority demands. Laws and practices were invoked that segregated people of colour, especially Blacks, from full and equal participation in Canadian society until the 1950s and 1960s. Racist groups such as the Ku Klux Klan have also relied on red-necked violence to cultivate an environment of fear and hatred against minorities throughout United States and Canada (Barrett, 1987).

Blatant expressions of red-necked racism in Canada are readily available. Racial violence in recent years has been perpetuated by White supremacist groups ranging from the White Aryan Nation and Western Guard movements to neo-Nazi skinheads in urban areas (Kinsella, 1994; Barkun, 1994). The beating death of a 65-year-old Sikh temple employee in Surrey, B.C. in mid-1998 by four "skinheads" has prompted calls to label Vancouver as Canada's racism capital (Wood, 1998). A group calling itself the Coalition for Humanistic British Canada has taken out full-page ads to endorse the protection of British culture, elimination of multiculturalism, and abolition of all immigration except from the United Kingdom. Its leader has referred to Blacks as "people with brutalistic, tribalistic instincts and patterns of thought and being. ...Essentially that means they won't fit in and no matter what you do to them—steam clean them or whatever—you can't make them White" (cited in Caldwell, 1999:A-1). Groups such as these are committed to an ideology of racial supremacy in which the White "race" is seen as superior to other races on the basis of physical and cultural characteristics. They are also prepared to transform society along White supremacist lines by seeking out converts to their ideology of hate (Li, 1995). The popularity and potential of White supremacist groups is difficult to gauge. Only a small number of hard-core supremacists are thought to exist in Canada; nevertheless, these extremists have the potential to destabilize a society by stoking dormant prejudices (McKenna, 1994; Howard, 1998). Many supremacists may see themselves as White Christians, fusing race and religion in a single nationalist crusade against the forces of "evil" (Jaret, 1995). Hate groups sustain their credibility and legitimacy by capitalizing on a poor economy and social instability. Disaffected youth are an obvious target because of their perception that the government is indifferent to their plight in a changing and diverse world. Demographic imbalances resulting from immigration are likely to ignite supremacist ire, as is the perception that certain minorities have hijacked government business for self-serving purposes. Hatred toward minorities is conveyed in different ways, but primarily through telephone hotlines, the internet, which allows dissemination without fear of reprisals or court challenges, and disinformation campaigns by hate-mongers recruited by the movement (see Kinsella, 1994). The combination of music, pamphlets, and the internet concocts a poisonous but appealing mishmash of neo-Nazi philosophies, KKK folklore, pseudo-Nordic mythology, and anti-government slogans (Wood, 1998). The courts in Canada have defined these diatribes as "hate propaganda" and a violation of Canada's criminal code. Technicalities, however, have often overturned such verdicts.

1b. Polite Racism

> In some ways I prefer to live in a society where they just say "You're Black, we don't like you. Here in Canada, people are hiding behind a mask (Kolawole Sofowora, cited in *Toronto Star*, 2 May, 1999).

Few people at present will tolerate the open expression of racial slurs. At one time, institutionalized racism was socially and politically acceptable. There was no need for pretense—everything was up front and openly visible (Griffin, 1996). But the risk of social or legal consequences, not to mention the potential for physical retaliation, serves as an inhibitor nowadays. The passage of constitutional guarantees, such as the Charter of Rights and Freedoms and Human Rights Code, has banished red-necked racism from public discourse. But while blatant forms of racism have dissipated to some extent, less candid expressions of bigotry and stereotyping remain in force. Instead of disappearing in the face of social reprisals and legal sanctions as might have been expected, racist slurs ("those kinds of people") are now couched in a way that allows people to talk around or disguise their criticism of others by using somewhat more muted (polite) tones.

Polite racism then can be seen as a contrived attempt to disguise a dislike of others through behaviour that outwardly is non-prejudicial in appearance. It often manifests itself in the use of coded or euphemistic language to mask inner feelings and attitudes. In contrast with the open bigotry of the past, racist attitudes are increasingly ambivalent or contradictory, and often coded in a way that invokes racism yet renders them deniable and difficult to prove as racist (Wetherell and Potter, 1993). This politeness is especially evident when people of colour are turned down for jobs, promotions, or accommodation (Henry and Ginzberg, 1985). For example, an employer may claim a job is filled rather than admit "no Blacks need apply" when approached by an undesirable applicant. Or consider how a general principle may be invoked to deny the legitimacy of a specific instance, as when refugees are criticized for "jumping the queue." Polite racism may appear more sophisticated than its red-necked equivalent; nevertheless, the sting of this hidden racism erects invisible barriers when visible minorities apply for jobs or promotions. This gap between the fairness that Canadians profess and the subtle discrimination they practise serves to sustain prevailing relationships of control, exclusion, or exploitation.

How does polite racism work? Evidence suggests that Canadians as a whole are receptive toward the principles of multiculturalism and racial equality (Fleras and Elliott, 1992; Berry and Kalin, 1993). Many Canadians express sympathy for the plight of those less fortunate than themselves. For example, immigrants are frequently portrayed as industrious contributors to Canadian well-being. Yet negative and prejudicial attitudes continue to distort our assessment and treatment of the foreign-born. Minorities are acceptable as long as they know their place and act as the mainstream wants them to. Minority demands that fall outside conventional channels are criticized as a threat to national identity or social harmony (Dijk, 1987). People of colour are chided for making too many complaints or demands at odds with the character of Canadian society. Government initiatives to protect and promote diversity are acceptable as long as they don't cost money or impose burdens in terms of sharing power or cultural space. Affirmative, or employment equity programs for historically disadvantaged minorities are disparaged as unfair to the majority. Minority espousal of genuine cultural differences is criticized for attempting to be "too different"—especially if these are seen as interfering with the rights of individuals, violate the law of the land, or undermine core Canadian values or institutions.

In short, Canadian racism is often depicted as polite and subdued. Racism in Canada is rarely perpetuated by raving lunatics who engage in beatings, lynchings, or graffiti. Rather, racism among Canadians is unobtrusive, often implicit, and couched in political correctness or higher ideals ("everyone should be equal before the law"). Derogatory references to minorities continue to be expressed, but they are usually restricted to remarks in private or to friends. Polite racism is increasingly popular with an educated population. With higher education, individuals become more adept at compartmentalizing and concealing racist attitudes behind coded expressions, lest they blurt out statements at odds with career plans or a sophisticated self-image (Fleras, 1996). This subtlety makes it difficult to confront—let alone eradicate—the expression of polite racism.

2. Institutional Racism

Much of the discussion to this point has dwelt on racism as an individual attribute. Other types of racism go beyond the interpersonal in terms of scope, style, and impact. Racism at the institutional level represents such a shift in expression. Institutional racism refers to the process by which organizational practices and procedures are used either deliberately or inadvertently to discriminate against others. With institutional racism, the issue is not of individual acts of racism within the confines of an institution or workplace. Rather, institutional racism refers to organizational rules, procedures, rewards, and practices that have the intent (systematic) or effect (systemic) of excluding or denying some and empowering others.

2a. Systematic Racism

Systematic racism involves rules and procedures that directly and deliberately prevent minorities from achieving full and equal involvement within society. This institutionalized racism appears when discriminatory practices are legally sanctioned by the state and formalized within its institutional framework, thus reflecting the values and practices of the dominant sector. It consists of formal rules and official procedures that are embedded within the design (structure and function) of the organization to preclude minority entry or participation. These institutional norms and values may be based on ideologies that uphold the superiority of the mainstream. As well, informal principles and practices may also be accepted, either consciously or unconsciously, reinforcing the institutional adage of "that's how we do things around here" (Isajiw,1999).

Systematic institutional racism flourished in societies that endorsed racial segregation. The regime of apartheid in South Africa was a classic example, as was pre-civil rights U.S.A. Nor was Canada exempt from the tarnish of institutionally racist practices (Reitz and Breton, 1994). Institutional racism was once a chronic and inescapable component of Canadian society (Walker, 1998). Minorities were routinely barred from even partial participation in mainstream institutions. Predictably, they were subjected to verbal and physical harassment, without much chance of recourse or retribution. This racism ranged from the slavery of Blacks in Nova Scotia during the pre-Confederation era (Jones, 1978), to the disenfranchisement of Japanese-Canadians in British Columbia until 1949 (Sunahara, 1981), and the differential admissions policy for Jewish students at McGill University in Montreal during the 1940s (Draper, 1983). African-Canadians were routinely excluded from entry into theatres and restaurants until these odious distinctions were rescinded in the 1950s (Walker, 1989).

Evidence now suggests that minorities are unlikely to be directly victimized by blatant institutional racism. Openly racist platforms find little public acceptance or political support in Canada (Adam, 1992). This injunction applies across the board, from institutions to interpersonal relations. Institutions can no longer openly discriminate against minorities, lest they attract negative publicity, invoke a lawsuit, or incite consumer resistance. Nevertheless, institutional racism continues to exist. It can incorporate various discriminatory actions, from red-necked to polite, all of which combine to preserve the prevailing distribution of power. It can take the form of harassment from supervisors or co-workers, often defended as unintentional or not meant to harm, by way of ethnic jokes, racial graffiti, racist cartoons, with excuses ranging from "just a joke," "where's your sense of humour," "didn't mean anything by it," or "it's just the way guys talk" (see Henry, 1997). Or systematic racism may refer to the way in which organizations deliberately manipulate rules or procedures to deny minority access or participation. The revelation that both Denny's restaurant chain (U.S.A.) and Texaco went out of their way to discriminate against African-Americans provides proof that the more things change, the more they stay the same (see also Watkins, 1997).

2b. Systemic Racism

There is another type of institutional racism that comes across as impersonal and unconscious. Its unobtrusive and implicit character makes it that much more difficult to detect, much less to isolate and combat. Systemic racism is the name given to this subtle yet powerful form of discrimination within the institutional framework of society. It is entrenched within the structure (rules, organization), function (norms, goals), and process (procedures) of social institutions. The standards and expectations inherent within these organizations may be universalistic and ostensibly colour-blind. Yet they may have the unintended but real effect of excluding those outside the mainstream. In other words, the normal operations of an institution may culminate in a racialized division of power and privilege.

With systemic racism, it is not the intent or motive that counts, but, rather, the context and the consequences. Policies, rules, priorities, and programs may not be inherently racist or deliberately discriminatory; for example, institutions do not go out of their way to exclude or deprive minorities. However, rules that are evenly applied may have a discriminatory effect in that they exclude certain groups, while conferring advantage on others. Entry rules may be systematically biased. In refusing to hire a world-renowned physicist because of race, a leading university was charged by the Ontario Human Rights Commission with systemic bias, reflecting traces of "cronyism" and the power imbalances inherent in the dynamics of an "old boys' network" that had the unintended effect of stacking the system and screening out non-White candidates (Schmidt, 2000). If hired, minority women and men have no choice but to work in organizational settings that are not of their making, thus creating a poor fit between institutional structures and minority realities. In brief, we can define systemic racism as the adverse yet unintended consequences that result from applying seemingly neutral rules, but with dissimilar effects on identifiable minorities.

Systemic racism is defined by its consequences. It rests on the belief that institutional rules and procedures can be racist in practice, even if the actors themselves are free of prejudicial attitudes. Even explicitly non-racist policies and practices may be systemically racist by ignoring the importance of differences, not in the sense of celebrating diversity, but in terms of power-sharing (see also Simmons, 1998). Institutions are systemically racist when they ignore how organizational practices and structures reflect and reinforce White experiences as normal and necessary. These institutional barriers to minority success are unintentional, but hidden in institutional reward systems that penalize some individuals because of who they are, not what they can do. As such, systemic racism is rarely identified as such by those who benefit from such arrangements because it is (a) embedded within institutional rules and procedures; (b) beyond our everyday consciousness; (c) undetected and disguised by reference to universal standards; (d) taken for granted; and (e) powerful in reflecting an appearance of fairness and impartiality.

Even a few examples will demonstrate how the implicit bias of a system designed by the mainstream can create unintended yet negative effects on minority women and men. For years, a number of occupations such as the police, firefighters, or mass transit drivers retained minimum weight, height, and educational requirements for job applicants. In retrospect, we can interpret these criteria as systemically discriminatory because they favoured males over females, and White applicants over people of colour. Valid reasons may have existed to justify these restrictions; nevertheless, the imposition of these qualifications imposed a set of unfair entry restrictions, regardless of intent or rationale. No deliberate attempt is made to exclude anyone, since standards are uniformly applied. But these criteria have the net effect of excluding certain groups who lack these requirements for entry or promotion. Other examples of systemic racism include an insistence on Canadian-only experience—a catch-22 conundrum that ensnares many professionals, many of whom must also confront the devaluation of minority experiences and credentials, unnecessarily high educational standards for entry into certain occupations, and other demanding qualifications that discourage membership into professional bodies. The situation is particularly acute with medical doctors. It is estimated that there are hundreds of foreign-trained doctors who have settled in Ontario in hopes of qualifying as physicians in a province that acknowledges a shortage of doctors because of dwindling enrolments and emigration to the United States. Yet most overseas doctors have run into quota barriers which severely restrict the number of doctors that are allowed to sit medical exams or take retraining programs to become licensed (Keung, 1999). Even passing this labyrinth of tests and training does not guarantee a licence to practice medicine in Ontario. Interestingly, other provinces, such as Saskatchewan and Nova Scotia, offer provisional licences to qualified doctors to ease shortages in certain communities (Carey, 1999).

In short, rules and priorities that may seem neutral on the surface are not even-handed in terms of who gets what. Such a hidden agenda imposes certain handicaps on those who are inadequately prepared to cope with organizational demands and routines. For many immigrants, their professional qualifications appeared to be an important component for entry into Canada. Canadians have long extolled the virtues of an educated and accredited immigrant population as part of Canada's commitment to society-building. But once in Canada, neither their degrees nor their overseas experience appear to have much value (Carey, 1999). Most are having trouble even getting low-level entry jobs in their chosen profession, with the result that employment is often restricted to security guards, restaurant servers and dishwashers, gas bar attendants, and babysitters. Well meaning people may have drawn up immigration policies, with Canada's national interests at heart, and the policies may have been administered as even-handedly as possible. Nevertheless, the logical consequences of these actions are systemically discriminatory because of the power imbalances that underpin these initiatives and that have the effect of further marginalizing minorities from full and equal participation.

3. Societal Racism

As noted by many, racism is more than a structure or ideology (Essed, 1991). It also constitutes a process that is created, reflected, reinforced, and reformulated through everyday interaction and routine practices. Societal racism constitutes that level of racism that occurs in the general functioning of society. It consists of interactional patterns, often without people being consciously aware of how their actions may inadvertently deny or exclude. This notion of racism as routine is not intended to trivialize racism. As with any expression of common-sense thinking, societal racism represents the natural and normal way in which people view and interpret the world, process information, engage with others, and deal with the practicalities of everyday life (Essed, 1991). We make a distinction between cultural racism and everyday racism, with its emphasis on unconscious speech habits that have the effect of denying or excluding. Cultural racism, in turn, reflects ambiguities in our value system, whose ongoing tensions have the effect of reinforcing a racialized social order.

3a. Everyday Racism

Contemporary racism is no longer expressed in direct aggression but in more culturally acceptable ways that deny or exclude (Sirna, 1998). Certain ideas and ideals are widely circulated that explicitly or implicitly assert the superiority of some people at the expense of others. The internalization of these racist ideas and their expression in daily behaviour is called everyday racism. It entails racist practices that infiltrate everyday life and become part of what is accepted as normal by the dominant group (Essed, 1991). The mechanisms of everyday racism are well established. Individuals interact with one another in a way that tolerates and reinforces racism, sometimes explicitly, other times in an implicit or oblique manner. As a process and social practice, racism is created and reconstructed through daily actions that are repetitive, systematic, familiar, and routine. Racist discourse is "prestructured" (Essed, 1991) in a manner that constrains individual actors and everyday behaviour. This suggests that the structures and ideologies that underpin racism are produced and reproduced through a complex and cumulative interplay of attitudes (prejudice) and practices (discrimination). This combination is (a) diverse in manifestation, but unified through constant repetition; (b) permeates daily life to the extent that it is viewed as normal or inevitable; and (c) implies the notion that the potential for racism exists in all of us, rather than reflecting a division of society into racists and non-racists.

The role of language in perpetuating everyday racism is increasingly recognized. Many think of language as a kind of postal system; that is, a neutral system of conveyance between sender and receiver for the transmission of messages created independently through a process called thinking. In reality, language is inextricably linked with the social construction of reality. Language is intimately bound up with our experiences of the world and our efforts to convey that experience to others. Ideas and ideals are "trapped inside" language, with the result that they influence patterns of thought and behaviour. Language can be employed to control, conceal, evade issues, draw attention, or dictate agendas about what gets said. Words are not neutral; rather they have the capacity to hinder or harm when carelessly employed. Words also have a political dimension: They convey messages above and beyond what is intended. Inferences can (and are) drawn about who you are and where you stand in the competition for who gets what and why. Language, in short, represents an ideal vehicle for expressing intolerance by highlighting differences, enlarging distance, and sanctioning inequality through invisible yet real boundaries (Sirna, 1998). Language may be used to degrade or ridicule minorities, as Robert Moore (1992) demonstrates in his oft-quoted article on racism in the

English language, by way of obvious bigotry ("niggers"), colour symbolism (black = bad), loaded terms ("Indian massacres"), and seemingly neutral phrases that are infused with hidden anxieties ("waves of immigrants"). Negative meanings can become part of everyday speech as the following passage from Robert Moore (1992) demonstrates:

> Some may blackly (angrily) accuse me of trying to blacken (defame) the English language, to give it a black eye (mark of shame) by writing such black words (hostile)...by accusing me of being black-hearted (malevolent), of having a black outlook (pessimistic; dismal) on life, of being a blackguard (scoundrel) which would certainly be a black mark (detrimental fact) against me.

The association of "blackness" with negativity illustrates how certain values are embedded in our everyday speech. Daily speech patterns provide an example of racism as everyday and interactive. Words are a powerful way of conveying negative images and associations. For this reason and others, some Canadians of African ancestry prefer to be called "African-Canadians" rather than "Blacks." To be sure, the racism implicit in words and metaphors may not be intended or deliberate. Nor will the occasional use of such loaded terms explode into full-blown racism. Moreover, it is inaccurate to say that language determines our reality. More precisely, it provides a cultural frame of reference for defining what is desirable and important. In other words, perils await those who trivialize the impact of language in perpetuating racism through discourses of everyday life.

3b. Cultural Racism

Cultural racism suggests the existence of cultural values that reinforce the interests of the dominant sector at the expense of the subordinate. These values may be specific in terms of openly compromising the right of minority women and men to equal treatment. Alternatively, they may indirectly endorse dominant value orientations by characterizing them as necessary and normal, while dismissing others as irrelevant or defective, and a prime cause of minority failures. Cultural racism reflects a conflict of interest between the liberal-pluralist values of universality and minority demands to be different (Wetherell and Potter, 1993). Consider the primacy of liberal-pluralism in Canadian and American society. Liberal-pluralist principles are based on a belief that what we have in common is much more important than our differences; that what we do and accomplish is more important than who we are; and the content of our character is more important than the colour of our skin. Differences are tolerated only to the extent that everyone is different in the same kind of way. Compare this universalism with the particularism of ethnicity with its focus on difference rather than similarity as a basis for sorting who gets what. Cultural racism reflects a certain degree of ambiguity implicit in contemporary liberal-pluralist values. The "subliminality" of this dislike goes beyond the explicitness of old-fashioned racism, yet reinforces racial inequality, however inadvertently, through muted criticism of minorities for demanding change that falls outside what the dominant sector defines as acceptable. Critics of minorities may be oblivious to their participation in perpetuating patterns of inequality. Still, the net effect is the same; that is, minority groups are cast as troublemakers or problem people, whose interests or means are unacceptable in liberal-democratic societies.

This ambivalence in cultural values may be called subliminal racism. It is alternatively referred to as "democratic racism" (Henry and Tator, 1994); "non-racist racism" (Elliott and Fleras, 1991); or "aversive racism" (Dovidio, 1986). It tends to locate conflict and contradictions within the psychological complex of a person's emotional and cognitive makeup (Wetherell and Potter, 1993). Subliminal cultural racism is located among people who abhor openly discriminatory treatment of minorities. Yet these same individuals are incapable of escaping the cultural blinkers that may encourage a dislike of others because of what they do. Individuals may profess a commitment to the principle of equality, but at the same time oppose measures that would remedy the inequality without recognizing the inconsistency (see Henry et al.,1999). Even many of those who profess egalitarian attitudes may be incapable of seeing how their criticism of minorities may unintentionally reinforce a status quo that has historically compromised and controlled minority women and men. In acknowledging the circulation of messages beneath the level of individual awarenesss, the subliminality of cultural racism appears to reflect an inescapable dichotomy in our core values (see Myrdal, 1944). On the one hand, we place a premium on the public good, with its emphasis on collective rights, special treatment, equality of outcomes, and fair play. On the other, there remains a powerful commitment to competitive individualism, with its focus on personal freedom, self-reliance, meritocracy, and competition. This dichotomous orientation enables individuals to maintain two apparently conflicting values, one rooted in the egalitarian virtues of justice and fairness; the other in the universalistic notion that everyone should play by the same rules in an open competition. Yet those very values that promote a democratic right to compete may be revoked if minorities compete too vigorously or successfully (Henry et al., 1995). These aversive feelings are not about outright hostility or hate, but entail discomfort or unease, often leading to patterns of avoidance rather than intentionally destructive behaviour.

How then do we explain this ambiguity in cultural values toward minorities in Canada? Cynics would argue that Canadians are hypocrites whose deep-seated racism is camouflaged by platitudinous pieties. Opposition to multiculturalism or immigration by way of coded or euphemistic expressions is perceived as more acceptable than open expressions of intolerance (Palmer, 1996). Yet subliminal racism differs from polite racism. Subliminal racism is not directly expressed but embodied in "lofty" opposition to progressive minority policies and programs that rationalizes criticism of minorities on the grounds of mainstream values, national interests, or appeals to a higher sense of fair play, equality, and justice. For example, refugee claimants are not condemned in blunt racist terminology; their landed entry into Canada is criticized on procedural grounds ("jumping the queue"), or they are belittled for taking unfair advantage of Canada's generosity or ability to shoulder processing costs. Other examples, such as the decision by the RCMP to accommodate the mandatory turban worn by religious Sikh males, are denounced as "unCanadian," an affront to majority values, illegitimate, excessively demanding, too costly, unacceptably rapid, or outside due process (See and Wilson, 1988). Clearly, then, a degree of cultural ambiguity is apparent. Individuals may endorse progressive attitudes as a matter of principle, yet disapprove of policy implications (the "costs") or minority assertiveness to bring about substantial change (Essed, 1991). Values that endorse racial equality are publicly reaffirmed under a liberal pluralism; nevertheless, there is deep-seated resentment at the prospect of moving over and making space for these minority women and men.

EXPLAINING RACISM

"People, why can't we just get along?" (Rodney King, 1992).

Well, why can't we? Racism as a social problem exacts an unacceptable toll. It represents a blot upon Canadian society, with the capacity to squander our potential as an ordered and

CASE STUDY 4-2	Is Canada a Racist Society? It Depends...

Is Canada a racist society? Are Canadians racist? Is racism a major problem in Canada? Responses to these questions are much more complex and problematic than many give credit. What exactly constitutes a racist society? What is meant when accusing Canadians of being racist? On what grounds are judgments made? The charge that Canada is racist is not simply an intellectual parlour game, even though raising the question may seem unusual at a time when a commitment to diversity has never been stronger (Levitt, 1997). Accusations of such magnitude run the risk of besmirching Canada's international reputation. Fears also are intensified of a looming race relations problem which, if left unchecked, may prove the undoing of Canada as a society. How accurate are these accusations and appraisals?

Problematizing the Charges

Canada is widely regarded as a socially progressive society whose initiatives for engaging with diversity are second to none. Yet there is gnawing concern that things are not what they seem to be, and that racism continues to flourish in Canada, albeit in ways that are unlikely to conform to conventional forms of racist thought and practices. Even positive initiatives are given a negative spin. Consider how the inception of multiculturalism or employment equity may be predicated on the premise that Canada is fundamentally racist, and that Canadians are racists in need of government intervention to reverse the trend. Recent developments would appear to uphold this unflattering assessment of Canada as a "racist society" (cited in *National Post*, April 24th,

1999). The gravity of such a charge makes it doubly important to deconstruct the notion of a "racist society." After all, it is one thing to make this charge; it may be quite another to prove it by way of argument and empirical evidence.

First, what exactly is meant by the concept of racism? Racism is not a static entity, but is evolving and situational, and increasingly defined in terms of consequence and context, rather than intention or essence. The notion of racism revolving around swastikas or burning crosses is also losing ground. Pressure is on moving away from classic conceptions that equate racism with: (a) formally prescribed boundaries between groups; (b) opportunity structures defined by inherited racial attributes; (c) codification of prejudice and discrimination into laws that openly discriminate against identifiable minorities; and (d) conscious exclusion of others from full and equal participation in spheres that enhance social and material rewards (Holdaway, 1996). South Africa's apartheid regime may have been racist according to these criteria, but surely not Canada, at least not since the 1950s, when new Canadians were routinely racialized as different and ranked accordingly. Rather, racism has become increasingly subtle in terms of its process and effects, in the process becoming less visible as Canada becomes more racially visible. Racism is the glass ceiling that deters visible minorities from advancing in the workplace; racism entails those daily indignities that confront people of colour; racism is expressed in the differences that inadvertently yet adversely affect outcomes within the criminal justice system (James, 1998); racism is criticism of immigrants behind the camouflage of national interests; and racism consists of those tacit assumptions that bolster dominant ways of thinking or doing, while cavalierly dismissing minority ways as irrelevant or inferior. In short, racism in Canadian society has become overwhelmingly covert, beyond explicit slurs and putdowns, and is increasingly embedded in the normal operations of institutions, reflecting the context and consequences of actions rather than attitudes or intent. Such invisibility not only complicates the challenge of detection and eradication. It also detracts from any consensus over the magnitude and scope of racism in Canada.

Second, what exactly is meant by a racist society? To answer this question, we need to delve more deeply into societal racism. What criteria must be invoked in defining a society as racist, and on what grounds? Is a racist society defined by what it is or is not; by what people do or don't do to others; and by what is said or not said? How can racism be measured—by way of incidents that come to the attention of authorities or through victim self-assessments? To what extent are statistics or national surveys a valid measurement of racism in society? Is a racist society based on a minimum number of racial incidents per year (how many?), or should we look more closely at systemic biases that unobtrusively but systemically perpetuate a racialized and unequal social order? Statistical measures are known to be riddled with inherent drawbacks. Pollsters are cautious about drawing sweeping conclusions from a few survey questions on race or ethnicity, according to Donald Taylor of McGill University. Not only are polls a crude measure of public attitudes because of their superficiality in talking about complex problems, but in-

tolerance is difficult to measure because of the unacceptablity of admitting to being a racist. Indirect questions must be designed to reveal people's true attitudes, Jacquie Miller (1998), writes, even if such questions are confusing, subject to interpretation, or may be easily taken out of context. Statistics cannot reveal the number of unreported acts. An increase in reported acts may reflect: (a) growth in anti-racism awareness in school curricula; (b) greater public awareness and police willingness to press charges; (c) expanding media interest and reportage; and (d) more open access to grievance articulation, such as a hate-crime hotline with an 800 number.

What is a racist society? Conversely, what constitutes a non-racist society? Broadly speaking, a racist society is one that officially encourages or condones racism, either by omission or commission. A racist society is one in which racism is: (a) institutionalized as a normal functioning of society; (b) supported by cultural values and expressed through widely accepted norms; (c) tacitly approved by the state or government; (d) intrusive in many interpersonal relations; and (e) largely impervious to reform or eradication (Aguirre and Turner, 1995). A society is a racist society when it systematically oppresses others through denial, exclusion, or exploitation on the basis of race or ethnicity. Discrimination toward others is formally institutionalized as a basis for entitlement or engagement in society. Formal mechanisms are rarely enacted to prevent or to deal with the outbreak of racist incidents at individual or institutional levels. Mindful of these criteria, it may be necessary to reassess the charge that Canada is racist. Canada officially prohibits racism and racial discrimination at policy and statutory levels. It possesses human rights legislation, criminal codes against racial hatred, and sentencing procedures that severely punish hate crimes. On these grounds, Canada can no longer be regarded as a racist society—as was once the case in our not too distant past—even though racism does exist in Canadian society.

Third, are Canadians racists? Some would say that all mainstream Canadians are racist by virtue of living in a "White (man's)" world, and deriving disproportional benefits from exposure to institutions, values, and structures that exclude some, and privilege others. Others would say that pockets of bigotry persist in Canada. Four criteria are employed to define a conventional racist: (1) a belief in the existence of biologically different races; (2) ranking of these races along lines of superiority/inferiority; (3) conferral of fixed and immutable status to this hierarchy; and (4) differential treatment because of membership in these groups (D'Souza, 1995). Still others would label many Canadians as "closet racists," given the degree of their thinly veiled hostility toward immigration, employment equity, or multiculturalism. While professing a commitment to equality and inclusiveness, these fair-weather racists criticize any initiative to improve minority life chances as too costly, too quick, too accommodative, too pushy, too "unCanadian," or contrary to national interests. Yet there is no proof that a dislike of government policies or minority initiatives is automatically indicative of racism, even if the unintended consequence of such criticism may reinforce a racialized social order. In fact, critics may argue that it is supporters of special programs who are racist, by treating others differently because of race, and that to be criticized for being wary of such programs is racist in its own right, since such "political correctness" suggests that mi-

norities are immune to criticism. Moreover, the very idea of an non-racist population or society may be an anomaly in its own right, given the range of publics that exist in society. Racism and intolerance are unavoidable, since Canadians are not perfectly consistent or logical in their actions, with pockets of resistance or resentment inevitable during periods of change and diversity. A certain level of ethnic friction in liberal-democratic societies is inevitable, in other words, and its existence may reflect the cost of living together with differences in a society that encourages freedom, equality, individualism, and rule of law.

Racist Society or Racism in Society?: From Either/Or to Both/And

What can we conclude? There is little doubt that racism exists in Canada, both personal and institutional, as well as open and covert. However accurate such an appraisal, this observation is not the same as saying that Canada is a racist society. The combination of racist incidents with racist individuals is not synonymous with or reducible to such labelling. Just as we must never underestimate the pervasiveness of racism in sectors of society, and exercise constant vigilance to that effect, so too is a degree of caution required in exaggerating the notion of a racist Canada. A sense of perspective is critical: Most racist incidents are instigated by a relatively small number of protagonists. The actions of a few are hardly representative of society at large and should not be manipulated as a measure by which to judge the inactions of many. Compare racism in Canada with the situation in Europe, where a European Union survey of 16 000 Europeans in 15 countries yielded staggering results: 55 percent of Belgians identified themselves as very or quite racist;

48 percent of the French, and 35 percent of the British (Bates, 1997). In Austria, a country where 70 percent dislike Jews and 20 percent actively loathe them, 26.9 percent voted for an extreme right-wing party in 1999, propelling its leader, a self-avowed Hitler devotee, into a coalition government. Comparable figures for hardcore bigotry in Canada are not available, given the notoriously unreliable responses to survey questions in this area, but evidence suggests a figure of about 15 percent (see Henry and Tator, 1985; Reitz and Breton, 1994). Nor can reference to racism or racial discrimination account entirely for the structural barriers that interfere with minority equality or participation in society. A host of factors from culture and history to misguided government policy may also contribute to the racialization of unequal relations (see also D'Souza, 1995; Loney, 1998).

It's been said that the smallest indiscretion in a society of saints would be sufficient to incur capital punishment (Levitt, 1997). In societies where hatred toward others is the norm, even the most egregious form of racial intolerance will go unnoticed or unpunished. In a society such as Canada where racism and racial intolerance are widely repudiated and legally unacceptable, the slightest provocation becomes cause for public remorse or social rebuke. And it is precisely these high standards that encourage yet complicate the process of debating Canada as a racist society. Canadians may not be racists in the conventional sense of close-minded bigots that deny or exclude. Racism in Canada is more likely to embody seemingly neutral acts of behaviour that have the unwitting effect of perpetuating a racialized social order. The unanticipated consequences of universally applied institutional rules and practices—largely created by Whites (and males) to normalize the preservation of power and privilege—may inadvertently have the cumulative effect of privileging some, disadvantaging others. White experiences continue to be defined as the norm by which others are measured and evaluated. When combined with the power to put these normative expectations into practice, an arrangement prevails that empowers some while disempowering others. In other words, Canada is racist in endorsing tacit assumptions that privilege mainstream values and institutions as natural, superior, and inevitable rather than discourses in defence of mainstream ideology. Racism is manifest in the articulation of policies and ideologies, reflected in the collective belief system of the dominant culture, and woven into the language, laws, rules and norms of Canadian society (Henry et al., 1999). Inasmuch as the structures, values, and institutions of the mainstream may "inadvertently" advantage some, while minority experiences and alternatives are dismissed as irrelevant or inferior, Canada may be regarded as racist. It is also racist in that foundational structures, from constitutional first principles to the "way things are done around here," remain anchored in a Eurocentric colonialism that resists debate or challenge. The unconventionality of racism that is systemically structured may make it difficult to detect, but no less real and powerful in denying and excluding. In short, perhaps, answers to the question of the nature of Canadian racism must avoid the framework of "either/or" (yes or no). A position that concedes "both/and" (yes and no), depending on circumstances and criteria, may provide a better insight into living with our paradoxes.

tolerant country. Racism costs all Canadians in the following ways: (1) it perpetuates inequality by infringing on fundamental human rights; (2) it reduces the number of people who can contribute to Canada; (3) it expends useless energy that otherwise could be funnelled into more productive channels; and (4) it diminishes Canada's competitive edge both domestically and internationally. The costs of racism are absorbed unevenly across society, with some capitalizing on racism to preserve privilege or power, while others suffer. Racism also adds an additional burden to minority lives (Ford, 1994). Minorities live in perpetual fear of physical retaliation. The loss of personal security intensifies isolation or self-defensive behaviours; a restricted set of economic and social opportunities constrains options and life chances. And many are dismayed by negative media messages that they are less worthy because of who they are (Thomas, 1998). Moreover, racism is known to intersect with and be constitutive of other forms of exploitation related to class, gender, ethnicity, or sexual preference, in ways both mutually intensifying yet often contradictory. To add insult to injury, exposure to racism may contribute to poor health, both physical and psychological. A few may even lash out in violence from frustration.

That racism in one form or another exists in Canada is widely accepted. With the benefit of some prodding and sharp reminders, Canadians are increasingly facing up to our checkered past, with its bewildering mixture of tolerance and repression (Satzewich, 1998). Racism may be equated with a particular psychological complex of emotions, feelings, and thoughts; it also entails the symbolic, cultural, and institutional expressions of society that are systematically and systemically organized around the suppression of some, and the privileging of others (Wetherell and Potter, 1993). Some forms of racism are now widely condemned and detested, even by those who are indifferent to the principle or promotion of diversity. Other varieties of racism continue to be endemic to Canada, with few signs of relinquishing their tenacious grip. Canada was founded on racist principles and continues to be racialized in consequence if not in intent, despite a tendency toward collective denial and historical amnesia (Philip, 1995; Henry et al., 1995; Walker, 1997). No less worrying is the persistence of racism: Even removal of openly discriminatory barriers does not appear to have had an appreciable effect; nor have government policies and legislative initiatives to guarantee equal rights and full participation. Yet the threat of social condemnation only seems to have propelled racism to go underground or seek new ways of expressing itself. The fact that racism continues to persist despite debilitating costs and destructive effects is cause for concern, and raises the question of what if anything can be done to eliminate racism.

How do we account for this anomaly? Is it because of societal inertia or public disinterest, with the result that racism drifts along, irrespective of its dysfunctional effects on society? In the same way that people appreciate the need for ecological sustainability, yet do not always act on that awareness, so too has public knowledge of racial harmony not necessarily resulted in behaviour modification. Some attribute the pervasiveness of racism to our genetic wiring from an evolutionary past, when outsiders posed a threat to survival in an uncertain environment. This adaptive reaction continues to operate in the present so that recoiling from what is different seems only natural. Such a visceral dislike of outgroups is purported to explain the universality of racism. Some like to think of racism as the by-product of ignorance or fear of the unknown because of improper socialization. Racism will vanish with improvements in people's stock of knowledge about differences and minorities. Others believe that racism persists because of its self-serving properties. Put bluntly, racism has a way of making the mainstream feel good about itself. Racism bolsters individual and collective self-images, whether people are aware of it or not. It also has the effect of enhancing majority privilege by reducing uncertainty and imposing control. Racism, in short, provides simple but effective explanations to justify why people get what they deserve or deserve what they get. This notion of racism as "functional" for Whites is captured in these words by Julian Bond, head of the NAACP, when referring to the tenacity of White supremacist racism (White, 1998:25):

> It's still White supremacy. It stills means so much to those who practise it. It defines who they are. It makes them feel that they are better than others. It ensures them positions in employment and college admissions they otherwise might not have. It still puts a lid on the dreams of Black people...

Still others look to social institutions as the primary culprit responsible for racism. Mainstream institutions are crafted by dominant groups, and either deliberately or inadvertently reflect dominant values, priorities, agendas, and practices, and normalize these as superior, necessary, and inevitable. The power imbalances inherent in such institutional dynamics have the intent or effect of racializing others.

Each of these explanations of racism is accurate. But reference to racism as a function of biology or psychology is secondary to most sociological analyses. Racism does not exist solely in the minds of demented individuals; nor is it an error of perception or belief. The roots of racism go beyond the conduct of aberrant individuals, even though individuals are the carriers and targets of this outgroup hatred. Racism persists because of its location within the capitalist structures of society (Bolaria and Li, 1988; Satzewich, 1991). The economic well-being, standard of living, and cultural history of Canada are constructed around a contrived hatred towards others, both in the formal and informal sense (McKenna, 1994). Through its ideological underpinnings, racism has played and continues to play a formidable role in establishing and maintaining patterns of inequality and control. Racist ideologies are employed as rationalizations to foster acquisition of a cheap and disposable labour supply; to destabilize minority movements by undermining any potential show of unity or strength; and to justify intrusive devices for regulating the activities of troublesome minorities (Satzewich, 1991; McKenna, 1994). The interests of capitalism are also served by a degree of inner turmoil—from racial unrest to class conflict—as long as racism does not unduly interfere with wealth extraction or public order. Rather than a departure from the norm, in other words, racism exists because it is supportive of a system designed to augment White power and privilege. Those in positions of power take refuge in racism to preserve privilege in the competition for scarce resources. Sowing the seeds of racism provides this advantage without drawing unnecessary attention to the contradictions and dysfunctions within the system.

In short, racism is linked to patterns of social control in contexts of inequality. Racism in Canada is neither a transient phenomenon nor an anomolous and unpredictable feature. The origins of racism have deep roots in Canadian society: That is, racism is intrinsic to Canada's historical and economic development; embedded within the institutional structures of society; endemic to core cultural values; and integral to Canadian society-building. Racism continues to flourish because of its positive functions in support of White, ruling class interests. Not unexpectedly, cultural values and institutional structures have evolved on the strength of racially-based social cleavages. It is not a case of false consciousness, moreover. Racism has a basis in real material conditions of social life and the concrete problems of different classes, providing ready explanations to ideologically construct a world in change, under stress, and increasingly uncertain (Henry and Tator, 1994). That fact alone should remind us that racism as a social problem is a majority (White) problem, not a minority problem. It also raises the possibility that racism and racial hatred are not always perceived as dysfunctional (abnormal or deviant). Racism's "normalcy" within the context of a commodity-oriented society only complicates the process of solution.

Not surprisingly, responses to the question of why racism persists continually miss the mark. The reason why there is no right answer is that people have been asking the wrong question. Perhaps the question should not be "Why does racism exist?" but "Why isn't there *more* racism, in light of structural pressures to preserve an unequal status quo?" Why, indeed, should racism *not* exist, in light of the benefits it confers on those in positions of power and privilege? Rephrasing the question in this way alters our approach to solutions. Racism-bashing initiatives that focus on racism as a self-evident social problem are doomed to fail. So are those aspects of government policy that are predicated on the assumption that racism is an irrational feature of an otherwise fundamentally sound system, judging by the language ("cancer," "scourge") employed to describe racism. Misreading the problem creates inappropriate solutions, especially when disregarding the social conditions that give rise to negative beliefs and behaviour. Racism, therefore, cannot be understood apart from the social, cultural, economic, and political contexts in which it is embedded and nourished. Racism is not a departure from society and its ideals, but is constitutive of the existing social order, whether by intent or in consequence. To the extent that institutions are irrevocably tainted by racism, both covert and overt, personal as well as institutional, formidable barriers stand in the way of eliminating racism.

SOLVING THE PROBLEM: ANTI-RACISM

Most Canadians are no longer racists in the classic sense of openly vilifying different races. Yet racism continues to exist in unobtrusive ways, deliberately or unconsciously, by way of action or inaction. Racism exists in tolerating practices and arrangements that have the intent or effect of discriminating against others. Doing nothing to confront such racial discrimination is racist in consequence because fence-sitting (through inactivity or silence) is not impartiality, but tacit acceptance of the status quo. Yet the cost of doing nothing is tacit acceptance that may have the effect of affirming and supporting the very structure of racist domination and oppression that many profess to want eradicated (hooks, 1995). By contrast, anti-racism can be defined as the process that isolates and challenges racism through direct action at personal and institutional levels (see also Dei, 1996). Anti-racist measures may include: fighting racist hate groups; direct action through protest or civil disobedience; boycotts, litigation, or legislation (Jaret, 1995). An integrative anti-racism constitutes an educational and political, action-oriented strategy for institutional and systemic change to address racism and interlocking systems of social oppression related to sexism, and classism (Dua and Robertson, 1999). It is egalitarian in outlook insofar as it seeks equality, not in the liberal sense of everyone being equal in the same way, but through structural changes that foster power-sharing, in an attempt to challenge historically constituted relations of domination that are embedded within societal structures (Dei, 1996:25).

Minorities in Canada have relied on different strategies to resist racism (Allahar, 1998). In addition to civil disobedience, the social processes of accommodation and assimilation have been employed as strategies of resistance, at least from the point of view of the powerless. To be sure, neither accommodation nor assimilation pretends to go to the root of the problem; both provide a defence against discrimination as well as a platform from which to criticize, negotiate, and advocate. In short, solving the problem of racism can take different forms, depending on how racism is defined (as race, culture, or power) and the level of racism under consideration (interpersonal, institutional, or societal). Two styles of anti-racist strategy can be discerned. One is concerned with modifying individual behaviour through education or interaction; the other with removal of discriminatory structural barriers by eliminating their systemic roots, either democratically through political channels, through institutional reform, or by revolution through protest and forcible seizure of power (Bonilla-Silva, 1996).

Personal Anti-Racism: Taking a Stand

Positing a distinction between personal and institutional anti-racism is useful. Taken at its most obvious level, racism is normally envisaged as a personal problem of hatred or ignorance. There is an element of truth to this assertion. Racism is generally expressed through the thoughts and actions of prejudiced individuals. Prejudice consists of a prejudgment of others because they are different or threatening. Thus, strategies for containment or control are called forth that focus on modifying inappropriate behaviour based on prejudice and stereotyping. Three of the more common personal anti-racist strategies for improvement are interaction, education, and law.

Interaction

Learning through interaction represents one of the many anti-racist techniques available for individual change. Interaction with others will remove barriers that stem from ignorance or fear. Lack of knowledge is replaced with mutually reinforcing understanding. Yet contact in its own right is not necessarily beneficial (Tilbury, 2000). It is doubtful if the millions of tourists who pour into the Caribbean each winter have done much to ameliorate race relations, given that such interactional patterns entail a pandering to White interests. Under these potentially degrading circumstances, the degree of resentment and contempt escalates as the indigenous populations recreate colonialist patterns of servitude and deference.

Reduction of racism through interaction depends on the nature of the interactional setting. For any positive effect, interaction must be conducted between individuals who are relatively equal in status; who collaborate on a common endeavour in a spirit of trust and respect; whose interaction receives some degree of institutional and societal support; and who derive mutual benefit from cooperation (Jaret, 1995). Interaction between unequals simply upholds the status quo by perpetuating stereotypes and confirms the worst prejudices in a negatively charged environment.

Education

It is widely assumed that formal instruction can reduce racism. Racism is viewed as a case of individuals subscribing to an irrational belief; thus the cure lies in educating people to realize that racism is wrong. Once aware of what they are doing and why, people are deemed sufficiently rational to make the appropriate adjustments. This notion of enlightenment through learning has put schools in the vanguard of institutions dealing with diversity. Education has long been seen as the most popular policy prescription for curing us of racism (Bonilla-Silva, 1996).

Two styles prevail in accommodating diversity within schools: multicultural and/or anti-racist (see Chapter 9). Multicultural education refers to a philosophy of "celebrating differences." It consists of activities or curricula that promote an awareness of diversity in terms of its intrinsic value to minorities and/or society at large (Ontario Ministry of Education and Training, 1993). The aim of multicultural education is largely attitudinal; that is, to enhance sensitivity by improving awareness about cultural differences. Emphasis is on becoming more aware of ourselves as cultural carriers; of the customs that underpin non-Western cultures; and of the role of ethnocentrism and cultural relativism in supporting or denying diversity. It is also aimed at fostering tolerance. In contrast to acceptance and understanding, tolerance is putting up with something that one does not like in order to improve interpersonal interaction or social harmony (Vogt, 1997). Strategies for this kind of sensitivity awareness are varied, spanning the spectrum from museum approaches to immersion programs, with cross-cultural enrichment in between.

Multiculturally based training sessions have proliferated also outside of school settings. Training sessions may involve workshops for new and established employees, with content ranging from cultural awareness modules to cross-cultural communication sessions, to pointers about prejudice and ethnocentrism. Police forces in the larger metropolitan areas are increasingly involved in multicultural-relations training programs for cadets, patrol officers, and management (Fleras and Desroches, 1989). Program sessions are generally geared toward the elimination of discrimination in policing; promotion of cultural diversity within the police force; development of sensitivity to culturally diverse constituencies; improvement of cross-cultural communication; and implementation of community-based policing principles. Yet diversity training programs can be counterproductive in the hands of poorly trained and inadequately motivated instructors. Blame-and-shame programs can backfire because they are openly confrontational or preachy, tend to make people defensive, and often foster resentment among participants because of humiliation, embarassment, guilt, or shame (Jaret, 1995). Even in the hands of skilled practitioners, there is no guarantee of positive change in attitude or behaviour, given the difficulty of isolating, let alone unlearning, something that was internalized unconsciously and is perceived as positive rather than irrational or inappropriate.

Anti-racist education seeks to overcome the limitations of multicultural education, arguing in effect that cultural solutions (multicultural education) cannot adequately address structural problems. Anti-racist education takes a critical view of power relations in society, and directs its attention to how the dominant sector exercises power over subordinate groups within and beyond the school system (Cheyne et al., 1997; Dei, 1998). Anti-racist education links racism to politics and economics, against a backdrop of policies, practices, and social structures. The historic relations of domination are analyzed and assessed at the level of individuals and institutions, thus exposing both minorities and the mainstream to the structural sources of oppression in society. Anti-racist education is also focused on encouraging individuals to look inside themselves and their culture as sources of racism. Whites are encouraged to examine their own racism and privileged positions, on the assumption that White awareness is critical to understanding personal privilege and taking responsibility for disempowerment of others (McIntosh, 1988). In short, anti-racist education differs from multicultural equivalents in several ways; namely, it: (a) privileges power at the centre of any reconstruction; (b) acknowledges institutionalized power to establish hegemonic dominance; (c) provides a discursive framework for analyzing how different oppressions intersect and overlap; (d) problematizes the notion of "culture" in multicultural education as a basis for transformative change; and (e) challenges the notion of what is valid and legitimate knowledge, and how other forms of knowledge can be incorporated, given the racialized practices in schools that have the intent or effect of erasing others (Dei, 1998). It remains to be seen if an anti-racist initiative can challenge the state and its educational institutions to live up to their self-defined democratic ideals of freedom, equality, and social justice.

Law and Legal Sanctions

Recourse to law is sometimes upheld as an effective personal deterrent. Laws exist in Canada that prohibit the expression of racial discrimination against vulnerable minorities. The scope of these laws is broad. Some legal measures consist of protection for identifiable minorities through restrictions on majority behaviour. For example, the Supreme Court of Canada has ruled repeatedly that prohibiting racial propaganda is a justifiable and reasonable limitation on the freedom of speech. Other measures are aimed at removing discriminatory barriers that deter minority participation in society. The objective is to make it illegal to discriminate by making people aware of the consequences of breaking the law.

Passage of these and related laws is not intended to alter people's attitudes, at least not in the short run. A democratic society such as ours entitles people to their own private thoughts, however repugnant or anti-social. But this right disappears when private thoughts become discriminatory behaviour: Legal sanctions apply at this point. To be sure, laws are limited in their effectiveness for modifying individual thought or behaviour. The legislative advances of the U.S. Civil Rights Act in 1964 neither resolved African-American inequities nor eliminated prejudice and discrimination. Section 319 of Canada's Criminal Code prohibits the promotion of hatred against identifiable minorities; yet this hate law may well have the outcome of: (a) driving racism underground; (b) reinforcing the in-group's belief in the rightness of its actions; and (c) fostering a sense of hero-worship or martyrdom in defence of the cause (Kinsella, 1995). Nor can laws eliminate disadvantages by dispersing the concentration of wealth or distribution of power. Passage of laws may be designed to minimize majority inconvenience, rather than to assist minorities. But laws can modify people's behaviour through the imposition of sanctions. On the assumption that most individuals are law-abiding because of the threat of punishment or social ostracism, passage of anti-racist laws ensures compliance with the letter of the law, at least outwardly, if not by personal conviction. In time, however, people's thought may converge with behaviour in an effort to reduce the dissonance between thought and action.

Institutional Anti-Racism: Moving Over and Sharing Power

There is room for cautious optimism when discussing the effectiveness of individually tailored anti-racist programs. But are these initiatives of sufficient scope to expunge racism at its roots? Are the structures of society amenable to reform through personal transformation? Perhaps a word of clarification is needed about the sociological point of view. With the possible exception of socio-biologists (see van den Berghe, 1985), most sociologists would argue that individuals are not biologically programmed to act in a racist manner. There are no genes that express themselves in racial discrimination. Nor is there reason to believe that people are born with a propensity to hate. To be sure, biological or psychological perspectives are not dismissed outright. There may be good reasons for an evolutionary approach that acknowledges the fear of others as a survival value. Our preferences are directed at social explanations: People are conditioned to be racist by environments that foster ethnocentrism, outgroup antipathy, and racism. Racism is inextricably linked with the process of social control for preserving the status quo in complex societies. This assertion is consistent with fundamental sociological premises: that the social is real; that it transcends individual personalities; that behaviour is contextual and constructed, and is amenable to analysis and reform; and that the social environment helps to account for differences and patterns in attitudes and behaviour. Racism may be expressed in and through people (who may be regarded as precipitating causes), but individuals are merely the conduits of racial antipathy. It is the social context that counts.

Racism can only be resolved by attacking it at its source; namely, the institutional structures that support a capitalist society. Racism is not just about individuals with regressive beliefs or dormant prejudices, but is rooted in institutional structures and provides a justifying ideology and practices in those contexts where the social order is structured around the placement of minorities in racial categories (Bonilla-Silva, 1996). Personal solutions such as anti-racist training are comparable to applying a bandage to a cancerous growth — compassionate and humane to be sure, but ultimately self-defeating in light of the magnitude of the disease. The symptoms are addressed, not the cause or source. The problem of racism cannot be eliminated except by confronting it within the wider confines of political domination and economic control. The only practical solution to a problem that cannot be solved by personal intervention is to institutionalize anti-racism by way of prudent race management, such as employment equity or multiculturalism (D'Souza, 1996). This comprehensive approach will entail a different set of assumptions and tactics than those focusing on personal initiatives.

The promotion of employment equity is one such measure. Employment equity programs are based on the premise that racially discriminatory barriers do not stem from ignorance, fear, or arrogance. These barriers are systemic and entrenched within existing structures: That embeddedness makes them amenable to reform only through institutional rather than personal change. Equity initiatives are directed at hidden rules and unconscious procedures that inadvertently distort the process of recruitment, entry, treatment, promotion, or reward allocation in favour of one group rather than another. These initiatives hope to identify and eliminate offending practices; they also intend to remedy the effects of past discrimination, to remove systemic barriers in pursuit of equal outcomes, and to ensure appropriate representation of identifiable groups at all workplace levels. The ultimate goal is the creation of a workplace environment where differences are embraced as a legitimate and integral component of "business as usual."

In short, anti-racism strategies consist of measures and mechanisms for dismantling the structural basis of institutional racism. The removal of discriminatory barriers is central: Selection and recruitment procedures as well as rules for promotion and reward are scrutinized for hidden bias, in the interests of promoting accessibility. Values and practices are monitored that historically have propelled the organization, but are irrelevant in a changing and diverse context. Anti-racist strategies must focus on dominant beliefs and values within the institution, the organizational system related to rules and practices, and the experiences and behaviours of organizational actors. These systemic biases are most apt to occur at the level of mission statement, culture and subculture, power and decision-making, structures (including rules, roles, and relationships), and the distribution of physical, financial, and human resources. Any institutional enterprise will foster racism intentionally or unintentionlly when it perpetuates mission statements that are exclusionary; refuses to share power or decision-making; promulgates a monocultural set of values and beliefs as normal and necessary; maintains an inflexible or unresponsive set of structures and operations; and endorses unequal distribution of resources (Chesler and Crowfoot, 1989). These multi-pronged, anti-racist initiatives sound plausible in theory; their implementation may be another story.

Toward a Comprehensive Solution: Think Socially, Act Personally

Dealing with racism in Canada demands that we recognize our colonial past, that we come to terms with the historic and violent oppression of aboriginal peoples, and that we talk about the race-based inequalities that pervade nearly every sphere of society. Racism is a messy matter, and if we are really interested in challenging it, we can't afford to just keep trying to tidy things up.

Andil Gosine, *Toronto Star,* March 21st, 1999

It's relatively easy to dismiss racism as a personal problem. It is equally tempting to situate racism within a system of vast and impersonal forces that are largely beyond individual responsibility and outside the bounds of human agency. Racism is deeply embedded in Canadian society, as well as in the tradition of liberal-pluralism upon which Canada is secured. Dismantling racism is also complicated by the interlocking nature of social oppressions such as gender, race, ethnicity, and class. Neither of these positions—racism as personal, or racism as institutional—is entirely correct. Individuals may not be the root cause of racism, but racism is located within and is carried by the person. Systems may generate root causes, but institutions do not exist apart from individuals who interact to create, support, maintain, or transform patterns of racism. Racism is implicit in our daily encounters through the perpetuation of countless actions, gestures, and speech patterns. Each of us must be held accountable for our actions, no matter how powerful the social context and social forces. This much is critical: Unless there is an awareness of people's contribution to the problem, it becomes difficult to be part of the solution. Put differently, when applied to the realm of racism and proposed solutions, the personal is indeed the political. The political in turn defines the personal. That is, changing the system invariably changes people's attitudes; changing people's attitudes may result in corresponding alterations in people's behaviour and revisions to society.

Racism is also a structural feature of contemporary society, although often beyond our awareness or consciousness. As individuals, we must reflect critically upon our degree of complicity in perpetuating racism. Racism is embedded in our capitalist society by way of social, economic, and political institutions and practices. This societal racism may be deliberately invoked to control, deny, or exclude. It may also flourish inadvertently in privileging Eurocentric norms, values, practices, and institutions as necessary and superior, while ignoring minority experiences as inappropriate. To combat the root cause of racism requires a sociological analysis and critique of how and why racism as ideology is widely perpetuated. Thus, strategies to combat racism must obviously take into account the interplay of social forces and the subjective experiences of individuals. Only a comprehensive approach can deliver the goods with any hope of success. It remains to be seen whether any system driven by private profit and money as the measure of all can ever hope to solve any of its problems, since the goals of making money may detract from the promotion of social values related to diversity, inclusion, and equality. In the final analysis, then, the objective of anti-racism is not simply to purge racism from our midst, but to create a new society that is based on living together with our differences in ways that enhance diversity without sacrificing equality.

GENDER RELATIONS

FRAMING THE PROBLEM

In 1963, Betty Friedan published *The Feminine Mystique*, a scathing critique of American women that proved as revolutionary in galvanizing women's consciousness and mobilizing women into action as had Rachel Carson's *The Silent Spring* in launching the environmental movement. Friedan labelled the unhappiness and boredom of middle-class women in their "comfortable concentration camps" as the "problem with no name." According to Friedan, a profound sense of emptiness and disillusionment, rather than contentment, confronted those women who sought fulfillment and identity by being "sexually passive," accepting male domination as natural and normal, obsessing over children and husbands, and fixating on their housework to the exclusion of looking after themselves. Two years earlier, another groundbreaking book by Simone de Beauvoir, *The Second Sex*, reinforced the perception of women as the subordinate gender. The subordination of women as service-providers could be directly attributed to the devaluation of women's work and worth. This subservience was unwittingly captured by the caption on the front page of the March 17th, 1943 edition of the *Globe and Mail* in which the RCAF Women's Division proudly proclaimed, "We Serve That Men May Fly." Gender options were clearly articulated: Boys were to taught to do and accomplish, whereas girls were conditioned to forfeit choices and possibilities, except to look after others while keeping unwanted dirt at bay. So pervasive and internalized was this presumption of women as "natural born nurturers" that few dared to step outside the rigidly sculpted gender script for fear of rebuke or rejection.

Women have "come a long way, baby" since publication of these books. In a relatively short period of time, gender relations have evolved beyond the days when women and children were regarded as male property for his disposal; rape within marriage was dismissed as a contradiction in terms; a woman's place was in the home or between the sheets; a working woman was pitied as irresponsible or an embarrassment; unwed mothers were stigmatized and shunned; and universities were institutes for snaring husbands rather than for higher learning. But the inception of legal equality has created the basis for court challenges to remove sexist and discriminatory barriers. Increasing numbers of women are in paid work, while women are fording the corridors of power to the refrains of "grrrl" power and "sisters doing it for themselves" (Walter, 1998). Women have made notable gains in occupations traditionally perceived as male. The income gap between women and men continues to close, albeit slowly; in fact, certain categories of women, namely, single, university-educated women, outperform their male counterparts in the same age/marital/education bracket. Women are taking control of many aspects of their lives, including: (a) deciding if and when to have children; (b) raising children on their own or with novel combinations of partners; (c) suing employees for harassment and discrimination; and (d) exerting pressure on hidebound institutions to embrace female realities or risk bottom-line credibility. This "gender quake" of change has transcended all age groups. Girls are doing better than boys at school, prompting public concern over a crisis in boyhood should contemporary trends persist. And buoyed by the success of the seemingly unsinkable *Titanic*, marketers are increasingly looking to young preteens ("tweens") as a fecund source of buying power. Amidst this sea-change of transformation that has all but banished the most egregious expressions of sexism, many are questioning the relevance of feminism in a world allegedly dominated by women.

How do we account for such progress? Perhaps the reason why women have come such a long way is because there was such a long way to go. Old fashioned assumptions and gender stereotyping had the effect of marginalizing women, undervaluing their achievements and contributions, relegating them to lesser-paying jobs in lower-ranking institutions, ghettoizing them into less prestigious corporate domains such as staffing functions (human resources), and excluding them from positions of power even when there was no malice or blatant intimidation. Despite obvious gains in opportunities and choice, however, women as a group still have a way to go to achieve economic parity, social equality, and political power-sharing. Women are more likely than men to be on benefits, to suffer from abuse and violence at the hands of men, and to be excluded from the higher echelons of corporate or political decision-making. They continue to be taken less seriously, judged on the basis of what they look like rather than what they do, and assumed to dote on their roles as caregivers and on their relationships to others. Politics remains a no (wo)man's land. Nowhere is this silencing more deafening than in the corridors of political power where women could not vote or hold office until 1916 in Manitoba, 1918 at the federal level, and 1940 in Quebec. In the 1997 federal election, women were elected in 62 of the 301 ridings, or 20.6 percent of all ridings, an increase over previous years, but still a significant underpresentation (Greschner, 1998). Stereotypes continue to prevail: Women continue to be perceived as passive, emotional, weak, and obsessed with appearances, in contrast to men who are thought to be assertive, ambitious, competitive, and goal-oriented. In a sense there is nothing inherently wrong with holding these stereotypes; problems occur when they serve as a basis for reward or relationships. The term "women's work" continues to resonate with a coded subtext, either as a way of describing maternal-domestic work both in and outside the home, or the relegation of women to largely low paying "girl ghettos" such as service, sales, or clerical (Kornblum and Julian, 1995). Opportunities for women continue to be restricted by the persistence and pervasiveness of the "second shift," with the nerve-wracking demands of balancing paid employment with unpaid household work (Hochschild, 1983; *National Post*, June 18, 1999). Double standards are alive and well: Women are criticized for undermining family values when they are employed outside the home, then chastised for "betraying the cause" by working at home. In short, the verdict is frustratingly mixed. The end of the millenium is proving a confusing mixture of progressive and regressive as the scripts of the past persist in practice if not always in principle. Women may have more freedom and choice, as Natasha Walter (1998) concludes, but they remain unequal in terms of being poorer and less powerful than men.

Men, too, are being buffeted by the gender quake that is challenging gender relations. Men in general have experienced as much change as women with respect to reconceptualizing who they are and what they must do. Social forces have combined to erode a man's sense of identity and importance, writes Susan Faludi in her book, *Stiffed*. Others, including Angela Phillips, in *The Trouble With Boys*, argues that men have been effectively neutered by a feminist-dominated status quo. In *Blood Rites*: *Origins and History of the Passion of War*, Barbara Ehrenreich contends that men are no longer central to women's and children's lives as hunters and providers. The legitimacy of malehood has suffered accordingly. Similarly, Lionel Tiger, in his book, *The Decline of Men*, posits that discriminatory public policy initiatives have emasculated men from significant involvement in family life. In a classic case of gender reversal, Fay Weldon (1997) writes, it is men who now complain of being slighted by "grrrl" power, and condemned by virtue of gender to put-downs and insults as lazy bastards, irresponsible louts, socially disconnected, and emotional blanks. To add injury to insult, a survey of 1000 male and female managers published in the magazine, *Management Today*, warned that traditional male skills and leadership qualities (such as hierarchy rather than teamwork, or motivation by command rather than persuasion) would no longer be applicable in the lean, fast-changing, and customer-driven organizations of the new millenium, and that only female-linked attributes would prevail (Baker, 1999). For young men approaching adulthood, in other words, the very definition of being a man is being transformed before their eyes. The transition from an alpha male ("competitive") to a beta male ("compassionate") is littered with cultural landmines and mixed messages about rethinking their relationship to women, to other men, and to children. Men no longer have the right to "have it all," as was once routinely the case; rather, male power and privilege are being whittled away by a combination of demographic shifts, changes in intellectual fashion, government initiatives, and female assertiveness. Insofar as the gains by women are perceived to be at the expense of men, the mounting resentment is reflected in palpable hostility and acts of destruction. To be sure, among younger, more educated men, there is growing acceptance of the principle of gender equity, especially in once female-dominated spheres such as child-rearing and housekeeping. But, generally, men appear unhappy about having to share power and privilege with those once defined as inferior or irrelevant, preferring instead to secure as much of the status quo as possible, without looking like a knuckle-dragging Neanderthal in the process (Johnson, 1997).

For all the talk of a gender quake, with ominous predictions of men as second-class citizens, rhetoric may not match reality. Canada remains arguably a (White)man's world in terms of foundational structures, core values, institutional frameworks, and constitutional principles. The entirety of Canadian society is not culturally neutral. More accurately, it is organized around a culture-specific agenda, with the result that other cultures and genders must work within the framework established by male privilege. There is nothing natural or normal about the way Canadians engage in societal routines. Rather, structures in society are socially constructed conventions designed by those with the power and resources to make choices that embody their interests rather than the aspirations of others. Of course, the most egregious expressions of sexism and patriarchy have been dismantled. Nevertheless, the values and infrastructures of society continue to bolster male needs, experiences, and realities, either by intent or by default. In monopolizing most of the powerful positions of authority, men as a group remain firmly in control of those decisions that shape political, economic, social, and cultural outcomes, with just enough exceptions to prove the rule. Such a scenario may be paradoxical for women: They must buy into the system if they hope for mainstream success; yet incorporation along these lines may prove difficult or costly in personal terms. Even those women who manage to crash the glass ceiling by scaling the corporate ladder find that acceptance is contingent on playing the male game, despite costs to female sensibilities. To be sure, women are challenging those ready-made scripts that historically secured the foundation of patriarchal society. Yet moving into uncharted territory is fraught with uncertainty and confusion. Women find themselves in a transitional state, in which new ideas must conform and coexist—however awkwardly—with traditional forms of responsibility related to family, marriage, parenting, and working (Heilbrun, 1999).

Thirty years of robust social and demographic changes have dramatically altered what Canadians say they think about gender. Women are no longer automatically assumed inferior or submissive; roles are not nearly as rigidly scripted as before; rules defining masculinity and femininity are increasingly contested; differences among women are accepted as empowering; and domestic relations are gradually embracing a commitment to the principles of partnership. Feminism has helped to redefine this shift in the balance of power by expanding the chances and choices open to women in contemporary society. Nevertheless, cultural beliefs have not always kept pace with social changes, with the result that Canadians are increasingly unsure of the expectations associated with gender roles, rules, status, and relationships. Many are aware that the old rules don't apply; nevertheless, new ones are difficult to define or implement without explicit guidelines. Traditional rules about gender relationships no longer seem applicable, even as new norms have yet to be formulated to everyone's satisfaction (Smith, 1998). For example, women are seen as having a rightful place in the workforce, with an obligation to contribute to household income; paradoxically, however, most Canadians believe that children suffer with two working parents. As a result, women find themselves damned if they do (irresponsible), and damned if they don't (welfare) (Mitchell, 1997). Of course, women are not the only ones undergoing change and adjustment. Men too are victimized by double standards: No sooner is a "softer" side shown, than they are precluded from female-dominated professions, discouraged from working with children, and criticized for acting "wimpy" around the guys. Many of the traits once negatively associated with "femininity" are now perceived as strengths; conversely, male virtues of independence and control are defined increasingly as vices, especially in the workplace environments of a freewheeling global market economy. Not surprisingly, men are experiencing an identity crisis and crisis of confidence in trying to figure out who they are and what is expected of them in this topsy-turvy world. Table 5–1 below attempts to capture some sense—in an ideal typical fashion—of the changes from the tightly scripted expectations of the 1960s to the more loosely phrased prescriptions in gender rules, roles, relations, and status at the end of the millenium.

How do we analyze and assess a situation in which women have made remarkable progress, yet continue to lag because of systemic biases? Conversely, while men appear to

TABLE 5-1	Gender Relations: Now and Then			
	1960s		**1990s**	
	Women	**Men**	**Women**	**Men**
Roles	"The lady of the house" * narrowly restricted to domestic-maternal roles as wife and mother	"king of the castle" * primary role = breadwinner and head of household as father and husband	"having it all" paid work (career) and unpaid work	breadmaker + breadwinner
Rules	"be a lady" * expectations = * passive * obedient * deferential * dependent	"act like a man" * expectations = * aggressive * independent * competitive * leadership material	"enlarging the script" * choice* with option of having it all — career/kids/ independence (feminine with an assertive centre)	"feminization of men" masculine traits are devalued + addition of select female attributes (macho with a soft centre)
Relationships	"stand by your man" supportive of and in service to men	"movers and shakers" in charge and taking control	"MS" partnership + egalitarian	"new age guy" attuned yet assertive
Social Status	subordinate "no status outside maternal domestic or in relation to some male"	dominant "privileged status at home, work, and community"	"I am Woman" different but equal	"The Descent of Men" move over and share space (and power)

* status = positions in the social system
* roles = patterns of behaviour associated with a position in society
* rules = ideas and ideals that shape behaviour in a particular context

have lost ground in the gender wars, do they remain firmly in control? The juxtaposition of these intersecting yet contradictory trends not only elicits a mixed message, but also generates a host of social problems that have proven difficult to solve. In such uncharted and contested territory, social conventions are up for grabs, and it is precisely this indeterminancy that is both a danger and excitement (Heilbrun, 1999). Insofar as gender constitutes a constructed and contested site of progress and regress, of empowerment and disempowerment, this chapter explores the evolving and enigmatic relationship between men and women from a social problem perspective. Gender relations are defined as unequal relations, and, inasmuch as this inequity is social in origin, definition, and treatment, emphasis is focused on how these relationships of inequality are constructed, expressed, maintained, challenged, and transformed. Gender is construed as a social problem in three ways: First, gender is a social problem when inequities between women and men continue to persist in a society that espouses gender equity. Gender inequities are couched in the greater exclusion of women from economic and political realms, and their incorporation into the category of the disadvantaged is shown to be structural and utilitarian, rather than personal and situational. Second, gender is problematic because the growing estrangement between men and women is likely to create unhealthy competition at great interpersonal costs and risk to social stability. Third, the problem with gender revolves around the scripting of masculinity and femininity into roles, rules, and relationships that may stifle personal choice while fostering unhealthy outcomes. The chapter explores the notion of gender from a conditionalist and constructionist perspective: as a condition with causes, consequences, characteristics, and cures; as a claims-making activity involving social movements known as feminism. In defining gender as social construction, central issues include some of the following questions: How different are women from men? Are differences one of degree or kind, of culture versus biology? What does it mean to be a man or a woman in a cross-cultural perspective? Efforts to explain gendered inequalities are examined by way of an extended case study of women in the corporation as they bump into glass ceilings and bounce off brick walls. Paradoxically, gender is not always the most important dimension of inequality for women. Gender may be superimposed on class, race, and ethnicity to create intersecting and interlocking patterns of inequality that have the intent or effect of denying or excluding women of colour, immigrant and minority women, and aboriginal women (Evans and Wekerle, 1997; Andersen and Collins, 1998). Also addressed is the notion that men are a gender too, one whose precipitous decline in status is simultaneously lamented or celebrated. Since gender issues are male issues, and gender problems are really male problems, the section on masculinity will demonstrate how and why the crisis in male identity confidence is proving both a problem and an opportunity. Finally, efforts to redefine gender relations are explored. Both the state and feminist movements have taken steps to create a society that upholds the principle and practice of equality. To the extent that the gender problem is differently defined by diverse feminisms, with different problem definitions and proposed solutions, answers to the question, "Is there a future for feminism?" are likely to be lively ones in the foreseeable future.

(DE)CONSTRUCTING GENDER

> We are told that the social gap between the sexes is narrowing, but I can only report that having, in the second half of the twentieth century, experienced life in both roles [male and female], there seems to be no aspect of existence, no moment of the day, no contact, no arrangement, no response, which is not different for men and women. The very tone of the voice in which I was addressed, the very posture of the person next in [line], the very feel of the air when I entered a room or sat at a restaurant table, constantly emphasized my change...
>
> - Transsexual British journalist, Jan Morris, after her surgical change from male to female

Interest in the dynamics that define male-female relations has escalated in recent years, thanks in part to the feminist movement and in part to changes in the workplace. The growing prominence of women in previously male-dominated domains has riveted public attention and political response as have few other contemporary issues. For personal and professional reasons, individuals express a consuming interest in the cultural meaning of womanhood ("femininity") or manhood ("masculinity"), together with how masculinity and femininity vary from time to time and place to place. Sociologists take as axiomatic the notion that neither manhood nor womanhood qualifies as the purely biological attributes of individuals. Biology may determine our sex as male or female (or one of at least three others sexes). But culture shapes the content and conduct of what it means to be a man or a woman (Strate, 1992). Those socially constructed and culturally specific attributes that are acquired by individuals through socialization are known as gender. Gender entails the culturally prescribed rules that define masculinity or femininity in a specific society. Masculinity consists of that package of attributes that is associated with an ideal typical male; femininity exemplifies the cultural characteristics that define the ideal typical female. As social and cultural constructs, concepts of femininity and masculinity are known to vary spatially (from culture to culture), laterally (within culture), historically (from one period to another), and longitudinally (across a person's lifespan) (Kimmel, 1992). The fact that gender is cultural and prescribed rather than biological and given confirms the centrality of social constructions in understanding human social existence (Ferree and Hall, 1990).

Gender is not a natural consequence of sex differences; it constitutes a culturally defined prescription about what is or should be (Nelson and Robinson, 1996). Moreover, it is precisely the notion of gender as socially constructed that creates the potential for social problems, since the imposition of these gendered social constructions confers more power, privilege, and wealth to some at the expense of others. Gender is not simply a social variable assigned to men and women that varies from one culture to another (Harding, 1986). The concept of gender is now recognized as a key variable that shapes how we think about ourselves and our relationship to the world. Our gender experiences constitute a central element in our personal lives; they also provide a primary point of contact with the world about us (Renzutti and Curran, 1999). Gender constitutes a primary axis around which social life is organized and maintained (Kimmel, 1992), ranking alongside the categories of race and class in defining who gets what in society. Its centrality in determining patterns of entitlement and engagement further reinforces the primacy of gender relations, and how these relationships are subject to the same kinds of inequality, hierarchical distinctions, and (dis)advantages as those of social class or race and ethnicity (Harris, 1993). This invariably leads to questions about how these relations are constructed, kept in place, challenged or resisted, or subjected to modification and change.

Men Are From Mars/Women Are From Venus?

This notion of gender and gender roles as socially constructed raises a host of related issues. First, how different are women and men? Are differences based on degree ("superficial") or kind ("fundamental")? Are women more cooperative and consensual compared to the aggressiveness of men; or are these differences superficial and reflective of situational adjustments irrespective of gender? Some would argue that women and men are basically alike: Similar outcomes will result if women and men are equipped with the same opportunities and expectations, situated in a comparable context, and exposed to similar pressures and competition (Kanter, 1977). Others propose a radical difference between women and men. For some, the differences are rooted in biogenetic wiring; for others, differences reflect the radically different social and cultural experiences that each encounter in society. For example, most men tend to separate their minds from their bodies in a way that is alien to many women, particularly since women continue to judge and be judged by their appearance more harshly than men, and they know it (Wolf, 1990; Harrison, 1995). Or consider how theories that depict society as a remorseless struggle for power are not neutral or objective in their analysis. Embodied instead is a gendered perspective that reflects male experiences, interests, and agendas instead of anything inherent in society itself. Belief in the existence of radical differences raises several questions. To what extent should people be treated the same if they are fundamentally different? Should women attempt to get ahead in the world of politics or economy by demonstrating traditional male virtues of aggressiveness, toughness, and competitiveness (Fukuyama, 1999)? Or should women try to shift the political and economic agenda away from the male obsession with hierarchy, competition, and domination? The fact that responses to these questions remain as contested as ever is itself indicative of the difficulties in agreement.

Second, what is the nature of female-male differences? Are behavioural differences between women and men the result of biology or culture, or both? To what extent do the brains of women and men process information differently? Is there any biological basis to the allocation of roles and rewards along gender lines, either in the past or at present (Brettell and Sargent, 1993)? Is it possible to resocialize men to be more like women or women to be more like men, or is what is "bred in the bone" largely unalterable by modifications to culture, socialization, or situational circumstances (Fukuyama, 1999)? Many continue to believe that gender relations reflect innate and inherited qualities; for example, that women's brains are more adept at solving problems involving spatial relations. According to Francis Fukuyama, virtually all evolutionary biologists believe differences between women and men to be profound and genetic, reflecting differential reproductive strategies. These differences extend to the mind as well as to the body and behaviour, thus making it extremely difficult to alter deeply ingrained patterns of behaviour such as male violence and aggression. Most sociologists reject the idea of genetic hard-wiring as a basis for explaining gender differences and similarities. While acknowledging that the genetic is not synonymous with fixed or predictable, but subject to modification or override, the denial of the biological is consistent with sociological assumptions. That is, similarities and differences in behaviour are the result of social forces, such as cultural values, socialization processes, structural constraints, group dynamics, and situational cues. Applied to gender relations, the concept of what it means to be a woman or a man ("femininity" and "masculinity") is socially constructed, relative to a particular time and place, and responsive to broader societal changes. As a social construction, gender does not refer to anything natural or normal about the world we live in, despite efforts by vested interests to make it appear so. Gender is a convention created at a particular point in time and place by those in positions of power to enforce these scripted notions of right or wrong.

What do cross-national studies say about gender and gender roles? Anthropology has performed a yeoman-like service in expanding our horizons on the social and cultural basis of gender relations. Evidence suggests that difference in our perceptions about women and men—in terms of skills, strengths, and capacities—are greatly exaggerated and reflect a lack of motivation rather than ability or talent (see Pearson, 1999). Differences are also culturally relative (Peoples and Bailey, 1997). Cultures not only construct gender by defining what it is to be a man ("masculine") or women ("feminine"). All societies construct distinctions between women and men, and assign certain rules, roles, meanings, values, and responsibilities to the categories of women and men (Gilmore, 1990). The socially constructed nature of female-male relations virtually ensures global variations in cultural notions of masculinity and femininity. The seeming inequality of gender relations is no less subject to debate. Men are defined (or have defined themselves) as superior to women in terms of authority, prestige, and access to power. Women's activities, no matter how significant to the local economy, are often devalued compared to male endeavours. Practical options for dealing with violence and abuse are limited, given women's economic dependency and lack of educational/employment opportunities (Nussbaum, 1996). A complex set of ideologies and symbols are also employed to denigrate women as irrelevant, dangerous, polluting, or untrustworthy, a view not necessarily shared by women who have learned to work around these restrictions even as they pay lip service to male domination (Harris, 1993; Abwunza, 1997; Chagnon, 1999).

Three key issues appear to animate much of the controversy surrounding gender relations from a cross-cultural perspective. First, the so-called "universality" of male dominance and female subordination despite the centrality of women to production and reproduction; second, a worldwide sexual division of labour in which men hunt and women gather; and third, the pervasiveness of gender-linked attributes pertaining to men as aggressors and women as nurturers. However, these things are not what they seem, given the exceptions to the rule that exist around the world. No less impressive is a growing awareness of the nuances and subtleties that characterize gender relations around the world. Gender differences and inequities are not an either-or phenomenon, but often reveal how those with even nominal amounts of power can work the system to their advantage. The need to reinterpret the past in light of the present may say more about anthropology and anthropologists than anything about "tribal people."

"DANCING BACKWARDS": GENDER INEQUALITY

The persistance and pervasiveness of gender inequality is central to any discussion of gender as social problem. In a society that aspires to equality between genders, problems arise when women and men align themselves along hierarchical lines. Gender inequality refers to the asymmetrical relationship between women and men based on the unequal distribution of power, privilege, and wealth. It also refers to the ranking of categories of women and men in ascending and descending order of differential access to the good things in life. These inequities are not random, but patterned, predictable, persistent, pervasive, and resistant to change. Gendered inequities are especially problematic when discrepancies in power and privilege are persistent and resistant to solution. These inequities do not necessarily reflect individual shortcomings, but stem from power relations, opportunity structures, discriminatory barriers, and workplace practices (Agocs and Boyd, 1993).

The relationship between women and men in all human societies is characterized by disparities of various sorts, although the intensity and scope of this gender gap is subject to cross-national variation. Throughout the world, politics remains a "no (wo)men's land," where women are routinely excluded from most involvement in government, state, or political life. Similarly, women languish near the bottom of the socio-economic ladder, despite making a disproportionate contribution to most economies. To be sure, women around the world have taken strides in uprooting ideals and practices surrounding their status in society. But patterns of inequality remain deeply entrenched. That is, women represent about half the world's population, perform nearly two-thirds of the work, earn about one-tenth of the income, and own less than one one-hundredth of the property (Ward, 1992).

Canada is no exception. By virtue of all standards of measurement (especially income), women continue to do less well than men, and to be excluded from preferential access to the good things in life. In a United Nations survey of 160 countries that put Canada on top in terms of overall life expectancy, education, and national income, the ranking of Canada slipped to 4th, once gender empowerment was taken into account. Evidence of disadvantage is difficult to refute: Canadian women live in a climate of fear of violence and poverty; are marginalized into occupational ghettos; have fewer job options and earn less income; are discouraged from excelling in traditional male pursuits; are subjected to harassment; and routinely confront discriminatory barriers and double standards. Their contribution to society is undervalued in some circles, except in terms of appearance ("adornments") or as objects

CASE STUDY 5-1   Shattering the Glass Ceiling

In 1977, Rosabeth Moss Kanter published what has become a modern-day classic in sociology. *Men and Women of the Corporation* received accolades by the bushelful for its excellence, including the coveted C. Wright Mills Prize for critical thought. The significance of Kanter's book went beyond its persuasiveness in explaining gender-based organizational behaviour within corporate America. The book provided an insightful, yet practical, application of how social forces impacted on human behaviour since, as Kanter observed, organizational actors tended to respond predictably when confronted by similar structural circumstances. Capitalizing on a sociological dimension symbolized a major departure from conventional studies of organizational behaviour, with their emphasis on psychological attributes and attitudinal predispositions.

Kanter attempted to explore the structural determinants of organizational behaviour by concentrating on the dynamics of a particular corporation. For Kanter, organizational behaviour stems from unconscious responses of actors to their status (or "placement") within corporate structures. Kanter concluded that, as a group, men prevailed in corporate settings, not necessarily because of male personality features or predispositions. Domination was derived instead from advantageous placement with respect to preferential opportunity structures, access to power, and numerical superiority. Women, by contrast, were often excluded or put down for precisely the same reasons that groomed men for success. For Kanter, in other words, the prominence of structure was critical in

understanding organizational behaviour. Organizational structures embodied something more than a passive backdrop for corporate games. These structures were logically prior and external to the individual; they also reinforced the benefit of a head start for those whose interests, experiences, and aspirations coincided with those of the corporation.

Opportunity Structures: "Nothing Succeeds Like Success"

The behaviour of corporate actors reflected their placement within the opportunity structures of the organization. Those who were labelled as having potential and streamed into the fast-track behaved differently from those saddled with limited opportunities. High achievers acted in a manner that reflected and reinforced a commitment to the corporation, with sights firmly locked on entry into the upper echelons. Those bent on upward mobility and corporate ladder-climbing could hardly afford to squander time in socializing or office politics. Conversely, those without high expectations acted accordingly, by displaying behavioural patterns consistent with marginality. In a classic reenactment of a self-fulfilling prophecy, they related to the corporation by way of hostility to management, displayed an unwillingness to put out for the company, a refusal to take risks to enhance upward mobility, and conducted themselves with an air of resignation and defeat.

From this, Kanter explained, opportunity structures were precisely that. Those on the fast track of opportunity acted in a competitive, dedicated, and instrumental manner. The expectations of others were confirmed by their confidence and assertiveness, subsequently opening even more doors for corporate scaling. Those on the slow track behaved predictably: Because of their "stuckedness," they were inclined to be peer-oriented, to exhibit signs of complacency and resignation, and appeared bereft of ambition, in the process reinforcing their peripheral status, both real and perceived. Problems also arose from confinement of women to the velvet ghetto of public relations, advertising, staff support, and personnel. The fact that few were streamed into key positions such as finance or research spoke volumes about a patriarchal legacy whereby women excelled in people-handling and emotional fine tuning, but men took care of business. The few exceptions merely confirmed the rule.

The significance of structures for corporate gender behaviour should not be underestimated. Corporate structures have the potential to reduce or enhance organizational commitment; they can also dampen or accelerate enthusiasm and aspiration. Men do not monopolize these fast opportunity tracks simply because of superior work habits or heightened ambition. Nor are women shunted aside because of their skills or lack thereof. Rather, men find themselves in positions where they are encouraged and rewarded more often to move upwards, whereas women are located in structures that inhibit career enhancement. As proof, even men derailed from the fast-tracking express tended to exhibit many of the same symptoms as those on the track to nowhere. Conversely, nothing succeeded like success for women on the fast track. In sum, individuals are successful not necessarily because they have the "right stuff" (although that is obviously im-

portant). The fact they have been centred out for success has a tendency to elicit the right corporate stuff. The person, in other words, does not make the job; more to the point, the job makes over the person.

The Structure of Power: "Powerlessness Corrupts"

Those who possessed power tended to act in a powerful fashion. They could take advantage of power to get things done, define situations, propose solutions, establish agendas, draw on resources when necessary, enhance performance, and improve productivity. These objectives were often achieved through discretionary decisions that went beyond the "rulebook." Powerful individuals also knew how to delegate responsibility without having to check with superiors. They were in a position to enforce decisions, yet were rarely victimized by second guessing, in effect, reinforcing the idea that power is most powerful when people are least aware of it.

Conversely, those without power displayed behaviour patterns at odds with corporate goals. Even when occupying positions of formal authority within the corporate chain of command, the powerless resorted to excessive authoritarianism or displaced aggression, reinforcing yet again the observation that the most powerful are those least inclined to flaunt it. Powerless people concentrated on what little residual power they had over subordinates through rigid, coercive, and vindictive displays. Throwing this "weight" around may have achieved the goal of compliance and ritual subordination, but ultimately sabotaged productivity while eroding cooperative manager-labour relations.

The power of power, in short, cannot be lightly dismissed: Power is indispensable for corporate success, especially when manipulated without fanfare or heavy-handededness. By way of conclusion, Kanter asserts that it is not so much that power corrupts; rather, that powerlessness is corrupting. Those unsure of their power, minorities and women, tended to act in a manner that underscored their peripheral status. Without power, a person's credibility was in doubt and openly contested, making it doubly difficult to receive deference, ensure compliance, and impress superiors.

The Structure of Relative Numbers: "Token Effects"

Relative numbers refer to the proportional distribution of certain categories of persons within the corporate setting. They also refer to how organizational hierarchies reflect differences in the social composition of the institutional workforce. The behaviour of those who constituted the majority differed from members cast as minorities (measured statistically). The former did not have to worry about being excluded, since they set the norm and established the standard by which others were judged. Majority members were exempt from double standards that plagued minorities. Conversely, minorities and women of the organization behaved differently. Differences did not necessarily stem from variation in corporate acumen or the human capital they brought to the company (although these may have been important), but resulted from different expectations and diverse pressures brought to bear on those on the margins.

Many of the problems minorities confront stem from a combination of double standards, tokenism, and stereotyping. It is commonly assumed that women and minorities have to work twice as hard as the average White male for success (Kanter, 1977:239). Minorities are likely to be treated as to-

kens, a situation that is patently disruptive because of inherent contradictions. A partial list of contradictions that distorted minority experiences regardless of what they did include:

1. Minority tokens are viewed as representatives of their race when they fail, and exceptions when they succeed.

2. Tokens are constantly reminded of their differences, but must conduct themselves as if these differences were immaterial.

3. Tokens tend to occupy the limelight, and anything they do is thoroughly scrutinized and evaluated. Expressions of behaviour are viewed in terms of reinforcing stereotypes or as typical of the community at large.

4. Tokens are extremely visible and the most dramatized of corporate performers, yet they are rendered invisible by exclusion from centre stage where props are set, scripts are rehearsed, and casts are assembled.

5. Tokens find the organizational settings stressful and constraining, even more so during times of relaxation or socializing (such as office parties), largely because of intensified levels of scrutiny.

6. Tokens, as relatively "unknown" commodities, are undervalued as potentially disruptive to the firm. Yet this perceived disruptiveness is primarily a function of their historic exclusion from meaningful participation within the organization.

The repercussions of this token effect are obvious in shaping how minorities behave and what is expected of them. Damned if they do and damned when they don't, minorities find upward movement a lonely and alienating experience, as forces conspire to exaggerate their uniqueness, yet depersonalize their individuality. Constant exposure to scrutiny and monitoring inevitably takes it toll on those hand-picked as standard-bearers for their "kind." Their imposed status as ambassadors and role models practically guarantees that any missteps will confirm the worst in reinforcing stereotypes and the expectations of others. Worse still, they carry around the guilt that the future of others depends on them. The combined impact of this token effect, Kanter explains, is anything but token in its impact and implications.

Sizing Up the Situation: Walking Up a Down Escalator

What can we conclude from Kanter's work? First, organizational structures are important in shaping differences in behaviour between men and women. Maleness or femaleness is not the issue; nor are personality characteristics or attitudinal predispositions. What appears to be critical is the location of individuals in certain structures that shape perceptions, interactions, and responses. Women and minorities occupy the lower echelons of a corporate hierarchy not because of personal deficiencies that make them a liability to the organization. Rather, any passivity and non-commital orientation is largely a behavioural response to structural inequities involving denied opportunity, an inadequate power base, and numerically induced tokenism.

Gender differences do not count as much as responses to the structures of opportunity, power, and relative numbers. Kanter, of course, did not focus exclusively on structural determinants. Cultural factors are also important. For example, mainstream culture values will influence who is eligible for access to organizational opportunity or rewards. Organizational behaviour is also derived from situational circumstances. Corporate actors from top to bottom define situations according to their perceptions and interpretations of the surrounding context. They then develop lines of action that are consistent with their assessment of where they stand in the corporate hierarchy, compared with what is expected of them. But structural limitations restrict the range of behavioural options, primarily because the system "...set limits on behavioural possibilities and defined the context for peer interaction" (Kanter, 1977:239). These structures were systematic and deliberate in some cases; in others, they were systemic and unintended, but nevertheless had a controlling effect on behaviour and outcomes.

Second, Kanter's work was directed at dissecting behaviour patterns within organizations. Much of her analysis is equally applicable to understanding the behaviour of women and minorities in society at large. For example, just as corporate dynamics are unmistakably male in structure and ethos, (men are the prime beneficiaries of continuous employment and minimal domestic responsibilities (Sydie, 1987), so too is society an essentially male construction, a "White man's world." Despite a shift toward greater inclusiveness, those who do not fit the straight, White, male mould are subject to criticism or second guessing. Pressures for conformity lead to frustration and despair, as well as disinterest in coping with the androcentric demands of contemporary institutions. A seeming lack of ambition and commitment among minorities is not necessarily a sign of inferiority. Unproductive responses stem from minority perceptions of themselves as undervalued and irrelevant to society. In such a situation, behavioural responses, from deviant acts to passive resignation, appear to be consistent with the structural circumstances in which people are located.

Third, what can be done about transforming organizations in a manner consistent with minority needs and female aspirations? It is insufficient to introduce programs and policies that focus on attitudinal changes or personality modifications. Organizational structures themselves need to be overhauled if any substantial change is anticipated. Productivity and satisfaction are contingent on structural arrangements that either facilitate or inhibit the best from each worker. For example, if the goal is to improve productivity, then structures must be altered to empower workers, improve meaningful consultation, and enhance their contributions to the corporation. The path to reform is all too clear. The restructuring of organizational priorities and procedures is mandatory. A proposed replacement of males by minorities or women without any corresponding structural changes is unlikely to alter the status quo. Only the players would change, while the corporate game would merrily roll along.

Then and Now: "Business as Usual"

Ten years after the publication of her book, Rosabeth Kanter provided an update on the intervening years in the journal *Management Review* (1987). On the one hand, modest organizational reforms had materialized, some of which came about because of her book, Kanter added. Women and minorities began to chip away at the glass ceiling that had inhibited upward mobility. Yet it was pretty much "business as usual." Male stereotypes continued to extol deeply held values about a woman's "rightful place" that pigeonholed women into communications, human resources, and corporate cheerleader jobs, thus denying them the line

experience that they needed (Smith, 1998). As far as Kanter is concerned, the combination of constraints of power, lack of opportunity structure, and relative numbers remain as formidable as ever. The traditional image of a company, a small number of highly paid White males in charge of an army of poorly paid clerical workers (mostly women), remains the reality in many cases, despite modest initiatives for improving the employment and promotion of targeted minorities.

Admittedly, a loosening of the corporate structures had encouraged upward mobility among women and minorities. Beyond a certain point, however, movement upward had ground to a halt, leaving women to ponder whether to persist or resign in the face of subtle and not-so-subtle pressures. Over and over again, women spoke of upward mobility patterns that hit a "brick wall" because of male refusal to take them seriously. Women cited an inability to fit into a competitive corporate mould as an obstruction. As well, there was burnout from the conflicting and impossible demands of the double shift. Not surprisingly, many have pointed a finger at uncooperative spouses, not bosses, as a major impediment. To the surprise of no one, women and minorities are fleeing corporate cut-throat competition for the friendlier confines of small business and individual entrepreneurship.

Corporate Patriarchy: "Double Days and Wasted Nights"

Drawing attention to structural barriers and determinants provides a useful corrective to personal and attitude studies. This is not to suggest that structures explain everything. For example, it is quite obvious that certain individuals are denied opportunity structures because of personality differences and social skills.

Likewise, discriminatory barriers that preclude minorities from equal access are a powerful deterrent, as are cultural images that invariably pigeonhole women and minorities into preconceived slots. In addition, all corporations are cultural entities in their own right; that is, they provide guidelines for behaviour which serve as standards by which to evaluate organizational behaviour, and furnish an ex post facto rationalization with which to condone corporate actions.

What is equally clear is the unmistakably androcentric logic at the core of organizational cultures. Corporations are very much a White man's world, with masculine value and male priorities embedded into organizational styles and agendas. This gendered corporate reality extends from managerial styles on outward to include standards for appointments, entitlements, and conduct. Even in the best of times, Kanter claims, pressures for a climate of conformity prevail. Managers gravitate toward appointments much like themselves in terms of age, gender, race, or social background. The presence of such trustworthy colleagues facilitates control, reduces uncertainty, enhances predictability, and perpetuates security within a closed, exclusionary circle. Those unlike themselves are excluded, thus perpetuating the cycle of homogeneity and conformity. The maleness of organizational cultures is recognized by women who feel compelled to deny their femaleness for success. During interviews, women have been known to remove wedding bands, or to deny having or ever wanting to have children. Even new workplace philosophies are proving to be a problem. With growing emphasis on teamwork and co-operation, the informal network of peers has assumed even greater importance. Yet these existing networks are difficult to access for minorities and women. A greater reliance on participatory democracy in the workplace sounds good in theory. But "hands on" involvement tends to be time-consuming, especially for women who must shoulder the demands of double days and sleepless nights. Many must cut back from total involvement because of domestic-maternal responsibilities. This, in turn, raises eyebrows over their purported lack of commitment to the corporation.

Core organizational values are typically male-linked, including a commitment to aggressiveness, competitiveness, achievement orientation, individualism, analysis and an emphasis on rationality and logic, toughness, and lack of emotional display. Values pertaining to connectedness and other-directedness are shuffled aside in the rush for success at all costs. Even organizational conduct is unmistakably androcentric. Survival techniques focus on the need to be unemotional (avoid feelings); depersonalize issues (never point the finger at anyone); be subordinate (never challenge authority); be conservative (better the devil you know); isolated (mind your own business); and competitive (people prefer to compete). Routinely dismissed as career-limiting (at least until recently) are female styles of discourse, with their adherence to accommodation, relationships and communication, supportiveness, deference and approval seeking. Not only are women refused recognition, they are also perceived as a threat in the competition for scarce resources. Who, then, can be surprised that women and minorities have found corporations user-unfriendly, and have experienced difficulties in navigating their way through the cultural mine fields of male-dominated institutions? That in itself raises the question whether women bosses should even bother to bring humane values into a corporate culture that is essentially alien to human values.

"Dancing Backwards and Doing It in High Heels"

Ginger Rogers and Fred Astaire appeared in numerous movies during the 1940s and 1950s as a gifted and graceful dancing team. Ginger was known to have once quipped that she was every bit as good as Fred, but she had to dance backwards and do it in high heels. That astute observation may apply to gender relations in general, corporate contexts in particular. Structures and values continue to pervade reality in a way that secures the advantage of men even if no intent or sexism is involved. According to the report, "Closing the Gap," by Judith MacBride-King and Sheila Wellington on female executives' progress in Canada, many of the barriers are unintentional but continue to have the effect of favouring men over women in the corporate rat race. This undervaluation of women is unfortunate and counterproductive. Corporations are losing quality women because of sexist values, androcentric mindsets, and patriarchal structures. This bleeding takes place at precisely the time when companies can least afford to ignore the competitive potential of a wider talent pool. For women the challenge is two-fold: They must cope in a cultural environment created essentially for males instead of individuals trying to juggle a career, children, and social life, a perilous path because corporate Canada continues to be structured around a military model of hierarchy and power-seeking. Career progress is rendered doubly difficult by increasingly intense pressures (from workplace harassment to global economies) that subject women to additional restrictions. Despite these structural barriers, few appear ready to abandon hard-fought economic gains in exchange for the reassuring but increasingly unrealistic confines of hearth and home.

("trophies") for male gratification. Women's self-confidence is under perpetual seige by vested interests, including those who would like nothing better than to endorse "family values" while keeping women "barefoot and pregnant" (Faludi, 1991). The net effect of linking workplace success with perpetual makeovers has led to unrealistic expectations about what is attainable, an obsession with appearance at the expense of health, and a preoccupation with weight loss and body image that borders on the pathological.

The reality of the situation is somewhat more complex, despite disparities that stubbornly persist. Women's employment climbed 3.7 percent in 1998, compared to 1.6 percent for men; as a result, women constituted 46 percent of the total employed in Canada. Nearly 58 percent of all adult women in 1996 were in paid employment, compared to only 24 percent in 1950. Still, Kendall et al. (1999) remind us, 70 percent of working women are concentrated in four occupations, teaching, nursing/health related, clerical, or sales/service. According to the 1996 census, women held 22 percent of the 25 jobs/professions with the fattest pay checques (only 17 percent in 1990). By the same token, women dominated 68 percent of the 25 lowest-paying jobs. In the *Globe and Mail's* list of the 100 highest paid CEOs, only one woman, Micheline Charest, a co-CEO of Cinar Corp., made the list at $927 000. Peter Munk, chair and CEO of Barrick Gold Corp. topped the list at $38.9 million. The message is most mixed when income differences are analyzed. Overall, women earned about 61.5 percent of what men earned. Women in full-time employment earned 73 percent of what men did in full-time employment. Single women earned 95.5 percent of what single men earned, whereas married women earned only 67.5 percent of what married men earned. Women between 15 and 24 earned 90.9 percent of what men earned. Women between 45 and 54 earned only 67.2 percent. However, women between 45 and 54 who were single and university-educated earned 102 percent of their male counterparts. And, with girls out-performing boys across the board in math, writing, and reading in Ontario primary schools (Galt, 1999), the income gap is likely to shrink.

Inequities in the Workplace

One of the more extraordinary developments in recent years is reflected in the changing composition of the corporate workplace. Women, people of colour, and individuals with disabilities have moved to challenge the once-exclusive male domain for status and rewards. Corporations have had to rethink the rules, structures, and priorities associated with the formerly reassuring expression, "That's the way we do things around here." The concept of institutional change may sound good in theory and have the best intentions at heart, but efforts for reform confront a host of barriers that historically resist even minor adjustments (Fleras and Elliott, 1996). Every concession is met with an equally powerful counterforce. Relations between women and men have become more political and antagonistic, as previous male strongholds must move over and share space with those once perceived as social inferiors.

Case Study 5–1 explores the politics of gender within a corporate workplace. But, rather than arguing that males are deliberately colluding to control women, the case study suggests that systemic biases associated with organizational structure are largely responsible for discrepancies. It also argues that women and men display different patterns of organizational behaviour not because of inferiority, either innate or acquired, but because of differential expectations and opportunities. Variable access to opportunity structures, the prevalence of ingrained cultural values, and situational adjustments invariably result in a process by which some prosper, others falter. The case study serves not only as a primer for thinking sociologically about social problems. In helping to account for gendered inequities, Case Study 5–1 provides insight into the logic behind who gets what and why in the corporate scheme of things.

Explaining Gendered Inequality

Few sociologists would deny the assymmetric quality of gender relations in Canada. Gender relations are anything but abstractions between categories. What we have instead are patterns of interaction between unequals involving power and control in contexts pervaded by inequality. Women continue to be "put down" because of institutional and systemic bias, or to be "put in their place" by way of outright harassment or subtle forms of intimidation. Many are denied equality in the workplace or deprived of the human capital and support to compete equitably with men in the corporate boardroom. By the same token, many men believe that women have achieved equality or are gaining ground at male expense, and that any further concession is both unfair and unnecessary. The net result is a conflict in interests between the "half fulls" (those who focus on how far woman have come) versus the "half empties" (those who focus on how far women still need to go).

A gap can be discerned between men's perceptions and women's experiences in accounting for the magnitude of the problem. Take sexual harassment: Sexual harassment involves attention toward individuals, both deliberate or inadvertent, that is unwanted,

CASE STUDY 5-2   Unmasking the Masculine Mystique

The question of gender is elusive and slippery. Only recently have we come around to appreciate the complexity of masculinity and femininity in our changing and diverse world. A host of questions spring to mind. Are men genetically programmed to be different from women because of evolutionary pressures (Fisher, 1998)? What precisely does it mean to be a man in contemporary society? How do we define masculinity? What do men want, and what are women looking for in men? Answers to these questions have proven elusive and illusory. Clichés as answers are common enough, involving references to proposed virtues such as "balance" and "nurturing," without any indication of the appropriate mix in what kind of context. There is less agreement than ever on defining manhood, with the result that men are experiencing a crisis of confidence with respect to identity. Their stereotypical role as "knights in shining armour to their ladies" has lost its lustre, creating a vacuum that is proving difficult to fill (Mawhinney, 1999). According to Susan Faludi in her book *Stiffed*, men are being denied the opportunity to have any real impact on society. Moreover, as Rutgers anthropologist, Lionel Tiger, points out, what is a man worth, if without one women can get pregnant, raise a family, and support themselves? And, as women have gained more control over their lives and life chances, men have had to rethink the once unimaginable: To move over and share public space and social power with those once assumed to be publicly irrelevant or innately inferior.

In other words, men are now to be pitied rather than scoffed at, writes Susan Faludi, as they stumble about in a society where testosterone no longer rules the roost, if it ever did. The great male identity crisis shows no sign of abating as pressure mounts to dislodge men from their lofty pedestal at the centre of the universe (Tannen, 1995). If anything, the pursuit of the male ideal is further complicated by conflicting images of what men long to be in terms of their relationship to themselves, other men, and woman in general. In that being a man (masculinity) is no less scripted into a set of roles and rules than being a woman (femininity), the cultural forces that shape both masuliniity and femininity deserve closer attention.

"From Marlboro Man to Postmodern Male": From Ruling the Roost to Roasting a Chicken

Revolutionary changes have challenged the place and privilege of men in the overall scheme of things. Males entered the 20th century in firm control of themselves and the world around them, including obedient wives, dutiful children, jobs for life, and security in society. But they are exiting the same century in a more precarious position because of disempowerment at home and the workplace as (a) women have seized more power; (b) children are asserting rights; (c) computers are taking their jobs; (d) their value to society is eroded by technological advances; and (e) their command and control skills are becoming obsolete in a global economy that emphasizes leadership by negotiation and diplomacy (Mawhinney, 1999). Perched at the top of the political, economic, and social ladder, men as a group have had it good for such a long time that most cannot change or refuse to do so. For most men, these changes have diminished their status and stature; instead of respect and deference, men are increasingly criticized as deadbeats or dolts who cannot be trusted, much less looked up to. Not surprisingly, men find themselves beleaguered on all sides by those who demand an end to male privilege. Those males with education and emotional resiliency will survive under these conditions; others for whom the slope of life is slippery have reacted to this emasculation by lashing out in a last ditch effort to secure meaning and satisfaction over their lives, family, and community (Edsell, 1995). Threatened by sudden changes and loss of control and power over their lives, still others respond by withdrawing deeper into themselves. The very social fabric that holds us together as a tolerant and open society may well rupture under the strain of genders in disarray.

Men, historically, were not troubled by questions about who they were. Their status as social superiors furnished them with ready-made answers that rarely evoked comment or debate. A "real" man embodied core cultural values, including that of a rugged heterosexual individual with a penchant for action, accomplishment, and competition, but not at the expense of unquestioned loyalty to country, corporation, and family. The John Wayne model for men—tall, tough, and silent—secured generations of male wannabes. To be sure, entry into a "man's" world did not come easily or automatically. To become a man entailed a struggle involving formidable odds and deceptive barriers, it was

thought, unlike the "ladies" who were viewed as passive and submissive, and naturally inclined toward motherhood through normal biological maturation. Male identities were constituted around gender inequalities and the perception of women as inferior. Whereas men congratulated themselves on having the "right stuff," women assumed the status of trophies that symbolized male conquest of competition. Women were defined in terms of their relationship to men as doting mothers, loving wives, hero-worshipping daughters, and "girlfriends." But this image of men and their relationship to women is undergoing change, despite its popularity in many circles. Rather than a utilitarian culture that bolstered male self-esteem and accomplishments, men no longer have useful roles to play with the emergence of a celebrity culture and a consumer-driven society that measures people by possessions (Faludi, 1999). These challenges to this largely scripted portrayal have resulted in a broader range of appropriate images, some of which flatter, while others don't. As portrayals of women have become "harder," so too have images of men "softened" and "diversified," ranging in scope from sex objects to family men and sensitive types, with an array of buffoons and boneheads in between.

From "Father Knows Best" to Deadbeat Dads Know Zilch

The post-Vietnam era has been unkind to men in terms of identity and relations (Gilmore, 1990). Nowhere is this more evident than in media treatment of men. The scripting of manhood has evolved over time with a shift from fairly rigid and singular representations to those more consistent with contemporary realities (Craig, 1992). Benign portrayals of men as tough, aggressive, independent, stoic, and in control have given way to extremely unflattering images. Playing by the rules no longer guarantees success or admiration. Former strengths are now defined as weakness or vices to be challenged and discarded. Where once men were synonymous with toughness and control, they are just as likely to be depicted as supercilious twits or natural-born killers. In reality, the media covers the entire spectrum from Mr. Moms to chauvinist swine. Sitcoms tend to depict men as neurotic, inadequate, incompetent, superfluous, or foolish, with an unmistakable whiff of irresponsibility about these men who prefer the refuge of sports and bars. By contrast, action dramas involving police or doctors prefer more positive portrayals (Zurawik, 1996). Class can also make a difference. Middle-class men continue to be portrayed as intelligent and sympathetic, while working class males, from Ralph to Fred to Archie to Homer to Al, continue to be depicted as buffoons for bemusement or scorn (Butsch, 1995). Other males pose as cynically sexist (Seinfeld) and think nothing of dumb jokes and the company of even dumber women while mocking the sexist inanities of television (Doyle, 1993). Ads increasingly depict men as incompetents whose goofiness is played for laughs. A variation of this entails the depiction of men as sex objects. The concept of an ideal body image for men has undergone substantial change. The new male image is definitely oriented toward a sleeker body shape, including square-shouldered, V-shaped torso, narrowed waist, pumped-up pecs, and washboard abs. Any sign of intelligence is superfluous in this drive to eroticize the male image (Lindsey, 1997). As messages about men shift from what they do to how they look, males too are set up for failure. In an appearance-based culture, measuring

manhood by usefulness or what men do has been challenged by consumerist principles that measure men by their display-value, sex appeal, and appearance as a winner (Faludi, 1999).

Both the domestication and eroticization of men in the media reflect the growing economic clout of women in society. With financial independence, women can afford to be selective about the kind of male images that appeal to them (Aguino, 1994). Not only are women more selective about what they find attractive, as images of women diversify, media representations of men have responded accordingly to accommodate these changes. Marketers and advertisers have been quick to capitalize on these trends by creating a new market for products that play upon male guilt, vanity, self-doubt, and narcissism (Cobb, 1993). Advertising now relies on male bodies to sell products. A crew of sleek, sculpted, poster boys are now achieving the fame equivalent to supermodels. Men are being encouraged to admire the male body and to want to look better on the grounds that this yearning is natural and normal rather than vain, narcissistic, or feminine. They are lured into the same fantasies that have seduced women for decades; that is, a perfect body (toned, thin, and muscled) will deliver happiness, success, and love (Avenoso, 1996). Yet men are also about to find out what women have long known about the media: They will be constantly under observation and scrutiny (Douglas, 1994). Whereas media males once engaged in actions, they are about to learn what it's like to be looked at and, like women, will have to learn to look at themselves as designer sex objects to be scrutinized by others. It remains to be seen how men will respond to the dubious pleasure of remorseless self-consciousness—the awareness that they must constantly watch themselves being watched by others (Douglas, 1994:17). The objectification of men by men may be viewed by some as egalitarian progress. Reducing men to the same level of insecurity and self-consciousness as women is perceived by others as a regressive step that can only deter the attainment of gender equity.

Unzipping the Facade

The forces of change and diversity have been relentless and disruptive, in the process fanning male anxieties, as once reassuring images continue to crumble and erode. For many men, the challenge of change is precisely that. They must not only change perceptions and beliefs about themselves and their relationships to men; behaviour patterns with women have to be altered as well, in a yet to be determined fashion depending on the context (Abraham, 1999). Subsequent surveys of popular books and magazines continue to extol the virtues of the ideal male, a sensitive family type on the one hand, a successful career on the other, with an undiminished sex appeal and sexual appetite in between. Values pertaining to caring and nurturing have emerged as central in the mindset of perceptive males, even to the point of forsaking career plans if necessary. Nevertheless, the support systems for such a change are not in place, with the result that progressive males are defined as "weak" and many are subject to slander or ridicule.

In sum, there is nothing wrong with men per se. Only the masculine mystique has been unzipped and exposed for what it is, a social construction in defence of power and privilege. For too long men have been the primary beneficiaries of a world unmistakably male in norm and White by standard. But male ways of doing things are no longer automatically assumed the best. Gender scripts are being fiercely contested. The rules of the game have undergone change because of feminism and pressures of diversity. Male leaders prefer a command and control style, in which they view job performances as a series of transactions with subordinates, with power defined as an end in itself, according to Judith Rosener (cited in CP, 1999). By contrast, female leaders tend to see power as an means to an end, appear more willing to share information and encourage participation, prefer to motivate by negotiation, diplomacy, and compromise, and are more comfortable with ambiguity. In theory, neither style is superior, although the female style is no longer devalued as weak and vacillating, but is increasingly valued as a preferred style for the new millennium. Yet there is no clear direction as to what the new gender relations rules should look like, much less how they should be put into practice. Such a massive gender quake has left both women and men in disarray as both genders fumble about in securing the scripts by which to live together with their differences.

unwarranted, and persistent in terms of actions or words. While a sexual component may prevail in some cases, the common element in most harassment is power and control over the workplace, either though quid pro quo (sex for favours) or creation of a "poisoned climate" to demean women by making them feel uncomfortable about their place in the institutional setting. Harassment is widely misunderstood by men because, as a rule, they fail to connect specific instances of sexual harassment with broader patterns of sexual inequality and power relations; ignore how both abuse and harassment constitute strategies of dominance and exclusion that have the effect of keeping women in place and out of men's; and have a corresponding reluctance to challenge workplace structures and underlying cultural values that would make women less vulnerable (Rhode, 1997). Not surprisingly, there is growing estrangement between women and men in Canada, in some cases bordering on "gender wars," as males seek to secure privilege and power, while women struggle for a more equitable redistribution of scarce resources.

How do we account for gendered disparities? Are they the result of innate differences or market forces? Should the blame be laid on capitalism or patriarchy (and its correlates, androcentrism, sexism, and misogyny)? Biological theories are generally discounted; psychological theories of maturational development are best left to psychologists. Sociological theories emphasize social factors as key explanatory variables. These social factors are not necessarily intentional, but the logical consequence of a system designed around the principles of preserving male privilege. The structure of capitalism has long been acknowledged as a key source of gender inequities. Under capitalism, women are subject to inequality because of the need to maintain a cheap and disposable workforce, to ensure divisions within the existing workforce, and to secure the domestic life for nurturing male labour. In conjunction with capitalist structures, the prominence of patriarchy is a central principle of organization. Patriarchy refers to a society that is designed by and organized around male interests. It can be defined as a system in which: (a) the social, political, economic, and cultural are controlled by men; (b) masculinity is more highly valued than feminine values; and (c) males have preferential access to the good things in life because of their gender (Kendall et al., 1999; Renzutti and Curran, 1999). Patriarchy itself consists of several interrelated constituents. Misogyny refers to hatred of women. Sexism covers that constellation of beliefs and practices that openly assert the superiority of one gender over the other because of preconceived notions of what is normal, acceptable, and superior. Androcentrism, by contrast, is the inclination to automatically and routinely interpret reality from the point of view of male interests and experiences; to posit this interpretation as natural and normal, while assuming that others will think so too, if given half a chance; to judge others on the basis of this masculinist standard; and to dismiss alternate interpretations as irrelevant or inferior. With androcentrism, men are defined as natural-born leaders from heads of households to heads of state, while women are defined as natural-born nurturers.

THE MASCULINE MYSTIQUE

Turn to the gender chapter in any sociology textbook. Virtually all focus on issues related to women as a "social problem," with particular emphasis on women and inequality, the devaluation of women's experiences, violence against women, changes in women's status and identity, and sexist, discriminatory barriers at odds with full and equal participation in society. A section on feminism and different types of feminist movements is routinely included. While this focus on a female dimension is timely and overdue, such a one-sided look glosses over the male component of gender and gender relations. This exclusion is unfortunate: Not only are male contributions to the gender equation excluded; after all, "men are gender" too, and, besides, it does take "two to gender." Also ignored is how men are undergoing a profound transformation in terms of status, roles, expectations, and responsibilities.

What does it mean to be a man in today's rapidly changing environment? Both women and men have experienced confusion about male roles in light of changing definitions of masculinity and femininity. The days of the Marlboro Man (a rugged individualist) are rapidly disappearing; so too has the Sturdy Oak model personified by the "Duke" (John Wayne). Even the quintessential 1980s man, Alan Alda (Hawkeye Pierce) of the television series "M*A*S*H," appears to have fallen into disrepute. Nothing seems to have taken the place of these earlier models except for vague and contradictory appeals for men to be sensitive yet manly, successful yet family-oriented, warmly intelligent yet well-chiselled, and good-natured yet decisive. No wonder contemporary males are in a quandary over ideas and ideals of manhood. Uncertainty and pressure will continue to mount even further as men, too, begin to want it all—a fast-paced career, nurturant father, sensitive and reflective confidantes in touch with their inner selves, insatiable sexuality, fabulous pecs and washboards abs, and the keys to a BMW. The resulting frustration may trigger even greater imbalances in how men relate to women and to themselves.

The next case study focuses on the crisis in masculinity. Emphasis is on how changes to the conventional meaning of "maleness" have played havoc with the masculine mystique. The case study also points out the elusiveness of defining a desired male model, in part because traditional rules no longer apply, while new rules have yet to be accepted by a diverse and demanding public. Context appears critical. A take-charge kind of guy is appropriate at times, especially in boardrooms and bedrooms, but so too is the sensitive and thoughtful type who can relate equally well to women or to children without sacrificing his masculinity in the process. This fractured and complicated picture may prove an opportunity in disguise for some, or a recipe for chaos for others, given the difficulties of "operationalizing" the concept of "new age guy." Such a conclusion would be amusing, perhaps, were it not for the fact that such confusion can erupt into hostility and violence as men grope around for the meaning of masculinity in an unyielding and unforgiving world. To be sure, women too are casting about for new images of what it means to be a woman. Yet their experiences and tribulations have received greater exposure from contemporary critics and authors, and a discrepancy of this nature justifies a case study on the politics and perils of being a man in today's image-conscious society.

RE-SCULPTING THE SCRIPT

All varieties of feminism agree that the history of women has been one of subordination due to the pervasiveness of patriarchal and sexist rules, roles, and relationships. There is less consensus on how to solve this problem. How effectively has the Canadian state responded to the plight of individuals victimized by race and gender? Does the solution reside in social movements that are by women and for women? This final section will explore the extent to which the different feminisms have addressed the problem of gender inequality together with corresponding solutions in the search for a society both diverse yet inclusive.

The State: Solution as Problem?

Is the state the solution? The double-edged nature of state involvement reveals its status as a tool for reaction as well as for progressive change. For some the state is the quintessential embodiment of patriarchy, thus eliminating any possibility of its challenging a gendered status quo. For others, the state is a contested site of openings and slippages in which challenges can originate (Wisel, 1998). For some, involvement with the state is preferred in terms of providing positive outcomes by way of policy and initiatives. For others, state involvement has resulted in cooptation and control, particularly with the restructuring of society along market lines. Women bear a disproportionate share of the costs associated with trade globalization, labour market shedding, hollowing out of the welfare state with respect to expectations and comprehensiveness, and cuts to social spending to reduce deficits. Such a double-edged impact demonstrates the role of the state as simultaneously supportive of and yet opposed to women's interests (Evans and Wekerle, 1997).

The legal framework for gender equality includes many components ranging from constitutional guarantees to federal and provincial statutes to policies and programs. In 1947, Saskatchewan was the first province to enact a comprehensive bill of rights. The first human rights commission was created in Ontario in 1962 to enforce anti-discrimination legislation. The grounds of prohibited discrimination expanded from the original ones of race and religion to cover such areas as gender and marital status (Flanagan, 1985). The Charter of Rights and Freedoms was heralded as an advance over human rights codes. Unlike parliamentary statutes (of which human rights codes are an example), Charter provisions are constitutionally entrenched and cannot be easily repealed. Gender relations are addressed in the Charter in the context of "fundamental freedoms" (s. 2), and especially Sections 15 and 28. Section 15(1) provides for "equal protection...without discrimination...based on...sex," while Section 15(2) provides for what are often referred to as employment equity programs; Section 28 states that Charter rights and freedoms are guaranteed equally to both sexes. Employment equity policies are permitted by the Charter in Section 15(2) and were enacted in the 1986/1996 federal *Employment Equity Act*. Since 1988, companies employing over 100 people under federal jurisdiction have been compelled to file yearly reports on the number of women, aboriginal peoples, people with disabilities, and visible minority members they employ, and to provide information on their occupation and salary levels. However, nothing in the legislation requires the companies to improve; there are no goals or timetables, while the removal of barriers is voluntary. Without "teeth," in other words, one cannot expect social change to occur in the wake of the *Employment Equity Act*.

Social Movements as Solutions

Women have not only looked to the state for support and change, they have also organized themselves into groups to bring about a more equitable state of affairs. The study of social movements has long been a staple of sociological thought (Carroll, 1997). Its popularity has expanded even further because of contemporary dynamics in reshaping the contours of Canadian society. Canada has emerged as a site of many social movements that range in scope from the 1960s civil rights and feminist movements, to the AIDs and breast cancer advocacy groups of the 1980s, with the recent rise of neo-Nazism and quality of life movements as markers for the 1990s. Other examples include newer movements that focus on the environment; denounce fur and leather as clothing apparel; decry the use of alcohol and tobacco in public; engage men in the search for the male within; and question the wisdom of a meat-based diet. Social movements vary in terms of scope, organization, and style (Aberle, 1966). Some are concerned with partial change (reform), others with a total revamping (revolution), still others with reversing current trends by reasserting conventional values or traditional structures (reaction). "Old" social movements often entailed labour issues; by contrast, "new" social movements may be concerned with the politics of identity or community renewal in light of rampant urbanism, overwhelming globalization, innovations in telecommunications and technology, and the tide of modernization (Adam, 1993). Tactics and strategies may also vary. Certain social movements advocate peaceful change (conventional channels and be-hind-the-scenes); others involve civil disobedience or flamboyant, media-catching actions; and still others endorse violence as a preferred course of action for achieving visionary goals.

Such diversity is a healthy sign. Yet it can hamper the creation of a coherent body of thought for analyzing the magnitude and scope of social movements. When the range of phenomena spans everything from well-financed international organizations such as Greenpeace to spontaneous street activists such as Queer Nation, the prospect of gleaning some broad generalizations may appear daunting. Social movements can be defined as conscious, collective efforts by a group of aggrieved individuals who initiate (or resist) social change through actions that fall outside institutional frameworks (Wilson, 1973). Such movements arise when individuals become disenchanted with select aspects of society, and are willing to do something constructive about their disenchantment. Involvement comes about not only be-cause people know something is wrong. They must also be mobilized into action groups under recognizable leadership for the deliberate and sustained pursuit of shared goals.

One social movement whose impact on society has proven nothing short of revolutionary is feminism. Feminism as a social movement has altered how we think about gender rela-tions. It has also reshaped the status and role of women in society, while striking at the very foun-dational knowledge of social existence. Some have vilified feminism as a source of all social problems including family breakdowns; others have praised it for its emancipatory qualities in releasing both women and men from rigidly scripted expectations; still others question the wisdom of portraying women as innately good (men by contrast are portrayed as depraved or deprived) and perpetually destined to victim status, in effect denying the truth about the multi-dimensional qualities of women, warts and all (Fillion, 1996). For example, an en-slavement to the beauty myth teaches women that one's self-worth and contribution are based on physical appearance and relationships to males (Wolf, 1991). To be sure, all feminists strive for some degree of equality between men and women; they also seek to eradicate pa-triarchy with its imposition of scripted gender roles (Gray, 1995). But feminism is not a sin-gular social movement, and the next section reveals the different waves of feminist thought in terms of premises, content, and objectives. Each style of feminism defines the problem in a dis-tinct way, and proposes solutions consistent with the assessment. A comparison makes it clear that feminism is much more than a criticism of the existing order. At the core of all femi-nisms is a proposed vision of society in which women and men can learn to live together with their differences. The proliferation of feminisms also suggests a variety of choices for women who want to politicize the personal in a way that is workable, necessary, and fair.

FEMINIST MOVEMENTS

> I myself have never been able to find out precisely what feminism is. I only know that peo-ple call me a feminist whenever I express sentiments that differentiate me from a doormat or prostitute. Rebecca West, English author and critic, 1913. (Cited in Gibbs, 1992:39).

Women in Canada and the United States have long struggled to address issues about gender inequality. Marching to the slogan that the "personal is political" enabled various women's groups during the 1970s to politicize the problem "with no name," as Betty Friedan aptly called it. Feminism took off when women escaped dependence on men for their living and claimed control over their fertility (Weldon, 1997). Emboldened by civil rights and anti-war activism, feminism originated when women began to seek social solutions to hitherto ignored or seemingly unimportant personal problems pertaining to restricted roles. Once the women's predicament was shared with other women, it quickly became a matter of social significance with respect to individual rights. Moreover, once women began to compare notes, says Fay Weldon, it was no longer possible for men to pick them off one by one, or to bully, insult, and assault them behind closed doors. Henceforth, women's issues would no longer be boxed into the personal and private. Imbalances over power would now be openly challenged in the public realm because of their rootedness in the structures of society, not simply in individual acts (Tweedlie, 1995). The impact of this collective protest has been unprecedented. Not only have feminist movements transformed the basis of gender relations. Women think about their sexuality and right to pleasure in different ways as well. The emergence of feminism has also been instrumental in changing cultural values and reshaping structural arrangements, while redefining entitlement patterns that historically characterized female-male relations.

Feminism in general consists of ideas and ideals pertaining to the goal of gender equality, even though the magnitude and scope of this equality is open to debate. It constitutes the so-called "preposterous" proposition that women are human beings whose normalcy and moral worth are equivalent to those of men (Gray, 1995). Feminism attacks androcentric mindsets that evaluate and assess according to marketplace perceptions and male fantasies. Central to feminism is the direct challenge to the status quo, together with the rejection of a scripted division of labour that is rigid and determined (Nelson and Fleras, 1995). Women are treated as a central point of reference by bringing their experiences into practical and research contexts in a way that involves their thinking and acting (Burt and Code, 1995). Yet feminism is not a single voice, much less a singular voice of experience, but a multi-vocal movement of criticism and activism. Feminisms differ in terms of how they define the problem of gender inequality, as well as how best to solve this problem. Disagreement is about whether women and men are fundamentally similar or different, and how the answer influences the choices of solution for eliminating gender differences. Failure to appreciate the range of voices within feminism not only diminishes our understanding of a complex social phenomenon. It also demonstrates how a single term can evoke different meanings.

Liberal Feminism: Levelling the Playing Field

Liberal feminism arises from classical liberal principles that extol the freedom of individuals to pursue interests and objectives (Macionis, 1995). Yet women as a group rarely enjoy equal rights or equality of opportunity, much less equality of outcomes. Women in Canada are devalued because of their unequal participation in institutions outside the family or pink-collar ghetto jobs. For liberal feminists, this inequality arises from imbalances within an essentially sound system. Liberal feminists do not propose to dismantle the system or rearrange the basic institutions of society; their aim is to equalize the distribution of individuals (women and men) within the existing institutions. Liberal feminists endorse the basic integrity of the system. Equality can be achieved if women are allowed the opportunity to compete on level terms with men. Achievement of equality between women and men is based on the elimination of sexism and removal of discriminatory barriers. It is also grounded in improving the cultural capital of women through education and improved training.

The inevitability of inequality in society is widely accepted. Any society organized around the principle of merit (one must earn one's reward) cannot avoid some degree of hierarchy in the sorting out of winners and losers. What liberal feminists dispute are injustices imposed on the system or personnel practices that preclude equal participation and equality of opportunity. The equality phase of feminism emphasizes equality of opportunity for women in the public domain. Liberal feminism also rejects any proposal of essential difference between women and men, at least none that could justify the differentiation of employment or opportunities. Emphasis on difference may have the effect, if not necessarily the intent, of reinforcing inequities through sex-role stereotyping.

Marxist Feminism: "Workers (Women + Men) of the World Unite"

A Marxist feminism corresponds to a conflict perspective in situating inequality within the framework of capitalism, with its correlates of profit, private property, and class relations. Under capitalism, women are oppressed, contend Marxist feminists, in the same way as men because both must sell their labour power to ensure physical survival. However, women, as a group, constitute the more exploited "fraction" within the working class, and this division is exacerbated by the forces of patriarchy and the contradictions of the nuclear family arrangement. Because the problem is chronic and structural, a system devoted to the principles of private property and rational pursuit of profit is viewed as hopelessly flawed and inimical to female interests. In contrast to liberal feminism, Marxist feminism insists on a complete restructuring of society before true gender equality can kick in. Tinkering with the system, they argue, merely feeds into the status quo, albeit under the guise of apparent change. With its focus on contradiction and change, Marxist feminism embraces a conflict perspective of society, with its view of society as basically exploitative.

Radical Feminism: "Hey, Ho, Patriarchy Has To Go"

For radical feminists, the key forces in society are domination and control of others through symbolic manipulation. The basic source of oppression for women is not the capitalist system. The root cause is the subjugation of women by men under the guise of patriarchy. Patriarchy is ultimately rooted in patterns of male superiority as it pertains to female subjugation and servitude. Just as the subordination of the proletariat is made natural under capitalism, so too is the subordination of women "naturalized" by the assumptions of patriarchy (Code, 1995). While capitalism and patriarchy are linked, even though analytically separate, the starting point for radical feminism entails a challenge to patriarchy, with particular emphasis on how male hegemony is constructed and construed through everyday actions. The focus is on deconstructing the components of this patriarchal oppression in order to eliminate both institutional and systemic biases. Social institutions that historically have enslaved women as women are criticized, but in particular the nuclear family, which is seen as little more than domestic servitude in disguise (see Macionis, 1995).

Cultural Feminism "I am Woman..."

The celebration and politicization of women as different and valuable is central to cultural feminism. Gender differences are neither superficial nor the result of social conditioning that causes men to be aggressive and competitive in contrast to the nurturant qualities of women. Women and men are not interchangeable in terms of work preferences, with the result that any discrepancies are the result of discrimination. Women and men possess different interests and strengths, together with different aspirations, in part because of biology, in part because of different experiences pertaining to inequality, the threat of violence, and demeaning media images (Gilligan, 1982; Nelson and Fleras, 1995). Women speak in a different voice and are defined by their relationships to others, their ability to nurture and cooperate, and to engage in contextual thought. Men, by contrast, are thought to be locked into abstract analysis, and are defined by their engagement with competition and individual achievement. Women and men approach leadership differently: A women's voice is potentially transformative because of its commitment to connection, community, and communication; men's voices dwell on combativeness, hierarchy, and self-interest. The problem resides in the suppression of the distinctiveness of female experiences and values. The solution resides not in eliminating these differences, but in celebrating them as positive in contributing to society.

Rainbow Feminism: Coats of Many Colours

White feminists are perceived to have a specific agenda. Concerns are rooted in issues pertaining to sexism or to classism, with men portrayed as the "enemy." Women of colour confront an additional set of pressures related to racism and ethnicity that are superimposed on and intersect with gender and class in creating overlapping and intersecting patterns of subordination that simultaneously amplify yet contradict. Consider the contrasts: White women focus on issues ranging from glass ceilings, the cost of daycare facilities, job and pay equity, and workplace harassment; by contrast, women of colour worry about basic survival skills related to employment, rather than employment equity; about getting and holding a job, rather than harassment on the job or barriers to promotion; and about access to any childcare facilities, rather than shattering the glass ceiling. These differences are sufficient to foster a growing estrangement between mainstream feminism in general and feminism of colour, whose realities and experiences are different. Problems are defined in such a way that solutions and proposed outcomes are inconsistent with mainstream perceptions.

Conservative Feminism: The Good Old Days

The last feminism is perhaps the most contentious, and many would prefer to exclude it altogether because of its seemingly regressive stance on the status and role of women in society. Conservative feminism, as exemplified by the initiatives of groups such as "R.E.A.L. Women," espouses a view of equality that acknowledges women in traditional, maternal, domestic roles. For conservative feminism the real problem involves too much change, rather than not enough, with predictable costs to family and traditional values. The solution rests with bringing back a traditional society in which "men were men" and "women knew their place" within the domestic-maternal spheres of life. In short, the world would be a much better place if women reverted to their natural role in society ("barefoot and pregnant") through acceptance of women's scripted and scripturally ordained status.

Table 5–2's survey of feminist movements represents only a small portion of the different feminisms. Consider the alternatives: socialist, developmental, lesbian, psychoanalytic, standpoint, multicultural, multiracial, construction, and postmodern (Renzutti and Curran, 1999). Men's movements and male-rights groups have also attempted to enter into dialogue with feminist movements. Some of these movements seek to advance feminism through support and empathy. While being aware of women's oppression provides a useful start, respect through sympathy is not the same as challenging the system. Other male movements are more interested in preserving any further erosion of male privilege, rather than advancing the concerns of women. And still others are willing in theory to address issues pertaining to power-sharing. For most men, however, privilege and power are hard to relinquish to those once perceived as inferior or irrelevant. Moreover, for many men the path of least resistance is to do nothing, especially since the status quo is organized around their image and their gendered interests (Johnson, 1997). Time will tell if men's movements can take the next step in accepting feminist values as a basis for living together with differences, both equitably and inclusively.

TABLE 5-2	Comparison and Contrast			
	What is the Problem	**Root Causes**	**Proposed Solutions**	**Vision of Society**
Liberal Feminism	unequal opportunity	sexism	removal of sexist barriers	level playing field
Marxist Feminism	exploitation	class relations	collective ownership	power to all people
Radical Feminism	patriarchy	hegemony	ideological transformation	an oppression-free society
Cultural Feminism	silenced voices	male voices	female voices	celebrating differences
Conservative Feminism	breakdown in conventional order	social change	reinstitute maternal domestic roles	"the good old days"
Inclusive "Rainbow" Feminism	whiteness	racism	removal of racial barriers	an inclusive society

6

CRIME AND CONTROL

FRAMING THE PROBLEM

The society we live in is a paradoxical place, sociologically speaking. On the one hand, there are people who routinely obey traffic signs, pay their bills on time, do as they are told, and would never think of shoplifting or ripping off the system even if their life depended on it. On the other hand, there are those who would rather cheat than conform, routinely ignore traffic signals, engage in misadventures that invariably bring them into contact with the law, and think nothing of ripping off the establishment at every opportunity. In between these admittedly extreme types, with the law-abiding on one side and the criminally-oriented on the other, are those who will tempt fate by cutting corners if the opportunity arises. From a sociological point of view, this continuum of commitment to the social order is perplexing. Why do some conform? Why do others commit crime and act uncivilized in a civil society? Why do others obey, but only if the price is right? Why do some get caught and pay the price for breaking the law while others get off scot-free? And most paradoxical of all: Why do those who normally conform engage in criminal acts that bring them into contact with the criminal justice system? Answers to each of these questions suggests social context as a key variable in shaping people's behaviour. Not unexpectedly, solutions too must focus on the broader picture (including structures, values, and institutions) if we are to win the fight against crime, assuming, of course, that the fight is winnable!

Sociologists have long acknowledged the pervasiveness of conformity or "rule-following." The vast majority of people observe the roles expected of them while playing by the rules in coping with the challenges of everyday life. Both a stable and coherent social order are dependent on a shared cultural "blueprint" and its transmission from one generation to the next. Yet deviance and crime are no less integral a strand of the social fabric, albeit in a perverse way. Just as people are conditioned by a culture of conformity and restraint, so too are rules internalized that encourage them to skip corners, take shortcuts, bend rules, rip off the system, and take advantage of others—all the better if they think they can get away with it. Deviance and crime are remarkably commonplace, rather than being restricted to a certain class of individuals. Even so-called "normal" people can act out of character by resorting to actions at odds with social norms or the laws of the land. Jaywalking or speeding are but two deviant activities whose violations are the "rule" rather than the exception, despite their illegality in many jurisdictions. In other words, the idea that "everybody's doing it" would imply that deviance and crime are extremely widespread. The same pressures that encourage conformity and consensus may also have the effect of fostering criminality, depending on the context, criteria, and consequences. Deviance and crime may be interpreted as the "norm," according to this line of thinking, with the result that anti-social behaviour is to be expected in a society that endorses a dog-eat-dog mentality.

The prospect of controlling crime is no less problematic. Many Canadians believe that the fight against crime has been lost, despite massive outlays. Public fears are mounting over being victimized by crime, although these fears are often misplaced or baseless. The effectiveness and cost of controlling crime by way of the criminal justice system have endured intense scrutiny. Both the police and the courts have been taken to task for responding inappropriately to the prevention and control of crime, even though neither is directly responsible for creating the problem in the first place. Corrections are increasingly seen as an expensive and inappropriate response to the problem of crime; so too is the processing of certain individuals through the criminal justice system. For some, crime is increasing because the system is too "soft" on offenders; for others, the system is too rigid and unaccommodative, thus manufacturing more crime than necessary; and for still others, the enormous expenditures do not justify the outcome. Certain sectors of society appear disproportionately inclined toward crime, at least judging by arrests and convictions. Yet what is known about crime is based on who is caught and what is reported. Do minorities or youth commit more crimes, or are they just more likely to appear on crime reports because of greater visibility and selective police surveillance? Do police apply the law uniformly, or are they abusing their discretionary powers by victimizing some while turning a blind eye to others? How is it that specific types of deviant activities (for example, street crime of the dispossessed) are vigorously enforced, while white-collar crime is relatively immune to the discretionary arm of the law? The list of questions could go on; suffice it, however, to conclude with a warning to the wise. While many Canadians regard crime and control a pressing social problem, there is little unanimity about what is going on, and why, or how to solve the seemingly insoluble problem of controlling the uncontrollable.

Fascination with the topics of crime and control is not only restricted to the general public. The entertainment industry has also capitalized on the troika of "cops," "courts," and "corrections." The combination of "cops 'n robbers," together with "nuts, sluts, and perverts," has proven a money-making winner with Hollywood since the inception of the movie-making machine. The sensationalization of crime on TV is mega-business, with no sign of letting up or easing its grip, despite mounting concern and criticism over its impact on society. News is no less hooked on crime and the criminal justice system in the competition for audience ratings and advertising revenues. In light of such massive and relentless exposure, the public is increasingly worried that a crime-storm is brewing, and that the social stabilizers of society are collapsing under the remorseless onslaught of gun-toting punks and cowering authorities. Of particular concern is the growing fear over the perceived lawlessness of some new Canadians, in effect prompting yet more calls for punitive measures in stamping out crime. Sociologists are equally interested in crime and control, albeit for different reasons. Sociological emphasis is focused on the social dimensions of "anti-social" behaviour, together with the impact of crime and deviance on society. A sample of sociological questions includes the following: What is crime? What causes it? By whom? How is it conceptualized within society? What is the relationship between crime and deviance? What strategies are employed to prevent crime? How effective are formal responses to crime? Why do people violate norms and break laws in the face of personal penalities or social sanctions? Conversely, why do people conform when the criminal opportunities may be potentially rewarding and readily accessible? Is it possible to construct a single explanatory model to account for seemingly pointless crimes, such as defacing public monuments, as well as to explain actions that deprive or destroy? The conceptual distinction between "social" and "anti-social" behaviour or between "deviance" and "crime" is further complicated by the fact that, under some circumstances, rule-following can be interpreted as deviant, while certain deviant actions are "normative," depending on context or consequences.

Sociologists prefer to analyze the topic of crime and control along sociological lines. Analysis is rarely interested in the singular or isolated events, however revolting or tasteless these may be. Approaches that dwell on the psychological dimensions of the "criminal personality" are rarely pursued. Sociological approaches tend to emphasize the social dynamics behind (a) socially constructing (defining) deviance and crime; (b) defining who is deviant and under what circumstances; and (c) applying appropriate responses to crime. Emphasis is on those social dimensions of crime with respect to causes, patterns and rates, and cures. Crime is interpreted not only as a legal problem, but as a social problem involving an unequal distribution of power, privilege, and resources. As a social problem, crime (a) originates in a social context (namely that of poverty and powerlessness); (b) is defined as a problem by laws that themselves are socially constructed in defence of the powerful and rich; (c) exerts a disruptive impact on society with respect to the status quo; and (d) is amenable to solution by way of treatment, at least in theory, if not always in practice. For sociologists, then, deviance and crime are not defined as a "thing" per se, but rather a property that is attributed to an action by those in a position to make these labels stick. Sociologists are also interested in the social relationship of crime to society; for example, do deviance and crime contribute positively to society through clarification of norms, enhancement of social bonds, reinforcement of moral foundation, or as an outlet for creativity and change? Alternatively, how are deviance and crime both disruptive to society and injurious to its members? Much, of course, depends on the sociological perspective that is employed. For functionalists, who see society as fundamentally sound and deserving of protection, deviance and crime are social problems because of dysfunctional effects. Conflict theorists, by contrast, interpret society as essentially unjust because of structural inequalities. As a result, crime is not only inevitable under such circumstances, given the power of the ruling class to criminalize some, but potentially subversive in challenging the foundations of an unjust system. Finally, symbolic interactionists are not interested in the functionality or dysfunctionality of crime and deviance. They prefer to see crime as a socially constructed exercise involving a host of definitions and jointly linked lines of interaction that eventually coalesce around a human accomplishment called society. While these perspectives are diametrically opposed in assumptions and outcomes, each has the benefit of casting light on certain aspects of crime and control that others tend to underplay, thus contributing to a comprehensive picture.

This chapter explores the concept of crime and control as a major social problem in Canada. It takes the position that, while crime can be problematized as a social problem, the really interesting questions focus on the "who" and the "why" behind crime as a social construction and as socially constructed. No less interesting is a concern with the perils and promises of the criminal justice system as a "solution" to the social problem of crime. The chapter is organized around a "conditionalist" perspective on crime and control, with its emphasis on causes, characteristics, consequences, and cures. It begins by looking at the magnitude and scope of crime in Canada, particularly in contrasting past and present trends, and continues by defining the key terms of reference in the chapter. The causes of crime are examined next, including the different sociological theories for explaining crime. This is followed by a look at the characteristics of crime, but especially who is most likely to engage (or to be perceived to engage) in criminal activity. The criminal justice system as a "cure" to controlling crime is then discussed at the level of "cops," "courts," and "corrections." Evidence suggests that the criminal justice system as currently structured may be as much of a social problem as a solution to the problem of crime. The chapter concludes by exploring several initiatives to reform the system, especially in the field of aboriginal justice. The fact that people continue to commit crimes for reasons and in contexts that are not readily open to solution or reform by the criminal justice system suggests continued employment for sociologists and those employed by the criminal justice system (Carrington, 1999). Three key objectives are addressed in this chapter: First, to inform readers about crime and control in Canada by debunking widely accepted myths that feed into people's fear of crime. Second, to improve an understanding of Canada by examining Canadian society through the prism of crime and control. Third, to sharpen our knowledge of social problems as a concept, without necessarily trivializing the costs of crime to society and consequences to victims.

CRIME IN CANADA

There are two lines of thought about crime in Canada. For some, Canada is widely regarded as a relatively safe place to live. Rates of crime, especially those involving weapons and violence, are perceived as low by international standards. To be sure, there is a growing perception of crime surges in major cities as youth turn to guns, gangs, and "ganja" for fun and profit. Others are concerned with immigrants who allegedly import criminal practices into Canada. To its credit, however, Canada is seen as an oasis of tranquility when compared with the anarchy in parts of the United States. How does this square with the facts? Comparisons across time and place pose problems. Each country may use different categories for inclusion. As well, different systems of reporting may also be utilized. Nor is it clear whether rates of crime are based on arrests, charges, or convictions. As commonly expressed within crime control circles, most crimes do not result in arrests, most arrests do not result in convictions, and most convictions do not result in imprisonment.

There is yet another perception of crime in Canada that paints a different picture. Canadians are routinely bombarded with references to crime. Public fear of crime continues to escalate because of media-driven moral panic. A crisis of confidence in the criminal justice system is escalating: Police are not catching enough crooks; sentencing and enforcement are too lenient; recidivism continues to baffle the best minds; and laws are not tough enough, especially on the young (Makin, 1999). The media are largely to blame for these misconceptions. Commercial media rely heavily on narratives involving crime and criminals. Newscasting is saturated with grisly accounts of depraved behaviour, while surveys and statistics point to unacceptable rates of personal and property crime. The news media tend to focus on the sensational; as a result, media depictions of random violent acts by strangers tend to be disproportionate to their occurrence in the real world. TV programming is no less guilty of valourizing crime. Not only is crime a staple of many prime-time shows. Crime is also glamourized as a way of solving problems that is likely to elicit respect and deference. Not surprisingly, Canadians appear poorly informed about the magnitude of crime in Canada. They are even less well-informed about the often-beleaguered efforts at crime control and social order. This ignorance or confusion not only makes it more difficult to solve a major social problem; it also bolsters public anxieties about the scope of criminal activity, even to the point of social paralysis or excessively punitive sanctions. Such a glaring omission makes it doubly important to understand the magnitude of the problem before applying solutions.

UNDERSTANDING THE CRIME PROBLEM

Is the face of crime changing?

Yes. Twenty-five years ago, gambling was illegal, robberies were rare, as were auto thefts, and sexual assaults were reported to the police only as a last resort. Today, gambling has become socially acceptable, robberies are commonplace, auto thefts doubled to 177 286 between 1986 and 1996, and both domestic and sexual assault are routinely processed by authorities (Barrick, 1998).

Is crime increasing?

No. Canada's crime rate, at 8102 per 100 000 population in 1998, fell to its lowest level since 1980. However, this figure is still about triple the rate of about 3000 per 100 000 population in 1962. Since peaking in 1991, according to the Canadian Centre for Justice Statistics, the national crime rate has fallen 19 percent. Nevertheless, certain types of organized crime (including drug-dealing, prostitution, and fraud) continue to buck the downward trend.

Are most crimes of a violent nature?

No. In 1998, 2.5 million crimes were reported. Of these, 56 percent were property crimes, 12 percent were violent crimes, and 32 percent fell under other Criminal Code offences. Of violent crimes, about 56 percent are of a common assault variety, while homicides or attempted murders constitute about 1 percent of the total.

Are violent crimes increasing?

No. Murders, robberies, assaults, and youth crimes have fallen for six consecutive years. Sexual asaults have also decreased by 25 percent, following 4 consecutive years of decline.

Crimes involving firearms are dropping as well; for example, the use of guns in robberies has dropped from one in three in the 1970s to one in five in the 1990s.

Are homicides rates increasing?

No. In 1998, Canada's homicide rate per 100 000 dropped to 1.92, or 555 murders (31 fewer than in 1997), according to the Homicide Survey, Canadian Centre for Justice Statistics. A twenty-year decline is noticeable: the 701 murders in 1975 represented a ratio of 3.09 per 100 000.

How does Canada's homicide rate of 1.92 per 100 000 population compare with other countries?

Homicide rates in Canada put it around the middle. Australia's homicide rate is 0.86 and England and Wales is 1.00. At the opposite end is the United States at 6.70 and Hungary at 2.79 (National Central Bureau-Interpol Ottawa).

Are most homicides by firearms/guns?

Yes. Guns continue to be the weapon of choice, according to the 1997 annual homicide survey by Statistics Canada, with 33.2 percent of the deaths, followed by stabbing (28.9), beating (19.8), and strangling (9.0). The rate for gun deaths in the United States is 14.24 per 100 000 people, compared to Japan at 0.05 deaths per 100 000. Canada ranked around the middle of the pack at 4.31 gun deaths per 100 000, while England/Wales bottomed out at 0.41 per 100 000. Still, the number of homicides by firearms is declining, from 283 in 1974 (or 47.2 percent of the total) to 193 deaths or 33.2 percent in 1997. Of all firearms, handguns figured in 99 deaths in Canada, whereas the handgun total in the United States was 9976 of the total of 12 397.

Do strangers commit the majority of homicides?

No. Friends, spouses, and acquaintances commit most of the homicides, with 53 percent of the victims killed in their home. Strangers commit comparatively few random acts of murder, despite media portrayals to the contrary.

To sum up: Evidence points to a gradual decrease in reported crime in Canada. Yet this statement needs to be qualified. People's perception and fear of crime continues to escalate. Such tenacity of thought suggests that public attitudes are not necessarily affected by statistics, but by media coverage and political electioneering. Perhaps fear is generated by the nature of violence rather than by its quantity, says Larry Gravill, Waterloo Regional police chief and member of the Canadian Association of Police Chiefs. That is, the number of violent crimes might be decreasing, but violence within these crimes is increasing and receiving more publicity because of its shock value (cited in the *Globe and Mail*, 22 July, 1999). Media preference for focusing on the sensational ensures that random violent acts are overrepresented in the public mind. Nor is there any evidence to suggest that smarter policing is having an appreciable effect on reducing rates of criminal offending, although the impact of community-based policing initiatives should not be dismissed. The drop in criminal offending may reflect declining numbers of younger people than in the past, according to David Foot, author of *Boom, Bust, and Echo*. Changes in rates of criminal offending may also say more about changes in police behaviour than about changes in public behaviour.

DEVIANCE AND CRIME

Even casual observation confirms the obvious: The vast majority of people play by the rules in coping with the demands of everyday life. Most observe the roles expected of them, defer to norms that underpin a variety of circumstances, and accept punishment as the cost of breaking widely accepted rules. Those of us who routinely follow the rules tend to congratulate ourselves on being integrated, well-adjusted, and law-abiding. Conversely, those who stray from the straight and narrow are condemned as misfits or degenerates. How can people act in such profoundly uncivilized ways in a widely admired civil society that professes equality, tolerance, and freedom? Deviance is remarkably commonplace, given the universality of rules in society, with few ever exempt from behaviour that does not infringe upon social norms or legal statutes. Jaywalking or driving above the speed limit are but two deviant activities that few would give much thought to, despite their illegality in many jurisdictions. Such universality makes it futile to divide the world into deviants and non-deviants (conformists). Even the most saintly or sanctimonious engage in some deviant acts, often inadvertently, and do so for the same reasons as "hardcore" deviants: namely, to achieve certain goals without excessive cost, disruption, or effort. Conformity and deviance, in other words, are not diametrically opposed, but simply different dimensions of the same behavioural coin. Reactions to deviance can vary from gentle rebukes and mild disapproval to ridicule or outright rejection, depending on the magnitude of the misdeed. Disapproval is mild at best for acts that do not inflict serious injury, while others, such as drinking and driving, are condemned as serious infractions worthy of formal attention. Responses to de-

---

BOX 6.1   **Defining Crime**

Norm

A widely accepted rule or expectation about how to act in a given situation or what is right in a particular context

Law

A formalized (legalized) norm

Deviance

Recognized violation of a widely accepted norm

Crime

Violation of a norm that has been formalized into law

Social Control

Both formal and informal practices to ensure conformity with norms or laws, prevent anti-social behaviour, or deal with incidents of deviance or crime

Criminal Justice System

Institutional (or formal) response to violations of law by way of the police, courts, and prisons

viance also vary with the context, since similar actions may elicit different reactions. Killing someone on a battlefield is defined as defending your country. "Offing" a person in the street is a deviant act called murder. Inflicting a serious injury on a sports field may or may not get you in trouble, depending on the circumstances. Finally, deviance and crime vary with time and place, so that what is normal in one society may be deviant in another place or time. Chewing gum is socially acceptable in many circles, but regarded as mildly deviant in formal settings, is discouraged in public venues such as schools, and is punishable by law in countries such as Singapore.

With this in mind, we can define deviance as public reaction to a violation of a widely accepted norm. It entails a breach of a norm that is widely endorsed, followed by some kind of negative reaction or application of sanctions. Norms themselves consist of rules or ideas about how people should act in light of what is widely considered as "right" in a particular situation. Violation of a norm does not come without cost to organized social life. Flagrant breaches to social norms may erode the trust that is central to social existence. The erosion of trust may also have the effect of undermining confidence in personal efforts, while compromising future involvements as hazardous or pointless. Serious acts of deviance may destroy the moral authority and public morality upon which society rests. As others have noted, public disfavour of an act of deviance will vary with: (a) how harmful or dangerous the violation is considered to be; (b) the intent of the deviant; (c) repeated violations; (d) the competence of the person committing the act; and (e) the degree of group consensus regarded the seriousness of the violated norm. A norm that is formalized into an official statement of right or wrong is called a law. Breaking the law is called a crime, and is subject to control by formal state agencies because it poses a threat to society or vested interests. Viewed in this light, crime is a subset of the broader category of deviance, while law is a subset of the category of norm. Conceptual problems are inevitable with these definitions, thanks to the looseness of terms such as "widely accepted" or "violation." A changing and diverse society may also complicate attainment of consensus; after all, what may be defined as deviant by one group may be upheld as normal and conventional by another, and dismissed as different by yet another.

To sum up: Deviance is not something inherent within the individual or intrinsic to reality, with a readily fixed label that reads "deviant." It is socially defined and constructed through widely held norms, imposition of laws, and establishment of agencies for control by those with the power and resources. Deviance is a label assigned to certain individuals or groups of activities because they threaten authorities, undermine tradition, challenge privilege, or upset the status quo. Many examples abound, but take the case of smoking in public. As recently as a decade ago, consuming tobacco in public was viewed as only mildly deviant—in some cases even as mature and sophisticated—despite some evidence of smoking as an unpleasant and destructive habit. As some measure of its acceptance, consumer advertising during the 1930s and 1940s depicted smoking as healthy (for example, assisting digestion), a claim that was confirmed on the printed page by the testimony of doctors. At present, however, smoking in public has progressed beyond the social condemnation stage (deviance). Growing awareness of the health risks of second-hand smoke has transformed what once was a personal decision into a public safety issue that is enforceable by law in some jurisdictions. Not surprisingly, even smoking in private or in designated areas is perceived increasingly as deviant and deplorable, so much so that smoking in bars and restaurants since January 1, 2000 in the Regional Municipality of Waterloo is now an illegal (criminal) act, subject to prosecution and punishment.

This example confirms the main point: Actions are neither deviant nor criminal by nature, but assume those qualities through human agency. Few people or things in this world are inherently deviant, as far as sociologists are concerned; rather, deviance is an attribute that is assigned to a wide variety of actions and things by those with the power to make these decisions. Deviance is not something that is natural or normal, although interests may make it seem inevitable, but a social construction or convention that is created by individuals who make choices in contexts not of their own making. This "constructionist" mentality puts an onus on the process by which specific activities become defined as deviant and subject to sanctions. As a rule, sociologists are less interested in what is right or wrong, much less in what is moral or immoral in the ethical sense, except as perceived as such by the public. Their interest revolves around people's perception of right or wrong, how these perceptions undergo change, and how agencies are enlisted to remove these disruptions. Sociologists are also interested in how individuals become deviants, sustain their involvement in deviant subcultures, and come to be labelled as deviants by the dominant culture, and how they respond to societal efforts to control them through sanctions and punishment. Finally, sociologists are drawn to the means by which individuals are processed through the criminal justice system—from police to courts—as one way of dealing with deviance in society.

CAUSES OF CRIME

Behaviour that is defined as criminal in one context may be regarded as normal and acceptable in another. Yet deviance and crime exist in all human societies, despite pressures and sanctions for conformity. Sociologists rely on a number of "theories" to explain something seemingly basic and fundamental. These theories try to account for the fact that certain forms of deviance become institutionalized as criminal acts. They also attempt to explain why certain individuals turn to crime, while others do not. The explanatory models themselves vary in the centrality of structures as formative influence. They differ in fingering who or what is to blame: poverty, bad influences, warped values, personal defects, or structural constraints. Differences also arise in their perception of crime either as integral and necessary or as an unintended dysfunction that demands control and surveillance. Each of these theories is useful in terms of what it sets out to explain. Difficulties arise because of what is excluded from each explanation. For convenience we can reduce explanatory models to three broad categories: biological, psychological, and sociological. For the most part, sociologists tend to stay clear of biological explanations (ranging from chromosomal disorders to biochemical/neurological impairment). Nor are they particularly enamoured with psychological reductionism (from psychopaths to alcohol damage). Preferred instead is a focus on social and cultural factors as more adequate to the task of explanation.

Biological Explanations: Natural-Born Criminals

Biological theories of deviance have varied over the years, but generally rely on genetic-physical explanations. Criminals are not made, but born, and often carry physical stigmas as "proof" of their depravity (Himmelfarb and Richardson, 1991). These explanations range in scope from the cranial measurement hypothesis of Cesare Lombrosa, to the proposed correlations between criminality and body size. Other studies include the notion of an extra "Y" chromosome lurking about in the criminally-bent. Still others have emphasized variations in physical strength and energy levels as key variables (Gove, 1985 in Stark). Gove suggests that criminal behaviour is most common among men, and drops off dramatically from the late twenties onwards because of differences in physical strength and energy peaks. Similarly, women are less likely to turn to crime because of anatomical differences.

Psychological Theories: Superegos out of Whack

Psychological theories tend to approach crime as a pathological disorder that symbolizes arrested personality development, childhood disturbances, frustration-aggression impulses, and maligned superegos ("conscience"). Deviance is seen as common among those with poor self-esteem. It is also common among those with an obsessive desire to repress rage or hostile urges under the guise of self-control (over-superego). Conversely, those with poorly developed superegos because of arrested childhood development are equally prone to deviate and stray (under-superego). Of course, not all psychologists portray crime as twisted or demented. Psychoanalytic theories may posit deviance as essentially a "normal" state of affairs. Conformity, by contrast, is defined as "unnatural" because it represents an unrealistic imposition that distorts inner urges and craven desires. On the plus side, we are reminded that crime rather than conformity may be the path of least social resistance. Conformity and obedience are not always in our best interests, in effect making a commitment to comply and conform akin to walking up a down escalator. Finally, there are rational, thinking-based arguments to account for deviance and crime. An economic approach operates on the premise that individuals engage in rational behaviour to achieve certain goals, within a range of choices constrained by the natural and social environment. According to this economic model, most criminals are rational beings who choose to commit crimes by weighing expected costs against benefits. When the benefits of deviance outweigh the costs, a criminal act is likely.

Sociological Explanations

Sociologists generally stay clear of biological or psychological explanations. Sociological explanations tend to focus on defining rates and explaining patterns over time and space. Sociologists are rarely interested in why one person committed a particular act of deviance. They prefer to look at the bigger picture in terms of what constitutes deviance, which deviant acts attract formal authorities, and what causes deviance and crime. To be sure, there is a psychological dimension to all human activities; nevertheless, all human thoughts and actions occur in a social context. A few have cast about for reconciliation. Rodney Stark (1987) suggests that we distinguish between intentional deviance, with its degree of self-awareness and conscious motivation (learning), and impulsive deviance, which is sudden, unprepared, and unreflective. Intentional deviance is intrinsically sociological, whereas impulsive deviance needs to be explained in terms of psychology and personality.

Sociologists tend to focus on the root causes by examining the social and cultural context in which deviance is constructed, defined, and controlled. Generally speaking, the sociological perspective reflects a view of deviance and crime as situated in structures, values, and institutions. Putting too much emphasis on individual responsibility for crime is seen as absolving society of what is essentially a social rather than a legal problem. Explanations are geared toward locating deviance within the framework of society and culture; emphasis is also on interaction that is patterned and predictable, and whose rates are amenable to analysis. Deviance, moreover, is treated as "normal" and "necessary" (that is, inevitable) to society, given the inevitable conflict of interest in a complex society, even though many sociologists find certain actions to be repugnant, and recognize their deleterious consequences (Himmelfarb and Richardson, 1991). Finally, sociologists differ in how they define the relationship of deviance and crime to society. What is defined as dysfunctional by some is defined as "functional" by others, and inevitable by still others. For convenience, these explanatory perspectives include functionalism, symbolic interaction, or conflict.

Functionalist

Functionalist approaches toward deviance and crime revolve around breakdowns in culture, society, or socialization, particularly during periods of rapid social change. For various reasons, certain individuals fail to internalize normal patterns associated with conventional values, beliefs, and practices. This maladjustment and absence of conformity "compels" individuals to turn to crime for attainment of their goals. Or, in some cases, crime is just as likely to stem from "oversocialization"; that is, excessive identification with cultural norms and values that may bring the perpetrator into conflict with the law. In other cases, crime may arise from exposure to subcultural values at odds with the standards of the dominant culture. Finally, crime is rooted in the process of relative deprivation. When expectations outstrip the reality of achievement, individuals fall back on alternative (unconventional) means to acquire those scarce resources they feel entitled to.

Conflict Theory

The second major perspective is known as conflict theory. Conflict theorists differ from functionalists in the way in which they assess the status and role of crime in society. For conflict theorists, society itself is a structured system of inequality and domination. Competition and conflict between social groups become inevitable as each attempts to advance, defend, or consolidate its position. Certain groups are more favourably positioned in this competitive struggle for adaptation and survival. Dominant groups possess both the power and the resources to define patterns of behaviour as criminal; they also possess the power to punish those who break the law. Class interests determine which acts are defined as criminal and subject to punishment. In addition, class inequities create economic imbalances that induce property crimes by the poor and peripheral (Samuelson, 1998). Corporate practices involving capital accumulation, from fraud to unsafe working practices, are rarely treated as a problem, let alone defined as illegal and prosecuted accordingly. By contrast, crimes by the working classes, many of which stem from life circumstances and rarely match the costs of corporate crime, tend to be punished more vigorously. In the final analysis, crime is not intrinsic to society, but is inherent in capitalist societies with their class divisions and private property. Crime is defined and imposed by the affluent to safeguard their interests from the encroachment of the poor and disempowered.

Symbolic Interactionism

Symbolic interactionism takes a different approach to crime and control. As a major perspective in sociology, symbolic interactionism rejects a view of society as a straitjacket of social forces for conformity or conflict. For symbolic interactionists, society is neither good nor bad; it just is. Symbolic interactionists argue that social realities are ongoing and evolving human accomplishments. Rather than some durable force out there, society and social reality are socially constructed through individuals engaged in meaningful and jointly linked interaction. Social actors define situations in a certain way, and then interact with others on the basis of these definitions. Both crime and control, in other words, are the by-products of interaction and interpretation within contexts that are shifting and situational. Criminal activity is acquired in the same way as conformity. It is learned through interaction with others in intimate personal groups (Sutherland and Cressey, 1977). Exposure to a deviant subculture reinforces rules and values that are likely to bring someone into trouble with the law.

Labelling represents one of the more popular interactionist theories of crime and control. Labelling theory begins with the premise that social actions in their own right are neither deviant nor normal, but take on those attributes through a collective definition process known as labelling. Through labelling, members of society create crime by making rules about behaviour whose infractions are defined as deviant or criminal. Formal mechanisms of control are thus established to reduce deviance. Paradoxically, however, labels that are affixed to persons by the criminal justice system may have the effect of amplifying criminality, since those labelled as such may act in conformity with these public expectations. Once they are labelled and stigmatized as criminal, in other words, individuals are inclined to act in a self-reinforcing manner because of restricted occupational opportunities, limited interpersonal relations, and reduced self-concept. In addition, those who have been stigmatized by a criminal label are prevented from engaging in conventional patterns, in effect encouraging and amplifying recourse to crime by default. Briefly then, crime is not a quality intrinsic to an act, person, or situation. It consists instead of an attribute conferred on an action or person, often resulting in a reinforcement of those actions intended for control. Laws may be established to curtail crime; yet crime flourishes, not because of anti-social persons, but because of laws that have created the problem in the first place.

A Sociological Conundrum

Various theories attempt to explain deviance and crime as complex and multi-faceted dimensions of anti-social behaviour. Each of these theories fits into a sociological perspective: functionalist, interactionist, and conflict. For functionalists, society is basically good, therefore, crime is bad; for conflict theorists, society is fundamentally bad, hence, crime simply reflects inequities in society; and for interactionists, society just is, and crime needs to be analyzed as a social construction. Notwithstanding differences in emphasis and scope, however, each theory shares a common sociological commitment. That is, crime is a socially constructed process, and as such must be analyzed in sociological terms, either by reference to culture and structure, or to situation and context.

Acknowledging perspectives is important beyond just understanding for sociological sake. What is at stake here is how specific definitions of a problem will shape particular types of solutions. If deviance and crime are the result of defective socialization, then solutions must focus on improving value internalization. If the problem is rooted in the structure of society, a restructuring of cultural norms and societal arrangements is in order. The focus on structures leads to a paradox of sorts. When a crime is committed, who is at fault? Do we pin the blame on the individual, since we are all responsible for our actions? Or does the fault lie with the system, in effect absolving the individual of direct blame and immediate responsibility? What precisely is the nature of the relationship between personal responsibility and societal context? To what extent are individuals the by-product of their social environment? Or is it more correct to see individuals as essentially autonomous persons with a capacity and responsibility to transcend social and cultural constraints? The question of whether the individual or society is responsible is frequently couched in debates over blaming the victim or blaming society. It is also framed in the discourse of free will versus determinism or agency versus structure.

Locating the balance between agency and structure has challenged sociologists over the years (Giddens, 1990), with only bland clichés as a compromise solution. The corrective of blaming the system rather than the individual may be taken too far if people refuse to accept responsibility. Individuals are ultimately responsible for their actions and need to be held accountable for what they do. Yet these actions do not arise in a social vacuum, and need to be interpreted within the social context, as Case Study 6–1 demonstrates.

CHARACTERISTICS OF CRIME: WHO DUNNIT?

Sociologists are interested not only in studying the causes of crime by way of theoretical models. Their interest extends to looking at how certain groups become involved in criminal behaviour. While deviance in general is common across the entire population, criminal activity appears to be concentrated in certain sectors of society. The major categories or key variables in explaining who commits crime are age, gender, ethnicity, and region. (See Statistics Canada, 1999)

Age

Which age group is most likely to be accused of committing a crime?

Those between the ages of 18 and 34 are most likely to be accused of a criminal code offence, according to Statistics Canada, constituting about 63 percent of the total.

Kids are impatient, impulsive, and imprudent, and this is reflected in criminal activity.

According to Statistics Canada, less than 5 percent of people aged 12–17 were charged with a criminal code offence in 1997, about the same as in 1987, but a drop from almost 7 percent of all youths in 1991.

Is youth crime on the upswing?

Youth crime in Canada has remained fairly stable during the 1990s, according to Statistics Canada. In 1997–98, youth courts processed 110 883 cases (down 9 percent from 92–93). Of these, property crimes were most common, at 49 602, followed by violent crime at 23 711(a slight increase from 21 653 in 1992–93), and other criminal code offences, including traffic crime, at 19 316. The number of youths charged with sexual assault (1438) dropped for the fifth consecutive year.

CASE STUDY 6-1   Being Aboriginal: Excuse or Constraint?

This debate over agency versus structure has assumed a new twist with a controversial ruling involving an aboriginal woman and the criminal justice system. At the core of the controversy is the degree to which the broader context can contribute to a mindset that produces actions at odds with the law. Equally important is the growing commitment to community-based criminal justice. In contrast to a "tough on crime" endorsement, with its focus on more police, more arrests, more prosecutions, and more prisons, this solution emphasizes the community ties that deter crime in the first place, correct the interpersonal imbalances created by the offence, and involve the community in punishment and rehabilitation by reintegrating offenders into the community (Cole, 1998).

First the facts: A Metis woman, Deanna Emard, 28, received a conditional sentence of two years less a day in the B.C. Supreme Court for stabbing her common-law partner, Wilfrid Shorson, 39, in January, 1997. She was sentenced to perform 240 hours of community service and to refrain from consuming alcohol. Defence counsel, Peter Wilson, argued that Ms. Emard, because of her "Indianness," should receive a lighter sentence for the stabbing death, despite the absence of domestic abuse in the relationship. In saying that past injustices contributed to the crime, her lawyer argued that she suffered from the systemic problems that plague Canada's First Peoples, including substance abuse, racism, and poverty. The presiding judge agreed: Although her aboriginal background did not absolve her of blame for committing the crime—after all, the jury did find her guilty of manslaughter—the woman had endured an unhappy life through "no fault of her own." The sentence also reflected sentencing guidelines introduced in 1995 to the Criminal Code (S718.2(e)): "All available sanctions other than imprisonment, that are reasonable in the circumstances, should be considered for all offenders, with particular attention to the circumstances of aboriginal offenders." Judges are now required to consider the social, cultural, and historical background of offenders, particularly the circumstances of aboriginal offenders as a group, to justify a sentence other than imprisonment, as long as the sentencing arrangement does not pose a risk to the public.

Second, the reaction: Reaction to this controversial ruling appeared negative. Some contemptuously dismissed the conditional "discharge" as a "Get Out of Jail Free" card for aboriginal offenders, in effect suggesting that aboriginal people have a diminished human capacity and are incapable of being treated equally. Others, such as columnist Lisa Birnie, dismissed the ruling as a clumsy, irresponsible, and racist attempt to assuage White guilt and defuse political pressure. In expressing concern over the effects of the amendment on the constitutional principle of fairness and equality before the law, Mike Scott, native affairs critic for the Reform Party, said: "You can't right historical wrongs by creating new injustices. When you move away from the principle that we're all entitled to the same treatment in the eyes of the law, you're going down a slippery slope." For still others, such leniency posed a risk by encouraging aboriginal people to commit similar crimes. The victim's family also accused the system of bending to political correctness; after all, the accused was Métis and a woman. As to her intoxicated state at the time of the crime, the victim's sister was quoted as saying: "Alcohol is not an excuse, and neither is being a native. There should be justice for everyone, not one system for Indian and Métis people and one for White people." Further outrage was clearly evident when a 37-year-old Saskatchewan Métis with a lengthy history of violent crimes dating back to 1979 was spared life imprisonment for an armed robbery that included a sexual assault because his aboriginal background contributed to his inability to function in civil society (Mickleburgh, 1999).

Third, the interpretation: This incident raises a number of key issues about the changing relationship of Canada to its citizens, but particularly its first citizens. While the ruling may single out certain races or categories of people for differential treatment, all Canadians now have the multicultural right to have their social and cultural circumstances incorporated into the sentencing process. The ruling does not undermine the concept of one law for all, nor that everyone is equal before the law, at least no more so than the Young Offenders Act absolves youth of guilt or responsibility. In the case of Ms. Emard, the question of guilt was not the issue, only the appropriate level of punishment. This judgment is consistent with other forms of cultural defence such as the "Black rage" strategy, which acknowledge the importance of social context and historical factors in shaping states of mind that may culminate in criminal actions. In other words, individuals are responsible for their actions; nevertheless, even offensive actions do not occur in a social void, but reflect options and choices that are constrained by extenuating circumstances.

Nor can this ruling be framed as a race issue. The intent is not to define a group of people on the basis of fixed biological features, while hierarchically ranking these racial categories in a way that denies or excludes. The ruling is not concerned with excusing the criminal acts of aboriginal people or getting them out of jail because of their aboriginality. Central to the debate is the privileging of aboriginality as principle and practice. As fundamentally autonomous political communities, aboriginal peoples have indigenous rights related to culture, land, and political voice that have yet to be extinguished. These rights not only articulate a special relationship with the Crown and the Canadian state; indigenous rights also provide a rationale for differential treatment when employed to enhance, bolster, improve, or advance. Finally, the broader context needs to be considered. Initiatives to keep aboriginal peoples out of jail may have nothing to do with aboriginal rights, but everything to do with reducing the number of aboriginal people in overcrowded jails. In a 1996 report, aboriginal peoples were eleven times more likely than non-aboriginal peoples to be in provincial jails, and five times more likely to be in federal penitentiaries. Prisons for many aboriginal inmates are little more than "barbed wire" universities that confer revolving-door degrees in criminality. At a time when community-based alternatives to traditional imprisonment are gaining in popularity, the decision to postpone jailing aboriginal offenders suggests the possibility of alternatives to better meet the needs of the community and the offender. This focus on re-establishing aboriginal connections to their community and culture may also concede the obvious: that the criminal justice system is not working, and that aboriginal communities can't possibly do any worse in stopping the bleeding.

Fourth, putting it into perspective: In a multicultural society such as Canada, everyone has the right to equality before the law. Each person also has the right to be culturally different without being penalized. Neither of these "rights" is more "right" than the other. The paradox lies in the "rightness" of both, and the fundamentally irreconcilable nature of this conflict between two mutually opposed but equal rights. Herein is the challenge for the twenty-first century: How much diversity can be tolerated in a multicultural society? How do we reconstruct a Canada that

is safe for diversity, as well as safe from ethnicity? Too little acceptance makes a mockery of multiculturalism; too much diversity precludes any possibility of living together with our differences. Nobody is quite sure of where to draw the line, and the essence of being Canadian may lie in constantly adjusting the line. In any case, Canadians will need to accept a certain level of ambiguity and compromise if we hope to constructively engage with diversity in the new millennium.

Sources: Cori Howard, "Racial Background Key Part of Argument at Sentencing Hearing." *Globe and Mail*, 11 Jan., 1999; Lisa Birnie, "An Ill-Advised Native Rider." *Globe and Mail*, 15 Jan., 1999; Editorial, "Crime, Time, and Race." *Globe and Mail*, 16 Jan., 1999; Jonathan Rudin, "Aboriginal Offenders and the Criminal Code." the *Globe and Mail*, 9 Feb., 1999.

Is violent crime increasing among youth?

Violent crime (assaults, robberies, and homicides) increased from 275 per 100 000 juveniles in 1980 to about 500 per 100 000 juveniles in 1996. Youths between 12 and 17 account for one in six of those charged with a violent offence in Canada. Of the violent crimes, 43 percent were of the common assault variety, 21 percent aggravated assault with a weapon, and robbery 14 percent. Murder, manslaughter, and attempted murder account for only one percent of youth violent crimes—a figure that has remained constant for the past ten years.

Who are the victims of youth crime?

Nearly 60 percent of violent crime victims were acquaintances of the accused youth, and 52 percent were youths themselves. Only 2 percent of victims of violent youth crime were 55 or over (DiManno, 2000).

Young people are often depicted by the media as more offending and law-breaking than was once the case. Evidence would suggest otherwise: According to Statistics Canada data, there has been virtually no change in the level of youth crime since 1980 (Carrington, 1999). In Canada, the rate of youth offending between 12 and 17 escalated from a low of approximately 8000 per 100 000 to a peak of 9300 in 1989, but back down to 7700 per 100 000 in 1997. In Ontario, the figure dropped from 8900 in 1980, to 7600 in 1996, based on the number of crimes reported to Statscan by the police. Even here caution is necessary. Allegations of increased youthful offending may reflect enlightened public awareness and willingness to report certain incidents, as well as more vigorous laying of charges by authorities. For example, what may have been a schoolyard scuffle followed by an after-class detention may now result in charges and arrests. Even parents of unruly children may be willing to transfer responsibility to the proper authorities for punishment and rehabilitation.

For the most part, both violent and property crime that come to the attention of authorities are concentrated among young, unmarried males (Tepperman and Rosenberg, 1991). The reasons are many and open to dispute, but may include relatively unstructured lifestyles that encourage aggression and the acting out of violence for public display. Cultural reasons may reflect a desire for adventure and nonconformity, a craving for the respect of others, a defence of status or turf, or an expression of virility. Fascination with guns has long been part of male youth culture. But, whereas possession once meant maturity and responsibility, young men now tend to associate guns with power and heroics. Precipitating causes are apt to include drink or drugs, while root causes stem from broken families, child abuse, and exposure to violence in the media. Additional root causes may extend to defective socialization, breakdowns in informal pressure, and inefficient formal agencies. Young men may be disconnected from society because many are caught in the conflicting demands of the new economy, feminism, government policy, and the erosion of traditional privileges and definitions of manhood.

Gender

Do men commit most of the crime?

Yes. Men continue to commit about 90 percent of the crime, even though the rates for women are increasing.

Are young women committing more crime?

They appear to be. Young women between the ages of 12 and 17 accounted for 22 percent of those charged in 1997, up significantly from 16 percent in 1987. The rate of violent crime by female youths (5652 charged in 1998) has increased twice as fast as for male youths (16 493 charged in 1998).

Who commits the homicides?

Men constitute 85 percent of the accused, with the median age of the accused rising from 26 in 1974 to 32 in 1997. Half of those accused, and a third of the victims, had consumed alcohol or drugs.

Who are the primary victims of homicide?

Men continue to be the primary victims, constituting nearly two-thirds of the total. In terms of age brackets, children under the age of two suffered the highest murder rate in Canada. At 33 per million children, according to Statistics Canada in its 1997 homicide survey, this was seven times higher than the rate for those between 2 and 17, 5 times higher than for those between 18 and 64, and 8 times higher than for those over 65.

Crime is gendered. Males tend to dominate in virtually all crime statistics categories. According to Lydia Miljan, director of the Fraser Institute's national media archive, most crimes are committed by male adults against other males, usually involving drugs or alcohol, and often late at night. Men, especially those between 18 and 34, commit nearly all the violent crimes in society, prompting a report on crime in Europe to conclude that if men behaved like women, the courts would be idle and the prisons empty. To be sure, women and girls do commit crime, particularly as young women adopt illegal means for fun and profit, but not nearly to the same extent as males. Even the rationale for crimes may be different. When women kill (Silverman and Kennedy, 1998), for example, almost 64 percent of the victims are spouses or children. Women may kill in reaction to domestic violence or to protect themselves and their children from further male violence. By contrast, males' violence toward others is aimed at controlling or subjugation. Other studies indicate that women reject self-defence as a motivating factor in violently abusing spouses, although women are twice as likely to suffer greater physical consequences of a brawl (Sullivan, 1999). Research studies also suggest that violence in intimate relationships is a two-way street, writes Donna Laframboise of the *National Post*, with both men and women sharing equally in behaving aggressively toward their partners. Still, the dynamics appear to be different. According to Michele Landsberg, in her Life section column each Saturday in the *Toronto Star*, the battering of women is more like organized crime through its control of victims by systematic, deliberate intimidation, and terror. In short, male violence toward women is a reflection of the power imbalance within a relationship. In contrast to men, who can walk away from an abusive relationship, women may be economically dependent because of their children or have to confront the possibility of being murdered if they dare to leave.

Region

Does crime vary across Canada?

Sure does. Canada averaged 8 102 incidents per 100 000 population in 1998. Of the provinces, Newfoundland had the lowest rate at 5 803 per 100 000, while British Columbia, with 12 141 per 100 000, and Saskatchewan with 12 403 per 100 000, had the highest. Ontario's rate stood at 7020 per 100 000, a drop of 5.8 percent since 1997. The North-West Territories had the highest rate of crime at 23 266 per 100 000 population.

Do the biggest cities tend to have the highest crime rates?

When it comes to reported criminal code crimes, the opposite seems to be true. In 1998, Regina led the list of selected cities with 14 785 total incidents per 100 000 population. Vancouver, Saskatoon, Victoria, and Thunder Bay followed behind. Quebec City had the least number of incidents at 5 348. Toronto was right behind with 5 839.

Which cities have the highest violent crime rate?

According to 1998 Statistics Canada data, Thunder Bay had the highest number of violent crimes, at 1740 per 100 000 population, of Canada's 25 census metropolitan areas, followed closely by Regina, Saskatoon, Victoria, and Winnipeg. Toronto was one of the safer cities, at

836 per 100 000, while Montreal had 827 per 100 000. The safest metropolitan area in terms of violent crime rates? Sherbrooke, Quebec at only 411 per 100 000 population.

Are homicide rates highest in the largest urban areas?

No. In 1997, the three highest metropolitan rates per 100 000 population were Saskatoon (3.59), Halifax (3.15), and Edmonton (3.0). The three lowest metropolitan rates were Chicoutimi-Jonquiere (0.0), Kitchener (0.69), and London (0.71), with Calgary (1.02) and Ottawa-Hull (1.15) close behind. The rate for Toronto was 1.71 per 100 000, according to the Homicide Survey, Canadian Centre for Justice Statistics, October 1998.

Are homicide rates in American cities much higher than in Canada?

In 1992, Seattle had the lowest murder rate of major American cities with 11 per 100 000. New York had 27, while Miami was 34.2. Washington and Detroit scored the highest rates at 75.2 and 57 per 100 000. Compare these to Toronto, at 2.3 per 100 000. Since 1993 to 1997, however, there has been a 25 percent drop in violent crime rates and a drop of about one-third in the rates of murder, largely because of the decline in the crack trade.

Class

Crime rates also appear to be distributed by class. Historically, working classes were assumed to be more criminally inclined because of denied opportunities and harsh social circumstances (Hagan, 1992). Others have proposed a correlation between social class and type of crime: Serious crimes involving drugs and guns are more common in the lower classes, while "less serious" crimes are more evenly distributed through all sectors. White-collar crime is perceived as the domain of the middle classes. For still others, such as conflict theorists, even the nature of the criminal activity reflects a class bias. A class bias can be detected in the application of criminal justice in terms of what constitutes crime, who and what are singled out as criminal, and how individuals are processed through the system. Laws that define crime tend to reflect the interests of the rich and powerful; there is a class bias in the preference to detect street crime rather than corporate crime; and class bias is reflected in differential conviction and sentencing for street crime and working class offences (Samuelson, 1998). In other words, the poor do not necessarily commit more crime. They are simply more likely to be caught and convicted than the affluent.

Of course, there is no need to blame inherent tendencies or psychological predispositions as factors in offending by the poor. Social explanations are more than equal to the challenge. Poverty is not necessarily a cause of crime; nevertheless, the root causes of criminal offending reflect the reality of being poor, unemployed, under-educated, victims of subsistence addiction, and a history of abuse (Consedine, 1999). Prejudice and discrimination within the criminal justice system have a way of disproportionately targeting the lower classes for control. Certain crimes are pursued and punished more vigorously (petty street crime) than others (white-collar crime) (Samuelson, 1998). Because of preconceptions, police are more likely to patrol densely populated areas, in effect resulting in higher charge and arrest rates. The poor and marginal are also prosecuted more often for criminal acts or juvenile delinquency. Further caution is necessary before jumping to conclusions because of the high rates of white-collar crime that are either undetected or treated more leniently by the courts. Conventional statistics also overlook the consequences of middle-class crimes, involving as they do huge sums of money or high costs with respect to human lives or environmental destruction.

Ethnicity

Does race or ethnicity have anything to do with criminality? Or has it more to do with background or circumstances (Siddiqui, 1999)? Is what we know about minority offending a reflection of reality or is it based on what is reported and recorded by the police? Do minorities commit more crime, or are they just more likely to be caught and charged because of their visibility, the visibility of street crimes, and the prejudices and profiling of police officers? The selectivity and bias that are inherent in processing minority women and men tend to distort the level and pattern of offending within minority communities. They also have the effect of racializing crime along race and ethnic lines, thus further amplifying the risk of detection and apprehension.

There is remarkably little information in this area that is not based on anecdotes, reflects prejudice, or conforms to political correctness. Studies suggest that, while immigrants commit less crime than the Canadian-born, some immigrants groups, such as those from certain Caribbean countries, tend to be jailed at higher rates than their proportion in the population. Young Black males in Ontario are also jailed more often, according to a 1995 study on systemic racism in the criminal justice system. For example, between 1993 and 1995, 43.2 percent of the respondents stopped by the police were Black. Only 23.8 percent of the respondents were White, and 19 percent Chinese. In each case, statistics cannot answer the key question. Are these rates a reflection of reality or of police prejudice in profiling minorities?

Ethnicity may be a variable that accounts for certain types of crime, according to the Canadian Centre for Justice Statistics, (cited in Galloway, 1999). Canada's five major organized crime groups are divided along ethnic lines, with each having its own area of criminal expertise, despite a common preoccupation with the drug trade. Eastern Europeans are thought to specialize in counterfeiting; Asian groups prefer extortion; aboriginal groups are focused on firearms trafficking and smuggling of cigarettes and alcohol; White motorcycle gangs tend to smuggle both guns and explosives; and Italians are linked with money-laundering through the use of legitimate businesses. Finally, aboriginal peoples are also more likely to be apprehended for crime. Among the general attributes of aboriginal crime that can be gleaned from research studies are the following:

1. Crime rates are higher on aboriginal reserves and communities in northern Canada than for the general population. There is considerable variation in the patterns of crime from one community to another.

2. High rates of violent crime, especially assaults against women and children, are common on aboriginal reserves and communities.

3. Alcohol is often involved in aboriginal crime.

4. Aboriginal people constitute 3 percent of Canada's population, but make up about 12 percent of the inmates in federal prisons. In western Canada, aboriginal peoples constitute upwards of 75 percent of the inmates in provincial jails.

How do we account for these disparities? Many minorities and aboriginal peoples are economically disadvantaged groups, with few resources to beat charges or avoid prison. Prejudices and stereotypes mean they are likely to attract an inordinate amount of police attention. Their visibility and cultural lifestyles may also foster negative encounters with the police. In an era of cash-strapped budgets, the police may have an ulterior motive for inflating the figures by feeding into the fear of crime and fanning public panic. The presence of open and systemic discrimination is a contributing factor as well. In short, the law appears to be protective of the White middle class, but is a source of worry for people of colour. For minorities, the criminal justice system is perceived as racist in intent or by consequence; most Whites reject this charge, although they acknowledge the existence of some racists within the system. In other words, there is no reason to believe that minorities are committing more crime than the general population. Even if minorities do commit more of a certain crime, these offences are not the result of their race or ethnicity, at least not any more than white-collar crime can be attributed to the racial attributes of Whites (Siddiqui, 1999).

CONTROLLING CRIME

Is policing in Canada undergoing change?

There were 55 300 police officers in Canada in 1998, costing the taxpayer $6.3 billion. On a per capita basis, there were 181 officers per 100 000 population, with Yukon the highest at 388, and Newfoundland the lowest at 142. The face of policing is slowly changing. Female police officers now account for one in eight police officers (7149), up from one in twenty a decade ago. However, only 7.5 percent of Toronto's Police Services are visible minorities, despite the fact that people of colour constitute over 31 percent of Toronto's population.

How does Canada's rate of imprisonment stack up internationally?

Russia has an incarceration rate of 690 per 100 000 population, followed closely by the United States with 672 per 100 000 population, and rising rapidly because of the emergence of private prisons. Canada's total is 115 per 100 000.

Is the prison system working?

In 1993, the average number of adults in prison in Canada on any given day was 31 709. The average annual cost for inmates in a federal penetentiary reached $51 202 in 1998 (but $70 326 for maximum security, and $91 753 for female prisoners). It cost $43 734 for each inmate in the provincial/territorial jail system.

How colour-blind is the criminal justice system?

Not very, at least judging by the number of visible minorities that are processed through the criminal justice system. The 1995 Report on Systemic Racism in Ontario's Criminal Justice System indicated that Blacks and aboriginal peoples are much more likely to end up in prison. Prison admissions per 100 000 members of the total population stood at 827. By comparison, the rate for Blacks was 3686; for First Nations, 1993; for Whites, 706; for Asians, 353. In 1986, Blacks constituted 7.1 percent of Ontario's prison population; by 1992–93, 15.3 percent, an increase of 203.6 percent (compared to only a 23 percent increase for Whites), although Blacks were only about 3 percent of the population.

Is the criminal justice system too soft on young offenders?

Canada is a world leader in incarcerating teenagers. With nearly 25 000 young people sentenced every year to closed or open custody, Canada's rate is more than twice that of Americans, 10 times that of Europeans, and 5 times that of Australians.

How do aboriginal peoples fare in the criminal justice system?

Aboriginal males and females are disproportionately represented in prison. In 1997, aboriginal adults accounted for 17 percent of federal jail admissions—up from 11 percent in 1991—despite constituting only 2 percent of Canada's adult population. In the prairie provinces, aboriginal peoples occupy 50 percent of the federal and provincial prison space, but less than 10 percent of the general population. Although aboriginal women constituted only 3 percent of the population of women in Canada in 1991, Carole LaPrairie (1996) writes, they formed 50 percent of the female inmates in provincial and territorial correctional institutions. A female Treaty Indian is 131 times more likely to be admitted to a provincial jail than a non-aboriginal person, while a male Treaty Indian is 25 times more likely, according to Professor Tony Hall of Aboriginal Studies at the Lethbridge Community College.

   Broadly speaking, social control consists of collective efforts to enforce conformity to norms. Control can be achieved through socialization, informal pressures, and formal agencies. Socialization is a key factor, and its impact can extend to the deliberate (family, education) or the inadvertent, including friends or the mass media. Informal pressures for ensuring compliance often entail approval or disapproval by family, friends, or peer groups. Ridicule, gossip, shaming, or social ostracism are some of the more common means for informally ensuring compliance, especially in pre-industrial societies or in rural areas where face-to-face encounters are the norm rather than the exception. As a result, social control functions are inherent in all institutions, since all are involved in some degree of socialization or resocialization, as well as internalization, compliance, and sanctions (Stebbins, 1990). When informal pressures are ineffective, especially in serious disturbances or in secondary contexts, then formal methods of control are applied. But "courts and cops" as well as mental hospitals and the military as sources of control are instruments of last resort because of the costs and logistics involved (O'Donnell, 1988).
   The effectiveness of the criminal justice system is under scrutiny. Is the system working? For whom? On what grounds? Is the system fair? Who says so, and why? Debates are focused on the role of formal sanctions as a deterrent to crime. Evidence suggests that punishment can serve to deter criminal activity when applied immediately and with certainty (Gibbs, 1975; Stark, 1987). But the fact remains that the chances of getting caught for any low-level crime are quite unlikely. Even more remote are the odds that a first-time offender will be punished for her or his actions, especially if the accused is White and affluent. Charges themselves may be dropped for various reasons, including flaws in the arrest procedure, problems of evidence, witnesses that fail to materialize, and plea-bargaining. In other words, punishment is uncertain, not swift, and rarely severe, reducing its potential as a deterrent. No small wonder, then, that while 2.5 million crimes are reported in Canada each year, an equivalent number may go undetected or unreported.
   The topic of social control raises a number of perplexing questions. Foremost among these is the question of why some deviant actions become defined as problematic and subject to

control both formal and informal. How is it that certain categories of drug-taking are regarded as an offence (although this was not always the case as recently as the turn of the century in North America); conversely, other drugs, such as tobacco and alcohol, are legally permissible, subject to certain constraints? Even here we might want to ask why and how public opinion is gradually turning against both alcohol and tobacco consumption. An additional example: Why are the affluent in the corporate world less likely to be charged (and even less likely to be convicted)? To be sure, white-collar corporate crime may lack the flair or flamboyance of everyday criminal behaviour. But who can underestimate its capacity to pollute the environment, violate consumer health, and risk worker safety? These questions are not easily answered; nevertheless, their very elusiveness does reinforce the notion of social control as a socially constructed artifice, often in defence of vested interests, but at the cost of impartiality and legal equality.

How do we account for this bias and selectivity in the processing of criminal justice? The criminal justice system is directed primarily at the type of street-crime that is more easily detected and punished. Conversely, there is less emphasis on crimes that stray outside that context, such as crimes that many police cannot relate to (such as domestic abuse or white-collar crime dealing with forgery, embezzlement, and work safety violations (Tepperman and Rosenberg, 1991). White-collar crime in particular is difficult to detect, still harder to prevent or punish once uncovered. Most white-collar crimes are performed by individuals with higher status in the community, making it difficult to bring criminals to justice because of a closing of the business ranks or the possession of resources to fight the charges. Two conclusions stand out: First, greed is as much a cause of crime as are poverty and need. Second, the criminal justice system tends to punish those crimes that are more readily detected, while waffling over more destructive forms of criminal activities in boardrooms and computer networks (Tepperman and Rosenberg, 1991).

The Criminal Justice System

Canada's criminal justice system evolved from the eighteenth century system of England. It also has much in common, procedurally speaking, with the system of criminal justice in the United States (Cunningham, 1998). Differences exist, of course, not the least of which is the universality of Canada's criminal code across the country, rather than the state-to-state variability of criminal law in the United States. Nevertheless, Allison Hatch Cunningham (1998) observes, the constitutionally defined division of power and responsibilities between federal and provincial jurisdictions ensures provincial control over administering justice, culminating in provincial differences over policing, prosecution, court management, and corrections. Critics in both countries have taken to task the criminal justice system for stumbling in the fight against crime. For some, the system is too lenient, particularly with respect to sentencing; for others, the system is too strict and insensitive to differences. For many, however, the system is seen as too costly for the returns. Not surprisingly, Canadian policy-makers have sought ways to reduce reliance on a cops-courts-corrections approach to crime, and to develop alternatives to custody or imprisonment for low-risk offenders.

Policing

One of the primary sources of formal control is the police. The police in Canada are a component of the criminal justice system (which includes courts and prisons) for the express purpose of social control and community service (McDougal, 1988). A wide range of roles and duties are encompassed under this protect-and-serve mandate, most of which revolve around the goals of protection (of life and property) and service through law enforcement and public order maintenance. As the "thin blue line" that separates civilization from disorder, police are empowered with the right to apply force in discharging their obligations, but only to the extent that its use is reasonable and demonstrably justified in light of Canada's democratic and legal traditions. This monopoly of force on behalf of the state makes police work "political" in the sense that policing is perceived as supportive of some sectors, but detrimental to others (see McDougal, 1988; also Neugebauer, 2000).

The police in Canada are big business. With an annual cost of $6 billion, or $195 per capita, police costs take the biggest bite out of the criminal justice budget each year. Nearly 55 000 police officers work at federal (RCMP), provincial (OPP), and municipal (Waterloo Regional) levels. This works out to about 181 officers per 100 000 population, or, alternatively, one police officer for every 554 Canadians, a decrease of 11 percent since 1991 (Cunningham, 1998). Police departments vary in size from 5000 uniformed officers in the Toronto Police Service to one-member detachments of RCMP officers in remote communities. Nearly forty percent of all police officers belong to the RCMP, making it one of the largest police services in the entire world. This growth in the number of police officers reflects a major trend in Canadian criminal justice, away from order maintenance by the community at large, and its replacement by formal agencies of social control. A corresponding decrease in community involvement in preventing crime and responding to offenders has proven a problem. Police functions have also evolved. From fairly limited tasks related to night watchmen, the police have assumed a variety of goals related to preventing crime, apprehending criminal offenders, maintaining local order, regulating traffic, responding to emergencies from crowd control to missing persons, and providing information of relevance to the community. These goals can be reduced to three major functions: crime control, order maintenance, and public service.

This expansion of functions is not without difficulties in shaping police-public relations. Questions abound: What is the relationship of the police to the public? Are they servants of the people who must submit to civilian control, or are they a law unto themselves, and accountable only to the uniform? What can police really accomplish in society? Many of the demands made on the police reflect social problems of such magnitude that they are virtually resistant to solutions. Are the police in a position to address the underlying causes of conflicts that come to their attention (Verdun Jones, 1994)? With their limited resources, the best they can do is address the symptoms of crime rather than the root causes of societal or personal problems. Or as put by Verdun Jones (1994:71), the police cannot prevent crime, they can only respond to it.

Crisis in Policing

Police-minority relations are undergoing a profound reassessment because of changes in public expectations. The sensibilities of many Americans and Canadians were deeply offended by the Rodney King-inspired riots that killed 50 people in Los Angeles in early May of 1992. The fact that a similar, smaller-scale riot was re-enacted in Toronto, with considerable property damage to the Yonge Street strip, laid to rest the fabled superiority of Canada's race relations. Shock, outrage, and sadness greeted news of the destruction in what many had seen as a model city of multicultural engagement. Elsewhere across Canada the police came in for biting criticism. In Montreal, a coroner's inquest castigated the police for their callous and racist indifference to human life following a display of sheer incompetence in the bungled shooting of an unarmed, Black male. Criticism has also uncovered a reliance on police strip searches as a way of humiliating the loud and uncooperative, or of punishing those likely to slip through the system (Editorial, 7 Nov., 1998). This "crisis" in police-minority relations has had the effect of eroding the legitimacy of the police in certain multicultural communities (Baker, 1994; Neugebauer, 2000).

Disruptions to police-minority relations often entail incidents involving young, urban, male African-Canadians (see also Holdaway, 1996). Many believe that Blacks are harassed more often because of double standards; they are also charged, arrested, convicted, and jailed at a rate far beyond their proportion in the community. Police, in turn, are accused of being excessively preoccupied with the belief that minorities are predisposed to crime ("overpolicing"), yet negligent in their attention to ethnic communities ("underpolicing") (Henry et al., 1999). Not surprising, police continue to be despised as tools of the White power establishment in communities of colour (Kivel, 1996). The police would dispute this assessment of their relationship with targeted minority communities. Racially motivated actions may exist, they concede, but excesses can be attributed to a small number of "rogue" officers rather than to any institutionalized racism. The apprehension of minority youths is not a case of discriminatory policing, according to the police, but a response to the spate of street crimes that invite police attention. By contrast, African-Canadians often see police as racist and trigger-happy, concerned only with protecting their turf against intruders. The fact that neither side can understand the other—much less engage in cooperative actions—intensifies the potential for crisis and confrontation. The result is a strained mutual avoidance: Minority youth stake out their patch by withdrawing legitimacy from the "big blue machine." The police, in turn, circle the wagons even more securely against what they perceive as unwarranted attacks by stroppy youths, community activists, an unsympathetic press, opportunistic politicians, and the forces of political correctness.

Police initiatives to "bridge the gap" by improving lines of communication with the community have proven uneven. Attempts to initiate positive reform in preventive policing are undermined by entrenched subcultural values among police that revel in a "kick ass" style of policing. The police as an institution appear reluctant to engage community involvement, preferring, for the most part, to remain a "closed shop" (Cryderman et al., 1998). The interplay of defensiveness, suspicion, and hostility is likely to isolate police from the community they serve and protect. This estrangement is reinforced by bureacratic structures that endorse conservatism, distance from the community, hierarchy, division of labour, and a paramilitary chain of command. Any potential for positive police-minority relations is diminished by the realities of incident-driven policing, with its focus on charges and arrests. Interactional patterns are further hampered by ineffective race-awareness training. What little most officers receive has been conducted by poorly trained, sometimes unmotivated officials. Much of the education has been geared toward cultural sensitivity, yet such a focus may have the effect of reinforcing stereotyping while doing little to improve police-minority relations (Ungerleider, 1992). Educating police officers about different cultures may have the opposite effect of reinforcing a view of "them" as really different and deserving of differential treatment (Holdaway, 1996). Few police services have the resources—or the courage—to conduct anti-racist training that seeks to uproot the racist and discriminatory aspects of police behaviour (see Kivel, 1996).

In short, police in Canada have come under pressure from different quarters. Urban police work under stressful conditions: Split-second decisions have to be made over matters of life and death in environments that rarely appreciate the pressure cooker of contemporary policing. Compounding the pressures of police work is the need to appear efficient and in control at all times (James and Warren, 1995). Allegations of harassment, brutality, double standards, intimidation, abuse, corruption, and racism have fuelled the fires of criticism of police. Additional questions arise over police effectiveness and efficiency in a society that is increasingly diverse, ever-changing, and more uncertain. Loss of public confidence raises certain questions over breakdowns in police-minority relations: Is police misconduct an isolated act or is it pervasive and structurally rooted? Is policing marred by a few "bad apples" or is the system "rotten to the core"? What is it about policing that creates "bad" officers? Does the "badness" reside in: (a) the recruitment and selection process; (b) the nature of police work; (c) the organizational framework; (d) negative work experiences; or (e) the type of personality supposedly attracted to policing?

The concept of multicultural policing is seen as one way of deflecting this potential crisis in police legitimacy, while restoring public confidence in policing a multicultural society (Fleras et al., 1989). Recruitment of minority police officers is widely heralded as a first step in restoring community confidence in law enforcement. Specific initiatives have been designed and implemented to secure a proportion of visible minority officers commensurate with their numbers in the local population. Additional attempts to "multiculturalize" the police have incorporated looser weight and height restrictions which traditionally discriminated against minority applicants. Of those initiatives at the forefront of multicultural policing, few have had the profile or potential of community policing (Fleras, 1998). Broadly speaking, community policing is about redefining police work by reworking its relationship to the communities the police serve and protect. More specifically, community policing can be seen as a reaction to the limitations of conventional policing styles that had the effect of distancing police from ethnic community involvement (Bayley, 1994). Professional crime-fighting models promoted a view of police as a highly trained and mechanized force for crime control and law enforcement. Police work could be described as incident-driven and complaint-reactive, and its effectiveness was measured by random car patrols, rapid response rates, and high conviction and clearance rates. Structurally, police were organized into a paramilitaristic model of bureaucracy involving a top-down chain of command and control. Rewards and promotions were allocated on the basis of the big catch or unswerving loyalty to the force. The fortress mentality at the heart of the policing subculture fostered a police sensitivity to outside criticism, reinforcing a commitment to protect one another and a reluctance to police themselves, and helped to create an institutional working environment that encouraged paranoia and distrust rather than co-operation with the community (Eng, 2000).

By contrast, community policing is about transforming the police from a "force" to a "service." It can be defined as a strategy that police have adopted to deter crime by successfully engaging the public as partners in crime prevention (see Moir and Moir, 1993). Community policing is about establishing a closer and meaningful partnership with the local community as part of a coherent strategy to prevent crime through proactive efforts at problem-solving. The community is defined as an active participant in crime prevention rather than a passive bystander. The police, in turn, are expected to shed their "crime-buster" image in exchange for proactive styles that embody a willingness to cooperate with increasingly diverse communities through establishment of liaison and communication (see Shusta et al., 1995). Five principles undergird the concept of community-based multicultural policing.

1. Partnership Perspective: A partnership status entails adjustments in police perception of the community. A partnership is committed to the ideal of police working with the community to prevent crime. A working partnership rejects a view of the police as experts with exclusive credentials for crime control. In its place is an image of police as "facilitators" and "resource personnel" who cooperate by working alongside citizens.

2. Prevention/Proactive: Arguably, all policing is concerned with crime prevention. Whereas conventional policing endorsed law enforcement as the main deterrent to criminal offending, community policing endorses prevention through community partnership as the preferred alternative. Proactive approaches attempt to deal with problems before they arise rather than after the fact ("an ounce of prevention = a pound of cure"). Prevention strategies revolve around proactive mechanisms designed by the community in consultation with the police.

3. Problem-solving: Problem-solving cuts to the core of community policing. Many have criticized the futility of continuous responses to recurrent incidents in the same area by a small number of repeat offenders. What is required is a style that diagnoses the underlying causes rather than just responding to symptoms (Saville and Rossmo, 1995). A problem-solving strategy seeks to: (a) isolate and identify the underlying causes of recurrent problems; (b) evaluate alternative solutions; (c) respond by applying one or more solutions; (d) monitor the impact; and (e) redesign solutions if feedback is negative.

4. Power-sharing: A commitment to power-sharing with the community is essential to community policing (Doone, 1989). Without a sharing of power, community policing is simply tokenism or a publicity stunt to offload responsibility for burdensome tasks. Police are under pressure to share power by loosening up organizational structures, transferring authority and resources to communities, and implementing mutually agreed-upon goals. The ability to identify, prioritize, and apply creative solutions to problems by way of meaningful input into the design and delivery of programs is also predicated to some degree on a sharing of power.

5. Pluralism:The crime control model, with its one-size-fits-all mentality, cannot possibly define police arrangements that are acceptable to minority women and men (see LaPrairie, 1992). In reaction to this standardization, community policing is thought to be more capable of reflecting the social and political conditions of a wide range of minority communities, because its principles of organization are more flexible and pragmatically oriented. The objective is a culturally safe policing, one that acknowledges the pervasiveness of the cultural factors of both providers and recipients in influencing outcomes.

To sum up: A commitment to diversifying policing cannot be taken lightly. With Canada in the midst of a demographic revolution, it is only a matter of time before mandatory measures are imposed to improve effective multicultural policing for all sectors of Canadian society. Policing from top to bottom must become better acquainted with the multicultural community in terms of its varied needs, entitlements, demands, and expectations. A commitment to diversity also compels the police to view cultural differences as a resource of potential value in preventing crime. The principles of community policing appear to offer the best multicultural option for doing what is workable, necessary, and fair. But until there is a collective mindset shift toward acceptance of multicultural communities as partners in preempting crime, confidence in policing will continue to be contested.

Courts and Corrections

The court system in Canada is similar to the United States. Both are adversarial in principle and practice; each also utilizes the same key doctrines, including presumption of innocence, the right to trial within a reasonable period of time, and reasonable doubt as the burden of proof. Differences exist, to be sure, including no statute of limitations for most crimes in Canada. Court sentences are different too: While state-federal distinctions in the United States reflect the type of offence (Cunningham, 1998), Canadians are sentenced to provincial or federal prisons on the basis of sentence length, with federal institutions reserved for sentences over two years.

Additional similarities reflect the processing of young people through the courts. Few jurisdictions have attracted as much attention or notoriety as the enactment of the national Young Offenders Act in 1994. Canada, like the United States, adopted a separate court for juvenile offenders at the turn of the 20th century. Initially based on a paternalistic model of early intervention and individualized sentencing, the YOA bestows all due process rights afforded to adults as well as some additional protections for youths between 12 and 17 years of age (Cunningham, 1998). Aspects of the original juvenile system remain in place: limits on the length of custody (two years maximum for most crimes); a ban on publication of the names of offenders and the destruction of all incriminating records; sentencing based on the characteristics of the offender rather than solely on the severity of offence; and absence of jury trials except for charges of murder. Since the 1990s, however, both Canada and the United States appear intent on redesigning the youth system along more adult lines, emphasizing protection rather than rehabilitation, particularly in response to perceived lenience in sentencing (Makin, 1999).

The corrections system in general is equally prone to criticism. Of Canada's 30 million population, about 34 000 can be found in prison at any given time, reflecting an adult population rate of 115 per 100 000 of population. The vast majority of the 119 000 adult admissions each year go into provincial prisons (114 600), with federal penitentiaries for those serving sentences of two years and over. Prisons are expected to carry out a variety of often conflicting functions, including:

- punishment: retribution for those who break the law
- protection: isolate offender from society
- rehabilitation: to reform the offender and preclude future offending through education
- deterrence: serve as a warning to the rest of society.

Efforts to balance each of these functions have proven largely unsuccessful. Punitive measures tend to prevail, and this retributive mentality has drawn criticism (Law Commission, 1999). Moves to reform the prison system are currently in place, with emphasis on replacing the somewhat sanitized and depersonalized procedures of the state with a more personal and interactive dimension (Lozoff, 1998). Rather than obsessing on retribution or punishment, there is a shift toward a restorative approach in the trial and sentencing which stresses responsibility, restitution, and healing. Offenders not deemed to be a risk to the public can be released under conditions that include house arrest, restitution, treatment, or community work. Nevertheless, confusion and skepticism are mounting regarding the effectiveness and regulation of conditional and alternative sentencing (Makin, 1999).

Corrections in Canada are widely criticized. Yet the prison system in the United States strikes many as a classic example of a solution gone amok. Prisons are now the fastest growing segment of the U.S. economy. Despite falling crime rates, a whole prison-industrial complex has evolved to replace the military-industrial complex of the Cold War (Lozoff, 1999). As a world leader in incarcerations, despite a booming economy, some 2 million Americans are locked up in state and federal prisons, another 3.4 million are on probation, and .7 million are on parole. National incarceration costs total $60 billion per year, in contrast to a national welfare budget of $25 billion. As prisons flourish, spending on rehabilitation inside the prison and prevention outside (for example, job training and early childhood education) has declined, with the result that states such as California spend more on prisons than on higher education. Nearly half of those imprisoned are minority women and men, and minority communities now constitute 70 percent of all new admissions (Kenna, 1999). Nearly one in three young Black men in the mid-1990s was under criminal justice supervision, including prison, probation, parole, or pretrial release. Chances of imprisonment are 30 percent for Black males, according to Kathleen Kenna (1999), 16 percent for Hispanics, and 4 percent for Whites. While the United States lectures other countries on human rights abuses, the American prison system has been widely condemned for tolerating repressive control methods and physical and sexual abuses that also violate international treaties on human rights. And while major and violent crimes have dropped to their lowest levels since 1973, prison construction is soaring to record levels, particularly private prisons that have become a profitable business that cash-strapped communities are eagerly courting.

RETHINKING CRIMINAL JUSTICE

The criminal justice system is under pressure to revise procedures and sentencing for aboriginal peoples. In response to the disproportionate number of aboriginal persons in correctional institutes, in part because of systemic discrimination, in part due to socio-economic deprivation, the courts have acknowledged the need for greater aboriginal control over responses to crime in the community. Measures include separate justice structures such as band policing with jurisdiction over the reserve, to the use of restorative justice principles in which the community cooperates with the judge to find non-incarceration alternatives as sanctions, while upholding culturally sensitive programming within the prison system (Cunningham, 1998). The more holistic approach to crime endorsed by aboriginal peoples would appear to be in conflict with the abstract and adversarial approach implicit in mainstream courts.

Rationale

Nearly four hundred years of sustained contact and interaction have left aboriginal peoples-government relations in a state of disarray and despair. The imposition of a colonialistic framework in this country exerted a powerful negative effect on aboriginal peoples (Alfred, 1999). In some cases, government policies deliberately undermined the viability of aboriginal communities in the never-ending quest to divest aboriginal peoples of their land, culture, and tribal authority. In other cases, the demise of aboriginal peoples came about through unobtrusive, yet equally powerful measures pertaining to education and missionization. In still other cases, the often unintended effects of possibly well-intentioned but ultimately misguided programs—for example, residential schools—have had lingering repercussions on marginalizing aboriginal peoples (Milloy, 1999).

To say that Canada's criminal justice system has experienced a profoundly troubled relationship with aboriginal peoples would classify as a classic understatement (Royal Commission, 1996; Green, 1998). Aboriginal involvement with the criminal justice system is deplorable as well. Nearly three-quarters of aboriginal males will have been incarcerated in a correctional centre at some point by the age of twenty-five. Aboriginal inmates occupy 64 percent of the federal penitentiary population in western Canada, according to Statistics Canada, but only about 12 percent of the prairie population (*Globe and Mail,* 2 Feb., 1998). Admittedly, some degree of caution must be exercised: Statistics may be misleading, since offenders may be convicted for relatively minor offences and serve time for offences that require only a fine. As well, only a small number of individuals may get in trouble with the law, but on a repeated basis (Buckley, 1992). Nevertheless, the statistics are damning: The revolving door of incarceration and recidivism has stripped many aboriginal peoples of any positive self-concept, in effect leading to self-fulfilling cycles of despair and decay. Nor can we disregard the sometimes disastrous consequences of often well-intentioned, but misguided government policies and programs (Shkilnyk, 1985). For too many, prisons are an ominous and terrifying experience; for others, their level of indifference to White justice stymies the deterrent or stigma value of prisons (Waldram, 1997). For others, the court process is an alien process. On one side are the values upon which Canada's White criminal justice system is based, including an emphasis on punishing the deviant to ensure individual conformity and to protect other members of society. On the other side are aboriginal concepts of justice, with their emphasis on healing and reconciliation as a way of restoring peace and equilibrium within the community. While the dominant society seeks to control actions that are regarded as potentially harmful and disruptive to society, aboriginal justice is concerned with reconciling the individual with his or her conscience and with the family and community that has been wronged. The punitive and adversarial focus of conventional Canadian criminal justice stands in sharp contrast to a more conciliatory approach that emphasizes restoration of peaceful relations between offender and the community. Rather than isolating the crime and judging it on the basis of abstract principles of justice, there is a significant emphasis on a holistic approach to justice that integrates the spiritual with the social, cultural, and economic (see Green, 1998 for additional information). This discord between fundamentally opposed principles of justice is reflected in different ways, but especially in the disproportionately high rates of aboriginal incarceration and recidivism. The limited recognition of aboriginal needs and values is best exemplified by the fly-in circuit courts that visit communities once a month, pronounce judgment on the cases presented to them, and then depart. Moreover, jails are neither the solution nor can they be considered a safe place which encourages disclosure, openness, and healing. As one Yukon elder explained (cited in Green, 1998:18):

> Jail doesn't help anyone. A lot of our people could have been healed a long time ago if it weren't for jail. Jail hurts them more and then they come out really bitter. In jail all they learn is "hurt and bitter."

Such bitterness undermines the very purpose of contemporary sentencing, given its emphasis on respect for law and the maintenance of a just, peaceful, and safe society.

Efforts to improve the relationship of the criminal justice system to aboriginal peoples have taken several routes. The possibilities fall into four categories: (1) modify the existing system to ensure equal treatment through removal of discriminatory barriers and prejudicial attitudes; (2) create a more inclusive criminal justice system through the inclusion of aboriginal values and personnel where appropriate; (3) create a parallel system of criminal justice for aboriginal peoples, one that is modelled on the conventional system but run entirely by aboriginal people; and (4) establish an indigenous criminal justice system by aboriginal people for aboriginal people that reflects, reinforces, and advances aboriginal needs, concerns, and aspirations. Most initiatives to date entail an inclusiveness model: Enhanced community participation in the sentencing and supervision of aboriginal offenders in aboriginal communities is encouraged by way of alternative measures both inside and outside of the criminal justice system (Green, 1998). Exploring sentencing alternatives for aboriginal offenders may reduce incarceration rates by diverting offenders from the court to community-based mediation committees such as sentencing circles. For those in prison, aboriginal peoples are demanding recognition of their right to religious freedom by incorporating their spiritual practices as therapy throughout the healing process (Waldram, 1997). However, no one should underestimate the challenges of incorporating a system at odds with Western principles, given that neither law nor the criminal justice system can be regarded as a neutral set of principles innocent of meaning or intent (1999, Law Commissioner of Canada, Discussion Paper, "From Restorative Justice to Transformative Justice": Ottawa). A comparison of aboriginal versus conventional criminal justice systems is illustrated in Table 6–1.

Time will tell whether restorative justice principles are effective in advancing the healing and renewal process. Many questions remain unanswered in redefining the relationship of aboriginal peoples to the criminal justice system. Should there be one set of rules for all

TABLE 6–1 Comparison of Criminal Justice Systems	
Canadian CJS	**Aboriginal CJS**
crime is transgression against the state	crime is rupture in the relationship between victim, community, and wrongdoer
criminal justice system is primary source of social control	community is primary source of social control
crime is framed in legal terms and abstract principles of right and wrong	crime is framed by how it affects community, victims, and wrongdoers. Emphasis is on context and consequences of the action, taking into account the social, cultural, and spiritual
process is adversarial, passive in outcome	process is conciliatory and cooperative, and offender involvement is encouraged in healing the breach
restitution is to the state	restitution is to victim and to community in hopes of restoring social order
punishment focus	focus is on healing and rehabilitation
victim ignored	victim is foregrounded by restoring sense of control over one's life, while encouraging offenders to take responsibility for their actions
focus on mental state of offender to determine guilt and assign punishment	holistic focus on the social and spiritual needs of offender to determine what went wrong, what can be done to ease the suffering, and how to deter future occurences.
benefits reflect the principle that the criminal justice system is a law unto itself	benefits are to capitalize on the transformative potential of restorative justice to create a more just society.

Canadians, or should justice be customized to reflect the diverse realities of aboriginal peoples? Should individuals take full responsibility for their actions, or must historical and social circumstances be incorporated into any assessment of wrongdoing? Should all crime be punished equally, or is best to ensure that differences are taken into account when decisions are made? Is it racist and paternalistic to imply that a racial or ethnic background merits special consideration in sentencing? Or does such an enlightened concession acknowledge the importance of the social and the cultural in securing a truly multicultural society? Efforts to bring about reforms have proven a problem, and time will tell if a rethinking of the criminal justice system will pay off for aboriginal peoples.

FAMILY AND DOMESTICITY

FRAMING THE PROBLEM

Families are generally conceded to be one of the oldest and most durable of all human institutions. Their centrality to human social existence is widely acknowledged. Most of us are born into a family; our primary point of contact with the world is filtered through family experiences; many are involved in establishing and nurturing new families, and younger family members may assume responsibility for the elderly or infirmed. Like many other institutions, the family constitutes an interrelated system of rules, roles, and relationships for meeting the universal human needs of security, subsistence, and survival. These needs reflect two levels of analysis. For society, these functions extend to include: producing new members; socializing and controlling children; serving the economy by consuming goods; conveying cultural values and beliefs; and regulating sexual relations. For individuals in search of intimacy, a family setting promises a context of security and self-actualization by virtue of its rootedness in one place. Families also serve as a primary social environment for learning about the facts of social life, including: gender relations; diversity and minorities; the care and treatment of the elderly; and patterns of intimacy. Of particular importance is the primacy of the family in the process of identity formation. Notions about who we are or would like to be are first nurtured within the supportive confines of the family (McAdoo, 1999). Not surprisingly, the domestic context is often regarded as one of the most satisfying and fulfilling aspects of human existence.

Yet another picture is apparent, and the flip side of family as haven cannot be casually brushed aside. The same aspirations that foster self-esteem may be crushed by the very pathologies that erode domestic arrangements. Violence and spousal abuse are as common as domestic bliss, while inequities within domestic arrangements are deeply entrenched and resistant to reform. The modern nuclear family is structured around an untrained and isolated pairing of strangers, both of whom may be poorly equipped even to look after themselves, let alone to carry a heavy functional load under trying circumstances. By the same token, some of the historic functions associated with the family, such as education, have been co-opted by state agencies, with a corresponding diminishment in status and role. To add insult to injury, there is mounting concern over the relevance of parents and parenting: Studies suggest that parental impact on children's behaviour is minimal compared to the role of peers or the media, especially outside the home context (Harris, 1998). Yet evidence is equally compelling in pointing out that poor parenting, rather than class, is the prime cause of problem children (Carey, 1999). And pressures continue to mount, especially on the financial front, where the average after-tax family income, at $45 605 in 1997, is still five percent less than what families earned in 1980 (Carey, 1999). Not surprisingly, a majority of Canadians in a national survey of 2499 adults agreed that the family is in a "national crisis" (Mitchell, 1999). Canadian parents are adrift, depressed, and stressed out; all mired in a confusing patchwork of family policies and conflicting expectations; most are desperately seeking a balance between home and work; and many are unsure whether parents (including themselves) are fit for the job of raising children (Shellenbarger, 1999).

There is much to commend in the observation that: (a) families are central to our social existence; and (b) the reality of family life is far more complex than the sugar-coated fantasy portrayed by politicians who bandy the term about to reassure or intimidate (Kendall et al., 1999). Nostalgic images of the family continue to be circulated by the media where the family has long served as a repository of moral values and a refuge from a chaotic world. Some of the more popular images include the family as suburban, materially endowed, socially embedded, and well adjusted, with parents in high-powered careers and in charge of precociously bright and self-reliant children. Perception of this ideal family type is often endorsed as the bedrock of social morality. The decline of family values, accordingly, is viewed by many as symptomatic of moral decay and social disintegration. Yet there is another image of the modern, urban family. This made-for-TV spoof, "Married...With Children" image is characterized by an absence of kinship circles; split by divorced parents; destroyed by domestic abuse; hounded by mouthy kids; tainted by bored wives and philandering husbands; and ridiculed by critics of society. With the breakdown in boundaries and scripts, moreover, life choices are constrained even further by a need to balance career, family, and personal choices, while attending to childcare, elder care, family-unfriendly bosses, burnout, job sharing, and daily emergencies (Shellenbarger, 1999). Complicating this picture is yet another contemporary snapshot. Conventional family structures are not necessarily havens in a heartless world. Some constitute regressive forces at odds with contemporary human aspirations, especially in perpetuating violence toward women and authoritarian control over children. The decline of this "hell on earth" is not to be lamented, in other words, but applauded at every turn.

The institution of family and domesticity is so pivotal to human social existence that any changes are likely to elicit passionate responses. Changes within the family and patterns of domesticity are known to reflect as well as be reflective of broader societal transformations (Furstenberg Jr., 1999). That is, the institutions of family and marriage are socially constructed and evolving in response to social changes, political debates, and ideological shifts. The majority of Canadian families a half of a century ago consisted of two adults in a permanent union with three to five children. At present, blended or reconstituted families are as much the rule as the exception because of divorce and remarriage (Vanier Institute of the Family, 1998). And for most Canadian adults, marriage and family will be the most political institution they will enter, a commitment of a more highly calibrated complexity than the gushy "diamonds are forever ads" would have us believe (Kingston, 1999). For all the turmoil and handwringing dismay, the family remains the central institution in the lives of most Canadians, with an overwhelming majority declaring its importance to their lives (Kendall et al., 1999). For better or worse, for richer or poorer, the family provides satisfying emotional experiences of importance to many. A 1994 survey by the Angus Reid Group found that 83 percent of Canadians named family life the greatest joy in their lives, with 94 percent of married couples with children (and 78 percent of single parents) hopping aboard the happiness bandwagon (*Transition*, 1994). Even young people are highly supportive: Of the 774 185 Canadian students who responded to a UNICEF-sponsored national survey on rights, 24.2 percent proclaimed their families as most important to them (Canadian Press, 1999). When young adults were asked in a *Time* magazine survey what they would want most if stranded on a desert island, 29 percent stated their parents, 24 percent said music, 21 percent their computers, 15 percent their books, and 10 percent their television (*New Zealand Herald*, "Fill in the Blanks Generation," August 10, 1997). Despite this groundswell of support, the contemporary family is proving hazardous to people's health, and the crisis in the family is widely acknowledged (Mitchell, 1999), with fears of disappearance unless corrective measures are invoked.

Few terms have managed to elicit such a wide range of emotion as the "f-word." From its endorsement as the cornerstone of a healthy society to its vilification as evil personified, the family continues to reassure and be revered by some, while provoking and dismaying others, with confusion and uncertainty sandwiched in between because of social changes and public demands. But it has yet to be determined whether such disarray or debate is positive or negative, or "simply transitional" (Eichler, 1988). Tension and conflict are inevitable in any transformational process, but "family values" are especially contested and challenged. This chapter attempts to put a positive spin on this crisis by suggesting that what humans have socially constructed may be de-constructed should the arrangements prove inappropriate. Our collective genius lies in this ability to reconstruct institutional arrangements to meet the emergent realities of a diverse, changing, and postmodern world. In the process a host of questions are raised in determining the magnitude of family and domesticity as a social problem, including:

- Is the family in crisis? Evidence suggests a declining birthrate (in 1997, 1.55 children per woman, but replacement rate is 2.1) partly because young Canadian couples cannot afford the luxury of having children (Cherney, 1999).

- Does the family matter in light of contemporary developments and demands? Have media and peer groups overtaken family as the primary agents of socialization?

- What is the nature of the changes to the rules, roles, expectations, and relationships within the family—demise, transition, reincarnation, or opportunity? For example, what is the point of parenting in light of theories that suggest a child's peer group rather than parents (other than genes and subsistence) prevail in shaping personality, attitudes, and relationships (Harris, 1998)?

- In what ways has the traditional nuclear family evolved into a contested site, involving a terrain of political struggles and resistance because of diverse expectations and oppositional ideologies (McDaniel, 1998)?

- How does the structure of a modern nuclear family contribute to domestic abuse and spousal violence? What cultural factors have distorted the dynamics of family violence behind the cliche, the "stranger is danger, the familiar is safe" (Miller, 2000)?

- What are some of the contemporary family unions that are challenging the primacy of so-called "natural" family structures (*The Report*, "Save the Family, Save the World," Dec. 6th, 1999)? Why are alternative family arrangements often regarded as deficient or deviant, subject to criticism and control, while blatant weaknesses within nuclear families are widely ignored or excused (Miller, 2000)?

- What is the nature of the family in crisis? Is it a case of families changing too much or social institutions having changed too little?

- Are escalating divorce rates a sign of progress or regress, or simply an indication of an institution in transition? Is human nature "socially constructed," and to what extent is this nature deformed and distorted by oppressive institutions such as the patriarchal family?

- How "natural" to humans are institutionalized forms of marriage, family, and domesticity, given that: (a) there is nothing natural or normal about two strangers establishing a permanent and monogamous household to discharge a host of functions pertaining to life and love; (b) humans may be predisposed to loosely informal arrangements (including what we call infidelity or adultery), and the institutionalization of such arrangements goes "against the grain," (Fisher, 1997); and (c) contemporary culture, especially the media, conspire to foster disenchantment with the present in exchange for fantasies about the future?

Responses to these questions provide an organizational framework for analyzing the family and domesticity from a social problems' perspective. These responses also furnish a basis for deconstructing an institution that is being buffeted by the winds of change, while casting light on the reconstructing of new domestic arrangements. This chapter begins with the premise that neither marriage nor the family is dying or irrelevant. Rather, contemporary families embody institutional arrangements that are experiencing a crisis of confidence in what they are, a crisis of legitimacy in what they are doing, and an identity crisis in what they are supposed to do. In shifting from the scripted formats of the past to the increasingly provisional arrangements at present, families are now seen as contested sites of many social problems with potentially powerful implications for society. And a host of new problems is created by this transformation in marriage, family, and domesticity from practical arrangements because of social duty, to increasingly egalitarian partnerships in search of personal fulfillment. This chapter addresses the extent to which families in Canada are evolving into a variety of diverse arrangements that not only reflect viable options in their own right, but also challenge the cult of patriarchal domesticity (Miller 2000). In normalizing the nuclear family ideal as natural and inevitable, while "problematizing" alternatives as inferior, unstable, or irrelevant, people are being set up for failure (Baker, 1996; McDaniel, 1998). Anti-social reactions to perceptions of failure make it doubly important to approach the family as a social problem.

The notion of the family as a social problem is conveyed in five ways: First, the modern nuclear family is defined as a site of social problems, ranging in scope from domestic abuse to arrested personal development, since individuals are expected to conform to roles that are inappropriate with the onset of the 21st century. Second, the family is a problem because of people's inflated expectations about domestic life, together with the inevitable disappointment that results from falling into this delusional trap of trying to live happily ever after. Third, despite diversity and change within families, cultural norms are failing to keep pace with social changes, and this perceptual gap invariably diminishes the status and viability of non-conventional families. Fourth, the family itself constitutes a site of inequality, given the disparities in power and privilege between partners and parents and children. And fifth, families are the building blocks of society in terms of social control and regulation of behaviour. Their demise may have a disruptive impact on society as individuals are cast adrift without a firm moral compass to guide, define, or criticize. Two assumptions prevail: If families are the site of social problems, the causes of these social problems must reside in the institutional structures of society rather than in individuals. Second, the normalcy of family structures is problematic in its own right. Domestic problems are not an aberration or departure from some ideal norm, but a "normal" component of a functioning partriarchal, male-dominated power structure (Miller, 2000). Insofar as family contexts reflect relationships of inequality within contexts of power, these unequal relations need to be explored in terms of how they are created, expressed, maintained, challenged, and transformed. The conclusion is unequivocal: Any solution to the social problems of family and domesticity depends on challenging social structures and inequities that created the problems in the first place (McDaniel, 1998). This position does not absolve individuals of responsibility when things go wrong. Rather it acknowledges the contextuality of people's choices in a world in which options and opportunities are more restricted than many would like to believe.

FAMILY AS SOCIAL CONSTRUCTION

Sociologists are very good at analyzing the structure and dynamics of contemporary modern societies. They are less adept at proving whether their conceptualizations are cross-culturally valid. They are even less keen on assessing the universality of human thought or behaviour, given their largely singular focus on the West. This dearth of a comparative mindset is evident from the study of family and domesticity. Questions are left unanswered: To what extent do marriage and family constitute universal categories of human institutional experience? In what ways does the logic of family and marriage differ from that of the West? Are current descriptions of non-Western families an imposition of ethnocentric discourses upon unsuspecting realities? To what extent are family types a series of socially constructed conventions rather than something natural or normal about the world?

Admittedly, the processes associated with establishing a household may be universally applicable. All societies must find ways of regulating sexual behaviour, procreating, socializing children, dividing labour, and transmitting property and inheritance. These relationships are sometimes formalized into institutions and practices called marriage and family. Yet few formal institutions exist in traditional tribal societies that resemble their Western counterparts. Moreover, the rationale behind non-Western families differs from a Western logic, making it doubly important to put things into a global perspective. The ideas and practices associated with marriage and family have evolved over time, with the result that different forms and functions are evident, depending on time and place. Even our concept of a nuclear family, with its explicit division of labour and reciprocal obligations between a restricted number of people, may be of relatively recent vintage, bolstered by nostalgia and a powerful myth-making machine (Stacey, 1990; 1997). Moreover, as a *Life* magazine special on the family concludes, no particular family form guarantees success, and no particular form is doomed to failure, reinforcing the fact that how a family functions on the inside is more important than how it looks from the outside. Diversity rules, in other words, and a relativist attitude toward cultural differences and similarities is indispensible in unlocking the logic behind this most basic of human institutions. Such an orientation also confirms the socially constructed nature of family—not as something naturally out there—but as a convention and human accomplishment that varies across time and place.

Defining the Family

Even the most obvious of social phenomena can pose definitional dilemmas. The concept of family is an especially instructive example, since the term is applied to different interactions, identities, and relationships. Consider the cross-section of family households taken from the U.S. Bureau of the Census (1980). They include households with a father as sole wage-earner, a mother as full-time homemaker, and at least one child; a household in which both husband and wife are wage-earners, with more than one child at home; households of married couples with no children at home or who are childless; households headed by a single parent (mother or father) with one or more children at home; households of unrelated persons living together; single person households; and households that include relatives other than children. If we add same-sex couples and ethnic families to this already teeming category, the perils of collapsing such variation into a single definition become obvious.

Defining a family is not merely an academic exercise. Revenue Canada relies on a definition for various tax purposes; Immigration Canada depends on one to determine who qualifies to get in under the family category (Owens, 1999). Despite increased demands for a definition, says Anne Mason, a project coordinator with the Vanier Institute of the Family, the family is a messy concept that is difficult to pin down because it is constantly changing in response to legal challenges in a rights-driven society. Complicating the definitional process is a growing politicization in defining the concept of family. To ensure inclusiveness by incorporating as many arrangements as possible, the Vanier Institute defines a family as "any combination of two or more persons who are bound together over time by ties of mutual consent, birth, and/or adoption/placement, and who together, assume responsibilities for variant combinations of some of the following: physical maintenance and care of group members; addition of new members through procreation or adoption; socialization of children; social control of members; production, consumption, and distribution of goods and services; and affective nurturing love" (cited in Owens, 1999:A-7). Others, including the Social Sciences and Humanities Research Council, prefer to define the family as "a group of individuals who are related by affection, kinship, dependency, or trust." To get around this politically fraught notion of family, the term "household" may be employed, albeit not to everyone's satisfaction.

Most would have little difficulty in recognizing diverse domestic arrangements as broadly "family" or "household." Many are tempted to define "family" as an enduring social entity composed of a male and female, together with their 1.7 children. Yet not all households conform to this model of domesticity. As Margrit Eichler (1983) has noted, the family (or household) will vary in definition depending on which dimensions are emphasized, including procreative (production of children), socialization, sexuality (sex both premarital and extramarital), residential (where the family resides), economic (financial obligations and interdependence), and emotional or companionship. To avoid the taint of ethnocentrism, this text defines a family as a relatively durable relationship between individuals who are conjoined in some kind of domestic arrangement for practical and/or personal reasons. This domestic arrangement involves those persons who are related by blood, marriage, or adoption; share a common residence or partake of shared meals; experience a sense of separateness from other domestic units; define a division of labour; and possess a set of mutual obligations and responsibilities (between spouses, and between spouses and offspring). This definition is broad enough to encompass a diverse range of practices and images, yet sufficiently specific to retain a focused subject matter, thus averting the paradox of defining everything as family, with the result that nothing is family. Deconstructing this social construction yields a host of interesting variations in family arrangements and types, each of which reflects a distinct logic and situational adjustments.

Deconstructing Families: Global Perspectives

The social and constructed dimensions of human families confirm their relativity to time and space. There is nothing natural and normal about family arrangements, despite vested interests to make them appear so. Rather, families constitute conventions that have been created through adaptation to particular environments. A global and comparative perspective is important in framing the socially constructed conventionality of the family. Logically, a family is constructed around the irreducibility of a mother-child relation. The incorporation of males (father, husband, brother, son) for protective, procreative, or productive purposes completes the picture. Still, there is nothing inherently natural about creating a household by conjoining a "husband" and "wife." It is just as natural (and logical) for a woman to rely on her brothers for protection as to marry a stranger, with all the accompanying risks of the unknown. This comparison between conjugal vs. consanguineal ("blood") families accomplishes three objectives: It demonstrates the variation in logic and dynamics underlying the expression of marriage and family; it puts the monogomous, nuclear family in Canada into a sharper relief, both historically and spatially; and it normalizes the presence of both diversity and change by deconstructing those customary practices that we routinely take for granted. And, in a multicultural society such as Canada, a commitment to understanding diversity is hardly a luxury or option: Personal success and social survival depend on it.

The logic of non-Western families appears to be at odds with Western practices. Family and marriage in our society entail a relationship between individuals, voluntarily entered into on the basis of free choice and romantic love. Such an arrangement was hardly the case in the past when parents and relatives of the bride and groom were involved in matchmaking decisions. Even at present, marriages involving high-ranking families involve less personal choice than would normally be the case (think of the royal family in Britain). This freedom of choice is reflected and reinforced by the evolution of romantic love. More so than in the past, North American society is consumed by the ideal of love as a prerequisite for a long-term relationship. Elsewhere, however, the concept of love (or lust) as a basis for a practical, lifelong relationship is dismissed as aberrant at best, compulsive foolishness at worst, especially when taking political and family considerations into account (Skolnick, 1978). Marriages were much more likely to be arranged on the strength of kinship obligations, economic calculation, or political expediency. Contrary to popular belief, even North American marriages are hardly random or capricious. Statistically, there is a high probability that people will marry someone of similar socio-economic status, religious background, and geographic proximity.

Many non-Western societies do not conform with Eurocentric ideals of family and marriage as a binding but voluntary compact between consenting adults. Marriages are much more likely to be interpreted as a pragmatic relationship involving a transaction (or exchange) between two corporate, kinship groups, encompassing a reciprocal and practical exchange of rights, duties, and obligations. Of particular note in these transactions was the transfer of rights over the productive and reproductive skills of women from her birth family to her new family. Unlike the situation in North America, the decision to marry was rarely left up to the concerned individuals. Too much was considered at risk in abdicating such weighty matters to flighty youth. Nor was the proposed relationship conducted between individuals, but reflected a conjoining of kin groups with a corresponding exchange of obligations and goods. Moreover, the concept of family in many non-Western communities is an open and public affair with regard to child rearing and sharing of resources. Compare this with the much more private and individualistic nature of the nuclear family. The role of the group in deciding who establishes households is critical in the closely knit confines of traditional communities. This is not to say that personal choice is non-existent or unimportant. Relatives may be less concerned with relatively unimportant proposals for marriage, while the introduction of a wage economy has loosened the grip of elders in determining who can marry whom. Still, few would deny the existence of a logic at variance with the Western ideal of family and domesticity.

Extended Family

Extended families are by far the most common type of family, if measured cross-culturally. They tend to proliferate in contexts with a relatively secure source of subsistence, low levels of geographical mobility, and the presence of immovable property as a primary source of wealth creation and inheritance. They also are common in agriculturally oriented societies where cooperative hands are critical to productivity and success. The extended family can be defined as a complex household of smaller family units of at least three generations, consisting of parents, one or more of their married children, their spouses, and their unmarried offspring. This combination of conjugal and consanguineal bonds cohabits in the sense of occupying a single dwelling while cooperating to achieve subsistence goals. Variations can occur on this basic model, such as the "modified" extended family, in which people cooperate but live separately.

The benefits of an extended family should be clear. The larger the size of the family, the more equitable is the workload. Expanded size also broadens the range of role models to emulate; enhances the circle of intimacy and support, especially in times of emergency; reduces the strain of sustained interaction with a small number of intimates; and encourages the pooling of resources for survival or wealth creation. Compared to a small but intense circle of spouses and offspring, extended families offer variety, flexibility, and a "diffuseness" that may work to the advantage of individual members. Polynesian families reflected an ideal of practicality and resourcefulness. The whanau (or extended household) was composed of a domestic unit of three or four generations of families who cooperated with one another in economic pursuits and child rearing (Ritchie and Ritchie, 1978). Children up to the age of two were indulged by attentive parents; shortly thereafter, they were weaned away from parental control, and put under the charge of older siblings and age mates. Girls as young as six as well as the community at large assumed primary responsibility for the discipline, care, and supervision of the children. In time, children become dependent on age mates rather than their family for social and emotional needs, with the result that the unit of socialization was not the family per se, but rather the extended household as well as the "community" of peers and siblings. Children were perceived as part of a larger collectivity, in other words, rather than the exclusive property of the natural parents.

Children were highly valued in Polynesian society, and large families proved the norm rather than the exception. The importance of children rested not on their value as individuals, but as members of a productive community. Large numbers of children served as symbols of status and prestige; they provided extra hands for social support and economic activity; and in time they furnished a resource base for inter-tribal competition. Among the Maori as well as most Polynesian societies, adoption was extremely common, often viewed as a normal exchange with many positive benefits for everyone involved (Metge, 1976). Invariably, it took place between relatives (it was unthinkable to give your children away to strangers), was conducted in the open to assist unfortunate couples or to provide companionship for older couples. Not surprisingly, the institutional practice of adoption has been widely misinterpreted as excessively callous and immoral or as a sign of neglect. In the context of Polyneisan society, however, the adopting of a child represented a practical arrangement for dealing with the vagaries of human social life.

Plural Marriage Family

Plural marriage families are extremely common, particularly in those parts of the world where survival is not dependent on physical mobility. Families of this nature are more likely when the source of wealth or inheritance is immovable or unable to be divided. These two criteria are likely to be found in horticultural or agricultural societies. The preferred arrangement of polygamous partnered families "permits" a person to have several partners, although this ideal is not necessarily reflected in how many spouses an individual will have, given the demands of status, costs, and demographics (Peoples and Bailey, 1997). Two types predominated: In polyandrous families, a woman is allowed two or more husbands simultaneously (or is it a case of a man sharing his wife with another male?), while in polygamous families, it is the man who can have two or more wives. A productive unit is created by plural marriage families in which the different members pool their resources to enhance adaptation or success. Contrary to Western mindsets and the perception of pervasive jealousy in polyganous unions, relationships between the husband and his wives as well as among the wives may be relatively tranquil. Co-wives may cooperate across a range of activities, often encouraging husbands to take additional wives not only to alleviate the burden of their workload, but also to bolster the status and prestige of the household. In other cases, where rivalry or jealousy prevail, adjustments may be required to compensate older wives for displacement by younger wives. Polyandrous families may circumvent interpersonal strife and the ruinous division of male property by ensuring that women marry two or more brothers. In both types of family settings, a broader circle of intimacy may create a more supportive environment for raising and socializing children.

The Nuclear Family

In his classic study of marriage and family, George Peter Murdoch (1957) confirmed the universality of the nuclear family either as an independent unit in its own right or as the basic constituent of more complex households. This conclusion raises a host of questions: Do polygamous families constitute a unique arrangement? Or are they essentially two or more nuclear families who happen to share a common spouse? Similarly, to what extent are extended families a distinct type of household? Or are they merely a configuration of relatively independent nuclear families or fragments thereof, connected by ties to a common parent and shared living arrangements? Structurally, there is much to commend in establishing the nuclear family as the foundation stone of more complex arrangements. Yet such an assessment ignores the psychologically different realities implicit in extended or plural marriage families. Nor does it take into account new family types based on single parents and same-sex unions. It also overlooks the possibility of differences in the logic and dynamics that distinguish nuclear from non-nuclear families, despite similarities in function and process.

Nuclear families can be defined as a social and residential unit consisting of a married couple and their unmarried children who reside in a single dwelling apart from their immediate relatives (Gee, 1990). This observation is consistent with the Statistics Canada definition of a nuclear family as a relatively self-contained domestic arrangement involving parents and dependent children. Childless couples, single parents, and common-law unions are treated as nuclear types by Statistics Canada, in the sense that these alternatives are catalogued as temporary "departures" from the standard. The nuclear family is a popular type of arrangement in urban-industrial societies where: (a) the family ceases to serve as the unit of production; (b) the state assumes a number of key functions related to socialization and elderly care; (c) kin are less important because of comprehensive social security systems; and (d) geographical mobility is central in pursuit of subsistence and wealth (Gee, 1990; Tepperman and Richardson, 1991). It is interesting to note that nuclear-type family arrangements prevail at the other end of the evolutionary spectrum since a foraging lifestyle, too, is dependent on mobility for subsistence survival.

The inevitability or desirability of nuclear families is no longer taken for granted. The nuclear family continues to be celebrated by many as an ideal living arrangement that yields support, mutual assistance, nurturance, emotional satisfaction, protection, and positive socialization. Others are not so sure, and critics have depicted the nuclear family as contradictory and oppressive. Nuclear families are reproached as largely unstable arrangements at odds with individual needs in a changing society. To be sure, the very isolation and privacy of the nuclear family may have its benefits pertaining to social and physical mobility. Yet these intense emotional attachments can provoke conflict and violence when individuals are forced to rely on a small support group for a host of functional needs in contexts of relative isolation (Peoples and Bailey, 1997). In short, because of economic isolation and social dependency on few individuals, the "hothouse" quality of nuclear families can produce extremes of behaviour, from passion on the one hand, to raging hostility on the other, with unremitting boredom or indifference in the middle.

Not surprisingly, innovative ways of thinking about domesticity and the family are currently in vogue. There is growing acceptance of the nuclear family as historical and evolutionary rather than a natural (and eternal) domestic arrangement of the West. Its entrenchment as the Western ideal can be traced to the Industrial Age. Pre-industrial families tended to be larger, rooted in economic needs and social necessity, and based on material interests rather than on romance, love, sexual attraction, or companionship. They constituted a large and diverse household of kin, lodgers, and servants, in which the community often played a key role (Miller, 2000). With industrialization, as Marx and Engels noted, however, the face of the family shifted. Men became increasingly estranged from the domestic realm; conversely, women tended to withdraw from the public. Both became intensely dependent only on each other, unlike the past when husbands and wives constituted a cooperative economic unit of production within the context of the community. Even attitudes toward children are historically defined.

Children in the past may not have received the same attention, since few parents could afford to invest emotionally in time or concern. In contrast to a time when childhood was viewed as an insignficant transition, the modern family is child-centred. Childhood is a distinct social category, and parents are assigned the responsibility of nurturing and protecting children, thus reinforcing the concept of homemaking as the central mission of modern womanhood (Miller, 2000). The much-touted traditional nuclear family of a working dad, homemaking mum, two kids, with a house in the suburbs of "Pleasantville" is a product of our myth-making imagination (Stacey, 1990; 1997). That individuals are being asked to live up to this distortion in reality is nothing short of irresponsible, setting families up for failure, according to Stephanie Coontz in her book, *The Way We Never Were: American Families and the Nostalgia Trap* (Basicbooks, 1991).

Postmodern Families

The institutions of marriage and family come wrapped in packages of different shapes and sizes. The term "postmodern family" seems to capture this sense of diversity. In 1981, for example, married couples with children constituted 55.9 percent of all families in Canada; married couples without children, 28.1 percent; common-law couples with children, 1.9 percent; and common-law couples without children, 3.7 percent. Single-parent families constituted 11.3 percent. By 1995, married couples with children constituted 44.5 percent of all families, while married couples without children stood at 29.8 percent; common-law couples with children were at 5.2 percent, while common-law couples without children were at 6.7 percent. Lone-parent families had increased to 13.8 percent. Extended families (three-generation households) increased by 39 percent between 1986 and 1996, and now constitute 3 percent of the total. Similarly in the United States: The most common living arrangement is unmarried persons with no children, constituting about one-third of all households, double the percentage in 1972, according to the National Opinion Research Centre at the University of Chicago (Rueters, 1999). The traditional nuclear family constituted 26 percent of all households, down from 45 percent in 1972. These patterns may reflect the combination of more women in the workforce and relaxation of social norms regarding cohabitation, divorce, and children outside marriage.

In rejecting the normalization of modern nuclear families as the ideal or standard by which to judge others, the postmodern family does not posit a single alternative. A multiplicity of family arrangements is recognized instead that are inherently unstable and reconstituted, frequently in response to changing circumstances. Postmodern families include arrangements such as adult children returning to live at home (nearly 50 percent of unmarried men and women between 20 and 35 return to live at home); blended or reconstituted families; and same-sex families. This provisionality is not intended to diminish the legitimacy of these families as bona fide domestic arrangements. There is no intention of downgrading their status to that of a default option, either deviant or transitional. Nor is it sufficient to simply acknowledge the existence of these often expedient arrangements. Families that depart from the cult of the domestic ideal of "one-size-fits-all" are not problems. Nor should these families of "commitment" or "conviction" be labelled a deviation with no claim to legitimacy as real families (Miller, 2000). To the extent that such arrangements are just as capable as conventional families of assisting individuals to fulfill their full potential as humans, their status as bona fide families is widely accepted. Insofar as they represent departures from the tightly scripted notions of family a generation ago, postmodern families may be seen as a solution to a problem.

Single-Parent Family

Single-parent families are an emergent phenomenon in those contexts with sufficient infrastructure (state support) for supporting a parent-child relationship. The proliferation of single-parent families reflects a fundamental shift in attitudes in North American society. It also heralds a growing array of options for women because of increased economic independence and a more supportive social climate. Nearly half of all children in Canada and the United States may spend all or part of their childhood in a single-parent arrangement. Yet living with a single parent may have a negative effect on children, mentally and emotionally (Carey, 1998). According to a long-term study by Statistics Canada involving 23 000 children, guardians, and teachers, single-parent family children tend to be in poorer health, have more behavioural problems, do less well in school, and have poorer interactional skills with their peers or adults. Other studies disagree, arguing that anything is an improvement over an abusive domestic context (Milstone, 1999).

A common type of single-parent family among African-Americans is organized around the principle and practices of matrifocality. A matrifocal family is based on the centrality of a mother and her children. According to Ian Robertson (1987), nearly 59 percent of Black children in the United States by the mid-1980s lived with a single parent (usually the mother). About one-half of all children were born out of wedlock. While many males have taken their familial responsibilities seriously, others have not. Tough economic conditions, especially punishingly high unemployment rates for young men, have complicated the process of settling down and moving in. In place of a male as protector and provider is a circle of close kin that the mother-centred family relies on for assistance on a daily or emergency basis (Liebow, 1967). This network of kin (relatives) combine their resources and resourcefulness for security and survival in an unforgiving environment. Without reliance on extended family networks and patterns of cross-residential cooperation, most female-headed households would be in more dire circumstances (Sudarkasa, 1999).

In principle, there is nothing inherently wrong with these arrangements as a means of raising children and making ends meet (but see Murray and Herrnstein, 1995). Nevertheless, single-parents families, both Black and White, tend to be especially vulnerable to poverty. They also are subject to manipulation and control by state agencies, to the detriment of society at large. But female-headed households are not the cause of Black poverty, crime, or homelessness, since marital stability is not the same as family stability, and female-headed households may be stable over time (Sudarkasa, 1999). In short, it is important to discard the notion that only nuclear families can provide stability and support to survive in the 21st century. The cooperation and reciprocity that allow female-headed households to thrive within an extended family context may prove equal to the task.

Blended Families

Blended families are increasingly common because most divorced people end up remarrying or cohabiting, in the process reconstituting domestic arrangements that combine the old with the new to create a unique domesticity. The combinations are endless, from the relatively simple, in which only one partner has children from a previous relationship, to more complex arrangements in which there are children from both marriages who live in both their new home with their step-siblings and in the homes of their biological parents. There are arrangements in which men in a second marriage are paying child support to their first wives, while the children they actually live with are being supported by their partner's former husband.

Such arrangements are both an opportunity and a danger: an opportunity for exploring novel scripts; a danger in creating unscripted relations that may confuse or provoke. Blended families do lend themselves to considerable tension and conflict between step-siblings; mixed emotions toward the new arrangement; hostilities toward the stepmother who must replace a child's most revered figure, her natural mother (Sachs, 1999); separation anxieties; general ambivalence about the divorce; and financial problems related to child support payments. Not surprisingly, second marriages run a higher risk of divorce, in effect creating the conditions for even more innovative blends of reconstituted domesticities.

Gay and Lesbian Families

Gay and lesbian ("homosexual" or same-sex) families are increasingly part of the Canadian social landscape, and provide a controversial alternative to the norm of the heterosexual family. The presence of gay and lesbian families may rankle or provoke, including denunciations from politicians and the pulpit about the "unnaturalness" of this "sexual perversion" as a threat to society. Nevertheless, these families are here to stay, judging by their popularity and recent court actions. To be sure, most jurisdictions in Canada do not yet recognize marriage between same-sex partners, allowing only heterosexual partners to be legally married. But court decisions in recent years have recognized the legitimacy of common-law, same-sex unions by granting spousal entitlements comparable to those of opposite-sex, common-law relations. These rulings are having the effect of eroding arbitrary and pointless distinctions that have existed for no other reason than the tyranny of custom and historical prejudices (Coyne, 1999). Partners registered under domestic partnership arrangements enjoy many of the benefits of married couples, despite lacking status as full-fledged marriages (Knopff, 1999). In Ontario, for example, provincial employees in same-sex relations receive the comparable pension benefits or spousal support rights of an opposite-sex, common-law relationship. Not surprisingly, in light of these trends toward inclusiveness, the government is considering the possibility of extending legal rights to economically dependent relationships such as widowed sisters or brothers (Tibbetts, 1999).

Reaction to gay and lesbian unions is mixed. Some would concur with recent court rulings disallowing same-sex marriage, arguing that marriage by definition is heterosexual. For example, lawyers for the province and Ottawa contend that same-sex marriages are unnatural and illogical as well as a violation of common law (practices according to tradition or practice). Marriage must be restricted to heterosexual relationships since that alone institutionalizes the survival of society (see Knopff, 1999). Interest groups, such as the Canada Family Action Coalition, also maintain that only heterosexual marriage provides the core relationship around which the family is established; is the only natural union that has the ability to procreate and sustain a strong society; and fosters the best environment for raising and nurturing children. But others have argued that denying marriage to gays and lesbians constitutes a further violation of the Charter's equality provisions and human rights commitments. The definition of a family expands to encompass more than sexual partners, according to this line of thinking, but to include those who want to establish long-term, live-in relationships. After all, it is argued, most people are social by nature, and those who seek stable relations tend to live longer, healthier, more productive, and happier lives than those dependent for their care on an impersonal state (Macdonald, 1999; Knopff, 1999).

The politics of same-sex marriage have proven interesting. Despite demands for recognition, many gays and lesbians are not interested in an institution that many "straights" are leaving in droves. The objective is to secure the same status as spouses, together with the equal treatment and legal rights that flow from being in a lawful relationship, including tax breaks, pensions, health care benefits, inheritance and property rights, and rights to alimony, custody, and adoptions that are automatically conferred on married heterosexuals and common-law cohabitation (Giese, 1999). Why should same-sex couples not have the same entitlements as heterosexual couples, given that procreation is no longer the sole purpose of marriage; marriage is no longer based on the exchange of property; equality between and among genders is assumed; interracial marriages are no longer illegal; and intimate relationships are not about hierarchy or biology (Graf, 1999)? The key may lie in acknowledging same-sex relations *as if* they were a marital relationship for purposes of entitlement and engagement. That makes it doubly important to rethink which relationships deserve government support and whether marriage should remain the basis of social policy and entitlements (Macdonald, 1999). In any case, lesbian and gay people are no longer just tolerated in Canadian society, but recognized as full and equal members who are capable of forming intimate relationships of economic interdependence (Newman, 1999). It remains to be seen whether same-sex couples can prosper with a smattering of state-controlled benefits and responsibilities, or if they require the less tangible but immensely powerful legitimizing and normalizing societal supports that come with legal marriage (Joanis, 1999).

Ethnic Families

Canada is a society of extreme diversity, particularly in the larger urban centres of Toronto, Montreal, and Vancouver. Nearly 33 percent of the population in Toronto are visible minorities, while the percentage of those who were not born in Toronto is rapidly approaching 50 percent. This racial and ethnic diversity is reflected and reinforced in the proliferation of diverse family arrangements. The connection is clear: Both family and ethnicity help to establish the core of a person's being, her sense of uniqueness and identity, and of being rooted in place to one group (McAdoo, 1999). Nevertheless, people of colour have long been denied the right to have the family form of their choice because of racism and assimilationist pressures that imposed a one-size-fits-all mentality (Gupta, 1998).

Ethnicity patterns pertaining to marriage and family are highly varied and occasionally at odds with mainstream practices. In the area of parenting and child rearing, ethnic families may subscribe to permissive or authoritarian styles, or both depending on circumstances, and reflect variation in practices such as punishment, reasoning, setting of limits, and reinforcement (Martinez, 1999). Tensions within ethnic families reflect the mainstream emphasis on independence versus ethnic values of interdependence, the stress on universalism versus an ethnic focus on particularism, and mainstream emphasis on husband-wife relations as primary compared to the primacy of the parent-child relationship (Lin and Lin, 1999). Gender relations may be problematic: Ethnic families may be uncomfortable with the concept of loosely scripted gender relations (from dating and premarital sex to equality in husband-wife relations). Violence may be tolerated in some ethnic families: Men are expected to be aggressive, and this aggressiveness is tacitly accepted as a regrettable component of a marital relationship, thus reinforcing the notion of domestic abuse as mechanism of social control rather than personal pathology (Cribb and Barnett, 1999). In traditional ethnic families, a woman as wife and mother must know her place if domestic peace and social harmony are to be maintained. To be sure, differences in status and role between husband and wife may not be perceived as a dichotomy of power and inequality, but complementary. Women and men are acknowledged as different, deserving of respect and fairness rather than of formal equality, with different strengths and contributions to make (Sherif, 1999).

No less problematic are relationships between parents and children, especially in first-generation domestic arrangements. Communal values of some ethnic families may not conform with the child-focused styles of middle-class parents who employ rational, issue-oriented discipline techniques to establish firm limits within a loving context (Martinez, 1999). Different groups may use different child-rearing orientations, especially if different expectations are applied to boys and girls, but similar techniques. Children may be taught to value relatives and tradition, to sacrifice personal needs for the greater good of the family or group, and not to question the authority of parents (Sherif, 1999). Yet efforts to maintain these customary practices may be undermined by the absence of institutional support, while the pervasiveness of mainstream values challenges such practices at every opportunity (Lin and Lin, 1999).

FAMILY IN CRISIS: WHOSE CRISIS?

> At the core of the 1990s TV sitcom "Home Improvement" is an underlying creed: Men and women were not meant to live together and, therefore, married life is a series of consequences couples face for having defied fate (cited in the *New York Times,* Sept, 18, 1994).

The family has long been a staple of entertainment and politics. Reference to family values conjures up reassuring images of a refuge of last resort in a chaotic and calculating world. This centrality for individuals and society may explain public concern over its apparent demise in contemporary Canada. There is no doubt of the turmoil and transformation that have shaken institutions to their very foundation. The growing legitimacy of personal choice in marriage and family is reflected in outcomes as seemingly disruptive and varied as the following: rising divorce rates, more satisfying relations, single parenting, declining birth rates, same-sex unions, and working mothers. Variations on the theme of the family are undergoing a bewildering array of everyday discourses, from "blended" families to "same-sex" families, with a raft of cohabiting arrangements in between. Reactions to these changes are no less varied. Many regard these trends as evidence of an institution in trouble or decline. According to this line of thinking, neither society nor many of its victims can expect to recover from the onslaught of dysfunctional families, domestic violence, sexual abuse, and juvenile delinquency. Others are pleased that conventional forms of marriage and family are ceding ground to more humane alternatives. The patriarchal logic of modern families is contemptuously dismissed as little more than "slavery" in defence of male power and privilege. That this arrangement routinely encourages abuse and/or indifference is further justification to hasten its demise.

Still others believe that talk of crisis and decay is misplaced or premature. The institutions of marriage, family, and domesticity are not experiencing a crisis in the negative sense of the term. There is no evidence of some decline from some mythical past when everyone knew her place and performed accordingly. Families such as the depression-era "Waltons" or pioneer families such as the one in "Little House on the Prairie" series rarely existed except in the minds of media moguls, fundamentalist Christian sects, or advertising jingles. Nor were extended families as extensive in Canada and the United States as once thought (Gee, 1990). References to idealistic portrayals of family life are especially noticeable when applied to parent-child relations as well as husband-wife relations. Yet such idealism may lead to frustration and confusion in cases where people defend, emulate, or aspire to institutional ideals that do not match social reality. A key question comes to mind: Is there a crisis in the family, or does the crisis reflect an increased awareness of the gaps between egalitarian ideals and unequal realities, between the unrealistic portrayals of made-for-TV families and the banalities of everyday reality? The crisis also reinforces a growing belief that a 19th century invention may not be equipped to meet 21st century challenges. In brief, the "crisis" in the family should not be interpreted as a collapse, however disruptive to certain interests, but as "growing pains" in the transition from the old order to a new.

For sociologists, the concept of roles is useful in explaining what has happened and why. Simply put, women and men are bewildered by the conflicting demands associated with being a husband or wife or parents (LeMasters, 1977). Changes in the norms and expectations have had discordant consequences for established patterns of interaction. Consider the following dilemmas when individuals are thrust into marriage and family: Parental and spousal roles are poorly defined (what is a perfect parent or perfect spouse?); there is little margin for error, especially when you hedge your bets on one partner and 1.7 children; parental and spousal roles cannot be discarded without payment of penalty; parents have responsibility, but increasingly are losing authority to schools, children's aid societies, and peer groups; parents are judged by professionals according to abstract ideals; parents often feel they must follow fashions and fads that experts endorse, then discard; parents and spouses are often victimized by poor advice regarding communication and interaction; parents must raise children who are better off than they were as youth; parents do not receive training for parenting, but must learn as they go along; and parents and spouses are conditioned to pursue personal self-interest without straying from the collective needs of the family. Yet poor parenting (including everything from put-downs to physical punishment) is more likely to produce problem kids than growing up poor or with a single or teenage mother (Carey, 1999). Of particular concern is parental lack of basic knowledge about child rearing and child development, according to a survey of 1645 fathers, mothers, and single parents with children under six. The dearth of awareness is especially acute in the formative years, when parenting exerts a powerful influence on children's development. Parents rarely have the training to deal with developmental problems; for example, upwards of 25 percent of children at the age of four have serious aggression problems, while 20 percent have emotional problems (Arnold, 1999). Not surprisingly, there have been suggestions that, in the interests of protecting children, parents should not be allowed to raise children until they have finished high school, completed a parenting course, and obtained a licence (Andrews, 1999). Others disagree, arguing that parenting is natural for most adults, that parents know better than experts what their children need, that incompetent parenting can never be proven to cause anti-social behaviour, and that people have been parenting successfully for centuries without government interference.

Rules, Roles, Relationships:
From Traditional Script to Contested Site

The modern family cannot be interpreted as neutral or devoid of interest. Inasmuch as the family is a social institution that shapes and is shaped by other public institutions, the ideal family in Canada originated and continues to exist to reflect national interests, advance the demands of capitalism, bolster male experiences and ideologies, and embrace masculinist definitions of the world (McDaniel, 1998). Rules that establish a relationship between the roles of husband and wife have evolved over time in the context of capitalist patriarchy. From the Industrial era onward, the traditional relationship was based on the male as breadwinner, the female as homemaker (Skolnick, 1973; Eichler, 1983; and Mandell, 1987). This script positioned the husband as provider and decision-maker, with wives predominantly in passive domestic-maternal roles. Gender roles were fixed for the most part, and scripted along traditional patterns associated with the ideals of masculinity and femininity. These scripted roles contributed to and shaped the nature of family interaction, including domination, control, and dependency.

But new relations are emerging that embrace more egalitarian ideals. Family roles are much more flexible, determined in part by experience and choice, and in part by dual-income careers and a freedom that comes with financial security. Relations between the roles of husband and wife are not nearly as rigid or authoritarian as in the past. Decisions to stay together are voluntary and personal, and based on balancing duty with companionship and personal growth (Kinloch, 1989). Even relationships between parents and children have shifted to embrace a more enlightened set of "rules" that pertain to rights, duties, and expectations. Both the family and images of the family are evolving at the level of normative values and structural constraints, as well as by way of legal principle (de jure) and everyday practice (de facto). This shift is not complete by any stretch of the imagination: As a result, families can be interpreted as sites of contestation in varying stages of transition, involving individuals in a competitive struggle to impose their interests through negotiation and compromise. Many of the rules that governed patterns of interaction within the family are now being contested, with the result that conventional norms are increasingly less applicable than once was the case. Roles within the family are undergoing change as part of the gradual decolonization of society and emancipation of women and men from tightly scripted rules, roles, and relationships. The family is no longer a nested hierarchy in which everyone knows her place and what to do. What we have instead of a "script" is a contested "site" that is subject to negotiation and compromise. Even family relationships are changing. Patterns of interaction within domestic arrangements are increasingly varied as people look for ways of balancing their roles as career persons with obligations as family members, without necessarily discarding personal aspirations and goals. Interactions are also changing the relationship of parents to children as the concept of human rights is expanded to be more inclusive than in the past.

His Family/Her Family

How can changes to the family be assessed? One might argue that modifications to the family are cresting the wave of social changes at large. The transition from an elitist (authoritarian) society to a more egalitarian society is reflected in the contested set of rules, roles, and relationships that constitute a modern family. Conversely, one might suggest that neither the traditional authoritarian family nor its modern-day counterpart represents an accurate reading of what is really happening. Most families fall somewhere in between these ideal forms, with the result that many family types incorporate confusing mixtures of the authoritarian and egalitarian. For example, most Canadians would endorse the principle of an egalitarian partnership with respect to duties and responsibilities. The reality is much different in practice: Most relationships continue to reflect fundamental inequalities, even in situations in which women work outside the home. In effect, the labour-force status of women does not necessarily mean equality at home. It is more likely instead to double the workload, with corre-

CASE STUDY 7-1 — Children Are People, Too

The roles, rules, and relationships associated with being a spouse and parent are confusing and contradictory. Spousal roles are not the only ones to undergo redefinition. The role of parent and the rules that govern this relationship to children are no less subject to change and confusion. Consider only the case of physical punishment. Until recently it was routinely accepted that sparing the rod would spoil the child, and that parents who did not apply such discipline were derelict of duty. But the tide is shifting, together with the underlying assumptions that justify physical punishment. Spanking children in public is likely to be greeted with social disapproval or stern rebuke by passersby, perhaps even a charge of assault, in contrast to the past when most conformed to the dictum of sparing the rod and spoiling the child. This situation was highlighted recently by a high profile court case in which an American tourist, David Peterson, was charged and tried for spanking his five-year-old daughter, Rachel, when she slammed the car door on her baby brother's hand, then retaliated by kicking her father. An enraged Mr. Peterson threw Rachel over the hood of the car, pulled down her pants, and spanked her bare bottom. A concerned citizen tried to intervene, but after an ensuing argument called the police who charged the father with assault and detained him overnight where he was fingerprinted and strip-searched (Donna Laframboise, "Lets Keep Spanking in Perspective," *Toronto Star*, 1 May, 1995). A medical examination revealed no bruising or redness on the child's bottom. Mr. Peterson was eventually acquitted by virtue of Section 43 of the Criminal Code which allows parents (or guardians such as teachers) to apply reasonable force as a way of correction. Ironically, another judge on that very day convicted a man for raping his wife, a charge that would have been unthinkable even a generation ago. What is proper role behaviour in one context is inappropriate in another, and is greeted with disapproval or sanctions. Conventional guidelines are subject to even further second guessing as a result of social changes.

Sparing the Rod...Spoiling the Parent

Reaction to the charge and the verdict were mixed (Margaret Wente, "The Anatomy of a Spanking," *Globe and Mail*, 29 April, 1995). Some felt Mr. Peterson (and all parents and guardians) possesses the right to physically discipline children as long as this force is applied judiciously, without malice, and with care and compassion. Others were outraged by the terrifying experience that Mr. Peterson (and by extension all parents) was exposed to because of the "whims" of a "nosy" citizen who could enlist the machinery of the state to push her agenda. Still others questioned the so-called right of parents to punish children physically or to lash out indiscriminately (even though the law condones "necessary force"). Such discipline is seen as ineffective, publicly degrading to a child or to the parent, and conveying mixed messages about violence as a problem-solving alternative. Children need to be disciplined or forewarned of pending danger, to be sure, but resorting to physical blows is by definition abusive. Besides, how can we justify using force against the most vulnerable members of society when social norms are endorsing zero tolerance toward others? Or, as put by the concerned citizen who says she would report such an offence again:

> You just don't throw your wife on the trunk with her pants down. Why do you think that it's right to do it to a little girl? It sends a mixed message to a child that it's okay to be humiliated in public, in broad daylight with your pants down, especially if you are a female (*Toronto Star*, 1 May, 1995, A-3, "Woman Defends Reporting Spanker").

Still others wondered about the implications of this chain of actions: Would the incident have gone to court if the father had admonished his son rather than daughter? Would there have been a problem had he spanked his daughter privately or fully clothed? Would the case have received as much attention had the mother inflicted the punishment? What exactly constitutes the dividing line between excessive versus judicious force, and how do law authorities make the distinction? Was it the man's defiance of outside interference rather than the act that precipitated the chain reaction?

Criminalizing Conventionality?

According to section 43 of the Criminal Code, "reasonable" force may be used to correct a child. As a result, children remain the only class of Canadians who can be corrected by reasonable force under certain circumstances by parents, teachers, guardians, and babysitters. To one side, section 43 is criticized as a violation of children's rights under the Charter of Human Rights and Freedoms, especially when pertaining to equal protection under the law. And, while the Supreme Court of Canada in 1983 attempted to define the criteria for reason-

ableness (including the nature of the child's offence, age and character of the child, likely effect of the punishment on the child, the type of punishment resulting in injury, and whether the punishment was motivated by anger or arbitrariness (Silver 1999), the vagueness of the concept "reasonableness" is itself open to abuse, insofar as parents are equipped with an escape clause if children are harmed under the guise of correcting them (Robertshaw, 1999). To the other side are fears that repealing section 43 may undermine parental authority and deny protection to parents and teachers who are behaving reasonably but find themselves charged with assault for applying force without consent (Silver, 1999). The dilemma is all too palpable: how to protect children without exposing and criminalizing parents to frivolous charges (Editorial, 1999)?

This case raises a number of issues related to parent-child relations in the new millennium. For sociologists, the interest is not in Mr. Peterson's case per se, but in exploring the social dimensions of this once-private problem that now stands as a public issue. First and foremost are shifts in the rules that guide appropriate behaviour. What once was seen as conventional wisdom, even virtuous, ("spare the rod and spoil the child") is now dismissed as irrelevant or deviant. Second, there are questions about what it means to be a good parent in a world where the rules, roles, and responsibilities of parenting are increasingly contested. Is physical punishment a useful way of raising children, or is it a way of making parents feel better while inflicting emotional and physical scars on the victim? With parents already experiencing guilt over their decreased involvement with children, the fact that no one seems to have the answers in a post-spanking era only intensifies the confusion. Third, to what extent is parenting a private rather than public affair? Historically it was viewed as a private matter between parents and children, in the same way that husband-wife relations were regarded as a closed business. But the politicization of family violence has changed all that. The moral panic over widespread child abuse has implicated state authorities and the general public, in effect destroying any clear-cut boundaries between private and public. Finally, can children no longer be viewed as property, that is, commodities at the disposal of parental displeasure? Children do have human rights, with the same protection from physical harm and assault.

Repercussions from this precedent-setting case are stunning to say the least. They portend a revolution not only in the nature of parent-child relations, but also in the field of human rights as applied to children. Contesting the terrain over parent-offspring relations may also herald an era of even more flux and fluidity in the search for optimal living arrangements. Should parents be more permissive and run the risk of inflating children's self-esteem to the point where

spoiled kids call the shots, lack real world coping skills, have little concern for others, and lack any moral compass for distinguishing right from wrong? (Underwood, 1999). Parents demand so little respect for authority in the push for bolstering so-called "positive" parenting, according to Ronald Morrish in his 1997 book, *Secrets of Discipline*, that children lose any sense of responsibility. To be sure, parents will continue to shoulder the responsibility for setting limits, curbing destructive behaviour, and making children aware of the consequences of unacceptable behaviour. Nevertheless, parents will also have to adopt non-violent alternatives within the framework of conventional family structures. Such a challenge may also remind the general public that parenting within a conventional family is an extremely underrated job for which few are properly equipped (Laframboise, 1995). Given the personal anguish and societal costs of poorly raised children by those without resources, training or commitment, who can be surprised by the call to license parents in the art of child rearing (Laucius, 1999)?

sponding frustration and resentment because of role conflicts. Admittedly, men are more likely to "assist" with domestic activities, especially in the care of children, but this is perceived as "helping out," rather than any fundamental restructuring of the division of labour. For example, women spent 138 minutes each day on household cleaning, laundry, cooking, and washing up. Men spent 35 minutes, while just 10 percent of Canadian men in dual-earning couples shared housework equally with women. Society may be responsible for this double standard: Women and men appear to be caught in an unforgiving vise between traditional role models and a changing world. Once they decide to have children, there is a corresponding tendency to backslide into traditional arrangements that intensify women's dependency on maternal-domestic roles but reduce economic power (Carter and Peters, 1996). Refusal to take domesticity seriously may suit male interests and resistance, but is a major source of tension in contemporary families.

The hidden costs that separate "her" and "his" marriage cannot be dismissed. Tension and disagreement are inherent components of any relationship, even more so in contexts that isolate individuals and make them highly dependent on each other across a broad range of needs and concerns. But there is a much darker side that puts women and children at grave risk. Despite images of comfort, coziness, and security, the family is now considered possibly one of the most dangerous environments for dependents. Violence and abuse within families is of epidemic proportions, according to numerous surveys. Between 1974 and 1992, a married woman was nine times more likely to be killed by her spouse than by a stranger. Of the 164 women murdered in Canada in 1993, 77 were killed by a current or former partner. According to the 1992 Violence Against Women survey, 29 percent of women who were or are married or in a common-law relationship have experienced at least one incident of physical or sexual abuse at the hands of an intimate partner (Nelson and Fleras, 1998).

Nor can anyone derive much satisfaction by rationalizing away current rates as an improvement over the past when domestic violence was neither openly discussed nor defined as a public problem. Few had perceived patriarchy as a problem; its perception as normative behaviour persisted well into the 1960s. Violence of course has always existed, but until recently was accepted as an inevitable if regrettable component of the nuclear family. The premier journal for the sociological study of marriage and family did not have a single article with the word "violence" in its title or even a single article on domestic violence between 1939 and 1969 (Nuefeld, 1993). Authorities, from police to physicians, refused to intervene out of deference to a man's personal and private affairs. It was assumed that men had certain passions and aggressions in need of release; women and children were offered as appropriate targets for male virility. Assaults against women were trivialized; for example, a husband could not legally rape his wife. Violence against women was accepted as normal, even necessary, and reflected a view of children and women as property that could be punished with a stick no thicker than a man's thumb ("rule of thumb") (Thorne-Finch, 1993). The private nature of violence and abuse has created difficulties in gauging its historical extent. Such is also the case at present despite more awareness of domestic abuse, less acceptance of its presence, and greater willingness to report violations to authorities. There are few assurances that statistics and national surveys are telling the whole story, or merely exposing the tip of the iceberg. That fact that many men are reluctant to acknowledge the reality or magnitude of the problem, much less do something about it, is proving as violent as recourse to words, fists, or guns. Still, the question must be asked: Is family violence increasing (including violence against women, the elderly, children, and between siblings), or has it always been a concern and only now is getting the attention it deserves because of broader definitions, zero tolerance, and stricter enforcement (Tepperman and Blain, 1999). Whereas 42 percent of Canadians in 1983 agreed that the father of the family must be the master of his own house, that figure dropped to 17 percent in 1998 (*Maclean's,* Jan. 25, 1999). This raises a disturbing paradox: How could a social unit that furnishes the potential for love and intimacy simultaneously incite aggression, abuse, and violence?

Patriarchy: The Binds That Tie

Women and men experience marriage and family from different vantage points. For women, the family is dangerous to mental and physical health. Risks may be greater if a woman is not employed outside the home. Class differences, moreover, may play a role in sorting out the quality of the spousal relationship. Profiles of abusive men suggest they are more likely to be unemployed or blue collar, between 18 and 30 years of age, dropped out of school, engage in drugs or binge drinking, come from abusive families, and have cultural or religious backgrounds that differ from their partners (Goleman 1995). By contrast, men who are successful and self-confident in personal or public life may feel less compelled than their working class colleagues to explicitly dominate and control (Skolnick, 1978). That in itself poses some serious questions about the necessity and viability of marriage and family as meaningful institutions for the 21st century.

Sociologists have responded to "the dark side of the family" in several ways. Those of a functionalist persuasion see domestic conflict as an aberration (a deviance from the norm) in a system in which consensus and cooperation are necessary for social stability. For functionalists, a functioning society is an orderly one, and the dynamics and design of society are geared towards creating, maintaining, and restoring equilibrium. A healthy and functioning family is perceived as pivotal for the maintenance of a cohesive and stable society (Yoest, 1994). Strong, stable family ties can reduce the incidence of violence, poverty, substance abuse, educational failure, and social dropout. Societal stability and regulation are achieved by carrying out the basic functions of the family, including reproduction, socialization, sexual control, economic production and consumption, and emotional satisfaction. Fulfillment of these functions enhances the integration of individuals into society. Not that everyone benefits equally from this "functional" arrangement. Spousal relations were constructed around norms that reaffirmed the patriarchal-androcentric values of the male as "lord" and "master of his castle," with women and children as his property for disposal as long as these controlling functions were conducted with tact and compassion. Such inequities did not necessarily detract from the contribution of the family to the maintenance of a cohesive social order. Order was ensured as long as everybody knew their place in the family system and complied with the script.

Conflict theorists agree that marriage and family are functional, but such an assertion simply raises the question "Functional for whom?" and "For what purposes?" According to conflict theorists, inequality is a central feature of society, and institutional arrangements are designed to secure class-based inequality. As Frederick Engels (a lifelong collaborator of Karl Marx) remarked over a century ago, nuclear families exist to serve the interests of the capitalist class, in part by creating a division of labour between women and men modelled along a private (women = home) versus public (men = work) domain. The consequences of this gender-based segregration by occupation proved disruptive to women's lives and life chances. The status of women deteriorated as many were isolated and marginalized by a patriarchal arrangement that reinforced their status as chattel and roles as slaves. Abusive relations and domestic violence are inevitable in situations involving an unequal distribution of power, wealth, or status. Others, such as Shere Hite (1994), argue that the conventional family arose for political rather than economic or religious reasons. With urban-industrialism, the new political order was confronted with the problem of ensuring the flow of inheritance through males. The modern patriarchal family was created to establish male control over a woman who would produce children for "him." Restrictions were placed on women's lives and sexuality to ensure that "his" children were on the receiving end of the inheritance process. Male control over children completed the confinement of women within the patriarchal framework of a nuclear family (Hite, 1994). Table 7–1 provides an overview that compares functionalist with conflict perspectives on evaluating changes to the family.

Have Conventional Families Outlived Their Usefulness?

There are more myths surrounding the family than about most human endeavours. The myth-making machine may exist to paper cracks that may trigger deep problems. Of the many myths, few are as pervasive or debilitating as the popular beliefs about the normalcy and in-

TABLE 7-1 Family in Crisis?	
'FAMILY IN CRISIS' **Functionalist Perspectives**	**FEMINIST PERSPECTIVES** **Conflict Perspectives**
• changes in family to be resisted	• family change = sign of progress
• family = haven/cornerstone	• family = hell/patriarchy
• there is one and only one type of family; any departure from ideal = dysfunctional or deviant	• families are diverse and changing, and should not be expected to conform to only one model
• people lived in big happy families, thus, family change is new and crisis-bound	• family instability has always existed, and family has changed in form and function due to changes in environment
• women should know their maternal-domestic place	• equitable treatment and equal opportunity for women
• families are essential to society survival	• family life is central to most people's lives
• family is basically private, but needs public policy to strengthen it	• family is a social institution that articulates with other institutions (adapted from McDaniel, 1998: 190–191)

evitability of conventional nuclear families. Consensus is growing that conventional families don't work any more. Heightened anxieties over the family may reflect challenges to its status as the cornerstone of society, coupled with a belief that further relapse will undermine the quality and order of human social life. Critics and concerned citizens point to a number of indicators that suggest the family is indeed in trouble. Among these trends are rising divorce rates; dysfunctional domestic arrangements; a proliferation of family types, especially single and same-sex unions; and alarming levels of domestic violence. New reproductive technologies may have an even more revolutionary impact on the nature of the family, what it means to be a parent, and the rights and obligations of family members (Eichler, 1988; Baker, 1996). To be sure, stresses and strains are inevitable in an arrangement that unites two untrained strangers for a demanding lifetime of diverse functions under conditions of change within contexts of inequality. Not surprisingly, efforts have focused on propping up the structure and dynamics of the nuclear family through threats or encouragement.

Talk of the family as dysfunctional or predictions of its demise may be greatly exaggerated. Conventional families will not disappear in the future since core images and the moral authority of nuclear families continue to be bolstered by both formal and informal messages, thus making them resilient and difficult to dislodge (Miller, 2000). Perhaps the so-called "crisis" is not really a problem, but an opportunity of yet unknown dimensions. The family is not necessarily in decline, but experiencing a transition from a modernist ideal to a postmodernist reality. As well, one might argue that these changes are not automatically regressive or deserving of ostracism. Rather the traditional patriarchal family is giving way to more democratic forms that not only encourage different styles but also foster more egalitarian and loving relations. But no institutional arrangement will please everyone. The institutional basis of human social life is constraining and restrictive by definition, and those who insist on seeking the perfect arrangement are setting themselves up for failure. Are marriage and family obsolete? Is the family disappearing? Yes, if we think of it as a scripted set of rules and roles in defence of patriarchy and control. No, if the "crisis" in the family may be seen as natural and inevitable in a society undergoing diversity and change. No, if families are regarded as socially constructed and contested sites in pursuit of companionship and fulfillment. Perhaps it is not a case of decline and disappearance. Families are not declining, but only a particular type of post-war ideal family that in turn idealized the urban, patriarchal family of the 19th century (Tepperman and Blain, 1999).

Nowhere is the crisis in conventionality more evident than in divorce. The emergence of divorce as a viable alternative lifestyle enables the "crisis" in the family to be evaluated in different ways, depending on the perspective of society, either functionalist or conflict. Relatively high divorce rates are viewed by some as symbolic of the decline in the health and vitality of the contemporary family. Most divorces, it is argued, are accompanied by emotional stress and financial strain, with children often experiencing disruption and distress, while the challenge of single parenting becomes even more burdensome because of responsibility overload, task overload, and emotional overload (Kornblum and Julian, 1995). Escalating rates and the de-stigmatizing of divorce are applauded by others as the demise of rigid and colonialistic family structures, and their replacement by more humane alternatives. Still others see escalating divorce rates as inevitable for an institution in transition. Rather than a rejection of family and marriage as institutions, divorce can be interpreted as an affirmation of core values and key institutions. They also criticize how divorce rates can be manipulated by vested interests. We leave it to the reader to decide—on sociological grounds—whether contemporary families are experiencing a "positive" or "negative" crisis, and if divorce should be interpreted as "good" or "bad" or "in between."

RE-SCRIPTING DOMESTICITY

The institutions of marriage and family have come under increased scrutiny and criticism. The critique is mild in some cases, and aims at drawing attention to inconsistencies between ideals and reality. In other cases, the critique has been withering and severe. Family and domesticity are depicted as a "chamber of horrors" that personifies everything evil about "man." Nothing is left unscathed in castigating the ideal of a monogamous, nuclear family as little more than a "comfortable concentration camp" (Frieden, 1963). The conventional family serves as a training ground for conformity and control, with an oppressive set of rules and roles that lock both women and men into scripted relationships. Women, particularly those restricted largely to the domestic maternal sphere, are robbed of individuality and a sense of self-worth outside that realm, and are implicated in patterns of dependencies that may deny or demean. Similarly, men are locked into behavioural patterns that preclude alternative definitions of masculinity. Contradictions abound because of this inequality. For example, men have the final say in critical matters, but prefer to remain aloof from involvement in domestic affairs except to "help out," while women continue to shoulder the bulk of unglamourous domestic labour without much reward or recognition. Admittedly, patterns of dominance are less obvious than in the past because of the breakdown in boundaries and scripts. Yet evidence suggests that it is wives who adjust their careers in deference to maternal responsibilities and spousal priorities.

What can we conclude from this assessment? Families are neither a heavenly interlude, as implied by sitcoms, nor are they a punishment from hell, as implied by critics and statistics. Perhaps the answer lies somewhere in between the poles of bliss and brutality. Changes and challenges to the conventional family need to be reassessed. The future of marriage and family as institutions is not necessarily in jeopardy. What is being challenged are the traditional and rigid scripts associated with family and domesticity, with their built-

CASE STUDY 7-2	De-Stigmatizing Divorce

In 1980, the crude marriage rate in Canada was 7.8 per 1000 population. By 1995, the rate stood at 5.5 per 1000 population. The number of marriage ceremonies conducted in 1997 was 153, 306, according to Statistics Canada, down 2 percent from the previous year and 22 percent from the peak year of 1972. More than two-thirds of the marriages involved first-time marriages, and these are lasting longer, at 13.2 years in 1997, compared to 12.2 years in 1993. The average age for first-time brides was 27.4 years, and 29.5 years for first-time grooms. Yet a third of marriages are destined to dissolve, according to a comprehensive study by Statistics Canada. How accurate is this assessment? In 1997, there were 67 408 divorces in Canada, or 34.8 percent of all marriages in that year, with Newfoundland lowest at 20.2 percent and Yukon highest at 47.7 percent. To be sure, divorce rates are beginning to fall, from 1600 divorces for every 100 000 married couples in 1987, to 1222 divorces for every 100 000 legally married couples in 1995. Still, Canada's divorce rate, which is thought to be a main index of social stability and health, is one of the highest in the world (Mitchell, 1997). The probable cause of this decline? Fewer marriages, as women abandon marriage with growing economic freedom, according to a Statistics Canada study of 5000 women (cited in Mitchell, 1999). Nor can we ignore the costs: A total of 1.8 million Canadian children (or one in five) are growing up in single-parent households. According to a 1998 Human Resources Development Centre report, more than half the single-parent families earn less than $20 000 per year, compared to only about 5 percent of two-parent families. Eighty percent of these single parents were women, and 60 percent lived below the low-income cut-off line. Hence the expression the "feminization of poverty" (the fact that women confront a higher risk of poverty and represent a higher percentage of the poor than men, in part because of domestic arrangements that kept women "barefoot" and "pregnant"). Lone father families do better than single mother families, but still earn only about 54 percent of two-parent family incomes.

For some, the high rates of divorce in Canada are a sign of moral decay and social disintegration. Many allege that escalating divorce rates originate from and contribute to sexual permissiveness, juvenile delinquency, deterioration of "family values," and trivialization of key human relations. For others, the higher rate of divorce can be attributed to a variety of factors. These might include: higher expectations of the marriage partners; easier access because of relaxed grounds for divorce; longer lives, thus eliminating early death as a means of dissolving an unhappy marriage; a commitment to personal growth and self-actualization as a sign of a good marriage; a growing willingness to leave an empty or abusive relationship if emotional needs are unsatisfied; discontent with an existing partner because of shifting expectations; increased economic independence of women; access to birth control and sexual freedom without the "obligations"; and both social and legal acceptance of divorce as inevitable and necessary. What can we infer from these alternative interpretations? Divorce is not a social problem per se, but rather a possible solution to problems that invariably arise in a changing and diverse society.

Changes in people's perceptions of what they expect from marriage reflect broader changes in society. Primary emphasis in the past lay with the discharging of role obligations and moral necessity. People did what was expected of them out of duty or fear of social disgrace and public ostracism. In a life filled with drudgery and economic uncertainty, the pursuit of marital happiness as an explicit goal may not have even registered on the social radar. With lowered expectations, a happy marriage and family life may have been defined as reflecting an absence of mutual antagonism. A shortened life span may have eased the burden of unhappiness without having to resort to divorce. But attitudes toward marriage are shifting because of the increased value placed on personal contentment and emotional satisfaction, a marked relaxation in patterns of authority and convention, and the growing assertiveness of women at political, economic, and ideological levels (Theodorsen and Theodorsen, 1990; Tepperman and Rosenberg, 1991). In a study that appeared in the *American Psychologist*, Louise Silverstein and Carl Auerbach of New York's Yeshiva University argue that most children do not suffer significant long-term effects from divorce, especially when leaving high-conflict marriages, but those who do suffer tend to land in poverty, lose contact with extended family, and are uprooted in neighbourhoods (cited by Milstone, 1999). Children do not need both parents to flourish, according to Silverstein and Auerbach, but one responsible adult with a positive emotional connection and a consistent relationship. In short, rather than viewing divorce as a sign of failure or marriage breakdown,

it may well become defined as a sign of personal growth and emancipation. In what may turn out as one of the more ironic inversions of postmodernism, those who remain married may be labelled and stigmatized as stagnant or self-deluding!

For others, divorce is not nearly as disruptive as the doomsayers make it out to be. For example, it is incorrectly repeated with mantra-like monotony that between one-third and one-half of all marriages will end up in divorce. That figure is extremely misleading: First, it applies to certain jurisdictions in Canada and the United States, with little applicability to national patterns. Second, the figures themselves cannot stand up to scrutiny. They are derived from tallying the number of divorces in any given year, then dividing that figure into the total number of marriages for the same year. For example, in 1996, a total of 156 642 Canadian couples married, while 71 528 divorces were granted (Statistics Canada, 1998). But comparing the number of marriages and divorces in each given year is misleading since the couples who divorce in each year are unlikely to come from the group that married that year (Kendall et al., 1999). What becomes ignored in these tabulations is the overall number of marriages that stay intact from year to year. By taking into account both new and existing marriages, nearly 85 percent of first-time marriages survive until death unravels them. It is the activity in the remaining 15 percent that inflates the divorce totals. Nor is there any proof that higher divorce rates signify an institution in decline. The fact that many remarry (3/4 of men remarry, 2/3 of women; 20 percent of marriages in Canada are remarriages) (Gee, 1990) suggests that most accept the concept of marriage. What they are looking for is not something outside marriage; greater satisfaction or emotional fulfillment is sought within the framework of a less-scripted format. This suggests that pursuit of human relations is a primary motive in marriage and family rather than legal obligations (O'Donnell, 1988).

This ambiguous status of divorce proves again that facts rarely speak for themselves. Interpretations of these data reflect a particular outlook. For some, galloping divorce rates are a sign of society and its institutions in distress. For others, high rates of divorce confirm that the institutions of marriage and family are as resilient as ever. There is a much higher commitment to the relationship than to the institution than once was the case. The pursuit of happiness would have deferred to obligation and duty, with divorce less of a going concern or a viable option (Stark, 1987). Such is hardly the case for many contemporary relations. People now define "happy" marriages and family life in terms of positive predictors pertaining to support, personal satisfaction, and individual growth. There are less compelling bonds for supporting a doubtful relation when these qualities are not forthcoming. This emphasis on relationships and emotions creates a more unstable and unrealistic condition, amenable to rupture and dissolution. It also creates the basis for a more satisfying and egalitarian partnership by relieving the pressure to stick it out, for better or for worse. And when women have the social, economic, and cultural freedom to leave an unsatisfactory relationship, they will take advantage of these life choices. In other words, given the rate and declining social stigma in Canada, divorce should no longer be viewed as a perversion, but as a normal part of people's lives to terminate destructive relationships, achieve personal growth and identity, and to alleviate

stress because of fear, violence, and squabbling (Church, 1996).

Sociology as a discipline offers a variety of different perspectives for analyzing the social world. Such a multi-perspective approach is especially applicable in studying marriage and family as a social problem. While the decline of scripted family arrangements is widely lamented as a recipe for social disaster, contemporary changes to the conventional family may reflect a restructuring of an antiquated arrangement rather than its untimely demise (Widdison, 1995). Escalating divorce rates may not necessarily reflect greater unhappiness or institutional rejection. Their proliferation may be inseparable from evolving notions of domesticity in the shift from "scripted" duty (where everything is in its place) to "contested" satisfaction (where everything is up for grabs). Divorce may also be the inevitable by-product of the bottlenecks that invariably complicate the decolonization of a 19th-century patriarchical institution in its transition toward an egalitarian partnership. Rather than a personal failure or social pathology, divorce may be rethought as a challenge with unlimited opportunity for personal growth and social survival. Divorce is not a rejection of marriage or family as institutions, but a dismissal of the unfortunate choices that individuals make, and a yearning for personal fulfillment or healthy relationships within the institutional framework of society. To be sure, suggesting that divorces are a "healthy" sign is not the same as endorsing them; nor should we casually dismiss their impact at large, especially on the lives of children or grandparents.

In short, the lack of institutional stability in contemporary families is not necessarily a sign of a dispirited and

alienated society. This crisis and confusion may be attributable to structure and norms that are inappropriate as tools for coping with the demands of the 21st century. Rigidly scripted structures such as the nuclear family may make it difficult to foster intimacy and domesticity in a world at odds with domestic arrangements in the first place. Think about it: There is nothing inherently natural about two strangers making a lifelong commitment only to each other along a broad range of fronts and responsibilities. Similarly, there is nothing unnatural about two people not being able to conform to such highly demanding and challenging social constructs. According to Rutgers anthropologist, Helen Fisher, comparative evidence from 62 countries indicates that relationships are genetically programmed to self-destruct after four years (cited in Harlow, 1999). Perhaps divorces are one way of reminding us that social conventions may be necessary for social order, but contrary to human needs or emergent realities. That many marriages do survive until death rents asunder what "man" has put together is a credit to the tenacity and compliance of social actors.

in weaknesses and high costs. The instability of nuclear families is inherent in the structure. Two strangers are thrown together in a kind of structure that tends to isolate a small number of individuals in a highly dependent relationship without much support, guidance, and training for carrying out the high functional load across a broad range of domestic fronts. Moreover, family relations, like all relations—even the most intimate and egalitarian—are pervaded by power and inequality, both blatant and subtle. Thus, the reassuring confines of marriage and family are as likely to induce control and oppression as they are to foster emotional gratification. The same context that may generate passion and intimacy can unravel into fits of hate. Abuse and exploitation coexist uneasily alongside expressions of intimacy and caring (Mandell, 1987, in Rosenberg et al., 1987). In short, the domain of marriage, family, and domesticity has come under pressure. Social, demographic, and ideological changes challenge the status and role of families while contesting the rules governing relations and expectations.

It is apparent that the institution of family and marriage is undergoing change. Uncertainty prevails under such disruptive conditions. Many believe the family is worse off than ever, in part because people compare the complex and diverse families of the 1990s with 1950s families, a unique era when every long-term trend of the 20th century was reversed and a national consensus on family values and norms emerged, albeit in a climate of coercion, censorship, deprivation, and discrimination (Stacey, 1997). In part, as a *Life* magazine special on the family indicates, many worries about the family reflect how much better we want to be, rather than how much better we used to be when problems from spousal rape to housewife depression were routinely swept under the rug. In each era, in other words, families have solved one set of problems only to face a new array of challenges, since families invariably play catch-up with a changing world. To be sure, there is still no clear-cut answer with regards to what women and men want from each other in a spousal relationship. Do women look at marriage and family as an opportunity to be taken seriously as a productive partner in an equitable relationship? Do men look for old-fashioned virtues, coupled with modern skills, but with none of the hang-ups? Male double standards continue to perplex and provoke, as Jan Mannette (1966:11) observed a generation ago: "Nobody objects to a woman

TABLE 7-2	Trends in Family and Domesticity	
from **SCRIPTED** • rules, roles, relationships, status, and expectations	to **CONTESTED SITE BECAUSE OF BREAKDOWNS IN BOUNDARIES** (+ choice, diversity, and change)
from **INEQUALITY/AUTHORITARIAN/COERCIVE**	to **EGALITARIAN/DEMOCRATIC**
from **DUTY & OBLIGATION**	to **CHOICE + RIGHTS**
from **KING OF THE CASTLE**	to **PARTNERSHIP**
from **PRIVATE /SOVEREIGN**	to **PUBLIC DOMAIN**
from **PRACTICAL GOALS**	to **PERSONALLY SCULPTED**

being a good writer or sculptor as long as she manages to be a good wife, mother, good looking, good tempered, well dressed and well groomed."

However pervasive and far-reaching in implications, the crisis in the legitimacy of the family and domesticity is not reflected in a wholesale of abandonment of principles or practices. National surveys clearly indicate that the vast majority of Canadians marry, raise families, and remarry when the opportunity arises. For many Canadians, according to Zeitlin and Brym (1991), a happy and emotionally satisfying family life ranks as one of the most important goals in life, surpassing even career and popularity. At the societal level, moreover, marriage and family remain key building block institutions in securing stability and support. Despite criticism and abandonment of specific and scripted styles of domesticity, nothing appears to be on the horizon as a replacement. In other words, fewer marriages and higher divorce rates are not necessarily indicative of a pending demise in the family or marriage. Nor is there evidence of a wholesale desertion of these institutions by individuals in search of alternatives. The content of marriage and family, as well as their expressions and functions, will continue to evolve and diversify. In light of the limitations within existing structural arrangements of nuclear families, the rescripting of the rules, roles, relationships, and expectations associated with living together should be embraced rather than resisted.

8

MEDIA

FRAMING THE PROBLEM

Is there any Canadian who has not capitulated to the lure of the media or succumbed to the persuasiveness of media messages? Probably not. For if there is a common denominator that underpins Canadian society, it is our absorption into a media culture, either as producers or consumers. Contemporary lives are awash in the media; their pervasiveness is such that media infiltrate into our lives without awareness or resistance. Incidents that matter become media events; media events matter, by definition. Reality is not lived per se except through images and representations that shape the reality of lived experiences (Gray, 1995). Personal identities and interpersonal relations are so inextricably saturated with media messages about normalcy and acceptability, media analyst Neal Gabler writes in *Life the Movie* (1998), that human existence is reduced to an entertainment medium. A craving for media attention is particularly true among those whose lives revolve around media images. Not surprisingly, in an image-based world of media where life imitates art rather than vice versa, the ability to distinguish reality from its fabrication can no longer be taken for granted because of media messages that reformulate the very reality under observation (Fiske, 1994; Abercrombie, 1995; Owen, 1997).

Interest in the media accelerated in the aftermath of highly publicized events involving violence in high schools. Words can barely capture the pain and bewilderment—much less convey the indignation and outrage—of knowing that innocent people were slaughtered only because they happened to be in the wrong place at the wrong time. Finger-pointing was inevitable under such duress, if only to pluck a measure of meaning from the meaningless, while asserting control over the uncontrollable: Bad parenting came under blame; so too was ready access to guns; youth subcultures that glorified nihilism and alienation as "cool," rebellious, or self-expressive; an amoral capitalism that has commodified violence as a lifestyle option; and the class structures that transformed high schools into cultural time bombs (Kogan, 1999). Of those culpable, however, only the media drew universal condemnation for their complicity in causing violence to run amok among youth. From *Natural Born Killers* to *The Matrix*, from *Heathers* to the *Basketball Diaries*, films were singled out as the "usual suspects"; the Internet was criticized for its accessibility to seductive anti-social sites; popular music from gangsta rap to Marilyn Manson endured the usual slings for corrupting youth; also vilified were point-and-shoot splatter video games, including "Quake" and "Doom," the latter involving people on a room-to-room killing spree. And for misleading the nation's youth, television violence bore the brunt of public anger. To the extent that few would blandly dismiss media impacts and effects as fictitious, the ensuing debate proved useful in drawing attention to a major social problem in Canada and the United States. Insofar as this debate tended to be emotional and impressionistic, however, there is additional urgency to explore the relationship of the media to society at the turn of the millennium.

Concern over the media and their impact on society continues to escalate. At the centre of this controversy is a realization that the media not only construct realities by shaping people's perceptions of the outside world. Young people increasingly rely on media as models for thought and behaviour; after all, nothing in their lives is of sufficient import to neutralize the impact of television, movies, or video games as substitute parental authorities. The media constitute a constructed reality in their own right, with specific agendas and biases—both explicit and systemic—many of which are at odds with audience interests and the needs of a moral society, both inclusive and sustainable as well as compassionate and progressive. In a strict sense, the media per se are not a problem. Problems arise from failing to situate media within the broader context of society: To what extent do the media reflect and reinforce prevailing cultural values and social patterns, or do the media define the social and cultural contours of society? Of particular note are discrepancies over what is expected of the media, that is, to (a) inform, (b) entertain (c) challenge or (d) transform. Contrast these expectations with what the media prefer to do, namely, to (a) make profits, (b) defend ideologies, and (c) secure thought control. Problems also arise from underestimating the media as socially constructed systems of communication in their own right. Media are not simply passive or neutral channels for delivery of content; more accurately, media are the message insofar as they are loaded with ideological values in defence of the status quo and vested interests. Failure of the media to foster a particular vision of society is seen as problematic as well, and the media may be criticized for bolstering an amoral society of self-serving individuals rather than a civil community of communities. Media are also implicated in hastening the transformation of society, from a vertically structured hierarchy to a more horizontally layered system in which deference to convention and authority is challenged by commitments to the here-and-now of multiple identities (Friedman, 1998). This transformation has had the effect of gutting traditional authority with respect to who gets what and why. To their credit, many Canadians generally seem cognizant of the media as a powerful social force, with the capacity to distort, conceal, or evade reality. Few, however, possess the critical skills necessary to delve into media dynamics and to analyze the techniques behind mass persuasion. Even fewer are equipped to put these skills into practice in a way that challenges and resists.

Reaction to the ubiquitous presence of the media has been mixed. Media are endorsed as a positive force for the advancement of human progress. The media are touted as indispensable in the construction of an open and cosmopolitan society, firmly rooted in the principles of free enterprise and liberal democracy. Others are less sanguine about media effects. Media are deplored as (a) an insult to the human spirit, (b) an instrument for promoting mediocrity or stifling creativity while encouraging anti-social behaviour, (c) a system of social control, reinforcing racism and sexism, (d) a cultural frame of reference at odds with social goals, and (e) a discourse in defence of privilege. In Canada's multicultural society where diversity is endorsed as integral to society-building, mainstream media have come under additional criticism for not reflecting, reinforcing, or advancing the goals of a pluralistic society (Fleras, 1995). To be sure, the media cannot be blamed for all the social problems in society; nor can they be expected to provide all solutions (Peart and Macnamara, 1996). Yet media-bashing has become a favourite pastime among those looking for a quick fix to society's problems. A "tropism toward blaming" may make it easier to "shoot the messenger" by castigating the media for fostering a social climate in which capitalism is synonymous with consumerism while individualism is reduced to an indulgent narcissism (Rieff, 1999). Scapegoating the media may have the virtue of simplifying the problem for blame. Unfortunately, it does little to advance our insight or offer a solution.

Between these two extremes are those who are inclined to dismiss such debates as puerile and unproductive. Accusing the media for society's faults is no more realistic than absolving the media of any complicity, given the reach of a multi-billion dollar advertising industry that operates on the principle of behaviour modification. Rather than pigeonholing the media into slots of good or evil, the media are portrayed as a complex social construction of contradictory roles, ambiguous messages, multi-faceted functions, and diverse impacts (see Stone, 1993). As "contested sites" of varying struggles, the media are neither good nor bad but simultaneously both, depending on the criteria, context, and consequences. Media processes and their outcomes appear to be sufficiently complex and contradictory that they often blur any distinction between positive and negative. On the one hand, media are accused of deliberately employing violence to shock or titillate; on the other, violence strikes at the heart of all media story-telling. Conflict and confrontation are integral to the narrative structure of news, even as newscasts condemn violence in society or the media (Pevere, 1998). To one side, the media are known to embrace a largely conservative and commercial agenda; to the other side, a combination of investigative journalism and ethnic/alternative presses wields the power to criticize and challenge, raise awareness, mobilize the masses, and spark social change. This ambiguity is expressed in the love-hate relationship people have with the media; that is, people will buy, consume, and condone even as they curtail, block, and condemn (Katz, 1997). Moreover, as the media continue to be upbraided for shortchanging society, developments in communications technology have enlarged people's accessibility—and enjoyment—of the media (Davies, 1996). The enigmatic character of media-society relations is nicely captured in this quote from Raymond A. Morrow (1994, 189), who reminds us that even the most pleasurable activities are not without damaging consequences:

> How can "having fun" be a social problem? Without falling back on any puritanical moralizing about the sinful nature of pleasure, the response is easy enough: My having fun or your having fun can be destructive to you or me or the community now or in the long run. ...Having sex without birth control or protection in risky situations can be great fun, but it is also a potential threat to the unborn or oneself or future partners.

Clearly, then, we must go beyond the knee-jerk reaction of reducing all media to a social problem. The challenge lies in accepting the media as a normal and important component of contemporary life, without necessarily ignoring a powerful potential to harm, deny, or exclude. The pervasiveness of the media ensures that virtually no part of our society or culture is untouched as a point of reference, debate, or comparison (Davies,1996). In their ability to redefine normal conduct and reshape behavioural standards, popular media discharge a double duty: They not only change people's notion of what is accepted, but also alter popular ideas of what is expected (Medved, 1996). This formidable power reinforces the absurdity of reducing the media to simply a mechanical transmission of information on a massive scale. The media are this and more, with consequences as disturbing as they are revealing.

This chapter explores the possibility of media as a social problem at odds with the realities of a progressive and multicultural society. The media are framed as a contested site of competing agendas whose inner logic, institutional values, and commercial imperatives have the effect of creating social problems, in consequence if not by intent. Emphasis is directed at the social dimensions of the media, rather than on technology per se. The ambiguous and strained relationship between media and society is analyzed, together with how this contested relationship is defined and secured or challenged and transformed. The concept of media as "enlightened propaganda" is also advanced by discussing the quality of media images of minority women and men that continue to demean or demonize, despite modest improvements in media representations. Select aspects of the media, namely, newscasting, advertising, and TV programming, are examined with respect to the consequences of the information they convey. Central here is the notion that media are not simply neutral conveyors of disinterested information. Media are actively involved in shaping the content of information by privileging some points of view and denying others. The paradox of computer-mediated communication reinforces the ambiguity at the heart of media impacts, given its divisive yet integrative functions, thus compromising the search for solutions that are workable, necessary, and fair. Before problematizing the media as a social problem, it is necessary to deconstruct the media to understand what they are trying to do, why, and how.

DECONSTRUCTING THE MEDIA

The media constitute a socially constructed system of technologically driven communication that are anything but neutral or passive in delivery. Media are actively involved in shaping messages and circulating meanings. As a social construction the media encapsulate within themselves a number of hidden agendas and dominant ideologies in advancing vested rather than common interests. The constructed character of the media is rarely conveyed to audiences, many of whom are often unaware of the production process behind the apparent "naturalness" of media products (Abercrombie, 1995). Not only are the media constructed through human agency, they also construct realities by "naturalizing" our perception of the world as necessary and normal rather than conventional and constructed. Cultural frames of reference are imposed that define some aspects of reality as acceptable and others as unacceptable.

Discourses in Defence of Profit

Of those dynamics that animate media content or process, few are as pervasive as the commercial imperative and the perpetuation of values consistent with conspicuous consumerism. The media do not exist to inform or to entertain or even to persuade. As a rule they are not interested in solving social problems or fostering progressive social change unless profit margins are directly involved. The media are first and foremost business ventures whose devotion to the bottom line is geared toward advertising revenues by attracting the largest possible audience. At the same time, the ideological dimension of the media cannot be discounted. The media are loaded with ideological assumptions that not only reflect the ideas and ideals of a dominant discourse, but preclude the values and views of those that might contest an unequal order (Abel, 1997). As discourses in defence of ideology, the media are effective because they can encode particular values by pretending to be something they are not (see also Abercrombie, 1995). Media messages combine to "normalize" contemporary social arrangements as universal and superior rather than as self-serving social constructs (Maracle, 1996). For example, media messages (a) represent dominant interests as universal and progressive rather than particular and parochial; (b) deny contradictions such as those related to capitalist production and distribution; and (c) naturalize the present as "common sense." Media are hegemonic, in other words, inasmuch as they secure consensus and control through consent rather than coercion (Apple, 1996).

There is little question that the media are powerful agencies with the capacity to dominate and control. In some cases, the exercise of power is blatant; in others, media power is sustained by an aura of impartiality, objectivity, and balance. An ability to frame issues and set agendas in ways that bolster the status quo is central to the notion of media as thought control in democratic societies (Hermann and Chomsky, 1988). This agenda-setting property also reinforces a view of the media as systems of (enlightened) propaganda by virtue of their impact. Yet the media are not monolithic structures with conspiratorial designs on the general population. Media represent a contested site, a kind of ideological battleground where different interests struggle for control over media agendas (Wilcox, 1996). It is precisely this area of the "in between" that is crucial in exploring the ambiguous properties of the media.

Thought Control as Enlightened Propaganda

Few would dispute the ability of the media to shape how people look at the world, how they understand it, and the manner in which they relate to it. A media-dominated society tends to elevate electronic and print media to a privileged status in deciding what is right or wrong, acceptable or unacceptable. Those in control of the media define the beliefs, values, and myths by which we live and organize our lives. They impose a cultural context for framing our experiences of social reality, in the process sending out a clear message about who is normal and what is desirable in society (Abel, 1997). Our dependence on the media for reality construction assumes even greater relevance in the absence of direct experience. For instance, what we know about the world has been filtered through the prism of several interpretive layers. Without necessarily impugning the integrity of the media, how do we know what really happened, except as interpreted by the press? Whose interpretation made it onto the screen or into print? For many, the whiff of propaganda is real, and may reflect a bias integral to (rather than peripheral to) the media process.

The concept of enlightened propaganda may be helpful in explaining the nature of media-society relations. Propaganda can be defined as a process of persuasion by which the few influence the many. Symbols are manipulated in an organized and one-sided fashion to modify attitudes or behaviour (Qualter, 1991). By contrast, enlightened propaganda dismisses the element of intent or consciousness as part of the persuasion process. Proposed instead is the idea of consequence or effect: That is, the organization and distribution of information has the effect of controlling our perceptions by promoting one point of view to the exclusion of others. In taking this perspective, propaganda is not equated with blatant

CASE STUDY 8-1	Portraying Minorities: Propaganda in Multicultural Land

The world we inhabit is pervaded and transformed by images. The control of knowledge and its dissemination through media images is fundamental to the exercise of power in society. Media images are critical for conveying shared cultural beliefs and underlying assumptions in organizing our way around society. These images not only assist in the identification and construction of ourselves as social beings, they also serve as "windows" which provide insight into social patterns and cultural values of society. The proliferation of media images makes it impossible to distinguish fantasy from reality, as Angus and Jhally (1989) explain, especially since the "real" is so mediated through media images that any separation of the two (except for analytical purposes) is futile. For minority women and men, the circulation of images is both a strength and weakness, depending on the context:

> Visual images in that sense are congealed social relations, formalizing in themselves either relations of domination or those of resistance. The politics of images is the same as any politics; it is about being the subjects not the objects of the world that we live in (Bannerji, 1986:20).

With images as powerful as they are, the onus falls on minority women and men to reclaim control over representations of who they are and what they want to be. Several questions strike at the heart of media portrayals of minority images. How do the media portray images of aboriginal peoples and minority women and men? How do media reflect and represent minorities in Canada? Are prevailing media images the result of conscious or unconscious decisions? What if anything can be done to improve this level of representation (Jakubowicz et al., 1994)? Four themes appear to characterize media (mis)treatment of minority women and men across all media outlets.

(1) Minorities as invisible

Numerous studies have extolled what many regard as obvious. Canada's multicultural diversity is poorly reflected in the advertising, programming, and newscasting sectors of the popular media (Fleras, 1994). Visible minorities are reduced to an invisible status through "under-representation" in programming, staffing, and decision-making. An informal survey by *Toronto Star* media critic, Henry Mietkiewicz (1999), confirms the cliché that "the more things change..." Based on 1787 television commercials in 114 hours of programming on Canadian and American channels in February of 1999, the following was revealed: of the 1314 commercials monitored on Canadian TV, 30.8 percent employed minority actors, however briefly, while 10.4 percent provided minority actors with more than a token appearance of at least 3 seconds of screen time. Whether these figures are consistent with Canada's evolving demographic depends on the point of reference: visible minorities constituted 11.2 percent of Canada's population in 1996, but 15.8 percent of Ontario's population and 31.6 percent of Toronto's. Even substantial presentation in the media may be misleading if minority women and men are slotted into a relatively small number of programs such as TV Ontario's "Polka Dot Door," or reduced to victim/assailant in reality-based programming. Nor is there much sign of improvement: In 1989, Robert MacGregor acknowledged the invisiblity of visible minority women in Canada's national newsmagazine (*Maclean's*) when measured by the quantity and quality of their appearances over a 30-year span. A follow-up study indicates that women of colour continue to be "couched in compromise" by virtue of mixed messages (Kunz and Fleras, 1998). Or consider the plight of African-Americans on television. All-Black cast shows are common enough, but most TV sitcoms continue to be segregrated; dramas are rarely built around Black actors (in the belief that there is no sizable demographic audience for this kind of material) (Onstad, 1999); and Black theme programs border on the demeaning or stereotypical (Braxton, 1997). For example, of the 26 new shows scheduled by the 4 major U.S. networks in 1999, not a single one featured a minority lead, despite the fact that African-Americans consume up to 70 hours per week (Allemang, 1999). Nevertheless, a recent report for the Screen Actors Guild conducted by George Gerbner of Temple University has reconfirmed that, Blacks notwithstanding, minorities such as Hispanics, Asians, and Native Americans are under-represented compared to their numbers in real life (*Toronto Star*, 23 Dec., 1998).

It would be inaccurate to say that the news media ignore minorities. Rather a "shallows and rapids" treatment is a more accurate appraisal. That is, under normal circumstances, minorities are ignored or rendered irrelevant by the mainstream press ("shallows"). Otherwise, coverage is guided by the context of crisis or calamity, involving natural catastrophes, civil wars, and colourful insurgents ("rapids"). When the crisis subsides, media interest is suspended until the next big thing. Conflicts and calamities occur in minority communties, of course, but the absence of balanced coverage results in distorted perceptions of needs, concerns, or aspirations. This distortion may not be deliberately engineered. Rather, the misrepresentation reflects media preoccupation with audience ratings and advertising revenues. When asked to account for media whitewashing, veteran TV producer Aaron Spelling did not mince words: "Our industry is not about Black or White. It's about money... the only colour that matters in TV is green" (cited in *National Post*, 26 July, 1999:B-7). The flamboyant and sensational are highlighted to satisfy audience needs and sell copy, without much regard for the effects of sensationalism on the lives of those sensationalized. The media may shun responsibility for their discriminatory impact, arguing they are reporting only what is news. Nevertheless, such an exclusive focus has the effect of portraying minorities as "subhuman" and less than worthy of our sympathy or assistance.

(2) Minorities as stereotypes

Minorities have long complained of stereotyping by the mainstream media. Historically, people of colour were portrayed in a manner that did not offend prevailing prejudices. Liberties taken with minority depictions in consumer advertising were especially flagrant. In an industry geared toward image and appeal, the rule of homogeneity and conservatism prevailed. Advertisers wanted their products sanitized and bleached of colour for fear of lost revenue. People of colour were rarely depicted in the advertising of beauty care and personal hygiene products, so entrenched was the image of "Whiteness" as the preferred standard of beauty (Bledsloe, 1989). Elsewhere, images of racial minorities were steeped in unfounded generalizations that emphasized the comical or grotesque. This stereotyping fell into a pattern. People from the Middle East continue to be portrayed as sleazy fanatics or tyrannical patriarchs (for example, "Islamic guerrillas" in the film, *The Seige*) where terrorism and religion are inextricably linked; Asians have been type-cast either as sly and cunning or as mathematical whizzes. Blacks in prime-time shows remain stuck as super-hero/athletes or sex-obsessed buffoons and are surrounded by a host of secondary characters such as hipsters or outlaws (Cuff, 1997). Newscasts continue to portray Blacks as athletes, entertainers, or criminals, according to studies by Francis Henry and another by Scot Wortley (cited in Siddiqui, 1999).

Consider how media have historically portrayed Canada's aboriginal peoples as the "other," a people removed in time and remote in space. This image of aboriginal peoples as the "other" has been filtered through a Eurocentric lens and has ranged in scope from their portrayal as "noble savage" and "primitive romantic," to their debasement as "villain" or "victim" or "comical simpleton," with the stigma of "problem people" or "menacing subversives" sandwiched in between (also Blythe, 1994; Wall, 1997). Images of tribalism continue to resonate with a spicy mixture of meanings, from backwardness to spiritual mysticism to ecological custodians (Jakubowicz et al., 1994). Most portrayals embraced a mythical image of an imaginary warrior who occupied the plains between 1825 and 1880 (Frances, 1992). Depictions revolve around ingredients from a so-called "Indian Identity Kit" (Berton, 1975) that consisted of the following items, few of which even were indigenous to aborigi-

nal peoples prior to European settlement: wig with hair parted in the middle into hanging plaits; feathered war bonnet; headband (a White invention to keep the actor's wig from slipping off; buckskin leggings; mocassins; painted skin teepee; and armed with tomahawk and bows and arrows. This "one-size-fits-all" (seen one, seen them all) image applied to all First Peoples, regardless of whether they were Cree or Salish or Ojibwa or Blackfoot. These images could be further divided into a series of recurrent stereotypes, in effect reinforcing a "seen one Indian, seen 'em all" mentality. Collectively, these images reinforce the notion of aboriginal peoples as a people from a different time and place, whose histories began with European colonization, and whose reality only makes sense in terms of interaction with Whites. Collective resistence to their colonization is rarely depicted, athough individual acts of protest may be valorized, in effect de-politicizing aboriginal concerns and contributions to Canada. The net effect ensured an image of aboriginal peoples as "safe, exotic, and somewhere else," as Philip Hayward writes with respect to the music industry co-optation of aboriginal artists.

Negative portraits inflict a degree of symbolic and psychological violence on aboriginal lives. Any sense of self-worth plunges because of images that devalue aboriginal status as that of the "other." To be sure, media have begun to invert conventional stereotypes of Whites and First Peoples, with much greater emphasis on the courage or durability of the indigenous people of the land versus the rapacious greed of White settler colonization (think of *Dances With Wolves*). Nevertheless, there is a long way to go, as Maurice Switzer, a member of the Elders' Council of the Mississaugas of

Rice Lake First Nations at Alderville, Ontario writes (1997:21-22):

> The country's large newspapers, TV and radio news shows often contain misinformation, sweeping generalizations and galling stereotypes about natives and native affairs. Their stories are usually presented by journalists with little background knowledge or understanding of aboriginals and their communities... As well very few so-called mainstream media consider aboriginal affairs to be a subject worthy of regular attention.

Why stereotyping? Simplication is at the heart of media, but particularly advertising and TV programming. Stereotyping simplifies the media process. Media movers and shakers prefer to tap into a pool of aboriginal stereotypes as a kind of convenient shorthand. Reliance on these simplistic and reductionist images creates readily identifiable frames (tropes) that impose a thematic coherence that audiences can relate to because of a shared culture code (Taylor, 1993; Ross, 1996). Over time these stereotypes solidify into definitive statements about "reality" and, while not "real" in the conventional sense, they are real in their social consequences.

The social dimension of stereotyping should not be overlooked. Rather than an error in perception, stereotyping constitutes a system of social control through the internalization of negative images. Stereotypes are employed to keep aboriginal peoples in their place and out of sight, thus sanitizing the colonization of First Peoples by assuaging White guilt (Churchill, 1994). With stereotypes, it becomes progressively easier to disregard their humanity and status as a distinct people. The racially coded discourses that constitute stereotyping not only tap into public fears, but also feed public demands

for tougher measures of social control. Paradoxically, such stereotyping may also contribute to the formulation of White identities (Davis, 1996). Imaginary Indians are filtered through the prism of European prejudice and preconception, in the process projecting Euro-Canadian onto the "other." To the extent that Whites have long resorted to certain images of the "other" as a basis for collectively defining who they are in relation to the world around them, these images about the other say more about the "creators" than the "created."

(3) Minorities as problem people

Minority women and men are frequently singled out by the media as a "social problem"; that is, as "having problems" or "creating problems" in need of political attention or scarce national resources. As problem people, they are taken to task by the media for making demands that may imperil Canada's unity or national prosperity. Consider the case of Canada's aboriginal peoples when they are depicted as: (a) a threat to Canada's territorial integrity (the Lubicon blockade in 1988 or the Oka Mohawk confrontations in the summer of 1990), or to national interests (the Innu protest of the NATO presence in Labrador); (b) a risk to Canada's social order (the violence between factions at the Akwesasne Reserve or occupation at Gustafsen Lake, B.C.); (c) an economic liability (the costs associated with massive land claims settlement or recent proposals to constitutionally entrench inherent self-governing rights); (d) a thorn in the side of the criminal justice system (ranging from the Donald Marshall case to police shootings of aboriginal people, including the killing of Dudley George at Ipperwash, Ontario), or an unfair player (cigarette-smuggling or rum-running across borders). Aboriginal activism is framed as a departure from established norms. Protestors are frequently framed as dangerous or irrational. The subsequent demonization marginalizes the legitimacy of dissent, trivializes minority issues, and distracts from the issues at hand. As a result, many news stories involving minority assertiveness are couched as a conflict of interest between destabilizing forces on one side and the forces of order, reason, and stability on the other (Abel, 1997). Compounding this negativity are reports of an excessive reliance on welfare, a predilection for alcohol and substance abuse, a pervasive laziness and lack of ambition, and an inclination to mismanage what little they have. The combined impact of this negative reporting paints a villainous picture of Canada's First Peoples. Time and again they come across as "troublesome constituents" whose demands for self-determination and the right to inherent self-government are contrary to Canada's liberal-democratic tradition. Success stories are rarely reported, and those that make it are portrayed as an exception to the rule.

Minority men and women are also problematized by the media. People of colour, both foreign- and native-born, are targets of negative reporting that dwells on costs, threats, and inconveniencies. Media reporting of refugees usually refers to illegal entries and the associated costs of processing and integration into Canada. Immigrants are routinely cast as potential troublemakers who steal jobs from Canadians; cheat on the welfare system; take advantage of educational opportunities without making a corresponding commitment to Canada; engage in illegal activities such as drugs or smuggling; and imperil Canada's unity and identity by refusing to discard their culture. This negativity may be coded in different ways, from content to positioning and layout of the story, length of article and size of type, content of headlines and kickers (phrases immediately after the headline), use of newspeak or inflammatory language, use of quotes, statistics, and racial origins. The cumulative effect of this largely one-sided portrayal reinforces the wedge between "them" and "us."

(4) Minorities as adornment

The media tend to portray minority women and men as mere adornments to society at large. This decorative aspect is achieved by casting minorities in roles that are meant only to amuse or embellish. Minorities are associated with the exotic and sensual, portrayed as congenial hosts from faraway destinations, enlisted as superstar boosters for athletics and sporting goods, or ghettoized in certain marketing segments related to "rap" or "hip hop." Most minority roles on television consist of bit parts, usually restricted to sitcoms or dramas which stereotype minority women and men as superfluous to society. Blacks on television are locked into roles as entertainers, criminals, or athletes (Siddiqui, 1999). Rarely is there any emphasis on intellectual or professional prowess, much less recourse to positive role models to which youth can aspire outside of athletics or entertainment (Cuff, 1997). Such a restriction may prove inherently satisfying to mainstream audiences who historically have enjoyed laughing at Blacks when cast as comics or buffoons. The depoliticizing of Blacks as "emasculated" cartoons ("playing 'em for laughs") has the effect of reassuring nervous audiences that the world turns as it should (see Farhi, 1995).

Media relations with minority women are no less demeaning (Jiwani, 1992; hooks, 1992; Creedon, 1993;

Graydon, 1995). Both women and men of colour are vulnerable to misrepresentation as peripheral, stereotypes, problem peoples, and the "other." Women also are subject to additional media mistreatment because of gender. The intersection of gender with ethnicity and race relegates aboriginal women, women of colour, and immigrant women to the status of decorative props. Minority women are generally reduced to commodities; this objectification equates women with objects for control or consumption. They are sexualized in a way that equates "the good life" with "snaring" and supporting a man to the exclusion of anything else. This sexualization is thought to infantilize women by casting them as silly or childlike, obsessed with appearances, and devoid of intelligence. They also are racialized in a manner that draws inordinate attention to their status as "other," together with the demeaning implications associated with being "otherized." Their bodies are gratuitously paraded to sell everything from esoteric fashions and sensuous perfumes to a host of exotic vacation destinations (see Graydon, 1995). Minority women are cast in roles of domestication, a process that tends to diminish their status and contributions to society. Finally, women of colour are portrayed as dangerous or evil, with potential to destroy everything good about society or civilization (Jiwani, 1992). In short, gender is superimposed on and intersects with race to perpetuate patterns of inequality in ways that are mutually reinforcing yet contradictory (Stam, 1993). These complex articulations tend to trivialize the realities and contributions of minority women to the level of adornments in an environment in which style prevails over substance.

To sum up: Visible minorities are rendered invisible through under-representation in programming, staffing, and decision-making. Conversely, they are visibly over-represented in areas that count for less, including tourism, sports, international relief, or entertainment. Media portrayals tend to depict minorities as the other. While Whites are portrayed as the norm and standard by which others are judged and found wanting, minority women and men are given short thrift as humans removed in time and space and outside the pale of civilization. Minorities complain of being treated as "foreigners" or "outsiders," whose lives seem to revolve around their "defining" status of race or religion, to the virtual exclusion of other attributes. They serve as a foil with which to praise or condemn contemporary values in society. Images of "them" as "those people" are filtered through the prism of European prejudice and preconceptions, in the process projecting mainstream fears or yearnings onto the "other." Such demeaning images serve as lightening rods to absorb public hostility over unpopular changes in society. What is taught by these racist depictions? Overtly negative representations are combined with the absence of complex characterization to create an impact that is racist in consequence if not always in intent. The need to frame all stories around the theme of conflict puts an onus on dividing the world into "good guys" and "bad guys." Through images and codes, children are taught that cultural differences outside the imprint of White, middle-class culture are inferior, deviant, irrelevant, or threatening. Children of colour also learn to dislike who they are because of these depictions. A spokesperson for an American Islamic association said this about the film *Alladin* (quoted in Giroux, 1995:40):

All of the bad guys have beards and large, bulbous noses, sinister eyes and heavy accents, and they're wielding swords constantly. Alladin doesn't have a big nose; he has a small nose. He doesn't have a beard or a turban. He doesn't have an accent. What makes him nice is they've given him this American character. I have a daughter who says she's ashamed to call herself an Arab, and its because of things like this.

Ethnocentrism and White superiority may not be openly articulated by media "whitewashing," but are assumed and normalized as the standard that disparages the "other." Portrayal of minorities as the other typically entails a cultural Catch-22: They are criticized for being too different, yet may be chided for not being different enough; they are taken to task for aspiring to be the same, yet denounced when they falter or refuse (Stam, 1993). Or, as Brian Maracle (1996) puts it, mainstream media are so steeped in Eurocentric values (including liberal pluralism and universalism) that the perception of bias is elusive, especially bias against those who don't share these values or ideals. The fact that media bias exists is not the problem; problems arise from the refusal to admit this bias while claiming to be neutral, fair, and objective.

The media in Canada are under scrutiny to make appropriate adjustments. Multicultural minorities and aboriginal peoples have asked some tough questions of the media regarding their commitment to accommodate Canada's ethnic diversity. Proposed changes include the incorporation of minority perspectives into the media process, multicultural programming, balanced and impartial newscasting, and sensitivity training for journalists and decision-makers (Abel, 1997). Alternate arrangements include the creation of separate minority networks for enhancing minority input into media process and outcomes (see also Spoonley and Hirsch, 1990). Responsible coverage of minority interests and concerns is predicated on the need to stop: (a) selective and sensationalistic accounts; (b) images and words that demean and malign; (c) portrayals that are biased and unbalanced while lacking any sense of context; and (d) stereotyping that inflames hatred and fear (Rees, 1986). But a conflict of interest is inevitable: The commercial media do not see themselves as reform agencies to promote progressive change or accommodate, even if others think they have a social responsibility to do so. They are a business whose raison d'etre is simple: to make money by connecting audiences to advertisers. Institutional practices that historically generated revenues (eg., stereotyping) will be retained; those that don't will be discarded. Such a bottom-line mentality will invariably be at odds with minority demands for balanced and contexted coverage, given media preference for "morselization" over context, conflict over cooperation, and personalities over issues (see Atkinson, 1994).

brainwashing or crude displays of totalitarian censorship. Nor is propaganda equivalent to deliberate lying. Propaganda is not necessarily something deliberately inserted into the media. Rather, it is inherent in media rules and intrinsic to daily operations, in the same way that systemic discrimination reflects the negative but unintended consequences of even-handed rules or well-intentioned procedures (Fleras and Elliott, 1999). The net result is the same in both cases: a one-sided interpretation of reality that normalizes even while it marginalizes. Redefining the media as propaganda may not be flattering to the industry, but the evidence is compelling, especially when applied to media representation of minority women and men in Canada, as demonstrated by Case Study 8–1.

Media objectives are directed towards the goals of "manufacturing consent" and "generating compliance" (Herman and Chomsky, 1988). Their very unobtrusiveness in achieving these goals has the effect of transforming the media into a powerful agent of domination and control. Media images about what is desirable or acceptable are absorbed without much awareness of the indoctrination process. The media fix the premises of discourse by circumscribing the outer limits of acceptability for discussion. This is accomplished in many ways: by suppressing information at odds with powerful interests, and through the perpetuation of stereotypes and ethnocentric value judgments. As Herman and Chomsky (1988) remind us: (a) powerful interests can fix the parameters of debate and narrow the range of information; (b) government and the corporate elite have monopolized access to what eventually is defined as news; (c) major advertisers can dictate the terms of newscasting; and (d) media owners can influence what will or will not appear. Distortions can be attained by the placement of articles and their tone, context, and fullness of treatment. Admittedly, the media do not act in collusion when presenting a monolithic front. Nor are media biases driven by a cabal of conspirators. Media authorities are known to disagree with one another, criticize powerful interests for actions inimical to the best interests of society, expose government corruption and corporate greed, and rail against measures to restrict free speech and other rights.

However, internal conflicts of this sort are more apparent than real, suggest Herman and Chomsky (1988). To the extent that disagreement appears, it generally reflects differences over the means by which to achieve commonly agreed-upon goals. Thus, the illusion of diversity and debate is fostered. Yet few bother to disagree over the underlying agenda, with the result that debates are limited to squabbles over details, not substance. Spirited discussion and lively dissension may be encouraged, but only within the framework of assumptions that constitute an elite consensus. The fundamental premises driving our society—the virtues of materialistic progress and competitive individualism—are generally off limits. For example, the media provide a venue for debating the pros and cons of free trade or global competitiveness; nevertheless, conspicuously absent from these discussions are questions about the desirability of capitalism as a system that destroys as it enriches. Also unexamined are the tacit assumptions underlying the interpretation of reality from a predominantly White, male, middle-class, heterosexual, and able-bodied orientation. However unintentional the consequences, the effects are anything but inconsequential. Propaganda can lead to the exclusion of alternate points of view, a reduction in dissent and disagreement, the creation of consensus and compliance with dominant ideologies, and the restriction of free debate. For these reasons, the media can be interpreted as systems of thought control in democratic societies. By securing majority interests without explicitly violating the practices of a free and open press, the one-sidedness of this thought control represents a case of enlightened propaganda, by consequence if not necessarily by intent. To the extent that social inequality is invariably portrayed by the media as a matter of individual choice rather than structured experience—not as social and constructed by way of power differences, but natural and normal—the media may be interpreted as propaganda. That every ad and all TV programming tell us that it's better to buy than not to buy if one wants to be saved also constitutes propaganda. The fact that minorities are invariably stereotyped as problem people who have problems or create problems may be seen as an exercise in propaganda. In short, the media define situations and impose "frames" of interpretation that "normalize" media priorities or corporate imperatives rather than consumer needs. The cumulative effect of such persuasion is to cast doubt on the reliability of media as a source of information.

PROBLEMATIZING THE MEDIA

Who says the media are a problem and why? On what grounds, and by what criteria can such an assessment be made? If the media are a problem, how is this problem manifest? In what ways do the media create problems, yet provide solutions? And what, if anything, can be done to minimize media damage? Responses to the question "Are media a social problem?" are thought to be contingent on a particular vision of society, and the role of the media in achieving that vision. Should media foster a pluralistic and socially responsible society, or should priorities be assigned to market-driven society and competitive individualism, even at the risk of eroding the social fabric? Three themes prevail in problematizing the media as a social problem: namely, (1) what are the media about? (2) what do the media do compared with what they are supposed to do? and (3) what are the media doing to us and society? First, the media are interpreted as being problematic in their own right. Their commitment to inform and entertain is riddled with hidden agendas that benefit some, handicap others. The media establish standards of performance, then fail to live up to these expectations, in effect creating a disjuncture between expectations and reality, both at institutional and public levels. Second, the media are known to generate social problems by virtue of their existence as a big business, their status as discourses in defence of profit, and their role as an instrument of thought control in a democratic society. This complicity makes it doubly imperative to explore how media contribute to the way in which inequities in society are created, expressed, maintained, challenged, and transformed. Third, problems arise due to the double-edged nature of media relations to society and society-building. By examining newscasting, TV programming, advertising, and "Internetting," the media are shown to exert a negative impact by eliciting mixed message at odds with the ideals of a progressive society.

THE PROBLEM WITH NEWS

Quickly now! Define news. Isn't it astonishing that something so simple and routine can pose such difficulties in definition? Problems of consensus result because people define news in different terms. It can be considered in terms of functions (the role news plays in society), by way of structure (its nature and properties), or at the level of processes (that is, whatever it is the news media do). With respect to functions, for example, news can be viewed as a system of communication that facilitates dialogue and interaction. News can also be viewed as a body of knowledge for expanding our understanding of the world as it unfolds in time and space. In some cases, this knowledge is not necessarily consistent with official doctrines and dominant ideologies; in many cases, it is. The notion of news as a professionally defined set of news values may not be a problem, but its potential to be problematic cannot be discounted (Miller, 1998). News becomes a social problem when it (a) detracts from fostering a democratic society of critically informed citizens, (b) obsesses over cosmetic redesign and market research rather than improved newscasting to capture market shares; (c) endorses a marketing concept that treats news as a commodity to be manipulated and sold as cheaply as possible; (d) provides a largely one-sided point of view rather than balanced coverage; (e) is driven exclusively by commercial interests and corporate agenda rather than the interests of service; (f) it is framed exclusively as entertainment rather than a source of information and knowledge; (g) relies exclusively on conflict and violence as a basis for storytelling and narrative structure; and (h) fails to acknowledge diversity in its personnel, process, and output (see also Miller, 1998). News that fails to conform to its standards and expectations is also problematic, and this failure to be a public service rather than a profit machine provides a starting point for framing news as a social problem.

Defining News

At the level of structure, what passes for news is normally associated with a property called newsworthiness (Abel, 1997). Generally speaking, news in North America is regarded as an "event" with one or more of the following characteristics: It must be immediate; be proximate (events further away are less likely to be reported); feature prominent individuals or flamboyant personalities; employ direct quotes and authoritative (although often unnamed) sources; involve magnitude in terms of cost or loss of life; embrace the odd or the deviant; be obsessed with conflict, anguish, and tragedy; and be easily labelled and condensed for quick reference and recall (Fuller, 1996). Unexpected or discontinuous events that constitute a break from norms and the routine also qualify as news values (Madger, 1997). Not surprisingly, in a profession consumed by negativity and the "un-normative," coups and earthquakes get top billing, as do crimes, clashes, and crises (McGregor, 1996). Situational factors may account for why one news item takes priority over another. Time and budgetary constraints may intrude (Abel, 1997). An item of local interest may take precedence over a global issue in a regional paper; conversely, a large urban daily may ignore regional interests. On balance, however, conflicts involving Hollywood celebrities are more newsworthy than mass killings in Africa. The media appear mesmerized by the deaths of royalty, under-age beauty contestants, and fashion designers rather than an analysis of why such incidents should consume so much space. Items for inclusion also depend on their "presentability," and this is determined by the media's access to visuals, easily identifiable protagonists, the availability of quotable reactions, and the novelty of the sound bites. Adversity and adversarial situations are preferred over the cooperative; so too are angles involving the unusual or the perverse. The dangers of applying a conflict framework to most news items is nicely captured by Gwynne Dyer, a London-based journalist and historian whose 3300 articles have been published in 45 countries. According to Dyer (1998), the world is not nearly as "stupid" or "nasty" as the news would have us believe, despite the heavy predominance of bad news, but is a far more "rational, less violent, and even kinder place than it used to be."

News as Social Construction

What passes for news is not simply a formulaic process; it consists of a series of judgment calls within the framework of organizational values and commercial commitments. The pervasiveness of these biases subjects newscasting to charges of bias (Hackett et al., 2000). In purporting to present only the facts, mainstream media have long endorsed the goals of objectivity in terms of fairness, accuracy, balance, and impartiality (Hackett and Zhao, 1998). However admirable such objectives may be, barriers are ignored that interfere with their attainment. Objectivity itself is a human impossibility, since no one is so utterly disinterested as to be transparent (Fuller, 1997). News is not something out there waiting to be plucked for placement as newsworthy. Rather, news is a constructed reality and, as a human accomplishment, is susceptible to various demands and pressures, both intentional and in-advertent. Collectively, these constraints blunt the media's capacity for balanced and accurate coverage. Many of the difficulties arise from the corporatization of the news media, the selectivity inherent in news collection and coverage, and the politics of news presentation. Each of these factors—rationale, coverage, collection, and packaging—undermines the potential of an informed citizentry.

Rationale: News as Big Business

Contemporary news (both print and broadcast) originates from several large corporate sources (Winter, 1994). This is certainly the case in Canada, where independent news sources are a vanishing breed. In lieu of independents are chains such as Hollinger or Thomson. Often transnational in scope, these corporations approach the news sector as nothing more than a profit-making business venture. Even publicly owned networks such as the CBC appear to be increasingly market-driven. A commercial imperative exerts a considerable strain on the integrity of the news media. It sharpens the potential for a conflict of interest between corporate needs and consumer concerns. A preoccupation with profit can lead to erratic (or non-existent) coverage of issues that require exhaustive investigative journalism. This "bottom line" mentality ensures a version of the news that is anything but impartial or detached. More to the point, news becomes whatever the industry defines as news, especially when consistent with majority interests of affluent agendas. The cumulative effect of this implicit collusion between news and big business (and the government) is not necessarily conspiratorial in intent, but rather a disquieting convergence of interests. Nor should we ever lose sight of the self-censorship at play in the news media. For, in the final analysis, mainstream news is as conservative as any other big business, with one eye cocked to audience ratings, the other to corporate revenues (Miller, 1998).

Consider the situation in Canada. As recently as late 1995, Hollinger Inc., a Vancouver-based mining consortium owned by Conrad Black, was a relatively minor player in the newspaper business. That all changed in the space of several months in the mid-1990s when Black went on an unprecedented buying spree that secured majority ownership of Canada's daily newspaper circulation, while transforming the media landscape in ways that rankled or dismayed. By 1996, Hollinger Inc. had emerged as a major player in Canada's newspaper sweepstakes, with ownership or control of 58 papers out of a total of 106 nationwide, 37 percent of the total daily circulation, and 42 percent of this country's readership. In addition to Canadian holdings, Hollinger Inc. has been active on the international front, with a slew of newspaper buy-outs, ranging in profile from London's *Daily Telegraph*, The *Jerusalem Post*, The *Chicago Sun-Times*, and Sydney *Morning Herald* to *Punxsutawney Spirit* in Pennsylvania. With worldwide daily circulation of over five million, Hollinger now ranks only behind News Corp. Ltd. of Australia, the global communications empire owned by Rupert Murdoch (7 million) and the Gannett Co. Inc. of Arlington, Virginia (6.6 million).

Is media monopoly a problem? Canada's 1970 Special Senate Committee on Mass Media lamented that control of the media was passing into fewer hands, with a corresponding conflict of interest. It also predicted that this trend was likely to continue. Twenty-five years later this observation appears extremely astute. Corporate groups account for about 93 percent of all copies of daily newspapers sold in Canada, up from 77 percent in 1970. In 1958, Canada's three largest dailies controlled around 25 percent of the daily newspaper total; in 1996, the figure had risen to 66 percent (Winter, 1997). Whereas 41.5 percent of the daily newspapers in Canada were independently owned in 1970, the figure had fallen to 17 percent by the mid-1990s. Of Ontario's 42 dailies, only Brockville's *Recorder and Times* can be regarded as independent. (Saunders and Mahood, 1996). Corporate concentration has reached the point where four provinces are without English-language daily newspaper competition, three of which are under the control of a single owner (Saunders and Mahood, 1996). The Irving estate continues to control the English-speaking dailies in New Brunswick, while Conrad Black's Hollinger Inc. owns both of the dailies in Newfoundland and P.E.I., in addition to the four dailies in Saskatchewan. Such concentration of circulation poses a potential for a conflict of interest.

Coverage

There is a lot going on in the world at any particular point in time. How do the news media decide what is worthy of being reported? The news industry is nominally committed to the principle of selecting only what is newsworthy (Miljan and Cooper, 1999). In reality, the industry is equally bound to making a profit by "selling" as much copy as possible through advertising and subscription rates. This dual commitment puts a premium on bolstering audience size and network ratings by appealing to the broadest possible audience. The news collection process is driven by a focus on the dramatic and spectacular, with particular emphasis on conflict, calamity, and confrontation. Newsworthiness is enhanced by the presence of flamboyant, preferably corrupt personalities with a knack for the outrageous or titillating. The non-controversial and cooperative are often ignored because they lack intrinsic appeal for an audience with a short attention span and an "action" mentality.

The "jolts" and "jiggles" mentality inherent in the news process has been widely criticized. Tabloid-style journalism is taken to task for fixating on the spectacular, such as the Clinton-Lewinsky fiasco or the murdered prepubescent beauty, Jon Benet Ramsay. Mundane but important topics are pushed aside, in the process denying the realities of the everyday world. Religion may be important to many Canadians and Americans, but few would glean that impression from the paucity of articles that appear in newscasts. The lack of context is especially disturbing. It not only imparts a sheen of superficiality to news, but also robs events and developments of any meaningful reality. Minorities in Canada and abroad have complained about news portrayal of them as belligerent, ruthless, or indifferent towards human life. No less flattering is their depiction as victims, vulnerable to social decay and societal disorder, enmeshed in graft and corruption, and without much capacity for cooperative, productive activity. Stereotypes, prejudice, and discrimination become easily entrenched under these circumstances.

A preoccupation with conflict is no less problematic. A relentless barrage of conflict, atrocities, and suffering may have the effect of diminishing people's capacity for genuine outrage, compassion, or committed activism. Nowhere is this more evident than in references to "compassion fatigue" (Moeller, 1998). Advances in technology, especially the Internet, enable viewers for the first time in history to witness slaughter in the more remote corners of the world, from Bosnia and Rwanda to East Timor and Chechnya. But rather than fostering a response that reinforces the primacy of a moral order of cooperation and compassion, the proliferation of images of suffering and death has tended to numb the sense and dull sensibilities. Instead of educating or informing by analyzing context, causes, and consequences, the press appears content with pandering to the lowest common commercial denominator through sensationalized chronologies of conflict or calamity (Rieff, 1999). The collective response to this tour package of war, genocide, and misery is that of confusion, cynicism, disengagement, and callousness. And this collective inability to experience compassionate may induce despair or indifference without eliciting any humanitarian response. Even higher thresholds of violence may be demanded to attract the attention of jaded palates.

Collection

Another source of bias is in the news collection process itself. The investigative journalist with a nose for news may also be an unwitting agent in relaying bias. Social and professional assumptions create particular frames of reference that do not reflect a neutral view of reality (Abel, 1997). Even a fierce commitment to objectivity and neutrality does not preclude the possibility of bias in news collection and packaging. All human beings, including those in the news industry, are embedded in social contexts that shape perceptions and interpretations. Neutrality can be difficult to achieve, according to Roger Landry, publisher of *La Presse* (*Globe and Mail*, March 4, 1997), especially since journalists are invariably influenced by personal interests or aversions. Words may be manipulated (unconsciously in many cases) when drawing attention to certain aspects of reality and away from other dimensions that are deemed less significant. The camera lens or tape recorder may not "lie" in the conventional sense of the term; however, each instrument only records a minute portion of what occurs around us. The ubiquity and pervasiveness of this bias undermines any pretext of objectivity and value-neutrality. For that reason alone, members of the public must cautiously approach what they are told to see, hear, or read, especially if they lack first-hand knowledge of the situation in question.

Bias also arises from news sources. Reporters are heavily dependent for their livelihood on official sources in the government, bureaucracies, police forces, and corporate sectors. Collectively these sources are difficult to access and prone to secrecy. Yet they are highly sought after because they lend credibility to stories and sometimes offer the promise of a "scoop." Not surprisingly, many organizations employ professional public relations and media consultants whose job description rarely includes telling the truth. They appear more interested in impression-management than in providing the facts (Peart and Macnamara, 1996). What emerge from these news "scrums" are highly selective bits of information that make the organizations look good at the expense of balance and accuracy. Even unofficial sources of information can be suspect. On-site reporting seeks to conjure up an image of painstaking and meticulous objectivity. Reality is reported as it unfolds before our eyes without the filter of interpretation. In fact, however, what passes for reality may be as contrived and manufactured as official reports. Demonstrations and protest marches may be staged and managed for the benefit of the evening news slot. The rhetoric produced by these telegenic displays is concerned with manipulating sympathy or extorting public funds, not with accurate reflections of the facts.

Packaging and Presentation

Bias in newscasting is compounded by problems in presentation. Distortions can be attributed to a variety of factors. Problems arise from the very act of packaging a complex and fluid reality into the straitjacket of visual images and sound bites, with a beginning and end, separated by a climax. An adversarial format is frequently superimposed to give some "bite" to the presentation. Isolated and intermittent events may be spliced together into a story, in the process accentuating the magnitude of crisis or urgency where none actually existed. The impact of "serious" news is blunted by and swamped with trivial news and advertising (Orwin, 1999). The presentation can be twisted in other ways. According to David Taras (1991), for each edition of CBC's *The National*, up to 1 million words and 40 hours of videotape are collected. This volume needs to be distilled into 20 minutes of news and enough verbiage to fill about one-third of a newspaper page. This example demonstrates the importance of understanding the grounds for editorial decisions: What is kept and what is discarded? Who decides and why?

To sum up: It should be clear, then, that the news is not an objective exercise in information transmission (Hackett et al., 2000). What eventually is defined as news is not something intrinsic to reality, with clearly marked and widely agreed-upon labels. Neither an impartial slice of reality reported by trained professionals nor a random reaction to disparate events, news as "invented" reality is shaped by organizational values and commercial concerns (Parenti, 1992). The concept of news as socially constructed is important: Rather than representing anything natural or normal about the world out there, despite efforts by vested interests to make it seem so, news is a product or convention, created by individuals who make choices in specific contexts. To define news as socially constructed is not intended to imply that news is a fiction or fabrication. The intent is to draw attention to news, not as a thing, but as an attribute that is applied to something by those with the power to make this application stick. In short, what eventually is "distilled" as news is expected to run a "reality" gauntlet in which truth is the victim. This is not to suggest, as Conrad Black has, that working journalists are "ignorant, lazy, opinionated, intellectually dishonest, and inadequately supervised" (cited in Hackett and Zhao, 1999:11). Nevertheless, the news process is subject to numerous biases and hidden agendas. It is formatted to attract audiences and secure advertisers, then filtered through selective mechanisms that only serve to enlarge the reality gap. News becomes a manufactured commodity in which any semblance of reality is accidental. In place of objectivity, there is an "invented" reality that embraces media priorities rather than any commitment to consumer needs or an honest appraisal of what actually exists. Interestingly, television no less than newspapers is selective in coverage or presentation. Reality is beamed into our homes, not in the sense of an exact replica, but as a form of realism purged of its sordid and messy elements lest it rattle nervous advertisers. This ambivalence has turned the news into an electronic equivalent of Orwellian doublespeak, a process whereby two opposing thoughts (entertainment and information) are accepted simultaneously without contradiction. In effect, then, TV news is packaged to meet audience demands and advertising priorities. In an age of zappers and satellite transmission, what is passed off as news are visual bites for fun and profit. Without visuals, a story is unlikely to get on the air, while complicated ongoing issues with unclear protagonists are likely to be shunned (Madger, 1997). There is nothing wrong with having news packaged in an entertaining fashion. But, when all subject matter is presented as entertainment, as Neil Postman (1985) writes in his biting commentary on television, it makes it increasingly difficult to separate fact from fantasy.

TOXIC TV

Some issues defined as social problems may catch the reader by surprise. For those not versed in media literacy, for example, the concept of newscasting as a social problem may have caught them off guard. Even those suspicious of the news industry may not have appreciated the magnitude of the disservice rendered to the viewing public. Other issues, however, are almost too obvious to mention as social problems. Television (and the programs it offers) falls into this category, even if the occasional study exonerates it as a positive or relatively benign force in society.

Is the banality of TV programming a deliberate attempt to insult the audience? Are audiences perceived as incapable of understanding complicated plot lines or complex characterizations? Is there a creative void in programming decisions? Is it part of an elaborate hoax to fool all of the people all of the time? Despite appearances to the contrary, the content of TV programming is driven by commercial imperatives rather than audience concerns. Programming is created to please advertisers who prefer programs that create the right atmosphere for product amplification. To the extent that audiences are important to programmers, they are seen as products (or commodities) for sale to advertisers. The bigger the audience, the merrier the profits (Tehranian, 1996). If this line of argument is true, and evidence supports these assertions (Andersen 1996), the relationship between advertising and programming may need to be inverted (see Ellul, 1965). Programming is not the normal function of television, with advertising as an interruption to the norm. Rather, programming may be interpreted as an interruption to television's normal function of advertising. Programming is the filler between commercials. Television itself is one long commercial for connecting advertisers by way of programming breaks with the right kind of audience. Yet another inversion: It is not the case that audiences watch TV; more to the point, television watches us to monitor our interests, habits, and concerns. Even the distinction between programming and advertising has blurred ("commercialtainment") with the proliferation of placement ads, programming environments (certain products will advertise only on certain types of programs), MTV (music videos are ads), and tie-ins (especially on children's shows). In short, the quality of programming is aimed at pleasing advertisers, who are its main consumers, rather than audiences. And those who pay the piper get to select the tune.

TV as Pleasantville

For many, television is a major social headache. Commercials are denounced as irritants, while programming is caricatured for insulting the viewer's intelligence, particularly with so-called "reality programming" (Who Wants To Marry a Multi-Millionaire?). Some are disturbed by the prodigious amount of television (23 hours per week) consumed by the average Canadian, excluding the VCR and video games. Time spent watching TV, so the refrain goes, is time away from constructive activities. This loss of connectedness with the real world invariably is thought to breed indifference and insensitivity (see Tate and McConnell, 1991). Children who watch television for prolonged periods appear to be less skilled at coping with stressful situations because of exposure to harmful actions that appear to be free of any consequence or rely on conflict to solve all problems (Leigh, 1999). Not surprisingly, the American Academy of Pediatrics has recommended that children under two not watch television in order to improve social/intellectual development and interaction with parents (cited in *Maclean's,* August 16, 1999). The report also criticized the use of television as a babysitter while recommending the banning of television from the rooms of teenagers to ensure better monitoring. The toxicity of television is expressed in other ways. A kind of "dumbing down" occurs by dissolving the boundaries between adulthood and childhood, as television makes the content of an adult world available to everyone (Meyrowitz, 1986). Adulthood has lost much of its aura and appeal as a result, with a corresponding decline in deference to authority or hierarchy that once existed simply because of age differences. A television-inspired commitment to instant gratification is held responsible for eroding the social trust and civility at the heart of any moral system, and replacing them with an aggregate of loosely connected individuals without central purpose or social responsibility. Other critics are bothered by the effects of television on otherwise normal individuals. With its predilection for conflict to drive plots or organize storylines, both television news and programming have created a cultural climate in which political and military crises are encouraged to attract audiences and bolster advertising rates (see Marchand, 1999). Still others flinch from the amount of sex and violence on television, not only during prime time, where it is supposed to be carefully monitored, but on children's shows, newscasts, sporting events, and music videos. With that kind of negative publicity and community concern, it is not surprising that pressure is mounting to censor television violence.

Television is arguably the most powerful yet enigmatic of contemporary social forces (Andersen, 1996). For some it is a "revolution in a box" with a capacity to enlighten and reform; for others it is a "tyranny of the trivial" with few redeeming qualities. Once a device for celebrating consumerism as an acceptable lifestyle after the Second World War, television continues to promulgate the virtues of a consumerist lifestyle. Since the logic of capitalism is derived from the systematic pursuit of profit, Chris Barker (1997) reminds us, a capitalist mode of production is dynamic and expansionist in its pursuit of new commodities and markets, with television an increasingly important component of this world-marketing strategy. Television is bound up with capitalism both as a set of economic activities as well as a cultural force that is constituted by and constitutive of the conditions of capitalist modernity. It also furnishes an outlet for those in search of convenient babysitting, companionship, solace, a sense of community, and escapism. No less worrying for many is television's role as a nemesis of democracy. Instead of substance and stance, the art of politics now revolves around telegenic candidates, stage-managed platforms, and eight-second visual bites. Television tends to portray a nasty and dangerous world, according to noted communications theorist George Gerbner (Stossel, 1997), further undermining the cohesion and interaction required of a democracy. With such multiple functions at its disposal, television has replaced religion as an important arbiter of who we are, what we want to do, and where we want to go. Its impact as an opiate of the masses is even more pronounced for those without access to alternate sources of information. Few issues over reality programming have garnered as much attention as the relationship between television and violence in society. Strictly speaking, there is no conclusive evidence linking television with violence, either on the street or at home. Still, the negative conclusions from more than 3000 studies cannot be discounted. Equally controversial is reliance on censorship as a solution to violent programming.

Violence on TV/Violent Society

The statistics have been trotted out before, but they continue to disgust and concern. Judging by the incidents of violence reported by the police and covered by the media, violence levels in Canadian society continue to reflect historic highs. Beatings and shootings are perceived as relatively routine, even outside major urban centres. There is another set of statistics that can trigger shock and indignation, and it relates to the disturbing amount of violence displayed on television. The average Canadian watches about 23 hours of television a week, that is, we spend about 20 percent of our waking hours around the TV. People "die" to be on television, and the killing of others is seen by some as a ticket to 15 seconds of TV fame. Programs designed for adults are violent enough, but the violence in children's programs is even more prevalent, with estimates ranging to ten times the violence in adult shows. And rather than subsiding in response to growing concern or outrage, prime-time television in the United States is getting more violent particularly among pay cable networks, according to a $3.5 million study conducted between October 1994 and October 1997, and commissioned by the National Cable Television Association (Associated Press, 1998).

In addition to the numbers, concerns are raised about how violence is portrayed and its acceptability as a problem-solving device. Graphic portrayals of violence as pathological are one thing; depictions of random and explicit violence as a joke in itself (think of *Reservoir Dogs*, *Pulp Fiction*, or *Natural Born Killers*) is quite another. Violence for the sake of violence no longer has shock value, but simply encourages people to see more without experiencing more (see Giroux, 1996). Violent excitement is the key, and no amount of hollow moralizing about doing the right thing or punishing evil seems to diminish the glamour or appeal. The degree to which this violence is "sugar-coated" is also disconcerting. Violent encounters are glorified as humorous, exciting, and glamorous, in part to suit the entertainment demands of prime-time audiences. TV routinely takes what is harrowing about reality and sanitizes it into something cosy and reassuring for the benefit of audience ratings and advertising revenue. Thus, what would by all accounts be a sordid and grisly event is transformed into something relatively painless or of little consequence, even ennobling, thus promoting its usefulness for solving interpersonal problems. Negotiation and compromise tend to be time-consuming and inconclusive; by contrast, violent solutions are clear-cut and unambiguous.

In recent years, the role of video games and the Internet in fostering violence has come to the fore. The passive experience of watching television is one thing; the act of acting interactively with violent video games or Internet sources is deemed quite another. A study by S.F.U. communications professor Stephen Kline found that one-quarter of 650 B.C. youth reported playing between 7 and 30 hours per week, a level of addiction that left many of them isolated and feeling helpless (Sankar, 1998). How do we assess a $600 million industry that caters almost exclusively to males under 25 years of age? Harmless fun? Release valve for dark fantasies? Or deadly conditioning for a violent outburst? Escalating levels of gratuitous violence in video games are a concern: To cater to increasingly jaded appetites and to maintain market shares, splatter video games such as "Dukem Nukem" are giving way to a new breed of games that enable players to manipulate photorealistic images of people in acts of torture, mutilation, and prostitution (Mandel, 1998). Even more disturbing is the perception that military conditioning and video games operate along similar lines. Soldiers are conditioned (desensitized) to be at ease with weapons and killings by repeatedly firing at human targets as second nature and without a second thought. The dangers in encouraging a violent mindset are all too evident, as acknowledged by an American educator:

> In video games, you're inflicting pain and suffering. Some of the games have characters who beg you to spare them. But you have to ignore them to get to the next level and score more points. Young people often can't distinguish that fantasy from reality. It doesn't process. (Cited in Cribb, 1999:B-2)

The fantasies and physical arousal of killing cyber-zombies may be transposed to the outside world, according to Stephen Kline, director of Media Studies Laboratory at Simon Fraser University, with the result that the shocking realities of mass murder are simply fictionalized in impressionable minds (Cribb, 1999). With adolescents, moreover, even the most repulsive act of aggression may be interpreted as an act of rebellion or self-expression. Dr Liss Jeffrey of Toronto's McLuhan Program in Media Studies, refers to this aggression as a "sicko star syndrome: that is, a sociopathic lack of compassion that gives a person the right to wreak revenge by turning the immediate environment into an immersive lethal video game" (see Flynn, 1999). And this combination is a recipe for disaster in a setting where violence is considered cool because, as the media constantly remind us, control over others brings deference and respect (Cribb, 1999).

Relation or Correlation?

How do we interpret the increasingly violent behaviour among youth and the proliferation of violent images on television? Is there a causal relationship? Will increased exposure to violence on TV activate aggressive behaviour in the viewer, as many are prone to believe? If so, what precisely is the nature of this cause-effect relationship? Does TV provide the cues, establish the models, serve as reinforcement, or stimulate the learning of violence patterns? Or does the causality work in reverse? That is, it is possible that more aggressive individuals are drawn to violent fare on television; if TV violence has any real effect on these people, it is merely to reinforce a pre-existing disposition. Even more intriguing is the possible absence of any direct relationship between TV and violence. TV violence does not exist in a social vacuum. In a violence-drenched society such as ours, violence becomes the norm from which there is no escape. In a society saturated with violent images and symbols, it is difficult to separate out one component as the causal factor. In fact, the media-violence relationship may be correlational simply because of the difficulties in isolating causes (TV violence) from effects (violent behaviour) in a society in which competition and aggression are the norm rather than the exception. To isolate TV as the prime culprit while ignoring other sources is sociologically irresponsible and socially dangerous.

Additional questions come to mind when analyzing this relationship: Does TV exert a similar influence on everyone who watches it, or is its impact dependent on personal differences and social circumstances? For example, the amount of television that people watch varies by region (those in Atlantic Canada watch the most), by gender (women watch more than men), and by age (older people watch more than younger people). Other important variations pertain to socio-economic status and levels of education, in addition to race or ethnicity. Finally, the entertainment industry has defended its depiction of violent excess by: (a) denying conclusive proof of any relationship; (b) claiming only to be reflecting society; (c) giving the public what it wants; and (d) reminding people of alternatives such as switching channels if the brutality persists (Medved, 1996).

Rethinking the Relationship

Sociologists are confronted by a host of questions when problematizing the link between television and violence. Foremost is the question of whether prolonged exposure contributes to anti-social behaviour in society. Most published results in this area—more than 3000 since 1940—support a direct link between media violence and violent behaviour. Prolonged exposure to TV violence is thought to generate several negative side-effects, including: (a) learning about aggressive behaviour; (b) a calloused indifference to the suffering of others, together with an inability to feel outrage or to do something about even the most depraved atrocities; and (c) exaggerated fear of becoming a victim of violence in a world that is increasingly perceived as mean and dangerous. The harmful impact of screen violence is intensified when associated with humour, an attractive or exciting perpetrator, and without consequences such as pain or punishment.

Common sense would have us believe that such conclusions are reasonable. Not all sociologists would agree with them, however, and the basis for this disagreement may well reside in the different research strategies of different disciplines. Most experiments and survey research conclude that those who consume screen violence tend to behave in anti-social ways. But this relationship is not as direct or as predictable as is frequently implied. Many of the studies in this area have lacked what researchers call external validity. That is, the studies were conducted in artificial contexts in which social significance and sanctions did not apply, and for this reason the individuals being tested lacked any incentive to act normally. In other words, these studies, which often involved university students or preschool children, looked good on paper, but bore little application to reality. To overcome this lack of external validity, natural environments are sought that allow observation in an undisturbed setting. Naturalistic studies to date confirm the general pattern of evidence from the laboratory (Williams, 1995).

Prolonged exposure to explicit violence would appear to induce aggressive behaviour, especially among young males. Yet a causal relationship is not nearly as certain as many people would believe. A number of variables must be taken into account, since the influence of TV varies from person to person. Even more important is the reason for watching TV. Older people may watch it for entertainment and presumably are less affected by it. Younger people may turn to television as a source of information about how they should act; thus, they would be more impressionable. In other words, people may only see what they want to see; they may absorb only what they are predisposed to accept. Too mechanical an interpretation of cause-and-effect relations is equally problematic. Perhaps the media only create a social climate, with a corresponding cultural frame of reference that defines some things as acceptable, others as unacceptable. Whether a person chooses to accept one option rather than another depends on a complex array of factors. Finally, protracted exposure to media violence may influence people's attitudes or beliefs. Exposure to televized violence tends to desensitize people by decreasing their empathy toward others while enhancing their apathy and indifference. Yet negative attitudes do not lead to anti-social behaviour, and this disjuncture between beliefs and behaviour complicates any analysis of media impacts.

In short, research conclusions on the causal relationship between TV violence and violent behaviour are tenuous and inconclusive. A relationship may well exist, but a causal connection may be difficult to prove or disprove, suggesting a need to think in terms of probabilities. Despite advances in statistical analysis and qualitative research, Davies (1996) points out, there are difficulties in "isolating" media effects within the context of a complex environment. Too many factors are at play, and efforts to isolate one at the expense of others produces a misleading picture. This suggests a rephrasing of the original question. Instead of asking whether TV violence creates violent behaviour, it might be more advantageous to inquire, "Under what circumstances and for what group of people is prolonged TV exposure a contributing factor to violent behaviour?"

Censorship as Solution?

In times of convulsive social change, people frequently turn to quick-fix solutions to complex problems. But superficial responses are not the answer, given how they frequently ignore the context of the problem or the consequences to society at large. A similar line of reasoning (but on a grander scale) pertains to issues of censorship and televised violence. Censoring the bad and the ugly on television has a certain appeal: It is reasonably simple to introduce through rating systems or technological devices, monitoring is relatively easy, and public acceptance can be counted on. Consider Steve Allen's Parents Television Council appeal to Americans: According to the council's paid advertisement, TV is a "moral sewer" because of its "filth," "vulgarity," "courseness," "sex," and "violence," and only the return of "family-safe TV" can possibly save America. But censorship in a free and democratic society is as much a problem as a solution. Many regard the right to "freedom of opinion and expression" as enshrined in Article 19 of the United Nations' Declaration of Human Rights as the cornerstone of democracy. Grave doubts are raised about our ability to limit censorship once it is in place and about the chilling effect such restrictions can have on freedom of expression. For others, censorship is a minor but necessary irritant. Its restrictions are seen as reasonable limitations that are demonstrably justifiable, and a small price to pay to protect society from its own worst inclinations.

Everyone is against censorship, Philip Marchand wrote in the *Toronto Star* (21 October, 1999), yet everyone wants to censor something (if only to censor people who want to censor!). For our purposes, censorship can be defined as a deliberate interruption in the flow of information from a sender to a receiver. This definition is admittedly broad, but it reinforces the notion of censorship as a process applicable to a wide range of human activities. It also confirms censorship as an instrument of power that has the intent or effect of controlling the free flow of information (Petersen and Hutchinson, 1999). Censorship is based on a fundamental behavioural principle: that what we are allowed to say, hear, or see will shape how we think and act. Change what people see or hear, and their behaviour will change accordingly. This assertion implies a direct relationship between thought and behaviour, an assumption that does not appear to be valid in everyday life. Censorship is also endorsed by people with a particular view of society and a desire to muzzle those whose visions do not coincide with their own. In cases where it is associated with direct exercise of state coercion, the exercise of censorship has the effect of simultaneously legitimizing some group or activity as acceptable, while delegitimizing the other (Whitaker, 1999). Several conclusions follow from this definition and characteristics.

First, censorship is going on all the time. To be human and live in society implies entanglement in a web of restrictions. Interruptions in the flow of information, such as self-censorship in talking or writing, are a routine and constitutive feature of any system of social relations (Petersen and Hutchinson, 1999). Thus, the issue is not one of censorship per se, which is unavoidable, but of where to draw the line in its application.

Second, there is no such thing as absolute freedom of speech. Nobody anywhere has ever had the right to do and say exactly as she pleased. Rather, the right to free expression is relative to time and place. What is permissible in one era is not in another, especially in times of uncertainty, change, and diversity. Context is also important. Yelling "theatre" in a crowded firehall is not an arrestable offence, although it could get you "committed." Shouting "fire" in a crowded theatre is an entirely different matter. Context is important in another way. Almost everyone agrees on banning child pornography, but there is less agreement on what to do about "explicitness" involving consenting adults. However repulsive blatant sexual exploitation may be, not everyone concurs that scuttling free expression is the solution. In other words, some degree of censorship is necessary, but the question of drawing the line is still open to debate.

Third, there is no agreement on how effective censorship is in curbing the flow of unacceptable information. Is censorship a solution to problems or simply a knee-jerk reaction that dodges key issues and costly commitments? Does censorship accomplish what it sets out to do, in light of doubts about direct media effects? What proof do we have of this, either for or against? Are restrictions on media violence an effective way of improving attitudes, modifying behaviour, empowering women and minorities, and changing social structures? Will restrictions make people crave what has been censored more on the assumption that people want what they can't get? Will censorship deter and convince people to desist, or will it have the effect of creating the right kind of noise and provide a million dollars' worth of free publicity? For example, advertising a program that carries a warning of violence is likely to attract rather than repel young audiences; they are also more likely to express positive attitudes towards the products being advertised during that program (Strauss, 1997). In other words, if censorship is the solution, what problem is it trying to solve?

The lack of consensus on many of these questions and the paradox do not auger well for censorship as a solution to the problem. In a democratic society that cherishes freedom of expression, Alan Borovoy, the General Counsel for Canada's Civil Liberties Association writes, the challenge may not be to muzzle but to marginalize by way of more speech rather than less.

ADVERTISING IN SOCIETY

Many of us have a love-hate relationship with the world of advertising. We enjoy being massaged by the message of more, yet bristle at the banality and superficiality that this implies. Much of our uneasiness stems from the sheer volume of advertising we are exposed to: Most of us will see millions of ads that cumulatively squander months of our life. It may not be immediately obvious, but whether we think of advertising as a blessing or a curse really depends on a particular view of society. If society is envisaged as a vast marketplace of self-serving individuals in rational pursuit of their interests, advertising may be endorsed as expanding the circle of choice. If, however, society is seen as a moral community of individuals whose collective interests extend to protection of the weakest members and the environment, advertising is indeed a social problem at odds with this vision.

Public reaction to advertising is mixed. It is a problem for some, a benefit for others. Many endorse advertising as part of the cost of doing business in a capitalist society. As the link between mass production and mass consumption, advertising is itself big business, the propaganda of capitalism as it is sometimes called. Others are less sanguine about advertising as an industry, holding it responsible for everything from the decline of the West to intellectual dwarfism. Advertising is accused of fostering discontent and creating insecurity by exploiting our fears, hopes, and anxieties. By harnessing these emotions to the purchase of a product, advertising not only exploits an obsession with our self-image, but also encourages weakness and dependency because relief is defined as a purchase away. Worse still, advertising encourages waste, contributes to the disfigurement of the environment, and creates an imbalance in human values. Even so-called "green advertising" is no solution, since the underlying message is the same; that is, use more, not less. An environmentally friendly car, after all, is still a gas-guzzling, steel-bending commodity at odds with the idea of public transit. Even the widely acclaimed slogan "reduce, reuse, and recycle" has been co-opted by big business. Finally, many ads are under criticism for their treatment of minorities in a country that aspires to multicultural ideals.

Generating Discontent/Glamorizing Consumption

Sociologists are interested in the social dimensions of advertising. Their interest extends to exploring not only the relationship between society and advertising but the social consequences beyond the commercial aspects. Advertising encompasses a number of functions. Foremost is the need to generate profits by selling products, generating brand-name recognition, and fostering corporate legitimacy (Williamson, 1978). Central to all advertising is a simple message: For every so-called need, there is a product solution (Andersen, 1996). Widely regarded strategies are employed to ensure product amplification in solving this problem, including targeting a market, capturing attention, arousing interest, fostering images, neutralizing doubts, and creating conviction.

A distinction between manifest (articulated) and latent (unintended) functions yields insights into the logic behind advertising. The manifest function of advertising is to sell a product by symbolically linking consumers with a commodity or service. A social value component is added to the product by glamourizing it through images and messages that purportedly strike a responsive chord. A latent function entails the selling of fantasies. As recently as the mid-twentieth century, ads sold a product by touting its virtues and practical applications. But contemporary advertising sells fantasies by employing images that promise more of everything. By buying into fantasies of popularity, sex appeal, attractiveness, or success, people are transported by images into a world of glamour and popularity by way of consumer goods. Advertising is also associated with selling a lifestyle anchored in the pursuit of conspicuous consumption. Consumer advertising exploits audiences by preying on gaps in their self-esteem by way of seductive images and fantasies that remind us that we are never good enough. This association makes it difficult to separate advertising from discourses embedded in capitalist ideology (McAllister, 1995). Advertising is ideological in that it represents ideas and ideals that protect and preserve the existing social order while excluding values at odds with a consumerist philosophy (Andersen, 1996). Equating advertising with dominant ideology reinforces its links as enlightened propaganda on behalf of capitalism and confirms the hegemonic properties of advertising. By normalizing consumption within the framework of a capitalist society (McAllister, 1995), audiences are "hegemonically"involved in perpetuating patterns of control, by consent rather than control.

In short, advertising is much more than a process of moving goods off a shelf. It goes beyond a fact sheet about the product in question. Advertising, in the final analysis, upholds a philosophy of life commensurate with core societal values about the good life. As an enlightened propaganda in defence of glamorizing conspicuous consumption, advertising promotes a lifestyle dedicated to the pursuit of consumerism, and its cultural correlates of greed, envy, waste, materialism, and environmental destruction (see Linden, 1997). To the extent that every ad says it's better to buy than not to buy, advertising is propaganda; in that every ad reinforces the social ideals of consumerism as inevitable, advertising is propaganda; insofar as advertising teaches us that external appearance is more important than what's inside, it is propaganda; and by equating consumerism as a matter of individual choice rather than a socially structured process, advertising is propaganda (see also Jhally, 1989). The cumulative effect of advertising as propaganda is overwhelming. At the heart of this propaganda is the irrefutable message: "Buy and you will be saved." On its own and taken out of context, each ad may not make much difference. Collectively, however, their impact cannot be discounted. For, in the final analysis, advertising instills the essential cultural nightmare in our society: the fear of failure and envy of success. Only through conspicuous consumption can we escape this recurrent dilemma by buying into contentment and happiness, at least until the next consumer product comes along to foment further discontent.

Advertising and Society

Many of the social problems associated with advertising reflect issues of perennial concern within the industry (Singer, 1986). First, there are debates about what should be allowed in advertising. Should the industry tolerate the advertising of products that are legal but contrary to our concept of the common good? Both the tobacco and alcohol industries depend on advertising, in part because sales are directly related to transforming dubious products into desirable social commodities. However, many regard it as irresponsible to advertise products that are anything but healthy when used as prescribed. In addition to a virtual ban on tobacco advertising through broadcast media in Canada, restrictions have been implemented to reduce the amount of advertising that is overtly sexist or racist. Such ads are thought to create an environment inconsistent with basic human rights in an egalitarian society.

Second, questions have been raised about who should be given access to advertising. Corporate sponsorship has been singled out as a questionable style of advertising. In the case of tobacco or alcohol companies, event-marketing ads represent one of the few outlets currently available in Canada. Underwriting symphonies, sports tournaments, and rock tours is a favourite way of reaching out to audiences, while bolstering an image as a good corporate citizen. Corporate sponsorship of "high-brow" events may secure access to a sophisticated market that otherwise would shun conventional advertising. Yet a positive association with an ethically dubious product through corporate links is widely criticized. Even political advertising is frowned upon, since techniques perfected to sell consumer goods are applied to political candidates, in effect transforming elections into market exercises and voting into consumer options. Still, politicians have little choice except to play along; as Preston Manning, the leader of the Reform party, said in response to questions about his make-over during the 1997 election: "If your teeth are crooked or your voice is strange or your clothes are out of sync, or if you stand out with your old hairdo or the wrong suit, people will not hear what you are saying. I'm interested in getting my message out" (Wong, 1997).

Third, there are moves to regulate specific techniques and target groups. Product placements and promotional tie-ins are directed at children and families by subliminally manipulating the subconscious (Madger, 1997). For example, many critics are concerned about the use of children's shows—from G.I. Joe and Mighty Morphin Power Rangers to Sailor Moon and Pokémon—as a carefully orchestrated market strategy involving an imaginary world of consumer goods (Kline, 1995). Interestingly, marketers now focus directly on children to take advantage of guilt-ridden, purchase-happy parents. Of special concern has been the use of prepubescent girls to sell perfumes or sunscreens. In a society in which child abuse is of worrying proportions, the inclusion of youthful seductresses in ads sends out a mixed message about what is socially acceptable.

The use of women in advertising has long been subject to criticism for its tastelessness and the way in which it perpetuates sexist stereotypes (Lindsay, 1997). Women are portrayed in ways that have nothing to do with the product except to confirm that sex sells. They are depicted as obsessed with their appearance (thin, youthful, beautiful, fit, and white) or preoccupied with domestic-maternal activities (cleaner, brighter, and whiter). Not surprisingly, women tend to be defined in terms of their relationships with men (be it husband, father, or brother) or in terms of who they are or how they look rather than what they do. To be sure, women in ads are appearing in a broader range of roles. They no longer are cast only in domestic-maternal situations, but now appear as movers and shakers who need only consumer goods to make a point or stay in style. The lessons of feminism are so densely woven into the cultural fabric of society that media images implicitly buy into gender equality (Kuczynksi, 1999). This concession conceals more than it reveals. Put simply, advertisers have simply expanded the number of products they are pitching at working women. In addition to domestic consumer goods, women now require additional products for coping with the demands of paid employment. The challenge of "having it all" demands a look that exudes femininity, yet is consistent with all the "right stuff" for career satisfaction and advancement. Women also require more labour-saving devices for unpaid domestic work. When these new developments are coupled with women's anxieties over their children and home, the potential for the female market is expanded, paradoxically, by capitalizing on trends critical of the industry.

In short, the media harbour a love-hate relationship in their portrayal of women with respect to role and status. On the one hand, media depictions emphasize the wrinkle-free, pore-less, sexualized, and deferential; on the other hand, women come across as rebellious, tough, and enterprising. Confronted by these conflicting and compromising messages, who can be surprised by the emergence of women as bundles of contradictions regarding who they are, what they want, and what is their proper place in society? Susan Douglas (1994:286) writes:

> Women are hardly immune to the svelte images, guilt trips, and all other normative messages that come at us courtesy of America's media moguls. But we are not putty in their hands either. Our interactions with sitcoms, the news, women's magazines, popular music, and movies are dynamic, a contested push and pull, in which they have most of the power but not all of it. While we can't assume that every woman who saw *Fatal Attraction* or *Pretty Woman* moaned "oh, pleeze" and cursed a lot throughout, neither can we assume that they just got down on their knees at the end and offered to lick their boyfriend's or husband's boots. And don't think, for a minute, that only upper-middle-class women with Ph.Ds who study semiotics and discourse analysis can debunk a misogynistic piece of crap like *9 1/2 Weeks*.

In short: Critics from Jean Kilbourne to Germaine Greer tend to admonish the media for refusing to reflect the multi-faceted realities of contemporary women. Yet the media do not claim to reflect reality: Only a degree of realism is required. Nor are the media in any position to address the diverse realities occupied by women, from domestic drudge to career leader. The media can only attempt to combine elements of fantasy and realism in a way that embraces realistic images for commercial or ideological purposes.

THE NETWORKED SOCIETY

A truism of contemporary society is the pervasive influence of computer-mediated communications in advancing the much-touted information age. Emergence of information as basis for wealth creation and reality construction is heralded as one of the more radical innovations in recent times, comparable in social impact to the invention of the wheel or the domestication of plants and animals. The information revolution may have an even more powerful effect on society, given the combination of the speed of its innovations, global scope, direct impact on individuals, and capacity to deal with corresponding problems (Editorial, 1996). Contemporary societies appear to be in the throes of a transition from an industrial society to a post-industrial (or information) era.

The future has begun to reformulate into what many call a "networked" society (*Time*, 1997; Webster, 1995). We live in a "wired world" in which human social existence is inseparable from the instantaneous exchange of information across vast distances. Commentators increasingly refer to the "informatisation of social life" (Webster, 1995, 1) as a definitive component of the modern world. Financial markets will rarely rely on paper, business will tap into global markets, hackers are poised to defraud computerized accounts, and bureaucrats will cast for ways to balance information with freedom. This global interconnectivity heralds an information revolution whose consequences are transforming how we go about our business in society. The increase of computerization and the power of networked communication is reconstituting social dynamics through changes in the workplace, family life, and social relations (Johnston, 1997).

Those who dismiss the potential of the digital revolution do so at their own peril. Computer-mediated communications are more than a quick-fix solution in search of a problem. They are not simply a machine for doing what print does, only more quickly and less expensively (Max, 1994). Nor can they be dismissed as a more efficient instrument for data retrieval or distribution, despite public perception of digital technology as just another labour-saving device for simplifying repetitive tasks. What we have instead is a fundamental shift in how we relate to the world "out there," as radically different in laying the foundations of a new society as the urban-industrial system was from the feudal agricultural order. Signs of this transformation include challenges to the organization and legitimacy of many traditional institutions, overwhelming established methods of goverance that originated in a world of clearer boundaries and limited information flows (Rosell, 1999). Even conventional understandings of mass-media communication are recast into sharper relief because of the microchip revolution, in effect confirming McLuhan's observation that the advent of a new medium tends to expose the premises and practices of traditional media (McLuhan, 1960; Morris and Ogan, 1996). It will also reinforce the view that creation of new media themselves (not just the content) will profoundly reshape the relationship of individuals to society (de Kerckhove, 1995). The possibilities are so vast, in other words, that reducing the discourse about computer-mediated communication to the level of good or bad, progressive or regressive, has the effect of trivializing both process and impact.

Cyberheaven or Internet Hell?

Much has been said in praise and condemnation of computer link-ups (Internet), satellite transmission, and microchip technology. Who cannot be impressed by a medium that compresses large amounts of data for rapid transmission via fibre-optic cables, thus, according to John Vivian (1997), heralding the death of distance and time? Supporters of digital communication tout its virtues in enhancing democracy and freedom through delivery of information power to people without pre-screening by central authorities. Through this "anarchic" dissemination of information, modern communication systems are able to strip large organizations of their monopolistic access to information, thereby eroding the hierarchies around which institutions are created and maintained. The potential for broader participation in political and policy-making decisions is also enhanced through two-way flows of information. This digital era of free-flowing electronic communication will spell doom for the forces of regulation (Barlow, 1997), even as controllers of information are learning to fight back (Wise, 1996). Rather than killing jobs through jobless economies and robotic automation, computer-mediated communications may enhance opportunities at home and abroad by tapping into unharnessed potential. Finally, in a world where people are losing faith in traditional institutions (from government to religion), computer-mediated communications provide a sense of empowerment that bridges the social gap between ourselves and the world at large (Roberts, 1996).

Yet detractors remain skeptical. It is one thing to advance the free flow of information; it is quite another to conclude that much of this information is subject to manipulation by elites with hidden agendas who prefer prevailing patterns of power and privilege while fostering the illusion of power-sharing with the masses. A computer-driven information society may accentuate social fissures that already exist, in effect relegating the computer illiterate and disconnected to the margins (Editorial, 1996). Anarchy is not the same as freedom; as a result, what is on-line for some is offside for others. That is, the rich, educated, and English-speaking will monopolize access to the Internet, while freedom from government censorship may pave the way for everything from harassment to disinformation (Wise, 1996; UN Development Report, 1999). Equally worrisome are the commercial implications. The hype behind computer-mediated communications is one thing, reality may be another (*Interrogating the Internet*, 1996). The democratizing of information may play a secondary role to the creation of a vast medium for advertising. In the same way that "TV programming really is just baling wire strung up to exhibit the commercials" (Turner, 1997, 63), so also is the Internet a medium for linking audiences with advertisers. Theodore Roszak (1996, 12) writes:

> In contrast, the Web is a creation of the entrepreneurial worldview. It favours high-tech effects and attention-grabbing tricks. The key forces behind it are seeking desperately to transform the medium into the new television, the new movies. Their objective is to get millions to look at their site so that they can make a lot of money. This is no secret: The main, ongoing story of the Web is how much profit its backers are (or are not) making. What passes through the medium is bound to be shaped by those values, not by any significant regard for quality, truth, or taste.

In addition, there are problems of access, interaction, privacy, regulation, and copyright. Damage that hackers can do to Web sites (from corporate secrets to national security systems) is widely known and feared (Ward, 1997). The unfettered flow of digital information complicates the preservation of cultural borders, to the detriment of national decision-making (see Shields, 1996). The proliferation of hate sites with their espousal of neo-Nazi White supremacist dogmas is proving no less disturbing (Visanta, 1996). Computer-mediated communications can also lead to loss of freedom, individual surveillance, invasion of privacy, centralization and control of power, and reduction of human contact. Computer technologies may be the most powerful forces at work today, in other words, but they are also among the most isolating for a species that is social by nature and has evolved through interaction in primary communities. The hidden costs of deepening inequality, social alienation, and community dissolution cannot be taken lightly (*New Internationalist*, 1996).

Not everyone agrees with this assessment of good or bad. In arguing that both positions are overstated, they tend to define computer-mediated communications as trivializing to the point of banality. Of particular note are doubts about the content that accompanies digitalized information. Neil Postman (1995) points to our movement from a society with an information deficiency to one mired in a glut of decontextualized data untied to human needs. The end result is more and more information, but less and less knowledge (Webster, 1993). Yet knowledge without context is little more than a game of trivial pursuit. Without a coherent or meaningful framework, people may become more informed about economic indicators, but less knowledgeable about assumptions that underlie the economy, particularly about work, wealth creation, and human dignity (Roszak, 1994). Worse still, the information produced by multimedia may constitute a kind of "garbage" (GIGO—garbage in/garbage out) by virtue of its sheer volume, lack of context, incoherence, and meaninglessness. The dissociation between information and ideas, between data and knowledge, is likely to widen further as computer-savvy children equate research with little more than a point and click. Even more distressing is the loss of learning through first-hand experience, as lamented by Stephen Talbot in *The Future Does Not Compute:*

> The most critical element in the classroom is the immediate presence and vision of the teacher, his [her] ability to inspire, his devotion to truth and reverence for beauty, his moral dignity— all of which the child observes and absorbs in a way impossible through electronic experience. Combine this with the excitement of a discovery shared among peers in the presence of the actual phenomenon occasioning the discovery (a caterpillar transforming itself into a butterfly...) and you have the priceless matrix of human growth and learning.

Between these extremes are those who dispute some of the hyped excesses of digital media, without necessarily disclaiming the social benefits of modem technology. This intermediate position acknowledges the inherent ambiguities in computer-driven information. Computer-mediated media are increasingly the norm in our society; yet this technology is useful when informative, user-friendly and interactive, but regressive when intensifying existing patterns of one-way, top-down interaction (Gooderham, 1997). Like any technology, the Internet possesses contradictory impulses towards liberation and domination, colonization or emancipation, oppression or resistance (*Interrogating the Internet*, 1996). The same digital forces that compress data may coerce people; they may control, yet provide a catalyst for resistance. In other words, every new link to the Internet in a plugged-in world has the potential for good or evil. Computer-mediated communication may produce a life that is profoundly democratic and emancipatory in levelling the playing field between big and small, rich or poor. Or people may lose their humanity as they become "netizens" (citizen-terminals) and take their cue from the pallid virtues in a virtual reality (Airhart, 1998). Perception is key, especially in defining a vision of society: Those who fear the government denounce the Internet as yet another arrow in the quiver of Big Brother; those who fret about anarchy are concerned by the potential of the Internet to attract everyone from mild eccentrics to cold-blooded terrorists (Stephenson, 1997).

What will happen to societies because of this revolution in communication? In theory, computer-mediated technologies imply an infrastructural potential for a distinct global culture that transcends the concept of the nation-state. They also promise an intensely democratized society in which information is readily accessible and interchangeable. Yet freedom for individuals may pose problems for the integrity of nation-states, as claimed by John Perry Barlow (1996, 43), ex-Grateful Dead lyricist and co-founder of the Electronic Frontier Foundation for the protection of civil liberties in cyberspace:

> The real issue is control. The Internet is too widespread to be easily silenced by any single government. By creating a seamless global-economic zone, borderless and unregulatable, the Internet calls into question the very idea of a nation-state. No wonder nation-states are rushing to get their levers of control into cyberspace while less than 1% of the world's population is on-line.

What the Net offers is the promise of a new social space, global and anti-sovereign, within which anybody, anywhere can express to the rest of humanity whatever he or she believes without fear. There is in these new media a foreshadowing of the intellectual and economic liberty that might undo all the authoritarian powers on earth. The declining significance of borders may be a problem for countries such as Canada, with their concern for control over communication and broadcasting (Pike, 1995). But controlling information will prove increasingly difficult in the borderless world of multimedia.

SCHOOLING
AND EDUCATION

FRAMING THE PROBLEM

All societies must socialize their children for participation in adult life. The means for achieving this goal are diverse, both formal and informal, and vary with time and place. Pre-European contact societies survived without formal arrangements for education and schooling, relying instead on informal socialization procedures such as parental or peer instruction. Opposed to this are urban-industrial systems in which education has become increasingly formalized. Formal institutions for schooling are characterized by several defining characteristics including: a constellation of norms, values, and practices; a team of specialists both in the class and out; a specific location for systematic instruction; and appropriate equipment and apparatus (Robertson, 1987). The universality of formal institutions is largely the rule rather than the exception, as a literate population is seen as a precondition for progressive development. Three major functions of schooling and education continue to prevail: (1) to impart knowledge and skills; (2) to prepare individuals for citizenship and the work world; and (3) to foster individual development through intellectual cultivation.

Canada is no slouch when it comes to expenditure on formal education. Canada invests more on education than almost any other society, according to Statistics Canada Report "Education Indicators in Canada" (cited in Beauchesne, 2000). Spending per student at all levels of education was $9274 in 1995 (second to the U.S.A. at $ 11 462) or 7 percent of its GDP, the highest among all industrial societies. Where Canada shines, however, is in tertiary spending. At 8 percent per year, it ranks near the top of industrial countries in the amount spent. Canada devotes more of its GDP to higher education (1.7%) than the OECD average of 1.2 percent, or than the United States with 1 percent (Editorial, October 1, 1997). As a result, 48 percent of Canadians aged 25–64 had some post-secondary education, while the percentage of Canadians aged 25–29 with a university education rose to 26 percent by 1998 from 17 percent in 1990 (Beauchesne, 2000). Such a commitment provides Canada with the edge in being repeatedly judged by a UN Development Agency as the best country in the world to live in. Nor is there any easing in sight: Despite escalating tuition fees across Canada and punishing debt loads, students continue to flock to universities and colleges, including a 13 percent increase in university undergraduate enrolment during the 1990s (Statistics Canada, cited in the *Globe and Mail*, 26th July 1999). Full-time enrolments in the 1997/98 academic year stood at 498 036, up about 0.6 percent from a year earlier, according to data compiled by the Association of Universities and Colleges, with B.C. and Newfoundland reporting the largest gains, at 2.5 and 2.9 percent respectively. Undergraduate enrolment included 274 950 women, with 30.6 percent of their enrolments in the social sciences, 13.6 percent in the general arts, 10.8 percent in education, 9.3 percent in humanities, and 9.2 percent in engineering and applied sciences. Full-time graduate enrolment increased slightly to 76 000, while part-time undergraduate enrolments at 203 500 continued a 6-year decline to their lowest level since 1980.

Yet these largely positive figures are misleading. Education is undergoing a revolutionary transformation from a print-based knowledge base to a digitally-driven system, with a corresponding set of challenges in the aims of education, conventional divisions of knowledge and disciplines, methods of teaching and learning, the role of teacher and nature of the student (Spender, 1997). Nevertheless, much of Canada's education and schooling seems stuck in the past. Too much of what passes for schooling and education remains anchored in the 19th century, in effect creating tensions within the system itself while shortchanging students in preparing them for the realities of the digitally-driven, knowledge-based, post-industrial economy (Spender, 1997). Whereas schools were once expected to forge a coherent, stable and unified culture out of diverse students, Neil Postman (1995) writes, the situation is now different. Contemporary education is focusing increasingly on economic utility and career prospects, consumerism as an inescapable lifestyle, reliance on technology and technological solutions rather than critical judgment, and information rather than knowledge and wisdom. Not surprisingly, education systems are experiencing an identity crisis. Unsure of their roles and responsibilities in contemporary society, yet resigned to plod along as best they can with diminishing resources, all levels of schooling find themselves under pressure to do more with less. Controversies and contradictions abound, many of which detract from public confidence in formal schooling. Education is often touted as the path to personal growth and social progress; unfortunately, the opposite appears equally true. For many, education or schooling is neither creative nor progressive, but a process both inflexible and bureaucratic, at odds with the fast-paced demands of a hyper-technological era (Spender, 1997). Robertson (1987, 383), captures this paradox: "Not all schooling is educational. Much of it is mere qualification earning...ritualistic, tedious, suffused with anxieties, destructive of curiosities, and imagination; in short, anti-educational." In place of small, intimate environments are sprawling, bureaucratic organizations where routine and regulation prevail in pursuit of efficiency and standardization. Students, parents, and teachers are expected to abide by ministry decisions, even when educational bureaucracies are remote and removed from local concerns and needs (Orpwood and Lewington, 1995). Parental involvement is encouraged in theory, but discouraged in practice for fear of disrupting the smooth implementation of board policy. Lip service to the creative and the critical is betrayed by the harsh realities of authority, dogma, routine, conformity, cost-cutting, and credentials at all costs.

Administration comes in for its share of blame. In terms of literacy or numeracy, Canada may rank first among English-speaking countries, yet up to 40 percent of Canadians lack basic literacy skills to function effectively at work or to adapt to workplace changes, including some 20 percent of recent high school graduates (Bolan, 1997). Students are sorted into categories for placement from advanced to basic; teachers are increasingly specialized and excessively accredited; curricula reflect philosophies of senior administration or popular pedagogies; administrative convenience supersedes student needs; credentials prevail over learning and have little relation to intelligence or parental concerns; and procedures are standardized to ensure order and predictability. The fact that educational authorities are aware of these flaws, yet appear unwilling or incapable of addressing the issues in any substantial fashion—notwithstanding constant mantras about empowerment or partnership—attests to the power of inertia in defence of the status quo.

No level of education is exempt from scrutiny (Keith, 1997). At the primary level, there is growing parental concern over declining educational standards, deteriorating pupil performance levels, laxity in discipline, and learning without the "basics." Teachers must increasingly cope with the results of poor parenting, a tendency to dump all social problems on the schooling system, and intense competition with instant forms of electronic gratification (Crispo, 1997). Educational philosophies continue to waver (or flip-flop): One of the more durable pedagogical debates reflects the demands of an outcome-oriented, curriculum-driven schooling versus that of a process-oriented, "child-driven" system which aims to bolster individual self-esteem through customized learning rather than competition for high grades through standardized testing and measurable performance indicators. Ministerial directives tend to confuse, anger, or alienate both teachers and parents, creating bottlenecks in debates over what to teach and how. Not surprisingly, parents are worried that students are unschooled in basic literacy skills, but awash in pedagogical mumbo-jumbo about self-esteem and personal creativity. Stroking the ego is fine to a point, they might argue, but how does it prepare children to cope with the demands of a knowledge-based, global economy?

The secondary level is no less prone to recrimination, finger-pointing, and second-guessing. High schools are demonized as ticking time bombs because of alcohol and substance abuse, teenage pregnancy, sexual activity and disease dissemination, racism and right-wing recruitment, and overt sexism. Violence appears to be a major problem, its ugliness seared into our consciousness by the recent shootings at Emery Collegiate in North York, Tabor, Alberta and Littleton, Colorado. Students are accused of suffering from a terminal overdose of media exposure, resulting in: (a) diminishing attention spans; (b) a discomfort with the written word; (c) acceptance of discontinuity and fragmentation as normal conditions of existence; and (d) a disrepect for the past as a source of inspiration or wisdom (see Keith, 1997). Equally worrying are the erosion of respect for custom and the defiance of convention or authority. Most young adults are so attuned to peer group pressure and so seemingly indifferent to adults that parental involvement in youth issues is generally resented or openly scorned (Eckhler, 1999). At the same time that young people are expected to excel academically, they must also adjust to bodily changes, separate themselves psychologically from parents, develop a working network of friends and allies, commit to education or vocational goals, and establish their sexual orientation.

Even post-secondary institutions are subjected to scrutiny or criticism. Universities are depicted as imperious ivory towers, not only out of touch with business realities and globalizing forces but impervious to the demands for diversity and change. According to Bercusson et al. (1997), the university enterprise is being buffeted by relentless pressures because of a dumbing down of curricula, grade inflation, a chilly climate of political correctness, and general irrelevance to contemporary realities. Rationalization and routinization have had the effect of "McDonaldizing" the university system into something safe, sanitized, and predictable (Bitzner, 1998). Like any oversized corporation, universities too are bureaucratized, insular and over-administered to do not much more than encourage the big drones to produce new drones for the future (Bercuson et al., 1997; Good, 1998). The deteriorating health of the post-secondary system is lamented in light of chronic underfunding, dwindling resources, increased commercialization, mounting workloads, inadequately prepared students, and impossible teaching conditions. Others pine for the days when a university degree was a mark of distinction—a proof of achievement—rather than just a rite of passage in the maturation process. Widespread belief in a decline in academic standards has done little to allay fears about the future of the university as a centre of learning (Bercuson et al., 1997). Still others fear that corporate interests are calling the shots, thus upsetting the balance that historically anchored the relationship between the practical and the contemplative. Although some degree of relevance to the economy is necessary, if only to retain support and students, many balk at the notion of universities as corporations for delivering products and services to the market rather than for developing critical and creative skills of benefit to society at large (Flynn, 1997). Talk of a fiscal crisis and corporate links camouflages a deeper malaise pertaining to rules, roles, and relationships; namely, a crisis of identity, as elitist assumptions jostle with the demands of democratization, while career concerns supersede a commitment to higher learning (Price, 1993; Reading, 1996).

To be sure, the labelling of education and schooling as a failure or social problem can be challenged. Even how schooling and education are interpreted may vary, with functionalist approaches focusing on goals of personal growth and social integration, while conflict perspectives see hidden agendas that control, dominate, and perpetuate inequities. Widespread criticism of schooling and education indicates a need to rethink the label of "failure." Who says schools are failing, why are they saying this, and on what grounds are these accusations being made (Barlow and Robertson, 1993)? The "lets-solve-it-through-schools" mentality tends to inflate the importance of education as an agent of socialization, and to underestimate the significance of the media and peer pressure as forces for change or conformity. Such a mindset also allows primary caregivers to wriggle out of responsibilities while scapegoating schools for shortcomings that rightfully belong to parents. To add insult to injury, education is being blamed for the miscalculations of Canadian business when it fumbles opportunities to compete globally. Such a multi-dimensionality of perspectives reinforces the notion of education as a "contested site," with progressive and reactionary forces aligned opposite each other. Ambiguity and paradox are inherent in a system that is neither homogeneous nor monolithic, but contradictory, ambiguous, and subject to internal dissonance (see Stone, 1993). Schools espouse democratic values, yet routinely revoke the principle of democracy in everyday practice. Learning is encouraged, but from within structures that inhibit rather than stimulate (Sleeter, 1991). Promoting equality of access, participation, and outcomes may be high on the list of priorities, yet the opposite is likely. Diversity is embraced, then discarded when priorities shift or costs are too high. In short, schools are designed for conformity rather than change, for consensus rather than disagreement, for social reproduction of the status quo rather than the reconstruction of social reality, and for preparing people to cope with the demands of the industrial age (traditional workplace, nine-to-five jobs) rather than those of an information-driven global economy. Many of these paradoxes are neither superficial nor transitory, but chronic and embedded, yet resistant to facile solutions.

Moreover, in those cases where problems are deeply embedded within the educational system, proposed solutions that only skim the surface may inadvertently exacerbate the situation by creating new imbalances. Rightly or wrongly, only one thing is certain: Criticism will continue to escalate because of the impossibly high standards expected of education by a demanding and diverse public. Not surprisingly, education and schooling are experiencing a crisis of identity, with a corresponding crisis of confidence in figuring out what they should do or be in a changing and diverse society.

This chapter explores the ideas of schooling and education as social problems in their own right. The education system as a principle or practice has come under sustained criticism. In a world convulsed by the dizzying pace and scope of social change, schools are faltering under the pressure to be all things to all people—parent, guardian, moral guide, social worker, and babysitter (Webber, 1994). The external world is changing faster than internal mechanisms can cope with in light of rising expectations and shrinking budgets (Orpwood and Lewington, 1995). In this context of turmoil and second guessing, the social dimensions of education and schooling are analyzed as a social problem in terms of their relationship to society. Three problems are uppermost: first, the problem of inequality. Education has long been endorsed as an instrument for the attainment of social equality. Yet the educational system has proven a site of inequality as competing interests struggle for control. The system may also perpetuate patterns of inequality because of differences in class, family expectations, cultural background, language competence, teacher attitudes, and peer group influences (Bowles and Gintis, 1976; Giroux, 1996). Second, the challenge of diversity is proving problematic.Schools have become demographically diverse as a result of robust immigration. Engaging with this diversity has elicited a variety of responses normally associated with different styles of multicultural and anti-racist education (Fleras and Elliott, 1996). Nevertheless, this engagement process would appear to run against the grain of education and schooling as instruments of assimilation and control. Third, problems arise from the mismatch between ideals and reality, as schooling and education don't always do what they are supposed to do. The crisis in post-secondary education is especially instructive of this conflict of interest between the old and the new, with the result that post-secondary institutions are losing their sense of identity in light of shifting government priorities and ideological changes. Admittedly, there is no shortage of ideas for reforming classrooms and boosting achievement, including reducing class size, raising teachers' pay, and new pedagogical theories about what works in the classroom. Yet research on the effectiveness of reforms is weak, inconclusive, or difficult to implement in a context where educators have yet to agree on what the purpose of school is (Miller, 1999). Under such conditions, schooling and education are social problems because of the gap between past and present; they create social problems by way of outcomes that are inconsistent with institutional ideals; and they constitute sites of social problems, as vested interests seek to modify and transform in ways that are likely to provoke and antagonize.

RESCRIPTING SCHOOLING AND EDUCATION:

People tend to take the social world for granted. Common sense dictates a view of society or social institutions as durable and enduring, timeless realities that have existed without change since time immemorial. However reassuring, this perception is frequently wrong. Human realities are socially constructed conventions rather than anything natural, normal, or inevitable. Insofar as these realities are conventions created by individuals interacting with others to make choices in contexts that constrain, the values and customs that shape people's lives are neither impervious to social changes nor divorced from the realities of a diverse and changing context. Institutions, too, are in a constant state of turmoil and flux in response to social challenges and political demands. Institutions emerge because of criticism, reform, or need; they persist and undergo modification because of internal and external pressures; and they decline because of ineptness or disinterest. This interpretation would appear true of all institutions, with schooling and education no exception to this rule. An overview of formal education in Canada from the 19th century onwards provides a look into why schooling is a social problem. For a century, as many have noted, the central task of schooling was to prepare children to be workers and citizens of an ever-changing world. The tools toward this goal have not changed (teachers still stand in front of the class), but gadgetry has (computers rather than slate boards). So too has the underlying assumption about how to prepare children: In a society based on rigid expectations of class and gender, drill and obedience shaped the school day; in a contemporary society that extols freedom and human rights, the cultivation of the individual supersedes other considerations. The democratization of schooling has proven of benefit to those Canadians once excluded. Yet this achievement has not been without costs, and many of the social problems attributed to schooling and education may reflect this commitment to be all things to all people.

Elitist Education (Pre-1900)

Compulsory mass education under state auspices is a relatively recent phenemenon. This is true of the primary level, and even more so at secondary and post-secondary levels (Johnson, 1968; Nock and Nelson, 1993). Prior to the mid-1800s, education for the most part was a privilege restricted to ruling-class children. Education and schooling had little practical value for the masses; its existence was justified for the express purpose of cultivating the minds of those with money for "idle" pursuits (Robertson, 1987). Religious instruction was paramount, with reading and writing directed at the Bible rather than preparation for work. Estimates suggest that perhaps only half of all children in Upper Canada (Ontario) attended school in the 1830s, and even then for a total of 12 months (Johnson, 1968; also Macionis, Clarke, and Gerber, 1994). Ordinary Canadians were excluded from schooling for various reasons, including: a reliance on labour-intensive agriculture as a basis for making a living; direct involvement in food production as a means of wealth creation; concentration of the population in rural areas; a highly stratified system that emphasized a hierarchical gulf between gentry and the masses; and the prominence of the church (and parents) as agents of socialization. A pervasive elitism may also have inhibited any inclination for mass, compulsory, state-supported education except for the privileged classes. As a result, education for the masses consisted of direct parental observation or entry into an apprenticeship for some trade (Nock and Nelson, 1993).

Taking it to the Masses (1900–1960)

The principle of mass schooling evolved with the onset of an urban, industrial Canada. By Confederation, both Protestant and Catholic schools systems had been established; the principle (if not the practice) of universal education was accepted; teacher training was in force; and text and curricula were under board control (Johnson, 1968). The Constitution Act of 1867 outlined a national system of local school boards to be governed by municipaliies (Flynn, 1999). Traditional forms of socialization (churches or extended families) were no longer as relevant in urban environments, in effect creating a demand for the state to assume responsibility through a regulated school system. In 1883, Toronto became only the second jurisdiction in North America to incorporate kindergarten into the school enterprise. By 1920, compulsory education was instituted to the end of elementary school (or about 16 years of age). Schools were designed to reflect the dominant mode of economic organization, namely, the factory, with its assembly-line outlook and one-size-fits-all mentality. Schools were places where rules mattered: Learning by rote was commonplace; emphasis was on the awe and majesty of the British Empire; and a military character predominated, involving high levels of regimentation, standardization, and discipline (Flynn, 1999). The rationale for taking education to the masses reflected additional social concerns. Curriculum remained basic and geared toward employment, including math, reading, writing, spelling, and history. Compulsory education was also endorsed as a means of distracting the attention of crime-oriented, unemployed children. Many of these custodial functions persist into the present where the potentially disruptive costs of unemployed youth are all too real. Mass primary education not only prevented the outbreak of class conflict or ethnic strife; it also legitimized the values and norms of a competitive, hierarchical society. Then as now, a concern with the "moral character of pupils" was paramount. In seeking to socialize or civilize, a one-size-fits-all model of education prevailed to foster obedient, God-fearing children.

Several additional points deserve to be mentioned. First, the commitment to mass education extended only to the primary level. Even by the 1950s, only about half of all 14 to 17 year olds were enrolled in secondary schools (Nock and Nelson, 1993). Resistance to mass post-secondary education stemmed from resentment over increased costs, the loss of cheap labour, and fear of contamination by contact. Second, the introduction of mass education altered our perception of children. As long as farming provided a primary employment for the masses, children were viewed as a productive addition to the household. Even early industrialization did not really question the morality of employing young children in mines and factories. Children who outgrew infancy and achieved the "age of reason" were expected to assume adult status and responsibilities. With primary education, however, the notion of children as an age-grade was reinforced, ultimately leading the way to post-war acceptance of adolescence as a specific age group with lifestyle outlooks. Third, for some Canadians schooling proved a collective nightmare rather than a learning process. From the late 19th century onwards, numerous aboriginal children were removed from family, communities, and culture, and placed in residential schools where many were abused, humiliated, and deprived of dignity, culture, and skills. In 1998, the federal government apologized for its part in the residential school system and allocated some resources to atone for the neglect (Milloy, 1999).

It is generally assumed that the technological changes associated with industrialization put a premium on skilled workers. Yet there is some question whether the expansion of 19th century manufacturing prompted the "massifying" of education. The scientific management philosophies of the early 20th century tended to treat workers as mindless extensions of an assembly-line machine. In some cases, vocational skills demanded a rudimentary level of literacy and numeracy; in other cases, they did not. Many jobs required only basic entry-level skills; further skills-training was built into the job. The credentials associated with education may have evolved instead as a device to deter unwanted masses from certain occupations. An emphasis on accreditation allowed professionals such as doctors or engineers to consolidate their privilege against indiscriminate entry. In short, schooling and education became universalized for reasons only partially related to manufacturing. Compulsory education may have sought to keep youth off the streets; reduce unemployment and crime rates among the young; instill optimism for the masses in an oppressive society; inculcate obedience and submissiveness to authority; and reproduce the social order through patriotism and citizenship. The regulatory functions overrode other considerations; hence, the popularization of education cannot be disassociated from a perennial concern with controlling the potentially unruly.

Democratizing Education (1960 to present)

Primary and secondary schooling for the masses were firmly in place by the early 1960s. While elementary school enrolments increased by about 50 percent between 1951 and the early 1990s, preschool numbers increased sixfold, while secondary schools increased by a factor of four. The notion of mass education for post-secondary levels came into being shortly afterwards, although entry restrictions remained in countries such as Japan and Britain. Historically, higher education was restricted to ruling class elites (Price, 1993). Universities served as finishing schools for the well-heeled and upwardly mobile. Post-secondary education was aimed at creating a trained professional class: This cadre of pampered elites was expected to staff the private and public bureaucracies of an expanding dominion, as well as preserve the cultural assumptions of Christian civilization through knowledge and research. In short, as Susan Mann, former president of York University notes, universities have educated elites for service to the power at the time, from the church to monarchy to bureaucracy to the state and now to the economy (see Galt, 1997).

University enrolments accelerated dramatically in response to a growing democratization of society, with its commitment to equal opportunity for everybody, not just the elites. In 1939, only 3 percent of 18 to 25s were in university; by 1963 the figure had risen to 7 percent; by 1994, the figure had increased to 30 percent. Between 1951 and 1971, there was a fivefold increase in full-time enrolments, followed by another doubling between 1971 and 1996. Students continue to flock to universities (from 8.3 percent of Canadians age 19 to 24 in 1975, to 18.6 percent in 1995), despite tuition fees that rose by 86 percent between 1983 and 1995, while the ratio of government grants received by universities per dollar of student fees dropped from $5.02 in 1975 to $2.97 in 1995 (Mitchell, 1997). Costs appeared irrelevant as governments channelled endless resources into universities in Canada. The forces behind this shift were complex, but invariably included: a burgeoning baby boomer population; changes in the Canadian economy; continued rural–urban movement; advances in technology; consolidation of the welfare state coupled with a government willingness to underwrite educational costs; and a growing belief in education as a key to socio-economic success. This commitment was further bolstered by competition with Communist Russia for Cold War supremacy and space age advantage (particularly following the launching of the Soviet Sputnik into outer space in 1957).

The democratization of education was first experienced by women. That a gender bias existed in schooling and education was widely acknowledged. Female students were objects of discrimination not only because of personal bias by indifferent teachers and bullying males, but because of structural factors related to curriculum and testing procedures. But gender has played an important role in the democratization of a traditional male institution. Women continue to excel as a percentage of university enrolment: They have accounted for over three-quarters of all university enrolment growth in the past 15 years. In 1978, 10 percent of all women between 18 and 21 attended university; by 1997, the figure had increased to 20.5 percent. Men by comparison saw their participation rate increase only slightly, from 12 percent to 14.2 percent. Women are graduating in much higher numbers: In 1997, 99 616 women received a degree compared to 72 120 men. Men earn more PhDs than women, 2519 versus 1395, but women earned slightly more MAs and considerably more BAs, 86 264 compared to 58 261. Women have also overtaken men in many disciplines: Women outnumber men in biology and pharmacy as well as medicine, dentistry, law, and biochemistry. Engineering remains a problem for women: Women were granted 35.6 percent of all doctoral degrees in 1997–98, but only 9.5 percent in engineering and applied science. Still, most universities are implementing proactive programs to ensure higher enrolments (Simpson, 1999). Full-time faculty by gender and rank in Canadian universities in 1997 has also shown a modest increase, with tenured males at 20 580 and tenured females at 6616. (*SWC Supplement*, 1999). And these trends are likely to continue, given that young women between the ages of 13 and 16 have achieved near parity with young men in math and science, while pulling even further ahead in reading and writing, according to a study by Statistics Canada and the Council of Ministers of Education (cited in Seeman, 2000).

The Paradox of Democratization

This democratization process has had a profound effect on higher education. Universities have become more inclusive by accommodating the historically disadvantaged, including members of the working class, women, and people of colour. Yet success has unleashed many of the problems associated with underfunding and overcrowding (Keith, 1997). According to Solway in his *Education Lost*, the levelling trends of an inclusive university are contrary to the somewhat elitist principle at the core of post-secondary education (cited in Keith, 1997). The democratization of post-secondary education has destroyed these elitist assumptions, in effect leaving the university enterprise perplexed and rudderless (Price, 1993). Overcrowded classes and overworked professors have resulted in a diminished capacity to foster excellence. In its place is a tedious ritual entailing memorized input and scheduled regurgitation, an exercise not dissimilar in consequences to intellectual bulimia. Egalitarian democratization is accused of sabotaging deference to authority, esteem for hard-earned accomplishments, reverence for heritage and knowledge of the past, a commitment to rationality and science, and a willingness to assert the superiority of one idea or standard over another (Henry III, 1994).

The democratization of education has trickled down to primary schools. The rigidity and regimentation of the past have evolved into an accommodative system that is more diverse, receptive to freedom of choice, and amenable to reform. The logical culmination of these trends is the replacement of a curriculum-oriented (outcome) schooling with a "child-oriented" (process) system. Debate rages over "What should schools teach?" "How and why?" "How to assess and monitor student progress?" and "How should students be prepared for the future?" On the one hand are conservative forces, consisting largely of concerned parents with an eye on the three Rs. For example, in Ontario, teachers are expected to implement a tough, fact-filled curriculum that provides detailed lists of specific and mandatory expectations (not vague outcomes) that are tested on standardized exams in hopes of raising standards to international levels, while encouraging greater accountability (Small, 1997). On the other hand are progressive forces who endorse a "life-skills" philosophy. Proponents of "process" are critical of "outcomes," arguing that any return to basics is obsolete and inconsistent with the demands of a changing and diverse reality. Students, they contend, already receive too many facts, but need more understanding to ensure: (a) that they can apply what they know to explain other events, and (b) a framework for thinking historically and comprehending important relations rather than Trivial Pursuit-type information about Vanna White (Chamberlain, 1999). The "outcomes" reply by pointing to process education as irresponsible and soft. Those streamed in process are accused of being improperly equipped to meet current challenges; they are also portrayed as rebellious and defiant of authority, with no respect for custom or convention. Those versed in outcome-schooling are dismissed as intellectual robots with few redeeming social attributes. What we have, in other words, are radically different perspectives, both of which appear immune to comparison or evaluation because of opposing assumptions about human nature and its relation to schooling and society. Neither is right or wrong, since each defines differently the roles and responsibilities of formal education. This controversy is interesting in its own right: It also symbolizes the struggle in Canada between the proponents of free-market principles, with their commitment to institutional adaptation in the direction of global competition, versus those must live with the consequences of systems increasingly directed toward the rational pursuit of profit and privilege (Barlow and Robertson, 1994). Under such circumstances, perhaps a compromise is in store, with both positions edging toward a middle ground.

MULTICULTURAL AND ANTI-RACIST EDUCATION

The educational system has for the most part reflected a fundamental commitment to monoculturalism. Historically, education was inseparable from the amalgamation of diversity into the mainstream. This conformist ideology sought to absorb immigrant children directly into Canadian society by stripping them of language and culture (Berryman, 1988; Allingham, 1992; McAndrew, 1992; Moodley, 1993). All aspects of schooling, from teachers and textbooks to policy and curriculum, were aligned with the principles of Anglo-conformity. Anything that veered outside this Anglo-centric framework was ignored as irrelevant or dangerous, and punished accordingly. Special curricula or references to other languages or cultures were rejected as inconsistent with the long-term interests of Canadian society-building. Schooling, in short, had evolved into a site for the reproduction of social inequality in that it denied equal opportunity and fostered outcomes at odds with the concerns and aspirations of minority students (Dei, 1996).

The explicit assimilationist model that once prevailed within educational circles is no longer officially endorsed, even though assimilation remains an unspoken yet powerful ethos at all schooling levels. These opposing dynamics have transformed schooling and education into a contested space, involving the struggles of those who endorse the status quo versus those who have historically been excluded and are seeking to multiculturalize the agenda (Giroux, 1994). In theory, the impetus for multicultural education constitutes a departure from conventional ways of doing things. Its introduction has not only challenged how schools should relate to diversity, but also raised questions about the form, function, and processes of formal education in a changing and diverse society. Multicultural education initiatives wrap themselves around the rhetoric of "cross-cultural communication," "racial awareness and sensitivity," and "healthy identity formation." By fostering a learning environment that acknowledges the culture of its students (Henry et al., 1999), multicultural education emphasizes cultural diversity as a basis for challenging and relativizing the basic principles associated with dominant and subordinate cultures in hopes of establishing a more dynamic schooling culture (Turner, 1994). The more demanding forms of inclusiveness are expressed in an anti-racism education that not only challenges those relationships of power that racialize the school social order, but also invoke direct actions for dismantling the structural roots of educational inequality (Giroux, 1994). To the extent that multicultural education seeks to institutionally engage diversity, it is eminently worthwhile. The fact that multicultural education may not accomplish what it sets out to do is indicative of the entrenched interests that seek to blunt, deflect, absorb, or crush any move to accommodate.

Monocultural Education: Socialization as Social Control

Education and schooling are secondary agents of socialization whose social functions are often at odds with formal mandates. The following functions of education prevail in society: (a) socialization, or transmission of culture; (b) self-actualization and individual self-development; (c) preparation for workplace, consumerism, and citizenship; (d) improvement in Canada's competitive edge; and (e) reproduction of the social order. Education plays both a conservative and progressive role in society depending upon the level of schooling under examination. For example, elementary school education discharges a conservative function whereby cultural assumptions are tacitly inculcated along with the three Rs. Post-secondary education, by contrast, endorses a more creative and informed debate as a basis for progressive change, at least in theory if not practice. Yet a tacit commitment to assimilation remains a central objective. Alok Mukherjee (1992:73) writes:

> Traditionally, the school has been a conservative institution. Its function, on the one hand, is to legitimize the dominant social, political, economic, and cultural ideas of society and, on the other, to perpetuate existing relations. The ownership, organization, and activities of the school reflect this dual role.

From daily routines to decision-making at the top, education is organized to facilitate cultural indoctrination and social control of minority students. These reproductive functions can be accomplished in a direct manner by the selection of textbooks that reflect mainstream experiences or values. The streaming of minority students into lower-level programs restricts access to higher education and useful employment. Indirect and largely unobtrusive measures are also employed. The school system screens out certain information by projecting certain views of the world as necessary and normal, and others as inappropriate. Diminished teacher expectation may be a problem for some. The widely accepted practice of grading students may have the effect of reinforcing competitive individualism to the exclusion of traditional cultural values. Through schooling, in other words, the reproduction of the ideological and social order is realized without much public awareness or open debate. In linking power with culture, schools tend to perpetuate prevailing distributions of power and resources (Apple, 1987). This "hidden curriculum" is aptly described by Apple and Franklin (1979):

> Schools...help control meaning. They preserve and distribute what is perceived to be "legitimate knowledge"—the knowledge that "we all must have." Thus schools confer cultural legitimacy on the knowledge of specific groups. (quoted in Mukherjee, 1992:76)

The assimilationist dynamic imposes constraints on expanding a multicultural agenda. A commitment to diversity and change may be fundamentally compromised in a context in which monoculturalism prevails. Rarely do schools seriously contemplate the magnitude of commitment to foster substantive changes at the level of curriculum, language, and culture programs for children, placement and assessment, employment and promotion, teacher training, and relations with community (McAndrew, 1992). Ad hoc adjustments are more common than a restructuring that goes against the grain. Nor does there appear to be any wholesale move to reject the assimilationist ethos of the school system (Cummins and Danesi, 1990).

Discriminatory structures are not easily dismantled in light of entrenched interests and ideologies, many of which are unlikely to tolerate significant changes without considerable resistance. Changes, when they do occur, apply to the cosmetic realm, and rarely impact on the key domains of decision-making, agenda-setting, and power-sharing. These impediments should warn against any excessive expectations regarding the potential of multicultural education. Still, the fact that pluralist initiatives have materialized at numerous schools suggests that multicultural education is here to stay in principle and in practice.

Multicultural Education:
Enriching, Enlightening, and Empowering

Multicultural education encompasses a variety of policies, programs, and practices for engaging diversity within the school setting. It may encompass the study of many cultures or an understanding of the world from diverse perspectives; alternatively, it may convey how power and politics are inextricably connected with unequal group relations (see Schuman and Olufs, 1995). Different styles of multicultural education can be observed, ranging in scope and comprehension from moderate to radical approaches. Three of the more common moderate approaches include enrichment, enlightenment, and empowerment (Fleras and Elliot, 1999). An anti-racism approach is constitutive of a fundamentally different style.

An enriched, multicultural education is aimed at all students. Students are exposed to a variety of different cultures to enhance a knowledge of and appreciation for cultural diversity. The curriculum is enriched with various multicultural add-ons. Special days are set aside for multicultural awareness; projects are assigned that reflect multicultural themes; and specific cultures are singled out for intensive classroom study. Additional perspectives include a focus on healthy identity formation; cultural preservation; intercultural sensitivity; stereotyping awareness; and cross-cultural communication. Desirable side effects of the enrichment process are greater tolerance, enhanced sensitivity, and more harmonious intercultural relations. A less beneficial consequence is a failure to initiate sweeping institutional changes because of reluctance to challenge the racism within and outside the school.

The enrichment model is widely acceptable because it is non-threatening. Yet this very innocuousness has brought it into disrepute with critics. Enrichment styles have been criticized as too static and restrictive in scope. They tend to focus on the exotic components of a culture that everyone can relate to, rather than to more substantive issues such as values and beliefs, and when taught by poorly trained teachers may inadvertently trivialize or stereotype (Henry et al., 1999). Diverse cultures are studied at the level of material culture, stripped of their historical context and discussed from an outsider's point of view (Mukherjee, 1992). There is also a danger of romanticizing minorities by focusing on a timeless past or, alternatively, of crippling them as social problems when doting on the present. Even sensitive presentations must grapple with dilemmas as varied as: (a) how to discuss elements of other cultures that are fundamentally opposed to Canada's democratic principles; (b) how to emphasize the positive features of minorities to the exclusion of problems that many confront; (c) how to present cultural differences without reinforcing stereotypes or reflecting an "us" versus "them" mentality; and (d) how to convey the idea that everyone is basically different in the same kind of way or, alternatively, everyone is fundamentally the same in radically different ways (see MacAndrew, 1992). Henry Giroux (1994: 327) puts its smartly in acknowledging the dilemma of particularist approaches: "A viable multicultural pedagogy and politics must also affirm cultural differences while simultaneously refusing to essentialize and grant immunity to those groups that speak from subordinate positions of power." The fact that these questions have yet to be answered to everyone's satisfaction is reflective of the magnitude of the problem in engaging diversity.

A second approach entails an enlightenment model of multicultural education. This approach is similar to enrichment insofar as both seek to modify people's attitudes by changing how they think about diversity. Enlightenment models are less concerned with celebrating differences as a basis for attitudinal change. The focus is on informing ("enlightening") students about race relations in society and their impact on education and schooling. Enlightenment models go beyond description of specific cultures. Advocated instead is a broader, analytical approach toward diversity not as a thing, but as a relationship, both hierarchical and unequal. Attention is directed at how minority-majority relations are created and maintained; it also is aimed at what would be required to challenge and transform these predominantly unequal relationships. Stronger versions may expose students to Anglo-European complicity in crimes of racism, dispossession, and imperialism, and the corresponding concentrations of power in White hands. Specific group victimization may be included, for example, genocide against First Peoples, while emphasizing the achievements of indigenous and immigrant peoples as a corrective to their marginalization in history, society, and culture (see Dinesh, 1996). Applied to education, the enlightenment objective is to analyze those arrangements that have the intent or the effect of compromising minority success in schools, including: (a) school policies and politics; (b) the school culture and hidden curriculum; (c) languages—official, heritage, and other; (d) community participation; (e) assessment, testing procedures, and program tracking; (f) instructional materials; (g) the formal curriculum;(h) the ethnic composition of the teaching staff; and (i) teacher attitudes, values and competency.

Both the enrichment and enlightenment style of multicultural education concentrate on the needs of non-minority pupils. In contrast is a third model, called empowerment multicultural education, which is directed essentially at the needs of the minority student. A minority-centred, or minority-focused, school provides an alternative learning environment that caters to students for whom mainstream (Eurocentric) schools are inappropriate and alienating, even with the incorporation of "other centred knowledge to achieve a multicentric, inclusive school" (Dei, 1996: 106). For example, an Africentric, or African-focused, school arrangement seeks to improve academic and social achievement by emphasizing the centrality of Black experiences in social history and cultural development. The minority-focus empowerment model is predicated on the belief that monocultural school systems are failing minority pupils. Minority students do not see themselves at the centre of culture and history in a Eurocentric curriculum that rarely acknowledges minority achievements and contributions to society. What minority students require is a school context that capitalizes on their strengths and learning styles as a basis for achievement. Empowerment models have proven controversial, since not everyone shares the assumption that separate but equal is the appropriate multicultural path to take (Dei, 1996; also Smith and Smith, 1996).

An example of empowerment education can be seen in the struggle by aboriginal peoples to gain control of aboriginal education. Since the early 1970s, aboriginal peoples have sought to implement a variety of reforms involving the need to: (a) decentralize the educational structure; (b) transfer funding control to local authorities; (c) devolve power from the centre to the community; and (d) empower parents to assume increased responsibility for their children's education. Aboriginal grievances and concerns over education are understandable. Historically, the government's educational policies have embraced an explicit commitment to assimilate aboriginal children through segregation and indoctrination. Federally-directed native education sought to disrupt the cultural patterns of aboriginal children, then expose them to the values and priorities of the West, often in schools off the reserve and away from community, friends, and relatives. The abusive consequences of residential schools have been widely documented. Other consequences are less direct but no less real in denying aboriginal experiences, as the Metis scholar, Paul Chartrand (1992:8–9) says, "It is easy to assert power over others if they are made to feel they have no identity, they have no past, or at least no past that matters." Only a relatively separate education system controlled by aboriginal people for aboriginal people is viewed as a corrective to these historically imposed disadvantages.

The aims of aboriginal-controlled education are twofold. First, it seeks to impart those skills which aboriginal children will need to succeed in the outside world. Second, it hopes to immerse children in an environment that is unmistakably aboriginal in content, style, and outcome. After all, overall outcomes for aboriginal youth are unlikely to change if they are expected to operate within a framework designed by the needs and priorities of the dominant sector. The key is to produce children who possess a strong sense of who they are and where they came from, without foresaking the skills to compete in the dominant sector. With its emphasis on empowerment through behavioural changes and institutional restructuring, aboriginal-focus may well have more in common with anti-racism styles of education. To put this into perspective, Table 9–1 provides a succinct comparison and contrast of the focus of enrichment, enlightenment, and empowerment models of multicultural education.

Anti-Racism Education

Multicultural education revolves around a philosophy of celebrating differences. It consists of activities or curricula that promote an awareness of diversity in terms of its intrinsic value to minorities and/or society at large (Ministry of Education and Training, Ontario, 1993). The aim of multicultural education is largely attitudinal; that is, to enhance sensitivity by improving knowledge about cultural differences (enrichment) or race relations (enlightenment). Yet there is no proof that enriched or enlightened attitudes will lead to behavioural changes. By contrast, anti-racism education is concerned with the identification and removal of discriminatory barriers at interpersonal and institutional levels. It begins with the assumption that minority underachievement is not necessarily caused by cultural differences. Cross-cultural

TABLE 9-1	Styles of Multicultural Education		
	Enrichment	**Enlightenment**	**Empowerment**
Focus	celebrate	analyze	empower
Objectives	prejudice	discrimination	success
Goals	diversity	equality	achievement
Outcome	lifestyle ("heritage")	life chances	biculturalism
Means	cultures	race relations	cultural renewal
Style	experience	understand	immersion
Target	student	institution	minority students
Scope	individual	interpersonal	collectivity

understanding will not contribute to any fundamental change in uprooting the structural roots of inequality unless they are directly and openly challenged (Kivel, 1996). Improving minority status is contingent on removing the behavioural and structural components of racial inequality, along with the power and privileges that sustain racism through institutional policies, practices, and procedures (Ministry of Education and Training, Ontario, 1993). Sweeping changes in the curriculum are called for, not simply a tinkering with multicultural concessions.

Anti-racism education is constructed around the commitment to actively challenge and transform those discriminatory aspects of education through direct action. Anti-racist education can be defined as a proactive and process-oriented approach that seeks to balance a focus on difference with a sharing of power (Dei, 1996). Four dimensions are implied: (1) critical insight into the interlocking differences that are brought into the classroom; (2) a critical discourse that focuses on race and racism as issues of power and inequality rather than matters of cultural difference; (3) an interrogation of existing school practices to uncover the structural roots of monoculturalism and inequality; and (4) challenging and changing the status quo through political and social activism (Dei, 1996). Put bluntly, the goal of anti-racist education is to deconstruct and to delegitimize the colonialism at the core of contemporary society by challenging the system of power relations that continues to racialize the social order and bestow privilege on Whites.

Anti-racism education differs sharply from multicultural education. While multicultural education is merely intolerant of racism in its practice, anti-racism seeks to actively eradicate racism through awareness, challenge, and confrontation (Kivel, 1996). Anti-racism education shifts attention away from subordinate cultures and focuses on how racism in its different forms is historically created, symbolically expressed, and institutionally embedded at various levels in society (Giroux, 1994). It goes beyond acknowledging differences (enrichment) or analyzing stereotypes (enlightenment) to understanding, engaging, and transforming the structural roots of racism and racial discrimination. The pedagogy becomes political, Giroux points out, when challenging the production of knowledge, social identities, and social relations that inform the schooling and education. Under an anti-racism education, both students and teachers are offered an opportunity to see how culture is organized; who is authorized to speak about different forms of culture; which cultures are worthy of valorization; and which cultures are seen as unworthy of public esteem. They also come to understand how power operates in the interests of dominant social relations, and how such relations can be resisted, challenged, and transformed (Giroux, 1994).

Different styles of anti-racism education can be discerned. Anti-racism at individual levels concentrates on behaviour modification through education and training (Stern, 1992). Institutional anti-racism strategies are aimed at dismantling the structural basis of school racism. These systemic biases are most apt to occur at the level of mission statement, culture and subculture, power and decision-making, structures (including rules, roles, and relationships), and distribution of financial and human assets. At one level anti-racist education is concerned with shifting minority presence into the centre of the curriculum. Emphasis is on providing a platform for minority stories to be told in their own voices, while repudiating the White-centredness of school knowledge as the only legitimate form of culture (Allingham, 1992; Mukherjee, 1992; McCaskill, 1995). An inclusive or multi-centric emphasis seeks to incorporate all students and the values they bring to school as a basis for improving successful learning outcomes while bolstering a truly multicultural curriculum (Dei, 1996). Table 9–2 provides a summary comparison of multicultural and anti-racism education in terms of focus, objectives, concerns, scope, and outcomes.

TABLE 9–2	Multicultural and Anti-Racism Education: Comparisons and Contrasts	
	Multicultural Education	**Anti-Racism Education**
Focus	Culture	Structure
Objectives	Sensitivity	Removal of Discriminatory Barriers
Concerns	Ethnocentrism	Systemic Racism
Scope	Student	Institutions
Styles	Accommodative	Challenge/Uproot
Outcomes	Understanding	Equality

CHALLENGING POST-SECONDARY EDUCATION

The workings of society can be interpreted from a variety of perspectives. Society is seen by some as essentially sound and productive, and any disruptions to the status quo are to be resisted in the interests of stability and order. Others pounce on society as fundamentally immoral and evil, so that any challenge or disruption is to be endorsed. Functionalists prefer to think of society as a set of interrelated institutions, each of which contributes to the order and survival of society by fulfilling essential "functions." The conflict perspective portrays society as an arena of competing institutions and groups in constant struggle for scarce resources. Such competition has a way of bringing the new into conflict with traditional patterns—with predictable costs. Problems are inevitable as (a) the new attempts to dislodge vested interests; (b) the untried rarely meshes smoothly with the conventional; and (c) expectations are raised that may be unattainable because of resistance from the old school. Nowhere is this upheaval more evident than in current debates over the role and functions of post-secondary schooling and education in terms of their relationship to a changing and diverse society.

Universities were once the most pampered and privileged of all institutions (*Economist*, 1993/1994). They represented communities both distinct in mission and values that fed into the mainstream of society by shaping law, diplomacy, policy, politics and civil bureaucracy. In defending the status quo, the university served as a socializing, civilizing, and even moralizing agent (Logan, 1997). The university and society were pointed in the same direction, shared consensus about the roots of culture, and concurred on the criteria for truth. Rarely subjected to public scrutiny or widespread criticism, post-secondary institutions were recipients of limitless dollops of cash by governments who revered them as engines of economic growth, social equality, cultural sophistication, and political democracy. Intellectuals flocked to them as sites of enlightenment and research. Taxpayers didn't mind the extra burden since universal access to post-secondary education opened avenues of social mobility for their baby-boom offspring. To a large extent, this perception of a post-secondary education as a sound financial investment for both individuals and society remains unshakable, judging by historic high levels of enrolment (Editorial, May 25, 1999). In 1995, nearly 300 000 students graduated from post-secondary schools: Within two years, 79 percent of trade and vocational grads had full- or part-time jobs, 83 percent of university grads, and 85 percent of college grads (Canadian Press, July 29, 1999).

But not all is well, and universities are under seige from various sources: They are distrusted by governments as an expensive luxury in a no-frill economy, lampooned by politicians for perceived excesses in political correctness and pandering to minorities, ignored by decision-makers as irrelevant to intellectual life in a world of thinktanks and information technologies, criticized by the private sector for inappropriate graduate material, and taken to task for trying to be all things to everybody. They no longer possess the moral and intellectual high ground to be either critic or the conscience of society, but appear to be driven by their own impulse for power and money (Logan, 1997). Martin Loney (1999) takes the universities to task because of their producer capture: "Funded by taxpayers and student fees, they are run in the manner of a medieval guild for the benefit of tenured academic staff whose jobs-for-life guarantee requires no commensurate commitment." It is impossible, he writes, to think of another occupation that offers such generous rewards for such minimal output. Rising costs and declining revenues have led to calls for rethinking the post-secondary enterprise. New faculty are not being hired; sessionals and contract workers are replacing full-time faculty; and students are shouldering an increased burden of operating costs by way of spiralling tuition fees. While there was an increase in the number of PhDs to 3914 in 1997 from 2937 in 1991, according to the Association of University and College Teachers (cited in *University Affairs*, Jan., 1999), the number of full-time faculty has declined by 11 percent between 1997 and 1992, while the average age increased slightly to 49 years. There is growing reluctance to regard post-secondary education as an investment in the future, writes Carol Goar, the editorial page editor of the *Toronto Star*, but as a highly subsidized service to students who should pay more up front. And while per capita spending on university students in the United States has increased by 20 percent in the last 20 years, Canada's funding of post-secondary institutions has declined by 30 percent to 1.6 percent of the GDP in 1999 compared to 3.6 percent two decades ago (Mickleburgh, 1999). Government grants to colleges and universities dropped 14.1 percent between 1993 and 1997, with the result that government revenues now make up only 57.7 percent of total revenues, down from 66.2 percent in 1993. Such declines not only erode the effectiveness of higher education in Canada, but also undermine the competitive advantages of Canada in a global and research-based world. Provincial variations are evident: Ontario ranked in the bottom third of provinces, according to Statistics Canada, Financial Management System, with spending of $275 per capita (a drop from $350 in 1992/93), compared to Quebec's $440 per capita (which also extends to community colleges). Not surprisingly, tuition fees have escalated to offset this loss of revenue. With annual costs of about $11 000 for fees, books, rent, and transport, the average debt burden of each student at graduation is between $17 000 and $25 000 compared to about $8000 in 1990, according to the Association of University and College Teachers.

The crisis goes beyond dollars and cents. Both politicians and the public are demanding more accountability and transparency from universities, especially with increased moves toward community college training for skills or trade (Galt, 1999). Universities are accused of being boring places because of greying faculty whose refusal to move over and make space for "new blood" bolsters the credibility gap between professors and students (Carey, 1995). Pedagogical styles have not kept up with student skills or outlooks (Giroux, 1996). Students are inundated with more information in classrooms at a time when they already are immersed in more raw data than they can possibly process. They continue to be exposed to irrelevant material and antiquated teaching methods, with the result there is a mismatch between faculty and student perceptions regarding skills for coping with the outside world (Renner, in Carey, 1995). Teaching techniques that worked well eight centuries ago when the professor owned the only book in the land are hard to justify in multimedia society (McSherry, 1993). Post-secondary educators are dismissing online learning as little more than crass commercialism in the hallowed

BOX 9.1 Escalating Tuition Fees: Gouging or Investment?

University tuition fees have escalated at a rate of 11 percent annually throughout the 1990s, according to Statistics Canada. In 1999/2000, a University of Waterloo arts student will pay $3874, while an engineering student's fees will climb to $4626 per year. For those in dentistry across Canada, the figure is closer to $7000. Compare these figures with the total of $1640 per undergraduate student in 1990–91, or about $470 per year in 1971. Averages for undergraduate arts and science programs range from $1668 at Laval to $5450 at Acadia, according to the 1999 *Maclean's* annual survey of universities. Provincial averages are noticeable, varying from Nova Scotia, with the highest average tuition fee for undergraduate arts students at $3903, to Quebec at $2292 for students from that province (Editorial, May 25, 1999).

It is obvious the Ontario government intends students to foot the bill for a revamped post-secondary system that links funding to job-related programs. Whereas student fees funded 24% of the operating costs in 1992/93, they now contribute 30 percent to many programs and 50 percent in some (Furey, 1999). Government contributions have diminished accordingly, in some cases to as low as 40 percent of operating costs, exerting even greater pressure on universities to find alternative sources of funding. But while university administrators may criticize rising costs, many like the idea of less reliance on government funding and interference from meddlesome politicians; politicians are elated to balance budgets by cutting back funding; professors prefer classes of highly motivated students; and ideologues are pleased that post-sec-

ondary education is now conceived of as a private gain rather than a public good, and as such price should be determined by supply and demand (Klassen, 1999).

Are high tuition fees worth it? According to Bruce Little (1998), from 1990 to 1997, the number of jobs for those with a post-secondary certificate increased by 1.83 million, while total employment for those who didn't finish high school dropped by 962 000. In 1997, 73.3 percent of all Canadians with a post-secondary degree or diploma had a job, whereas the employment-to-population ratio for those with less than a high school diploma was only 35.1 percent. And income figures still favour the educated. Findings from the "Class of '95: Report of the 1997 Survey of 1995 Graduates (cited in *Applied Research Bulletin,* Summer 1999, vol. 5, no. 1) demonstrate how higher education continues to be a sound investment. Interestingly, even the much-maligned arts degree appears to be holding its own in a world of highly skilled workers as employers look for candidates who are flexible, adaptive, and capable of lifelong retraining. Not surprisingly, perhaps, the communicative and analytical skills of arts students often culminate in higher-paying careers over the long run and in greater job satisfaction (Lewington, 1998; Cook, 1999). Median earnings increased significantly with education level in 1997, with median earnings of $23 400 for trade/vocational graduates, college graduates at $25 700, university BAs at $32 000, and MA and PhDs at $47 000. Similarly in the U.S.A: An average high school graduate earned $22 895, while the average college graduate earned $40 478 (Bowman, 1999).

halls, thus ignoring the '"wiredness" of the world out there and the necessity for ivory towers to get connected (Lynch, 1999). According to the president of Teachers College at Columbia University, Arthur Levine, the crisis is exacerbated by gaps between the way students like to learn (practical applications and active learning) and the ways in which faculty prefer to teach (abstract and theoretical material with passive teaching). Some criticize university faculty and administration as spineless cowards and "cringing conformists" who cave into political correctness at the expense of academic freedom (Furedy, 1995). Others accuse the university of not being sufficiently diverse and inclusive (Fleras, 1995). Universities are portrayed as assembly-line factories in which faculty manage while student-drones perform in pursuit of credentials and careers. Still others deplore the demise of exclusivity and the belief in education as a privilege rather than right with the economic utility of contemporary mass education (Bercuson et al., 1997). Growing reliance on tuition fees and private sector contributions rather than government funding may create universities that are more entrepreneurial, more results-oriented, and more student-directed. It remains debatable whether this should happen at the expense of their role as disinterested creators and disseminators of knowledge.

The Politics of Academic Freedom

A growing commitment to institutional inclusiveness is also contributing to the crisis in post-secondary education. Universities and colleges are now confronted by the postmodernist paradox of preserving academic freedom without trampling on gender or minority rights for inclusion within a bias-free environment (see Drakich, 1994). Post-secondary institutions are under pressure to foster environments in which all individuals can enjoy the freedom to study, teach, and conduct research. Yet such inclusiveness may compromise the historic role of higher education. Critics have argued that universities are losing their status as bastions of freedom by curbing free expression, abdicating an attendant "right to offend" if necessary, or caving in to unproven allegations of racism and sexism without due process (Fekete, 1994; Furedy, 1995). Others contend that academic freedom for all is impossible without creating an inclusive environment. Efforts to reconcile mutually exclusive yet seemingly valid perspectives may compel a rethinking of the university enterprise. Instead of providing autonomous space for the calm cultivation of rational thought and analysis, as many have tried to claim, higher education is better viewed as a complex and complicated political system where things happen for various reasons, from benign neglect to clumsy expediency, because of constructive logic, compassion, or moral precepts (Arthurs, 1993).

The principle of academic freedom is central to the post-secondary enterprise. Other values pale by comparison, as confirmed by the CAUT when it adopted its Policy Statement on Academic Freedom in 1977:

> The common good of society depends upon the search for knowledge and its free exposition. Academic freedom in universities is essential to both these purposes in the teaching function of the university as well as in its scholarship and research...Academic members of the community are entitled, regardless of prescribed doctrine, to freedom in carrying out research and in publishing the results thereof, freedom of teaching and of discussion...in a manner consistent with the scholarly obligation to base research and teaching on an honest search for knowledge (cited in *McGill*, 1994:12–13).

For many, the centrality of academic freedom as a foundation principle is beyond contention (Berger, 1993). Yet central to any understanding of academic freedom is the question of who owns the university? The community of scholars? Some church groups? The government? The board of governors? Students? (Horn, 1999). A capacity to pursue impartial truth and value-free knowledge without fear of reprisals is seriously compromised without guarantees of non-interference by intruders or do-gooders. The higher learning process is grounded on the commitment to academic freedom. Support for free expression presupposes that your adversaries have something useful to say, with every right to articulate it, provided a similar right is extended to others (Dickson, 1993). The principle of "agreeing to disagree" is not simply a luxury or post-secondary perk; it is critical to the process of sorting out competing truth claims as a precondition for intellectual discoveries. Impartiality and objectivity are seriously compromised without guarantees of non-interference by political or outside interests. Moves to "muzzle" open inquiry through outside interference are criticized and openly resisted as fundamental infringements to academic freedom and institutional autonomy (de Toro, 1994:15). The establishment of the Society for Academic Freedom and Scholarship, with nearly 300 members from coast to coast, has struggled to confirm the right of faculty to conduct classes or do research as they choose, and to speak freely on or off campus (Granatstein, 1994).

Commercializing the Enterprise

The rules, roles, relationships, and structure of the university are changing in response to internal and external pressures (Reading, 1996). Historically, the university was linked to the destiny of the nation-state which it served by promoting the idea of a national culture. But nation-states are declining as the prime creator of wealth. The protection and promotion of national culture is less urgent than in the past, given the increasingly tenuous relationship between higher learning and nation-state status in a globalizing era. No longer does national culture provide an overarching ideology and ideological reference point for what is the university. As a result, universities are turning into bureaucratic corporations with focus on a market-driven excellence rather than culture. Reading writes (1996:5): "The university, I will claim, no longer participates in the historical project for humanity that was the legacy of the Enlightenment and the historical project of Culture." Without a firm centre to hold their focus in place, universities are losing the sense of historical mission that defined and legitimated their status in society.

The increasingly close links between business and education are controversial (Lewington, 1997). In an era of dwindling resources and increased competition, universities are increasingly corporatizing the three Rs—restructuring, refocusing, and retrenchment (Lewington, 1997). Hard-pressed universities have little choice but to balance the pursuit of truth with the demand for corporate dollars, according to the CAUT, and with pervasive corporate-university links this is the rule rather than exception. This commercialization may well emerge as the major social problem of post-secondary education (cited in Canadian Press, *Kitchener-Waterloo Record*, Oct. 30, 1999). Debate also focuses on the so-called benefits of this partnership between boardroom and classroom. For cash-strapped universities, these links provide a much-required dose of relief from relentless government underfunding. Businesses, in turn, look to universities for connections, personnel transfers, and contract work arrangements. Commercialization continues to infiltrate universities, ranging from ads in washrooms to corporate donations to foreign buyouts of campus bookstores (Klein, 1997). There are lingering fears over loss of academic freedom because of unwarranted interference from business agendas. Questions abound: Can a commitment to job creation and product development be balanced with the university's historic purpose of knowledge creation rather than as sources of technology for immediate commercial gain, without necessarily foresaking the role of universities as idea factories for the new information-based and globalizing economy (Crane, 1999)? To be sure, a university disconnected from the real world is hardly an option that Canadians can afford. Yet if universities are too closely identified with established powers and measurable outcomes, they risk sacrificing their independence and creative scholarship. If they are too divorced from the outside world, they risk losing students, relevance, and support.

Still, all signs are pointing to a growing consolidation of industrial-educational links. Universities have had little choice but to reprime their relationship with the private sector to defray operational costs as governments cut back on funding —a situation that has split academics over potential conflicts of interest. Consider how Simon Fraser University has turned to the private sector to raise $25 million for its downtown Vancouver campus and $18 million for a conference centre (Drohan, 1999). To stave off insolvency, universities are closing down departments and programs in hopes of saving money and proposing to become more efficient and focused since they can't do everything. Even more controversial are moves by the Ontario government towards a performance-based, market-driven system of funding that is tied to the number of graduating students and subsequent employment (Furey, 1999). No one should be surprised: The rationalization of primary and secondary schools across Canada with more effective public control over finances and curriculum is likely to ripple outwards to universities and colleges (Thorsell, 1998). According to the Ministry of Training, Colleges, and Universities, students will become primary customers who must be secured and catered to; they will also continue to pay more tuition as part of this move to link funding with job-based academic programs. This in turn will force administrators to reshape programs to fit the needs of the job market or lose funding and/or students, especially if the government decides to fund students directly through some sort of voucher system for cashing at the university or college of their choice (Ibbitson, 1999). By attaching performance-based strings to the source of funding in the name of efficiency, the autonomous liberal arts university may well vanish, John Ibbitson argues, to be replaced by a provincially controlled polytechnic system, both consumer-driven and market-sensitive.

The privatization of universities is proving no less contentious. Two trends are noticeable: the creation of private industries and the commercialization of public institutions. To ease pressures on provincial treasuries and reduce post-secondary costs, the concept of private universities is being circulated (Loney, 1999). The fixation with numbers—from public opinion polls and cost-benefit analyses to a preoccupation with the bottom line—is exerting a powerful and privatizing effect on existing universities (Giberson, 1999). Universities now resemble money machines: They are equipped to file for patents, to develop licensing arrangements, to provide real estate for development, and establish new companies (Rohman, 1999). The "bean counters" of the world have managed to convince decision-makers that everything in the world, including universities, is quantifiable, and that failure to measure something is tantamount to being unaccountable. Such a shift may explain the popularity of *Maclean's* annual "measurement of excellence" ranking of Canadian universities to help prospective customers make a more informed choice of where to study. But, as Mark Giberson observes, education and schooling are not a commodity for consumption or comparison shopping but embody unique personalities in shaping people's lives, challenging their minds and imaginations, nurturing a sense of self-worth, and transforming them into good citizens. For example, educational "outputs" related to the creation and dissemination of knowledge are notoriously difficult to measure; not surprisingly, in its annual review of excellence in university education, *Maclean's* can only base rankings on measurable indicators that imply educational quality, such as library holdings, entrance standards, and alumni support (Cameron, 1997). Yet this preoccupation with numbers and accountability is to be expected, given that universities are no longer growth industries but mature industries that government treats in a different way. As Arthur Levine writes in "How the Academic Profession is Changing": "It seeks to regularize or control them. It asks hard questions about their cost, efficiency, productivity and effectiveness. It attempts to limit their size and funding. It diminishes their autonomy and demands greater accountability." Not surprisingly, Levine writes, the government is shifting the terms of the relationship between universities and the public, from a focus on teaching to one on learning (student-focused), from one on process (credits) to that of outcomes.

IDENTITY CRISES: WHO ARE WE?

The emergent crisis in post-secondary education is hardly a secret. In his article entitled "How the Academic Profession is Changing," Arthur Levine points out five forces that are driving this transformation, including: (1) changing political and economic relationship to the government in terms of funding, priorities, accountability and transparency procedures, and outcomes; (2) changing characteristics of university students (older, more diverse, ongoing); (3) evolving conditions of employment off campus; (4) emergence of new technologies and information highways; and (5) growing privatization of universities. The fact that universities appear to have fumbled the challenge seems to confirm the degree of organizational inertia (Nelson, 1999). Universities are criticized for doing too much or too little, depending on perspective or expectations. Much of this criticism is misplaced: The modern university is neither the source of Canada's social problems, nor an all-purpose solution to the paradoxes that confront a changing and diverse society. Those who pounce on it as a curse from hell are no less misguided, although students might be forgiven for making that association when a slew of assignments and tests converge. This fortress mentality has not robbed universities of the capacity to reinvent themselves, and collectively they have done so twice by becoming more meritocratic and democratic (*Economist*, 1993/94).

Yet the relationship of higher education to society at large remains ambiguous. On the one hand, the ivory towers prefer to remain detached and aloof from the cultural wars outside the ivy walls. On the other, they are implicated in social ferment that invariably challenges the mission and goals of post-secondary education. Universities are in crisis not only because of budgets or high enrolments; rather, they are experiencing a crisis of identity because they are no longer sure of what is expected of them in the midst of confusing and changing times (Price, 1993). Put simply, universities at present are experiencing a crisis of identity because of growing uncertainty over roles and responsibilities in a rapidly changing and increasingly diverse world (Price, 1993). Contrasting positions are now aligned in a way that may contest the very legitimacy of the post-secondary enterprise. This ambiguity is encapsulated in debates over post-secondary institutions as (a) enlightened sites of higher learning; (b) empowering instruments for social action; and (c) credential mills for career success. For institutions that historically have enjoyed the equivalent of diplomatic immunity from public scrutiny, the call for accountability and adjustment is as disruptive as it is dismaying. And in trying to be responsive to everything, there is a danger of being irrelevant to everybody.

Universities are currently experiencing a crisis of identity. They are perched at a crossroads with a variety of different options to pursue. Historically, universities have been both contemplative and practical, but the shift in focus from education to training has destroyed the balance between knowledge for its own sake and knowledge for immediate purposes. Consider the options: Must education improve the human condition by advocating a critically informed citizenry? Should it foster intellectual curiosity and encourage curiosity-driven research, or should schools emphasize the transmission of skills to ensure productivity? At present, universities are perceived in terms of three mutually exclusive yet discordant mandates: as centres of higher learning, as instruments of social action, and as launching pads for career success. The fact that all three are superimposed upon and intersect with the others creates a bewildering hybrid.

Higher Learning

Universities have historically prevailed as institutions for the acquisition and transmission of knowledge. They have evolved over time into a distinctively modern way of exploring the world out there that not only transcends the specifics of different academic disciplines, but also imparts a coherent unity to the whole scholarly enterprise (Berger, 1993). A distinct means of organizing and conveying knowledge is often inseparable from the university enterprise itself. At the core of this knowledge is a reliance on data collection, empirical observation, testing, verification, analysis and explanation, and revision (i.e., true until further notice). This knowledge is also organized by means of classification, typologies, models, and theories.

Central to the higher learning enterprise is the unremitting search for dispassionate and objective truth, as reflected in the ideals of objectivity and conduct according to the canons of cognitive rationality (Martin, 1993). Such a commitment would liberate students from the givens of authority and tradition, and prepare them to be democratic citizens (Scott, 1997). A single definitive reality is thought to exist; this reality is subject to discovery and analysis by properly trained individuals with a capacity to transcend social and culture barriers in the quest for excellence. Such a positivist outlook embraces the logic and methods of the natural sciences. The focus on instrumentally technocratic rationality is encouraged under positivism. So too is an empirically based method of inquiry with its embrace of quantifiable objective facts and neutral observation (Darder, 1990).

A postmodernist turn in recent years has challenged the notion of truth or objective knowledge. Proposed instead are many interpretations of reality, each of which is socially constructed as culturally specific embodiments across time and place. Truth or knowledge are relative to an interpretive framework; nor is there any way of stepping inside a privileged observer framework to determine which is superior or correct. Truth, in other words, has little to do with knowledge or objectivity but more with "muscle." Those with the power to control cultural expressions can dictate their definition of reality, given the potency inherent in words and images. A similar line of argument applies to the "normalcy" of "conventional science": Does normal science represent a quest for truth or, alternately, a venue for self-serving privilege by White males, dead or alive? Postmodernists say yes, and most have abandoned cognitively binding standards of scholarship as irrelevant and immoral. Higher education is irresponsible unless it meets the following criteria: inclusive, rooted in political conviction rather than detachment, based on standards both intuitive and intersubjective instead of explanatory or objective, and supportive of the underprivileged rather than abstract empiricism with its separation of object from subject. In short, emphasis is directed at the subjective—including the experiential and personal—as valid forms of knowledge and intellectual discovery (Berger, 1993). The goal of institutional inclusiveness is no less paramount, and accorded equal status alongside abstract logic since, in the final analysis, truth is political and politicized.

Social Critic

An ivory tower view of the universities must share space with an alternate perspective. Universities and tenured faculty are viewed by some as radical strongholds who are more bent on pandering to minorities than advancing higher learning (see *Economist*, 1993/94). Others attack institutes of higher learning as handmaidens of the status quo, more concerned with careerism and empire-building than with progressive social change. These same critics have taken the universities to task as excessively rationalist instruments whose preference for abstraction empowers some while disempowering others. A preoccupation with cognitive rationality is viewed as exclusionary because of its potential for elitism, racism, sexism, and colonialism.

In recent years critical discourse has escalated to the point of delegitimizing higher learning as content or process. The perception of higher learning as illusory or oppressive is central to this transformationist critique of higher education (see Martin, 1993). Often this critique entails references to "political correctness" (with its restricted speech codes) or "multiculturalist" cant against post-secondary outputs by "dead White males." A commitment to social action has displaced the pursuit of objective knowledge and truth-seeking as guiding principles. Learning for learning sake is less important than the pursuit of equality and justice. Moreover, the validity of an idea is no longer based on its degree of truthfulness, i.e., on whether it upholds minimum standards of evidence and argument, but on its potential to address minority interests in the struggle for liberation and empowerment. To be sure, post-secondary education has always been implicitly political in terms of who gets what, and why. Advocates of the social critic position argue that the mission of higher education should be overtly political, with objectives directed at nothing less than comprehensive social change. Put bluntly, universities need to be retooled as agents of social action rather than intellectually "neutral" sites (Martin, 1993). Everything from curricula to teaching is geared toward the pursuit of radical egalitarianism, in large part by unmasking the tyranny of higher learning while reinforcing the salience of race, class, and gender as driving forces in society. The objective is not memorization or recall: The goals are to deconstruct assumptions underlying the organization and transmission of this knowledge, and to use this as a basis for renewal and reform.

Efforts to impose a "social critic" agenda by discrediting the legitimacy of higher learning has confounded the very foundation of the university as a cornerstone of Western society. After all, once the pursuit of objective knowledge is abandoned as legitimate or worthwhile, those supports underlying higher education—objectivity, reason, and science—are likely to collapse.

Credential Factory

During the early 1970s many students went to university to engage in a process of self-discovery through learning. Life was seen as an adventure to be savoured and experienced, while thoughts of a career were rarely contemplated or treated with startled disdain. A critical understanding of the world and a person's relationship to it was a key objective of this contemplative journey. Students, of course, could afford such lofty pursuits since jobs were readily available to anyone who decided to re-enter the establishment. A secure economic future enabled people to become reflective, Edward Renner (in Carey, 1995) reminds us, while learning for learning sake proved a luxury that anyone could afford only when jobs were plentiful.

At present many students flock to university to enhance career success. They know only too well that a degree is a prerequisite for a well-paying job. Education pays: Between 1990 and 1994, the economy created 957 000 jobs for those with post-secondary school achievements; at the same time it shredded 830 000 jobs for people with anything less (Little, 1995). As a result, people with post-secondary credentials held 48 percent of jobs in 1994, up from 41 percent in 1990. The share of jobs available to those who didn't finish high school fell to 21 percent from 27 percent. And the figures keep getting better for the educated: 91 percent of University of Waterloo grads secured jobs within six months of graduation (close to the provincial average according to government figures for 1996), while 96.4 percent were employed within 2 years. Fields such as optometry, architecture, and business and commerce had 100 percent placement rates within 6 months. Conestoga College in Kitchener was tops in Ontario with 94 percent of its graduates finding work (D'Amato, 1999). Moreover, even the kind of degree doesn't seem to matter: Across Ontario, 91.8 percent of people who graduated from the humanities had jobs within 6 months; after two years, the figure had increased to 96.1 percent.

The balancing of the contemplative with the practical may sound good in theory; putting it into practice may be something altogether different. Paradoxically, while students want more training for jobs, many faculty mistakingly continue to uphold the primacy and principles of higher learning. Consider the criticism at the CAUT's October conference of the commercialization that is shifting Canada's post-secondary education away from a commitment to public good and higher learning and increasingly toward the concept of the university as a private-serving mission that limits the quest for knowledge, undermines the integrity of research and researcher, and prepares students for a preordained future (*CAUT Bulletin*, 1999). Table 9–3 below summarizes by comparing and contrasting. Note that the column for postmodernism straddles the boundary between higher learning and social action.

To sum up: Canadian universities are under pressure, driven in part by government funding cuts and greater reliance on non-conventional sources of financial support. They are expected to abandon their esoteric scope and concentrate on training future workers for the globalizing, information-driven economy (Galt, 1997). This raises the question of whether universities should see themselves as vocational training schools, or should focus on educating creative minds, creating knowledge for the sake of knowledge, and performing a broader social role than preparing students for business. Of particular note is the role of university as social critic. As Bernard Shapiro, principal of McGill University, says:

> We must be able to hold up a mirror of society to itself in such a way as to make clear not only the gap that continues to exist between society's rhetoric of its soaring objectives and the less impressive reality of its achievements, but also the inadequacy of the objectives themselves compared to the alternatives that may be considered (cited in Galt, 1997:A-6). We don't want financial people who don't understand the human implications and social implications of what they do.

Still, the monastic or ivory tower model may be inappropriate in an information age shaped by technology and global rivalry. Universities are central to public policy; they also

TABLE 9-3	Perspectives on Higher Education			
	Higher Learning		**Social Critic**	**Credential Factory**
	"modern"	**"postmodern"**		
Mission	construct knowledge	deconstruct knowledge	political	economy
Purpose	explain/laws	interpret	transform	personal accomplishment
Mandate/Goal	objective knowledge	intersubjectivity	equality	practical
Focus	teach/learn	experience	engagement	self-referential
Style	value free	value relativism	partisan/value laden	training
Objective	truth	truths	radical change	credentials

are central instruments in public policy, with the result that universities will invariably be drawn into debates about the relationship of programs and commitments to the changing and diverse needs of society. The corresponding demands and challenges may play havoc with institutional stability, given the dynamics of playing off competing perspectives for a renewal and reform. Time will tell how a largely modernist (even medieval) institution will cope with the postmodernist, market-driven realities of the 21st century.

WORK AND WORKPLACE

FRAMING THE PROBLEM

The cliche "nothing is constant except change" resonates with meaning when applied to work and workplaces. The very concept of work has undergone a paradigm shift of startling proportions in responding to the demands of: (a) an intensely competitive and free-wheeling global market economy; (b) massive restructuring because of automation and "labour"-saving technologies that are eliminating jobs and entire occupations; and (c) a reconsideration of wealth creation in a networking and information-highway age. New technologies have transformed how people work, the skills they need, the knowledge they can contribute to the workplace, and the kind of careers that can be planned (Beckow, 1998). Workplaces, too, find themselves subjected to a constant barrage of demands and regulations, each of which has the potential to complicate or confuse. Pressures for transforming work and workplaces are often internally driven, spanning the spectrum from increasingly alienated workers in search of empowerment, to harried CEOs under the gun to maximize profit, with an increasingly diverse workforce equally adamant in demanding "space" through removal of discriminatory barriers. Further pressure is exerted by disgruntled clients who bristle at the prospect of tolerating shoddy goods or indifferent services. Radical shifts in the business environment because of globalization have also disconnected the moorings that once secured the "way things are done around here." Rather than espousing structure and routine, according to the authors of *Competing on the Edge*, Shona Brown and Kathleen Eisenhardt, businesses today are expected to abandon comprehensive strategic plans in exchange for risk-taking, flexibility, and daring.

Put bluntly, the very concepts of work and workplaces are under pressure to evolve or be rendered irrelevant. Institutional rules and workplace wisdom have taken such a "pounding" that what once were virtues are now regarded as vices, and vice versa. An upheaval of such magnitude will undoubtedly generate a host of social problems for some, yet opportunity for others. In coping with these challenges as expeditiously as possibly, workplace organizations have responded with a volley of proposals for renewal and reform. Four dimensions reinforce this perception of workplaces as increasingly contested sites of social problems: namely, (1) transforming workplaces; (2) diversifying the workforce; (3) working inequities; and (4) rethinking work. The fact that each of these dimensions can be construed as both an opportunity as well as a problem adds yet another wrinkle to the dynamics of work and workplace.

Transforming Workplaces

The winds of change pose a menacing and disruptive challenge to institutional life. In the midst of a free-market revolution, organizations and workplaces are under pressure to change and adapt. In response to intense global competition over capital and investment, rules and priorities that once governed work and workplaces are increasingly contested, exposed to uncertainty, and subjected to second-guessing. Global forces exert a powerful impact both internally and externally: internally, at the level of group dynamics; externally, through institutional links and customer relations. Workplaces are evolving as new philosophies influence management style and strategies, worker relations, and the design of work. A restructuring of the workplace has flattened the organizational pyramid. Layers of management have been peeled away, thus paving the way for more horizontal forms of decision-making and power-sharing. The combination of worker demands and consumer dissatisfaction has compelled companies to restructure from within or lose the flexibility for coping with change from outside. And, with younger workers valuing freedom and flexibility in addition to security and responsibility, it becomes more important than ever to foster workplaces in which people feel as though they make a difference, have a sense of purpose and fulfillment, and are valued for their contribution (Laver, 1999).

Innovative thinking about workplace organizations has also evolved (Chorn, 1991; Capon et al., 1991). Revisions are apparent in how we think and talk about the workplace with respect to structure, functions, and process. At one time, workplaces were dominated by a set of simple physical tasks that entailed mechanistic mindsets for maximizing productivity (Chorn, 1991). A managerial mentality prevailed, with its commitment to rationality, goal pursuit, and causality. Management-labour relations were organized around the principle that managers managed and workers worked. Such a clearly scripted arrangement posed problems, with those at the bottom suffering disproportionately, but such a division of labour did simplify organizational relations. The external world was intrinsically ordered as well. The prospect of stable markets and reliable suppliers simplified the process of doing business and making tidy profits.

Workplaces in the new millennium are no longer bound by such tightly defined scripts. Complex and contradictory forces have exerted a profound impact on organizational design and workplace practices. The effect has been twofold: For some workplaces, the logic of decentralization has replaced centrality as the key organizational principle in the modern workplace. The era of paternalistic management-subservient worker relations is drawing to an end. So too is the notion of lifelong employment and corporate loyalty, thanks to the troika of downsizing, restructuring, and delayering. While a one-size-fits-all managerial mentality once prevailed, according to Peter Drucker in his *Management Challenges for the 21st Century* (Harper Business, 1999), contemporary management styles now need to be flexible, reflect the specific task to be accomplished, and to capitalize (rather than manage) on change as opportunity rather than as problem. Reliable suppliers and manageable markets are virtually a thing of the past. Patterned and predictable environments have given way to fluid and dynamic contexts that appear impervious to regulation or control. Direct cause-effect relations as a basis for doing or explaining are now dismissed as naively simplistic. Acknowledged instead are the principles of multiple causation and complicated feedback loops. For other workplaces, however, the situation is depressingly similar. The principle and practices of a conveyor-belt mentality continue to dominate the workplace, no more so than in the fast food industry where the entrenchment of "McDonaldization" as process and organization (including a devotion to efficiency, predictability, calculability, and control) (Ritzer, 1998) has confirmed the obvious: Emergence of a two-tiered workforce of haves and have-nots will bifurcate social reality in ways that could breed resentment and destabilize society.

Diversifying the Workplace

In addition to the challenges of pervasive and intrusive social change, workplace organizations must engage with the demands of diversity both internally and externally. Almost every workplace has people from different generations, genders, and races working alongside one another, each of whom has her own distinctive set of values and expectations that govern organizational behaviour (Zemke et al., 1999). Workplace inclusion of people with disabilities and aboriginal peoples has further diversified the organizational mosaic, with corresponding pressure to formulate innovative ways of working together with differences. The movement of women into the labour force, as well as into the corridors of power, is but one dimension of this surging diversity (Little, 2000). Another sign of the times is the expanding presence of visible minorities. People of colour now constitute over 11 percent of Canada's population, with the majority concentrated in the largest urban areas. As a group they are no longer content to linger by the sidelines. Recognition and participation are expected in the multicultural scheme of things, even if demanding equality means getting "uppity."

The focus on diversity goes beyond a simple "celebration" of workplace differences. Debates over diversity are inextricably linked to the politics of difference within the context of hierarchy, inequality, and relationships. Applied to the workplace, rules for entitlement (who gets what, and why) are being revised in response to minority demands for a bigger slice of the corporate pie. The concept of institutional inclusiveness extends to maximizing productivity by capitalizing on international contacts. Business and bureaucracies have had little choice but to rethink the delivery of goods and services to an increasingly diverse and discerning public. It entails providing services that are culturally sensitive and community-based. Equally important is the challenge of engaging with diversity as a legitimate component of the multicultural workplace without repudiating the legitimacy of institutional structures and corporate bottom lines. Central to this inclusiveness commitment is the removal of discriminatory barriers that distort the processes of recruitment, retention, promotion, and reward. Of course, talk of more inclusive workplaces is one thing, action quite another, as resentment mounts over measures to improve minority access, representation, and equitable treatment (Loney, 1998).

As well-intentioned as these initiatives might be, moves to engage diversity pose a challenge to existing structures and vested interests. Women and minorities want to be seriously appraised as productive and vital members of the workforce. They are anxious to be taken seriously for what they do rather than for what they are or how they look. Yet the process of transforming workplace structures along minority and gender lines is fraught with ambiguity, tension, and hostility. A diversified workforce sounds good in theory, but differences are just as likely to divide and frustrate as they are to empower and enrich. Entrenched interests have not taken kindly to proposals for institutional reform. The end result is barely concealed anger in the workplace, and the recent spate of violence in the workplace may be attributable to "worker rage" over changes they cannot control (Girardet, 1999). To no one's surprise, there are no easy solutions in sight. Many companies balk at implementing the concept of "mainstreaming diversity," except when they are backed into a corner. Preferred instead is the implemention of the letter of the law to blunt the parry of legal threats or human rights complaints. Still, the demand for engaging with diversity is no longer a luxury or an option. In a diversifying Canada and the global marketplace, a commitment to diversity will pay dividends in terms of career enhancement, workplace survival, and national prosperity.

Working Inequalities

Inequities continue to pervade the workplace, despite initiatives to smooth the disparities. Rhetoric about worker empowerment notwithstanding, the lines of command and control remain firmly entrenched, except, perhaps, for knowledge-workers deemed indispensable. Record sales and profits have not deterred a tendency to downsizing: Canada's major banks earned record profits of $9.1 billion in 1999, but employee attrition continues, with threats to slash 17 000 bank workers from the payroll to ensure global competitiveness and corporate profitability. "Tier-ism" is rampant: In the current lean and mean business climate, companies will increasingly target raises to keep valued staff; by contrast, those whose skills are in abundant supply will be dismissed, marginalized, "casualized," or contracted-out (see Gibb-Clark, 1999). In short, the mantra of economic rationalism—"greed is good," "market rules," and "competition cures everything"—has emerged as an all-embracing ideology that justifies any bottom-line mentality, however disruptive or destructive. Paradoxically, companies that downsize rarely perform more productively; only on the financial markets do results register. Yet indiscriminate downsizing may induce absenteeism, cynicism, creative blockage, demoralization, passive resistance, open sabotage, and risk-taking aversion (Robertson, 1997).

Gendered inequities are increasingly contested. During the 1990s, women 25 and over gained 60 percent of new jobs (1.14 million for women and 746 000 for men); the unemployment rate dropped from 7.3 percent in 1989 to 6.2 percent in 1999, while the adult male rate climbed to 6.4 percent, and labour force participation rose to 54.1 percent of all adult women, whereas the proportion for men fell to 69.3 percent (Little, 2000). Younger women are finding that, unlike their mothers who pretended home life didn't exist and suppressed their gender at work, they do not have to erect barriers between home and work. Nor do they have to deny their sexuality to succeed (Pollock, 2000). And sexual harassment, the once-private shame of women and brunt of male sniggers, is increasingly the public disgrace of men (Gallivan and Bazilli, 1999). Yet women continue to be victims of workplace inequality. A few have shattered the "glass ceiling" (implying in the process that you can make it if you try), but most continue to eke out a living behind formidable barriers that deny, demean, or exclude (Malneaux, 1999). Women constitute 45 percent of the workforce, but only 32 percent of the managers, 15 percent of the senior private sector management, 6.2 percent of board seats, and 2 percent of the *Financial Post* 500 CEOs (Source: *Catalyst*, cited in *Toronto Star*, 19th Sept., 1999). Nearly half of Canada's major companies do not have any female corporate officers (Hanson, 2000). Working women as a rule tend to earn less than men, regardless of the type of employment, although differences largely disappear for female workers who are single, university-educated, and childless. And while corporate executives are proclaiming changes in rules governing the behaviour of women and men in the workplace, with women being the wave of the future, according to Shere Hite in her book *Sex and Business*, such announcements may embrace politically correct lip service rather than a genuine commitment to inclusiveness (cited in Flynn, 2000). A ten-year study of women's advancement in business by the *Harvard Business Review* concluded: Most workplaces are created by men and for men, and are based on male experiences, with the result that workplace structures and cultures rarely accommodate women's value systems, styles of interacting, or complexities in their lives (cited in *Globe and Mail*, "Throwing Stones at the Glass Ceiling," Feb. 12, 2000). For women of colour, the situation is more grim yet (Dwyer, 2000). Rather than bumping into a concrete ceiling when scaling the corporate ladder, many remain mired in the "sticky floor" of the workplace, often dealing with sweatshop conditions, low-paying jobs, unpaid overtime, and sexual harassment (Malneaux, 1999). Even the prospect of home-based self-employment is hardly the solution it was once deemed to be, according to a report by the Canadian Policy Research Networks Inc. (cited in the *Kitchener-Waterloo Record*, 11 Sept., 1999), given the realities of no benefits or the possibility of long-term income and skills upgrading, while earning only $15 000 a year (compared to men who earn $25 000 when working from home). And efforts to bring about solutions by way of pay equity initiatives are criticized as more of a problem than the original, on the grounds this kind of engineering offends the notion of free will (wage gaps result not from discrimination but from choices to drop out of the labour market), marketplace decision-making, and principles of natural justice (Loney, 1998).

Rethinking Work

Work and workplaces are undergoing change with respect to what they look like (structure), what they are supposed to do (function), and what they really do (process). The corporate air is filled with slogans extolling the virtues of the "new economy," "the information highway," "total quality," "empowerment," "total quality management," "quality circles," "downsizing," "restructuring," and "delayering." Traditional bromides such as "seniority," "job security," "company loyalty," and "benefits" and "pensions" are rapidly fading from memory. The centrality of work to the human condition cannot be denied. Historically, people's lives and identities revolved around work and their relationship to workplaces. But human labour is gradually being redefined or discarded because of computer-mediated automation and corporate reorganization (Rifkin, 1995). Much of the uncertainty can be attributed to changes in the rules that formerly governed "how work was done around here." Work is rapidly disappearing in certain quarters, as automation kicks in and corporations kick out. Robots are appearing on more assembly lines, elbowing out old-fashioned workers, in an attempt to reduce costs and stay competitive in global markets (Stinson, 2000). Changes are also evident in the nature of working. The prospect of job permanence is vanishing because of organizational restructuring, managerial delayering, and workforce downsizing. The days of lifetime job security are numbered. Both legally and psychologically, the employment contract is a thing of the past. Gone are the days when job security was linked with employee performance. Both individuals and corporations are continually shopping around for the best deal, resulting in turnstile operations where team composition varies from year to year (Capon, 1999). The ideals of loyalty and commitment are showing their age: Once cherished as a mark of virtue, corporate loyalty is now likely to be caricatured as a sign of weakness, lack of ambition, or a stalled career. To the extent that job-hoppers are no longer seen as unreliable and a poor employment risk, but ambitious and confident, the paradox of contempory work could not be more forcefully articulated (DeBare, 1999).

For those with skills and connections, work is not necessarily a penalty for pay as much as an opportunity for growth and empowerment (Chiose, 1997). For others, work will remain a dreary cycle of dead-end jobs, from fast-food floor to white-collar factory workers (for example, telephone operators who handle customer calls), with few rewards and fewer opportunities (Clement, 1997). Grievances about impossible working conditions in the nursing profession reflect high levels of burnout, depression, mandated overtime, and "casualization" of the workforce (Mickleburgh, 1999). Or consider the plight of the 8000 homeworkers in the Greater Toronto Area, according to Roxanne Ng in her report, "Homeworking: Home Office or Home Sweatshop?" Those interviewed toiled away in sweatshop conditions, earned salaries below minimum wage, never received overtime pay, and endured work-related injuries (cited in Ross, 1999). Others still consider themselves lucky to get a job. Access to adequately waged jobs is further jeopardized by a combination of people-displacing technologies and a globalizing economy with its outsourcing to lower-paid offshore workers (Lerner, 1997). The net result is a bifurcated workforce: Some have so much work that personal and family life suffer because of overtime; others have so little work that they also experience deprivation at personal and social levels (Gwyn, 1996). Even the public sector, once the employer of last resort, is increasingly adopting a downsizing mentality. Instead of a well-paid job for life as was once the case, public servants are exposed to slash-and-burn management whose bottom-line mantra is efficiency and zero deficits. Such a mean and lean mentality is wreaking havoc with career plans. Career patterns may entail a combination of contract work for a variety of companies, interspersed with periods of unemployment or underemployment. It is also transforming workplaces into danger zones, ranging from incivility and work-rage and, tragically, culminating in the killing of (ex)co-workers.

Work comes in all shapes and sizes, and its pervasiveness in people's lives is rarely disputed. Students engage in work when going to school; upon graduation many will begin to work at jobs or pursue careers. Some will continue to work at home by looking after children, but without formal payment. Others will work out of their homes by exchanging goods and services for payment. Still others will be paid for working outside the house, often in large corporate settings, but at the risk of losing their creativity, control, and individuality. A few see work as the crowning feature of a meaningful existence and source of identity; others prefer to shirk their jobs as a source of aggravation or humiliation. In short, working is so central to many people's lives and to society at large that a world without work is unthinkable, and it is precisely this tension between work as an opportunity and a problem that provides the impetus for this chapter. The topic of work and workplace from a social problem perspective is analyzed and assessed in terms of its impact on individuals and implications for society. The first part of this chapter surveys the evolving and contested nature of work and workplaces in contemporary society. The concept of work and working in the 21st century is examined next against the backdrop of a world that is diverse, changing, and uncertain. Work is not disappearing per se; but work as conventionally defined is being superseded by new forms that reflect a shift in doing work, workplace design, and dynamics of working. Inception of a human resources approach is widely approved in meeting the demands of a knowledge economy and knowledge workers. Nevertheless, many workers continue to be treated as little more than glorified machines, as demonstrated by the case study on conveyor-belt burgers. The chapter concludes by isolating the barriers that preclude workplaces from greater inclusiveness. A look at efforts to implement community policing will provide some insight into the difficulties encountered in attaining the goal of an inclusive institution.

Admittedly, the concept of work and workplaces is not necessarily a social problem in its own right, since much depends on context, criteria, and consequences. Even the problems that plagued workplaces in the 1990s may not apply in the new millennium. Previous editions of *Social Problems* focused on the impact and implications of a stagnant economy to work and workplaces. At present, however, Canada's economy is booming: strong job creation, surging consumer confidence, low inflation, receptive markets, and predictions of healthy growth in the future. Unemployment has declined to less than 7 percent nationwide; a total of 14.82 million Canadians were employed, an increase of nearly 750 000 in the last two years; the availability of full-time work is growing faster than part-time work; exports to the U.S. are piggybacking on the strength of a robust American economy and undervalued Canadian dollar; and the manufacturing sector is rebounding, with three-quarters of all job creation in this sector (Associated Press, cited in *Globe and Mail*, Nov. 6, 1999). Those who predicted the end of work because of technology, profits, and globalization (Rifkin, 1995), may have trouble accounting for the creation of nearly two million jobs since 1992, a labour force participation rate of 66 percent, and growth in self-employment to 17.6 of the total (Finlayson, 1999). Yet there is a downside, since not everyone is hopping aboard the "gravy train." Almost 1.1 million Canadians are looking for work, while upwards of 500 000 have given up the search (Canadian Press, 2000). Subdued growth in real wages and weekly earnings suggests anything but an idyllic time for workers. Problems arise when people's expectations do not match the realities of what is happening out there, when changes are having a differential impact in terms of who gets what, and when the consequences of work and workplaces contribute to the erosion of the societal fabric. Several themes provide an organizational framework for problematizing work and workplaces:

(1) Workplaces and organizations are social problems in their own right because of design and definition. Workplaces are particularly problematic sites for those who are exposed to dangerous, dehumanizing, or demeaning jobs. In cases where automation is eliminating jobs, people's right to work and to sustain themselves is being jeopardized. Violence in the workplace involving co-workers is of growing concern. In being beset with more change and complexity than ever, workplaces have evolved into "engines of conflict" that bode ill for society.

(2) Workplaces are thought to be responsible for creating social problems because of work-related stresses. Conflict-producing workplaces include the high demand/low control workplace as well as the high-effort/low-reward workplace, culminating in random acts of work rage because of burdensome workloads combined with a brooding sense of powerlessness and injustice in a mean and lean environment (Cole, 1999). Workers who are required to work longer than ever pose a higher health risk (they drink, smoke,

and weigh more) according to the National Population Health Survey between 1994/95 and 1996/97 (cited in Staseson, 1999). Stress may be especially acute when seeking to balance career plans with personal and family life (Laver, 1999).

(3) Workplaces are themselves sites of social problems because of their susceptibility to patterns of inequality. Workplace relations are unequal relations, and these inequities need to be examined in terms of who gets what, on what grounds, and with what impact.

(4) Workplaces are known to resist changes and solutions to problems. By the same token, proposed solutions to the problems of work and organizations often generate conditions that create more problems. Workplace solutions such as downsizing may be great for the bottom line; they may also have the effect of tossing thousands of workers out of work, with little or no chance of re-entering the labour market regardless of retraining.

(5) Workplaces are problems because of their relationship to the economy. What is the economy for? For some, the point of the economy is to make a profit; for others the economy exists to create meaningful and stable jobs (Laxer, 1999). Not surprisingly, critics respond differently to the prospect of even profitable corporations eliminating workers in the name of efficiency and profit (Bartram, 1999).

This chapter explores the concepts of work and workplaces as social problems. In a rapidly changing, increasingly diverse, and uncertain world, the social dimensions of work and organizations need to be examined and analyzed. Workplace organizations are interpreted not as concrete "things" in their own right, but as "sites" of "contestation" where confusion and uncertainty are the rule rather than exception in coping with diversity and change. Much can be gleaned by approaching workplaces as an ideological battleground involving different competitive groups in a constant struggle for control of the agenda. Diverse forces, such as labour and management, are locked in perpetual combat; in some cases, competing when pushed, but cooperating when necessary, because of differences in outlook regarding problem definition or proposed solution. The contesting of agendas with respect to problems and solutions ensures that workplace realities fall somewhere in between the poles of chaos and regulation, structure and agency, continuity and change, and resistance and control. Such an interpretation may not yield elegant models of organizations and neat workplace flowcharts. Nevertheless, it does capture the dynamics of workplace politics with the onset of the new millennium.

WORKING IN THE 21ST CENTURY: FROM CRISIS TO CHALLENGE

> Work is about daily meaning as well as daily bread. For recognition as well as cash; for astonishment rather than torpor; in short, for a sort of life rather than a Monday through Friday sort of dying... (Studs Turkel, *Utne Reader*, May/June, 1995).

Work has been around since the beginning of time. It remains the most essential of human activities in providing both physical sustenance and, more importantly, the basis for personal identity and self-esteem (Krahn and Lowe, 1994). But until the nineteenth century, people did not have jobs; more accurately, they did work (Keegan, 1996). As pointed out by William Bridge (1995), author of *Job Shift*, work was not something that a factory provided in exchange for pay. Historically, work was an activity that had to be done at a certain time and place. It often was difficult to disentangle work from the rhythm of a person's life. But organized work (having a job) evolved with the Industrial Revolution and the mechanization of the productive process. Even so, barely 50 percent of the workers in the industrialized world belonged to a company a century ago. Workplaces were small, family-owned, and rudimentary in organization (Campbell, 1996). It was not until the early 1970s that labour-intensive industrialization raised the job figure to 90 percent of the workforce.

But the concept of work has continued to evolve. No sooner did the culture of work begin to take hold—including the notion of a full-time job for life, well-defined career paths, and corporate loyalty in exchange for job security—than countervailing forces combined to dismantle the very nature of work and structure of the workplace (Keegan, 1996). Both the private and public sector embarked on a labour-shedding process that eliminated jobs because of automation and digital technology, particularly those that entailed repetitive aspects of production. In a market-oriented climate that defines greed as good, ruthlessness has proven a virtue rather than vice. Yet corporate downsizing is creating a bifurcated workforce; on the one hand, there is a core of a permanent employees (if stressed out and demoralized by pressures to produce or else); on the other hand, there is an outer perimeter of part-time or contract workers with little opportunity for security or success. The "work-rich" have secure jobs with continuous, high-value employment as a function of their skills; by contrast, the "work-poor" are relegated to semi-employment status with generally lower wages and few benefits (Gwyn, 1996). And, adding insult to injury, there is an untapped pool of hundreds of thousands of workers on the margins of society without even a hope of finding a job.

A World Without Work?

According to some social critics, jobs will become an endangered species with the onset of a new, information economy. The new economy is driven largely by the microchip as a basis for work, production, and wealth creation; based on knowledge rather than making goods; global, since money and information respects few boundaries; networked, in that all production and distribution is linked; and increasingly decentralized and difficult to control because of uncertainty and chaos (*Time*, Dec./Jan., 1998). Admittedly, not all jobs will disappear because of the new economy. A knowledge-based economy will produce jobs for scientists, engineers, software analysts, and biotechnology researchers (Rifkin, 1995). Those in the caring sector (from teachers to caregivers for the elderly) should prosper. But there is little hope for those on the margins. For them, part-time and temporary jobs will be the rule, together with a culture that dismisses casual or part-time labourers as dilettantes and failures. No amount of retooling or upgrading will help the millions who are discarded because of planned obsolescence. Blue-collar workers may become obsolete in a workerless world, with massive unemployment as computer-guided machines displace most workers from the production process. The hollowing out of the middle ranks of employment, both professional or skilled, will prove no less disruptive.

The creation of a two-tiered workforce is not without consequence. Those employees clever enough to seize the opportunity will prosper at the expense of the less fortunate, in the process rupturing the sense of community at the core of a sustainable society (Stewart, 1997). A large reservoir of underemployed (or never-employed) will intensify the gap between rich (skilled) and poor (unskilled), while tilting the balance of decision-making power towards owners and employers. A recipe for social disaster is ever-present as well, insofar as the disenfranchised (many of whom are young males) may see few options except crime and violence, for no other reason than having nothing to lose when nothing is at stake (Keegan, 1996). As Jeremy Rifkin says, "If the talent, energy, and resourcefulness of hundreds and millions of men and women are not redirected into constructive ends, civilization will continue to disintegrate into a state of increased lawlessness from which there may be no easy return" (cited in Goar, 1996). Finally, the very existence of capitalism may be threatened when nobody can buy what workerless factories produce. What indeed will happen when we don't want what they have, and they can't buy what we sell (see Rifkin, 1995)?

A rethinking of work and the workplace is urgently needed. The gradual decline of smokestack industries may be attributed to the internationalization of capital and labour, as profit-hungry companies seek offshore locations to reduce production costs. Introduction of a computer-driven microelectronic revolution has put the onus on information processing as a source of wealth creation. Computers may be creating more jobs than they absorbed, but this technology is undermining the security of unskilled workers in repetitive jobs (Little, 1997). The forces of automation and digital technology have also expanded the volume of work done by machines, without having to take into account coffee breaks or costly dental plans. Conventional wisdom advocates getting rid of costly workers in the rush to improve productivity and profits. As a result, even new skills or retraining may not help if there is a dearth of meaningful jobs. Even the service sector (from banks to retail) is beginning to automate in hopes of replacing managerial layers with (a) highly skilled professional teams, (b) outsourcing for specific needs, and (c) sophisticated technology (Rifkin, 1996). As Michael Dunkerley writes in his book, *The Jobless Economy*, "People are now the most expensive optional component of the production process... People are now targeted for replacement as soon as the relevant technology is developed to replace them" (quoted in Gwyn, 1996, F3). Young Canadians have been hit especially hard by this rupture. Unemployment rates for Canadians under age 25 stood at 13.2 percent in December 1999, but were closer to double that figure when including drop-outs, part-timers, and school-returners. Time will tell if the benefits of an e-economy will be distributed in a way that rewards both the "lucky" and "unlucky."

A Solutionless Problem?

> Part of the problem is the very American mindset that there's a solution to every problem, and then an end to it (Bruce Hoffman, director of the Centre for the Study of Terrorism and Political Violence, St. Andrews University, Scotland. (Quoted in Dickey, 1997).

Are we at the end of work, or of particular types of jobs? A globally based, knowledge-driven economy cannot possibly provide work for everyone. By the same token, the resiliency of a free-enterprise system should never be underestimated. The creation of some 750 000 jobs in 1998/99 attests to that. Is there a solution to this problem? Both pessimists and optimists concede the inapplicability of simple solutions to this complex problem. Notwithstanding the time and effort expended in freeing people from the drudgery of work, there is little consensus in dealing with the thousands of workers who have been cut adrift from the rhythms of the world, unsure of how to make their contribution in a society that defines a person's value by her work. Perhaps the solution lies in defining away the problem. Since full employment is neither attainable nor desirable, according to economists and policy-makers, proposed instead is a "natural" rate of unemployment of around 8 to 9 percent, in effect implying the acceptability of Canada's current unemployment rate of around 7 percent. Others suggest that the demise of work is greatly exaggerated (Matas, 1996). Both the government and economists cite the creation of millions of new jobs since 1993, including manufacturing jobs, with the result that employment now stands at 14 639 800, up dramatically from 12.8 million in 1992 (Little, 1999). Each new technological advance has the potential to create new products, invent needs never dreamed of before, and new employment patterns. In other words, the introduction of a computer-driven, knowledge-based technology is not the end of work so much as the end of work as we know it.

The rules of the new economy have altered the nature of work, how work is organized, and how wealth is generated by workers. The government is no longer convinced of a Keynesian need for investing in the economy to stave off depression or stimulate economic activity. Employment patterns that once reflected boom-bust cycles are drawing to a close. Job recovery does not automatically follow a recession; labour shedding continues even with economic recovery in the headlong rush to downsize regardless of the bottom line. A raft of solutions have been proposed in hopes of coping with the challenges of a knowledge-based, market-driven, and globalizing economy, including reducing the workweek to spread around the supply of jobs; abolition of mandatory overtime; pro-rated benefits for part-time workers; pay for voluntary service to the community; a redistribution of profits from the private sector to underwrite community service and voluntary sector jobs; and a conversion of excess wealth into job creation (Rifkin, 1995). A fundamental rethinking will be required to bring about changes in the workplace. Most would agree that Canada must remain internationally competitive. But surely the goal of economic competitiveness regardless of cost must be balanced by a preference for a better quality of life through reasonable standards of living, employment security, and opportunities for meaningful work (Krahn and Lowe, 1994). Solutions that rely on "letting the market decide" may need to be rethought. After all, should the discipline of the market provide a model for the public service sector or the government (Mintzberg, 1996; Stewart, 1997)? The balancing of profit with civic responsibilities through work policies not only protects citizens from uncertainties and dismissals, it also ensures a decent life for the many, not just for the fortunate few (see Krahn and Lowe, 1994).

Rethinking Work: Workerless Factories and Virtual Workplaces

A globalizing free market revolution has exerted bewildering pressure on organizations and workplaces, in part because of intense global competition and in part because of automation and technological innovations. Manufacturing jobs are disappearing; so too are white collar jobs, often being replaced by highly skilled professionals employing state-of-the-art computer technology and just-in-time support personnel as one way of squeezing labour costs. A rethinking of management–labour relations is taking place in the knowledge economy. A restructuring of the workplace has flattened out the organizational pyramid, with layers of management pared away for democratizing more horizontal forms of decision-making and power-sharing. The era of paternalistic management–worker relations is waning. Even the distinction between management and labour is increasingly fuzzy as humanistic paradigms challenge conveyor-belt philosophies. To be sure, the prospect of a more inclusive and democratic workplace is showing signs of modest improvement under equity directives. Yet appearances may be deceiving, because of the autocracy that remains entrenched within the workplace, sometimes discreetly, other times openly. Nor can the human costs and squandered potential be glossed over in chasing the "almighty dollar."

The Old (Fordist) Workplace

Rules that apply to work, workers, working, work environment, and workplace are rapidly changing. Marked differences reflect major shifts in the production process—from Fordism to post-Fordism. A mode of production named after Henry Ford and the practices he brought to car manufacturing, Fordism included the mobilization of masses of labour into huge factories to produce large batches of standardized goods for mass consumption (Holly, 1996). Fordist means of production dovetailed with Taylorist principles of scientific management, and became associated with mass production, standardized products, large inventories, strict division of labour, labour de-skilling, vertical integration, and global firms. For most of the 20th century, mass production was the dominant organizational framework, influencing both corporate strategy and the design of jobs. Central to the principle of mass production was a commitment to maintaining stocks of inventory and completed work as security against possible disruptions to production (Perry et al., 1995).

The old work environment sought to regulate and control both the internal and external environment by eliminating uncertainties from all facets of production or distribution. Fordist models were based on an integrated assembly line, rationalization of production and labour, product standardization, economies of scale, and principles of scientific management (Perry et al., 1995). The work environment was rigidly stratified and regimented, with managers who managed on top and workers who worked at the bottom. The conventional workplace could be described as autocratic in that it was organized around the bureaucratic principles of an authoritarian hierarchy where everything was in its place and done in a proper sequence ("just in place"). Work skills relied heavily on the physical strength or manual dexterity normally associated with smokestack industries. The mind, for all intents and purposes, could be parked at the factory gate. Workers were seen as cogs in the machine of industry. A specialized division of labour placed emphasis on workers with specialized training. It was assumed that workers were motivated primarily by extrinsic rewards (money) rather than job satisfaction. Work itself was seen as a full-time, lifetime activity. Company loyalty and commitment to its goals over the long haul (seniority) provided the stepping stone to career success. The work site constituted a large cohort of males rooted in one place and compartmentalized into cubicles or conveyor belts who produced something in exchange for rewards and promotion. The rigidity and regimentation of traditional work could be symbolized by the expression "nine to five." At the management level, company success was measured by its inclusion in the Forbes 500 survey of the biggest and the best.

The New (Post-Fordist) Workplace

The certitudes of the old work environment have been abandoned by chance and uncertainty. Post-Fordist models of production have shifted to production processes that incorporate more flexible means of wealth creation as applied to product types; delivery of parts as needed; availability of disposable labour; reliance on outsourcing (contracting out); small batch production to meet demand; and elimination of any operations (such as storage) that do not directly contribute to corporate value (Holly, 1996). New ways of organizing work are characteristic of the post-Fordist workplace, including reduced tiers of management, greater worker discretion, just-in-time production, and new approaches to industrial relations (Perry et al., 1995). Reliable suppliers and predictable markets are virtually a thing of the past. Instead of pattern and predictions, fluid and competitive environments prevail that seldom lend themselves to regulation or control but entail risk-taking. The creation of wealth is based on post-industrial employment patterns rooted in knowledge and services rather than in manufacturing (Castells, 1993). While the old work is organized around mass labour, the new work is advanced by knowledge elites, resulting in a two-tier system of labour: On the one hand are the knowledge workers, with high-paying, relatively secure jobs who are expected to serve as catalysts in generating wealth; on the other hand are the poorly paid and underemployed, whose jobs have been de-skilled by automation. Complicating these changes is the entry of women and minorities. Diversifying the workplace has allowed management to tap into a broader pool of talent and expertise; it also has meant adjustments in corporate rules and procedures to ensure equity in treatment. Equally noticeable is the disappearance of a large, permanent workforce. Companies are looking for ways to prune costs by shedding those layers of "fat" that do not actively contribute to the bottom line. CEOs prefer a workforce that can meet fluctuations in the business cycle: Just-in-time labourers can be hired quickly during business upturns and dismissed promptly when profits shrink (Lerner, 1997).

The concept of work is also undergoing radical change. Teamwork and reliance on outside expertise are increasingly commonplace and widely touted. The shift from lifetime employment and career aspirations to just-in-time employment (part-time) puts the onus on personal "reskilling" and lifetime learning. Workplaces are no longer characterized by a rigid pecking order, with the lowly worker at the bottom and a maze of management on top. Appearing instead is a flattened hierarchy that invites decentralized and participatory decision-making. Even the concept of a work site is losing its sense of physical locale. Corporate offices are being replaced by virtual offices/virtual corporations that exist only in name and modem address, in effect releasing contemporary work sites from the constraints of time or space (Arnault, 1995). Knowledge workers do not necessarily need on-site supervision; they are even less dependent on the regulatory measures of punch clocks, cubicles, and the nine-to-five workday. Without the constancy of a physical location, the new workplace redefines traditional relationships by forcing people to reorganize their lives and relationships accordingly. Not surprisingly, corporate bigness for the sheer sake of being big is losing lustre in an era of flexible specialization. Table 10–1 provides a brief synopsis of the differences that ideally distinguish the new work from the old.

Table 10–1 can only make sense as an opposition between ideal types. Or as Holly (1996) reminds us, a dualistic framework between Fordism and post-Fordism always distorts by oversimplifying; nevertheless, such a distinction provides a basis for analyzing differences and similarities. How then does the new (postmodern) workplace compare with the old (modern) workplace? Reality suggests that modern work is riddled with ambiguity, since it combines aspects of Fordism and post-Fordism. Perhaps it's more accurate to say that the new work is superimposed on the old without dislodging the latter. Since neither model is powerful enough to displace the other, the workplace may reflect a contested site involving competitive struggles between the new and the old. Contradictions also pervade the workplace: It is ostensibly more democratic and inclusive yet remains as autocratic as in the past because of its competitive pressures. Emphasis is directed at being more inclusive, flexible (less rigid, more participatory and discretionary), and worker-friendly (less harassment), yet the primacy of profit and productivity remain uncontested. Employees are touted as a company's greatest asset, but bottom-line calculations routinely compromise this commitment. Loyalty is disposable, since bottom line considerations are not averse to slashing these valued "assets" to cut costs and bolster profits. The introduction of modern technology is no less ambivalent. Labour-saving devices may reduce much of the drudgery associated with tra-

TABLE 10–1	Comparison of Old Work and New Work	
	Old (Fordist) Work	**New (Post-Fordist) Work**
Work Environment	Control, Order, Certainty	Chaos, Uncertainty
Work Skills	Brawn "McDonaldization of Work"	Brain The Information Highway Computer Literacy
Worker Status	Cog "Another Brick in the Wall"	Catalyst Two-Tier = Creativity + De-skilled
Working Style	Nose to the Grindstone Career-Oriented	Empowerment, Teamwork Re-skilling/Lifelong Learning
Workplace	The Bureaucratic Pyramid	De-layered
Decision-Making	Autocratic	Democratic
Work Site	"The Firm" 9 to 5	Virtual Reality ("Hotelling") Anytime/Anywhere
Management Philosophy	Full Employment Contract for Life	Downsizing = Leaner and Meaner Contract for a Job
Management-Labour Relations	Scientific Management	Human Resources
Workforce	Homogeneous	Diverse and Demanding of Inclusion
Work Ethos	In Its Place	Just-in-Time

ditional tasks. To the extent that they also eliminate labour or condemn people to new types of alienation, the paradox of the workplace will continue to perplex or provoke.

HUMANIZING THE WORKPLACE

The traditional workplace was authoritarian by nature. Not only did most workers exert little control over the production process, but the work itself was often alienating or exploitative, if not openly dangerous. Stress factors contributed to high rates of staff turnover and absenteeism, while mind-numbing routines could induce thoughtless complacency or open sabotage. Managerial interests took top priority at the expense of workers who were relegated to the bottom or the background.

Many have criticized the traditional workplace. Labour unions and worker advocates have denounced workplaces as places fit for machines rather than humans. Academics have pounced on organizational workplaces as inhumane and counter-productive by exploring the logic behind the process of exploitation and control. Proposals have been put forward for transforming the workplace into a worker-friendly environment that is still capable of functioning under budgetary limits. The introduction of a human resources approach to shop-floor dynamics is but one solution to the demands of a productive yet humane workplace. How, then, has this problem come about in the first place?

Scientific Management: Workers as Machines

The emergence of big business during the nineteenth century posed a series of logistical problems. Through mergers and vertical monopolies, organizations grew in size and complexity. Such expansion exerted additional pressure to develop the means for taking control of sprawling operations and far-flung empires. This, in turn, entailed a need for reducing the uncertainty created by expansion, enhancing the coordination of disparate parts into a smooth functioning whole, and maximizing productivity and profits during an era of financial expansion. Equally important was the need for controlling potentially disruptive workers. For the managerial class, the principles of scientific management proved to be fortuitous in furnishing the formula for maximizing production while controlling labour.

Scientific management as principle and practice is associated with Frederick Winslow Taylor. His ideas were introduced in the 1890s, quickly captured the soul of American industry after an initial period of resistance, and were firmly entrenched in Canada by the First World War (Campbell, 1996). Taylorism sought to make complex organizations more efficient and productive by shifting control of operations from family ownership to a professional class who relied on the principles of rationality (including intervention, regulation, precision, calculation, and coordination) as a basis for generating wealth. The drive for efficiency transformed the workplace into a glorified machine with mechanistic precision for control and profit. The workplace was also based on the notion that (a) workers did not require a skill to do a job; (b) workers didn't need to start and finish a job; (c) management could monitor and control what workers did on the job; and (d) the secret of efficiency lay in controlling costs (Campbell, 1996). The following procedures were thought to be elemental:

(1) A simple division of labour, best summarized in the aphorism, "Managers think, workers do." Managers assumed responsibility for all aspects of the planning and design of activities. By definition, they were best positioned to monitor and manipulate the organization at large. For managers, primary functions revolved around command, control, and coordination; workers were expected to demur and passively obey.

(2) The use of carefully calibrated methods to determine the most efficient work procedures. Through precise measurement and reliance on time-and-motion studies, scientific management sought to reduce waste or needless energy. An optimum level of performance could be devised, in large measure by dividing a job into its smallest constituent units for assignment to trained workers.

(3) Select and train the best person for each job. Each worker would receive the training for a particular job, and no other. Productivity was optimal when the right person could perform a specialized task without waste or loss of energy. Paradoxically, individual workers were expendable insofar as each cog could be replaced with a component of comparable value, without destroying the balance. Encourage productivity by increasing monetary rewards as the central incentive for hard work. Workers were perceived essentially as economic animals whose motivations were purely of material self-interest. Payment in high wages provided an incentive to work harder and reduced the threat of strikes or subversion. A new social contract evolved around a widely accepted truism; namely, company loyalty in exchange for secure, well-paid employment.

(4) De-skilling work. "Craftsmen" who took a manufactured product from start to completion were replaced with workers (robots) who did one job repeatedly for the entire shift. Workers and the machines they tended became cogs in the conveyor belt. Isolating workers from one another also minimized opportunities for waste or shopfloor sabotage.

(5) Routinizing work. Central to scientific management is the commitment to eliminate the human element (i.e., uncertainty, risk, or choice) in the production while improving control over the entire process.

The consequences of scientific management have been immense. Taylor's decidedly undemocratic principles gave rise to the moving assembly line that Henry Ford incorporated in 1913 for his Model T. Even today these principles serve as a model for workplace relations, despite altered circumstances and competing perspectives. The current mania for measurement and management (Mintzberg, 1996) is providing a rationale for improving productivity and profit by controlling costs through the elimination of uncertainties. Nowhere is this mindset more enthusiastically embraced than in the fast-food industry, which continues to extol the virtues of a conveyor belt mentality in dealing with customers and employees (Morgan, 1986; Reitzer, 1996; Ritzer, 1993). The next case study deals with the mechanization of this industry and the corresponding de-skilling of work in such a regulated environment. This portrayal of work experiences at a Toronto-based Burger King restaurant demonstrates how the preoccupation with standardization applies not only to food preparation but to customer relations and workplace dynamics. The fact that everyone is treated as little more than a cog in the fast-food machine confirms the tenacity of scientific management in the contemporary era.

Human Resources: From Conveyor Belts to Quality Circles

The 1980s heralded a new wave of management thinking in redesigning manager-worker relations. Impetus for this shift stemmed from the success of Japanese management techniques and the influx of women into the workforce. Contributing factors also included managerial concern over worker productivity, cost-cutting, and offshore competition. Changes to the economy have been particularly important in bolstering the profile of the human resources approach. A human resources approach is critical in preparing for an economy inundated by mergers and acquisitions, the blending of corporate cultures, corporate alliances, and global expansion, but, most importantly, as human intellect replaces warehouse inventory as a source of wealth, and as work moves to workers' heads from their hands (*Globe and Mail*, Nov. 15, 1999).

A human resources perspective challenges the principles of scientific management. Job enrichment and enlargement replace the notion of simplification and excessive specialization. Workplaces are seen as a collection of competencies rather than a hierarchy around layers of management (Schellhardt, 1997). Instead of defining workers as purely economic animals to be pushed or prodded at the convenience of management, they are seen as whole persons who crave psychological satisfaction and creative outlets. Metaphorically, the employment contract shifted from that of a conveyor belt to a quality circle involving a holistic and democratic environment of active and concerned participants. Rather than hiring workers to do a specific task in a specific place over a specific number of hours, knowledge workers have wrested a significant degree of control over their work, both in terms of where they work (at home rather than office) and how they work (based not on the number of hours worked, but on what they accomplish). The emergence of a knowledge economy and knowledge workers has further marginalized old-style management. Managerial control and power has weakened in part because many are incapable of monitoring highly skilled knowledge workers, let alone of providing close and highly evaluative supervision

CASE STUDY 10-1 — Conveyor Belt Burgers

"Any trained monkey could do the job" (Reiter, 1992, 167).

The contemporary fast-food industry in Canada and the United States is organized around the principles of scientific management. Central to this philosophy is a commitment to dehumanize the workplace. Rigid operational procedures and standardization are adopted not to improve food quality, but to eliminate the uncertainty—the human element—from the production process. Or, as one of the original McDonald brothers once said about his golden arches: "If we gave people a choice, there would be chaos" (Love, 1995, 15). Attainment of this dehumanization process is organized around the pursuit of quality (the ideal of standardization and predictability in the preparation of food), service (speed in the delivery of food to each customer), and cleanliness (associated with "order" and consumer "appeal" rather than healthfulness). Each outlet combines unskilled machine operators and auxiliary staff and sophisticated technology to produce a highly polished product through painstaking attention to design and planning (Reiter, 1992, 75). To the extent that these goals are achieved, each fast-food outlet conforms with the ideals of scientific management. Many of the examples below are taken from Ester Reiter's (1992/1996) book on a Burger King franchise in Toronto, *Making Fast Food: From the Frying Pan into the Fryer*.

A Burger King franchise is regulated to the most minute detail. Pots and pans, as well as chefs and dishwashers, have been replaced by automated routine and a crew of undifferentiated machine-tenders. With the aid of computer technology, Burger King can slot almost any crew person into any food processing function at the outlet by simply cross-training workers to conduct a number of simplified tasks. Both worker movements and emotions are considered to be at the disposal of the franchise. Those who work at counters and take customer orders are expected to display a ready smile, a cheerful yet energetic disposition, and clichéd lines in promoting the sale of meals. Kitchen workers are no less programmed in terms of appearance and lines of interaction.

Consider the preparation of food. All food enters the store in its final cooking stages: Hamburgers arrive as frozen precooked patties, while buns are precooked and caramelized to ensure an appealing image. French fries, chicken, and fish are precooked to ensure a standardized product. Condiments such as onions or pickles (with the exception of tomatoes) are presliced or pre-shredded. The instore preparation of these foods is essentially that of machine-tending—the incorporation of assembly-line technology in the food service industry. For example, hamburgers are placed on a conveyor belt that transports the frozen meat patties through a gas broiler in a space of 94 seconds. A worker at the other end of the broiler picks up the cooked patty with tongs and transfers it to the bottom half of the bun. The ungarnished hamburger is then placed in a steamer where it can remain for up to 10 minutes before being discarded. Workers at the burger board "assemble" the burger by adding the condiments (cheese slices, pickles, onions, mayonnaise, lettuce, tomatoes, ketchup, and mustard). Pickle slices are spread evenly over the meat or cheese (no overlapping is allowed). Ketchup is applied by spreading it in a spiral circular motion over the pickles. Mayonnaise is applied to the top of the bun in a single stroke, while three-quarters of an ounce of shredded lettuce is sprinkled over the mayonnaise. Two slices of tomato (three is permissible, but only with management's permission) are then put on top of the lettuce. The assembly process itself should take no longer than 23 seconds for a Whopper. The finished burger is placed in a box or wrapper, reheated in a microwave for 14 seconds, and put in a chute.

Numerous tasks are associated with food assembly. Jobs are divided and arranged in a way that is easy to master and measure for the sake of efficiency. Workers are treated as little better than commodities along a conveyor belt. A worker at Burger King is expected to place her or his responsibility to the franchise above family or friends. Each worker is asked to work as hard as possible, to come to work at short notice, or to put in irregular hours. The self-discipline and control required of workers contrasts sharply with the image of self-indulgence and convenience offered to customers. Customers are thus shielded from the exploitative work situation that confronts Burger King workers; they see only the benign image of benevolence and wholesomeness.

The fast-food industry employs work processes and labour-management relations in an unusually restrictive environment that reduces labour and work to its simplest components. The principle of formal rationality strikes at the core of this process and relationship (Ritzer, 1993). Rationality is characterized by a commitment to efficiency, predictability, and calculability, the substitution of non-human technology for human labour, and control over uncertainty. Applied to fast food, there is little question that the operation is predictable (consistent when it comes to taste, appearance, and speed of delivery) and calculable, since quantity is emphasized over quality (the bottom line is not in the taste of the food but in the number of customers processed, the speed with which they are processed, and the profits produced); that workers are expected to act in robot-like fashion (people are trained to work in an automatic, unthinking way whether preparing food or serving customers); and that control over the product is secured by enslaving the workforce. Customers are no less controlled in accepting such standardized fare as food.

based on a hierarchy of command (Crane, 1999). As knowledge workers assume even greater control over their work, a culture of trust will need to offset the old-style supervisory management that once prevailed. In contrast with the past when workers were thought to resemble wheelbarrows who worked best when loaded up and pushed around (Nisbet, 1994), employees were now seen as enjoying work and being productive, provided they were given the right conditions to flourish. Workers were expected to assume responsibility and control over the production process, rather than park their brains at home. In perhaps the most significant shift of all, workers (and customers) were redefined as assets and resources, not simply as a problem for solution, control, or replacement. The vaunted chasm between management and labour was displaced by a cooperative philosophy involving workers, management, and customers. Paradoxically, management was increasingly labelled as a problem by foreclosing patterns of communication and channels for creativity (Adams, 1996). Proposed instead for an increasingly interdependent global economy are managers who can think globally by acknowledging the reality of multi-level relationships and complex social and cultural realities (Lane et al., 1998).

Of the many initiatives encouraged by the human resources model, few have proven as alluring or as contentious as those subsumed under the umbrella of "participatory management." Once organizations represented hierarchies that comprised a complex division of labour among individuals. Workers were expected to be obedient and do as they were told in discharging their obligations. By contrast, worker participation is now defined as the cure for organizations that need to become more flexible (and profitable) in the face of rapid environmental change (Jackson and Ruderman, 1995). The goal of participatory management entails a reworking of the factory floor into work teams. The concepts of work teams and participatory management reflect a shift in assumptions about the natural inclination of individuals for creating groups and establishing standards of conduct. Self-managing teams (quality circles) of 6 to 20 workers assumed direct responsibility for immediate matters pertaining to their sphere of productivity and working conditions (Southerst, 1994). Inside these work teams, individuals could rotate jobs to stave off boredom or acquire multiple skills. Each worker has the option of attending after-hours meetings with other quality circles to discuss plant problems and quality improvements. Work teams from different departments then convene to plot strategy, improve productivity, and consult with senior management over a broad range of relevant issues. Everyone allegedly benefits from this arrangement since, collectively, it is in everyone's best interests to increase productivity, reduce costs, enhance quality control, and improve customer service and satisfaction. Case 10–2 examines community policing as a response to a particular type of human resources approach.

Many corporations have had little choice but to rethink the rules for survival in a rapidly changing world. The controlled reality of management-labour relations has begun to unravel as the competition for profit intensifies. Once-reassuring patterns of interaction are now subject to revision and reform, and openly contested in some cases by those at the margins. Once individuals were singled out for praise if they followed guidelines, avoided risks, minimized mistakes, justified action (or inaction) according to the book, and slavishly carried out what was expected of them. Under a knowledge economy, however, the shift from command and control to employee empowerment has rendered these virtues increasingly obsolete and secondary. Instead of clockwork obedience, Marti Symes (1994) warns, employers now want workers who are not threatened by change or diversity, but thrive on risk-taking and multiple tasks. Yet the promise of empowerment has left victims in its wake. Thousands of employees have been made redundant, despite rhetoric about corporate missions and shop-floor democracies, in effect sapping worker morale and making a mockery of any pretext to loyalty or participatory democracy.

The concept of human resources is widely regarded as a solution to the problems created by an approach to doing business. Yet solving one problem by way of innovative solutions often creates conditions for a raft of new problems. Even the concept of participation is being contested. The principle itself sounds good in theory, but participation may consume a lot of unpaid overtime and personal commitment. Company time can be particularly demanding on women who are torn between home and work. Nevertheless, refusal to participate may well have long-term consequences in terms of promotion and retirement benefits. Refusal may also be interpreted as letting down your team. Work teams can be problematic in other ways. They may exist to enhance flexibility, creativity, and productivity, yet the heightened level of diversity may preclude the possibility of working together effectively (Jackson and Ruderman, 1995). Nor is there any proof that participation involves a real say in decision-making or power-sharing. Appeals to the virtues of empowerment, partnership, participatory management, and quality circles may be interpreted as window-dressing. Illusions of meaningful involvement are fostered without actually relinquishing any of the levers of power. Substantial decisions regarding relocation or hiring remain firmly in the grasp of management. The irony is inescapable: That thousands of workers are losing their jobs in the midst of a human resources revolution makes references to worker empowerment an especially cruel hoax.

WORKPLACE CHANGE/WORKPLACE RESISTANCE

Workplaces are under pressure to change. Despite these pressures, facilitating reforms and achieving goals may prove difficult to achieve, given the magnitude of the challenges confronting workplace dynamics and design. For example, management-labour relations have evolved from a mechanistic mentality to a more organic approach that emphasizes quality, commitment, and cooperation. Changes in the workplace have altered the very nature of work and working in response to the demands of the new (post-Fordist) economy. The politics of diversity have proven no less challenging. Initiatives to engage with diversity by way of employment equity and racial/sexual harassment policies are indicative of major transformations within the workplace, even though there is still concern about resistance to reforms by entrenched interests and systemic barriers.

In short, there is growing awareness that things don't work like they used to. Environments are seldom controlled, individuals cannot be pre-progammed in a predictable way, and ground rules cannot be formulated in a way that will please all parties concerned. The most common of these obstacles are mistaken notions about workplaces themselves; namely, the pervasiveness of bureaucracy; the role of organizational culture and subcultural systems; questionable insights into human "nature"; and naiveté about the process of planned change. The implementation of progressive programs can be sabotaged by workplace resistance to changes that threaten individual livelihoods. But the pressure to change is relentless, and corporations that refuse to bend will find that they can no longer compete.

Towards an Inclusive Workplace

It is one thing to contemplate the concept of workplace change. It is another thing to put these principles into practice in a way that makes an appreciable difference. Perils and pitfalls await those who underestimate the complexity and uncertainties associated with planned change. Nowhere is this more true than in creating a workforce that is reflective of Canada, a workplace that treats all employees equitably, and a service that is responsive to the needs and concerns of the local community. Historically, the workplace tended to marginalize disadvantaged groups such as women, visible minorities, aboriginal peoples, and people with disabilities. At present, the historically disadvantaged are demanding full and equal participation through removal of discriminatory barriers and creation of more inclusive workplaces. The concept of an inclusive workplace entails a process by which diversity is incorporated at the level of structure, function, and process, but without undermining either profitability or cohesiveness in the process. Five components would appear uppermost in specifying the parameters of an inclusive workplace: (1) representation; (2) institutional rules and operations; (3) workplace climate; (4) service delivery; and (5) community relations.

First, the workforce should be representative; that is, the composition and distribution of its workers should be relatively proportional to that of the regional labour force, taking into account both social and cultural factors as extenuating circumstances. Such numerical representation applies not only to entry-level jobs, but to all levels of management, access to training, and entitlement to rewards. Second, institutional rules and operations cannot deny or exclude anyone from the process of job recruitment, selection, training, and promotion. This commitment to root out discriminatory barriers, both systemic and personal, demands careful scrutiny of company policy and procedures. Third, the institution must foster a working climate conducive to the health and productivity of all workers. At minimum, such a climate cannot tolerate harassment of any form; at best, differences are accepted as normal and necessary to effective functioning and creative growth. Fourth, an inclusive institution ensures that delivery of its services is community-based and culturally sensitive. Such a commitment requires both a varied workforce and a sense of partnership with the community at large. Fifth and finally, workplaces do not operate in a social or political vacuum. They are part of a community and cannot hope to remain outside of it in terms of accountability and responsibility if success is anticipated. Institutions must establish meaningful relations with all community members to ensure productive lines of communication and some degree of community involvement in the decision-making process.

Barriers to Inclusiveness

An array of personal and social barriers interfere with the process of workplace change. Debate in this field is polarized by those who advocate change without much thought to the costs and difficulties, versus those who are resolutely opposed and resist change at all costs. Theories of workplace change are known to operate on the 30–50–20 principle (Laab, 1996): 30 percent of workers will willingly accept imposed changes, 50 percent will resist initially but can be converted to the cause with arguments or threats, and 20 percent will resolutely oppose any change, and nothing can dissuade them. Such divergences are to be expected: implementing institutional change is not like installing a new computer technology. Institutions are complex, often baffling landscapes of domination and control as well as of resistance and rebellion. Conservatives and progressives are locked in a struggle for power and privilege. Conventional views remain firmly entrenched as vested interests balk at discarding the tried and true. Newer visions are compelling, yet many lack the singularity of purpose or resources to scuttle traditional paradigms. The interplay of these juxtapositions can be disruptive or disorienting, as workplaces become reconstituted into a "contested site" involving competing world views and opposing agendas.

Numerous barriers exist that interfere with the process of directed institutional change. Stumbling blocks include people, hierarchy, bureaucracy, corporate culture, and occupational subcultures. People themselves are a prime obstruction. Workers are likely to resist any appeal to move over and make space without an understanding of what is going on, why, and how changes will affect them. This should come as no surprise, as few individuals are inclined to relinquish power or privilege without a struggle. The dimension of hierarchy will also inhibit inclusive adjustments. Those in higher echelons may be highly supportive of institutional change for a variety of reasons, ranging from genuine concern to economic expediency, with an eye towards public relations in between. Yet publicly articulated positions in defence of internal reform may be long-winded on platitudes, but short-minded on practice or implementation. Middle and lower management may be less enthusiastic about changes, preferring to cling to traditional authority patterns for fear of rocking the boat through institutional adjustments. Corporate cultures may not be conducive to change, given a reluctance to change the way we do things around here. To be sure, many talk of changing the corporate culture toward greater inclusiveness, but talk is one thing, reality quite another, since corporate cultures tend to resist all but the most superficial of changes. Even more disruptive to an inclusive workplace are occupational subcultures. The subcultural values of front-line workers may differ from those of the higher echelons because of differences in experiences or expectations. This slippage may prove fatal to the transformation process, especially if resistance turns to open sabotage (see Gillmor, 1996).

Of the many impediments to the incorporation of diversity and change, few are as daunting as the presence of bureaucracy. The concept of bureaucracy is often associated with certain structures and sets of rules that are found within large-scale, complex organizations. All complex organizations are systematically organized by means of formal rules, with departments of trained experts coordinated around a hierarchical chain of command. They are also distinguished from informal groups by a centralization of authority, an emphasis on impersonal procedures, and a reliance on written documents (Weber, 1947; Blau, 1963). Bureaucracy can also be defined as a principle of control. Organizationally, bureaucracies are imbued with an explicit commitment to command, coordinate, and control through creation of a strict division of task, a supervisory hierarchy, and attachment to rules and regulations (Morgan, 1986; Hummel, 1987). Two themes prevail: First, bureaucracies resemble machine-like instruments designed for rational goal achievement or crisp efficiency in service delivery. Bureaucratic work can be partitioned into a coordinated set of specific tasks; each task is then assigned to trained specialists who are responsible for dealing with particular cases or issues. In this sense bureaucracies are the epitome of scientific management principles. The second feature entails a commitment to the routine, the standardized, and the predictable as the preferred way of doing things in the organization. Not only do bureaucratic principles conflict with the elements of improvisation and the unexpected, the essence of bureaucracy also revolves around reducing all human affairs to the rule of reason. Bureaucracies are in the business of stamping out the informal or discretionary aspects of reality at odds with efficiency or control. In their place are appeals to universality and professionalism, coupled with the application of uniform standards and formal procedures. This universality simplifies the administration of a large number of individuals (both workers and customers) without getting bogged down in paralyzing detail. Adherence to the virtues of rationality and standardization is critical. Rationality attempts to reduce human affairs to the rule of reason within the framework of formal regulations, clearly defined roles, and prescribed relations. As a system of rational control, any course of action is justified on the grounds of rationalizing workplace efficiency, organizational productivity, or corporate profits (Hale, 1990).

Such a commitment not only has a controlling effect on behaviour; it also raises the question whether a bureaucracy can respond to a change model that: (a) delegates responsibility and power to clients and employers; (b) encourages creativity and risk-taking; (c) establishes participatory decision-making and open lines of communication; (d) fosters a group-oriented climate involving trust and cooperation; (e) recognizes employee performance and promotes professional growth; and (f) monitors organizational performance to ensure commitment to mission and values (Report, Department of Indian Affairs,1991). The next case study provides a useful account of the challenges involved in attempting to redesign the worksite and work. As this study on community-based policing reveals, any transformation must occur at the level of institutional structure as well as within individual mindsets. It must also concentrate on the relationships within (the workplace environment), in addition to relationships without (clients).

CASE STUDY 10-2	Towards Community Policing: The Politics of Inclusiveness

One of the more innovative approaches within the human resources circle is known as "total quality." As a principle committed to greater inclusiveness, total quality seeks a wholesale transformation of workplaces that goes beyond the superficial or cosmetic. The organizational structure and culture are redesigned to ensure the primacy and needs of the clients or consumers; to maximize employee satisfaction and rewards through partnership and meaningful consultation; and to secure the involvement of both the community and management in spearheading a service culture that is locally-based and culturally sensitive (Perry et al., 1995). In contrast to impersonal and bureaucratic structures that routinely impose decisions without client involvement—alienating many who recoil from a process they cannot hope to influence—total quality seeks meaningful consultation with clients and workers that goes beyond mere rubber-stamping, but engages the public in the general problem-solving process. There is a commitment to de-layer unnecessary levels of management by delegating decision-making powers to workers, thus empowering the workforce with a say in those aspects of productivity pertaining to schedules, outputs, service delivery, working conditions, and shop-floor waste. Under total quality, operational style must change from inward-looking (law unto themselves) to an outward focus (client needs), from bureaucratic rigidity to organizational flexibility (Rawson, 1991). In place of stonewalling or indifference are citizens' demands for involvement in the design and delivery of community-based social services.

Related to this is the greater demand for public servants to be accountable for their actions by making decision-making more transparent.

This case study will examine the extent to which the police services in Canada have redesigned their relationship with the community along the lines of total quality. Interest in community policing has expanded to the point where it no longer symbolizes only a promising experiment in redesigning police-community relations (see Cryderman, O'Toole and Fleras, 1998). The principles of community policing have catapulted it to the forefront of contemporary Canadian policing, even if the rhetoric may outstrip reality. Its appeal may reflect an ability to evoke powerful emotional symbols that pluck at the core of contemporary cultural concerns, including "democracy," "power to the people," or "small-town morality" (Seagrave, 1997). This commitment to community policing has focused on transforming the police from a technically driven, bureaucratic, and professional crime-fighting force to a customer-inspired service that is community-responsive, culturally sensitive, problem-oriented, and "user-friendly." Such lofty ideals raise the question, What exactly is meant by community policing, and is it attainable?

Professional Crime-Fighting Force

Canada's police at federal, provincial, and municipal levels have relied for the most part on a "professional crime-fighting" model as a blueprint for appointed duties (Walker, 1987). Acceptance of this model drew its inspiration from developments in the United States. American police reformers adopted a professional ethic as one way of circumventing widespread corruption, questionable service, and political interference within local precincts. A commitment to professionalism defined the police as a highly trained force with a shared identity and code of ethics for crime control and law enforcement. Police effectiveness was measured by way of: (a) random patrol as a deterrent to criminal activities; (b) rapid response to calls for all services; (c) arrest, conviction, and clearance rates; and (d) citizen satisfaction surveys. An "incident-driven," "complaint-reactive" approach was bolstered by administrators who sought to bureaucratize policing by linking organizational procedures with technique and the latest technology. Structurally, the police were organized into a paramilitaristic model of bureaucracy involving a top-down chain of command and control, law enforcement by the book, a compulsion with internal rules and regulations, and an explicit system of checks and balances to deter corruption, enhance control, monitor activities, and maintain surveillance. Rewards and promotions were allocated to some extent on the basis of the "big catch," in addition to loyal and long-standing service to the "force."

Certain assumptions about the community prevailed under a professional crime-fighting model. The police envisaged themselves as a "thin blue line" between the community and chaos; their job was to keep disorder at bay. Community involvement was kept to a minimum; citizens were expected to report crime to the police by way of the 911 system, to provide information on possible criminal activities, and to co-operate in the apprehension and conviction of lawbreakers (Tomovich and Loree, 1989). Beyond that, however, police interaction with the community was

brief and to the point, idealized by the immortal words of Sergeant Friday of the TV series "Dragnet": "Nothing but the facts, ma'am." Oettmeier and Brown, (1988, 15) explain the rationale behind this "fortress mentality": Officers are not expected to look beyond an incident to attempt to define and resolve a particular problem. Once dispatched to handle calls, the patrol officers are encouraged to return to service as quickly as possible to resume random, preventive patrol. Little attention was directed toward the service needs of citizens that had become victims of crimes.

In short, community participation was dismissed as irrelevant to the social control process. Crime control was viewed as the prerogative of a professional and distanced bureaucracy. Just as too much community involvement had once compromised the principle of impartial policing, so would an arm's-length distance provide police with the latitude to professionally discharge appointed duties. Confronted by this indifference, the police and community drifted apart. Such a rift did not imply that all police departments embraced the perspective of "two solitudes." Not all police officers subscribed to a detached and impersonal style of policing (consider, for example, those with roots in small-town environments). Rather, conventional policing may be interpreted as a specific style that flourished at a particular time and place in the evolution of modern urban policing. This professional crime-fighting model has prevailed to the present as a cornerstone of policing. For better or worse, its values and visions continue to frame police experiences on a daily basis.

Towards Community Policing

The introduction and popularity of community policing reflects an increased disillusionment with conventional police styles, many of which are perceived as inefficient, ineffective, inappropriate, and inequitable (Rosenbaum, 1994). Critics have raised questions about the value of a "cops, courts, and corrections" approach to curbing crime, fear of crime, urban disorder, incivilities, and social decay. Police in Canada have come under pressure to change from different quarters. They are accused of losing the fight against crime because of outdated workplace styles. Complaint-reactive, incident-driven styles of policing are largely incapable of dealing with the precipitating causes of crime, of preventing crime at the source, or of fostering cooperative relations with minority communities. The remoteness of bureaucratic policing is also thought to breed passive and unresponsive communities that further depress police effectiveness. Allegations of harassment, brutality, double standards, intimidation, abuse, corruption, and racism have fuelled the fires of criticism of the police. Additional questions arise over police effectiveness and efficiency in a society that is increasingly diverse, ever-changing, and more uncertain. The concept of community policing is widely endorsed as one way of warding off this potential crisis in police legitimacy and restoring public confidence.

Community policing can be broadly defined as a discourse about the nature of police work and the place of police in society. As principle and practice, community policing consists of a strategy (including a set of principles, policies, and programs) by which police are engaged with community members in the joint pursuit of local crime prevention. This definition is consistent with Lee Brown's (1988, 78) reference to community policing as an "interactive process between the police and community to mutually identify and resolve community problems" (see also Royal Commission on Aboriginal Peoples,

1995, 91). Objectives include a framework for assisting police to help communities to help themselves by way of citizen-defined community problems (Seagrave, 1997). It envisions a demilitarization (debureaucratization) of police departments—a downshifting of authority through management rank—to enhance discretionary powers for police on the street in hopes they will go beyond arrests and will focus on analyzing problems through community cooperation. Five recurrent themes distinguish community policing from conventional policing: (1) partnership perspectives; (2) proactive/ preventative policing; (3) problem-solving orientation; (4) power-sharing; and (5) pluralism (see also Bayley, 1994). Community policing is about establishing a closer and meaningful partnership with the local community as part of a coherent strategy to prevent crime through proactive efforts in problem-solving. The community emerges as an active participant in crime prevention rather than as a passive bystander, with the potential to deal with problems before they criminalize. The police in turn are expected to shed their "crime-buster" image in exchange for proactive styles that embody a willingness to work more closely with increasingly diverse communities through establishment of liaison and communication (see Shusta et al., 1995). Policing from top to bottom must become better acquainted with the multicultural community in terms of its varied needs, entitlements, demands, and expectations. A commitment to diversity also compels the police to view cultural differences as a resource of potential value in preventing crime.

Impeding Inclusiveness:

Occupational Subcultures

People who occupy a similar occupation may develop distinctive ways of perceiving and responding to their social environment (Chan, 1996). They also are likely to endorse a common system of norms and values related to work. The police are no exception. They belong to a type of occupational subculture defined by the demands of the job and the constraints of public expectations (Desroches, 1992). A distinctive set of norms, values, and beliefs has evolved and become entrenched through shared experiences, similar training, common interests, and continual interaction.

The grounds for this police occupational subculture are not difficult to uncover. Most police officers in Canada are male, White, able-bodied, French- or English-speaking, and of working class origins. This homogeneity in sex, social class, and ethnicity is reinforced by similar socialization pressures related to common training and peer group influence. The resulting solidarity is reinforced by a sense of isolation from the community ("us versus them"), by police perception of the public as ignorant and unsupportive of law enforcement activities, and by the nature of police work, which encourages a degree of caution or defensiveness. Suspicion towards those outside the profession compounds the pressures of isolation, mutual distrust, and alienation. Adding to the divisiveness is the need to appear efficient and in control at all times as part of doing police work (James and Warren, 1995). Not surprisingly, police deeply resent those segments of the community that defy police authority or violate concepts of order and stability. Police solidarity and estrangement from the community are further reinforced by the requirements of the job, including shift work and mutual support in times of crisis and danger.

The values and priorities underlying the police occupational subculture are inconsistent with those of community

policing (Seagrave, 1997). These differences can be summarized by way of contrasting outlooks (see Seitzinger and Sabino, 1988, 45–46):

(1) Officers define police work as "man's work," in that they condone aggressiveness and a take-charge mentality as a means of conflict resolution and a path to career success (Worden, 1993).

(2) Officers feel comfortable reacting to crimes, but many are uncomfortable dealing with community organizations. Crime control continues to be defined as "real" police work, and everything else as a "soft option" or "luxury" for public relations reasons (Robinson et al., 1989).

(3) Officers have been trained to believe in rapid response and random patrol as key crime-fighting tools. Walking the beat, by contrast, is often perceived as a punishment, the preserve of misfits or those about to retire, or a sign of a "stalled" career.

(4) Community police officers tend to be isolated from their peers, in some cases actively disparaged as "traitors" or "phoneys" who jeopardize the lives of fellow officers by not pulling their weight (Chan, 1996).

(5) The lack of a career structure for community policing makes it a questionable measure of success and stepping stone for advancement.

This list confirms the lack of enthusiasm for a community policing option. The police openly resist those aspects of community service at odds with the reassuring confines of the traditional policing subculture. Evidence indicates that many police officers do not want to be seen as "facilitators," "resource personnel," or "peacekeepers." They see themselves as law enforcement agents who define success by the number of arrests and citations. Many resent a "social welfare" tag, preferring a "take-charge" identity that reinforces their self-perception as professional crime-fighters. Again, we turn to Oettmeier and Brown (1988, 15):

> The organizational culture of municipal policing has, in general, continued to condition police officers to think of themselves primarily as "crime-fighters." Traditionally, police departments have attempted to identify and recruit individuals into policing that have displayed bravado. Organizational incentives have also been designed to favour self-conceptions of machismo, conceptions that are reinforced through pop art (e.g., detective novels, "police stories," "Dirty Harry" movies, etc.). Many, if not most, of the approximately 500 000 law enforcement officers in policing in America today have strong opinions about what constitutes real police work.

With its focus on community, diversity, and service, the principles of community policing do not coincide with popular perceptions of police as professional crime-fighters. Community policing culture endorses the virtues of trust, familiarity, cooperation, and respect. The community is viewed not as a problem but as a "resource" with unlimited potential for dealing with local issues. Opposing this is the occupational subculture of the police with its detachment from the community. The community is dismissed as uninterested in social control work; indifferent and passive (waiting to be policed); incompetent to carry out even simple tasks; not organized to act in unison; and misinformed about the pressures and demands placed on the police. In other words, the community is perceived as irrelevant to the point of being an impediment to effective policing except in the most passive way by providing information (Gillmor, 1996). This clash of visions makes it difficult to imagine a situation more conducive to misunderstanding and distrust. Even the influx of women into policing is not likely to foster a more receptive climate for community policing. To be sure, women are known to see police work differently than men; to seek out different relations with the community; employ different concepts of morality and justice; prefer community service to law enforcement; and engage in communication rather than control through aggression (Worden, 1993). Yet these community-oriented qualities may be for naught in the face of pressures to join the "brotherhood" of "policemen."

Bureaucracy: May the "force" be with you

No less inhibiting of organizational change is the pervasiveness of police bureaucracy. The police as an institution are organized around bureaucratic principles. Police personnel from top to bottom play roles as bureaucrats whose primary obligation is to the "force." As a bureaucratic organization with paramilitary overtones, the police are governed by a central command and control structure, with a ranked hierarchy, complex division of labour, impersonal enforcement of formal rules, carefully stipulated procedures, and the provision of a rationally based service. Police bureaucracies exist to control a large number of persons (both internally and externally) without prejudice or explicit favouritism. This control function is attained through rational control procedures, standardization, conformity through rule-following, and accountability to the organizational chain of command. A commitment to control would appear consistent with a traditional professional crime-fighting model, yet complicates efforts to respond to community demands or to initiate positive changes in police-community relations (Clairmont, 1988).

The principles of bureaucracy and community policing appear mutually opposed. The partnership ethos and the reciprocity inherent in community policing are strikingly at odds with an entrenched bureaucracy and occupational subculture. Community policing emphasizes collaboration, creativity, joint problem-solving, accountability to clients, and co-responsibility for crime control and order maintenance (Normandeau and Leighton, 1990). Bureaucracies, by contrast, are destined to be remote, isolated, and case-oriented. They are also bound by rules, organizational procedures, and hierarchy. One model is programmed for control and routinization, the other for cooperation and consultation. In other words, a fundamental reorientation is called for that entails a de-bureaucratization of role, status, functions, reward structures, operational styles, training programs, and objectives. Yet fundamental questions remain: How can creative problem-solving techniques flourish under workplace conditions that expect obedience and compliance while discouraging questioning, self-motivation, and innovation (Tomovich and Loree, 1989)? Can innovative, even risk-taking solutions be reconciled with a mindset based on "not rocking the boat" or "shut up, and do as you're told"? Who can be surprised that community policing initiatives have withered under such intimidating conditions?

Rethinking the Thin Blue Line

Even the brightest proposals for change will not take hold without an adequate analysis of barriers and constraints. The introduction of new ideas is likely to encounter resistance from entrenched interests or established values, especially in a conservative bureaucracy renowned for its reluctance to move over and make space. The introduction of community policing principles represents such a threat. Community policing provides a conceptual framework for transforming the police service in a way that improves community involvement in the design and implementation of programs for crime prevention. But reference to community policing rarely acknowledges the barriers that stand in the way of successful implementation. It is likely to meet with resistance and resentment unless management finds a way to: (a) break down the barriers to social change; (b) educate all police officials about its benefits and advantages; (c) address manageable problems before embarking on widespread reforms; (d) convey that community policing is a natural outgrowth of developments within the department; (e) demonstrate the merits of community policing to the general public and elected officials; (f) give clear indications of changes in training, reward structures, and career enhancement; (g) indicate willingness to experiment with innovative ideas and structures; (h) reveal how administrative styles and management techniques will be redesigned to meet new concerns; and (i) clear up misunderstanding and misconceptions regarding the goals, content, and scope of community policing (Brown, 1989).

Community policing will not make its mark until police are convinced of its application to the "real world" (see Chan, 1997). Such a scenario is unlikely as long as senior administration are perceived by rank and file to be out of touch with reality and beholden to political rather than police interests (Gillmor, 1996). Much of what passes for community policing deals with appearances, not substance. It may constitute little more than an expedient repackaging of small-town policing to placate the public, curry political favour, and extract additional resources from the government, or a public relations exercise for damage control, conflict resolution, and impression management. Nor will it make much of an impact until the goals of community policing are shown to be attainable, realistic, and rewarding, especially for those officers who stand to benefit or lose from its introduction. As long as individual officers believe they have nothing to gain from community policing, and that rewards lie with "kick-ass policing," the prospect of attitudinal change is remote. In the final analysis, the success or failure of community policing depends on its capacity to bring front-line officers around to a vision of the thin blue line as an inclusive circle rather than assembly line.

11

ABORIGINAL PEOPLES AND THE CANADA PROBLEM

FRAMING THE PROBLEM

Aboriginal peoples constitute the indigenous (original) occupants of modern nation-states. They are highly varied in culture and custom; differences can also be discerned at levels of development and degree of absorption into Canadian society. Some aboriginal peoples are covered by the general provisions of a royal proclamation, others have ceded sovereignty in exchange for specific rights, still others have neither been conquered nor signed treaty rights, yet others were conferred benefits because of their role as British allies, and yet others still live in urban areas but identify themselves as aboriginal peoples (Christian, 1999). Despite legal, historical, and developmental differences, aboriginal peoples in Canada and abroad share much in common (Fleras and Maaka, 1998). Many, including American Native Indians (Cornell, 1988), Australian Aborigines (Lippman, 1996), New Zealand Maori (Walker, 1995; Durie, 1995), and the Saami of Scandinavia (Eidham, 1985; Paine, 1985), have long struggled to (a) retain control over the development of traditional lands and resources, (b) cope with government intervention in their lives, (c) survive as a culturally distinct population, and (d) sever the bonds of dependency and underdevelopment created by internal colonization (Stea and Wisner, 1984; Havemann, 1999). Aboriginal peoples do not regard themselves as immigrants or minorities. As involuntary "migrants" whose status was forcibly imposed, they prefer instead to see themselves as relatively independent political communities, each of which is sovereign in its own right yet shares in society by way of multiple, interlocking jurisdictions (Asch, 1997; Maaka and Fleras, 1997). Aboriginal peoples define themselves as descendants of the original occupants whose collective and inherent rights to self-determination over internal jurisdictions have never been extinguished but remain intact as a basis for entitlement and engagement (Fleras, 1996; 2000). In rejecting the colonial governance that denied and excluded them, aboriginal peoples are casting about for indigenous models of self-determination that have the effect of curbing state authority while enhancing aboriginal empowerment over land, identity, and political voice. The focus is on rewriting the social contract by shifting conventional notions of sovereignty along the lines of the "nations within" (Fleras and Elliott, 1992). Official acceptance of an inherent aboriginal right to self-government within a Canadian framework promises to further shift the relational status of aboriginal peoples from that of a "problem" to a "people" (Royal Commission, 1996; Fleras and Spoonley, 1999; Frideres, 2000).

Canada is widely praised as a paragon of virtue in engaging diversity. Yet Canada's treatment of aboriginal peoples is generally considered a national tragedy and an international disgrace (Royal Commission, 1996; Canadian Human Rights Commission, 1997). There is no dearth of betrayals to demonstrate the magnitude of the federal government's neglect and oppression of aboriginal nations (Long and Dickason, 2000). Historically, Canada's aboriginal peoples have been either pitied and condemned or denied and excluded by mainstream society. From the nineteenth century on, aboriginal peoples were dismissed as a "problem people" whose problems were exacerbated by refusal to discard the past in exchange for the realities of the present. They have also been castigated as "problem-makers" whose stubbornness and unreasonableness extract costly reparations at odds with national interests. This assessment raises several questions whose responses provide an organizational framework for this chapter. First, what exactly is meant by the expression "Indian problem"? Who says so, on what grounds, and why? Second, how is this problem manifest with respect to social and cultural indices? Third, why does the "Indian problem" still exist? Fourth, have government policy initiatives contributed to the problem or the solution? And fifth, what can be done to improve aboriginal peoples-Canada relations. As passage of the Species at Risk Act clearly indicates, the key issue will revolve about the government's right to regulate on behalf of national interests versus aboriginal rights to self-determination and development along a broad set of fronts, thus reaffirming that neither Crown nor aboriginal rights are absolute, but must be exercised in a way that acknowledges both rights as equally valid. To the extent that more of the same is likely to pose a greater challenge to national unity than doing something, the re-constitutionalizing of aboriginal peoples-Canada relations is both vital and overdue.

THE "INDIAN PROBLEM"

Aboriginal peoples comprise an extremely diverse constituency, with numerous tribes of varying size, access to resources, development levels, and social health. According to the 1996 Census, nearly 800 000 people reported they were aboriginal, of which 554 000 were "North American Indian," 210 000 Metis, and 41 000 Inuit (Canadian Press, 14 Jan., 1998). Social, political, and cultural differences among aboriginal tribes remain as real and divisive as they did prior to European contact (Frideres, 1993). Aboriginal communities vary in terms of development and socio-economic status; differences also exist between rural and urban aboriginals as well as between aboriginal women and men and aboriginal adults and youth. Even the term "aboriginal peoples" is misleading, since this constitutional status can be further subdivided into the categories of status Indians, non-status Indians, Metis, and Inuit.

Who Are Aboriginal Peoples?

The aboriginal peoples with the highest profile in Canada are status Indians. Membership to status Indians is defined by (a) admittance to a general registry in Ottawa, (b) affiliation with one of 605 bands, (c) entitlement to residence on band reserve lands, and (d) jurisdiction under the Indian Act. The current population of status Indians stands at 553 316, up from 230 902 in 1967. These numbers are expected to increase to about 750 000 by 2005, primarily through reinstatement of individuals who had lost status through marriage or other means. Ontario has the largest population of status Indians with 121 867, followed by British Columbia with 90 769 (Socio-economic Status, DIAND, *The Globe and Mail*, July 5, 1994). Status Indians reside on one of 2597 reserves across Canada, ranging in size from a handful of people on one Pacific coast reserve to nearly 19 000 at the Six Nations Reserve near Brantford, Ontario. The majority of status Indians (59.2 percent in 1992) live on reserves created by one of 61 treaties signed with the Crown. The interests of status Indians are represented by 633 chiefs who constitute the Assembly of First Nations.

The second category of aboriginal peoples is non-status Indians. The exact population is unknown, but estimates vary from 75 000 and up. Unlike status Indians, non-status Indians are exempt from provisions of the Indian Act and jurisdiction of the Department of Indian Affairs. Some individuals relinquished their official status in exchange for the right to vote, drink alcohol off the reserve, or (in the case of women) to marry a non-Indian. Others are non-status because of never having entered into any formal treaty agreement with the federal government. Non-status Indians do not live on reserves (only status Indians are entitled to reserve life and to receive band inheritance); they are scattered in small towns and large cities across Canada. Despite this formal estrangement from their roots, many non-status Indians continue to identify themselves as aboriginal peoples because of shared affinities. Inclusion of non-status Indians as aboriginal peoples by the Constitution Act of 1982 has legitimated the identity and concerns of non-status Indians. Still, relations between non-status and status Indians have been fraught with tension and disagreement because of competition over limited federal resources.

The third class, the Metis, constitute a contested category of the off-spring (and descendents) of mixed European-aboriginal unions. Numbering between 100 000 and 400 000 persons, Metis initially were restricted to those descendents of the Red River settlements in Manitoba who identified with the Metis nation. Many Metis at present dwell in relatively remote communities throughout the prairie provinces without much land base to secure economic prospects. Metis may be officially regarded as a distinct aboriginal peoples with constitutional protections and corresponding guarantees. But the lack of judicial recognition on a par with status Indians undermines the legal authority of Metis to negotiate claims over traditional lands, the assumption being that the constitutional rights of 1982 can only be enjoyed by those who can prove original occupancy, an exclusive relationship to the land, and can exercise the rights to aboriginal title (Bell, 1997; Spiers, 1998). The Metis continue to be hampered by difficulties in defining who is Metis and the jurisdictional debate between Ottawa and the provinces over who is responsible for off-reserve natives. In late 1998, the Ontario provincial court ruled that Metis and non-status Indians have as much right to hunt and fish for food as status Indians. The ruling also confirmed Metis as a culturally distinct aboriginal people (Anderssen, 1998). The Alberta government has also recognized Metis self-governing rights along with the right to limited institutional autonomy. The 192 000 Metis across the prairies are represented by the Metis National Council.

The Inuit constitute the final category. The 41 000 Inuit (or 55 700, according to DIAND figures) enjoy a special status and relationship with the federal government despite never having signed treaty arrangements. Vast changes in Inuit culture in past decades have not yet substantially altered subsistence and cultural patterns: Inuktitut is widely spoken in the 53 communities across the NWT and Northern Quebec and Labrador. Many continue to rely on hunting and trapping to secure food, clothing, and shelter (DIAND Information, Oct. 1996). Despite an enviable degree of cultural integrity, deeply rooted social problems are endemic, including soaring rates of teenage pregnancy, substance abuse, suicide rates, accidental deaths, and diabetes (Anderssen, 1998). At local levels, Inuit are governed by municipal councils, with various committees to take responsibility for health and education. Inuit interests at national levels are represented by the Inuit Tapirisat (an association of various Inuit leaders) of Canada. The Inuit have recently concluded successful negotiations with Ottawa for control over their homeland, Nunavut, in the Eastern Arctic. Since the 1970s, Inuit groups have negotiated several other comprehensive land claims, including the James Bay and Northern Quebec Act of 1975, the first of its kind in Canada, as well as the NorthEast Quebec Act of 1978, both of which involved transfers of land for cash, land, co-management bodies, and hunting and trapping rights.

Socio-economic Status

Nearly four hundred years of sustained contact and interaction have left aboriginal peoples-government relations in a state of disarray and despair. The imposition of a colonialistic framework exerted a powerful negative effect on aboriginal peoples (Bienvenue, 1985). In some cases, government policies deliberately undermined the viability of aboriginal communities in the relentless quest to divest aboriginal peoples of their land, culture, and tribal authority. In other cases, the demise of aboriginal peoples came about through less obtrusive, yet equally powerful measures pertaining to education and missionization. In still other cases, the often unintended effects of possibly well-intentioned but ultimately misguided programs, for example residential schools, have had lingering repercussions in marginalizing aboriginal peoples.

No matter how evaluated or assessed, aboriginal peoples as a group remain at the bottom of the socio-economic heap. Housing is inadequate or overcrowded on many reserves, failing to meet basic standards of amenities and structure. Fewer than 50 percent of aboriginal homes have sewer or water connections (Frideres, 1993). With rates nearly three times the national average, unemployment is a major cause of aboriginal distress, leading directly to poor housing, illness, a sense of powerlessness, cultural disintegration and social decay, and cycles of poverty (Drost et al., 1995). On certain reserves, up to 95 percent of the population subsist on welfare or unemployment benefits. The $2.5 billion the government spends just to offset poverty, including $1 billion on social assistance, is really closer to $7.5 billion if we take into account lost productivity and potential taxes. The awkward location of many reserves and their limited resources remain key problems, yet many are reluctant to abandon them for fear of losing reserve entitlements. The situation is equally grim for the one-half to one-third who have drifted into the cities. Many have few skills, experience high unemployment, live in derelict housing, and are exposed to inadequate services, yet are cut off from federal funding or reserve benefits. Only a small percentage (about 20 percent) of aboriginal students even finish secondary schooling, let alone go on to post-secondary levels. Nevertheless, enrollments in post-secondary education have escalated from about 200 in the 1960s to 14 242 in 1987, and doubled since then to 27 487 in 1997 (Simpson, 1998).

Equally worrying is the demographic time bomb that is ticking away in many aboriginal communities. The aboriginal population has been rapidly increasing since the 1960s because of high fertility and dramatic declines in infant mortality (Canadian Press, 14 Jan., 1998). With a birthrate that is 70 percent higher than the general population, the youthfulness of many aboriginal communities is causing concern, given the average age of 25.5 years compared to 35.4 in the non-aboriginal population. The aboriginal cohort aged 15 to 24 is expected to increase by another 26 percent by 2006; the demand for access to education and social services will increase correspondingly. Nearly a third of aboriginal children under 15 years live with a lone parent, often in cities, twice the rate in the general population. The implications of this demographic reality are staggering, no more so than in urban areas. Nearly two-thirds of the aboriginal population prefer to live off-reserve, including 44 percent of status, on-reserve Indians. About one-fifth of urban aboriginals live in seven cities: Regina, Winnipeg, Calgary, Edmonton, Saskatoon, Vancouver, and Toronto (Canadian Press, 14 Jan., 1998). Winnipeg, with the largest number of aboriginal residents at 46 000, might well be called Canada's largest reserve. Reasons for migration are numerous, but often reflect "push" factors (lack of resources, opportunity, or excitement) and "pull" forces related to employment, education, and lifestyle. Structural (band size, proximity to urban centres), social (poor housing, unemployment), political (misguided reserve policies and fiscal mismanagement), and cultural (socialization) factors are important in making the decision to leave or return (Frideres, 1993). For some the move to cities is positive. There are aboriginal lawyers, teachers, nurses, and successful entrepreneurs, many of whom earn high incomes and are actively involved in the community. For others, coping with the demands of a large urban centre is a disaster (Moore, 1995). Urban life is fraught with missed economic opportunities, abysmal living conditions and homelessness, exposure to substance abuse, discrimination and lack of cultural awareness, and repeated brushes with the law (Maidman, 1981). The federal government, for its part, offers little in the way of services to off-reserve aboriginals, citing jurisdictional problems with the provinces as a stumbling block. Established government institutions are ill-equipped (both in terms of resources or needs assessments) to provide adequate culturally sensitive services to aboriginal clients (Maidman, 1981). Many aboriginal-run voluntary agencies have been established to address issues of health care, traditional healing, shelter, and criminal justice.

The psychological effects derived from a sense of powerlessness, alienation, and irrelevance have been no less detrimental (Shkilynk, 1985). As noted by David Courchene, a former president of the Manitoba Indian Brotherhood:

> One hundred years of submission and servitude, of protectionism and paternalism have created psychological barriers for Indian people that are far more difficult to break down and conquer than the problems of economic and social poverty (quoted in Buckley, 1992:24).

Aboriginal individuals may transform this powerlessness and impotence into an expression of self-hatred. The internalization of White racism and/or indifference is reflected in violent death rates which are up to four times the national average. Infant mortality rates are about 60 percent higher than the national average. Alcohol and substance abuse are widely regarded as the foremost problems on most reserves, with alcohol-related deaths accounting for up to 80 percent of the fatalities on some reserves (Buckley, 1992). Domestic abuse is endemic within aboriginal communities, according to some observers (Drost et al., 1995). Few aboriginal children grow to adulthood without first-hand experience of interpersonal violence. Aboriginal youth are angry, bored, confused, and defiant. Many suffer from terminal self-loathing and pay the price throught suicide, violence, or substance abuse. Violent deaths and suicides are also disproportional when compared to the general population. With a suicide rate of six times the national average for certain age-specific groups, aboriginal peoples represent one of the most self-destructive groups in the world at present.

Aboriginal involvement with the criminal justice system is deplorable as well. Nearly three-quarters of aboriginal males will have been incarcerated in a correctional centre at some point in their lives by the age of twenty-five. Aboriginal inmates occupy 64 percent of the federal penitentiary population in Western Canada, according to Statistics Canada, but only about 12 percent of the Prairie population (*Globe and Mail*, 2 Feb. 1998). Admittedly, some degree of caution must be exercised: Statistics may be misleading since offenders may be convicted for relatively minor offences and serve time for offences that require only a fine. As well, only a small number of individuals may get in trouble with the law, but on a repeated basis (Buckley, 1992). Nevertheless, the statistics are damning: The revolving door of incarceration and recidivism has stripped many aboriginal peoples of any positive self-concept, in effect leading to self-fulfilling cycles of despair and decay. Nor can sometimes disastrous consequences of often well-intentioned, but misguided government policies and programs be disregarded (Shkilynk, 1985). And finally the plight of aboriginal women is gaining prominence as the most disadvantaged of the disadvantaged (Monture-Angus, 1999). Economically, they are worse off than non-aboriginal women and aboriginal men in terms of income levels and employment options, with the result that the feminization of poverty bites deeply, especially for lone parent women in cities (Williams, 1997). Social hardships are numerous, and include abusive male family members, sexual assaults and rapes, inadequate housing, squalid living conditions, unhealthy child-raising environments, and alcohol and drug abuse. Levels of violence directed against aboriginal women and children are extremely high, as explained by the Native Women's Association of Canada in a 1991 brief (quoted in Razack, 1994: 910):

> We have a disproportionately high rate of child sexual abuse and incest. We have wife battering, gang rapes, drug and alcohol abuse, and every kind of perversion imaginable has been imported into our lives.

Depression and self-hatred among aboriginal women is expressed in high rates of suicide, alcohol dependency, and neglect of children.

The abysmal circumstances that confront aboriginal peoples are a scathing indictment of the status quo. Aboriginal people tend to score poorly on those indicators that count and rank high on those that don't. Of course, not all aboriginal peoples are destined to fail, even when measured by mainstream standards of success or failure. Aboriginal peoples are gaining access to substantial sums of money and resources because of successful land-claims settlements. Success stories abound, including the recent selection of a formerly poverty-stricken Quebec Cree community (Ouje Bougoumou) as one of the 50 places around the world that best exemplifies the objectives of the United Nations (Platiel, 1995). There are currently 10 000 aboriginal businesses, 50 financial institutions, a native trust company and a native bank, thus confirming the relationship between possessing wealth and exercising power. Nor should success be evaluated on such narrow grounds. There are individuals who possess secure and satisfying prospects and exceptionally enriched lives without rejecting one or both cultures. As a group, however, most live under conditions that evoke images of grinding developing-world poverty.

ACCOUNTING FOR THE INDIAN PROBLEM: A CANADA PROBLEM

It is obvious the First Nations have problems. Yet focusing on problems may be a problem itself. The impression is created that poverty will disappear with better opportunities, thus ignoring structural problems and the fundamental changes required to a system that continues to deny or distort. Improvements will occur only with changes that provide aboriginal control over institutions and a share of revenue from reserve mineral resources and aboriginal title to land. Focusing on problems also has the effect of "framing" aboriginal peoples as a problem people who have problems or create problems. Such a focus also glosses over the fact that the aboriginal plight may arise from repeated Crown violations of treaties, misguided government policy, bureaucratic incompetence, racism, and a system of free enterprise (George, 1997). In other words, it is not a case of aboriginal peoples as problems. Instead of an "Indian problem" there is a "Canada problem" (Waldram, 1994). Several questions come to mind: How does Canadian society create problems for aboriginal peoples? Deliberate or inadvertent? To what extent are government policies and programs central to this Canada problem? What is it about Canadian society that makes it so problematic for the First Nations? Answers to these questions are not merely academic. Inasmuch as government policy continues to be predicated on solving "the Indian problem," the issue is of relevance for national unity and society-building.

What then is meant by the so-called "Indian problem"? How did the label come about? Who says so, and why? Is the labelling an accurate reflection of reality? Or are there different ways of talking about this problem? References to "the Indian problem" imply that aboriginal peoples bear full responsibility for their plight. First Nations have problems that many see as of their own making, compounded by a refusal to assimilate (see Waldram, 1994). This blaming-the-victim approach implies that aboriginal peoples do not know what is good for them; it also exempts the government from blame while condoning even greater control over aboriginal lives (Frideres, 2000). Any solution to the "Indian problem" can only come about by eliminating aboriginal culture through the assimilation of aboriginal peoples into mainstream society. The federal government has routinely subscribed to this view, and has employed several strategies to remove social and cultural "obstructions" to Western-style economic development and growth. Policies were formulated to deal with this conundrum in the hope that the indigenes would die out—physically or culturally—and thus solve the problem of their own accord. Band members were encouraged to renounce their Indian status by moving to cities from reserves, and both aboriginal culture and reserves were dismissed as nothing more than breeding grounds for violence, apathy, and alienation. Exposure to modern values and institutional involvement was proposed as the key to a brighter future. Alternatively, the government has been anxious to modernize reserves by upgrading facilities and infrastructures with federal funding and expertise. If this transformation were successful, the hypothesis held, the so-called "Indian problem" would vanish. Paradoxically, the opposite appears to have happened (Shkilnyk, 1985).

BOX 11.1 Peace, Power, and Righteousness: Decolonizing the Indian Problem

In a book that is destined to become a major work in thinking about aboriginal peoples-Canadian society relations, Taiaiake Alfred (1999) explores the root causes of the "Indian problem" in Canada. Alfred also offers valuable insights into how this problem is expressed and what must be done to solve it if there is to be any hope of forging a unity by which two people may peacefully coexist with their differences.

For Alfred, aboriginal people continue to be caught in the crossfire of colonialist structures and mentalities that constrain, control, and dominate. These colonialist structures have distorted aboriginal relations with society at large. The impact of colonialism on aboriginal communities is no less devastating, particularly since a colonialist mentality is so pervasive among indigenous and non-indigenous peoples, and is tacitly assumed necessary and normal as well as natural and inevitable. Aboriginal communities find themselves caught between two competing value systems: On one side are rooted traditional values; on the other are colonialist structures, values, and organizations, each of which espouses radically different systems of social organization designed to achieve different goals. Factionalism within aboriginal communities is rife because of leaders who are torn between the demands of servicing the system and serving the people. Some are blind to the reality of their co-optation; others are complicit in politically subjugating their people. To overcome the polarizing effects of colonialism, Alfred poses the following solutions:

- to isolate and challenge those structures imposed by colonialism, while exposing those beliefs and values that perpetuate the continued colonization of aboriginal peoples;
- to contest colonization by rejecting the values and structures of the colonizer while "heeding the voice of the ancestors" through traditional leadership and aboriginal values.
- to gain recognition and respect for the right to exist as self-determining peoples, unencumbered by the demands, rules, and identities imposed by a colonial compulsion for control and domination. The objective is not to destroy the state but to reconstruct it in a manner that secures the basis for indigenous self-determination.
- to shift politics to the primacy of aboriginal concepts, rules, and values that are grounded in aboriginal culture. Self-government structures that espouse possessive individualism or non-indigenous forms of leadership tend to compromise or distort indigenous peoples by coopting them into systems of domination. Rather, self-governance must be constructed around the traditional concepts of respect, harmonious coexistence, and quest for balance between opposites in advancing the goals and values of indigenous peoples.
- to employ ancestrally defined aboriginal differences as a power base for asserting aboriginal models, rights, and jurisdictions.

Progress to date has been mixed, according to Alfred. Only the most egregious forms of colonialism have been challenged, while the more subtle aspects go virtually unnoticed. Indigenous peoples may have exposed the iron cage of colonial oppression, articulated the injustices foisted on indigenous communities, challenged the Crown's self-proclaimed right to rule (by rejecting assumptions that legitimate their subordination), and revealed how those attitudes that sustain this subjugation can no longer be justified. Yet the Canadian state has shown considerable skill in shedding its most burdensome and costly aspects of colonial rule in which individuals are co-opted into the system of bureaucracy, without relinquishing its hold on the lands and resources. Government control is achieved in different ways, including: (a) promoting-neo colonial forms of self government; (b) integration into mainstream for purposes of entitlement; and (c) espousing principles and rules that define and constrain through references to market or national interests. To be sure, the state is willing to make concessions for preservation of the framework of dominance and basic power structure. But concessions are tolerated only to the extent that they serve or at least do not oppose state interests and agendas in any major way.

In some cases, the decolonization has removed aboriginal peoples from direct state control and established the framework for aboriginal-run jurisdictions. In other cases, a neo-colonialist framework has emerged in which aboriginal leaders and claims-making processes are manipulated to legitimize the Crown's longstanding goal of assimilation. In neither case is there any shift toward a post-colonial governance that re-engages aboriginal peoples with the state through aboriginal leadership and traditional values. Nor is there much hope of post-colonizing the relationship; after all, it is futile to work within the very system that created the problem in the first place. Without a sound traditional basis for constructively engaging with the Crown, involvement in Canadian society will have the controlling effect of subjecting aboriginal people to more subtle yet equally powerful forms of manipulation and control.

But one could plausibly argue that "the Indian problem" is not an aboriginal problem per se. It is essentially a "Canada problem" created by European expansion and settlement and perpetuated through systems of domination, control, and exploitation (Waldram, 1994). Many of the problems that exist today did not happen until European expansion transformed Turtle Island into a colonized settlement by dispossessing the First Nations of their land and cultural traditions (Stevenson, 1999). Problems arose from trying to impose an alien and alienating culture in the headlong rush to tranform aboriginal peoples into God-fearing, hard-working, and ultimately self-sufficient rural Canadians. Tensions also arose from fundamentally different world views and the interplay of culturally different values that go with them, one based on the principles of consumerism, competition, and progress, the other based on a commitment to spiritual values, community, peaceful coexistence, and balanced harmony (Alfred, 1999). The competitive struggle between a dominant sector and a subordinate one over power, resources, and status compounded the problem. Put bluntly, the so-called "Indian problem" must be placed squarely within a political-economy perspective and analyzed within a capitalist framework of institutionalized domination, legal control, and resource exploitation (Wotherspoon and Satzewitch, 1993). Logic suggests that solutions to this problem must entail challenging the colonialist domination that has framed aboriginal peoples-Canada relations, especially the bonds of dependency and underdevelopment that have a controlling effect (Calliou and Voyageur, 1998). Redefining "the Indian problem" as a "Canada problem" casts a different light on causes and cures, and draws attention to the barriers that preclude solutions, including racism, systemic bias, legal discrimination, and political duplicity (Calliou and Voyageur, 1998).

To what extent has the state, by way of government policy, contributed to or detracted from the "Indian problem"? Do state initiatives facilitate the achievement of aboriginal claims to self-determination and innovative patterns of belonging? Or do they have the effect of blocking or undermining aboriginal jurisdiction over land, identity, and political voice (Durie, 1998)? The role of state policy and administration in the dispossession of aboriginal peoples has been well documented. Little can be gleaned by rehashing the negative consequences of even the well-intentioned actions of Indian Affairs officials often more interested in careerism and empire-building than in fostering aboriginal empowerment (Ponting and Gibbins, 1980; Ponting, 1986; also Shkilnyk, 1985). What more can be added to the sorry legacy of official indigenous policy, with its focus on promoting "national interest" rather than protecting aboriginal concerns? Yet the verdict in assessing state performance may be more accurately described as ambiguous. The state is capable of progressive policies that enhance indigenous rights; it is equally capable of regressive measures that may exclude, deny, or exploit (Spoonley, 1993). Policies of disempowerment tend to diminish options of indigenous peoples; by contrast, enabling policies provide a window of opportunity for empowerment (Hinton et al.,1997).

A similar assessment can be applied across Canada where aboriginal relations with the state have long been mediated by legislation and policy, yet are marred by duplicity and expediency. Aboriginal affairs policy can be seen as evolving through a series of overlapping stages, with the focus never wavering from a fundamental commitment to foster aboriginal self-sufficiency (Fleras, 2000). An initial period of cooperation and accommodation gave way to a largely misguided and paternalistic policy of assimilation, with its underlying racist assumptions of White superiority as basis for control and coercion (Tobias, 1976). Treatment of aboriginal peoples as captive "wards" was intended to facilitate the eventual absorption of aboriginal peoples into the mainstream—but with little success, as Case Study 11–1 demonstrates.

A shift from assimilation to integration and "ordinary citizenship" gathered momentum after the late 1940s. Integrationist policies and programs sought to normalize relations with aboriginal peoples by terminating their unique relationship with the Crown and placing aboriginal people on the same footing as ordinary Canadians. Yet federal efforts to integrate by "mainstreaming" Aboriginal peoples had the catalytic effect of mobilizing aboriginal peoples in protest against the ill-fated White Paper of 1969. Federal policy discourses shifted toward devolution from the 1970s onwards, in part to acknowledge aboriginal jurisdiction over land, identity, and political voice, in part to confirm the legitimacy of aboriginal rights as a basis for belonging, rewards, and relations, and in part to defuse mounting resentment and international disapproval. Recent government and aboriginal initiatives have tended to endorse a conditional autonomy model by exploring the implications of aboriginal peoples as peoples with an inherent right to self-government, albeit within the framework of Canadian society.

CASE STUDY 11-1	"To Kill the Indian in the Child": Solution through Assimilation

The Canadian government recently apologized to the First Nations for decades of systematic assimilation, theft of their lands, suppression of cultures, and the physical and sexual abuse of aboriginal children. At the centre of this apology is the "profound regret for past actions" that destroyed aboriginal communities. For over a century, thousands of aboriginal children passed through the residential school system where many were exposed to an inferior education in an atmosphere of neglect, disease, and abuse. The government acknowledged its role in enforcing policies that forcibly removed children from their families and placed them in residential schools often hundreds of kilometres from their community, leaving behind a legacy of emotional scars because of intense homesickness and pain. "To those who suffered the tragedy of residential schools," the Minister of Indian Affairs, Jane Stewart announced, "we are deeply sorry." As a token of atonement, the government pledged $350 million to fund counselling programs and treatment centres for residential school victims of emotional, sexual, and physical abuse. To be sure, not everyone agreed with this assessment: To demonize all residential schools as symbols of cultural genocide, critics argued, tended to accentuate the negative at the expense of the positive, dismissed the testimony of those who enjoyed the experience, relied heavily on vague and unsubstantiated testimony, stigmatized the schools as scapegoats for aboriginal suffering, and fed into White liberal guilt by cultivating grievances (Donnelly, 1998).

Still, the statement of reconciliation caught many off-guard because of its unprecedented nature. Central authorities historically have been reluctant to apologize or even acknowledge responsibility for past misdeeds, since admitting liability may encourage lawsuits. Yet the government may have had little choice but to apologize, despite the risk of being sued, not necessarily to right the wrong or to accept responsibility, but as a plea bargain to limit damages from further revelations regarding the more sordid dimensions of the residential school experiment (Coyne, 1998).

Content

Founded and operated by Protestant and Roman Catholic missionaries, but funded primarily by the federal government, residential schools (or industrial schools as they were called initially because of the emphasis on manual skills acquisition) for aboriginal children were built in every province and territory except Prince Edward Island, Nova Scotia, and Newfoundland, with the vast majority concentrated in the prairie provinces. From two residential schools at the time of Confederation, the number of schools expanded until nearly 80 residential schools existed by 1931, shared among Roman Catholic (44 schools), Anglicans (21), United Church (13), and Presbyterian (2) (Matas, 1997). Between 100 000 and 125 000 aboriginal children (about one in six) entered the system before it was closed down in the mid-1980s, although four residential schools continue to operate, but under aboriginal jurisdiction (Miller, 1996). To be sure, Canada was not the only jurisdiction to remove children from their parents and resocialize them in schools or foster families. From the 1910s to the 1970s, about 100 000 Australian part-aboriginal children were placed in government or church care in the belief that Aborigines would die out, a practice that was tantamount to cultural genocide, according to Australia's Human Rights Commission.

Rationale

From the mid-19th century onwards, the Crown engaged in a variety of measures to assert control over the indigenous peoples of Canada (Rotman, 1996). The Indian Act of 1876 was ultimately such an instrument of control, a codification of laws and regulations that embraced the notions of European mental and moral superiority to justify the dispossession and subjugation of aboriginal peoples. The Indian Act provided a rationale for misguided, paternalistic, and cruelly implemented initiatives to assimilate aboriginal peoples into White culture. The mandatory placement of aboriginal children in off-reserve residential schools fed into these racist assumptions of White superiority and aboriginal inferiority. With the assistance of the RCMP when necessary, the government insisted on taking aboriginal children away from their parents and putting them in institutions under the control of religious orders. The rationale for the residential school system was captured in an 1889 annual report by the Department of Indian Affairs:

> "The boarding-school dissociated the Indian child from the deleterious home influence to which he would otherwise be subjected. It reclaims him from the uncivilized state in which he has been brought up. It brings him into contact from day to day with all that tends to effect a change in his views and habits" (quoted in Roberts, 1996:A7).

The guiding philosophy embraced the adage "that how a twig is bent, the tree will grow." Federal officials believed it was necessary to capture the entire child by segregating him/her at school until a thorough course of instruction was acquired. However, the residential school system had a more basic motive than simple education: The removal of children from home and parents was aimed at forcibly assimilating aboriginal peoples into non-aboriginal society through creation of a distinct underclass of labourers, farmers, and farmers' wives (Rotman, 1996; Robertson, 1998). This program entailed not only the destruction of aboriginal language and culture, it also invoked the supplanting of aboriginal spirituality with Christianity in hopes of "killing the Indian in the child." (Royal Commission on Aboriginal Peoples, 1996)

Reality

This experiment in forced assimilation through indoctrination proved destructive. Many of the schools were poorly built and maintained, living conditions were deplorable, nutrition barely met subsistence levels, and the crowding and unsanitary conditions transformed them into incubators of disease (Milloy, 1999). Many children succumbed to tuberculosis or other contagious diseases (Fournier and Crey, 1997). A report in 1907 on 15 schools found that 24 percent of the 1537 children in the survey had died while in the care of the school, prompting the magazine *Saturday Night* to claim, "Even war seldom shows as large a percentage of fatalities as does the education system we have imposed upon our Indian wards" (quoted in Matas, 1997). Disciplinary terror by way of physical or sexual abuse was the norm in some schools, according to the Royal Commission on Aboriginal Peoples (1996). As one former residential school student told the Manitoba Aboriginal Justice Inquiry:

My father, who attended Alberni Indian Residential School for four years in the twenties, was physically tortured by his teachers for speaking Tseshalt: They pushed sewing needles through his tongue, a routine punishment for language offenders. ...The needle tortures suffered by my father affected all my family. My dad's attitude became "why teach my children Indian if they are going to be punished for speaking it?"...I never learned how to speak my own language. I am now, therefore, truly a "dumb Indian." (quoted in Rotman, 1996:57)

Punishment also included beatings and whippings with rods and fists, chaining and shackling children, and locking in closets or basements. Reports of abuse appeared in anecdotal form by the 1940s, went public during the 1960s and 1970s, but did not capture the public imagination until Phil Fontaine, the National Chief of the AFN, disclosed his personal experiences in 1990. Admittedly some aboriginal children profited from the residential school experience. Others suffered horribly: children grew up hostile or confused, caught between two worlds but accepted in neither. Young impressionable children returned as older Western-educated people; having lost their identity and an ability to converse in their own language, many could neither communicate with older members of the community nor identify with their community ways (Rotman, 1996). Adults often turned to prostitution, sexual and incestuous violence, or drunkenness to cope with the emotional scarring from the residential school system.

Implications

This misguided and destructive experiment in social engineering makes disturbing reading when judged by contemporary standards of human rights, government accountability, participatory democracy, and aboriginal self-determination. Admittedly, it is easy to judge and condemn actions from a radically different time by people who may have genuinely believed in the superiority and universal applicability of Western culture. Negative impacts may stem instead from the logical consequences of well intentioned programs that were based on faulty assumptions ("progress through development"), or an inaccurate reading of the situation ("eliminate poverty by throwing money at the problem"), or cultural misunderstanding ("they want to be like us"). Advocates of residential schools believed that they were acting as good Christians by improving the lot of First Nations and welcomed government initiatives as enlightened or necessary (Editorial, *Globe and Mail*, 8 Jan. 1998). Nor should the role of aboriginal parents be ignored: According to Miller (1996), aboriginal leaders insisted on a European-style education for their children, while federal authorities acknowledged a fiduciary obligation to oversee such education. Finally, incidents of abuse and violence were likely, especially during an era when corporal punishment was routinely accepted as part of the "spare the rod, spoil the child" mentality.

Still, the Royal Commission concluded that the residential school system was an "act of profound cruelty" rooted in racism and indifference, and pointed the blame at Canadian society, Christian evangelism, and policies of the churches and government. The apology and proposed reparations may prove a useful starting point for acknowledging injustices in the past that denied recognition of the moral and political stature of aboriginal people as full and complete citizens and human beings (Editorial, *Globe and*

Mail, 8 Jan. 1998). It remains to be seen whether psychologically scarred natives, broken families, and dysfunctional aboriginal communities will respond to the balm of healing and counselling centres and establishment of programs to reverse the destructive consequences of the residential school experiment.

The emergence of three general themes, namely, renewing the partnership, strengthening aboriginal governance, and supporting strong communities, suggests a continuing commitment to conditional autonomy in the 21st century.

ABORIGINAL SOLUTIONS

In their misguided arrogance and entrenched ethnocentrism, Canadian policy-makers have long advocated certain solutions for eliminating the so-called "Indian problem." These solutions have varied over time, but are best embodied in government policies of assimilation, integration, and devolution. What is common to each of these (besides their built-in failure factor) is a refusal to formulate the issue except in terms reflecting, reinforcing, and advancing national interests (Boldt, 1993). In recent years, aboriginal peoples have finally succeeded in taking ownership of solutions to "the Indian problem," in part by redefining the terms of the debate. In place of a White agenda, aboriginal leaders have proposed a series of solutions they feel are consistent with their peoples' needs, concerns, and aspirations (Calliou and Voyageur, 1998). Three themes recur throughout this redefinition process: First, the reinstatement of "aboriginal-plus status" as a basis for redefining aboriginal peoples-Canada relations; second, restoration of inherent rights to self-determination through self-government; and third, recognition of aboriginal and treaty rights as grounds for reclaiming aboriginal jurisdiction over land, identity, and political voice. In each case, a common thread can be detected; namely, a belief in the inappropriateness of structures that once colonized aboriginal peoples. Proposed instead are indigenous models of self-determination that sharply curtail state jurisdiction while bolstering aboriginal empowerment (Alfred, 1995).

Aboriginal-Plus Status

In response to the question of what aboriginal peoples want, the most direct answer is, "the same things as all Canadian citizens." Aboriginal peoples are anxious to live in a just and equal society in which (a) their cultural lifestyles and languages are protected from unnecessary assimilationist pressure, (b) select elements of their culture can be preserved and interpreted within the framework of contemporary realities, (c) bureaucratic interference in their lives is kept to a minimum, (d) discrimination and racism is eliminated from their contacts with politicians, bureaucrats, state agents, and the general public, and (e) collective access to power, resources, status, and meaningful decision-making is within their grasp. Most of us would agree that these objectives and aspirations are not altogether dissimilar from what we expect as citizens of a democratic government.

Aboriginal peoples have also expressed a desire to be different. The objective is to transcend the constraints of formal citizen status and to explore novel ways of redefining who they are within the framework of Canadian society. The concept of "aboriginal-plus status" entails a recognition of pre-existing rights that have never been extinguished. These rights include:

1) the right to control land and resources;

2) the right to protect and promote language, culture, and identity;

3) the right to conduct their affairs on a nation-to-nation basis; and

4) the right to establish indigenous models of self-government.

For aboriginal peoples, the recognition of aboriginality is paramount. Aboriginality as a principle is based on rights, rewards, and relationships that flow from original occupancy. Equal opportunity or equality before the law is helpful but insufficient. On the premise that equal standards cannot be applied to unequal situations without perpetuating inequality, aboriginal leaders have demanded special status and preferential treatment as a basis for restructuring their relationship with the rest of Canada.

In short, aboriginal peoples have claimed the right to be different as well as the right to be the same (hence the expression, "aboriginal-plus status"). They want equality of treatment (formal equality), yet demand entitlements, such as a third tier of government with control over internal jurisdictions, consistent with their legal status as original occupants whose rights to be different have yet to be extinguished and whose problems cannot be solved in a conventional manner. Many are anxious to receive the benefits and privileges of Canadian citizens, but not at the expense of their rights as founding members of Canadian society. Nor is there any contradiction in making these demands. As far as they are concerned, aboriginal peoples paid for these concessions with the loss of land, lives, livelihood, and cultural lifestyles. Canadian politicians and policy-makers rarely dispute the validity of aboriginal arguments for unique status and preferential treatment. The entrenchment of aboriginal rights in the Constitution and the proposed recognition of the inherent right to aboriginal self-government are proof of that. Debate revolves instead around how to redefine the nature and scope of aboriginality.

Self-Determination through Self-Governance

A second step in solving the "Canada problem" is no less controversial. Without a power base to define and defend, aboriginal peoples cannot possibly take control of their destiny, and the attainment of self-determination by way of aboriginal self-governance is critical to aboriginal aspirations. Aboriginal peoples tend to reject a view of themselves as a group of Canadian citizens who happen to live on reserves. They see themselves instead as sovereign and self-governing nations that have a distinct political status within the Canadian nation-state. Certain inalienable rights follow from this fundamental recognition. As a "nation within," they are anxious to deal with federal authorities on a government-to-government basis. The rationale for self-government is further bolstered by (a) the belief that all aboriginal peoples have the right to control their destiny; (b) a recognition that international law stipulates the right to aboriginal self-determination; (c) the fact that the Royal Proclamation of 1763 affirmed and protected aboriginal nationhood; and (d) the faith in the notion of inherent self-government to avert the further erosion of aboriginal life and culture (see also Royal Commission, 1996). Aboriginal leaders have endorsed self-determination as essential in severing the cycle of deprivation, dependency, and underachievement that afflicts so many of their communities. While acknowledging various models of self-determination (for example, guaranteed parliamentary representation (Fleras, 1992), current appeals focus on the demand for aboriginal models of self-governance.

Even though the attainment of political self-determination through self-government is touted as a key aboriginal plank (Penner, 1983; Little Bear et al., 1984; Boldt, 1993; Royal Commission, 1996; McIvor, 1999), the concept of self-governance is proving difficult to define. There is no consensus among aboriginal leaders regarding an ideal self-governing model, and major differences are evident between models proposed by some aboriginal leaders and those favoured by government officials. Probably no single model can possibly be adequate, given the social and cultural diversities of aboriginal peoples. Possibilities will be restricted by government policy principles for negotiating self-government, including:

(a) the exercise of self-government must be within the Canadian Constitution, while the Charter of Rights and Freedoms will apply to all governments;

(b) federal and provincial criminal codes will prevail, while provincial, federal, and aboriginal laws must work in harmony;

(c) all third-party interests (such as municipalities) must be taken in account;

(d) self-governing arrangements must enhance the participation of aboriginal peoples in Canadian society.

Some models will involve a reinterpretation and revival of traditional structures, others will involve the creation of new structures, and still others advocate only greater control in the provision of government services (Royal Commission, 1996). Some will reflect a government model; others an aboriginal model; and still others will combine elements of both. Four self-governance models are theoretically possible, including: (1) statehood: acquiring complete independence and brooking no external interference; (2) nationhood, within the framework of society, yet retaining authority and jurisdiction over internal matters; (3) community-based (or municipality-based), retaining control over internal affairs by way of parallel institutions, but limited by interaction with comparable mainstream bodies; and (4) institutional, having meaningful decision-making powers through representation and involvement in the general political and institutional order. Table 11–1 summarizes these possibilities.

Self-governing structures are not delegated by federal authority or Canadian law. Aboriginal governance is thought to be rooted in the reality of aboriginal nationhood, which has never been extinguished. This right to self-government is inherent in the sense that it has always existed (but was usurped by European settlement) and will continue to exist because aboriginal peoples did not voluntarily relinquish these rights by conquest or through treaties. Finally, jurisdictional matters under self-government are expected to vary from band to band. In all likelihood, they will include (a) control over the delivery of social services such as policing, education, and health and welfare; (b) ownership of resources and use of the land for economic regeneration; (c) the means to protect and promote distinct cultural values and language systems; (d) a final say over band membership and entitlements; and (e) input into the federal budget expenditures according to aboriginal rather than White priorities. Also anticipated are political structures that reflect local decision-making or consensual styles, as well as a workable division of labour between the different levels of government. No one is predicting that aboriginal self-governance will solve the "Indian problem." But compared to the patronizing dependency of government structures, putting aboriginal peoples in control of their political destiny is likely to bring about positive changes.

TABLE 11-1   Levels of Aboriginal Self-Governance

Statehood
- absolute (de jure) sovereignty
- internal + external jurisdiction
- complete independence with no external interference

Nationhood
- de facto sovereignty
- self-determining control over multiple yet interlinked jurisdictions within a framework of shared sovereignty
- nations within/province-like

Community/Municipality-based
- conditional sovereignty
- community-based autonomy
- internal jurisdictions, limited only by interaction with similar bodies and higher political authorities

Institutional
- nominal sovereignty
- decision-making power through institutional accommodation
- parallel institutions

Aboriginal Title and Treaty Rights

The process of renewal and reform is anchored in the recognition, definition, and implementation of aboriginal title and treaty rights. Enforcement of federal treaty obligations is particularly important in advancing aboriginal interests and aspirations. Treaties were seen as a fundamental component of aboriginal diplomacy with European powers, and the medium by which aboriginal peoples and the state continue to regulate their relationship with each other (Rotman, 1997). The British in particular insisted on observing legalities: Treaties represented practical nation-to-nation relationships between European colonizers and tribes; they also provided a foundation for a system of private property in a free-enterprise economy, since only land that had been been properly acquired ("without encumbrances") could be sold, mortgaged, used as collateral, or employed in a productive manner (Walkom, 1998). Treaties continue to be regarded as ongoing and organic agreements that reaffirm the distinctive legal status of aboriginal nations. They also procure a meaningful basis for political interaction between the Crown and aboriginal peoples.

Aboriginal leaders have long upheld treaties as semi-sacred and binding documents. Land and resources were exchanged for a raft of treaty rights that guaranteed perpetual access to goods, services, and a reserve homeland. Yet a conflict of interest was evident from the start. For the most part, British governments saw treaties as legal surrenders of aboriginal land. Such recognition proved an improvement over those domains where the doctrine of "terra nullius" prevailed; that is, Europeans could claim aboriginal land if viewed as "empty" or "under-utilized," according to Christian precepts. Treaties would provide legal title to underoccupied land, foster peaceful settlement, avoid costly wars, and deter American annexation or expansion (Price, 1991). For aboriginal peoples, the treaties were viewed as solemn transactions involving a sharing of land and resources in exchange for Crown assistance to facilitate the transition to the new economy while securing traditional lifestyles and livelihood. While the Crown signed treaties to formalize surrender of aboriginal title, aboriginal peoples saw treaties as reaffirming their autonomy and territories by sharing resources in exchange for Crown assistance to pursue new economic opportunities without abandoning their traditional lifestyle (McKee, 1996; DIAND, April, 1997). As far as aboriginal leaders are concerned, the government remains bound to honour the contractual obligations of these treaties. Access to benefits and services (such as free education and tax exemptions) is not a charitable handout; nor can they be considered a benevolent gesture on the part of an enlightened authority. Treaty entitlements are a legally binding exchange that aboriginal peoples have paid for over and over again with their lives and life chances.

Two types of treaty rights exist: one is based on specific claims to existing treaty violations and the other involves comprehensive (modern-day treaties or regional) settlements. A series of treaties were signed between 1763 and 1867 involving the governments of Britain, those of Eastern Canada, and aboriginal nations. The earliest treaties resembled peace compacts to facilitate trade, secure allies, and preempt European rivals (McKee, 1996). Between 1867 and 1923, eleven numbered (1–11) treaties were signed, involving a surrender of aboriginal interest in land to the Crown across much of the Prairies, and parts of Northwest Territories, B.C., and Ontario (DIAND, April, 1997). These historic Indian treaties set out the promises, obligations, and benefits of both parties to the agreement. Aboriginal peoples surrendered title to land, and received in return reserve lands, agricultural equipment, ammunition, annual payment, and clothing. Their right to hunt and fish on ceded Crown land remained in effect as long as these lands remained unoccupied. The Crown also promised schools on reserves or teachers when requested. Yet treaties were often marred by wilful duplicity or a fundamental inequity in the relationship between the Crown and aboriginal treaty-makers (Price, 1991). Most grievances involved failure to live up to these promises by cutting back on benefits. Another source of grievance entailed the unauthorized and uncompensated whittling away of reserve lands because of fraud, expropriation, or government theft (Spiers, 1998). So too was the misappropriation of aboriginal monies from government sale of resources or mineral rights held in trust by the Crown. Ambiguities in the misinterpretation of treaties have also come under scrutiny, with the result that the government is expected to give a "fair, large, and liberal interpretation" by providing the benefit of the doubt to aboriginal peoples.

By contrast, comprehensive claims consist of modern day treaty arrangements over land whose ownership is in dispute. Comprehensive claims do not deal with lapses in a specific treaty. These modern day treaties address the need to establish treaty relationships with those who have never signed a treaty in the past, in hopes of clarifying the rights of ownership to land and resources (DIAND, May 1994). Securing certainty over control of land and resources is imperative: For the Crown, certainty of ownership is a prerequisite for investment and development; for aboriginal peoples, only a solid economic base can secure the principles for social and cultural self-determination. Negotiated settlements provide aboriginal communities with protection for traditional land-based interests related to wildlife harvests, resource management, some subsurface mineral rights, and regulated development. Economic benefits can be derived by renting out lands and resources at rates that are favourable to aboriginal interests. Benefits also can be achieved through local development (in tandem with public or private interests) at a pace that reflects community priorities and developmental levels. In short, any fundamental changes in the status of aboriginal people are more likely when negotiating from a position of economic strength and the political power that sustains it. To date, ten comprehensive claims settlements have been concluded since 1973, including the Nunavut Agreement which came into effect in April, 1999, and the Nisga'a settlement in early 2000.

The resolution of comprehensive settlements in Canada is predicated on the principle of aboriginal title. Broadly speaking, aboriginal title specifies aboriginal rights of use over land and resources whose ownership ("title") has not yet been legally extinguished and transferred to the Crown (Gray, 1998). The principle itself revolves around the question of who owned or occupied the land prior to the Crown's unilateral assertion of ownership: If aboriginal peoples can prove they had continuous and exclusive occupation of the land prior to sovereignty, aboriginal title belongs to them; otherwise the land reverts to Crown possession (Editorial, *The Globe and Mail*, 13 Dec. 1997). The concept of aboriginal title has no counterpart in English common property law (hence "sui generis"). With aboriginal title, land cannot be extinguished or transferred to anyone but the Crown, is sourced in original occupancy, and is collectively held in perpetuity for the benefit of future owners.

The *Delgamuukw v. British Columbia* ruling in 1997 affirmed the principle of aboriginal title. The ruling concluded a legal compaign by 51 Gitskan and Wet'suwet'en hereditary chiefs whose predecessors had struggled since the 1880s to reclaim aboriginal title to their lands. *Delgamuukw* recognized the validity of aboriginal claims to certain lands they had never ceded in treaties or agreements. Under *Delgamuukw*, the Court has ruled that aboriginal peoples have a constitutional and exclusive right of use and ownership to land they occupied prior to European arrival, in effect going beyond an earlier conception of aboriginal title that included only the right to traditional hunting, fishing, and food gathering. As long as aboriginal title is unextinguished and aboriginal peoples retain interest in the land, *Delgamuukw* ruled, aboriginal people can use the land or resources in almost any way they wish—traditional or non-traditional—except in a destructive way that might imperil future use (Gray, 1997). And until aboriginal title is settled, moreover, not a single tree can be cut by non-aboriginal interests unless the claimants are consulted, compensated, or cede it voluntarily. This applies even in cases where infringements on aboriginal title lands are for public purposes or national interests (Matas et al., 1997). Finally, *Delgamuukw* advanced the concept of aboriginal title by expanding the support base for proving title. Oral traditions are now as admissible as evidence as written documents in deciding aboriginal title, in effect tipping the burden of proof from the claimants to the Crown.

The consequences cannot be underestimated: Not only has *Delgamuukw* forever changed the ground rules that will shape the future direction of aboriginal peoples-state relations. The Supreme Court has also equipped aboriginal peoples with a powerful negotiating tool — the idea of clear, definable aboriginal title to their land in negotiating land claims (Gray, 1997). The concepts of aboriginal title and self-government have been put to the test with the Nisga'a settlement.

From "Cutting Deals" To Constructive Engagement

One of the more striking developments in aboriginal peoples-state relations is a growing reliance on claims-making settlements for sorting out who controls what and why (McHugh, 1998). The logic behind a claims-making approach is relatively straightforward: In an effort to right historic wrongs by settling outstanding complaints against the state for breaches to aboriginal rights, the government offers a compensation package of cash, land, services, and controlling rights to specific aboriginal claimants in exchange for "full and final" settlements of treaty-based

CASE STUDY 11-2

Nisga'a: Apartheid, or Standing Apart to Work Together?

The proposed settlement of B.C.'s first but longest-running land claims test promises to be one of those watershed events that will forever reconfigure Canada's political contours. For some, Nisga'a puts a nail into the national unity coffin; for others, the settlement offers an innovative basis for society-building. According to critics, an "extraordinary agreement" with the Nisga'a Indians of British Columbia has "raised the spectre of racially separate development across Canada." This precedent-making treaty is the first of its kind in B.C. in this century, and entails the following: (a) provides the Nisga'a with more autonomy and self-government than that accorded to Quebec; (b) empowers the Nisga'a to pass laws on any matter other than defence, currency, and foreign affairs; (c) ensures exclusive access to ancestral lands and total control over resources; (d) confers benefits unavailable to other Canadians, based solely on culture or skin colour; (e) is proceeding without public mandate; and (f) prohibits non-Nisga'a from voting for the region's administration, thus disenfranchising local residents. The agreement's principles are seen as re-contouring the constitutional basis of B.C., since aboriginal rights are seen as taking precedence over Charter rights and rights of Canadian citizenship (see Mickleburgh, 1998). The more extreme critics persist in pushing all the right buttons by demonizing this pact as the evil reincarnation of the much-detested apartheid, with its bantustans (separate homelands), and the only jurisdiction in Canada where some Canadians can be taxed without representation or cannot vote because of race.

Finally, even aboriginal leaders are upset with what some perceive as a sellout deal that extinguishes aboriginal claims over land, while further locking aboriginal people into mainstream governance (Alfred, 1999).

First, the background. Early relations between Europeans and aboriginal peoples rested on striking deals through treaties. Such, initially, was the case in British Columbia: The English governor signed treaties for purchase of Vancouver Island, but, when the Colonial Office refused to underwrite the costs of governing the Empire, Victoria found itself without a tax base or treasury to purchase land for White settlers. The governor simply and unilaterally declared the land and minerals to be property of the Crown, and ceased to sign any treaties (Mulgrew, 1996). Even when B.C. joined Canada in 1871, the federal government refused to enter into treaties, despite aboriginal bitterness at the legal theft of aboriginal land. In what amounted to a tacit admission of guilt, and to compensate in lieu of a treaty, the government allocated $100 000 per year (upped to $300 000 in 1979) to be distributed on a per capita basis. This state of affairs existed until 1973 when the Supreme Court Calder decision rejected Nisga'a land claims, but triggered a sea change in government policy by suggesting aboriginal peoples had a valid complaint over the possibility of aboriginal title. Still, B.C. refused to sign treaties or acknowledge aboriginal title until 1991, arguing that aboriginal proprietary rights to land were extinguished by virtue of discovery, declaration of British sovereignty and common law, and the realities of Crown rule.

Second, the facts: Nisga'a have looked to Ottawa for redress since 1885. They petitioned the British Privy Council in 1913 and in 1968 took their case to court. The Calder decision in 1973 ruled against the Nisga'a, but indicated that aboriginal title had never been extinguished in B.C., and that the government had to do something about it (Walkom, 1998). It was not until the mid-1980s that a tentative settlement was reached: Actual terms of the agreement (not a treaty) are commonly known. The Nisga'a agreement would provide the 5500 member band who live 800 km north of Vancouver a land base of 1900 sq. km (a fraction of the amount originally proposed), control of forest and fishery resources, $200 million in cash, release from Indian Act provisions, a municipal level of government, including control over policing, education, community services, and taxes, and eventually eliminate on-reserve tax exemptions (Matas, 1998). To pay for this culture, Nisga'a will receive forest and timber-cutting rights, oil and mineral resources, 26 percent of the salmon fishery, plus $21.5 million to purchase boats and equipment, and a fishery-conservation trust. It is expected that this transfer in wealth and control will help to alleviate the social conditions in the Nisga'a community, including high levels of unemployment, criminal offences, and crowded homes. Under Section 35 of the Constitution Act, Nisga'a also have the constitutional right to protect and promote their language, culture, and society in areas such as marriage or adoption.

Third, the reality: The Nisga'a agreement-in-principle (it was fully ratified in early 2000) is not the first this century. Canada has signed nearly a dozen comprehensive agreements with indigenous tribes since passage of the 1975 James Bay and Northern Quebec Act. To be sure, this proposed settlement is the first in British Columbia since 1859, and the first of fifty outstanding land claims encompassing the entire province. Second, to suggest that the Nisga'a will have more powers of self-determination than Quebec is inaccurate. Quebec is often treated as a distinct society in Canada, with wide-ranging powers from controlling immigration to establishing diplomatic relations with foreign powers. By contrast, Nisga'a self-governing powers are restricted to those of a "super" municipality, including policing, education, taxes, community services, with a few provincial bits thrown in for good measure. The settlement is worded to protect federal jurisdictions in criminal law and the Charter, and provincial authority over policing and justice. Although health, education, and child welfare services must meet provincial standards, Nisga'a government will have exclusive jurisdiction in matters related to language and culture and to citizenship and property, even when these conflict with federal/provincial laws (Walkom, 1998). Third, Nisga'a will not be the only jurisdiction in Canada to restrict voting rights. Admittedly, in most liberal democratic systems, individual rights are acquired by residence: that is, if you live in Toronto, you can vote in Toronto. In contrast, rights in Nisga'a nation are based on ethnicity, with the result that only Nisga'a can claim rights of citizenship or vote for government. For the first time in Canadian history, Thomas Walkom (1998) concludes, government is being established on a foundation that is fundamentally racial and ethnic rather than territorial. Yet this assertion is not entirely true: There are 2567 reserves across Canada that also restrict voting to membership in one of 633 bands. Besides, what is the point of self-government if non-aboriginals can vote and undermine the very principle of aboriginal self-determination?

Fourth, the interpretation: Criticism of Nisga'a reflect errors of interpretation that border on fear-mongering involving a worst-case scenario. The powers negotiated by the Nisga'a are vastly overstated by critics. Nisga'a self-governing powers may be constitutionally protected—a status that admittedly no municipality has—and not subject to override except by federal, provincial, and aboriginal agreement (Walkom, 1998). In reality, Nisga'a powers are circumscribed (a super-municipality) and are considerably less than those implied by federal recognition of Canada's aboriginal tribes as "peoples with an inherent right to self-government." Terms of all inherent self-government agreements are set out in a 1995 federal policy document: Inherent self-government is based on contingent rather than sovereign rights; that is, aboriginal self-governments must operate within the Canadian federal system, work in harmony with other governments, be consistent with the Canadian Charter of Human Rights and Freedoms, and enhance the participation of aboriginal peoples in Canadian society. In other words, Nisga'a self-government is firmly located within the framework of Canadian society where the right to be different cannot violate the laws of the land, the rights of others, or fundamental values of society. Nisga'a will not become a state within a state, but a people who remain citizens of the country, subject to constitutional override and federal and provincial criminal codes.

Even more disconcerting is the critics' penchant for racializing the Nisga'a pact. Nisga'a is not about racially separate development by restricting the rights of other "races." Nor is it about race-based governments in the mould of apartheid; after all, apartheid was forcibly imposed on South African Blacks to exclude, deny, and exploit, in contrast with self-government arrangements that work on the voluntaristic principle of standing apart in order to work together. Nisga'a is about indigenous rights and the right of indigenous peoples to construct aboriginal models of self-governance over jurisdictions of land, identity, and political voice. It is about the rights of six generations of Nisga'a who since 1887 have tried to achieve self-government and establish native title to ancestral land that had never been surrendered to European powers. And finally, Nisga'a is about deconstructing those colonial constitutionalisms that continue to deny or exclude, together with a new constitutional accord that reflects, reinforces, and advances Nisga'a rights as original occupants.

Fifth, the future: Canada is widely renowned as a country constructed around compromise. The Nisga'a settlement is but another compromise in crafting an innovative political order in which each level of government—federal, provincial, and aboriginal—is sovereign in its own right, yet shares in the sovereignty of Canada as a whole by way of multiple yet interlocking jurisdictions. A settlement of such magnitude is not intended to be divisive or racial, although this treaty reveals a major ideological rift between the principles of liberal-pluralism (especially commitment to individual rights) and the assertion of collective indigenous rights (Laghi and Scofield, 1999). The objective is to find some common ground for constructive re-engagement between founding peoples. The Nisga'a settlement is intended to dispel uncertainty over who owns what, since investment is deterred by uncertainty of ownership (see *Financial Post*, 1998). The point is to establish an element of certainty by balancing and reconciling the pre-existence of aboriginal societies with the sovereignty of the Crown in a way that is workable, necessary, and just.

grievances. In Canada these regional agreements range from the James Bay-Cree settlement of 1975 to the Nunavut Agreement in 1993, involving extinguishment of aboriginal title in a region in exchange for a package of (a) perpetual aboriginal rights to various categories of land, from absolute freehold title to usufructuary rights to hunt and fish; (b) co-management and planning in various socio-ecomic and environmental issues; (c) hefty compensation payouts for unauthorized use of land to foster aboriginal economic develop and political infrastructures; and (d) various self-management arrangements (Jull and Craig, 1997).

Governments have taken to regional agreements as one way of establishing certainty over land titles and access to potentially lucrative resource extraction (Fleras and Spoonley, 1999). Regional settlements are endorsed as a case of restorative justice in compensating historically disadvantaged peoples for unwarranted confiscation of land, while securing a resource base to offset corresponding social and cultural dislocations (see Wilson, 1995). Governments prefer a full and final settlement of past injustices, if only to eliminate uncertainty from any further governance or development (Graham, 1997). But a restitutional claims-making policy environment has proven a double-edged sword. Claims-making resolutions are undeniably important as part of a broader exercise in relations-repair, but, on its own and divorced from the bigger picture of rethinking relationships, such a preoccupation is fraught with hidden messages and underlying contradictions (Rotman, 1997). However unintended, the consequences of the claims-making process foster an adversarial mentality: Disputants are drawn into a protracted struggle between opposing interest groups over "mine," "yours," and "ours" that concedes as little as possible. Issues, in turn, are confined to a rigid format that complicates the process of securing a compromise without losing face. Reliance on claims-making as aboriginal policy in the absence of clear principles is counterproductive, and may accentuate power-conflict models that reinforce the very colonialism that is being contested. Grievances remain grievances no matter how much money is being exchanged. Without a corresponding state commitment to restore the relationship in a generous and unquibbling fashion (see Milroy, 1997), attempts to right historic wrongs by equalizing material conditions are insufficient because they ignore what aboriginal people were before the wrongs began: fundamentally autonomous political communities sovereign in their own right and existing in a government-to-government relationship to others (Asch, 1997). A preoccupation with contesting claims to the exclusion of engagement has also had the effect of glossing over the central element in any productive partnership: namely, the managing of a relation in the spirit of cooperative co-existence (Henare, 1995:49; McHugh, 1998).

Pressure may be mounting to transcend claims-making as an exclusive model for defining state-indigenous peoples relations. Proposed instead is a more flexible approach that emphasizes engagement over entitlements, relationships over rights, interdependence over opposition, cooperation over competition, relations-repair over throwing money at a problem, reconciliation over restitution, and power-sharing over power conflict (Fleras and Maaka, 1998). Advocated, too, is a policy framework that acknowledges the importance of working together rather than standing apart, even if a degree of "standing apartness" may be inescapable in the constructive partnering of two peoples. Emergence of a "constructive engagement" model of interaction to replace the claims-oriented "contestation" mode may provide a respite from the interminable bickering over "who owns what," while brokering a tentative blueprint for working together by standing apart (Fleras, 2000). Among the key planks in constructively reconstitutionalizing aboriginal peoples-state relations are the following acknowledgements:

(a) First and foremost: Aboriginal peoples are not minorities, but fundamentally autonomous political communities, sovereign in their own right, while sharing in the sovereignty of society at large.

(b) Aboriginal peoples do not aspire to sovereignty, but already possess sovereignty by virtue of original occupancy—at least for purposes of entitlement or political engagement. Only appropriate arrangements are required to put this sovereignty into practice.

(c) Appeals to sovereignty and aboriginal models of self-determination are, in the final analysis, discourses about relationships. Proposed as part of a partnership is a relation of relative autonomy within a non-dominating context of cooperative coexistence (Young, 1990; Scott, 1996). Aboriginal peoples are neither a problem for solution nor a competitor to be jousted with, but a partner or people with inherent rights to benefits, recognition, relations, and identity.

(d) Aboriginal rights must be accepted as having their own independent sources rather than being shaped for the convenience of the political majority or subject to unilateral override (Asch, 1997).

(e) Power-sharing is critical to advancing cooperative engagement and peaceful coexistence (Linden, 1994). Innovative patterns of belonging to society are necessary. Rather than a "one size fits all" citizenship, proposed instead are multiple affiliations and belongings by way of membership in ethnicity or tribe rather than as individual citizens.

(f) Dispute resolution, problem-solving, and negotiations must be entered into not on the basis of jurisprudence, but on the grounds of justice, not by cutting deals but by formulating a clear vision, and not by litigation, but by listening and learning.

In short, a constructive engagement constitutionalism goes beyond the idea of restitution as simply a righting of historic wrongs. It is focused on advancing a relationship on an ongoing basis by taking into account shifting social realities in sorting out who controls what in a spirit of give and take. A renewal in the relationship must be based on the principles of partnership, recognition, respect, sharing, and responsibility, while being anchored in a commitment to cooperative coexistence and a relative, yet relational, autonomy (Royal Commission, 1996). Policy outcomes with respect to jurisdiction cannot be viewed as final or authoritative, any more than they can be preoccupied with "taking" or "finalizing," but must be situated in the context of "sharing" and "extending." Wisdom and justice must precede power, in other words, rather than vice versa (Cassidy, 1994). In acknowledging that "let's face it, we are all here to stay," as Chief Justice Antonio Lamer has observed, is there any other option except to shift from the trap of competing sovereignties and contested jurisdictions to the primacy of relations between partners (McHugh, 1998)?

Contesting the Terrain

Aboriginal struggles to sever the bonds of colonialist dependency and underdevelopment appear to be gathering momentum. Several innovative routes have been explored for improving aboriginal peoples-state relations, including constitutional reform, indigenization of policy and administration, comprehensive and specific land claims, constitutional reform,

Indian Act amendments, devolution of power, decentralization of service delivery structures and, of course, self-government arrangements (Prince, 1994). Aboriginal demands are consistent with their claim for inherent self-determining rights over jurisdictions pertaining to land, identity, and political voice as a unique nation within a Canadian framework. In seeking to establish government-to-government relations, aboriginal peoples are confirming their status as fundamentally autonomous political communities, each of which is sovereign in its own right, yet shares in the sovereignty of Canada by way of multiple, interlocking jurisdictions. Aboriginal peoples are not seeking to separate from Canada. Nor is there any intent to impose their lifestyle on the non-native component. Instead, they are looking to find a middle way to strike a balance between extremes.

First, while there is little inclination to separate from Canada in the territorial sense, any move towards assimilation is categorically rejected. A commitment to the inherent right of self-government is endorsed instead as a compromise between the poles of separatism and absorption. Second, although aboriginal peoples don't want to preserve their cultural lifestyle in aspic for the edification of purists or tourists, they also refuse to abandon their language, culture, and identity in exchange for an alien and incompatible package of non-Aboriginal values and beliefs. As a compromise, they want to take relevant elements of the past and apply them selectively to the realities of the present. They want to be modern, in other words, but not at the expense of eroding their uniqueness. Third, aboriginal peoples are pragmatists who wish to achieve a working balance between tradition and progress. Balancing the cultural and spiritual values of the past with the technological benefits of modern society remains a pressing priority. Fourth, achievement of political and economic power is viewed as critical to restoring aboriginal communities as flourishing centres of meaningful activity. Yet these goals are unacceptable if attained at the cost of undermining their spirituality, collective and community rights, and cultural values. Whether aboriginal peoples can use the resources available to forge a "golden mean" between seemingly unworkable extremes cannot be answered as yet. Nevertheless, the healing process has begun, even though the journey promises to be a long and arduous one (Mercredi and Turpel, 1993).

Politicians and the public have reacted adversely to this rethinking of the "Indian problem." Deeply ingrained and difficult to dislodge is a perception of aboriginal peoples as a problem people who interfere with national interests, or as peoples having problems that entail costly solutions. Attempts to address aboriginal concerns from the vantage point of a liberal-democratic state have tended to reinforce the degree of miscalculation in addressing aboriginal demands (Fleras, 1989). As a result, conflicts and contradictions continue to pervade the interaction between political and aboriginal sectors. Some Canadians are confused or frustrated by what they consider to be the highly unorthodox nature of aboriginal demands. Aboriginal challenges to the very constitutionalism upon which Canada is constructed, for example, the absolute sovereignty of the Crown or state, are unlikely to win many converts. Nor is there much mainstream enthusiasm for aboriginal rejecting of those colonial arrangements that kept aboriginal peoples "down and out," followed by the establishment of a new social contract involving a new set of fundamental principles pertaining to governance, citizenship, and relational status. Others refute the validity of these demands altogether, preferring to maintain the status quo. Still others are in general agreement with aboriginal aspirations, but remain concerned about the long-term implications of the more radical proposals (Fleras, 1992).

At one level, Canadian politicians appear willing, in theory, to acknowledge the plausibility of aboriginal demands as a policy item, if only to avert a crisis of legitimacy and restore some semblance of political tranquility. Such an endorsement can be attributed in part to a desire to maintain credibility in the face of potential embarrassment and ridicule (Dyck, 1985). But this support also feeds on the fear of international censure and the threat of reprisals. Few politicians can afford to dismiss the existence of aboriginal rights or the validity of preferential status or treatment for fear of unleashing a powerful backlash. What is debated instead are answers over defining their limits, and how best to concede these rights without shredding the social fabric of society in the process. Also evident is a political willingness to negotiate issues related to self-determination, even self-government if necessary, although not to the extent of condoning territorial secession and constitutional dismemberment.

At another level, however, there are widespread misgivings about the concept of aboriginality and the corresponding assumptions underlying the distribution of power and resources in society. The principles behind aboriginality and aboriginal rights continue to confound and confuse Canadian politicians. National interests must take precedence over aboriginal interests, they say (Boldt, 1993). While the concept of aboriginal government may be tolerable, the idea of self-*governance* may be more problematic. Self-governance goes beyond government per se, but is concerned with the relationship between governments and other sectors of society, including those structures and values that determine how power is to be exercised, how decisions are to be taken, and how decision-makers are to be held accountable (Plimptre, 1999). And, given the government's refusal to acknowledge aboriginal rights outside of a context of a negotiated settlement (Walkem, 2000), the choices will continue to be based on the denial of aboriginal people as a people with an inherent right to aboriginal models of self-governance. Finally, there are irrevocable perceptual gaps. Aboriginal claims, with their focus on indigenous status and non-negotiable collective rights, are often in conflict with the individualistic and universal values embedded within liberal-democratic contexts (Weaver, 1984; Boldt and Long, 1984). Of particular note is the universalism inherent in liberal pluralism: that is, what we have in common as rights-bearing individuals is more important than membership in a group. Consider the question: Is it possible to politicize aboriginality as different yet equal in a society based on the universalizing principles of liberal-pluralism and internal colonialism? Not unexpectedly, both politicians and the Canadian public have been slow to acknowledge aboriginality as a guiding principle for solving the Canadian/Indian problem. Refusal to confront the most quintessential of Canada's social problems, namely, that aboriginal peoples continue to chafe under colonialist principles of control, manipulation, and assimilation, will surely inflame the national unity crisis. And without a fundamental rethinking of the constitutionalism that must underpin aboriginal peoples-Crown relations in a post-colonial Canada, the "Canada problem" will continue to fester.

THE QUEBEC QUESTION

12

FRAMING THE PROBLEM

"I've never met an English-speaking Canadian, but I'm sure they're as nice as any other foreigner."

(Alice Simard, mother of Lucien Bouchard, premier of Quebec, quoted in Report on Business, January 1996).

Canada may be regarded as the world's best place to live according to UN quality of life rankings. Yet for all its resources and resourcefulness Canada is in danger of splintering along ethnic fault lines. Canada is not alone in this predicament: The forces of ethnicity (as well as language, region, or religion) pose a greater threat to the sovereign integrity of states than the threat of invasion by outsiders (Simpson, 1996). Traditional cross-border wars, in the conventional sense of using force to capture coveted territory, have been replaced by threats "from within" because of aggrieved minorities. In this sense, Quebec's threat to Canadian unity is but one expression of a global drive for national affirmation, according to Anthony Smith in his book *The Ethnic Origins of Nations* (1996). The search for collective touchstones of identity by way of race or ethnicity may be the definitive challenge to the stability of our impersonal and homogeneous world. Yet existing states seem incapable of dealing with these ethnically-charged nationalisms because of structural constraints or constitutional limitations (Qadeer, 1997).

The question of Quebec's status within Canada—and vice versa—has consumed Canada's society-building agenda since Confederation (Meisel et al., 2000). French–English-speaking relations have coexisted uneasily since 1841 when Upper and Lower Canada combined into an incipient nation-state, a situation aptly described by Lord Durham as the equivalent of "two nations warring in the bosom of a single state." Interaction has vacillated, including stretches of sullen isolation ("two solitudes"), to periods of convulsive social change ("the Quiet Revolution"), with occasional flashes of violence in between ("two scorpions in a bottle"). Conflicts are varied, and range from interminable language rights battles to provincial-federal squabbling over resources and jurisdiction, but tend to focus on Quebec sovereignty aspirations as a "distinct society" within a vastly revamped federalist framework. The Québecois constitute a powerful political community of people who claim some degree of sovereignty (autonomy) by virtue of a shared history, a collective vision, a set of grievances, and collective goals of a people with a common ancestry (see Juteau, 1994). In contrast to a deep emotional attachment to their homeland of last resort, Quebeckers see English-speaking Canada as a remote, even unfriendly, place with its own set of priorities and preoccupations, few of which concern or apply to Quebec (Gagnon, 1996; Conlogue, 1997). Many Quebeckers resent those English-speaking Canadians who appear unwilling to accept even minimal concessions to confirm Quebec's distinctiveness. Such insensitivity is seen to reflect a lack of distinct anglophone cultural identity. While Québecois know who they are, English-speaking Canadians are perceived as bereft of common vision or grand design, except in opposition to something else, thus inhibiting their capacity to accept Quebec for its differences and history. Others argue that the federal system is no longer viable and that Quebec cannot possibly associate itself with a system that is incapable of dealing with its own problems (Castonguay, 1994). Federalism does not pay; rather, staying in Canada extracts a heavy economic cost because of extra layers of government and the perpetual gridlock between Quebec and Ottawa (Fournier, 1994).

The potential for misunderstanding reflects radically different images of historic relations between the French and English. English-speaking Canadians tend to support a Trudeauian vision of Canada, with its commitment to a strong central government, multiculturalism, no special status for Quebec, official bilingualism, individual rights, and equality of provinces. This vision has less currency in Quebec where the commitment lies in strengthening Quebec, enhancing the French language, assimilating immigrants into a Francophone culture, and seeking special arrangements for Quebec within a renewed federalism (McRoberts, 1997). English-speaking Canadians envision Canada as a social contract between a central authority and ten equal provinces. For French-speaking Quebeckers, the preferred vision is that of a covenant or compact between fundamentally autonomous political communities, each sovereign yet sharing in the sovereignty of Canada. While Québecois discourses appear to dwell on the wrongs done in the past and unfair treatment during two centuries of cohabitation, English-speaking Canadians believe Quebec has benefited from its status as a Canadian province, and that any indignities that have been inflicted are more than compensated by benefits (Meisel et al., 2000). Ambiguities in this relationship are animated by the politics of language. Debates over bilingualism as a means of solving the national unity crisis have infuriated and divided the country as have few other issues. Quebeckers dismiss bilingualism as an act of appeasement bereft of any moral legitimacy; English-speaking Canadians bristle at the inconvenience associated with bilingualism. The often passionate zeal of Quebec's language police has evoked howls of derision from English speaking Canada (White, 1997). Sensitivities are further inflamed when the English-speaking media pounce on minority language issues to portray Quebec as harsh and intolerant (Sniderman et al., 1993), in effect contributing to a siege mentality and the need for Quebeckers to be perpetually on the defensive.

In short, both sectors are locked into seemingly unflattering images of the other. Each regards its counterpart as the "problem." Francophones throughout Canada have depicted English-speaking Canadians as insensitive to Quebec's legitimate interests as a cultural homeland of last resort. Anglophones, in turn, have dismissed the Québécois as rabid nationalists, with little or no respect for liberal values or individual rights, much less any concern over "national interests" except for milking Canada as a treasure trove for plunder rather than as a community to nourish. Quebec has taken advantage of its status within Canada to milk it for what it's worth, as a former separatist premier put it (cited in Gwyn, 1998), yet it continues to chafe under federal containment and anglophone insensitivity (Gagnon, 1993). English-speaking Canadians appear increasingly opposed to fundamental concessions, preferring a status quo federalism of formally equal provinces (McRoberts, 1993). In suggesting that it's time for Canada to abandon Quebec (Scowen, 1999), they also fail to understand that restlessness is the psychology of a permanent minority, writes Jeffrey Simpson, in the Canada day issue of the *Globe and Mail* (1999). With their fierce pride, abiding attachment to language and culture, prickly sense of distinctiveness, shrewd sense of political interests, suspended between unrealized ambitions, and under perpetual threat by anglophones, Quebeckers expend considerable energy examining themselves and their relationship to Canadian society. And it is precisely this failure to foster a rapprochement between these two founding nations that strikes at the very core of Canada's survival. Yet even the close referendum decision in October 1995 (50.6 percent for federalism, 49.4 percent for sovereignty) does not appear to have stimulated any new vision of—or urgency about—how Quebec and Ottawa can get their act together (Honderich, 1996; Cohen, 1996). There is no shortage of conflicting messages: Quebeckers believe that separation is inevitable, yet many sovereignists prefer a renewed deal within Canada. Most Quebeckers think Canada is a good place to live, yet many would vote yes to separation in a future referendum (*Globe and Mail*, February 24, 1996). Given a choice of either/or, Quebeckers prefer a status quo federalism over complete independence by a margin of two to one. But support for sovereignty rises when integrated into a partnership with Canada (renewed federalism) (Stewart, 1999). In other words, Quebeckers are attached to Canada, but their attachment is conditional (Stewart, 1997). Similarly, English-speaking Canadians may be positively predisposed to Quebec, but recoil at the prospect of separation by extortion, and an ethnic concept of Canada. Still, there is no doubt that the "Quebec question" has challenged English-speaking Canadians to rethink the nature, purpose, and future of Canada as a society. For, as the Clarity Act (Quebec cannot begin to separate without a "clear" majority vote, and can only do so on a "clear" question) clearly demonstrates: Canada *is* indivisible in theory; in practice, the process will be difficult, if not impossible.

This chapter will explore the politics of Quebec against the backdrop of the national unity crisis. It is argued as in the previous chapter that the Quebec question is really a Canada problem, and, that as long as reforms are situated within a largely 19th century framework, lasting solutions to the problem of Quebec-Canada relations are unlikely to transpire. Central to the argument are the politics of recognition (Taylor, 1992). Is Quebec a province or ethnic minority? Or is it a fundamentally autonomous political community whose people see themselves as sovereign in their own right and sharing in the sovereignty of Canada at large? Failure to acknowledge the logic and dynamics behind this political reality will result in additional dialogues of the deaf. The chapter begins by examining how official bilingualism has proven an innovative but ultimately insufficient solution to solving the national unity problem. Much of the controversy reflects radically different visions of Canada, with contract views clashing with compact perspectives to create tensions—even more so with recognition of aboriginal peoples as part of a three nations-state arrangement. The way in which this problem has become more complicated yet paradoxically simplified is explored with the emergence of Quebec's First Nations as powerful political levers. The chapter provides a lengthy discussion of how Quebeckers would prefer to solve the Quebec question. A vast range of responses in redefining French-English-speaking relations reveals the formidable barriers to arriving at any agreed upon solution. The chapter concludes by way of a conundrum: Perhaps the national unity problem was never meant to be solved—after all, proposed solutions tend to create more problems—but rather to muddle along in a way that is quintessentially Canadian.

OFFICIAL BILINGUALISM: A FAILED SOCIAL EXPERIMENT?

Canada can be described as a linguistic duality whose national language policies are simultaneously a source of unity and disunity. Problems in communication and accommodation can be expected in a country of two major languages with three-quarters of the population speaking one language, one-quarter the other. The problem is compounded by a linguistic divide: The vast majority of English-speaking Canadians outside of New Brunswick and northeast Ontario cannot speak French; most francophones in Quebec outside of Montreal cannot speak English. Such a communications gap exposes the fragility of Canada as a society. A series of responses, including official bilingualism, has evolved to solve the riddle of national unity.

Bilingualism itself comes in different shapes and sizes. Under individual bilingualism, each person is expected to become proficient in one or more languages in the country. Territorial bilingualism is another option, and reflects a division of language use along geographical lines. For example, Belgium and Switzerland are divided into regions where one of the official language predominates (Linden, 1994). Finally, there is institutional bilingualism with its focus on institutionalizing official languages at organizational levels, including the creation of bilingual workplaces or delivery of services.

All three styles of bilingualism are found in Canada. There is an unofficial territorial bilingualism, namely, Canada is divided into two language heartlands—Quebec and the rest of Canada—with a limited number of bilingual districts adjacent to Quebec, such as Ottawa or New Brunswick. Increasing numbers are attracted to this type of bilingualism in light of demographic realities that show a rapid assimilation of francophones outside of Quebec in conjunction with the abandonment of Montreal by Quebec's anglophones. Individual bilingualism also exists in Canada; nearly 17 percent of the total population in the 1996 census possessed fluency in both languages, up from 13 percent in 1971, including 38 percent of the residents in Quebec, 33 percent in New Brunswick, and 12 percent in Ontario. Officially, however, Canada endorses an institutional bilingualism. It acknowledges the equal and official status of French and English as languages of communication in federal institutions across the country. How, then, do we assess official bilingualism as an initiative for national unity through minority language protection?

Federal Bilingualism: Institutional Style

Canada's experiment with federal bilingualism began in the 1960s. Efforts to strengthen French language rights in exchange for social peace resulted in the right of federal public servants in 1966 to conduct business in either French or English. Passage of the Official Languages Act in 1969 formalized linguistic duality as a fundamental characteristic of Canadian society. Provisions of the Act acknowledged the presence and legitimacy of both French and English as official and equal languages. Implicit in this unity formula was a vision of Canada that allowed speakers of either language to feel at home in all parts of the country (Goldbloom, 1994b; Commissioner of Official Languages, 1995). The Official Languages Act confirmed the right of Canadians to work in French or English in federal organizations, to receive federal services in either language, and to guarantee official language minority rights across Canada. The rights of official-language minorities would protect French-speaking Canadians in English Canada and English-speaking Canadians in Quebec. Official language minorities were entitled to federal services in either French or English in areas where numbers warranted or demand was significant. Federal employees won the right to work in the official language of their choice, while equal opportunities for French and English speakers in the public service were guaranteed as well. Bilingualism was expressed in federal documents, signs in national parks, parliamentary proceedings, court cases, and federally chartered passenger vehicles, from Air Canada planes to shuttle buses at Pelee National Park. The courts and parliament, in addition to the central offices of all federal government institutions, were to be bilingual. Recent efforts to update the Official Languages Act (1988) have reaffirmed Ottawa's commitment to bilingualism by strengthening official language minority control over education and school boards (parents who speak one of the official languages have a right to educate children in the preferred language) where they constitute viable communities. For example, minority language groups across Canada have been heartened by a Supreme Court decision that gives 150 francophone children in a P.E.I. community the right to French-language schooling (Hébert, 2000).

Bilingualism in Practice

Nearly thirty years of the Official Languages Act have proven inconclusive as a tool for national unity. Both political and public responses to national unity are polarized, involving an mixture of support, rejection, expediency, and indifference. Critics tend to exaggerate the magnitude and scope of official bilingualism; supporters prefer to exaggerate its benefits. Levels of support for bilingualism vary with the phrasing of questions on national surveys. A slight majority of Canadians appear to support Canada's language duality, the principle of bilingualism, and the provision of bilingual government services as a blueprint for intergroup relations—at least when issues are couched in terms of responsiveness and accommodation rather than government intervention (Commissioner of Official Languages, 1995). Popular too is the extension of French language social services into areas of high francophone concentration. As well, highly motivated parents have enrolled their children in language immersion programs across Canada.

Federal and provincial authorities have wavered in their endorsement of official bilingualism. Generally speaking, the reality of bilingualism is restricted to (a) federal institutions, (b) communities with a high proportion of French-speaking residents such as Eastern and Northern Ontario, (c) the delivery of some essential provincial services, and (d) some school children in larger urban centres. Only New Brunswick among the provinces is officially bilingual. Even here, unease simmers between French-speaking Acadians who want to expand French language services versus the English-speaking majority who prefer the status quo. The Northwest Territories has also acknowledged French and English as official languages, in addition to six aboriginal languages, for a total of eight official languages. Another six provinces are nominally unilingual. Resistance to official bilingualism is couched in economic terms ("too costly"), political terms ("too divisive"), cultural terms ("too irrelevant"), and social terms ("too undemocratic"). English remains the de facto language of communication in the delivery of service, although French language concessions have been introduced for a variety of reasons. Ontario is a good example of a province that has moved toward limited French language services. Its French Language Services Act (Bill 8) in 1986 enshrined the delivery of French-language services when warranted by numbers (namely, where the French-speaking population reaches a total of 5000 or represents 10 percent of the population). London, Ontario by virtue of its 5100 francophone inhabitants became the twenty-third region to qualify for bilingual provincial services. Despite this concession, Ontario refuses to constitutionally guarantee bilingual rights across the province. And Ontario's refusal to designate the capital of Canada as officially bilingual has managed to attract even federal wrath. Other provinces, including Nova Scotia and British Columbia, have implemented only minimal concessions to official minority language education, despite constitutional guarantees to that effect (Goldbloom, 1994a). Elsewhere, Franco-Manitobans have experienced difficulty in having their constitutionally entrenched rights recognized.

Three provinces are now officially unilingual in opposition to the spirit of the Official Languages Act. Alberta and Saskatchewan have enacted legislation making English the sole provincial language. This decree ensures the primacy of English for business, commerce, administration, and provincial court activities. In fairness, there exists limited but inconsistent access to French-language services, while ethnically powerful groups such as the Ukrainians have been successful in incorporating their language into the school curriculum. The third unilingual province is Quebec. Quebec has endorsed official unilingualism since passage of the French Language Charter (Bill 101) in 1977. Nevertheless, Quebec's 667 000 anglophones or just under nine percent of the population benefit from guaranteed English-language services in health and education. By all accounts, Quebec's French-only unilingual initiatives have proven a success. According to Professor John Richards, an economist from Simon Fraser University, in a paper to the C. D. Howe Institute, nearly 100 percent of all Quebeckers who learn French as infants speak it at home as adults. In 1996, French was the mother tongue of 81.5 percent of Quebeckers, up from 80.7 percent in 1971. English, by contrast, had declined from 13.1 percent to 8.8 percent. Yet Quebec's unilingual language laws appear to contravene constitutional and statutory guarantees for official-language minorities. Section 23 of the Charter stipulates that the "official language minority has the right to instruction in their mother tongue, the right to autonomous school facilities, and the right to the management and control of these schools." How does this apparent contravention stand up to scrutiny? The next case study will examine the slippery slope of language politics.

Official Bilingualism—Failure or Success?

Has thirty years of official bilingualism been a success or failure? Problem or solution? Has it contributed to national unity by keeping Quebec in Canada or will it provide the catalyst for further political turmoil? Are the costs justified in light of the modest returns, with

Many of the language issues that confront Canadians are based on efforts to reconcile conflicting rights as well as competing realities. Continued discussion and disagreement over Bill 101 constitutes one example. Passage of Bill 101 completed the initiatives of Bill 22 that transformed French into the preferred language of the province for work, education, commerce, and service delivery. Bill 101 went one step further and prohibited the use of English in public. This French Language Charter asserted French as the sole official language on the grounds that Quebec had as much right to be French as Ontario was English. The Act was prompted in part by a belief that the Canadian model of one country, two languages, will inevitably lead to the eventual extinction of the French language and culture; in part by fears over language loss due to declining francophone birth rates in Quebec and allophone preference to send children to English-speaking schools. English would be permitted in certain constitutionally designed areas such as education and health (and federal services would continue to be bilingual). But for all intents and purposes, English was restricted to the personal and private, thus robbing it of its usefulness as a language of public power (Daost-Blais, 1983).

Equally controversial was passage of Bill 178 in 1988. In 1985, Robert Bourassa regained power on a platform to promote the French face of Quebec from within a framework of bilingual federalism. The Liberals pledged to revoke the French commercial signs provisions of Bill 101 and institute bilingual storefront signs. Both Quebec's Superior Court and the Supreme Court of Canada had acknowledged Quebec's right (by way of Bill 101) to take necessary steps in promoting French as the working language of the majority in that province. But banning the use of English on storefronts was ruled by both as unconstitutional and in violation of Canadian human rights. In other words, although the Quebec government could promote the prominence of French on commercial signs, it could not expressly prohibit the use of other languages such as English without infringing on official language minority rights. Bourassa responded by invoking the notwithstanding clause within the Constitution to override both the Canadian and Quebec Charter of Rights and Freedoms for five years. Under Bill 178, French-only signs were permitted outside an establishment; bilingual signs were allowed inside provided the presence of French prevailed. Few were satisfied by Bourassa's inside-outside compromise for reconciling the demands of Quebec nationalists and anglophone federalists. Nationalists scorned any concession to the hated anglais as appeasement. Anglophones by contrast resented the supercedence of Quebec's collective rights over individual language rights. To be sure, protective measures for the survival of French could be justified, but surely not by trampling on the constitutional rights of official language minorities.

In Defence of Collective Language Rights

How justified were the Québecois in passing a law that violated both the spirit of official bilingualism in addition to the individual equality provisions of the

Canadian Charter of Rights and Freedoms? Does suppression of English language rights by the Quebec legislation constitute a justifiable limit on individual rights in a free and democratic society? Responses to these questions seem to begin with "it depends." Right or wrong depends on whose perspective is taken into account. As Victor Goldbloom, Official Languages Commissioner notes, Quebec's sense of collective destiny, including fears of being swallowed up by an English-speaking continent, continue to clash with English-speaking attachment to individual rights and freedoms. From an anglophone perspective, Bill 101 is a serious infringement on the Constitutional rights of individuals and official language minority rights. Anglophones perceive francophones as a bullying majority in the province who prop up their linguistic and cultural insecurities by picking on minority individual rights. No democratic government has the right to prohibit the use of another language in public, even if certain concessions may be possible under limited circumstances. From Quebec's point of view, the promotion of collective rights as implicit within Bills 101 and 178 is justified. Proponents have stoutly defended Bill 101 as the minimum necessary to neutralize the impact and assimilative pressures in a continental sea of English. Moreover, because Quebec is not a province comme les autres, neither English-speaking authorities nor the Charter of Rights has any right to interfere in determining the fate of North America's only French-speaking jurisdiction (Gagnon, 1993b).

Several lines of argument are employed in defence of collective language rights. First, the Language Act is not discriminatory because French and English are not on the same footing: One is

threatened, the other isn't, according to Quebec's minister of intergovernmental affairs. The 8 million Québecois see themselves as imperilled by a continental tide of 267 million North Americans with designs (both conscious or by consequence) to remove the French face of Quebec. The precarious status of French as the homeland of last resort demands special measures to promote Quebec's collective rights—even if these should infringe on anglophone individual rights. Second, with passage of Bill 101, Quebec is doing only what other provinces have historically done, which is to deny the right for francophones outside of Quebec to protect their language. If Quebec is restricting the language rights of anglophones, its actions are no worse than those of other provinces who routinely infringe on minority language rights. Even then, Quebec's anglophones already possess the best constitutional protection of official minority rights in Canada, unlike the French in other parts of Canada where services depend on provincial political whims or numerical calculations. Third, those who regard Bill 101 (and Bill 178) as blatant violations of the Charter's equality provisions have had to rethink the application of abstract individual rights in contexts of inequality. For the Québecois, the protection of their French culture and language is prior to individual rights. Without this collective guarantee there is no context for the expression of individual rights. Both political elites and High Court officials have defended the collective right of francophones to protect their language because of their status as a cultural enclave in North American society. This override of collective rights is permitted as long as the promotion is reasonable, set out in law, and demonstrably justified in a free and democratic society.

The Politics of Compromise

In late 1993, Quebec passed Bill 86 following the expiry of the notwithstanding exemption for Bill 178. Bill 86 watered down some of the controversial provisions of Bill 178 by allowing languages other than French on commercial signs, as long as the French was dominant (Picard, 1994; Francis, 1996). According to this compromise, French had to be twice as large as English on commercial signs; alternatively there had to be twice as many French signs. Outstanding charges against merchants who violated the French-only commercial sign law were dropped as a gesture of good faith. The bill also abolished the so-called language police, "Commission de Protection de la Langue Française." These compromises were rooted in pragmatism rather than ideology, according to Quebec's Language Minister, Claude Ryan. The "inside-outside" compromise may not have provoked the public outrage of its predecessors. But clashes are anticipated following reinstatement of the language police in 1997 to placate Quebec's "language hawks" (Ha, 1997) for non-compliance with commercial sign laws. An underlying message can be discerned: Quebeckers may be a majority that exerts power and control in their province. Outside this jurisdiction, however, they are a linguistic minority, and any concession to anglophones must be avoided on the assumption that if you give the anglais an inch, they take a mile (Ha, 1997). With the language hawks nipping at their heels, Quebec's political leaders simply cannot afford to look soft on the language question, although a recent Superior Court decision to strike down aspects of the language law as discriminatory may be used for political gain (Seguin, 1999).

Putting it in Perspective

Twenty years of what some regard as one of the most pivotal—and controversial—pieces of legislation in Canada continue to evoke strong feelings (Ha, 1997). Lauded by some, but reviled by others, passage of the bill on August 26, 1977 remains a lightning rod for English resentment, yet a beacon of pride for French speakers. Benoit Aubin (1997:D-3) captures a sense of the ambivalence when he writes:

> Bill 101 has represented the best and the worst....It has been called, variously, the beginning of a new era, a vile instance of state driven discrimination, and the most ambitious piece of social engineering ever attempted in Canada. It has given rise to petty and mean spirited abuse; language cops pouring over business cards or labels on kosher products to see if they contained the prescribed proportion of French words. It has led to ridiculous extremes, as can happen when controversial laws fall into the hands of lawyers.

Debates remain over whether to tighten, to ease, or to scrap Bill 101. All agree that the bill has proven an instrument of cultural affirmation and social change. With the stroke of a pen, businesses had to operate and offer services in French, immigrant children had to go to French schools, and English disappeared as public and commercial signs. Today, francophones are in charge of the province's economy, French is common in the workplace and the language of communications within companies, and French-speaking residents do not earn less than English-speaking counterparts (Fournier, 1994; Synnott, 1996). In short, Bill 101 has modified the cultural and political landscape of Quebec and Canada in ways that went far beyond what its proponents envisaged. And in perhaps the greatest irony of them all, by allaying the linguistic and cultural insecurities of many Quebeckers, while securing a better place for French within the Canadian federation, Bill 101 may have inadvertently saved Canada by cutting the main fuel line of discontent to the separatist engine (Aubin, 1997; Hébert, 1999).

estimates ranging from $549 million in 1996 to $2 billion annually if hidden costs are factored in. Or should its worth be measured in terms of fostering a new national identity and improved Canadian awareness of French-English relations?

Answers to these questions will depend on how "success" and "failure" are defined, by whom, on what basis, and what for. Responses will vary with the criteria employed, including location (B.C. vs Ontario vs Quebec) age, socio-economic status, gender, and ethnicity. A broad spectrum of opinion is evident: On one side, Max Yalden, a former Official Language Commissioner, has described the Official Languages Act as one of the most innovative and important social revolutions ever brought about peacefully in a democratic society (cited in Campbell, 1997). On the other, such critics as Scott Reid in his 1993 book, *Lament for a Nation*, chide bilingualism for its failure to bring Canadians closer together. In between are the critics who pounce on official bilingualism for not making Canadians more bilingual, in contrast with Quebec's success in advancing French in the province by way of admittedly controversial legislation (Auger, 1997). The number crunchers are equally outspoken. Some point to the 63 000 public servants who have taken bilingual courses as a sign of success, in addition to the 31 percent of federal service jobs that are declared bilingual. Others applaud the expansion of bilingualism across Canada, but worry that costs may not justify the results. Despite massive annual outlays, the number of bilingual speakers in Canada outside of Quebec has remained relatively constant, from 7 percent in 1971 to 10 percent in 1991. The figures in Ontario show an increase from 9.3 percent in 1971 to 11.6 percent in 1996.

How does official bilingualism contribute to or detract from Canadian society-building? Kenneth McRoberts (1997) suggests official bilingualism originated in large part to counter the surge of nationalism in Quebec. It arose to restore national unity by offering Quebec the promise of participation and opportunity throughout all of Canada. As a "society-saving" strategy, this national language policy responded to Quebec's discontent and threat of separation by depoliticizing language through its institutionalization at federal levels. Official bilingualism addressed the national unity question, not by making Quebec more distinctive or power-sharing, but by making the rest of Canada more like Quebec. In the words of William Thorsell, editor-in-chief of *The Globe and Mail*, March 30, 1991:

> In essence, Ottawa tried to dilute Quebec nationalism by dispersing it across Canada, most obviously in the form of official bilingualism. The strategy was basically this: Ottawa would deny Quebecers additional powers in their own province in exchange for additional rights in Ottawa and all the other provinces.

The intent was purely political: Official bilingualism sought to defeat Quebec separatism by the texture of Canada itself, and to advance national unity by making Quebec francophones feel more at home across Canada. Any wholesale power-sharing or promotion of collective rights was not on the table. Yet this Trudeau-inspired national unity strategy reflected a misreading of Canada (according the elite consensus and its expression in the Royal Commission on Biculturalism and Bilingualism). Measures such as official bilingualism were part of a strategy for francophones to discard their historically distinct national collectivity. In its place, Quebeckers would adopt a reading of Canada that included multiculturalism, individual rights, and the equality of all provinces. But this national unity strategy failed to dislodge Quebec's perception of its place in Canada. It also drew attention to inadequacies in a province-based, symmetrical federalism (Kymlicka, 1998). If anything, Kenneth McRoberts (1997) notes, official bilingualism has solidified Quebec's resolve to see itself as a people and nation.

There is much to commend in this view of official bilingualism as a conflict management device to diffuse Canada's national unity crisis. However effective in keeping Canada together during the 1970s and 1980s, recent events and polls indicate that federal bilingualism is increasingly irrelevant as response to Québécois assertiveness. Efforts to integrate Quebec into the national political community by way of language policies rather than power sharing appear inconclusive at best. This would suggest that solving problems by mis-defining the problem is likely a recipe for failure. It would also suggest that federal bilingualism is a necessary but insufficient component of a national-unity strategy, and must be supplemented by arrangements that address Quebec's political and politicized concerns.

THE PROBLEM WITH CANADA: PROVINCES OR PEOPLES?

Quebec is part of Canada's federalist system. The political compromises that culminated in the 1867 Constitution Act (BNA Act) established a centralized system. It incorporated Quebec's linguistic, legal, and social distinctions as part of the constitutional fabric, in effect confirming Quebec's special place in Confederation (Burgess, 1996). Yet federalism as a system of political compromise invites diverse interpretations. These interpretations or visions include federalism as a "contract" and federalism as a "compact." A third vision, Canada as a "three-nations" state, is slowly gaining acceptance.The coexistence of these competing visions generates much of the dynamic that animates French–English-speaking relations.

Canada as a Contract

According to this first interpretation, Canada constitutes a federalist system of ten provinces under a central authority in Ottawa. A contract exists between the provinces (including Quebec) and the federal government. The provinces (including Quebec), as well as the federal government, are sovereign within their own jurisdiction, as set out in the Constitution. Neither can usurp the authority or powers of the other. In 1867 the BNA Act specified the limits and scope of provincial versus federal powers. Competition over these powers is such that Canadian history can be interpreted as a struggle by provinces and federalist forces over who has control over what jurisdictions.

Two variations of the contract thesis exist. First, provinces (including Quebec) are equal to each other, but subordinate in status and power compared to the federal government. Conferral of federal priority is justified because of its responsibility for advancing Canada's national interests both at home (comprehensive social programs) and abroad (diplomatic or military initiatives). Second, federalism is defined as a network of relatively autonomous provinces that have freely entered into accord with the federal government. Under the terms of the agreement, Ottawa has assumed those duties and responsibilities that the provinces were unable—or unwilling—to discharge. As a result of this freely agreed-upon division of power, all 11 players are equal in status, with a corresponding division of jurisdiction as outlined by constitutional decree. Demands for greater decentralization with attendant powers and devolved levels of autonomy are consistent with this perspective. Quebec is perceived as equivalent to the other provinces in legal status; nevertheless, some concessions may be allowed for Quebec to pursue its language and culture objectives, even if these should regrettably interfere with fundamental Charter rights (Chodak, 1994).

Canada as a Compact

A second vision interprets Canada as a compact between English-speaking and French-speaking Canadians. This vision is strongly endorsed by the Québecois, who reject definitions of themselves as ethnic minorities or as Canadians who happen to speak French or live in Quebec. Even the notion of Quebec as a province in the conventional sense is dismissed. Canada is not a union of one central authority with ten equal provinces, of which Quebec is but one province, but a compact between the French (Quebec) and English (Ottawa). There is a fundamental dualism in Canada that is rooted in constitutional law and long-standing political agreement. The BNA Act recognized the right of Quebec to promote its distinctive culture and language without undue interference from Ottawa, except in cases involving national concerns. The notion of Canada as a "covenant" between two founding nations dominated political discourses prior to the appearance of Trudeau in 1968. But the dynamics shifted from compact to contract because of Trudeau's commitment to a centralized Canada with its espousal of liberal-pluralistic principles of unity before diversity.

A compact perspective endorses a vision of Quebec as a "nation within" the Canadian state whose self-governing powers are equivalent to those of Ottawa. Quebec entered into Confederation with assurances that it would retain its status as a nation and, as founding people, its entitlement and special citizenship into perpetuity. Quebec does not like to be viewed as just another province with equal rights and privileges. Nor does it want to be treated as an ethnic group with a need for solutions through government intervention or assistance. It is a nation not only deserving of recognition of its differences, but entitled to those powers for securing its distinctiveness against outside intrusion (McRoberts, 1997). Quebeckers are a "people" with a shared language and culture occupying a homeland of last resort. These self-governing powers include the right to establish immigration policies, conduct foreign policy, and initiate bilateral agreements that fall under provincial jurisdiction.

Interpreting French-English relations as a compact casts light on the logic behind Quebec's aspirations, concerns, and political moves. It also points to potential sources of conflict. Quebeckers perceive English-speaking Canadians as politically and economically powerful agents for assimilation whose agenda reflects a commitment to a unitary federal state by centralizing its powers at the expense of other provinces. Moves to strengthen federalism are frequently interpreted as assimilationist in consequence if not in intent. Not surprisingly, Quebec's leaders have sought to secure the gap between Ottawa and Quebec. They have looked for ways to transfer power and resources from Ottawa for fulfillment of Quebec's ambitions. Public support has been galvanized to legitimate their nationalist policies as well as to strengthen Quebec's hand in dealing with Ottawa. Québecois leaders have capitalized on the public's inclination to equate language issues with the status of French–English-speaking relations. Widespread public support for language issues is thus manipulated as leverage for extracting various concessions from the federal government.

Canada as a Three-Nations State

A new and equally provocative vision of Canada is slowly gaining ground. Canada is neither a contract between a centre and the provinces nor an exclusive compact between Ottawa and the French. Recognition of aboriginal peoples as a self-determining people is pushing Canada towards a three-nations state model; that is, it comprises three separate founding nations with overlapping citizenships, each of which possesses rights and jurisdictions within its sphere (Kaplan, 1993; Webber, 1994). To be sure, belated recognition of First Nations as a nation within Canada and a distinct society will complicate an already complex relation that exists between the two charter groups (Whitaker, 1996). Yet the inclusion of additional players may also create intriguing new political alliances whose combined effect may neutralize the possibility of radical actions. The survival of Canada will hinge on our ability to acknowledge and incorporate a plurality of ways of belonging because of these deep diversities (Taylor, 1993).

RETHINKING THE RELATIONSHIP

> "Le Quebec, ma patrie, Le Canada, mon pays" ("Quebec is my homeland, Canada is my country.")
>
> - Lysiane Gagnon, *Globe and Mail*, April 4, 1992).

French–English relations remain as fraught with tension as they were immediately before the 1995 referendum. There has been a lot of talk between the two sides, but little dialogue except between the deaf ("dialogue des sourds"), as both sides continue to talk past each other in a spirit of mounting animosity (McRoberts, 1997; Conlogue, 1997). The unthinkable— Quebec separating from Canada—is now actively entertained in the aftermath of the referendum that nearly brought Canada to the brink. Surveys conducted since the early 1990s point to a similar conclusion: A majority of Quebeckers are attracted to some form of renewal within the present federalist system and fewer appear to be inclined towards any outright separation. The diminishing appeal of separatism appears in most surveys, including a *Globe and Mail*-Léger and Léger poll in January 2000 which indicated 58.6 percent against sovereignty and 41.4 percent for (cited in *Globe and Mail*, Jan. 28, 2000).

A healthy skepticism towards polls and statistics is called for, without automatically dismissing their significance in gauging the mood of Quebec society. Much depends on how the survey questions are phrased, the number of options available, and the political climate at the time of the survey. Nevertheless, three scenarios are possible. First, we are presiding over a turbulent period of intensive social change from which Canada will emerge a strengthened and restructured union. Second, we are currently witnessing the breakup of Canadian society into a "Swiss cheese" federalism of relatively autonomous political entities along the lines of the European common market bloc. Third, it will be business as usual once all the sabre-rattling and politics of brinkmanship subside. We cannot predict which scenario is the most feasible, but the question remains: What then do the Québécois want, and what is being done to address the demands of Quebec's ethnic nationalism? In another context, we could just as easily ask, What do English-speaking Canadians want from Quebec, and what are the Québécois doing to accommodate these demands?

BOX 12.1

Duelling Nationalisms/ Intersectioning Sovereignties

The Cree people are neither cattle nor property, to be transferred from sovereignty to sovereignty or from master to master. We do not seek to prevent the Québecois from achieving their legitimate goals. But we will not permit them to do so on Cree territory and at the expense of our fundamental rights, including our right to self-determination.

(Mathew Coon Come, chief, James Bay Cree Nation, quoted in *This Magazine*, June, 1994.)

"If Quebec can separate, so can the Indians."

Kahn-Tineta Horn, quoted in *Windspeaker,* Nov.6, 1994.

"If there is one thing sacred in Quebec, as in any country, it is territory."

(Lucien Bouchard, Premier of Quebec.)

Ethnic nationalisms threaten the territorial integrity of every society. Central authorities fear the balkanizing effect of ethnic nationalisms, with their capacity to fractionalize the country like pieces of a jigsaw puzzle. From the vantage point of ethnic nationalisms, however, a centralized system that seeks to control by standardizing differences is equally divisive. Quebeckers may be politically divided, but many are unhappy with the current federalist arrangement that treats them as one of ten relatively equal provinces rather than a founding nation. Federalist and nationalist forces may agree on Quebec as a distinct society, with a unique and distinctive assemblage of cultural and linguistic characteristics. Disagreements tend to reflect different means—flexible federalism or secession—for preservation of Quebec as a

French-speaking homeland (Kymlicka, 1998). But Quebec is not alone in pushing for distinct society status. The indigenous occupants of Quebec have also staked a claim for ownership. The seeds of this discontent were planted with the Oka crisis and energetic opposition to Hydro Quebec's megaprojects. Quebeckers were forced to discard folkloric images of the first inhabitants as museum pieces for anthropological study, and confront instead the politics or sovereignty by those claiming to be legitimate owners of the land and resources (Leger, 1994). The furor over Quebec's future has escalated further following the election of the Parti Québécois in 1994, with its promise of a future referendum to determine the relational status of the Québecois. At the core of this debate are the politics of recognition (Salée, 1995). Peoples are increasingly in the vanguard of acknowledgement and respect of their particular identities, together with inclusion of these differences on their own terms rather than those dictated by others (Taylor, 1992). What happens when competing nationalisms come into conflict over who is more sovereign than the other?

Contested Claims

The ten nations that constitute the 60 000-strong First Nations in Quebec (including the Cree, Inuit, Mohawk, Huron, and Algonquin) are adamant that Quebec does not have a legal claim to their lands. They see themselves as sovereign nations, with as much right to remain in Canada as Quebec has a right to secede. According to indigenous leaders, up to 80 percent of Quebec is under aboriginal control: Certain lands have never been ceded while others have yet to be resolved through treaty or aboriginal rights claims. For that reason alone Quebec's aboriginal peoples cannot afford to abandon the financial security of remaining in Canada. The 1996 Cree document, *Sovereign Injustice*, reinforced their refusal to incorporate unwillingly into an independent Quebec, arguing that their fiduciary relationship with the Crown cannot be extinguished or unilaterally transferred from Ottawa to Quebec.

Quebec's aboriginal people are adamant: If Canada can be divided so can Quebec, especially if the original occupants exercise their international right to self-determination to stay in Canada (Grand Council of Crees, 1995). Any unilateral secession would abrogate constitutionally-protected aboriginal and treaty rights; hence any constitutional amendment on Quebec independence is contingent on aboriginal consent. Moreover, the special trustee relationship with the Crown puts the onus on federal government to protect aboriginal interests within the framework of Canada. Or, as Claude-Armand Sheppard, counsel for the Cree put it, just as the federal government has repeatedly indicated it wants to keep Quebeckers in Canada against their will, so too are aboriginal peoples asking that they not be taken out of Canada against their will (cited in Brydon, 1998). Agnes Laporte, counsel for Kitigan Zibi Anishnabeg, captured the politics of the situation when declaring that aboriginal peoples are not simply assets and liabilities that Ottawa and Quebec can negotiate away as part of any divorce settlement, but a people with an inherent right to self-determination over where they belong.

The Quebec government disagrees. Quebec's boundaries are inviolate, as far as the Québecois are concerned, and its territoriality is sovereign and beyond negotiation or dismemberment. Questions about Quebec's territorial integrity are not on the agenda even with recent provincial initiatives to establish a structure of self-government that would send aboriginal representatives to Quebec's legislature, provide taxation powers to aboriginal communities, and entail revenue-sharing schemes in new projects as part of a new partnership (Seguin, 1998). As far as Quebec's leaders are concerned, aboriginal rights to Quebec's land no longer exist; instead they were extinguished when the Canadian state transferred Ungava to provincial jurisdiction at the turn of the century. The James Bay Agreement in 1975 also signed away aboriginal "interests" (although a federal act in 1977 also said that Cree and Inuit would retain the "benefits and rights of all other [Canadian] citizens.") A hardening of Quebec's position is understandable. On the one hand Quebec believes its treatment of aboriginal peoples is second to none, given the government's willingness to recognize aboriginal self-government (within Quebec society), ownership of land and resources, and protection of language and culture (Gourdeau, 1993). On the other hand, Quebec can hardly afford to capitulate to aboriginal peoples (and indirectly to Ottawa) for fear of losing enormous reserves of surface and subsurface resources, both of which are indispensable for any newly independent state in search of economic viability and international acceptability.

These intersecting sovereignties are animated by duelling nationalisms. Aboriginal peoples constitute a form of ethnic (indigenous) nationalism with its focus on peoplehood. As peoples, they have the right to self-determination by virtue of the doctrine of popular sovereignty (sovereignty from the people). By contrast, the federal government prefers to define itself as a civic nationalism in seeking to establish a community of rights-bearing, equality-seeking citizens. Federal ministers such as Stephane Dion like to portray Canada's nationalism as democratic, pluralist, rational, universalist, and progressive in contrast with Quebec's ethnic, exclusivist, anti-democratic nationalism (see David Seljak, letter to the *Globe and Mail*, 8 Oct., 1997). According to federalists, Quebec's nationalism cannot respect diversity and fundamental rights because membership is inherently ethnic and reserved for those whose ancestors are of New France vintage (la pure laine). The "money and ethnics" post-referendum speech by Premier Parizeau that blamed immigrants for the defeat of sovereignist forces simply confirmed what many had suspected: Quebec's ethnic nationalism cannot be trusted to engage constructively with aboriginal peoples or ethnic minorities (McPherson, 1999).

But the distinction between civic nationalism and ethnic nationalism is not so simple. Canada's much-touted civic nationalism is a post-1970s emergence, and contains ethnic dimensions related to the idea of British nationality and Canada as a White dominion (McRoberts, 1997). Moreover, Quebec's nationalism is much more civic-oriented than many give credit (see Seymour et al., 1998). Quebec finds itself in a quandary since its nationalism touches on several dimensions: First, an ethnic dimension reflecting the original White French Québecois who constitute 82 percent of the population; second, a civic dimension that is anchored in the principles of inclusiveness. Most francophones appear committed to the creation of a modern, open, and technologically advanced society, yet must struggle with the demands of balancing modernity with preserving distinctiveness as a French-speaking jurisdiction and a desire to exist collectively as a "people" with a particular historical experience, shared sense of collective grievance, a will to survive, and aspiration toward collective historical destiny (Whitaker, 1996). To the extent this transition from ethnic to civic is proving more awkward than anticipated, it remains to be seen if Quebec can establish a new kind of identity from a synthesis of ethnic and civic ("territorial") nationalism. Inasmuch as the interplay of intersecting nationalisms will profoundly reconfigure the contours of Canadian society in general, and those of Quebec in particular, the society-building project in each of these jurisdictions is far from complete.

The Canadian state is precariously perched between these intersecting sovereignties and duelling nationalisms. It stands to lose because neither of these sovereignties is compatible with national interests. The federalist strategy rests on playing one group off the other in hopes of neutralizing the combined impact. Ottawa sees the Cree as allies and a negotiating chip in bargaining with Quebec, even though the government has, until recently, repudiated any recognition of aboriginal peoples as "peoples" with inherent rights to self-determination. John McGarry, a political scientist from The University of Western Ontario writes: [T]hey will be happy to use the Native position on Quebec as a club with which to beat the separatists, and a convenient tool to minimize the amount of territory they can take from Canada (The *Globe and Mail*, 15 October 1994). Yet Canada may have no choice but to close ranks with Quebec since neither side is anxious to transfer vast tracts of disputed land over to aboriginal ownership and control.

But dangers await whichever course of action federal authorities choose. Siding with the Québecois against aboriginal nationalism could spark a First Nations backlash that could make Oka seem a light-hearted reheasal. Yet playing off one against the other might play into Québecois hands; after all, if the federal government can recognize aboriginal peoples as "peoples" with an inherent right to self-government, why not Quebec?

Nevertheless, there is room for optimism. The perception of Canada as a binational society has proven problematic in the past. Such polarization has complicated the goal of compromise and accommodation, while the potential for conflict becomes more pronounced and more difficult to mediate when policy issues are perceived as a zero-sum game in which one side wins and the other loses. But the addition of another key player enhances the possibility of policy trade-offs; coalition shifts become increasingly less problematic. If several nations share power, David E Schmitt (1997) writes, it becomes possible to make less glaring compromises or to hide losses to each group behind more complex plans. The playing off of one group against another by central authorities may backfire, but demands of any one group can be deflected or resisted. It can also allow each party to be part of a winning coalition on particular issues. In that sense, the assertiveness of Quebec's First Nations may prove the glue that secures Canada's national unity.

What Does Quebec Want?

It is unfair to imply that the Québecois have a uniform set of expectations and aspirations. Reactions to the "Canada problem" are varied; so too are proposed solutions, reflecting to some extent Quebec's own two solitudes: Montreal as a modern, multicultural, federalist, and interconnected community whose residents define themselves primarily by employment and education *and* the pure laine francophones of Quebec's hinterland (Kay, 1999). Responses range from those who prefer only moderate changes to those who wish to radically restructure Quebec's relationship with Canadian society at large, even if outright secession is the only alternative. Responses to the "Quebec question" do not always reflect a perfect consistency; ambiguities often prevail, thus reinforcing the adage that nothing is simple and straightforward in the byzantine twists of Quebec politics. For example, the prospect of cultural security and political determination may be appealing, but the economic disadvantages of severing ties with Canada are sufficiently daunting to dampen sovereignist ambitions. A sizable majority want Quebec to be sovereign, while an overwhelming majority want Quebec to remain in Canada (Gagnon, 1996). In other words, the Québecois want the best of both worlds, or as quipped by Yvon Deschamps, a French Canadian comedian: "They want an independent Quebec inside a united Canada" (*Globe and Mail*, June 18, 1994).

Even terms such as sovereignty or separation are loaded or misleading, with meanings that vary with context and person. The distinction between separation and sovereignty is subtle but valid. Sovereignty is what the Québecois already possess, as far as many Quebeckers are concerned, because of their charter-group status and evolution as a distinct society. Like aboriginal peoples, Quebeckers seem themselves as fundamentally autonomous political communities that are sovereign in their own right yet sharing in the sovereignty of Canada at large. Arrangements are required that advance this recognition of a people with a homeland, cultural distinctiveness, and a collective right to self-determination. Separation, by contrast, is something that perhaps only a small percentage of Québecois are willing to entertain. Thus, sovereignty is not merely a softer version of separation, much less a sign of confusion in the minds of the electorate, but a nuanced reading of the Canadian federal system and Quebec's place in a globalizing and interconnected world. Quebeckers may not want to quit Canada, in other words, but neither do they want to appear weak or vacillating by capitulating to the demands of English-speaking Canadians.

Generally speaking, all Quebeckers are anxious to maintain the French character of their society. They want to create conditions, both political and economic, with which they can protect and preserve the distinctiveness of Quebec as their homeland of last resort in North America. As long as Quebec remains in Canada, it needs the capacity (power, recognition, and space) to protect and promote its threatened status as a minority culture in a wider context of an English-speaking sea (Burgess, 1996). Quebec's nationalism is rooted ultimately in the desire of the Québécois to exist collectively and to have this collective existence normalized at political levels (Balthazar, 1993). But agreement over goals does not always translate into consensus over means (Fournier, 1994).

On one side are the moderates, who generally prefer accommodation within Canada by strengthening Quebec's position within the federalist system, in large part by reinforcing Quebec's presence in Ottawa and expanding Quebec's access to power and resources. A new constitutional division of powers is also anticipated to ensure that each level of government controls what it does best (Johnson, 1995). Moderates prefer a kind of flexible federalism with sovereign control over internal jurisdictions of relevance. They continue to identify first and foremost with Quebec as their homeland, yet endorse affiliation with Canada as their country. The insights of Lysiane Gagnon are useful here: "What is wanted is a larger bed (more space for each partner) maybe even twin beds. But there is definitely a desire to continue sharing the bedroom. This is a marriage not of passion but of reason and convenience—a fine arrangement based on common history, shared interests, and mutual respect (Lysiane Gagnon, *The Globe and Mail*, July 27, 1996).

Radical perspectives entail some degree of separation from Canada. Many independantistes are tired of being labelled a minority group that English-speaking Canadians define as a costly problem people. They prefer a space that Quebeckers can call their own, where they are the majority and they call the shots. Quebeckers want to be in the "big leagues"—a state within a state—not just an administrative subunit of a political system of which Quebec is a province and Quebec people a mere minority (Bouthillier, 1999). Or, as put by Louise Beaudoin of the Parti Québécois, "I want to be a majority in my own country" (Editorial, *Globe and Mail*, March 1, 1995). The high risk of being permanently outmaneuvered (tyranny of the majority) is sufficient to justify a fundamental shift of power from the state to the people. The transfer of power and jurisdiction is as critical as it is radical, and was recognized a generation ago by a Canadian national-unity commission when it claimed: "Quebec is distinctive and should, within a viable Canada, have the powers necessary to protect and develop its distinctive character. Any political solution short of this would lead to the rupture of Canada" (Task Force on National Unity (Pepin-Roberts Report), 1977–79).

Separatists believe that Quebec is poised to make a move: It has a broad industrial base, a healthy government financial structure, shared language and culture, and autonomous sources of revenue. Only procedural questions remain: Can Quebec secede only with public opinion and international law on its side or must it abide by constitutional law and provincial consent? Secessionist moves come in different packages, from outright separation to sovereignty association, but most proposals entail some degree of political independence (including control over culture and language), without loss of close economic ties such as free trade and common currency (J. Laxer, 1994). To be sure, sovereignty will come with economic and social costs, but ethnicities everywhere have shown a willingness to make sacrifices for heroic ideals, and Quebeckers appear ready to engage in such a trade-off as part of a sacred duty (Olive, 1996). Sovereignty will not solve all of Quebec's problems, concedes Jacques Parizeau (1996), but it will "normalize" the situation by sharpening the lines of jurisdiction.

What does international law have to say in sorting out the validity of these contested claims? Under international law, colonial peoples (those who live in a defined territory but under a foreign power) have the right to secede. This right to independence and self-determination does not apply to either Quebec or the Cree because secession under international law applies only to "salt-water" (overseas) colonies. Since both international law and the United Nations are constructed around the inviolability of sovereign states, there is no enthusiasm for compromising state interests by extending sovereign rights of secession to internal cultural minorities. The obligation to respect minority rights but not to the extent of secession is clearly outlined in this passage from a UN declaration:

> States shall protect the existence of the national or ethnic, cultural, religious, and linguistic identity of minorities within their respective territories and shall encourage conditions for the promotion of that identity... Persons belonging to national or ethnic, religious, and linguistic minorities... have the right to enjoy their own culture, to profess and practise their own religion and to use their own language, in private and in public, freely and without interference or any form of discrimination...States shall take measures where required to ensure that persons belonging to minorities [are able] to express their characteristics...except where specific practices are in violation of national law and contrary to international standards...Nothing in the present Declaration may be construed as permitting any activity contrary to the purposes and principles of the United Nations, including sovereign equality, territorial integrity and political independence of states.
>
> UN Declaration on the Rights of Persons Belonging to National or Ethnic, Religious and Linguistic Minorities.

In other words, a "people" have the right to self-determination and autonomy. But they do not have the right to secession except under exceptional circumstances, and even then only through negotiation and compromise.

Living Together with Differences

The picture at present is transitional. Forging a workable accommodation between Ottawa and Quebec is unlikely without a major rethinking of Canadian society. Perhaps its too late: In response to a *Time* interview question regarding what Canada could offer to shelve the idea of a referendum and sovereignty, Bouchard responded, "I don't see anything. We're beyond that now." (March 17, 1997). Others believe that it is possible to explore creative solutions for living together with differences without resorting to outright secession or status quo federalism. And the current debate appears to have shifted toward the federalists. According to a 1998 Supreme Court ruling, Quebec does not have a right to unilaterally secede from Canada; however, if Quebec's voters "clearly" vote to go the independence route, federal authorities are obliged to negotiate the separation in good faith. Time will tell if framing French-English relations around what constitutes a clear question and clear majority is likely to prolong the national unity crisis rather than solve the problem.

The fundamental question is whether two communities with such divergent interests can share a common cultural space (Salee, 1995; Salee and Coleman, 1997). Flag-waving or finger-pointing may not solve what increasingly is perceived as a structural problem rather than a simple case of mutual pigheadedness. Unless the social, political, and cultural context is taken into account, there is not much hope of isolating the problem for analysis, let alone in working towards a solution. The Quebec question appears inseparable from structures in Canadian federalism. Put simply, just as the idea of provinces may be antiquated and irrelevant (Diamond, 1997), so too is a federal system based on a parliamentary process designed for an agricultural, unitary state (Gillies, 1997). Continued recourse to a nineteenth-century political framework for solving contemporary problems may be misguided or counterproductive in a 21st century world of freewheeling economies, global realignment, and national retrenchment. Engin Isan of York University writes of the need to reconsider the Quebec question within the rapidly changing and shifting identities in the new world order:

> [P]olitical boundaries no longer represent the social and economic realities facing Canadian provinces today. Loyalties of Canadian citizens and their sense of belonging are divided along other lines than the nineteenth century territorial boundaries represented by the provinces. There are many other territorial identities and regions that are articulated into the different spheres of the global economy, rendering provincial loyalties and identities increasingly not only banal but counterproductive (1996, 6).

Yet there is room for guarded optimism. The principles of federalism continue to unite an increasingly fractious Canada; namely, the acceptance of difference without ignoring shared values and an acknowledgement that survival and prosperity are attainable through cooperation (Saverimuthu,1999). Canada's federal system is remarkably flexible in its capacity to endlessly tinker with the balance of power between Ottawa and the provinces. By promoting government both responsible and responsive rather than massive and remote central government, federalism encourages the kind of flexibility that is foundational to and constitutive of democracy. De facto (informal) arrangements have been worked out that recognize the distinctiveness and relative autonomy of certain provinces. Quebec, for example, has its own pension plan, its own system of private law, levies its own income tax, and exercises a degree of control over immigration that is unprecedented in any federal system (McRoberts, 1996). As well, according to Stephane Dion, the intergovernmental affairs minister and the key constitutional adviser to the federal Liberal government, Quebec resembles a quasi-state in control of the powers for setting provincial priorities and controlling jurisdictions (Steward, 1994). With or without constitutional guarantees, Quebec is acting as if it were a distinct society by exercising powers of a relatively sovereign nation. Ad hoc arrangements, in other words, do not appear to be the problem. The stumbling block resides in moves to legally recognize Quebec's distinct-society status. As Charles Taylor (1993) notes, English-speaking Canadians may be willing to accept negotiated and pragmatic arrangements. Yet they may balk at the idea of formalizing those concessions at odds with conventional views of Canada (as a social contract) that violate certain values related to formal equality (the principle of equal provinces), and create imbalances within Canada's federal system because of preferential treatment. There may be an additional barrier: Explicitly formalizing Quebec–Canada relations may complicate the society-building process in the same way that three decades of addressing the national unity problem has had the effect of keeping the problem in existence. Perhaps it is time to rethink the problem as not a problem to be solved, according to David Cameron, political scientist at the University of Toronto, but a "tension to be accommodated, an arrangement to be lived with, and a practical situation which is not perfect, but tolerable" (cited in Gwyn, 1998 A-8).

IMMIGRATION AND OFFICIAL MULTICULTURALISM

FRAMING THE PROBLEM

Multiculturalism has established itself as a major framework for society-building and national unity. It is widely regarded as a uniquely Canadian way for engaging with diversity as different yet equal (Fleras, 1998). As a political strategy of ethnic inclusion and a focus for national identity, Canada's multiculturalism is built on the premise that the integration of all Canadians is possible without assimilation (Harles, 1998). Its inception as official government policy in 1971 has resulted in widespread international praise as an enlightened tool for the harmonious management of race and ethnic relations in an increasingly diverse and changing society (Berry and Kalin, 1995). In embracing a paradox that still is shaping Canada's future, recourse to multiculturalism furnishes Canadians with a practical alternative to the assimilationist policies of the past. It also empowers minorities to pursue the dual goals of ethnicity and equality without abandoning a commitment to society-building in Canada (Esses and Gardner, 1996).

Public reaction to Canada's official multiculturalism is extremely varied, ranging from acceptance to rejection, with indifference or ambivalence in between (Abu-Laban and Stasiulis, 1992; Berry and Kalin, 1993; Vasta and Castles, 1996). Much of this variation can be attributed to differences in terms of (a) what people think official multiculturalism ought to do or not do; (b) what people think multiculturalism does; (c) what multiculturalism was and is intended to do; (d) what multiculturalism actually does; and (e) what it should do in light of political realities. Confusion also stems from failure to distinguish between different dimensions of multiculturalism, including multiculturalism as: (1) demography; (2) ideology; (3) official policy;

(4) practice; and (5) resistance (Fleras, 1997). Thus, in response to the question, "Is Canada a multicultural society?," answers will vary depending on the level of meaning that is employed. In general, most Canadians would agree that multiculturalism is a defining feature of Canadian society. Yet multiculturalism is perceived to be as much a problem as a solution to the challenge of national unity and society-building. Can a society be built around a principle of living together with our differences—even if these differences are radical and incompatible wih widely accepted social norms? Or does the promotion of diversity undermine the centre, to the detriment of the whole? Is it possible to build a society around the recognition of difference as a basis for entitlement? Or is it a recipe for disaster to single out and reward people on the basis of ethnicity and membership in a particular cultural group?

For some, the problem with multiculturalism is in encouraging too much diversity at the expense of national unity. Public resentment of multiculturalism escalates when diversity is seen to be divisive and disruptive. For others, multiculturalism is a problem because it promotes too much unity at the expense of diversity and equality. As a hegemonic strategy of control and containment, multiculturalism undermines diversity by depoliticizing differences into a celebration or a commodity. For still others, however, multiculturalism provides a solution to many of the problems associated with ethnic diversity in a democratic society. The protective canopy of multiculturalism alleviates some of the inequities confronting minorities, in the process defusing the threat of society-destroying inter-ethnic strife. For yet still others, it is uncertain whether multiculturalism constitutes a problem or a solution. They prefer instead to acknowledge its ambiguous status as a two-edged sword that can contain and control or enhance and empower, depending on criteria, circumstances, and outcomes. On the one hand, multiculturalism can be conceived as social glue for bonding together Canadians in a way that is workable, necessary, and fair (Fleras, 1994); on the other hand, it can be viewed as a pair of scissors for shearing apart the social fabric of Canadian society (Bissoondath, 1994).

Such a cacophony of opinions is not altogether surprising (see Li, 2000). The politics of diversity complicate the very process of Canadian society-building at a time of change and uncertainty. Endorsement of multiculturalism has proven a boon to some, a detriment to others, and a source of confusion to still others. Such an assessment provides two insights into the construction of social problems. First, debate over the pros and cons of multiculturalism reveals how contemporary social problems are "contested sites." Competing groups with different priorities and unequal resources struggle to gain control of the agenda in hopes of defining the problem and solutions. Second, the definition of a social problem does not remain constant. Social problems change over time, with corresponding pressure to revise definitions and solutions to take into account emergent realities and oppositional tensions. There is a second variation on this theme. Solutions to social problems often trigger unanticipated consequences. Solving one problem may uncover additional but previously unmentioned grievances; alternatively, solutions may upset certain groups who previously were content with the status quo. Focusing on this dimension reinforces an awareness that the distinction between problem and solution is only an interpretation apart. It also accentuates the need to determine precisely what official multiculturalism is intended to do, and why, and whether it can be judged to have been successful in solving the problem of national unity, and on what grounds the judgment can be made. Inasmuch as official multiculturalism originated to address the national unity problems associated with immigration and diversity, the chapter will begin with a brief overview of "who are Canadians," and "how did we become this way"? The linking of immigration with multiculturalism is deliberately pursued: ~~Immigration provides the rationale for multiculturalism; multicultural-ism, in turn, secures a receptive social climate for migrant adaptation.~~

ETHNIC DIVERSITY

Canada embraces a diverse collection of immigrants and refugees from different parts of the world. The first of many movements was inaugurated by East Asian populations across the Bering Strait as far back as 50 000 years ago. Both French and English traders/adventur-ers/explorers constituted the second wave of immigrants. These colonizers eventually dis-placed the aboriginal populations and unilaterally assumed official status as the founding ("charter") members of Canada. The third wave consisted of various non-English and non-French-speaking immigrants who arrived en masse during the twentieth century as part of Canada's society-building commitments. In recent years, the magnitude and nature of im-migration has undergone yet another significant shift, thus profoundly altering Canada's demographic profile, while establishing a new set of dynamics and demands for living to-gether with differences.

Canada's demographic composition has turned on its head since inception of the BNA (Constitution) Act of 1867. Only 8% of Canada's population was not of British or French ancestry at the time of Confederation (Palmer, 1975). Between 1896 and 1914, the bal-ance began to shift when up to 3 million immigrants—many of them from Central and Eastern Europe—arrived to domesticate the west. Immigration increased substantially prior to and just after World War I, reaching a peak of over 400 000 in 1913. Another wave of Eastern European immigrants during the 1920s brought the non-British, non-French proportion up to 18%. The post-Second World War period resulted in yet another influx of refugees and immigrants from the war-torn European theatre. Sources of immi-gration since the 1980s have also shifted toward so-called non-conventional countries such as Asia, the Caribbean, and South and Central America. In 1997, 58.11 percent of immi-grants arrived from Asia and the Pacific, another 7.84 percent from Africa and the Middle East, while 33 percent of refugees came from Africa and the Middle East, and 31 percent from Asia and the Pacific. This infusion of immigrants of colour has rekindled contro-versy over the direction of Canada's immigration policies and programs. It has also fostered considerable debate regarding the role of foreign-born multicultural minorities in forging the demographic basis of Canadian identity and unity.

Of Canada's total population of approximately 30 million, about 50 percent report hav-ing some non-British or non-French ancestry, including 11.2 percent who in the 1996 cen-sus were identified as visible minorities. (The term "visible minority" refers to an official government category of native- and foreign-born, non-White, non-Caucasoid individuals, in-cluding Blacks, Chinese, Japanese, Koreans, Filipinos, Indo-Pakistanis, West Asians and Arabs, Southeast Asians, Latin Americans, and Pacific Islanders. This administrative cate-gory does not always square with popular perceptions of what constitutes visibility (Worthy, 1996). A breakdown of those reporting non-British and non-French ethnic origins reveals in-teresting patterns. Total responses from 1990's surveys indicated that those of German background rank highest (with 2 793 780), followed by Italians (1 147 775), Ukrainians (1 054 295) and aboriginal peoples (1 002 675). With the exception of Quebec and Ontario, where Italian-Canadians are more numerous, those of German descent are the most fre-quently reported ethnic origin in the other provinces. Of the 3.2 million visible minorities in Canada, those of Chinese origins are the most populous visible minority, with a total of

860 000 persons, or 26.9 percent of the visible minority population, followed by South Asian with 671 000, or 21.0 percent, and Black with 574 000, or 17.9 percent.

Canada is home to approximately five million foreign-born Canadians. The proportion of immigrants relative to the population at large (17%) has remained relatively stable since 1951, despite ebbs and flows in immigration totals. Regional and municipal variations in ethnic composition are noticeable. Ontario has the largest number of persons with non-British, non-French origins with over five million. This is followed by British Columbia and Alberta with just over two million each, and Quebec with just over one million. The Atlantic provinces have relatively small totals. The distribution of visible minorities continues to be uneven: In the early 1990s, 52.6 percent of all visible minorities lived in Ontario, 20.7 percent in BC, 13.6 percent in Quebec, and only 2.3 percent in Saskatchewan and the Atlantic provinces combined. By 1996, visible minorities constituted 17.9 percent of British Columbia's population, 15.8 percent of Ontario's population, and 10.1 percent of Alberta's population, but only 1.1 percent of the population in New Brunswick and PEI, and 0.7 percent in Newfoundland. Multicultural minorities continue to reside in large urban regions. Both absolute numbers and relative percentages make Montreal, Toronto, and Vancouver more diverse than provincial or national averages. In 1996, according to Statistics Canada, 85 percent of all immigrants, including 93 percent who arrived between 1991 and 1996, lived in census metropolitan areas. Toronto, Vancouver, and Montreal accounted for about three-quarters of all arrivals. These three metropolitan regions are also important centres for visible minorities: The percentage of Toronto's visible minority population by Census Metropolitan Area in 1996 stands at 31.6 percent (from only 1 percent in 1971), Vancouver's at 31.1, and Calgary at 15.6 percent. Compare this with the total percentages in Trois Rivieres at 0.9 percent and Chicoutami-Jonquiere at 0.4 percent. The vast majority of visible minorities reside in major urban centres for reasons related to opportunity, sociability, and transition. That concentration, in turn, proves irresistible as a magnet for the next wave of immigrants and refugees. Arguably, then, Canada can be best described as a moderately heterogeneous society, with relatively concentrated pockets of urban multicultural diversity interspersed with vast stretches of ethnically monochromatic hinterland.

IMMIGRATION POLICIES AND PROGRAMS

Canada is one of the few countries in the world that regard themselves as an immigration country (Ucarer, 1997). United States and Australia are two notable immigration countries, so too are Brazil and Argentina, several Latin American countries, and most recently, New Zealand. Three characteristics distinguish immigration countries from non-immigration countries. First, policies exist that attempt to regulate the flow of immigrants into the country. Second, programs are put into place to assist in the assimilation or integration of migrants. This absorption not only includes social and material adjustment; immigrants also receive all civil and political rights associated with citizenship in that country. Third, immigration is viewed as a key part of society-building. Immigrants are expected to assist in the social, economic, and cultural development by taking up jobs, filling in underpopulated areas, contributing to population growth, and making international linkages. Compare this with non-immigration countries such as Germany, given their commitment to policies that stabilize inflows, limit long-term stays, discourage permanent residences, label immigrants as guest workers, and withhold citizenship and attendant rights (Ucarer, 1997). Those of German parentage are automatically granted citizenship because of kinship ("bloodlines"); by contrast, foreigners and their children are generally excluded from citizenship even if born and raised in the country. Very simply, immigration in non-immigration societies does not fit into the long-term plans related to national identity or society-building.

Canada is frequently praised—or pilloried—as a country of immigrants. As one of a small handful of immigration countries in the world, immigration has played a pivotal role in Canada's national development, and will continue to do so in the foreseeable future. The increasingly unfettered movements of ideas, labour, and investment across cultural borders will see to that. With the exception of aboriginal peoples, all Canadians are immigrants or descendents of immigrants. On the whole, Canada has become a more vibrant and dynamic society because of immigrants. Immigrants have contributed to Canada's cultural diversity and economic prosperity without destroying its social fabric in the process. Canadians, for the most part, have embraced immigration with the kind of civility that is becoming a trademark of Canadian society (Siddiqui, 1998). Yet there is an undercurrent of concern or confusion over the social implications associated with a proactive immigration commitment (Avery, 1995). Canada remains a "reluctant host" whose ambivalence—even hostility—toward certain foreign-born is palpable beneath a veneer of tolerance. Migration into Canada is increasingly seen by some as a threat to internal security or scarce resources. Immigrants are viewed by others as an economic threat because of unfair competition. Not surprisingly, many immigrants encounter unacceptable levels of prejudice and discrimination in the process of settling into Canada.

Immigration has emerged as a pivotal dynamic at the end of the millenium (Thompson and Weinfeld, 1995). In capitalizing on their determination and drive, their family connections, global links, and financial support of community institutions, immigrants are reclaiming abandoned industries, derelict neighbourhoods, and declining services, and bringing hope to blighted areas of Canada (see also Millman, 1997). But the importance of immigration to society goes beyond the question of demography or economy. Patterns of immigration have irrevocably altered the very concept of Canada as a British colonial outpost and transformed it into a rich, English-speaking mosaic of different cultures and languages (Dyer, 1998). In the space of a generation, immigration has revolutionized the social face of urban Canada more quickly than an aging population or high aboriginal birthrates, with potentially profound implications for long-standing French-English relations (see Passaris, 1998). Immigrants continue to fuel the spark for rethinking and rebuilding Canada. As a former Minister of Immigration and Citizenship once commented when observing the relationship between society and immigration: "Immigration is fundamentally about nation-building—about deciding who we are as Canadians and who we want to become....we need a clear and practical vision of the kind of nation we want to build." (Sergio Marchi, Annual Report, p.iii 1994). The role of immigration in the re-envisioning of Canada is reflected in the kind of questions that invariably are raised by immigration, including:

- What does it mean to be a Canadian?

- What kind of country is envisaged for the future?

- What is Canada's perception of itself in relationship to the world at large?

- What core values must be protected, and which values are open for negotiation?

- How do immigrants contribute to or detract from a preferred vision of Canada?

- How many immigrants (if any at all), where from, which type, and what for?

Answers to these questions require careful deliberation beyond the realm of political slogan or public posturing. They involve debates over the future of society and the relationship of immigrants to particular visions of what is or should be. Disagreements over the degree of openness or restrictiveness often lead to provocations or partitions, thus necessitating a broader understanding of immigration in terms of policies, patterns, and practices.

Immigration Program: "Who Gets In?"

Immigrants to Canada have long experienced exclusion because of race (Avery, 2000). Preference for British and northern European immigrants ensured a hostile reception for those deemed to be unassimilable or who were perceived as threats to Canada. It was not until the 1960s that immigrants were accepted on the basis of skills rather than race or national origins. Passage of the 1976 Immigration Act consolidated the range of admissable immigrants. It also articulated the entry conditions for admission into Canada. Three possible avenues of acceptance exist: family, independent, and refugee.

(1) Family reunification class

This class recognizes the need for families to stay together, if only to stabilize the process of integration into Canada. Immediate members of the family, namely a spouse and dependent children under 19, are automatically allowed into Canada provided they are of good health and without a criminal record. Until recently, parents and grandparents were also included; a separate entry stream is currently under consideration. More distant relatives must "top-up" with points from the independent class to secure entry into Canada. Currently, the family reunification category accounts for about 30 percent of all immigration to Canada, a figure that has slowly declined in recent years.

(2) Independents

The independent class includes skilled workers and business (both entrepreneurs and investors). Skilled workers are assessed under a point system that emphasizes their suitability on the grounds of job-related skills, age, official language knowledge, and education, as well as a personal assessment by an immigration officer. The number of points required for entry varies: Business class (both investor and entrepreneur) requires only 25; self-employed and skilled workers need 70, although they are automatically entitled to a large bonus because of their talents. Assisted relatives also receive credit as nominated immigrants, but require additional points elsewhere to qualify for entry. To enter, skilled workers must pass the usual health and security clearances.

A subcategory of the independent class entails a transfer of funds as the price of entry into Canada. The business, or entrepreneurial, program selects immigrants with an ability to establish businesses that will generate employment opportunities for Canadians. Under the investment program, applicants must meet the usual immigration criteria and have a demonstrated net worth of $500 000. In exchange for investing between $350 000 and $450 000 in a Canadian fund for five years, a business applicant receives landed immigrant status (a permanent resident visa). This program has been used by about 14 000 immigrants since its inception in 1986, with a total investment of $3.75 billion and creation of 33 000 jobs, according to the Immigration Minister Lucienne Robillard (cited in the *Globe and Mail*, 22 March,

1997). But the program has also been plagued by abuse and mismanagement. Plans are in place to transfer more responsibility to the provinces for the monitoring of investment funds.

(3) Refugees

The refugee category is the third and perhaps most controversial of immigrant streams into Canada. Refugees are accepted as part of Canada's humanitarian and legal obligations to the world community. Canada has performed admirably by comparison with countries that perfunctorily deny basic human rights or deport refugees as part of a general crackdown. Since World War II, Canada has officially admitted over half a million refugees, with recent annual intakes in the 20 000-35 000 range. Canada's apparent generosity and support of international refugee programs has been amply documented, especially with receipt of the Nansen Medal in 1986—the first country ever to be bestowed such an honour by the United Nations.

Two categories of refugees are recognized, neither of which require points for entry. One category includes sponsored refugees. Sponsored refugees are pre-selected abroad by government officials, others by private agencies, individuals, clubs, or church groups, with private sponsors obligated to provide support for up to ten years. Both government and privately sponsored refugees receive landed immigrant status before arriving in Canada and assistance through government programs once they arrive (Jackson, 1991). A second category of refugees consists of refugee claimants who arrive unannounced by foot, boat, or plane, often without documentation such as passports, and claim refugee status upon arrival to Canada. Refugee claimants did not become an issue until 1982 when the numbers doubled from 558 to 1162, and again in 1991 when the numbers rose from 8328 to 29 092. Refugee claimants have outnumbered sponsored refugees in each year of the 1990s decade.

By world standards, Canada's refugee determination process is generous and regarded as one of the world's best by the U.N. Commission on Refugees, despite criticism from refugee lawyers and advocacy groups who believe the system is too tough on refugees (Simpson, 1997; Mawani, 1997). Others tend to think the system is too lax, including William Bauer and Daniel Stoffman, who point out that Canada accepts refugees claimants at six times the international norm and even approves claims from citizens of democratic societies such as Israel, the United Kingdom, and the United States. Of the 95 500 refugees who made claims to the IRB between 1993 and 1997, according to the auditor-general, 42 percent were accepted, 33 percent were rejected, and 25 percent were not finalized or declared ineligible. There are currently in excess of 29 000 claims waiting to be heard. Of the 31 200 claims rejected between 1993 and 1997, only 22 percent have confirmed their departure from the country.

Problem or Solution: Costs and Benefits of Immigration

All indicators suggest a continuation of Canada as a favourite destination for those fleeing political oppression, ethnic conflicts, demographic pressure, and economic stagnation. Immigrants and refugees are not only "pushed" from their homeland, but also "pulled" to Canada because of opportunity and freedom. Invariably this raises the question of whether immigration provides a benefit or extracts a cost. Canadians, in turn, have reacted to immigrants and immigration in different ways, ranging from enthusiasm and endorsement on one hand, to resentment on the other, with a combination of indifference, resignation, or indecision in between. A step back from the fray can help to keep things in perspective. Nevertheless, there is still much that is unknown about the impact of immigration. There is even less consensus about the benefits of immigration (Isbister, 1996). Such uncertainty raises the question of what kind of country we value, and how immigrants contribute to or detract from this vision.

Benefits

Increased immigration into Canada has been justified or vilified on various grounds. Canada is a land of immigrants whose prosperity and identity are dependent on the perpetual movement of people (Avery, 2000). Studies in other parts of the world, such as Australia, New Zealand, and the United States confirm the notion that, on balance, immigrants are a net contributor to society, demographically, socially, culturally, and economically (Isbister, 1996; Millman, 1997; Smith, 1997; Castles et al., 1998; Spoonley and Fleras, 1999). The same conclusions exist for Canada. These outcomes, however, are not distributed equally, with some provinces such as B.C. receiving a disproportionate slice of benefits because of more affluent immigrants (Matas, 1994).

Many tout the economic perks of immigration (Cohen,1997; but see Stoffman, 1998). Immigrants enhance Canada's ability to compete in the global economy, Gwynne Dyer likes to remind us, because Canada itself is a global society by virtue of its multicultural character, both domestically and globally. Immigrants create more jobs than they take; as consumers they provide markets for Canadian goods; they are more likely to start businesses than other Canadians; are better qualified in terms of education; and pay more in taxes than they receive in social services. Immigrants not only ease labour shortages during phases of capitalist expansion, but also find employment in jobs that other Canadians dislike. Immigrants tend to possess drive and vitality, with boundless energy and optimism, and a willingness to take entrepreneurial risks by capitalizing on international links to improve Canada's competitive position in a global economy. After all, a global economy requires a continuous two-way flow of skilled workers and capital for investment. In general, then, rather than hurting an economy, immigrants are apt to provide a much-needed kick start.

Social benefits can also be discerned. Immigrants are more likely to be married than the Canadian-born, and less likely to divorce, with rates below those of the Canadian-born. Most immigrants do not soak up welfare rolls or commit a disproportionate amount of crime. On the contrary, with the possible exception of one or two groups, they are less likely to end up in the criminal justice system or engage in criminal activity, despite the reports of irresponsible media. The demographics of Canada also work in favour of increased immigration. An aging population pyramid with declining birthrate totals (1.7 children per family, which is below the replacement rate of 2.1; and a growth rate of 2.3) puts the onus on younger immigrants for future support of social programs. Immigrants are also more likely to integrate into Canadian society by applying for citizenship.

Costs

Canadians as a whole possess ambivalent attitudes toward the presence of immigrants and refugees. Many people are supportive of immigrants and refugees as hardworking and positive contributors to society. But others dislike what they see as threats to Canada's economy and cultural identity. Immigrants are deeply resented and fiercely resisted as "scroungers" who steal jobs, housing, and education; who undermine moralities and foster crime; and who swamp access to increasingly scarce services (see Cohen, 1997). Others deplore immigrants for making unreasonable demands on Canadian society, when it should be Canadians who call the shots. Consider this statement by Ted Byfield in a July 18, 1996 issue of the *Financial Post* reminding immigrants that: (a) Canada possesses a distinctive culture; (b) this culture is superior and should supersede immigrant cultures; (c) immigrants may retain aspects of their culture that are compatible with Canada's and do not drain public monies; (d) immigrants know their place in society and prove themselves by starting at the bottom and working their way up; (e) immigrants are "guests" in this country, and they should fit into Canada rather than the other way around; (f) immigration should be shaped by national needs rather than by immigrant wants or ethnic lobby groups pressure; and (g) Canada should be able to cut back on immigration when it chooses to do so.

These ideas may or may not reflect concerns of many Canadians. Nevertheless, polls confirm that many believe there is too much immigration of the wrong kind from the wrong place. Canadians as a rule may accept the necessity or inevitability of immigrants and refugees, but bristle at legislative loopholes and unscrupulous stakeholders, especially when even dysfunctional government policies are resistant to change because of a small number of vocal clients ("clientele capture") with a vested interested in preserving the status quo (Stoffman, 1994). Some criticize what they see as excessively generous concessions to immigrants at a time of relentless cutbacks in services and benefits. The government should be looking after "our own," it is argued, rather than throwing money at refugee determination processes and immigrant resettlement programs (Sudol,1998). Others take exception to the integration costs of immigrants (for instance, the costs for language training which in the 1997/98 fiscal year amounted to $387.1 million dollars at the federal, provincial, and local levels (Galt, 1998). Still others are concerned about the "problems" that immigrants bring with them to Canada. These include allegations that immigrants are using their ties abroad to establish illegal international distribution systems for contraband drugs, loan sharking, prostitution, and smuggling of illegal aliens into Canada, while victimizing those already in Canada through extortion rackets (Madely, 1994). The growing fear of undermining the WASPish character of Canadian society through unrestricted entry is palpable as well. Finally, there is a perception of immigrants as a source of cheap labour. Immigrants provide a steady supply of customers for immigrant lawyers. They serve the intellectual convictions of those who believe virtually everyone outside Canada can qualify as a refugee. A powerful ethnic voting block may also explain why politicians are fearful of tampering with the status quo, despite a growing chorus of concerns over policy and practice.

Neither Good Nor Bad

Joel Millman (1997) provides a useful insight. He argues that no person, no matter how opposed to immigration in principle or practice, is without some sympathy for the plight of the world's poorest. Similarly, even the most enthusiastic booster is not without some concern over the negative impact of immigration on some sector of society. Somewhere between those who endorse and those who vilify immigration are those who are unsure of what stand to take. They acknowledge certain costs associated with immigration, and it is these costs that tend to make people ambivalent about aspects of immigration. Some Canadians, such as unskilled workers, may be penalized by immigration; others, such as real estate agents or immigration lawyers, may prosper; the vast majority of Canadians may be only marginally affected (Stoffman, 1998). Business may flourish, but taxpayers may be forced to foot the bill with respect to social costs and escalating pressure on existing services (Smith, 1997). The changing ethnic

mix is endorsed as enriching the Canadian landscape; yet fears mount over the potential for social friction or diminution of core Canadian values (see also Isbister, 1996). Costs are inevitable: A country cannot expect to have a policy of immigration-driven, sustained economic
growth without some social and economic repercussions. With an intake of approximately
200 000 new Canadians each year (but only 174 000 in each of 1998 and 1999), many with radically different lifestyles and outlooks, a degree of friction and annoyance is inevitable, given
the inevitability of crowding, pressure on existing services, inflated markets, and congested roads.
Cultural clashes are inescapable, but most controversies tend to involve modest demands or the
accommodation of outwardly superficial symbols such as the ever-contentious turban issue,
rather than any fundamental shift in power or resources. A sense of proportion is badly needed:
If Canadians value the cultural and economic benefits associated with immigration, they must
be prepared to make adjustments for these differences.

Criticism and dialogue are important. To be sure, opposition to immigration that is articulated solely on the basis of skin colour or national origins is racist. But people should be
able to express informed opinion on immigration and to criticize policies and practices that
are inconsistent with their vision of society. Concern over immigration because of Canada's
absorptive capacities or competition over scarce resources is legitimate, does not necessarily reflect bigotry or racism, and does not automatically trivialize the benefits of immigration. Critics acknowledge the partial validity of arguments, both for and against, and that
answers to questions about immigration are never right or wrong, but both right and wrong,
depending on the context. Few solutions to immigration questions are of an either-or variety, but rather a both/and. Inflated claims on both sides of the debate often conceal whatever
truths they contain. As well, people intuitively recognize that constructive answers with
operationalizable goals and realistic procedures are subject to never-ending debate. A balance is often required, with national interests on the one side and the needs of those in
search of opportunity or freedom on the other. And, with official multiculturalism, a potential balance is proposed that has managed to anger or excite Canadians.

OFFICIAL MULTICULTURALISM:
PROBLEM-SOLVING OR PROBLEM-MAKING?

Pluralistic societies confront a paradox in grappling with the question of how to make society
safe "for" diversity, yet safe "from" diversity (see Schlesinger Jr., 1992). A social and political framework must be established that can engage with differences as different yet equal,
but without eroding a commitment to national unity and social coherence in the process.
White settler dominions such as Australia and Canada have endorsed multicultural principles as a framework for accommodating immigrant minorities (Pearson, 1996; Vasta and
Castles, 1996). Yet staunch support for multiculturalism has not congealed into any consensus
over definition, attributes, or applications (Goldberg, 1994). Contradictions compound the
definitional process: On the one hand, multiculturalism may encourage the very thing ("ethnicity") that it sets out to control or discourage; on the other, it ends up controlling ("diversity") that which it purports to encourage. Multiculturalism simultaneously evokes a
preference for consensus, but does so alongside a platform of criticism and reform; of hegemony yet resistance; of conformity yet diversity; of control yet emancipation; of exclusion
yet participation; of compliance yet creativity (see Vasta, 1996). Both championed yet maligned, idealized as well as demonized, the term has absorbed a broad range of often conflicting social articulations that resist integration (Caws, 1994). In short, multiculturalism can

mean whatever meaning is assigned to it depending on context or criteria (see Pearson, 1995). Such flexibility can be helpful at times: It may also foster needless misunderstanding as people grope about for common ground to communicate.

The centrality of multiculturalism to contemporary discourses has yielded such an array of meanings that many despair of any clarity or consensus. Broadly speaking, however, multiculturalism can be defined as a process of engaging with diversity as different yet equal. More specifically, multiculturalism consists of an official doctrine, along with a corresponding set of policies and practices, for advancing the mutually related but analytically separate goals of cultural differences, social equality, societal integration, and national unity (Wilson, 1995). With multiculturalism, a framework is established for the full and equal participation of minority women and men through removal of discriminatory institutional barriers (both cultural and structural). Endorsement of social equality and cultural space confirms a minority right to be different yet the same ("equal"), depending on the circumstances. Under multiculturalism, a social and political climate is fostered in which diversity initiatives can be introduced without inciting a backlash or social turmoil. Inasmuch as multiculturalism engages with diversity by challenging society to move over and make space, its contribution to society-building is widely acknowledged. Insofar as the promotion of diversity without a unifying vision can prove disruptive, a commitment to multiculturalism poses a challenge to national unity.

To say that Canada is officially multicultural is stating the obvious: Official multiculturalism originated in 1971 as an all-party government policy; its status was secured with the constitutional entrenchment of multiculturalism in the Charter of Rights and Freedoms in 1982; and Canada become officially multicultural when the 1988 Multiculturalism Act was passed, making Canada the only officially multicultural country in the world then and now. As a political program to achieve political goals in a politically acceptable manner (Peter, 1978), multiculturalism originated around the quest for integrative society-building functions; it continues to persist for precisely the same reasons, namely, the "containment" of ethnicity by modifying the rules of engagement and entitlement in a modern democratic society. Only the means for managing diversity have evolved in response to demographic upheavals and political developments, with cultural solutions giving way to structural reforms and, more recently, the promotion of shared citizenship (Annual Report, 1997). An initial focus on "celebrating differences" as a means of eradicating prejudice and securing acceptance was superseded by an emphasis on "accommodating diversity" through institutional adjustment and removal of discriminatory barriers. The ground has again shifted in recent years to concerns about citizenship and belonging. For the sake of simplicity these shifts can be partitioned into three stages, including folkloric, equity, and civic multiculturalism—keeping in mind that overlap between these stages is the rule rather than exception. Table 13–1 compares and contrasts the different stages in the evolution of Canada's multiculturalism policies.

Multiculturalism in Canada is primarily a political program for pursuit of national interests. In shifting from colonialism to multiculturalism as a basis for a new moral order, official multiculturalism in Canada is a form of state legitimacy rather than a vehicle of broader emancipation (see also Goodman, 1997). It is more concerned with society-building functions of consensus and containment than with protecting social and cultural rights (see also Vasta, 1993). This political discourse in defence of dominant ideology endorses those policies and initiatives that often have the effect of subordinating minority needs to the greater good of society. The next insight compares multiculturalisms in Canada and the United States, and in the process reveals the true nature of Canada's "monocultural" multiculturalism.

TABLE 13-1	Multiculturalism in Policies		
	Folkloric Multiculturalism (1970s)	**Institutional Multiculturalism (1980s)**	**Civic Multiculturalism (1990s)**
Focus	Celebrating Differences	Managing Diversity	Engaging Diversity
Reference Point	Culture	Structure	Society
Mandate	Ethnicity	Race Relations	Citizenship
Magnitude	Individual Adjustment	Institutional Accommodation	Participation
Problem Source	Prejudice	Systemic Discrimination	Exclusion
Problem Solution	Cultural Sensitivity	Employment Equity	Inclusiveness
Key Metaphor	"Mosaic"	"Level playing field"	"Belonging"

PUTTING MULTICULTURALISM TO THE NATIONAL UNITY TEST

Criticisms abound about multiculturalism as a problem rather than a solution (Bibby, 1990; Bissoondath, 1994; Thobani, 1995). Of particular note is an assertion that official multiculturalism is a policy of containment rather than change that does little either to challenge the cultural hegemony of the dominant sector or to remove systemic discriminatory barriers (Fleras, 1997; Henry and Tator, 2000). For the sake of analysis, adverse reactions can be classified into four categories (Fleras and Elliott, 1991): (1) multiculturalism as "divisive," since it undermines Canadian society; (2) multiculturalism as "regressive," since it defuses minority aspirations and needs; (3) multiculturalism as "ornamental," since it manipulates symbols to foster the illusion rather than substance of change; and (4) multiculturalism as "irrelevant," since cultural solutions are inappropriate for structural problems. Each of these criticisms will be put to the critical test to determine its validity as problem or solution. In this way multiculturalism will be revealed for what it is: an imperfect but potentially progressive social experiment for engaging with diversity without challenging national unity or disrupting society-building in the process (Abu-Laban and Stasiulis, 1992; Fleras, 1994).

Is Multiculturalism Divisive?

Multiculturalism is widely denounced as an irritant to the goals of national unity and identity. The promotion of multiculturalism runs the risk of "balkanizing" Canada by fomenting conflict between ethnic groups. Construction of a national identity is next to impossible, according to these critics, when minorities are encouraged to pursue ethnic "tribalisms" at the expense of their duties as citizens (Bissoondath, 1994). Gina Mallet (1997, D2) captures this sense of doom when she writes:

> Although the drive to honour diversity through official multiculturalism was originally undertaken in order to promote tolerance, it is accomplishing the opposite. By setting Canadians against one another and emphasizing our differences rather than the many things we have in common, diversity has, in fact, gone too far.

A close analysis of these arguments suggests an alternative view. Multiculturalism originated and continues to exist as a pragmatic instrument for cementing Canadians into a "dis-

BOX 13.1 Duelling Multiculturalism Discourses

Multicultural principles and practices continue to animate the politics of society-building in Canada and the United States, albeit in fundamentally different ways. Canada may claim to be a multicultural mosaic, but its multiculturalism is geared toward integrating ethnic Canadians into the mainstream. The *e pluribus unum* of the United States seems conducive to conjuring up the melting pot, but an "insurgent"" multiculturalism has precipitated cultural wars involving identity politics and ethnic identities that threaten to undermine any coherent national vision (Simpson, 1998). References to Canada's official multiculturalism embrace a commitment to consensus by way of "conformity" and "accommodation." Multiculturalism in Canada is essentially a society-building exercise that seeks to depoliticize differences through institutional accommodation. Official multiculturalism seeks to transcend racial and ethnic differences by regulating their co-existence as part of a national mosaic, in which the English and French sectors provide the grout for keeping the tiles in place. A multiculturalism of this nature is grounded in the liberal-pluralist credo that what we have in common as rights-bearing, equality-seeking individuals is more important than what divides through placement in an exclusive ethnic heritage. Compare this with American multiculturalism, in which group differences and identity claims are politicized by challenging the prevailing distribution of cultural power for making cultural space (Goldberg, 1994). Attainment of these multicultural goals is varied, spanning the spectrum from promoting proactive measures to fostering tolerance toward diversity, reducing prejudice, removing discriminatory barriers, eliminating cultural ethnocentrism, enhancing equitable access to services, expanding institutional engagement, and improving intergroup encounters.

By contrast, the thrust of popular multiculturalism in the United States is critical in contesting the organization and control of cultural space. Admittedly, many are baffled by the emergence of any multiculturalism in a society whose ideological moorings had anchored a melting pot mentality. The recency of the transformation is staggering: A Nexis data base of major newspapers as recently as 1988 yielded no references to multiculturalism; by 1994, 1500 entries had appeared (Glazer, 1997). Expansion of multiculturalism has been applauded for reasserting people's control over their lives, detested as political correctness gone mad, deplored for "fetishizing" diversity at the expense of national vision and collective goals, and dismissed as a humanizing ideal that is somewhat prone to excessive zeal and "political correctness" (see Higham, 1993). But multicultural discourses have challenged the venerable *e pluribus unum.* (from many, one) principle that individuals are endlessly variable, yet fundamentally alike. Advocated instead is the distinctly "Unamerican" axiom that personal patterns of engagement and entitlement should reflect disadvantage or birthright rather than merit, identity rather than conformity, and diversity rather than universality (McLaren, 1994). Of course, not all multicultural discourses in the United States are cut from a critical cloth. Under a "happy face" multiculturalism, a universalist centre is promulgated that ostensibly celebrates diversity while simultaneously scaling it back for purposes of control or containment (Eisenstein, 1996; Hesse, 1997). Such a liberal-pluralism may pay lip-service to multiculturalism, but any commitment to diversity is devoid of critical content, historical context, or patterns of power (Giroux, 1994). Under a critical multiculturalism, a discourse of resistance is endorsed that challenges the authority and legitimacy of White supremacy by contesting the racism, sexism, and patriarchy embedded in American society (Giroux, 1994). In seeking respect and equality for all cultures, multiculturalism can be pictured as a social movement based on the denial of Western cultural superiority and celebration of the other. Differences do not merely exist under critical multiculturalism, they exist as part of the struggle to create a new public culture. Inasmuch as multicultural interests are openly contesting the power to shape the production and reproduction of knowledge in institutions from education to media, critical multiculturalism is challenging the conventional underpinnings that once secured national unity.

Canada's society-building multiculturalism differs from its American society-dismantling counterpart at several points of discourse (Canadian multiculturalism is featured first in each set of contrasts). One multiculturalism is directed at transforming the mainstream without straining the social fabric, the other multiculturalisms are concerned with empowering minorities by eroding the monocultural firmament of society. One is officially political, yet seeks to depoliticize diversity for society-building purposes; the other falls outside the policy domain, but politicizes differences as a catalyst for minority empowerment and entitlement. One is rooted in the modernist quest for unity, certainty, and universality; the other in embracing a postmodernist zeal for differences, provisionality, and fragmentation. Of particular note is how the Canada's official multiculturalism transforms cultural differences into a discourse about social inequality; critical multiculturalism reformulates social inequalities into a discursive framework about cultural differences and public culture. One is based on the outward-looking public goals of unity and consensus, the other on the inward-looking needs of victims for self-esteem, recognition, compensation, and role models. In other words, a "playful" inversion is called for in juxtaposing duelling discourses: Rather than making *society* safe from diversity, or safe for diversity, as is the case in a multicultural Canada, the underlying logic of critical multiculturalism is to make *diversity* safe from society as well as safe for society.

tinct society." Multiculturalism is not concerned with the promotion of diversity per se, as demonstrated in a careful reading of the Multiculturalism Act of 1988 (or of Trudeau's multiculturalism speech in 1971). It is even less concerned with the promotion of minority cultures. Rather, the goals of multiculturalism are firmly fixed in building a united society in which diversity is depoliticized and incorporated as an integral and legitimate component of society without undermining either the interconnectedness of the whole or distinctiveness of the parts in the process (Fleras and Elliott, 1996). In rejecting the promotion of self-sufficient ethnic groups with separate institutions and parallel power bases, multiculturalism emphasizes the right of individuals to identify and affiliate with the ethno-cultural tradition of their choice. Nor does multiculturalism encourage an "anything goes" mentality. Tolerance of diversity is accepted only to the extent that its practice does not violate the laws of the land, interfere with the rights of others, or discredit fundamental political and economic institutions. Put bluntly, every Canadian has the right to be different, but each of us must be different in the same kind of way, in effect neutralizing any potentially disruptive tendencies (Eisenstein, 1996). In other words, multiculturalism is not about creating a society along ethnic lines, but of establishing Canada as one big happy family by integrating (not assimilating) minorities into society through removal of individual prejudices and discriminatory institutional barriers.

Of course, there is always an element of risk associated with any policy that promotes a pluralistic framework for living together with our differences. At times, minorities may be singled out because of special needs; yet this preferential treatment is not intended to encourage social conflict, but to achieve positive social goals. Even the notion of multiculturalism as "celebrating differences" is directed towards intercultural sharing as a means of demolishing barriers. Similarly, the conferral of hyphenated citizenship (for example, Lithuanian-Canadian) should not be feared as divisive. A hyphenated identity can be interpreted as two strands of a single Canadian citizenship. The primary strand involves a commitment to core Canadian values and institutions, while the secondary strand allows an optional identification with the cultural values and symbols of a person's choice. In short, multiculturalism serves as the society-building buffer that makes Canada safe "for," but also safe "from," ethnicity (Moynihan, 1993).

What about Canadian identity? Does multiculturalism foster a "visionless coexistence" through the mindless promotion of endless diversity, as lamented by Reginald Bibby in his text *Mosaic Madness*? Perhaps this is sometimes so in practice, but an adherence to multiculturalism does not necessarily detract from a coherent Canadian identity. On the contrary, multiculturalism enhances a perception of Canadians as a community of communities that is held together by the one thing they share in common: their differences. In fact, one could argue that a commitment to multiculturalism (within a bilingual framework) is one of the definitive characteristics that distinguishes Canadians from Americans. Rather than undermining a sense of Canadianness, in other words, multiculturalism encourages a shared identity by furnishing a set of myths or symbols for binding Canadians into a moral community (Jamieson, 1993). The fact that immigrants continue to become naturalized citizens at greater rates than those in Britain or the United States (neither of which are officially multicultural) would imply a positive role for multiculturalism in forging Canadian unity and identity (Ungerleider, 1997).

In summary, it is not multiculturalism that divides Canadian society and excludes certain groups from full participation in it. More accurately, it is the imposition of "monoculturalism" that is the problem, given its potential to exclude or deny those who fall outside its preferred orbit (Mitchell-Powell, 1992). Under official multiculturalism, the expression of ethnicity is encouraged, but only to the extent that it reinforces core cultural values at the heart of Canada's society-building project. Nor is multiculturalism divisive in the same sense as the cultural politics of Quebec or First Nations. Most voluntary migrants are not anxious to dismantle Canada; rather they have a vested interest in strengthening the country of their choice. The divisiveness within multiculturalism—where it does exist—arises from its manipulation by some opportunistic politicians and minority leaders who have sabotaged pluralist principles for ulterior motives.

Is Multiculturalism Regressive?

Multiculturalism has been discredited by some critics as a regressive tool that distracts minorities from access to the corridors of power and resources. By promising much but delivering little, multiculturalism has the effect of marginalizing minority women and men into ethnic ghettos that preclude full and equal participation in society (Bissoondath, 1994). And this exclusion may foster an underclass of minorities who perceive themselves as having no stake in the system, with corresponding impact for society at large (James, 1999).

Racial and ethnic minorities are not uniformly marginalized in Canadian society. Certain ethnic groups earn more income than "mainstream" Canadians, while foreign-born Canadians often outperform native-born Canadians in areas such as education (Agocs and Boyd, 1993; Pendakur and Pendakur, 1995). Other Canadians, such as African-Canadians and aboriginal peoples, of course, are less fortunate, but their exclusion and exploitation long predated the appearance of official multiculturalism. Second, the explicit intent of multiculturalism is the removal of discriminatory barriers to equality. Since 1971, multicultural policies have sought to dismantle the cultural fences that block ethnic involvement in Canadian society. The current anti-racist thrust of contemporary multiculturalism focuses on structural rather than cultural blockages to minority participation. Consequently, programs and initiatives for righting past wrongs have been directed towards removing institutional barriers and expanding opportunity structures.

It should be obvious, then, that multicultural objectives are concerned with integrating minorities into society (Kymlicka, 1999). The concept of institutional inclusiveness looms heavily in this platform. In the past, immigrants and minorities were expected to fit into the existing institutional framework as part of the adjustment process. At present, however, institutions also are expected to move over and make space (Annual Report, 1997). Reforms are focused on rooting out systemic biases related to recruitment, hiring, promotion, and training. Admittedly, there is no conclusive proof of dramatic shifts in minority socio-economic status because of multiculturalism. The strength of this policy resides instead with the creation of a society that fosters acceptance of diversity as normal, necessary, and valuable (McLeod, 1987). Its strength reflects the creation of a supportive social climate in which proactive measures for managing diversity can be implemented without public backlash. Finally, multiculturalism equips minorities with an official platform through which they can articulate their grievances and hold the government accountable for actions at odds with multicultural principles.

Is Multiculturalism Ornamental?

Manoly Lupul (1983) once remarked that multiculturalism is not taken seriously by anyone who is a somebody. There is some element of truth in this observation (Jaworski, 1979). Multiculturalism comes across as little more than a frivolous political diversion whose currency is symbolic rather than substantial. Here the critics get it right—albeit for the wrong reason. There is no question that multiculturalism embraces a restricted, often symbolic endorsement of diversity. Yet multiculturalism is not interested in preserving the substance of ethnic lifestyles. The entrenchment of relatively autonomous minority groups—complete with parallel institutions and separate power bases—would pose a threat to national sovereignty. Instead, multiculturalism endorses a commitment to ethnicity that is symbolic and situational, rather than political. In this way, minorities are entitled to identify and affiliate themselves with the cultural tradition of their choice without incurring a social penalty or revoking a commitment to society at large.

Even dismissing the symbolic value of multiculturalism may be premature. Symbols have the power to move mountains, and the symbol of Canada as a fair and tolerant society secures multiculturalism with the moral authority to challenge and demand. By relativizing the powerful while contesting the taken for granted, multiculturalism has exposed the constructed character (rather than the normalcy) of the dominant culture, in effect advancing shared understandings of the politics of diversity in a changing and uncertain world (Eller, 1997). The symbolic value of multiculturalism also extends to the creation of a social climate in which diversity can flourish without penalizing its proponents. Besides, many Canadians prefer the limited responsibilities of a symbolic ethnicity over the rigours of full-time ethnicity. Critics may scold multiculturalism for focusing on the symbols of diversity rather than its substance, in other words, but their criticism simply chides multiculturalism for something beyond its mandate within the framework of a liberal-pluralism.

Is Multiculturalism Irrelevant?

The final criticism of multiculturalism is perhaps the most difficult to refute. It has often been denounced as impractical or irrelevant in a society organized around the principles of profit, private property, competitive individualism, and insatiable consumerism. There is some doubt whether cultural solutions can be applied to structural problems such as systemic discrimination (Agocs and Boyd, 1993; Satzewich, 1993). Can a policy directed at reforming society possibly address root problems, or is it yet another case of applying a bandage to a gaping wound?

There are two ways of countering this criticism. First, multiculturalism was never intended to do what international communism proved incapable of accomplishing, that is, to bring capitalism to its knees. Multiculturalism was devised to work within the existing system by softening its harshest blows for its marginalized members. A morally authoritative framework was established in which minority inequality could be addressed, debated, challenged, and transformed by holding governments accountable for actions inconsistent with multicultural ideals (Vasta and Castles, 1996). Second, it could be argued that multiculturalism "lends its weight to the social transformation of capitalism" by establishing the primacy of "equality rights" over "inequality wrongs" (Fleras, 1994). The reinvention of multiculturalism from a focus on culture to structure indicates a willingness to apply a human face to capitalism. And, as the globalization of capitalist market economies continues to expand, multiculturalism provides the mindset to confront the challenge of a shifting and increasingly borderless life that is likely to be our lot in the twenty-first century (see also Woodley, 1997).

Doing What Is Workable, Necessary, and Fair

There is little doubt that multiculturalism originated as a political program to achieve political goals in a politically astute way (Peter, 1978). Yet by now multiculturalism has assumed a life of its own beyond that specifically promoted by the state. It has evolved in directions never envisaged by its originators: A framework is currently in place that legitimates the normalcy of diversity at cultural and institutional levels without reneging on the right to full and equal participation. What originated as a policy for "European ethnics" has secured a Canada that is relatively comfortable with the presence of new Canadians from all parts of the world.

Has it been worth it? On balance, yes. Multiculturalism has resulted in the establishment of a policy and a corresponding set of initiatives for advancing minority interests that strikes many as consistent with Canada's liberal-democratic framework. That may not sound like a lot to those with unrealistically high expectations, but the contributions of multiculturalism should not be diminished by unfair comparison with utopian standards. A sense of proportion and perspective is required: Just as multiculturalism cannot be blamed for everything that is wrong in Canada, so too should we avoid excessive praise. The nature of its impact and implications prevails somewhere between the poles of unblemished good and absolute evil. Multiculturalism is neither the root of all Canada's social problems, nor the all-encompassing solution to problems that rightfully belong to political or economic domains. It is but one component—however imperfect—for engaging ethnic diversity, while at the same time seeking to balance the competing demands of individuals, minority groups, national unity, and society-building.

Multiculturalism remains the policy of choice for a changing and diverse Canada. As philosophy, policy, or practice, it symbolizes an innovative if imperfect social experiment for engaging diversity without compromising our collective self-image as a free, open, and tolerant country. Multiculturalism has done much to recontour the social landscape of Canada from an Anglocentric outpost to its current status as one of the world's most diverse societies. Multiculturalism has also bolstered Canada's much ballyhooed status as a trailblazer in the enlightened management of race and ethnic relations (Kurthen, 1997). Under the circumstances, it is not a question of whether Canada can afford multiculturalism. More to the point, Canada cannot afford *not* to embrace multiculturalism in its society-building search for political unity, social coherence, economic prosperity, and cultural enrichment.

GLOBALIZATION AND CANADA

FRAMING THE PROBLEM

The world is full of contradictions, conflict, and change. Whether we approve or disapprove, broad historical forces are establishing innovative scenarios for the new millennium. Not only are the ground rules changing, but so too is the game itself, as players and strategies reposition themselves in response to new challenges. Issues that engulf the world at present resonate with ambiguity and tension at a time when orthodoxies are reversed so rapidly that new expectations cannot take shape before being swept aside (Kanter, 1995). Past privileges and earlier priorities have been revoked or reformulated in a way scarcely imaginable even a generation ago. What once were seen as vices are now accepted as virtues, and vice versa. Such a cacophony of contradictions is as disruptive as it is opportunistic, even as many concede that significant change without conflict is a contradiction in terms. Governments and economies are reeling before the onslaught of forces seemingly beyond control or comprehension, says Alvin Toffler, as the third wave of global transformation trisects the world into agrarian, smokestack, and knowledge-based economies, all of which may collude, coexist, or collide. People, too, are becoming increasingly edgy over (a) the pace of change that renders obsolesence in its wake; (b) economic policies designed for profit rather than people; (c) politicians that no longer inspire confidence in systems that seem hopelessly archaic; and (d) fragmentation of society and loss of community because of market discipline (Aitken, 1997).

The global sources of this dismay and disarray are clearly before us. People around the world exhaled a collective sigh of relief with the Cold War thaw. Many assumed the collapse of superpower hegemony would usher in prosperity and peace among nation-states. The "end of history" thesis, as it came to be identified, predicted the worldwide triumph of liberal democracy by virtue of the free market economy, thus eliminating human conflict while securing salvation through consumerism (Fukuyama, 1989). But the euphoria turned out to be short-lived. A decade after the dismantling of the Berlin Wall and demise of the Soviet Union, the much-anticipated, brave new world remains mired in the throes of depression and despair. Western society may have taken refuge in the notion of human beings as fundamentally social and only lacking in opportunity to put this goodness into practice (Peters, 1999). But as the brutalities in Kosovo and Rwanda depressingly demonstrate, the world is witnessing a dreary and demoralizing round of random violence so stunning in its savagery and amorality as to question the very "nature" of human nature (Ignatieff, 1993). Parts of the world continue to be engulfed by lawlessness and to be shattered by dystopia of such unprecedented cruelty in the atavistic struggle for depleted resources that perhaps Thomas Hobbes was right: Human life is nasty, brutish, and short (Kaplan, 2000). Images of both emaciated refugees cowering in makeshift camps without hope, or mangled corpses of mass executions and ethnic cleansings have become so commonplace as to lose all shock value. Compounding the physical barbarism is a structural violence that underpins a worldwide system of segregation ("global apartheid") for enriching the affluent few at the expense of the impoverished masses (Richmond, 1994; Haviland, 1999). What passes for global civility is the collapsing of the world into an ideologically homogeneous market where the slogan, "greed is good" is the prevailing mantra, justifying even the most callous of cost-cutting measures. The global drive for growth is laying waste to the planet, since the earth cannot possibly sustain a consumer-driven lifestyle without major changes (Suzuki, 1999). Growing inequities between the "haves" and the "have-nots" have also escalated in spite of trade liberalization and developmental assistance (Vidal, 1996). Any hopes for progress in the poorer developing countries are being derailed by population explosions, urbanization, poverty, environmental degradation, and the revival of ethnic rivalries in the teeth of global monoculturalism (Jackson, 1992). Each of these problems has the potential to terminate planetary existence if left unchecked (Kaplan, 1994).

Equally provocative are global disruptions to the economy. Just as the Industrial Revolution signified a radical break with its feudal predecessors, so too has an information-driven, post-industrialism established a fundamentally different way of generating and distributing wealth. The new economic order is not simply a reorganization of widgets around a computer economy. A revolutionary shift in ways of "doing business" is now taking place, in effect offering an opportunity for some, marginalization for others, and confusion for still others (Daniels and Lever, 1996). In such an intensely competitive environment, both world currency markets and transnational corporations have revealed a knack for shunning countries that dare to maintain protective trade barriers or subvert investment opportunities through taxation, labour and environmental laws, or costly social programs (Laxer, 1996). In reminding audiences that business knows no national boundaries, Jane Fraser and Jeremy Oppenheim write in a 1997 issue of *The McKinsey Quarterly*:

> We are on the brink of a major, long term transformation of the world economy from a series of local industries locked in closed national economies to a system of integrated global markets contested by global players. (cited in Davies, 1999).

With the internalization of investment capital and the relatively free movement of goods and financial services across increasingly porous borders, the economy is becoming truly global, perhaps for the first time since the free-trading era prior to World War One. The new economy reflects a readjustment in how wealth is created: from smokestack industries to information processing; from a state-regulated national economy to a market-driven export trade; and from Fordist production to productive loops. Of particular note is the worldwide penetration of free market principles into previously undisturbed corners of the world. In the relentless quest for profits and expansion, globalization goes beyond the imposition of economic systems. Imposed as well is the replacement of cultural diversity and ecologically sensitive practices with a single set of values and relations that extol commercialism, consumerism, and a culture of disenchantment (Hahnel, 1999). In bearing out Marx's prescient observation of the 1850s that capitalism transcends spatial barriers because of its remorseless pursuit of worldwide markets (Scholte, 1997), the triumph of global capitalism has culminated in an integrated global system that differentially incorporates societies into a vast productive loop as cost-effective "links." Yet a global economy that transcends national borders is strewn with perils and pitfalls. The game board has no boundaries, the rules are always changing, the number of players is increasingly exponentially, occasionally the financial tap will dry up and move away, and every so often the playing field begins to tilt and gyrate wildly out of control (Davies, 1999). Such a scenario does not bode well for a functioning world order.

Canada is no more immune than other countries to the clash of contradictory trends. The crises that confront Canada can only be comprehended against a backdrop of a disruptive transformation created by the imposition of free market (laissez-faire) ideologies on world economies, political systems, social institutions, and local cultures. Canada's economic prosperity once rested on a commodity-based export sector, alongside a heavily protected domestic manufacturing industry and an extensive social welfare system (see Robinson, 1996). But major structural shifts in the global economy have exerted pressure for a fundamental reordering of the economy, dismantling of protectionist frameworks such as import-substitution industrial strategy, the deregulation of economic life, and calls for new international competitiveness. For better or worse, Canada is increasingly enmeshed in a globalizing world of free trade agreements, exposed to the harsh realities of a competitive marketplace, and rendered vulnerable to outside forces for its very livelihood. Incorporation of Canada into a transnationally driven, global marketplace is conditional on stripping the national economy of any unnecessary barriers at odds with export trade and investment. Governments are increasingly compelled to measure their success by introducing cost-cutting measures, structural adjustments, and inflation-dampening initiatives (Rizvi, 1996). As a trading nation with export trade accounting for 40 percent of its wealth, the prospect of freer trade in goods and investment is of potential advantage; nevertheless, each arrangement and accord runs the risk of imperilling Canada's culture and sovereignty (Ford, 1996). With 80 percent of its exports to the U.S.A., concern is mounting over how Canada will cope in the eventual meltdown of the superheated American economy (Nankivell, 1999). The conundrum confronting Canada is typical of many countries. Two challenges prevail: First, how to derive benefit from a freewheeling global economy without abdicating a commitment to community, justice, and equality (Barlow and Clark, 1996; Goar, 1997). Second, how to transform a resource-based economy into an aggressive global competitor without dissolving either its social conscience or the integrity of the constituent units that shape its distinctiveness.

This chapter examines the social dimensions of globalism by exploring its complex and contradictory relationship to society at large, Canada in particular. By focusing on the long-term social implications of global capitalism, the politics of globalization are defined as a potential social problem, given that any system devoted primarily to the pursuit of profit is potentially harmful to ordinary people, the environment, the social fabric, cultural values, or national sovereignty. Equally problematic is a business agenda that assigns priority to the rights of capitalists (from investors to private interests) over those of the public good as the appropriate framework for society-building (McQuaig, 1999). Moreover, despite signs of prosperity and surface civility, many Canadians are still learning to cope with the disorientations associated with rapid change, technological advancement, and the dynamics of globalism, particularly in those areas that (a) reveal how fragile society is; (b) expose the relentless trivialization of life and human values; and (c) yield a gnawing awareness of the growing irrelevance of core national values related to equality, justice, and community. On the assumption that globalization is proving a challenge in shaping Canada's destiny, for better or for worse, the nature of the global economy must be understood in formulating viable alternatives that balance profit with people, environment with economy, and consensus with chaos. However analyzed or assessed, the issue of globalization needs to be problematized, since there is nothing natural or inevitable about globalization despite efforts of vested interests to make it seem so. A movement toward free markets and away from state intervention as a basis for entitlement or wealth creation is not a natural process, but rather a political project by those who make self-serving choices by way of policy or programs in contexts that are not always of their making. In going beyond the notion of evaluating globalization as right or wrong, good or bad, the focus is typically constructionist, involving conditions that are defined as problematic because of their impact and implications for society. Problematizing globalization revolves around key questions, including: What is meant by globalization? What is its magnitude and scope? Is globalization working and for whom? To what extent does it imperil national unity and identity? What are its implications for prosperity and sovereignty? At the core of all debates is the question of whether Canada can be made safe for globalization, yet safe *from* globalization within the evolving context of free trade, transnational dominance, and ascendancy of markets over governments as the primary catalyst for wealth creation and distribution.

GLOBALIZATION: GLOBAL CAPITALISM IN ACTION

Modern industry has established the world market . . . All old-established national industries . . . are dislodged by new industries whose . . . products are consumed, not only at home, but in every quarter of the globe. In place of the old wants . . . we find new wants, requiring for their satisfaction the products of distant lands and climes.

- Karl Marx and Frederick Engels, The Communist Manifesto, 1848

The term globalization is one of those curious turns of phrase with a fathomless capacity to infuriate, confuse, or enlighten. As an inexact term for a wild assortment of activities and processes, globalization is often hailed as the defining historical moment of our times, despite suffering from overuse and lack of definitional clarity (Scholte, 1997). This ugly 13-letter word has become the mantra of business, politics, and culture, thanks to its potential to transform structures while influencing outcomes (Editorial, *Economist*, 29th Dec., 1998). Its existence may be used as an alibi by politicians who prefer to cite a force beyond their control to justify unpleasant policy options such as cuts in social spending. Its virtue as the single most influential international trend is widely touted: Globalization encourages governments to make foreign trade policies as effective and results-oriented as possible; offers real advantages to those economies and societies that are genuinely open to innovation; rewards flexibility and openness in institutions and government; encourages growth and development to pay for health care improvements, education, and housing; and fosters economic interdependence with positive flow on effects for wider security and strategic relationships (Downer, 1998). Globalization is thought to foster democratic political change, since corrupt and authoritarian regimes cannot cope with demands for transparency and cooperative competitiveness, without adjustments to their human rights record (Kristoff, 1998).

But there is an underside to globalization that rankles and provokes. Few find globalization exceptional or objectionable if employed to describe the process of international trade and investment that links many countries in an open-world trading system of exchange and transaction (Hirst, 1998). Difficulties arise when globalization is used prescriptively to explain, justify, encourage, and expand inequities: Globalization is generating gaping inequities as regions and states compete for corporate investment, in the process lowering wages, eroding environmental standards, and compromising human rights protections (Mander, 1996). Far from being global, moreover, the world economy is dominated by the elites of three major blocks of power and wealth: Europe, Japan, and the United States, in addition to a limited number of small, successful countries or specific regions (Hirst, 1997). Even the vast sums that are traded daily on the financial markets do little to enhance national economic performance, since these repeated dealings are largely divorced from trade or production. Nevertheless, their potential for creating national chaos or international crisis is legendary. Indeed, the global economy may be interpreted as a financial casino in which speculative investment has supplanted productive investment as the engine of global economy. Rather than buying shares in a company for enhancing production, hedge-fund speculators now invest in mutual funds where they can gamble on price fluctuations or the values of currencies. Currency speculators bet billions of dollars that they can overwhelm a country's central bank by dumping their investments and mutual funds when currencies begin to tumble, profiting from the resulting currency devaluation (Norman, 1998). In the process of trolling the bottom for dollars and profits, speculators and gamblers can make or break national economies and hold politicians hostage to their interests by moving vast sums of money around the world with a click of the mouse, thus sending exchange rates and stock markets into wild gyrations unrelated to any underlying economic reality (Clarke, 1999). Even corporate mergers do not result in productive gains. Only stock prices rise, providing corporations with more cash to buy up competitors.

In short, globalism is animated by contradictory forces with the potential to simultaneously create or destroy. Concentrations of political power and economic wealth are being contested by the decentralizing forces of a microchip information technology (Standing Senate Committee on Social Affairs, cited in the *Toronto Star*, July 8th, 1999). Support for the market is pervasive, reflected in booming trade and growth rates; yet state spending as a share of the GNP continues to escalate (Gray, 1997). Globalization is capable of being a problem or opportunity, depending on the criteria employed. It encapsulates the potential of bringing people closer together or driving a wedge between them, and it is this two-edged character that generates much of the concern and controversy over global capitalism. On one side is its capacity for bringing about universal harmony through a single global economy; on the other is a fear of anarchic global forces and the shrinking of a natural resources base that propels vested interests into more dangerous rivalries (Gray, 1997). A globalization that erodes national sovereignty to the detriment of self-determination may be lamented by some; others take comfort that globalization is exposing human rights violations while taming the lawlessness that hides behind the cloak of national sovereignty

(Editorial,1998). Are the impact and implications of globalization for Canada no less ambivalent? asks the Standing Senate Committee on Social Affairs. What force will hold Canadian society together in a context shaped by the interplay of intense global competition and expansion of a freewheeling digital technology against a backdrop of growing gaps between rich and poor and a government whose commitment to include the excluded is being eroded? The very forces that may strengthen Canadian identity may also simultaneously advance prosperity even as globalization erodes Canada's sovereignty, thus reinforcing a dialectical truth: The same forces that unite and advance may also divide and deter (Reid, 1998). The fact that potential drawbacks coexist with apparent benefits seems typical of social problems in general.

Hype notwithstanding, there is nothing especially new about globalization as a powerful force that is erasing national borders while integrating the world in an unprecedented web of trade and investments (Kristof, 1999). Consider the *Communist Manifesto* (1848) with its references to "constant revolutionizing of production," "endless disturbances of all social conditions," "constantly expanding market," "daily destruction of old established industries," "new wants," "universal interdependence of nations," and "intercourse in every direction" (cited in Joffe, 1999). Marx knew what he was talking about: Modern international trading systems had evolved by the mid-nineteenth century to enmesh wide swaths of the world into an interconnected commercial civilization, with several major powers having high trade to gross domestic product ratios. By 1913, for example, the ratio in France was 35.4 percent, in Germany, 35.1 percent, and in the UK, 44.7 percent, ratios that were not surpassed until the mid-1990s (Hirst and Thompson, 1996).

In short, what distinguishes globalization is not the importance of international trade in a borderless world which only now is approaching pre-1914 levels. What is new in this post-protectionist world is the striking speed, scope, and intensity of this transformation, thanks to the gravity-defying, leapfrogging ease of computer-driven communications (Kristoff,1999). In shrinking time, space, and borders by linking people more deeply and immediately than before, the economy is truly global insofar as it operates as one big domestic market, with the result that trade is competitive and international rather than complementary and compartmentalized (eg., Sudbury nickel for New Zealand sheep) (Friedman,1999). Also new about globalization is the manner in which these components are ideologically organized into a global framework that unabashedly extols the following virtues: unregulated free market dynamics, free trade as a catalyst for growth, elimination of import substitution economies that foster economic self-sufficiency, privatization of public enterprises, and an aggressive consumerism (Mander, 1996). As a result, the market is replacing governments as powerful forms of governance, in effect blurring a distinction between private and public sectors because of government compliance with the corporate sectors. The tight coupling of global capitalism with all aspects of social life is also a distinctive feature of globalization. Whereas economic arrangements were once removed from government, free market views are less restrained than in the past. The result? All citizens, institutions, and values must live within an ideological framework in which the quality of something is defined according to price rather than the intrinsic qualities it may have (Corson, 1999). Finally, globalization is new insofar as relationships are organized around and conducted through linkages that somehow go beyond national boundaries and render them irrelevant, rather than simply cross them to exchange goods or services. With globalization, in short, the whole is not only greater than the sum of its parts, but the whole is the site in which parts derive their meaning and value from a global capitalist system.

Conceptualizing Globalization

Public reaction to globalization tends to be varied, welcomed by some and lamented by others, and eliciting bewilderment in still others. Its effects may be interpreted as a problem, as an opportunity, and as both a problem and opportunity, depending on context and consequences. The worldwide reorganization of markets has dismantled trade barriers, but it has also meant "rationalizing" domestic markets in the scramble for global advantage; eroding the integrity of distinct local cultures; and challenging the legitimacy of nation-states as the sole source of political organization (Tepperman and Blain, 1999). Trade liberalization has been a bonus to some nation-states, but disruptive for those whose goods and services incur a "value-added tax" because of higher environmental, social, and labour costs. A more competitive money market has increased the availability of BMWs, yet the pressure for profit amplification has dampened employment prospects for those without the resources or resourcefulness to take advantage of a freewheeling global economy.

Such ambiguities undermine the definitional process. Consider the possibilities. To one side, globalization is viewed as a catalyst for national prosperity through the elimination of artificial barriers to free enterprise. The future lies in the creation of a borderless world of boundless prosperity, anchored in the promotion of global consumerism and the demise of market-meddling state institutions (see Capling, 1997). Freeing up global economies through the discipline of the market is thought to increase choice, reward risk, unleash creativity, and eliminate waste. To the other side are the critics. Market-motivated philosophies can throw people out of work and dissolve social service access, in effect foreclosing choices, widening disparities, diminishing diversity, and eroding national identity (Editorial, 1996). Women, particularly in dependent countries, have suffered because of austerity measures associated with structural adjustments that reduce national deficits but intensify local deprivation (Duggan and Dashner, 1994). In a strongly worded critique, William Robinson (1996) couches globalization in apocalyptic terms as a world war between the global rich and the global poor from which no economy can escape involvement, and whose human and environmental impact is comparable in predatory scale to nineteenth-century colonialism. Erosion of a civil society is but one cost of this neo-colonialism; environmental destruction is yet another in an era in which short-term profits take priority over long-term sustainable growth. The celebrated Canadian nationalist, Maude Barlow (1999), writes to this effect when she refers to globalization as the dominant economic paradigm of our time:

> ...a system fuelled by the belief that a single global economy with universal rules set by global corporations and financial markets... Everything is for sale even those areas of life once considered sacred. Increasingly, these services and resources are controlled by a handful of transnational corporations that shape national and international law to suit their interests. At the heart of this transformation is an all-out assault on virtually every public sphere of life... The most important tool in this assault has been the creation of international trade agreements whose tribunals and enforcements supersede the legal systems of nation-states...

Such a totalizing impact on all aspects of human existence makes the global economy inherently unjust, unstable, and unsustainable. Finally, there are those who are unsure of how to respond. For them, just defining the concept—let alone sorting out the mélange of pros and cons—is puzzling and infuriating.

Defining Globalization: A World Order

The term globalization encompasses everything from downsizing to deregulation and privatization, with free trade and sophisticated information highways thrown in for good measure. It can also encompass processes from the freer movement of goods, ideas, and capital, to the interconnectedness created by closer relationships, with the growing perception that people are enjoying the same food and drink, watching the same movies, and driving the same cars as everyone else. Many conceive of globalization as a single and logically coherent package of social, political, economic, and cultural changes that culminate in a more advanced stage of human history. In reality, it should be seen as a more fluid and less determinate process with often contradictory and contingent sets of possibilities (Currie and Newson, 1998). Socially and politically, globalization entails an intensification of worldwide social relations in which diverse localities are linked in ways that are mutually reinforcing yet contradictory (Giddens, 1990). Culturally, it acknowledges that our thinking is now electronically connected and governed by transnational organizations and supra-government bodies.

Generally speaking, globalization can be seen as a process of change in which the local and the national are amalgamated with the global to make a single integrated world system. It entails the relatively free exchange of goods and services through elimination of barriers, opening local markets to global capital flows. Globalization is inseparable from increasing interdependence and global enmeshment, as everything from money and markets to people and ideas move swiftly and smoothly across national boundaries (Hurrell and Woods, 1995). More specifically, globalization refers to the geographic penetration of capitalist market relations into new sites of production (Barlow and Clarke, 1996; Bromley, 1996). Combining the specific with the general, globalization can be defined as the process in which interlinkages are established across a broad range of fronts by way of relationships and organizations that transcend national borders (see also Scholte, 1997) This definition reflects the multi-dimensional nature of globalization, namely, globalization as economic phenomenon (reduced trade barriers, high volumes of international commerce and investment, worldwide competition, and mobility of production to cheaper sites), as well as political (erosion of sovereignty), cultural (homogenization of culture and values), social (disruption to communty patterns), and communicative (new and rapid information networks) (Reid, 1998). In conceding that the terrain in which these processes operate is global rather than national or local, globalization supplants the old world order with its discrete bounded units in favour of a new world order involving novel patterns of human organization, wealth creation, and social action (see Albrow, 1996). In other words, as Susan Sibley (1997) writes, globalization is a form of postmodern colonialism whereby the worldwide distribution and consumption of goods is removed from the contexts of their production, but organized instead through legal frameworks to constitute a form of domination by advanced capitalism in seeking an unfettered world in which to invent or invest.

Most definitions equate globalization with new forms of wealth creation by way of economic restructuring on a global scale (Laux, 1990/91). The forces of globalization are thought to arise from the interaction of several simultaneous processes, including (a) expansion of transnationals seeking markets and production sites, (b) mobility of financial capital because of deregulation in world currency markets, (c) erosion of state barriers to preempt movement of capital or expanding scope of operations (Macdonald 1997), and (d) growing faith in worldwide markets and unrestricted competition as a means of sorting out "who gets what." Openness in trade and investment flows are no less pivotal, given the demise of socialist ideals of self-sufficiency, liberalization of trade and tariff regulations, and the world-shrinking spread of information technologies (Editorial, *Economist*, 29 Dec., 1998). Under globalization, national economies are reorganized around an integrated system of production for the express purpose of maximizing profit and minimizing risk (Robinson, 1996). This reorganization of production into global loops of cost-effective sites compels economies to specialize or perish in the unremitting competition for markets, investments, and jobs (Laxer, 1991). In global trade parlance, this specialization conforms to the law of comparative advantage; that is, prosperity is best achieved when each economy specializes in what it does best (Clegg, 1996). The production process itself is transformed under globalization. On one side are Fordist models of production, with their emphasis on mass and standardized production, vertical integration, economies of scale, and de-skilled labour; on the other are more flexible systems for producing varied and specialized goods and services (Holly, 1996). Post-Fordist production is geared primarily to export rather than domestic consumption. Inefficient industries are abandoned, while foreign investment and onshore jobs are vigorously pursued through the creation of "business-friendly" environments. Finally, trading in financial services (from currency speculation to commodity futures) vastly exceeds trade in material goods (Swyngedouw, 1996). Money no longer exists only as a means for buying something, but as a valued commodity and an exchange value in its own right (Daniels and Lever, 1996).

Three implications follow from this spectrum of meanings. First, globalization is not simply a trend or fad. It constitutes an international system with its own set of rules, logic, structures, and procedures, often at odds with the principles of the cold war system (Friedman, 1999). The cold war system was static; globalization involves an integration of markets, nation-states, and information technologies into a dynamic that enables deeper penetration into all parts of the world. If the wall represents the quintessential cold war system, globalization is represented by the world wide web which connects everyone but with no one in charge. The cold war system was built around nation-states and balanced by two superpowers. Globalization is built around a balancing act involving states, bond and stock markets, and powerful transnationals. Second, globalization goes beyond a simple economic shift created by the cross-border exchanges of high technology, instantaneous communication, borderless investment, reduced subsidies, and free trade. The globalization of business has prompted a reorganization of products, markets, and finances of unprecedented magnitude and scope, in effect creating interdependencies that could not have existed in the past. No economy is left untouched in the ruthless compulsion to displace the old and traditional with a capitalist market economy (Robinson, 1996). Yet the resulting interdependency is uneven and fragmented, with gross disparities in the control of power, resources, and status. Globalization also entails a shift in values, with diverse and more human alternatives being replaced by a singular set of values revolving around commercialism, consumerism, and discontent (Haviland, 1999). Third, the interplay of world economic markets and globalization has undermined conventional thinking about national sovereignty. Borders have become increasingly porous with the advent of microchip technologies, while the salience of the nation-state as a relatively autonomous unit of political economy is challenged by the unimpeded flow of capital and investment. The once exclusive authority of the sovereign state is diminished further when stateless corporations, known as transnational conglomerates, replace domestic production as the engine for wealth creation.

| BOX 14.1 | **Transnationals: Engines of Injustice** |

The term globalization was coined relatively recently, but there has been a comparable trend in existence for several centuries, known as colonialism. Since the end of the Second World War, neocolonialist pressures have further intensified the concept of international trading links within a capitalist framework. The cumulative effect of this capitalist expansion is a global system in which the world is partitioned into unequal sectors of "haves" and "have-nots." All countries are now absorbed into a capitalist world system to the extent that production and distribution of goods and services are conducted along free-market principles. National economies are inextricably linked with a free-flowing international division of labour. Competition for markets, jobs, and resources is increasingly conducted without much interference from the regulatory mechanisms of national boundaries. The result? Affluent countries enrich themselves at the expense of the poor by taking unfair advantage through the control of investment, bank loans, hedge-fund speculators, trade and tariffs, and industrial dependency. The engines behind this uneven development and imbalanced international division of labour are transnationals (or multinationals).

Few will dispute the impact of transnational corporations in transforming the world along global lines (Clegg,1996). Once reviled in capitalist and communist countries alike, transnationals are now endorsed as the embodiment of modernity and progress, with governments around the world lining up to attract these money-making machines (Emmott, 1993). They are the foremost actors on the global stage, straddling national boundaries and generating sales in automobiles, oil, electronics, computers, and banking that often exceed the aggregate (GNP) output of most countries (Carnoy, 1996). The incursion of huge transnational corporations into genetically modified crops confers enormous power over the world's food supply through increased dependency on agrochemicals (Simms, 1999). Their spectacular growth in recent years can be attributed to different factors, including government failure to regulate overseas investment, rapid telecommunication and transport systems, reduction of tariffs and trade duties, and the softening up of domestic markets for international trade. Transnationals have taken advantage of largely American-driven moves to integrate the world market by exploiting wage and cost differentials among different regimes in the world (Palat, 1996). In rationalizing the production of goods and services for maximizing profits, transnational business is rapidly becoming a global affair, as reflected in largely expedient decisions regarding plant location, resource extraction, and market or investment futures. The ultimate goal is an integrated global production system in which individual countries constitute but one link in a vast production chain of transnationally controlled "stateless corporations" (UN World Development Report, 1993, in Crane, 1993).

Transnational corporations can be defined as multi-tiered networks that include parent companies, foreign affiliates, alliances with other companies, and contractual agreements that enhance control over the entire production process. This control extends from research and development to transport, assembly, marketing, and finance. The magnitude and scope of multinationals are undeniable. Globalization is being driven by about 60 000 transnational corporations with more than half a million overseas affiliates, accounting for about one-quarter of total global output, the most lucrative source of foreign investment for developing countries, and a key conduit for introduction of advanced technologies (Edwards, 1999). Currently, the world's largest transnationals include General Electric on top, followed by Ford and Royal Dutch Shell (others include Exxon, Coca Cola, Intel, Merck, Toyota, Novartis, IBM, Philip Morris, Proctor and Gamble, and BP) who together own about one-third of the world's private-sector assets (Clegg, 1996). Only three Canadian companies rank in the world's top 100 transnationals: Seagram at 23rd, BCE (the telecommunications company) at 49th, and Thomson (printing and publishing) at 52nd (Edwards, 1999). At present, 52 of the top 100 economies in the world are transnational corporations: Mitsubishi is bigger than the 4th most populous country in the world (Indonesia), GM is larger than Denmark or Norway, and Daimler-Chrysler outpaces both South Africa and Saudi Arabia. Canada's GDP now stands at $692 billion per year; the market value of Microsoft is $590 billion and is expected shortly to overtake Canada (Gwyn, 2000). The combined revenue of the 200 largest corporations is greater that of the 182 nation-states who continue to be responsible for the livelihood of 80 percent of humanity (Clarke, 1999). Only ten industrialized countries export more than the world's ten biggest transnationals, according to the *UNESCO Courier* (July/Aug.,1999), yet these increasingly powerful behemoths have little global responsibility for the environment or worker rights. Canada, of course, is not immune to this corporatization: Foreign corporate

holdings of Canadian companies stood at $217 billion in 1998, up from $148 billion in 1990 (MacKinnon, 1999). Of the 12 725 foreign-owned corporations in Canada in 1998 with revenues of $15 million or assets of $10 million, 53.6 percent were American-owned, and 26.6 percent were from the European Union, according to Statistics Canada, with chemical, transportation equipment, and electrical products the sectors with the highest degree of foreign control in 1996.

The global economic power harnessed by the transnational mobility of these stateless conglomerates is widely acknowledged. Unfettered as they are by national boundaries or loyalties, transnationals can move to whatever part of the globe promises the best return on their investment. They operate in a domain beyond the jurisdiction or accountability of any one country, in a global context that does not as yet have an adequate framework for regulating them. Both wealth creation and the means of production have been redesigned in response to the logic of transnationalism. Old economic boundaries around countries have given way to new centres of power in the private sector. Global systems of production are created, involving components and assembly in different countries, with a new international division of labour on the basis of job location (Crane, 1996). The transformation of the world into a global loop of cost-effective sites of production makes a mockery of the expression, "Made in country X."

The role of transnationals in advancing global systems is self-evident. Yet the integrity of sovereign states is being eroded by precisely this process. Thanks to the power of economies of scale, these stateless corporations now wield more economic and political clout than many national governments. Multinationals can shift production from one location to another when profits dictate because of increased capital mobility. In this way, they can play one country off against another by moving labour-intensive operations offshore to take advantage of cheaper labour and tax breaks (Marchak, 1991). The logic is impeccable, if amoral: What is the point of doing business in a country where industrial wages average around $15 per hour while people in developing countries are willing to work for $15 a day, with few worker benefits and even fewer workplace protections? Both rich and poor countries have little choice but to bargain with powerful capitalists who thereby gain leverage for controlling future investments. Impoverished countries are even more susceptible to transnational demands. In order to maintain reserves of foreign or "hard" currency for servicing their debts, developing countries will often exchange subsistence agriculture for cash crop production, with the simultaneous loss of livelihood for its people and of self-sufficiency for society at large (Goldenberg, 1997). Transnational investment in resource industries leads to a growth of capital-intensive resource extraction at the expense of a sustainable subsistence base. Existing companies may be crowded out, while nascent industries may never gain a foothold (Edwards, 1999).

Put bluntly, transnationals are in the economic driver's seat. As stateless transients in pursuit of profit in a global market economy, transnationals eschew national allegiance or loyalty, often putting their own interests ahead of local or national interests (Hitchcock, 1997). In rejecting any fealty except to themselves, they confirm an observation by George Grant in his *Lament for a Nation*, that smaller societies cannot secure their existence on the basis of the loyalty of capitalists (Gwyn, 1999). Zillah Eisenstein (1996) argues that multinational, global

capital can flow anywhere because of communication and transportation advances, in the process creating its own rules and escaping accountability and blame behind the cover of the global economy. Transnationals can shuffle factories around the world in search of cheap labour (a global economy has swelled the ranks of a reserve army of surplus and unemployed labour), and governments that won't bother them with details such as taxes, environmental laws, and safety regulations (Gwyn, 1998). The globalization of transnationals is rapidly transcending political borders, but also regulatory systems, since the greater the internationalization, the easier it is to slip between the cracks of national regulation (Gwyn, 1998). With this kind of power at their disposal, small wonder that the concept of sovereignty is being put to the test by these transnationals who continue to dominate and dictate, but this time through corporate protocol and trade agreements (Khor, 1996). Of particular concern is the corporate takeover of democratic life, as transnationals move in to take over social priorities on a for-profit basis that used to be the responsibility of the state, thus focusing their energies on restructuring the role of the governments to more directly serve their interests (Clarke, 1999). It remains to be seen if a growing backlash will compel greater accountability among transnationals in terms of responsibility to communities and employees (Crane, 1997). The recent riots in Seattle over the World Trade Organization meetings suggest a mounting aversion to transnational corporate dominance of the global economy at the expense of a civil society (Hahnel,1999). Time will tell if a restructuring of the corporate legal framework will render offending transnationals directly responsible for their injustices against humanity and the natural world (Lasn, 1999).

GLOBALIZATION OF CANADA

There is little doubt that capitalist globalization has redefined the way in which business is done around here. Advances in telecommunications and transportation have compressed the world into a globally integrated production loop of cost-effective sites. On paper, the economic benefits of globalization are too tempting to dismiss. There is merit in a logic that correlates national wealth with the removal of pesky tariffs for international trade, improving productivity through competition, enhancing the climate for jobs and investment, and reducing unwarranted government intervention and social spending. A fundamental restructuring of the relationship between society and the economy has taken place under globalization, and those with the resources and resourcefulness have been amply rewarded in the process. Yet the structural adjustments associated with globalization have not developed as many had hoped because of threats to national and cultural sovereignty, worker rights, and the environment, in effect abandoning a citizenry who feel increasingly betrayed or disillusioned (*New Zealand Herald*, August 7, 1997). Transfer of economic control from the state to the unfettered market is condemned by some as an unmitigated disaster and an open invitation to unhealthy competition and open conflict. Others have endorsed the shift as pivotal in creating a more open and prosperous society. To still others, the ascendancy of globalization has compelled a rethinking of what society is for. Not only is the concept of a sovereign society under attack, but globalization has sharpened the debate over the role of the market versus the state in creating and distributing wealth. And, as Marx predicted a century and a half ago, a solution has yet to be found to this problem.

From State to Market

Should societies be organized around the principle of a freewheeling market, thus reinforcing the Thatcherian notion of society as a collection of private, individual interests? Or should the state (or government) be in charge by focusing on public priorities and the perception of humans as fundamentally social animals (McQuaig, 1999; Fukuyama, 1999)? The state can be defined as a set of public institutions, including the government as well as courts and police that, as the final source of authority and coercion, make and enforce laws that are binding on all members of that political organization. For more than 50 years, Western democracies clung to interventionist philosophies as a means of managing the economy. There was broad consensus over the need to intervene in economies if the more vulnerable members of society were to be protected from the often harsh and unforgiving demands of the marketplace (Macdonald, 1997). The crudely competitive capitalism of the nineteenth century gave way to Keynesian policies of government intervention and state regulation. Throughout the many succeeding cycles of boom and bust, the regulatory duties of an interventionist state have included controlling employment levels, distributing incomes, encouraging consumption, protecting local industry, and establishing social security as a safety net. Strategies of state management have varied, of course, but often incorporated social investment, consumer subsidies, trade and tariff regulations, monitoring domestic growth and prosperity, and supervising collective bargaining sessions (Laux, 1990/91; Drache and Gertler, 1991).

A new social contract eventually shaped the post-World War Two economy. A nationalist-inspired industrial strategy took root, with an activist state at the helm to stimulate the economy and generate wealth through domestically controlled capital accumulation (Shields and McBride, 1994). The principle of collective bargaining took precedence over the practice of wages freely determined by a supply-side market. Linking wages with productivity and growth contributed to the material well-being of workers; as a result, consumerism and economic growth spiralled upwards. A second key policy initiative focused on servicing the domestic market. Export trade was not spurned outright; however, it served primarily as an extension of the domestic market rather than as an industrial strategy per se. Instead of overseas investments, capital had to be "domesticated" to ensure jobs for Canadians (see Daniels and Lever, 1996). Interventionist strategies involved protection (through tariffs) and procurement (by government purchasing) as well as state ownership of key industries as a basis for generating national wealth (Laux, 1990/91). To be sure, the shift from competitive to regulated capitalism did not profoundly alter the balance of power between labour and capital; capitalist ownership remained firmly in place. Nor did it question the fundamental premise of capitalism, namely, the rational pursuit of profit through private production. Nevertheless, a relatively high degree of security and prosperity evolved under this reciprocal arrangement.

The concept of an interventionist state has lost its lustre. The flow of international capital had already escaped national borders by the mid-1970s, followed shortly thereafter by the mobility of production in search of cheap labour (Trotter, 1995). As the biggest boosters of globalization, Americans embraced the Thatcher/Reagan vision that free people in unencumbered markets and private property will outperform those in protectionist big governments (Coxe, 1998). Laissez-faire ideologists argued that free markets were self-sustaining and self-correcting, provided, of course, that the government didn't interfere or disrupt (Soros, 1998). By the early 1990s, international trade had reached the point where transnationals sought to diminish the remaining manifestations of national sovereignty. A new industrial strategy for wealth creation has evolved in response to the transnationalization of global economies (Shields and McBride, 1994). The new economy drew its inspiration from Joseph Schumpeter's idea of capitalism as creative destruction: Globalization is about creatively destabilizing existing arrangements, with the result that whoever produces certain goods at the lowest price will prosper; those that can't will wither, unless government intervenes to artificially protect the weak (Coxe, 1998). The national agenda is now firmly planted in the narrow pursuit of commercial interests through foreign markets, unfettered trade, global competitiveness, and a deregulated state. In lieu of state intervention for regulating the economy for the benefit of the many, an open market is endorsed instead as a basis for conducting business to benefit the few—a scenario that raises the question, "What society is for"?

> Business elites have welcomed the prospects of unleashing the market on a world scale. They want new rights to invest and divest with minimal restriction and establish their businesses without regard to borders. Where existing programs are perceived as barriers to business, they have to be modified... If present standards stand in the way of harmonization and competitiveness, new standards have to be imposed (Drache and Gertler, 1991, 3).

With the decline of tariffs, international export trade has boomed, accounting for 37 percent of the global economy in 1998, compared to only 27 percent in 1980 (Stokes, 1999). The figures are even more stunning for Canada. Exports accounted for about 8 percent of Canada's GNP in 1950; by 1981 this figure rose to about 28 percent, and to over 40 percent by 1997 (Grady and Macmillan, 1999). By contrast, interprovincial trade has declined from 27 percent of the GNP in 1981 to 20 percent in 1997. According to Statistics Canada, export performance doubled in dollar value between 1992 and 1998, from $163 billion to $324.4 billion, with a trade surplus of $2.7 billion by the end of the year (cited in McKay, 1999). And despite Canada's image as a hewer of wood and drawer of water, natural resources only accounted for 32 percent of Canada's exports.

Since 1992, Canada's political agenda has been dominated by neo-conservative policies designed to eliminate deficits and spiralling debts, deregulate the economy, privatize the public, and reduce social benefits (Jeffrey, 1999). National economic policies have shifted toward a greater reliance on the market rather than the state as a source of wealth and its distribution. The triumph of neo-conservatism has not only resulted in budget surpluses, after years of deficits, but also a political and social transformation of privatizing, deregulating, or slashing services while appeasing the public with assurances of "quality" health care or "quality" education. In this new world order of triumphant transnational capitalism, the government's role has shifted from a public agenda to a catalyst for business deals, from a regulator of the economy to balancing budgets and fighting inflation, and from a protector of society against market excesses to a defender of corporate interests from public demands (Barlow and Campbell, 1996; Galbraith,1999). In a globalizing marketplace, all governments must find ways of paring down the costs they impose on the business sector if international competitiveness is to be assured. Key elements in this structural readjustment process include a raft of austerity measures, ranging from the sale of state assets and elimination of protective tariffs to the elimination of agricultural subsidies and a cap on welfare spending (Kelsey, 1997). References pertaining to sovereignty, cultural identity, social progress, and the common good are dismissed as market impediments, on the assumption that markets are always cleverer than governments; welfarism only cripples productivity by stifling individual initiative, and that taxes are punishing when there are too many layers of government, and wasteful expenditures on national programs such as bilingualism and subsidies for have-not provinces (Giddens, 1999; Francis, 1999). As a result, interventionist states have little role in a global economy except to enforce the structural adjustments that facilitate the flow of capital, labour, and investment.

For critics, then, global capitalism is not what it seems to be or to promise (Hahnel, 1999). In spinning a myth that capitalist commercialism is inevitable and superior to other alternatives, global capitalism glosses over other life-affirming options such as equitable cooperation as a humane, feasible, and politically achievable possibility. In theory, market economies are supposed to provide maximum incentives for socially useful innovations while allocating scarce productive resources where most needed or useful. In reality, bottlenecks appear that deny, exclude, or exploit, reminding us again that the velvet hand of the market cannot work without a hidden fist (see Friedman, 1999). In extending its reach for cheaper raw materials, less costly workers, and willing buyers, global capitalism degrades environments while demeaning the lives of the exploited majority. The tight coupling of capitalist relations with all aspects of social life not only distorts human values, but also diminishes cultural diversities and diverse identities (Corson, 1999). Cultural differences are commodified into a global mush, according to Friedman, while everyday life and national decisions are controlled by faceless market forces, both remote and removed. And the commercialism associated with global capitalism is not only about dollars and cents. It is a way of life and a system of values as much as a system for making economic decisions. It is a way of thinking and relating to others that is driven by fear, competition, and greed, a life whose motto is to "do in others before they do you in" (Hahnel 1999:9). Of course, not everyone agrees with this demonization of global capitalism. Adoption of a freewheeling global capitalism is widely endorsed as a springboard to prosperity not only for advanced economies but also for the developing world.

The intersection of endorsement with rejection strikes at the heart of the political debate over the primacy of state versus market as regulatory principles. On the one hand, governments are anxious to improve the competitiveness of domestic production in a globalizing market. On the other hand, they must impose limits on the movement of capital within their borders. Nevertheless, they must ensure some level of social spending for those likely to be victimized by the ruthlessness of the competition. Not surprisingly, the primary task of the state (which is still growing relative to the GNP in many countries) is to socialize risk and cost, while privatizing power and profit. For central authorities, the challenge is clear: They must reconcile the forces of market competitiveness with state concerns for protection of political sovereignty. Confidence in a freer and more open market must be balanced by a stronger government that advocates a more prudent regulation of the financial system, ensures freedom and basic services to citizens, and extols a commitment to social justice such as workers rights and social security guarantees (see also Kravis, 1999). In other words, an economic strategy must be devised that enhances state security yet attracts international investment, improving Canadian competitiveness abroad without shredding the social safety net. All this must be accomplished without the support of now-discarded ground rules of "doing business." The end result of these competing pressures is a delicate balancing act. Governments are caught in a bind as they juggle the opposing demands of the free market with those of national economic security, social conscience, and territorial sovereignty. How is this possible, and why has it happened?

Restructuring the Economy: From Local Production to Productive Loop

Canada occupies an awkward status as a powerful society. Its income puts into the rich category, but structurally it remains somewhat marginal because of reliance on primary resource extraction as a basis for wealth creation. It is relatively rich (core) compared to most developing world countries, but it is also poor (periphery) because of its colonial past, dependence on resource exports and branch plants, and control/dependency by high levels of foreign investment. Canada is rich when measured by conventional standards of GNP and manufacturing productivity but poor since the value of finished goods is low compared with that of exported raw materials. Canada is neither powerful enough to dominate the world's economic stage, nor so inconsequential a player that it is completely at the mercy of other nations. At present, aspects of the Canadian economy remain in the hands of American and other multinational corporations. The economy continues to be propelled by a resource-based export trade and branch plant industrial production, despite the growth of a knowledge-based industry as a source of wealth creation (Watkins, 1997). The combination of foreign ownership and internationalization of production has enabled Canadian capitalists to collude with American capitalists for control over a continental trade block (Clements, 1997). Collaboration with Canadian elites has been instrumental in creating a stunted industrial sector that has arrested Canadian development (Zeitlin and Brym, 1991). Lack of economic independence makes it difficult for Canadians to cooperate with Americans as equal partners in bilateral trading arrangements. The subsequent outflow of capital and profits jeopardizes domestic investment and local job creation, particularly with the creation of a network of branch plants with restrictions on what they can do (often limited to the assembly of goods from parts made outside the country) or to whom they can sell.

The vulnerable status of Canada ensures its involvement in globalizing changes, by choice and by default. Between 1984 and 1993 the Conservative government endorsed the principle of free market trade—despite public resentment and social costs—as the solution to all of Canada's economic problems (Drache and Gertler, 1991). A business strategy was devised for managing society and the national economy around private-sector models

(Barlow and Campbell, 1996). The objective was to improve competitiveness by removing unnecessary barriers to the free flow of capital, labour, and investment, in part by eliminating social costs, in part through job attrition, labour shedding, and plant closures. Also on the chopping block were inefficient industries once protected from outside competition. Slash and burn industrial strategies were introduced that stripped protection from uncompetitive workplaces. Workers were unceremoniously dumped in the ensuing downsizing.

Exposure to the logic and discipline of the global market economy constitutes a radical departure from the past. In the old system of branch economies, a foreign corporation would establish a branch plant (subsidiary) for the express purpose of manufacturing a product primarily for the Canadian market. For example, the 1965 Canada–U.S. Auto Pact stipulated that for every American car sold in Canada, one had to be built here (Laver, 1994). The big three auto makers, General Motors, Ford, and Chrysler, invested billions of dollars in Canadian plants to meet Canadian content rules. Later, when Toyota and Honda began Canadian production, they were assessed a 9.2 percent duty because of failure to meet the Auto Pact targets for Canadian production. Until recently, most car production was geared towards the domestic market, and Canada erected tariffs and duties to protect its domestic industry (Hiller, 1990). Higher Canadian prices reflected the costs of doing business in a country where smaller economies of scale prevailed. This protectionist mentality resulted in the manufacture of the same product in several different provinces to supply the needs of local markets. Such an arrangement may have ensured "full" employment and a measure of control over national decision-making, but it also encouraged inefficiency and duplication.

The rules of the game have changed in the wake of globalizing waves. With a new global division of labour and rapidly expanding foreign markets, a manufacturing strategy has emerged that focuses on export productivity rather than on protecting domestic industry. Of the three million cars, trucks, and minivans produced in Canada in 1999 (a figure that is likely to make Ontario rather than Michigan the car capital of North America), 90 percent are exported to the United States, thus accounting for $100 billion in annual earnings and 13.6 percent of total exports (Walton, 1999). Conversely, most of the cars that Canadians buy are imported (22.3 percent of Canada's imports in 1995 were cars or auto parts) from the United States and Europe! The branch plant mentality has vanished because of advances in technology and communication, followed by the disappearance of trade tariffs and investment barriers. On January 1, 1994, for example, the Canadian government slashed or eliminated duties on a wide range of auto parts, in effect burying the 1965 Auto Pact (Laver, 1994). The production process has also been revamped. Rather than being a branch plant economy both regulated and protected, each country such as Canada is now expected to become part of the production loop in which labour (jobs) and capital (in the form of goods, services, investment, and markets) are integrated under intense pressure to compete in a global market. Instead of making a product only for domestic use, a Canadian plant might make a component for export around the world; another foreign plant would make a different component. Outputs from these plants would be linked together in a worldwide operation. Borders count for little under such an arrangement.

Canada's industrial strategy is now centred on market-driven export trade rather than state-regulated expansion of domestic markets. Until the 1980s, a key principle of the Canadian nation endorsed economic independence and political sovereignty as inextricably linked, thus making it important to construct a strong industrial infrastructure to undergird autonomy and prosperity (see also Jesson, 1998). The role of the state in advancing national interests has shifted accordingly. Instead of bolstering domestic growth, the state is concerned with reducing barriers for investment and trade, while forging a social climate hospitable to international trade. Social spending as a percentage of the GDP has declined from historic highs in the pre-free trade era (Drache and Gertler, 1991). With few exceptions, social programs from health to education have suffered cutbacks and budgetary restrictions under budget-pruning, social contract arrangements. Post-secondary institutions have been particularly hard hit, with many receiving a disproportionately smaller slice of the economic pie, despite oft-quoted platitudes about advanced education as a prerequisite for economic prosperity.

There is nothing inherently *bad* about such an economic process. Problems arise from the loss of self-determination when corporate functions can be located anywhere. Canada can be banished from the production loop if it fails to reduce costs related to skilled labour, infrastructure, social welfare, and taxation. Transnationals will avoid locating in countries where barriers to investment or trade are maintained. What emerges from this competitive free-for-all is a global division of labour largely determined by corporate agendas rather than national interests. The costs of intense competition are tough on a socially progressive country such as Canada. The disappearance of branch plants is bad enough; erosion of national autonomy and loss of control over business decisions is tougher still, in the face of growing competition from developing countries over investment, jobs, and markets. As bluntly stated by Adam Zimmerman, chairman of Noranda, "If you are in a business that can move, why bother with the hassles of staying in Canada?" (as quoted in Hurtig, 1991). Why, indeed, when employees at the Bata plant near Trenton, Ontario, earn up to $10.50 per hour while Bata workers in Pacific Rim countries earn $2.20 for an entire day? The debate over free trade captures the dilemmas of globalization and its impact on Canada, as Box 14–2 demonstrates.

Canada is currently exposed to the chilly blasts of globalization in the competition for export trade. The seeming lack of viable alternatives to capitalism following the demise of the Soviet Union has reinforced the remorseless march of globalization and free-market principles. The globalization of Canada's economy has intensified competition with wealthy industrial giants such as Germany and Japan. Canada's ability to attract jobs and markets has been further blunted by inroads from aggressive newcomers such as the Asian "tigers" of Singapore and South Korea. Its social and political priorities will be altered even further as competition and export-led trade impose their own economic agendas on the Canadian state. A new set of challenges now exist. Canada must devise an industrial strategy that maximizes its global advantages, insulates it from the worst effects of pure competition, ensures a decent standard of living for everyone, and enhances its capacity as a sovereign and "distinct" society. The challenge, in other words, requires a tricky balancing act among the conflicting demands of economic restructuring, a reorganization of the labour market, incorporation of different production technologies, and retention of Canada's vaunted social programs. It remains to be seen whether these dynamics and demands can be reconciled to mutual advantage in sorting out the competing forces of global competitiveness, state sovereignty, and social compassion.

Whither Now Canada: Nationalism or Globalization?

Globalization is not a policy choice, it is a fact.

- Bill Clinton

Globalization is irreversible and irresistible.

- Tony Blair

Or is it?

- The Ecologist

To say that we are living in interesting times is something of an understatement. Global movements and interconnectedness have brought about benefits. But global capitalism is not without its problems, including the uneven distribution of benefits, the instability of a flighty and speculative financial system, the ambiguous role of the state, the potential threat of global monopolies such as transnationals, and the question of values, social justice, and national cohesion (Soros, 1998). Any period of change generates disruptions in people's lives, and the profound changes associated with globalization may be instilling a terrifying sense of insecurity in those without the skills or social support to buffer these changes. How then do we interpret global change? Are we on the brink of a precipitous decline because of (a) ruinous competition for scarce resources, (b) the polarization of the world into rich and poor, or (c) confrontations between "tribal" forces? Or is this disarray merely symptomatic of a transition from one social era to another? Perhaps the problems confronting societies are not pathological, but reflect the normal growing pains accompanying the unfolding of new realities. Or perhaps the world is proving much more complex and chaotic than often acknowledged by mechanistic theories of clockwork precision, according to Robin Bieronstock and Thomas Homer-Dixon in the *Globe and Mail* (Sept 3, 1998), with the result that even a small event such as the devaluation of the Thai baht in the summer of 1997 can trigger an avalanche of often unpredictable consequences.

It is widely accepted that the challenge of a truly global market economy is inevitable (Hirst, 1997). Advanced economies suggest they have little choice except to endorse demands of international competition or accept the consequences. Governments of these countries have had to revise or downscale distinct national strategies of social welfare and macroeconomic management. Political agendas are likely to be set by transnational corporations or international financial markets. Monetary policies that run counter to the market, including those that promote higher levels of direct taxation, extensive labour and environment rights, and generous social benefits, are dangerous: They render a country uncompetitive, while risking punishment from world currency markets. The market's ability to instantaneously transfer cash anywhere in the world with the click of a mouse is playing havoc with national policies: Any mistake by the government is punished with ruthless speed by the market. With the scale of economic activity no longer corresponding to the territory of the nation-state, but transnational and transcending national borders, central governments will become little more than glorified local authorities whose responsibility is to secure a compliant labour force. The best the government can do is to get out of the way of business by deregulating the economy and containing public spending.

Is the trend to globalization inevitable and ungovernable? Is capital beyond control? Is the nation-state powerless in the face of this onslaught? Do citizens have no choice except to capitulate to the system? Many believe the answer is yes to each of these questions. Nothing else is possible in a global economy in which the forces of globalization are undermining democratic options. Globalization and free-trade agreements have ensnared Canada in a way that diminishes its capacity to (a) govern itself, since it cannot establish industrial or economic plans; (b) create innovative labour force strategies; (c) regulate its monetary policy; and (b) focus on domestic markets (see Hargrove, 1998). Others disagree, believing that economic growth and trade openness can be combined with fairness within and between countries, provided there is a political will for concerted action to regulate, control, resist and challenge (Hirst, 1997). Is the government really powerless to regulate multinationals or does it simply use globalization as an excuse to avoid making electorally unpleasant decisions? The notion that things are unchangeable and inevitable is a convenient excuse for those who prefer the status quo, since it is better to defer to some law of nature than to justify or excuse a system that is creating more intense levels of inequality (McQuaig, 1998). But, while many believe that free trade is natural and normal in a global economy and defend it as the only solution to the problem of inefficient economies (Saul, 1995), there is nothing natural or normal about globalization; globalization is a social construction, a convention created by individuals who make choices. A new corporate feudalism is not a regrettable but unavoidable fact of global economy. The corporatization of the world is a socially constructed convention of primary interest to some rather than others, and is imposed by politicians and corporate decision-makers. People need to be convinced that the ambiguous effects of globalization are not a historical inevitability beyond challenge or change, but the result of conscious policies by vested interests, in the same way that high unemployment is not a regrettable necessity of the economy, but a ruthless decision that suits monied interests rather than the general public (Editorial, 1996; Sandbrook, 1997).

In short, the challenge for the 21st century will be to create an open and democratic society in which market freedom is balanced with social justice. Central to this challenge is a balance between markets and society: one that will unleash the creative energies of private enterpreneurship without eroding the cooperative basis of human social existence (Rodrik, 1997). A new humanism is required that places human needs and concerns ahead of global capital and corporate interests (McQuaig, 1998). Yet the prospect of retaining national sovereignty in a globalizing world of transnationals will be a challenge: As Eric Kierans put it, what is a borderless world except one that is emptied of every value and principle except greed and accumulation (cited in Peter Newman, *Globe and Mail*, April 11, 1998). Or, in the society-destabilizing words of the U.S. head of IBM World Corp (also cited in Newman): "The boundary separating your nation from mine is no more meaningful than the equator—a line on maps, void of meaning."

BOX 14.2   Free Trade? Bonus or Bogus?

The principle of open competition as a catalyst for Canada's industrial strategy is reflected in policy initiatives both market-based and trade-oriented. A substantial portion of Canada's wealth continues to depend on exports and international trade. Currently, two trading trends are noteworthy. On the one hand are agreements for loosening restrictions on the movement of goods and services across all borders. Negotiations over a General Agreement on Trade and Tariffs (GATT) since 1947 have been aimed at opening international trade by dismantling protective barriers and eliminating punishing tariffs. The principle behind free global trade rests on a belief in comparative advantage; namely, that prosperity follows those countries that maximize what they produce best because of history or geography. Free trade among these countries is the key to prosperity, especially when products of one country are matched with those of another without the distortion of tariffs or regulations.

On the other hand, there is the trend towards restricting trade to regions. Examples of this are regional trading blocks such as the European Union (EU) as well as regional blocks in Southeast Asia and South and Central America. Regional trading blocks are justified on the grounds of improving economies of scale by freeing the movement of goods and services among "natural" trading partners. The economic benefits of many regional arrangements are plausible. The creation of these regional blocks has compelled companies to set up plants in these regional markets to circumvent the tariff barriers they have surrounded themselves with, in effect making companies more multinational (Daniels and Lever, 1996). But social costs related to government assistance programs and local industries invariably raise debate about the desirability of free trade agreements in North America.

For Canada the dilemma is obvious. Since the mid-1970s and the loss of preferential access to European and British markets, Canada has had little choice but to explore alternate trading arrangements for its products and exports, particularly in North America. What could be more attractive than the prospect of trading with a regional block of 360 million consumers, with the potential for more as agreements are negotiated? But the opening of American and Mexican markets to Canadian exports has threatened to eliminate some programs and regulations that historically have bolstered the costs of doing business in Canada. For instance, certain environmental regulations and collective bargaining agreements that involve employment protection could well be scuttled in the interests of making Canadian businesses more competitive. Protection of Canada's cultural industries and social programs is likely to be challenged by American-style private-

enterprise models. Such concessions may appeal to those who live and die by the bottom line, but they may look a lot less appealing to those whose lives and life chances are negatively affected by pure economic calculation.

How does Canada stack up in the free trade stakes? The Free Trade Agreement (FTA), which was signed in 1988 by Canada and the United States, advocated the gradual abolition of trade tariffs as impediments to markets. Supporters argued that free trade would bring about national and regional prosperity; detractors feared the absorption of Canada into the U.S., with a corresponding threat to social programs and sovereignty (Conway, 1996). A continental free trade agreement secured American access to Canadian resources, while smoothing the path for increased American investment in Canada. It also enhanced the export of Canadian goods to the world's richest and largest market. As well, the FTA compelled the Canadian economy to harmonize its policies with the practices of a business-friendly U.S. by curbing unwarranted government intervention, regulation, and social spending. A similar commitment to bolster Canadian economic prosperity by liberalizing trade through open markets characterized the North American Free Trade Agreement (NAFTA), signed in 1994 by Canada, the U.S., and Mexico. NAFTA has the potential to create a trading block of 360 million persons, with $6 trillion gross in consumer products. This is likely to grow even further into a hemispheric trading block with the addition of other Central and South American countries. Under NAFTA, U.S. and Mexican investors must be treated no less favourably than Canadian investors, with a host of prohibitions on minimum levels of Canadian ownership or purchase from local suppliers (Shields and McBride, 1994; Barlow and Clark, 1996). In 1996 the intercontinentalization process was further extended when Canada and Chile signed a bilateral agreement for expansion of trade entry into Latin American markets (Ford, 1996).

As yet there is no consensus regarding the final outcome of NAFTA. The benefits of hitching Canada's wagon to the fifty stars of the USA have fallen short of the economic bonanza promised by proponents; but the cost envisaged by its severest critics have yet to materialize (Crane, 1999). One report indicated that Canadians to date have been the prime beneficiaries of NAFTA in terms of jobs and a predominance of Canadian exports over American imports (Beltrame, 1997). Exports have increased dramatically, and now stand at 41 percent of GDP, compared to 25 percent in 1991, as companies have restructured their operations in north-south line to take advantage of a healthy American economy. In terms of total value, Canadian companies exported $165.4 billion worth of goods to the USA in 1997, compared to a pre-free trade total of $69.2 billion in 1987 (imports more than doubled during this decade). Similarly, exports to Mexico rose to $918 million in 1997 from $639 million in 1993, before Mexico joined the free trade market (Swift, 1999). For better or worse, exports to the United States in 1996 constituted 79.1 percent of Canada's total, with Japan a distant second at 4.5 percent (Statistics Canada, cited in the *Globe and Mail*, June 24, 1999). Public support has grown as well: The same report quoted a Goldfarb Consultants tracking poll which indicated public support for NAFTA has increased from 37 percent in 1993 to 67 percent in 1998. Another bank survey contends that neither wages nor jobs have been adversely affected by NAFTA, as many had feared, with 47 percent of 631 firms indicating they had increased their workforce, 41 percent indicating it was

about the same, and 11 percent indicating a loss of workers (Kenna, 1998).

Critics of free trade are not convinced, and continue to believe the "giant sucking sound" called NAFTA is detrimental to Canada's national interests. Much of Canada's economic boom is directly related to the boom in the USA, and the lower Canadian dollar, and is based on exports rather than productivity-driven growth (Crane, 1999). Critics point to the loss of control over foreign investment in Canada, the growing privatization of key public services such as health and education, the shrinking of Canada's social programs, and the erosion of minimal protection for workers and the environment. Both Canadian and American industries have closed shop and shifted operations to more profitable locations because of lower wages and social security payments and poorer working conditions. In Mexico's booming maquiladores (export processing zones), NAFTA has created jobs, but many workers continue to experience exploitative wages, workplace abuse, and reprehensible working conditions (Stackhouse, 1999). Wages have been held in check by companies that threaten to move out every time employees ask for increases. Even the continued flow of investment into Canada is no cause for celebration. According to Mel Hurtig (1999), much of this investment is funnelled into company takeovers that provide few jobs. As a result, profits and dividends continue to be siphoned from the country at alarming rates, while Canadian jobs and investment are being diverted to lower-wage destinations (Eggerton, 1998). Canada's ability to control its destiny as a sovereign society is compromised because of this political and economic integration. With its colossal resource base, the United States can advance its interests by falling back on the courts or trade legislation to punish Canadian protectionist measures. Further integration into an intercontinental economy comes with a hefty price tag. The costs of closer economic ties could culminate in political union, according to James Laxer (1993), at the expense of social programs and an activist state.

In other words, NAFTA is not simply an exchange of commodities between countries. Its hidden agenda affects every aspect of Canadian life, curbing Canada's freedom to make decisions that reflect Canadian unity, identity, prosperity, and sovereignty. Nor are the costs of dependency and underdevelopment evenly distributed. The richer provinces have suffered least until recently, but poorer regions such as Atlantic Canada continue to bear the brunt, with the result that local and regional economies remain even more dependent on government grants as traditional jobs dry up in fishing, forestry, resource extraction, manufacturing, and defence. In this restructuring from a resource-based to a service-oriented economy, many Atlantic Canadians have been consigned to seasonal or makeshift work, supplemented by social assistance or E.I. benefits. The promised benefits—prosperity, jobs, and environmental regulation—have yet to materialize in Canada and the United States (Wallach, 1999). In other words, the jury is still out on the decade of free trade in Canada, but there is no question that NAFTA and FTA have radically changed the Canadian economy and prompted a major industrial restructuring by changing the focus and strategy of most Canadian businesses along a north-south axis (Scoffield, 1998).

The debate over free trade versus protectionism will never be resolved to everyone's satisfaction. Is it the path to prosperity and wealth that its proponents claim, or has it resulted in the demise of Canadian values and institutions, with a corresponding Americanization of Canadian society (Crane, 1999)? This lack of resolution stems in part from radically different perceptions of the economy, coupled with the government's role in generating wealth. Free traders believe that wealth is generated when the economy is driven by prices freely and competitively set according to the laws of supply and demand. Free trade ideologues believe that political units such as the nation-state are irrelevant or counterproductive when the economy functions internationally and is subjected to the liberating discipline of a competitive market. The government is rebuked as a meddlesome hindrance rather than a help in creating a corporate society. The government is seen as an impediment to the free play of unfettered market forces. Jobs, investments, and plant locations will materialize only in those countries whose national outlooks are business-friendly. A country's attractiveness is bolstered by lowering taxes, paring production costs, pruning government programs and spending, loosening government regulations, reducing the debt load, dismantling the welfare apparatus, dropping wage rates and related costs to competitive levels, and making trade as free as possible by cutting tariffs and artificial barriers (see Francis, 1993).

Protectionists disagree with the definition of the problem; consequently, they propose different solutions. For protectionists, the unfettered market is not a solution, but a problem to be controlled by an interventionist government. With its culture of greed that benefits few at the expense of many, free trade is denounced as contrary to a caring and compassionate society. Proposed instead is protection for Canadian industry and trading arrangements consistent with national interests, not just those of the wealthy elite. Such intrusion is costly, of course. Costs include raising taxes and security payments to ensure a level playing field, expanding capital projects for make-work activities, increasing government regulation in defence of worker rights, and establishing equity initiatives for inclusion of the marginal. Maximizing export trade is important in this equation. Equally significant, however, is Canada's survival as a humane and egalitarian society. As Canadians sacrifice more of their political and economic sovereignty on the altar of free trade, they have less control over internal matters. Canadians appear to be rebelling against the onslaught of government cutbacks, and look to government to protect their interests through job creation and social security (Walkom, 1997).

How do we assess free trade in terms of its impact on Canada? To what extent does globalization provide benefits exclusively to big business rather than to the workers who bear the brunt of cost-cutting, profit-bolstering moves? Critics say the free trade agreements have not delivered what was promised, including a jump in productivity; by contrast, supporters point to the overall positive contribution and the boom in export trade (which may reflect the lower value of the Canadian dollar) (Watson, 1999). For some, free trade has solved the problem of an underachieving economy, with its short production runs and frequent re-toolings (McCallum, 1999). For others, the bottom line can justify the onslaught on ordinary Canadians and the integrity of Canada as a society. On one side are those who believe that Canada's problem will be solved when it becomes more like the United States; on the other, those who believe the solution to Canada's problems lies in being as different as possible without provoking the colossus to the south (Andrews, 1999). Business would appear to have succeeded in establishing a pro-business agenda in government in hopes of "freeing" enterprise or enhancing business stability (from deficit-cutting to free trade). They also seem to have reneged on promises to deliver job security and real incomes for ordinary Canadians (Hargrove, 1996). The era of an interventionist welfare state is being replaced by a globally diffused, individualized, and unregulated system of power, and a selectively residual state whose prime function is to create the conditions for successful private enterprise and the internationalization of labour, capital, and investment (see Kelsey, 1997). Accompanying this change is the shift from a heavily protected and highly regulated economy to an open economy dominated by international money markets and financial speculators. The costs of restructuring are widespread: Just as Canada does not possess full control over economic decisions, so too many private citizens are helpless in the face of economic decisions that render them disposable. It makes little sense to blame a worker for loss of employment when the local plant has moved to Mexico where labour is cheaper and social costs are non-existent (Stackhouse, 1999). Instead of blaming the victims of economic restructuring, it is time to examine the social context for answers. What is the point, in other words, of improving Canada's global competitiveness if this results in the impoverishment of many Canadians? What do we gain when an obsession with market fundamentalism as a "metaphor for the meaning of life" (Soros, 1999) has the effect of transforming all social relationships into market transactions, while subordinating community and civic commitment to individual self-interest, in effect posing a greater threat to an open society than any totalitarian ideology (Collison, 1999)?

GLOBAL
PROBLEMS

FRAMING THE PROBLEM

The world we inhabit is in a shambles, or at least this would appear to be the case judging by media sensationalism and the accompanying howls of public anguish. Too many people exist, according to the headlines, and too many of them live in the wrong places, with too many problems and not enough resources to halt the hurting. Perceptions are loaded with contradictions. On one side, the developing world craves the material trappings of a modern society, with a comparable standard of living. On the other, it appears incapable of paying the price for economic progress because of an apparent tendency to relapse into tribalism, tradition, and ethnic chauvinism instead of pulling together for national unity and the common good. Human life is depicted by the Western media as cheap and disposable, and easily extinguished by interclan killings or natural disasters. Lip service to the ideals of democracy means nothing in light of the authoritarian rule of despots, military juntas, tribal cleansings, and religious fanatics. The sheer volume and intensity of this pending anarchy is disturbing, particularly as the social fabric of human societies is being shredded by a scarcity of resources, crime, disease, tribalism, and overpopulation (Kaplan, 1994). The cumulative result of these ungovernable forces must not be underestimated. Developing countries appear to be hopelessly mired in an endless cycle of crisis, conflict, corruption, and catastrophe, with no solution in sight (Kaplan, 1994). People live in a world that Yusuf Hassan Abdi describes as a "desolate moral vacuum devoid of the most basic human values . . . nothing is spared, held sacred, or protected" (Refugee, 1999). To add insult to injury, efforts to help may end up hindering: Many developing countries are recipients of Western generosity through foreign aid or favourable trade arrangements, yet opportunities for development are squandered because of corruption or gross incompetence, without even a murmur of gratitude to their beneficiaries.

The pervasiveness of this global problem is staggering (Elliott, 1998). According to the UN Human Development Report, about one-quarter of the world's population (or around 1.5 billion people) live on less than one dollar a day. Nearly a billion are illiterate; another billion go hungry; and about one-third of the population in the developing countries are not expected to live to 40. To the consternation of many, this gulf between rich and poor is expanding, culminating in a kind of "global apartheid," with its extremes of power and wealth combined with geographical and social separation (Richmond, 1994). Income of the top 20 percent of world economies was 30 times higher in 1960, but nearly 74 times the share in 1997, with the result that the world's poorest 20 percent own only 1.1 percent of the world's income, down from 2.3 % in 1960 (UN Human Development Report, 1999). The situation is particularly grim in Africa where the political and economic aftermath of colonialism continues to deny or destroy, despite attainment of nominal political independence (Kaplan, 1994). Statistics can only hint at the enormity of the problems. African countries occupy 9 of the bottom 10 positions in the United Nations' Human Development Index, notwithstanding "generous" levels of foreign aid, which in 1993 amounted to $38 per person compared to $8 per person in Latin America (Chege, 1997). Resources continue to be depleted at alarming rates, giving rise to further cycles of starvation, disease, or pestilence. The extraction of resources has resulted in only limited manufacturing, while living standards of the poor are rarely improved by the so-called trickle-down effect of wealth creation (Parris, 1997). Economically, the situation as a whole continues to stagnate. Since 1970, African productivity for the global market has shrunk by 50 percent; its debt is now equivalent to its GNP, having multiplied twentyfold in recent years; food production in the sub-Sahara is about 15–20 percent lower than in the late 1970s; and per capita income has plunged by 25 percent from 1987 (Parris, 1997). Contradictions abound: Despite savage inter-ethnic killings and deaths in refugee camps, the population continues to escalate, with projections of 1.5 billion by 2025. A combination of droughts, ethnic and clan killings, and armed conflicts under military juntas has created a refugee pool of between 5 and 10 million people. Put bluntly, the plight of Africa could well emerge as the world's most pressing social problem in the twenty-first century.

How valid are these perceptions of reality? Human diversity being what it is, there is an element of truth to these observations. Who could deny the pervasiveness of poverty, despotic rule, crowded living conditions, inter-ethnic and religious rivalries, and the threat of natural catastrophes in the developing world? This is not the entire story, however, and a sense of proportion is badly needed without discarding all compassion. First, not all developing countries in Africa are economic basket cases. Economic growth is substantial in certain areas, life expectancies are inching upwards as are school enrolments and rates of adult literacy, infant mortalities have halved since 1965, and democratic institutions are gradually gaining a foothold in once authoritarian regimes (d'Aquino, 1997; UN Human Development Report, 1999). Second, poverty, crowding, despotism, conflict, and disasters may be pervasive, but neither Canada nor the United States are exempt from such indictment. Consider the status of First Nations in Canada, whose living conditions on some reserves are comparable to standards in some developing countries. Besides, any civilization that spawned two world wars and continues to supply small arms and land mines for ongoing conflicts can hardly afford to hug the moral high ground. Third, too much of our understanding of life in the developing world as "nasty, brutish, and short" reflects a media preoccupation with "triggers" such as India (religious conflicts), Bangladesh (natural disasters), Somalia (clan killings), and South Africa (tribal hostilities). But not all developing world countries are patterned after these media hot spots. Many are relatively peaceful and reasonably well-adjusted to the surrounding environment. Moreover, fixation on the sensational tends to overlook the routines of daily life—the cooperation, consensus, and regulation—that must surely exist for community to survive. Fourth, the media are largely responsible for negative perceptions of the developing world. Racist personnel are not always the problem: Media preference for the flamboyant and telegenic as newsworthy are no less blameworthy in imparting the worst possible spin. Cooperation and consensus rarely sell copy or create compelling visuals for the evening news, exerting even additional pressure to troll the bottom for newsworthiness. This selectivity reinforces a predominantly one-sided view of the developing world as breeding grounds for death, destruction, and demise. In reality the picture is much more complex, and a balance sheet on human development between 1990 and 1997 reveals the two-edged character of global improvements (UN Human Development Report, 1999).

To what extent is the developing world responsible for the plight in which it finds itself? Centuries of exploitation under colonialism and transnationals have stripped many developing countries of the resources and resourcefulness for dealing with deeply entrenched problems. One of Britain's most notorious colonialists, Cecil Rhodes, wrote in the 1890s "We must find new lands from which we can easily obtain raw materials and at the same time exploit the cheap slave labour that is available from the natives of the colonies. The colonies would also provide a dumping ground for the surplus goods produced in our factories" (cited in Goldsmith, 1999:154). The colonialization process has evolved over time: initially, by direct colonial rule, then by the imposition of a developmental/modernization paradigm, and in its most recent incarnation as a corporate global market model that reinforces patterns of dependency and underdevelopment (Goldsmith, 1999). As a result, Western aggression and global greed must share the blame for developing world problems. To do otherwise, by holding the victims entirely accountable for forces beyond their control, is ultimately an irresponsibility of the highest order. In other words, the Western world must see itself as part of the solution to global problems because it is inextricably part of the problem.

This chapter explores the concept of global conditions from a social problem perspective. Conditions defined as problematic are examined at the level of causes, characteristics or expressions, consequences, and cures. Solutions to these global problems by way of developmental models are not dismissed outright, but caution is advised in dealing with issues that are complex, historically entrenched, and beyond simple explanation or solution. The chapter begins appropriately enough by looking at a host of global problems that are engulfing the planet at present; namely, overpopulation, urbanization, poverty, global monoculture, ethnic conflicts, and the environment. The characteristics and consequences of these global problems are discussed throughout the chapter. To be sure, placement of global problems in this section is not meant to blame the developing world as the architect of its own misfortunes. After all, there is no compelling reason to blame the victims of global colonialism for the problems of the world, much less to expect developing countries to make disproportionate sacrifices for solution. On the contrary, global problems are arguably Western problems, in light of past history and current events. Convenience, however, dictates a discussion of these global problems where they are most acutely manifest and where solutions are more desperately needed (Kaplan, 1994). Finally, proposed solutions to global problems are revealed for what many are: exercises in self-serving expediency. The politics and per-

TABLE 15-1	Human Development Between 1990 and 1997 (based on UN Human Development Report, 1999)	
	Global Progress	**Global Regression**
Health	life expectancies are rising because of reduced mortalities for infants and elderly	• life expectancy in Africa = 51, in North America = 77 • about a quarter of the population will not survive to 60 • AIDS is proving a major killer • many lack access to health services and sanitation
Education	both primary and secondary enrolments continue to increase	• lack of literacy and participation in schools remains a key problem in some areas
Food and Nutrition	• food production per capita increased • increases in per capita daily intake of calories and protein	nearly one in seven remains malnourished
Income and Poverty	slight increases in per capita GDP	• by 2020, there will be three billion poor people in the developing world • one-quarter of the world lives on less than a dollar a day • the share of global incomes continues to decline for the poorest 20 percent • the annual income of the 358 richest people in the world is greater than the total income of 2.3 billion people, or 45 percent of the world population
Status of Women	increases in both education levels and economic activity	women continue to be hampered by double standards, patriarchal attitudes and practices, abuse, and lack of participation
Children	infant mortality has declined dramatically largely because of immunization campaigns	• mortality rate in Sierra Leone is 170 per 1000 live births; in Norway and Germany, 5 per 1000 live births • many children remain malnourished • child labour remains a problem
Environment	significant reductions in the share of heavily polluting traditional fuels in energy use.	Millions continue to die from pollution and unsanitary water sources
Wealth Creation	real growth in certain sectors	• reliance on export of raw materials in a world that is less reliant on these than in the past

ils of foreign aid as a source of (mis)development are analyzed and assessed, and shown to be fundamentally flawed. Nevertheless, a growing commitment to human rights as a means of solving global problems provides a degree of cautious optimism of pending improvements in the lives and life chances of ordinary people.

SURVEYING GLOBAL PROBLEMS

In a world that appears to be convulsed by a barrage of conflicts and dilemmas, there is no shortage of global problems for study. While there is no consensus regarding which problems to select for analysis, certain conditions are of such gravity and scope that they cannot be ignored in any reasonable discussion. Of those global problems, the following have been deemed as important.

Overpopulation

There is a saying among sociologists: "The rich get richer, the poor get children." Despite its mocking tone, the expression latches onto a popular perception of the developing world as teeming with people who have neither the resources nor the space to support their own children. There is some truth to this perception. The world is experiencing a population explosion that is unprecedented in human history. From 1804, when the world population reached the one billion mark, it took 123 years to reach two billion, but only 12 years to go from 5 billion in 1987 to 6 billion on October 12th, 1999, in effect doubling in less than 40 years, with projections of doubling again to 12 billion by 2050 if current growth continues (cited in *NY Times*, 19 Sept., 1999). However, the growth is expected to taper off as fertility rates drop and the population ages. Virtually all of the growth is occurring in the poorest of developing countries; sixty percent of the world's population increase is in ten countries, with India, at 16 percent and China, at 11.4 percent, leading the way. It is estimated that as much as 95 percent of the future population growth beyond replacement level will occur in the developing world. Not surprisingly, many people are alarmed and for good reason. As far back as 1968, Paul Erlich had already articulated grave concerns over the world's carrying capacity—at a time when the world's population stood at "only" 3.5 billion.

Why this demographic explosion, given that half of the world's married women rely on family-planning techniques, with the result that in 61 countries, women's fertility rates have dropped below the replacement level of 2.1 children per woman (*Los Angeles Times*, Oct. 11, 1999). One major reason for population growth reflects the one billion teenagers that are entering their reproductive years. Longer life spans are another obvious answer. Life expectancies have increased substantially, while infant mortality rates have declined in response to improved medical care, the eradication of certain fatal diseases, and advances in technology. The growing impoverishment of the poor may also be a contributing factor. Family sizes continue to expand in reaction to mounting poverty. Larger families provide a margin of safety for survival in environments of grinding poverty, economic emergencies, and an absence of any safety net for the aged or unemployed. In other words, what is often defined as a global problem (that is, large families) may serve as a solution for survival when alternatives such as rudimentary social programs are non-existent.

The politics of population is proving vexing. Increasing population through control of diseases and death rates is a positive goal. Yet this creates additional pressure on dwindling resources and existing social services. Local environments are especially vulnerable to escalating demands. The depletion of basic necessities, coupled with the proliferation of waste, are worrying in their own right. Satisfying the food needs of 100 million additional persons each year will pose new challenges with declining outputs from grains, grasslands, and marine sources (Brown, 1993). The effects of overpopulation are not restricted to the developing world. Rich countries are also affected, as might be expected in an interconnected world, with impacts ranging from terrorist attacks to mass emigration.

Urbanization

Half of the world's population of 6 billion people are estimated to live in cities. In the developing world, the figure stands at about 23 percent of the population, up from 13 percent in 1950 (Bowring, 1993). Africa and East Asia have the lowest rates, while 71 percent of the

Latin American population is urban (including 86 percent in Argentina). The rates in Canada and the United States are about 80 percent at present. Singapore and Hong Kong are almost entirely urban. Yet even in areas with low urban-to-rural ratios, the presence of sprawling urban agglomerations is the rule, not the exception—from Sao Paulo at 17.4 million and Shanghai at 13 million down to Manila at 7 million and Bangkok at 6 million. Projected figures are equally formidable, with an estimated 30 million in Mexico City by 2020.

Despite obvious drawbacks for most newcomers, many people are attracted to the city by a process often called "push and pull." Migrants are pushed out of rural communities because of unemployment, limited land resources, lack of opportunity and employment, boredom, and dislike of social patterns such as factionalism. Migrants are pulled into cities for precisely opposite reasons. For some, economic survival for themselves and their children is a compelling reason; for others, the lure is that of glamour, excitement, and sophistication. The decision to uproot is not always productive. Newcomers may exchange intermittent agricultural jobs for low-paying urban jobs, often supplemented by proceeds from scavenging and involvement in the invisible economy. For many, however, perceived benefits do outweigh the costs.

In theory, many developing countries profess to discourage urban migration, citing problems related to employment, sanitation, limited transportation and traffic snarls, pollution, access to services, and crime. Most of these "instant" cities were not built for such number crunching. Even more daunting is the prospect of newly evolving but "infrastructureless" cities such as Surat, India, whose 1.5 million people must survive without garbage collection and waste-water treatment. The only constant is the ever-present threat of diseases such as bubonic plague. Despite difficulties, it's business as usual. Many countries gear public policy towards urban residents to distract the masses and keep them contented and subservient. Only lip service is paid to bolstering rural economies and social services. National pride is often at stake as well. Cities are viewed as symbols of progress as well as centres of industry and wealth, even though much of the city is blighted by slums and derelict housing projects.

In short, developing world urbanism would appear to qualify as a bona fide social problem. Potential damage to society and the environment is such that attention must focus on consequences. Resources are diverted to sustain the activities of people in cities, some of whom are becoming richer and consuming more as people's self-worth becomes increasingly defined by consumer goods (Honey, 1999). Yet inhabitants of these cities may not see it that way. There is not much point in returning to resource-depleted and socially stifling environments. Even the inconveniences and dangers of city life are a small price to pay for its opportunities and excitement. Solutions to the problem of global urbanization must reflect these differences in perspective.

Poverty

Many are aware of poverty as a major social problem in the developing world. What most do not recognize is the real magnitude of this problem, the reasons why it exists, and why eradication is a formidable, if not impossible, task. The globalization of world economies does not automatically confer equal access to the benefits of commercial success. Some prosper, others become increasingly impoverished. Even media portrayals of the developing world tend to ignore the presence of affluent classes, with glaring disparities in wealth, power, and status between the haves and the have-nots. Still, poverty remains the rule rather than the exception, with the poor eking out an existence in the midst of plenty.

Defining developing world poverty can be a problem. Many are absolutely poor when compared with North American standards of consumerism or measured by GNP per person. In emphasizing economic factors, however, such criteria overlook improvements in the general standard of living related to health or education. Measurements often gloss over how costs of living are considerably less because of reduced needs, cheaper infrastructures because of minuscule tax bases, and diminished expectations. Also ignored are how community networks and an informal economy can bolster standards of living, although this may not show up in the national ledger.

Why does developing world poverty exist? Overpopulation is widely regarded as a primary cause of developing world poverty. Conversely, the reverse may be an equally valid interpretation. It may be argued, for example, that poverty contributes to overpopulation by necessitating large families as a survival tactic (Brown, 1993). The fact that the poorest countries continue to be the fastest growing confirms the validity of this argument. Equally important as contributing factors are structural factors, including: unequal economic distribution, the lack of political will to correct this, and the legacy of colonialism with its reinforcement of dependency and underdevelopment (Skinner, 1988).

Expressions and causes of poverty vary from rural to urban regions. For urbanites, poverty is directly related to lack of jobs. It is most graphically expressed in squalor and derelict housing, a lack of sanitation or waste disposal, and the constant danger of violence. For farmers and peasants, poverty stems from inadequate prices for goods produced for export. International prices fluctuate wildly, or the demand for agricultural products or raw materials may collapse in the face of synthetics and substitutes. The presence of poverty in the midst of high expectations can create problems. The terminally impoverished, as Jacques Attali (1990) calls them, may rebel, and this rebellion can be channelled into religious movements at odds with secular rule. Others prefer to protest via terrorism or mass insurrection. These options may not strike us as valid or viable, yet what other choices are there for those with nothing to lose?

The face of poverty has shifted again in recent years. The AIDS epidemic has struck Africa with a vengeance, particularly in sub-Saharan Africa, accounting for 83 percent of all AIDS deaths since the inception of the epidemic here (Englund, 1999). An estimated 34 million people in this region have been infected, of whom 11.5 million have died, a quarter of them children. By comparison, there are around 890 000 people living with AIDS/HIV in Canada and the United States. IN 1998, AIDS killed 2 million Africans; at this rate, and amid the utter desolation that AIDS is wreaking on the continent, any material or social benefits derived from development may be lost (Herzberg, 1999). Poverty intensifies the suffering. While the US spent $880 million combating AIDS in 1998, despite "only" 40 000 new HIV infections, about $165 million was spent in Africa to offset some 4 million new infections (Schiller, 1999). The poverty of the people makes it difficult to get the kind of medicines that can prolong health and life, especially the AIDS cocktail (anti-retroviral regime) which can cost up to $60 000 a year to administer. According to Englund, much of what passes for medical care consists of a cot, a couple of aspirins, and a towel to wipe a victim's forehead. Also contributing to these figures is the stigma associated with AIDS. The shame and ostracism attached to AIDS is so powerful a deterrent that people will decline what little assistance there is since its acceptance implies acknowledgement. In some areas, between 20 and 50 percent of the women have been found to be infected. A third of these women will transmit the virus to their children. Yet these same women risk being beaten and thrown out of the house if implicated, even if infected by their husbands, and women are unlikely to force an issue on condoms or question partners about fidelity for fear of abuse or abandonment (Schiller, 1999).

Global Monocultures

The cultural dimension of globalization is no less ambiguous in impact and implications (see *National Geographic*, August 1999). As noted, the ideological principles of the global economy are not new, only now they are being applied globally, with the result that all human cultures are expected to comply with a global game whose rules include aggressive consumerism, replacement of import-substitution economic models for export-oriented models, primacy of free trade and unregulated investment, privatization of public enterprises, and obsession with exponential economic growth (Mander, 1996). To be sure, modern technology has prolonged human life spans and comfort zones in ways that could hardly be imagined even a generation ago. But a globalizing technology, in reflecting a Western corporate vision, also has the potential to destroy the varieties and vestiges of human culture (which may be defined as maps of meaning by which realities are negotiated). The world appears to be in the throes of worldwide transformation of cultures with a corresponding erosion of unique perspectives. The rapid disappearance of the remote and removed is part of a broader trend in which the basic dynamic remains the same: Goods move, people move, ideas move, and cultures change. Admittedly, human societies have always mixed and intermingled, but everyone is swept up by the dynamics of an urban-oriented, technologically based culture that moves faster and further, even the one billion people who are illiterate and living on less than a dollar a day.

Around the world, the pressure to conform to the expectations of global and consumerist monoculture is eroding regional difference and cultural identities. Conformity pressures are also intensifying levels of uncertainty, ethnic friction, and collapse (Norberg-Hodge, 1999). Media exposure to a one-dimensional fantasy view of modern life, with its sophistication, fast cars, designer clothes, and shiny white teeth invariably makes people feel stupid and ashamed of those traditions that lack glamour, entail hard work, and involve sacrifices. Although corporations do not plan the destruction of diversity, often lacking an awareness of the consequences of decisions and structures on real people in other parts of the world, a collateral destruction of cultural diversity appears inevitable under the circumstances (Suzuki, 1999). In castigating globalization as a step toward homogenous consumption, with a corresponding diminishment of self-sufficiency and dismantling of local traditions, Helena Norberg-Hodge (1996:20) makes a similar point:

> The myth of globalization is that we no longer need to be connected to a place on the earth. Our every need can be supplied by distant institutions and machines. Our contact with other people can be through electronic media. Globalization is creating a way of life that denies our natural instincts by severing our connection to others and to nature. And — because it is erasing both biological and cultural diversity — it is destined to fail.

However pervasive the lure of globalization, a global monoculture is not inevitable. People do not have an innate human desire to indulge in Westernized, urbanized cultural lifestyle, notwithstanding mantras that West is best, or consume and you be will be saved (Norberg-Hodge, 1999). Yet fears of global uniformity may be exaggerated. The very opposite may be in evidence, despite concerns over a cultural cloning that pollutes, assaults, and flattens every cultural crease into one large McWorld, especially among teenagers with time and money to spend in fulfilling their cravings for novelty and things American.

Cultures and the people who live in them are proving to be much more resilient, resourceful, and unpredictable. Evolving instead of a monoculture is a shifting hybrid of experimentation and innovation in which the new and old are precariously juxtaposed, mutually transformed, or syncretically reinterpreted (Zwingle, 1999). Rejection of a standardized, one-size-fits-all mentality may bolster the distinctiveness of local and regional differences (Quelch, 1999). As a result, two apparently contradictory trends are unfolding in the new millenium: Societies are converging because of globalization and consumerism; no less evident is a growing divergence because of global inequalities and increased reattachment to traditional values as oases of tranquility in times of turmoil. Playing one off against the other may not necessarily yield disarray, but provide an opportunity for creative growth.

Ethnic Nationalism

The integration of human societies into a global system is counterbalanced by an equally powerful surge of separatist-leaning ethnic nationalisms (Guibernau, 1996; Breton, 1995; Balthazar, 1996). Just as there is a growing convergence toward a single global monoculture, given the influences of transnationals, media, and rampant consumerism, so too is there evidence of a divergence based on tribal loyalties and maintenance of ethnic ties. In a globalizing world of standardization and homogeneity, people cling even more fiercely to whatever local customs impart distinctiveness, in some cases pushing the protection of these differences to politicized claims for sovereignty, autonomy, and self-determination. In a post-Cold War world, people do not divide themselves along ideological or economic lines, as Samuel Huntington points out in his book "The Clash of Civilizations," preferring instead to define themselves on the basis of perceived differences related to language, culture, or religion. World politics is being re-contoured along cultural lines, resulting in new patterns of conflict or cooperation that transcend the bipolar politics of the Cold War. As the traditional nation-state recoils from the challenges of capital mobility and international trade, ethnic nationalisms may rush to fill the political void created by the eclipse of sovereign states. That this reconfiguration is proving disruptive is of mounting concern. Conventional state sovereignties are under pressure from insurgent ethnicities to create a kind of global mosaic of mutually antagonistic homelands (Ignatieff, 1994). The invocation of "ethnic cleansing" in what was once a multi-ethnic Yugoslavia reminds us all too depressingly of the dangers implicit in this sort of jingoism. The imploding effect created by ethnicity threatens to divide even established democracies into squabbling factions. As a result, the nation-state may relinquish its legitimacy to act on behalf of its citizens, and concede ground to ethnic conflict every bit as demoralizing as that in Bosnia or Kosovo.

The politics of ethnicity are proving the catalyst behind a new world (dis)order. Ethnicity (defined as a shared awareness of perceived ancestral differences as basis for reward, recognition, or relationships) itself is not a social problem. Those who embrace ethnicity endorse it as a solution to many contemporary problems, both social and personal (Solomos and Black, 1996). Ethnicity is endorsed as a means of survival on a changing and diverse planet. A commitment to ethnicity allows an escape from feelings of irrelevance, powerlessness, alienation, and impersonality. Appeals to ethnicity foster a sense of continuity, belonging, and security, especially for those at the margins of society without alternate channels for coping with societal stress. It constitutes an oasis for meaning and commitment—even relaxation and enjoyment—in an increasingly complex urban-technological environment. At other times, it has furnished the impetus for mobilizing people into goal-directed action (Rex and Drury, 1996). The pooling of combined resources allows ethnic minorities to compete more effectively in crowded contexts. Under the banner of ethnicity, members of a group seek to maximize their social and economic advantages in a rational and calculated manner (Olson, 1965). Nowhere is this more evident than with indigenous peoples. Indigenous peoples are demanding levels of political autonomy that reflect their status as the original occupants whose collective rights to self-determination over jurisdictions from political voice to land and identity have never been extinguished, but remain intact as a basis for rethinking who gets what in society (Fleras, 1997).

What some see as an opportunity, others define as a problem. Critics have denounced the surge in ethno-cultural pride or identity as divisive, backward-looking, and counter-productive (Porter, 1965). With the onset of modernization and forces of globalization, ethnic attachments are rebuked as atavistic survival mechanisms and repudiated for being inconsistent with cultural rationality and national integration (Connor, 1972). Ethnically based nationalisms have been singled out as major contributors to international conflicts as well as a threat to the cohesion and integrity of states around the world (Brown, 1989). Ethnicity is condemned as an inexcusable reversion to tribalism in which blind conformity to the collective and an obsession to avenge past wrongs may degrade all that is noble in human progress. It runs counter to the liberal-pluralistic values that underpin globalization; that is, a belief that what we have in common is more important than what divides; that what we do as individuals is more important than what group we belong to; that the content of character is more important than the colour of skin; and that reason prevails over emotion as a basis for thinking and doing. Rejection of these values is thought to be bad enough; even more worrying are the implications of living together with radical differences. Instead of a shared humanity and common values, an insurgent ethnicity emphasizes a dislike of others and a refusal to cooperate in a state of ethnic coexistence.

For still others, the question goes beyond the notion of good or bad. Like it or not, they say, ethnicity is here to stay as a formidable presence in human affairs. The very forces of globalization are likely to intensify rather than defuse demands for more local attachments (Paz et al., 1996). The seeds of communal politics and ethnic and religious fundamentalism are sown by the economic totalitarianism associated with globalization which fosters homogenization, centralizes power, destroys livelihoods, creates displacement, and degrades environment (Shiva, 1999). Economic development not only exacerbates existing ethnic tensions (some of which were suppressed by superpower hegemony), but may create them by destroying bonds of reciprocity, mutual dependence, and sustainable lifestyles without providing substitutes (Norberg-Hodge, 1999). Instead of the nation-states we now know, boundary lines will be redrawn to reflect loose confederations of ethnic and indigenous communities tied together into regional or global trading blocks. In short, if the twentieth century was heralded as the age of ideological nationalism, the 21st century may well be defined or destroyed by the dynamics of ethnic nationalism. The challenge of making society not only safe for ethnicity, but also safe *from* ethnicity may well emerge as the key global problem confronting the new millenium (Schlesinger, 1992).

Environmental Crisis

The natural environment plays a prominent role in shaping each country's global agenda (Jackson, 1992). Consider the ways in which the following environmental problems could influence government policy or public perceptions: a shortage of raw materials, drought and crop failure, deforestation in the tropics, and pollution ranging from waste misman-agement and noxious emissions, to global warming and ozone depletion. Efforts to do some-thing about this crisis in global fragility are often lost in a haze of platitudes, rarely leading to concerted or coordinated cooperation. In 1992, for example, 150 leaders gathered in Rio de Janeiro, Brazil, and raised righteous concern over the deteriorating environment. The Rio Declaration promised that "[s]tates shall cooperate in a spirit of global partnership to con-serve, protect, and restore the health and integrity of the Earth's ecosystem." A document was signed by more than 1600 senior scientists, including over half of all Nobel Prize winners. Five years later, a follow-up summit of more than 60 leaders learned that, lofty rhetoric notwithstanding, the global environmental crisis has deepened in terms of forest destruction, fresh water shortages, worldwide overfishing, and mass extinction of species (Schoon, 1997). The gap between the rich and poor nations has increased, as has the division be-tween rich and poor within societies, with calamitous effects on the environment, as the poor of the world strip forests for warmth and cooking, while the rich install more air con-ditioning. Emissions of fossil fuels by rich nations have risen to the point where artificially contrived climatic shifts are a real possibility with the build-up of greenhouse gases. That the Rio Declaration was a failure is regrettable but understandable in light of political grand-standing. Public posturing in 1992 was cheap, especially since pronouncements of global part-nership were not legally binding. What is less forgivable is the thought that heads of state have reconvened in hopes of re-enacting their own version of gaseous emissions (reinforcing the problem in the process) without acknowledging their hypocrisy.

The world now confronts a global eco-crisis of frightening proportions. In a devastating indictment on the future of the human race, a UN-based report entitled "Global Environment Outlook 2000" indicated the main threats to human survival were posed by water short-ages, global warming (its impact on extreme weather events had taken three million lives in the past five years), and nitrogen pollution. Global catastrophe, it concluded, could only be averted through political will and ongoing citizen choices (cited in the *Guardian Weekly*, Sept. 23–29th, 1999). Equally important was the need to reverse the process of conspicuous over-consumption by 90 percent among the world's rich countries. The politics of problem def-inition and solution divide along "class" lines. The rich countries say that environmental degradation such as global warming is a global problem, and that all countries must do their part to combat it, and refusal to extract concessions from poor countries will result in refusal to ratify any deals. The poor countries argue that the rich are responsible for the problem, es-pecially the greenhouse gas problem, and they should be the ones to fix it rather than the poor countries who can ill afford to make the adjustments without sentencing millions to poverty and squalor (Editorial, *Globe and Mail*, 1997). Admittedly, chronic environmental degradation threatens the lives and life chances of the rich and poor alike, but the poor of the world have little choice except to exert additional pressure on the environment, while the con-sumption patterns of the affluent, by contrast, result in depleted stocks, less biological di-versity, and costs that are borne by the poor despite lesser access to the benefits (UN Human Development Report, Introduction, 1999). Consider only how the export of prawns and shrimp to the richest countries has destroyed massive areas of coastal mangrove forests to accomodate crustacean farms (Goldsmith, 1999). Or think of the environmental havoc cre-ated by our fixation on coffee. Modern plantation-grown coffee (unlike coffee that natu-rally grows in shade) requires huge amounts of chemicals, and can lead to deforestation and reduced habitat for natural species of birds and animals (Mittelstaedt, 1999).

Even Canada's image as squeaky clean does not stand up to scrutiny (Wallace and Shields, 1997). Canadians put a premium on protecting the environment over promoting economic growth (McArthur, 1997). Yet the political will is absent, together with public fears that thinking green may interfere with economic growth (Knox, 1997). A political obsession with the economy may pose more of a problem than a realistic solution, especially when Environment Canada has lost 30 percent of its budget between 1995 and 1997, with corresponding reductions in staffing to inspect and prosecute (Mitchell and Winfield, 1998). Environmentalists are criticizing Ottawa for reneging on a promise made in 1995 to reduce emissions to a pre-1990 level. Instead, greenhouse gases have risen by 13 percent, prompting the UN to identify Canada as one of the world's heaviest energy users. According to another study, Canada's environment has deteriorated dramatically in terms of air and water pollution, loss of wetlands, waste and nuclear disposal, and chemical poisons in soil and the food-chain (*Kitchener-Waterloo Record*, 1995). These assaults on Canada's environment are the result of global warming, automobile traffic, nitrates in rivers, reliance on pesticides, deforestation, toxic substances, and depletion of otherwise sustainable resources. Moreover, a growing reliance on global free trade is unlikely to enhance environmental concerns as competition at all costs takes hold (Abley, 1997).

Not surprisingly, the Canadian Institute for Business and the Environment has pinned a "C-" on Canada for its lack of progress since the Rio Declaration. The institute cites federal budget cutbacks in environmental protection as one problem; the other culprit is provincial refusal to do more in the face of slashing costs (Gallon, 1997). Ontario was named by the Montreal-based Commission for Environmental Cooperation as the continent's second worst jurisdiction for industrial pollution, after Texas and just ahead of Louisiana in third place (Armstrong, 1999). Treatment of waste is a national disgrace, says the Sierra Legal Defence Fund (Mittlestaedt, 1999). Major Canadian cities, including Victoria, St. John, Halifax, St. John's, and Dawson City, continue to dump more than one trillion litres of sewage and excrement with little or no treatment directly into the environment. Despite these threats to the environment, politicians in Canada continue to prattle on about jobs and deficits, as if sensible and somehow painless solutions to these problems might be implemented in a resource-depleted world (Suzuki, 1998). This suggests a need to reconsider whether the economy is the primary issue. Instead of seeing a booming economy as the solution to all of Canada's problems, Suzuki contends, we should question whether the profit-motivated private sector can possibly protect the "ecological capital" that sustains all planetary life. The virtual collapse of the ground fishing industry in the Atlantic provinces, coupled with widespread layoffs in west coast fishing, attest to the damage that can be inflicted by greed, carelessness, or indifference.

Proposals to address environmental issues must be couched as global social problems. We are all in this together, and together we have to make changes, with the rich helping the poor (Schoon, 1997). A mindset shift of monumental proportions is required. First, the natural world does not exist in isolation from human communities. One billion people live in unprecedented prosperity; another billion live in abject destitution. According to Durning (1991), both rich and poor engage in consumption patterns (one from greed, the other from need) that exert pressure on existing resources such as water, land, forests, and atmospheres. Recognizing the relationship of people to the environment helps to "frame" many of the global problems in play at present. Second, political decisions rather than the forces of nature are overwhelmingly responsible for defining the basis of this relationship. Much of the decision-making originates in the north rather than the south, and this observation puts the blame where it rightfully belongs (Jackson, 1992). To be sure, many will blame the developing world for economic ruin, but many of the world's economic problems stem from Western consumption patterns, obscene levels of waste and wastefulness, and an obsession with the "cult of the immediate" (Attali, 1990). In spite of this, the developing world is expected to disproportionately contribute to the protection of the global environment—even if this means curbing local consumption or curtailing regional economic growth (Durning, 1991). There is much to commend in balancing production with ecology, but those who point the finger at others should begin by first examining their own consumption patterns. Third, solutions to environmental problems are not simple. The relation of human beings to their environment is complex, with the result that changes in one area will affect another, even though there is no way of predicting precisely what will happen in each situation. A commitment to slash our addiction to lavish energy consumption may not materialize until Canadians suffer the consequences of "manmade" changes in climate such as extreme weather patterns or flooding and erosion in coastal areas (Dyer, 1999).

Root Causes/Structural Solutions

> The media have failed to connect the dots and show how many of today's international crises have their roots in globalization. (The *Ecologist*, Vol 29, no 3, 1999)

The world of today is inundated by an avalanche of deepening crises and open conflicts. Such a candid admission may seem counter-intuitive, given the promises of globalization, but does acknowledge the double-edged character of global development. The growing interdependence of world peoples through shrinking borders, time, and space, has the potential to create or preclude opportunities, to generate benefits as well as political, economic, social, and ecological securities, and to foster divisions, even as unity through conformity prevails (UN Human Development Report, 1999). World trade and global capitalism have the potential to deliver billions from poverty, create opportunites for choice and personal development, and reinforce democracies around the world. They also have the potential to deny, exclude, or exploit. Critics and supporters align themselves accordingly: On one side are concerns about global warming and the extinction of species; on the other are worries about the onset of a global monoculture, ethnic conflicts, and intensifying levels of poverty. As well there are incongruities that beg to be explained: Why do Canadians export most of the cars they produce, while importing most of the cars they drive at prices significantly higher than in the United States? Why will Britain export 111 million litres of milk and 47 million kilograms of butter, while importing 173 million litres of milk and 49 million kilograms of butter (Norberg-Hodge, 1999)? If these problems and paradoxes are perceived as isolated from each other, the challenge of solution seems insurmountable. However, if interpreted as diverse symptoms of the same root cause, the situation appears more amenable to reform (Editorial, *Ecologist*, 1999).

At the heart of most global problems is an economic system that separates producers from consumers, people from nature, and local decision-making from large institutions in a way that enriches some at the expense of others. The internal logic of this near-universal global economy ensures that virtually no problem is exempt from its operational dynamics. The dominance of the market at global levels has had the effect of dividing both people and nations, with winners reaping the rewards while victims cope with the effects (UN Human Development Report, 1999). Unrestricted global trade and imposition of Western developmental models are exacerbating environmental problems: Forests are depleted, seas over-fished, water awash with pollutants, and croplands seriously degraded (Goldsmith, 1999). Globalization of markets fosters a rampant competition in which countries compete to create the most attractive conditions for industry, even if this means running roughshod over environmental concerns or regulations. A global economy also requires the conversion of yet untapped rural populations of the developing world into consumers, with corresponding pressure on finite resources. The construction of transportation infrastructures from highways to airports, often at public expense, may be justified as a convenience for citizens, but is often tailored to the needs of the largest corporations and their vision of the world: one in which every society is dependent on a single, high tech, energy-intensive consumer economy under the control of a small number of transnationals (Gorelick, 1999). In other words, Edward Goldsmith writes, freewheeling development and global capitalism are a problem rather than a solution to the lives and life chances of the developing world. Moreover, this global dynamic may be eroding those very things that individuals and communities require in order to survive; that is, clean air, safe water, a unifying vision, and sense of security and community. Instead, as the lead editorial in the *Ecologist* concludes, a multibillion-dollar advertising industry is transforming children into voracious consumers, global warming is wreaking increasing havoc with our weather and settlement patterns, exotic goods and foods are routinely shipped to discriminating palates in the West, despite horrific costs to subsistence patterns and ecological zones; and everything from the meaning of work to the biological diversity of the world is defined in relation to the pursuit of efficiency through standardization.

A critique of global economy provides a vision of social and ecological renewal: about conserving communities, about providing children with a sustainable future, about renewing relationships with the natural world, about trade that meets people's needs rather than profits, employing resources that are locally available, and about encouraging diversity by escaping the clutches of a conformist global monoculture and an Americanization of culture (Editorial, 1999). Empowerment stems from understanding the global and economic roots of these impacts on the social and ecological environment. More importantly, an uplifting sense of optimism is made possible since the vast scope and magnitude of these global problems is rendered more manageable by the recognition of their prime cause (Editorial, 1999). The forces of global capitalism are not immutable or irreversible, with no alternatives to consumerism, free trade, or economic growth (Korten, 1999). Rather, these global forces are socially constructed, rather than natural, normal, or inevitable, and they are simply carrying out their instructions to put profit before people. The only way to alter this behaviour is to re-code it by reconstructing its charter, processes, and outcomes (see also Lasn, 1999).

THE PROBLEM WITH SOLUTIONS: FOREIGN AID AND (MIS)DEVELOPMENT

The global integration of national and transnational economies is an established fact. The magnitude and scope of this integration cannot be overestimated. Nor can there be any doubt about the unevenness of this process. These imbalances in the global process are especially evident by observing post-war trends in international assistance. Since the Second World War, affluent countries have transferred billions of dollars of assistance to the poorer, developing world. The rationale behind these initiatives is quite simple. While the average Canadian earned nearly $22 000 in 1995 (the figure for an American is closer to $27 000 per year), the

BOX 15.1	**Human Development**

The following is an edited excerpt from the introduction to the 1999 United Nations Human Development Report. The full text of the report is available on the internet at: www.undp.org/hdro

This 10th Human Development Report—like the first and all the others—is about the growing interdependence of people in today's globalizing world. This era of globalization is opening many opportunities for millions of people. Increased trade, new technologies, foreign investments, expanding media, and Internet connections are fueling economic growth and human advance. All this offers enormous potential to eradicate poverty in the 21st century—and continue the unprecedented progress of the 20th century. We have more wealth and technology—and more commitment to a global community—than ever before.

But today's globalization is being driven by market expansion—opening national borders to trade, capital, information—outpacing governance of these markets and their repercussions for people...When the market goes too far in dominating social and political outcomes, the opportunities and rewards of globalization spread unequally and inequitably—concentrating power and wealth in a select group of people, nations and corporations, marginalizing the others....The challenge of globalization in the new century is not to stop the expansion of global markets. The challenge is to find the rules and institutions for stronger governance—local, national, regional, and global—to preserve the advantages of global markets and competition, but also to provide enough space for human community and environmental resources to ensure that globalization works for people, not just for profits.

In the globalizing world of shrinking time, shrinking space, and disappearing borders, people are confronting new threats to human security—sudden and hurtful disruptions in the pattern of daily life. In both poor and rich countries, dislocations from economic and corporate restructuring and from dismantling the institutions of social protection, have meant greater insecurity in jobs and incomes. The pressures of global competition have led countries and employers to adopt more flexible labour policies with more precarious work arrangements.

Globalization opens people's lives to culture and all its creativity—and to the flow of ideas and knowledge. But the new culture carried by expanding global markets is disquieting. As Mahatma Ghandi expressed so eloquently earlier in the century, "I do not want my house to be walled in on all sides and my windows to be stuffed. I want the cultures of all the lands to be blown about my house as freely as possible. But I refuse to be blown off my feet by any." Today's flow of culture is unbalanced, heavily weighted in one direction, from rich countries to poor.

average annual income in Ethiopia was $120, and only $70 in Mozambique. Not only is this morally awkward for many, but such a disparity also has the potential to disrupt the international status quo, with long-term repercussions for global survival. Only a reduction in this gap can stave off the threat of global confrontations or deter the movement of asylum-seekers in search of economic opportunity. In this sense, any move to secure greater global equality is of benefit to the rich as well as the poor.

One strategy for achieving this goal has focused on expanding initiatives in foreign aid. A package of short- and long-term programs has been implemented in hopes of bolstering developing world standards to the level of developed countries. But after 40 years of development and assistance, the track record is mixed at best. On the one hand, life expectancy in the developing world has crept up to 63 years (compared with an average of 75 in the industrialized world). Much of this increase can be attributed to longer survival rates among children because of improved immunization programs. On the other hand, the downside is inescapable. Increases in life expectancy may compound the problem of overpopulation in many developing world countries, resulting in corresponding demands on scarce resources and sprawling urban processes. Once again the solving of social problems is subject to certain truisms. Elements exist only in relation to others, with the result that changes in one area may ripple out to others because of this interconnection. The complexity of these interrelations makes it difficult to predict events or control outcomes (Jackson, 1992). Solutions or problems rarely fit into an "either-or" category. Solving one problem may intensify existing problems or activate often unexpected difficulties whose combined impact could well undermine the original gains. Solutions that only superficially address the problem, rather than long-term prevention strategies that link people with resources, are also destined to fail.

These conundrums in problem-solving apply to the field of foreign aid. As the concept has come under intense scrutiny, criticism is mounting over the use of foreign aid to bring about renewal and reform. Critics prefer that development rely on liberalizing trade or the discipline of the market by way of structural adjustments and private sector reforms. The moral underpinnings of foreign aid pose an awkward dilemma. The effectiveness of foreign assistance is also being questioned, because of unacceptably slow or non-existent rates of progress in coping with the social problems of receiving countries. Megaprojects like superhighways or international airports have also been criticized because of their adverse effect on local economies and the environment (Culpepper, 1993). That doubts are escalating should come as no surprise. A backlash against foreign aid is inevitable as the rich countries wrestle with their own downsizing demons. Resentment smoulders when governments are seen as helping others while ignoring the plight of the poor through domestic deficit reduction or lack of job creation. Finally, public perceptions are playing a key role in cutbacks. Many believe developing countries are responsible for the predicament in which they find themselves. The developing world is also criticized for not doing enough to reduce inequities, defuse ethnic animosities or religious strife, or curtail military spending that consumes scarce resources at the expense of productive potential. In response to this criticism about its propriety and effectiveness, there has been a rethinking of developmental assistance in recent years. The shift to more human-centred assistance (focused on health, education, and ameliorating poverty) is widely touted, as is the emphasis on sustainability (locally owned development) and proactive initiatives (with an emphasis on prevention rather than cure). Increasingly, attention and funding are directed towards cooperative programs, often involving women in collectives, as catalysts for change. Still, questions remain about whether foreign aid reduces or magnifies the problems of the developing world. Even more disturbing is whether Canadians are part of the problem or part of the solution.

Underlying Logic

Foreign aid is based on the concept of improving a country's economy by modernizing its services and production facilities. The philosophical underpinnings of developmental assistance reflect the success of the Marshall Plan in the late 1940s. Conceived by U.S. Secretary of State John Marshall, the plan provided for the reconstruction of war-ravaged Europe through massive airlifts of supplies and the provision of technical assistance. The plan was so successful that it provided a blueprint for all future assistance strategies. The less fortunate (the south) receive assistance from the privileged (the north) through the transfer of wealth (resources, skills, expertise) in hopes of accelerating economic modernization. The objective of this so-called munificence is threefold:

1. to reduce inequality by eliminating dependency (especially dependence on those aspects of culture and society that inhibit growth and progress);

2. to encourage development at local and national levels; and

3. to fortify the grounds for a stable, capitalist, and democratic society.

The anticipated benefits of foreign aid are widely invoked. Political, economic, social, and moral reasons often serve to rationalize the transfer of aid from the rich to the poor. On the assumption that continued prosperity in Canada is directly related to prosperity abroad, foreign aid is endorsed as an investment in global security and international peace, rather than as an act of charity or chivalry (Culpepper, 1993). A reduction in local inequalities may forestall global tension, deter ecologically or ethnically driven conflicts, avert massive migration, and arrest environmental destruction. The rationale of most of these plans is based on improving the GNP of each society. By focusing on GNP, most foreign aid programs aim to increase domestic wealth through the transfer of capital and tools (resources, money, infrastructure, experts, and expertise). At one end of the transfer continuum are donations of emergency assistance when countries experience natural catastrophes such as floods or famines. At the other end are long-term investments, which can include donations of foodstuffs or finished products, investment and expertise for sustainable community development, bilateral trade exchanges, and infrastructure development related to roads, communication links, and hospitals. In recent years, the focus and scope of foreign aid and development have taken a new direction. From an earlier commitment to throwing money and experts at a problem, the underlying philosophy is now directed towards locally driven, sustainable development (best encapsulated in the aphorism "give people fish, and they will eat for a day; teach them how to fish and they will eat for a lifetime"). But what happens when the local fishing place becomes polluted or stocks are depleted? What sounds good in principle, in other words, does not always work in practice.

For Whom, for What?

Canada is widely admired as a generous contributor to the international scene. Under the auspices of the Canadian International Development Agency (CIDA), developing nations have been the recipients of billions of dollars in assistance. Funding has been funnelled into a variety of programs, both in the short term (emergencies) or long term, and ranging in scope from megaprojects to the locally driven sustainable development. But Canada's commitments do not match reality. In 1999, the government projected $2.3 billion for foreign aid, or about 0.25 percent of the GNP, a drop from about 0.5 percent in 1991, and far below the 0.7 percent that Canada once promised. With the possible exception of the Netherlands and Scandinavian countries, a comparable downward trend is evident elsewhere: Foreign aid, once a key component of American foreign policy, "free fell" from $27.1 billion in 1985 to $12.3 billion in 1997. World totals have plummetted as well to $47 billion (US) in 1997 from $58.9 billion two years earlier. Yet even these sums are deceiving, especially in Canada. The prominence of strings-attached bilateral trade arrangements ensures that nearly two-thirds of every foreign aid dollar is eventually spent in Canada. According to the 1997 federal report "Shaping Our Future," Canada's foreign aid policies were to be aimed at the poorest countries in an effort to help people to help themselves. In reality, less than 20 percent of Canada's foreign aid is directed at the neediest, with many Eastern European countries in receipt of large sums. Taken together, 33 percent of all aid is directed at "geographic programs" (including everything from infrastructure to lines of credit), 16 percent consists of cash transfers to international financial agencies (such as the International Monetary Fund), 12 percent is for food, 9 percent matches funds from other agencies (such as Oxfam), and 6 percent is for administration.

Despite such seeming generosity, the result of nearly a half century of assistance from the rich to the poor has proven mixed. Many have concluded that billions in foreign aid spending have had little impact on reducing global inequality. Nor has it had much effect on the economic policies of the developing world, despite the use of foreign aid as an incentive to reduce inflationary government spending, pare back subsidies, and eliminate bureaucracy (Blustein, 1997). How do we account for this singular lack of success? Does the problem reflect the fact that foreign aid has more to do with politics and commerce than with poverty or powerlessness? Is it a Band-Aid solution ill-equipped for dealing with fundamental issues related to structure and system? Are target populations inadequate to the task of assisting in their own development? Or is the problem one of expediency; that is, is the transfer of wealth organized around the needs of the donor rather than the target country? Is foreign assistance a tool for encouraging independence and growth, or a trap for fine-tuning the bonds of dependency and underdevelopment? Consider the case of Bangladesh, which came into existence when India was partitioned in 1971, and to this day receives half its national budget from foreign sources. It has been claimed that overseas contributions account for more than 90 percent of the government development budget—including everything from building bridges to paying teachers' salaries, while another $5 billion in foreign aid remains "stuck in the pipeline" (Miller, 1991). This aid transfusion is viewed by some as a necessary prelude to self-management; by others as an example of how "well-intentioned waste" aborts local growth by reinforcing a welfare mentality and dependency syndrome. In other words, foreign aid can be interpreted as much as a problem as a solution. It also has the effect of catching Canadians and Americans in one of their cultural blind spots; that is, a belief that there's a definitive solution to every problem (Dickey, 1997).

Perils and Pitfalls: A Trojan Horse

What conclusion can be drawn from this examination of disbursements under foreign assistance? On the surface, there is much to be said for the commitment to help others to eventually help themselves. In reality, too much foreign aid is concerned with political or commercial issues rather than with poverty eradication (Knox, 1996). The model of development that is foisted on the developing world is colonialist in seeking not to improve people's lives but to ensure markets, foster consumerism, extract resources, and create a pool of cheap labour

(Goldsmith, 1999). The rationale behind foreign aid has historically focused on political leverage for helping "allies." Expediency dictated that enemies would be overlooked regardless of need or duress. Foreign assistance was rationalized on the grounds of stabilizing—and rewarding—countries that were friendly to the West, thus allowing capitalist expansion without fear of unnecessary unrest or unwelcome takeovers. Second, most aid could not be separated from economic considerations. Foreign aid often materialized as a disguised export subsidy for the donor country, with strings attached because of "bilateral" political or economic concessions. Under "tied" assistance, countries would receive benefits provided they purchased Canadian-made goods in return. While this was of obvious benefit to Canada, developing countries were forced to purchase unnecessary goods at inflated prices as a precondition to qualify for foreign assistance from Ottawa (Drohan, 1996). Not surprisingly, the strings-attached mentality further ensnared the host country in the workings of a global economy (Nicholson-Lord, 1992). Other aid is contingent on making punishing structural adjustments to induce higher productivity in industry or agriculture through free-market pricing, private ownership, inflation reduction, pared-away government expenditures, elimination of food subsidies, and reduced social services. These austerity measures may please World Bank donors, but they often incite riots when suffering becomes acute (Chege, 1997). Third, the bulk of foreign aid is of an expedient rather than humanitarian nature. Generous offers of emergency assistance are often an excuse to discard surplus commodities without depressing international commodity markets. This has happened in the past. The fact that disaster relief may intensify the suffering of the victims (for example, sending powdered milk to relief victims who cannot comfortably digest milk enzymes) is unconscionable. That the government can get away with off-loading embarrassing and subsidized stockpiles of milk powder, butter, and wheat—and still look good in the process—is called "politics."

The failure of foreign aid programs may also reflect differences in the ways people think about social problems. Take the concept of solutions, for example. A central theme throughout this and other chapters is the inapplicability of simplistic solutions to complicated problems. Social problems are related to solutions in ways that are ambiguous, contradictory, and unpredictable. The world we live in is too complex and too interconnected to allow us to confidently predict outcomes or to control the shape of events. We may even have to confront the prospect that some problems have no solution. Still, we continue to be preoccupied by a quick-fix mentality. In times of rapid change, simple solutions take on a certain appeal to those who merely want to convey the illusion rather than the substance of change. However, our search for simple (as in simplistic) solutions may be partly the result of a dominant intellectual tradition that shapes how we think and experience reality (Rothenberg, 1992). Our intellectual tradition emphasizes a line of thought that partitions the world into mutually opposed categories (opposition thinking), linear models (cause-effect relations that reflect single causes and predictable effects in a straight-line progression), and the existence of a hierarchy (with a ranking of differences on a scale).

There is nothing wrong with patterns of thought organized around a line that connects and moves in a straight direction between points. However, an exclusive reliance on such rationality makes it impossible to consider alternative forms of thought that acknowledge complexity, relationships, and contradiction. Such a linear style of thought spells disaster in the design and implementation of foreign aid programs. It also compounds problems of communication when the host and donor communities do not have the same priorities or think along the same lines. A mindset is required instead that allows the coexistence of mutually exclusive alternatives. Mass industrialization and large-scale technological development are not the only model for development in a world characterized by new global economies, including decentralization, individual empowerment, local management, and environmental concern (Bennett Davis, 1998). Additional reasons relate to poor program design and implementation. Projects continue to be poorly planned by technical experts out of touch with the particular needs of a country. Efforts are sabotaged by poor delivery systems and a lack of communication with local experts about how best to modify Western-style showpiece programs for Third World consumption. Experts may be inclined by training to produce computer-based irrigation technologies when all the local community really needs is a hand-held well pump. The human factor is too often ignored. Lastly, problems of maintenance are rarely addressed. Sophisticated technology may require expensive upkeep and constant repairs, thus further alienating the masses from participation or benefit. In other words, the poor become poorer, partly because developmental programs deal with symptoms rather than causes, ignore the broader social and cultural context, and disregard the interconnectedness of society and the environment. This may not be the intent behind foreign aid; nevertheless, the consequences of assistance actions are such that, despite good intentions, they inadvertently harm those who need help the most.

Solution or More of the Same?

The string of foreign aid failures is now legendary. Developmental assistance has been criticized for fattening political elites and spawning a global array of non-governmental organizations, but doing little to improve living standards for the poor (French, 1996). Big cash outlays pave the way for corruption. That, in itself, is no reason to blame individual field workers for glitches in the process. There is even less reason to accuse the recipients of being lazy or corrupt. Rather, failure is often built into the principles and practices of foreign aid. As well, it is easy to criticize foreign aid as a disincentive to progress or growth. But few any longer deny the political and economic overtones of conventional assistance. Agencies such as CIDA have revised their mission to include sustainable development and community-based growth. Partnerships are being forged that focus on local projects and areas of poverty, with women increasingly being targeted as the beneficiaries. There has also been a move to decentralize and deregulate the procedures by which programs and projects are designed and delivered.

   Public reaction to foreign aid and development remains as vocal as ever, especially by those who denounce the exercise as morally dubious and economically doubtful. Foreign aid is perceived as wastefully tossing money into a bottomless pit. As the former editor of the *New Internationalist* sarcastically put it, foreign aid "transfers money from the poor people of the rich country to the rich people of the poor countries" (quoted in Nicholson-Lord, 1992). Many see foreign aid and development as a superficial solution that never gets to the root of the problem. Too much, they say, is spent on building bridges and roads but not on helping the poor, given that only three percent of foreign aid budgets are earmarked for health or education (Knox, 1996). For some, the concept of foreign aid reflects an old-fashioned liberalism; one identified the problem, then called in the social scientists to analyze it, the technicians to solve it, and the government to finance the program (*Economist*, 1996). By contrast, current neo-conservative thinking denies the existence of a problem in the first place—social scientists have misunderstood it, technicians can't solve it, and any effort by the government would only make things worse. Even more galling is an awareness that foreign aid may unwittingly abet conflict or suffering by propping up murderous regimes by playing politics with people's lives (Unland, 1996). Famines in parts of Africa are not caused by droughts but by civil war, according to this line of thinking, and pouring in more relief intensifies the fighting (Toolis, 1998). For still others it is the short-sightedness of foreign aid that rankles. A short-term problem is solved at the expense of creating a long-term solution or an additional set of problems. It is one thing to feed people during emergencies; it is quite another to furnish them with the tools to feed themselves; it is still another to appreciate how increased life expectancy will exert further pressure on dwindling resources and restricted land space.

What to do? The solution is not to discontinue foreign aid and development; after all, people need assistance to survive regardless of our moral qualms. The goal is to examine the problem in global terms and to apply local solutions that transcend dependencies and foster meaningful local development. This is accomplished in part by taking foreign aid out of official hands and putting it to use as directly as possible for those in most need. For if there is one thing we have learned, it is that social problems are rarely solved by telling others what to do or by doing it for them. Failure is inevitable unless steps are taken to deal with these problems holistically. Problems are even less likely to be solved if solutions fail to come from within the community, focus on the structures that created the problem in the first place, and provide a level of assistance that is consistent with that community's level of development.

HUMAN RIGHTS: TOWARDS A NEW GLOBAL GOVERNANCE

There is much that is terrifyingly depressing about the state of global affairs in the new millenium. Problems are appearing out of nowhere, and appear to be overwhelming the finite resources and resourcefulness at our disposal, while solutions appear hopelessly inadequate to do anything of substance. Yet there are flickers of hope that things are not as bad as they seem to be, and that solutions are being implemented as situations arise. Nowhere is this optimism more brimming than in the emergence of human rights as a global issue, with profound implications. By putting human rights, including liberty, life, justice, equality, tolerance, and mutual caring, at the forefront of global concerns, the reinventing of global governance may prove a turning point for the 21st century (UN Development, 1999).

The international legal framework for human rights originated with the Universal Declaration of Human Rights by the UN General Assembly in 1948. Article One declared that "All humans are born free and equal in dignity and in rights. They are endowed with reason and conscience and should act towards one another in a spirit of brotherhood." The declaration articulated a vision of the world in which all states were committed to the protection of all human rights (civil, political, economic, social, and cultural) under a rule of law anchored in the principle of equality and non-discrimation at a time when (a) self-determination was denied to colonized people throughout the world, (b) most women continued to be denied basic rights, and (c) racial discrimination remained legally entrenched in Canada and the United States. The International Bill of Rights was strengthened by the adoption of the International Covenant on Civil and Political Rights and Economic, Social, and Cultural Rights in 1966. Specialized human rights treaties by the UN included the prohibition of discrimination (1966), discrimination against women (1979), torture (1984), and the violation of children's rights in 1989. A high commissioner for human rights has been appointed. To atone for the 120 million people who have perished in wars, political persecution, genocide, and ideologically engineered famine, Canada and 120 countries are laying the foundation for an international criminal court, with jurisdiction over genocide, crimes against humanity, war crimes, and aggression. But problems are already evident: The lack of mechanisms for enforcement is glaring; only national governments can be held accountable rather than individuals or corporations; and international justice is restricted to the most egregious abuses against humanity while remaining oblivious to the banality of evils that hurt and hinder (UN Development, 1999).

The signficance of this international social movement cannot be lightly dismissed. As a result of these humanitarian initiatives, most of which have been ratified by numerous states, the post-Second World War era has been defined as the age of rights, involving the transformation of constitutionally protected rights within a few states to a universal conception of human rights and its basis in defining international policies, politics, and law (Chinkin, 1999). Fifty years after its proclamation, the UN Declaration of Rights has been called the "sacred text" and a major article of faith of a worldwide secular religion; a yardstick by which human progress is measured; and the foundational document that subsumes all other creeds directing human behaviour (See Ignatieff, 1999). The commemoration of the Declaration is a reminder that human rights constitute political and civil rights, as well as economic and social rights pertaining to the right to life, and rights to jobs, housing, health, and education. We also are reminded that the basic principles upon which human rights are based are universal, and, although the mechanisms that infuse life into them are shaped by features specific to each society, there is no justification for citing cultural relativism or respect for cultural identity as an excuse for violation of human rights (Mayor, 1999). In a world that holds nothing to be true, except the truth that remains trapped within us, Michael Ignatieff writes, the emergence of human rights over the primacy of state sovereignty is nothing short of astonishing. The internationalization of human rights is such that states can no longer justify mistreatment of individuals under their own jurisdiction as "internal matters." Gone are the days when atrocities inside the borders of a sovereign country were dismissed in the same way that domestic abuse was once in Canada, as a domestic matter that was nobody's business (Editorial, 1999). In other words, sovereignty is to be respected only when nation-states respect the rights of their citizens—an idea that was introduced by the Nuremberg Trials when it was proclaimed that a society's human rights violations were subject to international prosecution. To be sure, these aspirations were never implemented because of Cold War politics; nevertheless, the thaw has resulted in an assault on national sovereignty, no more so than on March 24th, 1999, when NATO began bombing Serbia, the first multinational attack designed largely to curb violations of human rights within a country's borders (Rosenberg, 1999).

In short, the world is developing a conscience. In a world of satellite television and the Internet, news of mass murder and atrocities travels quickly and fosters a sense of human solidarity that transcends national boundaries and ethnic differences (Editorial, 1999). In consolidating this international discourse that all human beings have basic rights and liberties, state sovereignty is being redefined: States are increasingly seen as instruments at the service of their citizens, rather than vice versa, while the fundamental freedoms and rights of individuals have been enhanced by a spreading consciousness of human rights (Annan, 1999). In the words of the UN Secretary-General, Kofi Annan, "Strictly traditional notions of sovereignty can no longer do justice to the aspirations of people everywhere to attain their fundamental freedoms. Massive and systematic violations of human rights—wherever they may take place—should not be allowed to stand."

This interventionism on behalf of human rights is not without problems: In global affairs, the security of individuals is critical as an international priority and impetus for international action. Yet the impunity of human rights violators throughout the world continues to mock the vision of the Declaration, in that violations continue to be committed in the name of religion, custom, tradition, or ethnicity. The social and economic human rights of developing countries are compromised by the structural adjustments programs imposed by the titans of economic globalization and global capitalism. Uniform globalism and its commitment to commerce will ensure that fundamental freedoms are fragile as long as poverty, exclusion, and inequality persist, and the role of government is restricted to mediator and security rather than protector of the general interest (Mayor, 1999). Non-state actors, including transnational corporations, may also compromise human rights by way of corporate decisions that deny, exclude, or exploit (Chinkin, 1999). Questions remain: Is intervention to be pursued everywhere or selectively? What price are people willing to pay for moral interventionism? Are moral universals useless unless countries are willing to sacrifice both blood and resources in their pursuit (Ignatieff, 1999). In other words, Christine Chinkin explains, the ideal of human rights standards has been achieved in principle. Now comes the hard work with respect to their scope, applicability,and implementation. Establishing the principle was one of the great accomplishments of the 20th century. Putting this principle of human rights into practice will be the challenge for the 21st century.

References

Abbate, Gay (1999). "Hate-related Crimes Rising, Police Say." *The Globe and Mail,* February 25.

Abbate Gay (1999). "Change in Police Views on Youth Urged." *The Globe and Mail.* May 20.

Abel, Sue (1997). "Shaping the News." *Waitangi Day on Television.* Auckland University Press.

Abella, Irving and Harold Troper (1982). *None is Too Many. Canada and the Jews in Europe 1933–1948.* Toronto: Lester and Orpen Dennys Ltd.

Abercrombie, Nichalas (1995). *Television and Society.* London: Polity Press.

Abley, Mark (1997). "Free Trade No Friend of Earth." *Toronto Star,* May 3.

Abraham, Carolyn (1999). "The Allure of a Man with Two Faces." *The Globe and Mail.* June 24.

Abu-Laban, Yasmeen and Daiva K. Stasiulis (1992). "Ethnic Pluralism Under Siege. Popular and Partisan Opposition to Multiculturalism." Canadian Public Policy 18(4): 365–386.

Abwunza, Judith (1997). *Women's Voices, Women's Power. Dialogues of Resistance from East Africa.* Peterborough: Broadview Press.

Agocs, Carol and Monica Boyd (1993). "Ethnicity and Ethnic Inequality." Pp. 330–352 in Jim Curtis, Ed Grab, and Neil Guppy (eds.), *Social Inequality in Canada,* 2nd edition. Scarborough, Ontario: Prentice Hall.

Ahenakew, David (1985). "Aboriginal Title and Aborgnal Rights: The Impossible and Unnecessary Task of Identification and Definition." Pp. 24–30 in Menno Boldt and J. Anthony Long (eds.), The *Quest for Justice. Aboriginal Peoples and Aboriginal Title.* Toronto: University of Toronto Press.

Airhart, Sharon (1998). "Will No Birds Sing in the Wired City?" *The Globe and Mail.* January 3.

Albo, Gregory and Jane Jenson (1996). "Remapping Canada: The State in the Era of Globalization." In J. Littleton (ed.), *Clash of Identities.* Scarborough: Prentice Hall.

Albrow, Martin (1996). *The Global Age.* London: Polity Press.

Alfred, Gerald Robert (1995). *Heeding the Voices of Our Ancestors: Kahnawake Mohawk Politics and the Rise of Native Nationalism in Canada.* Toronto: Oxford University Press.

Alfred, Taiaiake (1999). *Peace, Power, Righteousness.* Toronto: Oxford University Press.

Allen, Scott (1999). "The Planet Turns for the Better." *KW Record.* November 27.

Andersen, Robin (1996). *Consumer Culture and TV Programming.* Boulder, CO: Westview Press.

Andrews, Corbin (1999) "A License to Parent?" *National Post.* February 22.

Andrews, John (1999). "Holding its Own." *The Economist.* July 24.

Annan, Kofi (1999). "Two Concepts of Sovereignty." *The Economist.* September 18: 49-50.

Annual Report (1997). *Canadian Heritage.* Multiculturalism Division. Ottawa: Government Printer.

Apple, Michael W. (1996). *Cultural Politics and Education.* Buckingham: Open University Press.

Armstrong, Natalie (1999). "Ontario Named Continent's No. 2 Industrial Polluter." *National Post.* August 11.

Arnold, Tom (1999). "Parents Lack Basic Knowledge of Child-Rearing, Survey Finds." *National Post.* April 22.

Asbury, Kathryn E. (1989). "Innovative Policing: Foot Patrol in 31 Division, Metropolitan Toronto." *Canadian Police College Journal* 13(3): 165–181.

Atkinson, Joe (1994). "The State, The Media, and Thin Democracy." Pp. 146–177 in Andrew Sharp (ed.), *Leap into the Dark. The Changing Role of the State in New Zealand since 1984.* Auckland: Auckland University Press.

Attali, Jacques (1990). "Can Eastern Europe Move From the 19th to the 21st Century?" *New Perspectives Quarterly:* 38–41.

Bailey, Sue (1999) "$1.3 Million Will Hire More Women Science Profs." *KW Record.* May 9.

Baker, Peter (1999). "The Modern Office: Where Men are More Like Women." *National Post.* November 1.

Balthazar, Louis (1993). "The Faces of Quebec Nationalism." Pp 2–17 in A.G. Gagnon (ed.), *Quebec: State and Society,* 2nd edition. Scarborough: Nelson.

Balthazar, Louis (1996). "Identity and Nationalism in Quebec." Pp. 101–112 in J. Littleton (ed.), *Clash of Identities.* Scarborough: Prentice Hall.

Banton, Michael (1987). *Racial Theories.* London: Cambridge University Press.

Barlow, Maude (1999). "Global Rules Could Paralyze Us." *National Post.* August 31.

Barlow, Maude (1997). "Media Concentration is Reaching Crisis Levels." *Toronto Star,* May 2.

Barlow, Maude and Bruce Campbell (1996). *Straight Through the Heart. How the Liberals Abandoned the Just Society.* Toronto: HarperCollins.

Barlow, Maude and Heather-Jane Robertson (1993). *Class Warfare: The Assault on Canadian Schools.* Toronto: Key Porter.

Barrett, Stanley (1994). *Paradise. Class, Commuters, and Ethnicity in Rural Ontario.* Toronto: University of Toronto Press.

Barrett, Stanley R. (1987). *Is God a Racist? The Right Wing in Canada.* Toronto: University of Toronto Press.

Barrick, Frances (1999). "Face of Crime Has Changed Over 25 Years." *KW Record.* January 18.

Barthos, Gordon (1994). "Two Faces of Foreign Aid." *Toronto Star,* February 27.

Bartram, Jerry (1998). "The Left Talks." *The Globe and Mail.* September 26.

Bauman, Zygmunt (1999). "The Burning of Popular Fear." *New Internationalist.* March: 20-24.

Bayley, David (1994). "International Differences in Community Policing" Pp. 278–284 in D.P. Rosenbaum (ed.), *The Challenge of Community Policing.* Thousand Oaks, CA: Sage.

Beauchesne, Eric (1999). "Only 6 % of Canadians are Poor, UN Finds." *National Post.* October 7.

Beauchesne, Eric (2000). "Schools Cost More, Pay Less, Study Says." *National Post.* February 22.

Becker, H. (1963). *Outsiders.* New York: Free Press.

Beckow, Steve (1998). "The End of Employment." *The Globe and Mail.* July 11.

Behrendt, Paul (1996). "Aboriginal Australians: A Mirror of Attitude and National Conscience." Pp 6–15 in A. Pattel-Gray (ed.), *Martung Upah: Black and White Australians Seeking Partnership.* Blackburn, Victoria: HarperCollins.

Benzie, Robert (1999). "Hiring Guidelines." *National Post.* September 21.

Bercuson, David, Robert and J. L. Granastein (1997) *Petrified Campus: The Crisis in Canadian Universities.* Random House.

Berry, John W. (1993). "Cultural Relations in a Multicultural Society." Paper presented at a Community Psychology Seminar for Wilfrid Laurier University, Waterloo, Ontario, March 30.

Berry, John W. and Rudolf Kalin (1993). "Multiculturalism and Ethnic Attitudes in Canada. An Overview of the 1991 National Survey." Paper presented to the Canadian Psychological Association Annual Meetings, Montreal, Quebec, May.

Berry, John W and Rudolf Kalin (1995). "Multicultural and Ethnic Attitudes in Canada. An Overview of the 1991 National Survey." *Canadian Journal of Behavioural Sciences* 27(3): 301–320.

Berton, Pierre (1975). *Hollywood's Canada.* Toronto: McClelland and Stewart.

Best, Joel (1995). *Images of Issues: Typifying Contemporary Social Problems*, 2nd edition. Hawthorne, NY: Aldine de Gruyter.

Best, Joel (ed.) (1989). *Images of Issues: Typifying Contemporary Social Problems.* New York: Aldine de Gruyter.

Bibby, Reginald W. (1990). *Mosaic Madness. The Potential and Poverty of Canadian Life.* Toronto: Stoddart.

Bibby, Reginald W. (1995). *The Bibby Report: Social Trends Canadian-Style.* Toronto: Stoddart Publishing Company.

Biddiss, Michael D. (ed.) (1979). *Images of Race.* New York: Holmes and Meier.

Bienvenue, Rita M. (1985). "Colonial Status: The Case of Canadian Indians." Pp. 199–216 in Rita M. Bienvenue and Jay E. Goldstein (eds.), *Ethnicity and Ethnic Relations in Canada.* Toronto: Butterworths.

Bissoondath, Neil (1993/1994). "A Question of Belonging: Multiculturalism and Citizenship." Pp. 367–387 in William Kaplan (ed.), *Belonging. The Meaning and Future of Canadian Citizenship.* Kingston/Montreal: McGill-Queen's Press.

Bissoondath, Neil (1994). *Selling Illusions: The Cult of Multiculturalism in Canada.* Toronto: Penguin.

Blauner, Robert (1972). *Racial Oppression in America.* New York: Harper.

Blythe, Martin (1994). *Naming the Other. Images of the Maori in New Zealand Film and Television.* Metuchen, NJ: Scarecrow Press.

Boismenu, Gerard (1996). "Perspectives on Quebec–Canada Relations in the 1990s: Is the Reconciliation of Ethnicity, Nationality, and Citizenship Possible?" *Canadian Review of Studies in Nationalism* XXIII(1–2): 99–109.

Bolan, Kim (1997) "Canada Leads in Literacy." *KW Record.* November 11.

Bolaria, B. Singh (ed.) (1991). *Social Issues and Contradictions in Canadian Society.* Toronto: Harcourt Brace Jovanovich.

Bolaria, B. Singh and Peter S. Li (1988). *Racial Oppression in Canada*, 2nd edition. Toronto: Garamond Press.

Bolaria, B. Singh and Terry Wotherspoon (1991). "Income Inequality, Poverty, and Hunger." Pp. 464–480 in B. Singh Bolaria (ed.), *Social Issues and Contradictions in Canadian Society.* Toronto: Harcourt Brace Jovanovich.

Boldt, Menno (1993). *Surviving as Indians. The Challenge of Self-Government.* Toronto: University of Toronto Press.

Boldt, Menno and J. Anthony Long (1984). "Tribal Traditions and European-Western Political Ideology: The Dilemma of Canadian Native Indians." *Canadian Journal of Political Science* 17: 537–554.

Bonilla-Silva, Eduardo (1996). "Rethinking Racism: Toward a Structural Integration." *American Sociological Review* 62: 465–480.

Bouthillier, Eric (1999). "Ottawa's Low Blow." *The Globe and Mail.* November 26.

Bowles, Samuel and Herbert Gintis (1976). *Schools in Capitalist America.* London: Routledge & Kegan Paul.

Bowman, James (1999). "The Graduates." *National Review.* May 17.

Bragg, Rebecca (1999). "Toronto to Hire 55 New Firefighters." *Toronto Star.* July 28.

Brazier, Chris (1999). "The Radical Twentieth Century." *New Internationalist,* No. 309. January/February.

Breton, Albert (ed.) (1995). *Nationalism and Rationality.* Cambridge University Press.

Breton, Raymond (1998). "Ethnicity and Race in Social Organizations: Recent Developments in Canadian Society." In R. Helmes-Hayes and J. Curtis (eds.), *The Vertical Mosaic Revisited.* Toronto: University of Toronto Press.

Breton, Raymond, Wsevolod W. Isajiw, Warren E. Kalbach, and Jeffrey G. Reitz (eds.) (1990). *Ethnic Identity and Equality: Varieties of Experience in a Canadian City.* Toronto: University of Toronto Press.

Bridge, William (1995). *Job Shift.* Reading, MA: Addison-Wesley.

Brinkerhoff, David D., Lynn K. White, and Suzanne T. Ortega (1992). *Essentials of Sociology,* 2nd edition. St. Paul's: West Publishing.

Brodie, Janine (1997). "The New Political Economy of Region." In W. Clement (ed.), *Understanding Canada. Building on the New Canadian Political Economy.* Montreal/Kingston: McGill-Queen's University Press.

Bromley, Simon (1996). "Globalization?" *Radical Philosophy,* November/December, 80: 2–4.

Brook, Paula (1999). "Snakeheads or Globalism at Work?" *National Post.* September 13.

Brown, David (1989). "Ethnic Revival: Perspectives on State and Society." *Third World Quarterly* 11(4): 1–17.

Brown, Lee P. (1988). *Community Policing: Issues and Policies Around the World.* Washington, D.C.: National Institute of Justice.

Brown, Lee P. (1988). "Preface." *In International Association of Chiefs of Police, Developing Neighborhood Oriented Policing in the Houston Police Department.*

Brown, Lester (1993). "Facing the Crisis of Too Many Mouths to Feed." *The Globe and Mail*, August 9.

Brown, Paul (1999). "UN Report Warns of Environmental Crisis." *Guardian Weekly.* September 23-29.

Browne, Malcome (1994). "What Is Intelligence, and Who Has It?" *New York Times Book Review,* October 16.

Brym, Robert J. (1991). "Ethnic Group Stratification and Cohesion in Canada. An Overview." Pp. 49–78 in Robin Ostow et al. (eds.), *Ethnicity, Structural Inequality, and the State in Canada and the Federal Republic of Germany.* New York: Peter Lang.

Brym, Robert J. (1993). "The Canadian Capitalist Class." Pp. 31–48 in James Curtis et al. (eds.), *Social Inequality in Canada,* 2nd edition. Scarborough: Prentice Hall.

Bulla, Frances (1999). "No Place Like Home." Atkinson Fellowship Series. *Toronto Star*, October 26.

Bulletin, (1999). "Fall Conference Exposes Commercialism Trend." *CAUT* 46 (9), November.

Burgess, Michael (1996). "Ethnicity, Nationalism and Identity in Canada–Quebec Relations: The Case of Quebec's Distinct Society." *Journal of Commonwealth & Comparative Politics* 34(2): 46–64.

Burne, Jerome (1999). "Amazon Sisters Ruled the Cave." *National Post.* May 22.

Butler, Judith Davis (1998). *The Nurture Assumption.* New York: Free Press.

Butterfield, Fox (1999). "Rethinking the Strong Arm of the Law." *New York Times.* April 4.

CAFCA (Campaign Against Foreign Control) (1996). "News Media Ownership in New Zealand." Fact Sheet No 3.

Caldwell, Brian (1999). "Newspaper Ads Mask Racist Goals." *KW Record.* Oct 15.

Cameron, Silver Donald (1997). "The Way Maclean's Ranks Them." *The Globe and Mail.* November 24.

Campbell, Murray (1996). "The Shifting Line Between the Haves and the Have-Nots." *The Globe and Mail*, October 12.

Campbell, Murray (1996). "Work in Progress. A Century of Change." A Six-Part Series. *The Globe and Mail*, November 28.

Canadian Human Rights Commission (1997). Annual Report. Ottawa: Minister of Supply and Services.

Canadian Press (1999). "Class of '95 Does Well in Job Market." *KW Record*. April 29.

Canadian Press (1999). "Kids Vote for Families First." *KW Record*. November 11.

Canadian Press (2000). "More Jobs But More are Jobless." *KW Record*. January 6.

Canadian Press (1999). "Suicide Brings Heavy Financial Cost, Study Finds." *The Globe and Mail*. September 7.

Cannadine, David (1998). *The Rise and Fall of Class in Britain.* New York: Columbia University Press.

Capon, Dick (1999). "Today's Job Contracts Discourage Loyalty." *Toronto Star*. August 14.

Capon, Noel, John E. Farley, James M. Hulbert and David Lei (1991). "In Search of Excellence Ten Years Later: Strategies and Organization Do Matter." *Management Decision* 29(4): 12–21.

Cardozo, Andrew (1996). "Policy Works, Warts and All." *Toronto Star*, October 14.

Carey, Elaine (1999). "Despite Upturn, Families are No Better Off." *Toronto Star*. July 27.

Carey, Elaine (2000). "Family Incomes on the National Downward Slide." *Toronto Star*. January 13.

Carey, Elaine (1997). "'Glass Ceiling' Still Keeps Women From Top Jobs." *Toronto Star*. August 10.

Carey, Elaine (1999). "The Golden Years Really Are." *KW Record*. October 2.

Carey, Elaine (1995). "Is Graying of Faculty Turning Universities into 'Boring Places'?" *Toronto Star*, September 25.

Carey, Elaine (1998). "More Grads Finding Part-Time Work, Statscan Finds." *Toronto Star*. March 13.

Carey, Elaine (1998). "One-Parent Families Under Fire." *Toronto Star*. October 28.

Carey, Elaine (1999). "Parenting Strongest Influence on Kids, Study Finds." *Toronto Star*. December 10.

Carey, Elaine (1999). "Starting Over, South Asian-Style." *Toronto Star*. May 15.

Carnoy, Martin (1993). *The New Global Economy in the Information Age: Reflections on Our Changing World.* Pennsylvania State University Press.

Carrington, Peter (1999). "UW Researcher Finds Little Change in Canada's Youth Crime Rate." *UW Gazette*. Bob Whitton (ed.). April 28.

Carroll, William K (1997). *Organizing Dissent. Contemporary Social Movements in Theory and Practice,* 2nd edition. Toronto: Garamond.

Carter, Betty and Joan K Peters (1996). *Love, Honor, & Negotiate: Making Your Marriage Work.* New York: Simon and Schuster.

Carver, Lisa (2000). "Feminist Upheaval." *The Globe and Mail*. January 1.

Castells, Manuel (1993). "The Information Economy and the New International Division of Labor." Pp 15–44 in M. Carnoy (ed.), *The New Global Economy in the Information Age: Reflections on Our Changing World.* Pennsylvania State University Press.

Castonguay, Claude (1994). "Why More Quebec Voices Aren't Arguing for Federalism." *The Globe and Mail*, July 25.

Chamber, George (1997). "The Hypertextual Sea Change." *NZ Educational Review,* July 9.

Chamberlain, Art (1999). "Memorizing Isn't Learning, Education Conference Told." *Toronto Star*. April 23.

Chambliss, William J. (1973). "The Saints and the Roughnecks." *Society,* November– December.

Chan, Janet (1996). "Changing Police Culture." *British Journal of Criminology* 36(1): 109–133.

Chan, Janet B.L. (1997). *Changing Police Culture. Policing in a Multicultural Society.* Cambridge, UK: Cambridge University Press.

Cherry, Matt and M. Matsumara (1999). "Visions of Families for the 21st Century." *Free Inquiry* 19(1):25-26.

Chege, Michael (1997). "Time to Put Away the Heroic Stereotypes." *TLS,* January 3: 14–16.

Cherlin, Andrew J (1999). "I'm O.K., You're Selfish." *New York Times.* Sunday Magazine. October 17.

Cherney, Elena (1999). "Infants Prone to Violent Behaviour." *National Post.* July 30.

Cherney, Elena (1999). "Families Can't Afford the Luxury of Kids." *National Post.* December 23.

Chinkin, Christine (1999). "The Age of Rights." *LSE Magazine.* 4-5.

Chiose, Simona (1997). "You're Going to Make it After All!" *The Globe and Mail*, March 1.

Chisholm, Patricia (1996). "The Role of Parents." *Maclean's,* August 12, 109(33): 13.

Chodak, Simon (1994). "Review Essay: Voices on National Divorce." *Canadian Journal of Sociology* 19(3): 379–389.

Chorn, N.H. (1991). "Organisations: A New Paradigm." *Management Decision* 29(4): 8–11.

Christian, William (1999). "Justice For Canada's First Nations is Long Overdue" *KW Record.* August 28.

Churchill, Ward (1994). *Indians Are Us? Culture and Genocide in Native North America.* Toronto: Between the Lines.

Chwialkowkska Luiza (1999). "StatsCan Study Casts Doubt on Male-Female Wage Gap." *National Post.* December 21.

Clairmont, Don (1988). *Community-Based Policing and Organizational Change. Occasional Papers.* Halifax: Atlantic Institute of Criminology.

Clarke, Tony (1999). "Twilight of the Corporation." *The Ecologist* 29(2):158-161.

Clarke, Tony and Maude Barlow (1998). *MAI: The Multilateral Agreement on Investment and the Threat to Canadian Sovereignty.* Toronto: Stoddart.

Clement, Wallace (1997). "Introduction: Whither the New Canadian Political Economy?" Pp. 3–18 in W. Clement (ed.), *Understanding Canada: Building on the New Canadian Political Economy.* Montreal/Kingston: McGill-Queen's University Press.

Clement, Wallace (1998). "Power, Ethnicity, and Class: Reflections Thirty Years After The Vertical Mosaic." In R. Helmes-Hayes and J. Curtis (eds.), *The Vertical Mosaic Revisited.* Toronto: University of Toronto Press.

Cleveland, Harland (1985). "The Twilight of Hierarchy: Speculation on the Global Information Society." *Public Administration Review,* January/February, 45.

Cloward, Richard S. and Lloyd E. Ohlin (1960). *Delinquency and Opportunity: A Theory of Delinquent Gangs.* Glencoe, IL.: Free Press.

Cohen, Patricia (1998). "Daddy Dearest: Do You Really Matter? *The Globe and Mail.* September 15.

Cole, David (1998). *No Equal Justice: Race and Class in the American Criminal Justice System.* New York: Free Press.

Cole, Trevor (1999). "All the Rage." *Report on Business Magazine.* February. Pp.50-53.

Collison, Robert (1999). "Postcapitalism for Beginners." *The Globe and Mail.* March 6.

Conlogue, Ray (1997). "Time has not yet healed deep referendum wounds." *Globe and Mail*, January 1.

Connor, W. (1972). "Nation-Building or Nation-Destroying." *World Politics* 24(3).

Consedine Jim (1999). "Crime: Are the Answers Staring Us in the Face?" *Christchurch Press.* January 18.

Cook, Kathy (1999). "Arts Students Do Better in Life, New Studies Show." *Ottawa Citizen.* June 13.

Coontz, Stephanie (1992). *The Way We Never Were: American Families and the Nostalgia Trap.* New York: Basicbooks.

Corcoran, Terence (1996). "How Subsidies Ate Atlantic Region." *The Globe and Mail*, October 29.

Cordell, Arthur J. (1991). "The Perils of an Information Age." *Policy Options,* April: 19–21.

Cornell, Stephen (1988). *The Return of the Native: American Indian Political Resurgence.* New York: Oxford.

Corson, David (1999). "The Assimilation of Diversity." *Toronto Star.* January 27.

Cowan, Tyler (1999). "Cashing in on Cultural Free Trade." *National Post.* 24 April. B-1.

Coyne, Andrew (1999). "Prejudice from a Bygone Era." *National Post.* May 21.

Coyne, Andrew (1996). "We Need a Better Measure to Gauge Who is Living in Poverty." *Toronto Star*, December 15.

Coxe, Donald (1998). "Vanishing Act." *Report on Business Magazine.* November: 49–50.

Crane, David (1996). "Beware of Globalization Backlash." *Toronto Star*, February 1.

Crane, David (1996). "Multinationals Must Be Held Accountable." *Toronto Star*, September 26.

Crane, David (1997). "Building Backlash Over U.S. Globalization." *Toronto Star*, April 3.

Crane, David (1997). "Let's Not Give Up Culture." *Toronto Star*, February 9.

Crane, David (1997). "A Very Good State To Be In." *Toronto Star*, June 27.

Crane, David (1998). "Globalization 'The Only Way', Says WTO Chief." *Toronto Star.* Febuary 11.

Crane, David (1999). "Free Trade's Ambiguous Legacy." *Toronto Star.* June 7.

Crane, David (1999). "As We Celebrate, Canada at Crossroads Again." *Toronto Star.* July 3.

Crane, David (1999). "Don't Let the Rending of Social Fabric Go On." *Toronto Star.* July 4.

Crane, David (1999). "Can't Convert Universities into Factories." *Toronto Star.* August 1.

Crane, David (1999). "Knowledge Economy Redefines Work Ethic." *Toronto Star.* December 11.

Cribb, Robert (1999). "The Killing Game." *Toronto Star.* April 25.

Cribb, Jo and Ross Barnett (1999). "Being Bashed: Western Samoan Womens' Responses to Domestic Violence in Western Samoa and New Zealand." *Gender, Place and Culture* 6(1):49-65.

Crispo, John (1997). "The Teachers' Strike About Control and Power." *Toronto Star.* November 7.

Crone, Greg (1999). "Standard of Living to Return to Boom Levels, Banks Says." *National Post.* December 1.

Cryderman, Brian, Christopher O'Toole, and Augie Fleras (1998). *Policing in a Multicultural Society: A Handbook for the Police Services.* Markham: Butterworths.

Cudmore, James (1999). "Study Paints Bleak Picture of Canadian Employment Scene." *National Post.* June 3.

Cuff, John Haslett (1991). "Civil Wars That Nobody Wins." *The Globe and Mail*, November 18: C3.

Culpepper, Roy (1993). "Now is Not the Time to Forget Foreign Aid." *Toronto Star*, July 28.

Cummins, Jim and Marcel Danesi (1990). *Heritage Languages: The Development and Denial of Canada's Linguistic Resources.* Toronto: Garamond/Our Schools—Our Selves Education Foundation.

Cunningham, Allison Hatch (1998). "North of the 49th Parallel: The Criminal Justice System of Canada." *Criminal Justice* Summer: 1–27.

Curran, James and Michael Gurevitch (ed.) (1994). *Mass Media and Society.* London: Edward Arnold.

Currie, Jan and Janice Newson (eds.) (1998). *Universities and Globalization: Critical Perspectives.* Thousand Oaks: Sage.

Curtis, James, Edward Grab, and Neil Guppy (eds.) (1993). *Social Inequality in Canada: Patterns, Problems, and Policies.* Scarborough: Prentice Hall.

Curtis, J. E. Grabb, and N Guppy (eds) (1999). *Social Inequality in Canada: Patterns, Problems, and Policies*, 3rd edition. Scarborough: Prentice Hall.

D'Amato, Luisa (1999). "University Grads Get Jobs: Study." *KW Record.* May 15.

d'Aquino, Thomas (1997). "Outlook for Social Progress Bright." *The Globe and Mail*, January 1.

Dafoe, Chris (1999). "Fatherhood." *The Globe and Mail.* June 19.

Daniels, P.W. (1996). "The Lead Role of Developed Countries." Pp. 193–214 in P.W. Daniels and W.F. Lever (eds.), *Global Economy in Transition.* Harlow Essex: Addison Wesley Longman.

Daniels, P.W. and W.F. Lever (1996). "Introduction." Pp. 1–10 in P.W. Daniels and W.F. Lever (eds.), *Global Economy in Transition.* Harlow Essex: Addison Wesley Longman.

Darder, Antonia (1990). *Culture and Power in the Classroom: A Critical Foundation for Bicultural Education.* Critical Studies in Education and Culture Series. New York: Bergin and Garvey.

Dare, P. (1996). "Coming to a School Near You." *Kitchener-Waterloo Record*, January 29.

Das Gupta, Tania (1999). "Native People, Immigrants, and People of Colour." *In Canadian Families.* N. Mandell and A. Duffy (eds.). Pp 146–182. Toronto: Harcourt Brace.

Davies, Charles (1999). "New Worldly Ways." *National Post.* April 21.

Davis, Mark (1998). "Sick, Wicked Cultures." *AQ* Sept/Oct. 16–23.

DeBare, Illana (1999). "Job Hoppers No Longer Seen as Unreliable." *New York Times* News Service, reprinted in the *KW Record.* January 11.

de Beauvoir, Simone (1961). *The Second Sex,* translated by HM Parshley. Toronto: Bantom Books.

deSilva, Arnold (1992). *Earnings of Immigrants: A Comparative Analysis.* Ottawa: Economic Council of Canada.

DeGroot-Maggetti, Greg (1999). "Too Many Poor." *KW Record.* December 10.

Desroches, Frederick J. (1992, original 1986). "The Occupational Subculture of the Police." Pp. 39–51 in Brian K. Cryderman and Chris N. O'Toole (eds.), *Police, Race, and Ethnicity: A Guide for Law Enforcement Officers.* Toronto: Butterworths.

Diamond, Jack (1997). "Provinces are Archaic. More Power to the Cities." *The Globe and Mail*, May 26.

Dobson, Chris and Ian Jackson (1993). "Clayoquot Sound is Not Clearcut Sound." *Imprint,* October 8.

Doone, Peter (1989). "Potential Impact of Community Policing on Criminal Investigation." Pp. 84–106 in J. Robinson et al. (eds.), *Effectiveness and Change in Policing.* Wellington: Victoria University Institute of Criminology.

Downer, H. (1998). "Harnessing Globalisation's Power: Australia in the National Economy." Address to the Melbourne Business School and reprinted in the *Christchurch Mail.* April 20.

Drache, Daniel and Meric S. Gertler (eds.) (1991). *The New Era of Global Competition: State Policy and Market Power.* Montreal/Kingston: McGill-Queen's University Press.

Drohan, Madelaine (1996). "Dependency on U.S. Leaves Canada 'Vulnerable': WTO." *The Globe and Mail*, November 20.

Drohan, Madelaine (1996). "Rich Nations Urged to Cut Strings on Aid to Poor Countries." *The Globe and Mail*, September 20.

Drohan, Madelaine (1999). "Education Can't Be a Political Football." *The Globe and Mail.* December 10.

D'Souza, Dinesh (1996). *The End of Racism.* New York: Free Press.

Dua, Enakshi (1992). "Racism or Gender? Understanding Oppression of South-Asian Canadian Women." *Canadian Woman Studies*, Fall, 13(1): 6–10.

Dua, Enakshi, and Angela Robertson, eds. (1999). *Scratching the Surface: Canadian Anti-Racist Feminist Thought.* Toronto: Women's Press.

Duggan, Penny and Heather Dashner (1994). *Women's Lives in the New Global Economy.* The Netherlands.

Dwyer, Anna (2000). "Catalyst Examines Corporate Path for Women of Colour." *Women's Newsmagazine.* Winter: 16.

Dyck, Noel (ed.) (1985). *Indigenous People and the Nation-State. Fourth World Politics in Canada, Australia, and Norway.* St John's, Nfld.: Memorial University.

Dyer, Gwynne (1996). "Saying 'The World is a Mess' Is Just Not True." *New Zealand Herald,* September 4.

Dyer, Gwynne (1998). "Confessions of a Globe-Trotting Journalist." *Toronto Star.* December 24.

Ebner, David (1999). "Carleton Slashes Work Force by 18%." *The Globe and Mail.* June 24.

Eck, John E. and Dennis P. Rosenbaum (1994). "The New Police Order: Effectiveness, Equity, and Efficiency in Community Policing." Pp. 3–26 in D.P. Rosenbaum (ed.), *The Challenge of Community Policing.* Thousand Oaks, CA: Sage.

Eckler, Rebecca (1999). "We Know Who Did It." *National Post.* November 20.

Ecologist (1999). "Beyond the Monoculture: Shifting from Global to Local." Vol 29 (3). May/June.

Economic Council of Canada (1977). *Living Together: A Study of Regional Disparities.* Ottawa: Supply and Services Canada.

The Economist (1993/1994). "Towers of Babble." December 25–January 7.

The Economist (1996). "The Old New Right." September 14.

The Economist (1999). "Reflections on the Twentieth Century: Liberty, Equality, Humility." Sept 11–17.

Editorial (1996). "Canada, the Unfinished Country." *The Globe and Mail.* July 1st.

Editorial (1997). "The Rich, the Poor and Global Warming." *The Globe and Mail.* December 8.

Editorial (1998). "No Country is an Island." *The Globe and Mail.* October 9.

Editorial (1999). "Panning for Discrimination." *National Post.* April 24.

Editorial (1999). "Wrong Time to Skimp on Universities." *Toronto Star.* May 25.

Editorial (1999). "Brown of the Globe Got Canada Right." *The Globe and Mail.* July 1.

Editorial (1999). "Canada's Children Deserve Better." *Toronto Star.* November 20.

Editorial (1999). "Spare the Child." *The Globe and Mail.* December 2.

Editorial (1999). "The World is Developing a Conscience." *The Globe and Mail.* December 29.

Editorial (1999). "Introduction." *The Ecologist.* 29(3):153.

Editorial (2000). "The Revolutionary Western World." *National Post.* January 1.

Edwards, Steven (1999). "The Corporate Engines that Drive Globalization." *National Post.* September 29.

Eggerston, Laura (1998). "NAFTA woes." *Toronto Star.* January 12.

Ehrenreich, Barbara (1992). "Double Talk about Class." *Time,* March 2.

Eichler, Margrit (1988). *Nonsexist Research Methods: A Practical Guide.* Winchester, Mass: Unwin Hyman.

Eichler, Margrit (1989). "Reflections on Motherhood, Apple Pie, The New Reproductive Technologies and the Role of Sociologists in Society." *Society/Société,* February, 13(1): 1–15.

Eidham, Harald (1985). "Indigenous Peoples and the State: The Sami Case in Norway." Pp. 155–171 in Jens Brosted (ed.), *Native Power: The Quest for Autonomy and Nationhood of Indigenous Peoples.* Oslo: Universiteforlaget AS.

Eitzen, D. Stanley and Maxine Baca Zinn (1992). *Social Problems,* 5th edition. Toronto: Allyn and Bacon.

Elabor-Idemudia, Patience (1999) "The Racialization of Gender in the Social Construction of Immigrant Women in Canada: A Case Study of African Women in a Prairie Province." *Canadian Woman Studies* 19 (3): 38–44.

Eller, Jack David (1997). "Anti-Anti-Multiculturalism." *American Anthropologist* 99(2): 249–260.

Elliot, Patricia and Nancy Mandell (1995). "Feminist Theories." Pp 3–31 in Nancy Mandell (ed.), *Feminist Issues: Race, Class and Sexuality.* Scarborough: Prentice Hall Canada

Elliott, Larry (1998). *The Wealth and Poverty of Nations.* London: Little, Brown.

Elliott, Jean Leonard and Augie Fleras (1991). *Unequal Relations: An Introduction to Race and Ethnic Dynamics in Canada.* Scarborough: Prentice Hall.

Ellul, Jacques (1965). *Propaganda.* New York: Knopf.

Emmott, Bill (1993). "Multinationals. Back in Fashion." *The Economist*, March 27: 5–13.

Eng, Susan (2000). "Cop Culture: For Us or Against Us?" *The Globe and Mail.* January 27.

Englund, Stephen (1999). "Death in Africa." *Commonweal.* Aug 13.

Esses, Victoria M. and R.C. Gardner (1996). "Multiculturalism in Canada: Context and Current Status." *Canadian Journal of Behavioural Science* 28(3): 145–152.

Evans, Patricia M. and Gerda R. Wekerle (1997). *Women and the Canadian Welfare State: Challenges and Change.* Toronto: University of Toronto Press.

Evenson, Brad (2000). "Suicide Linked to Defective Gene." *National Post.* January 28.

Falk, Richard (1999). "World Prism." *Harvard Business Review* xxi (3).

Faludi, Susan (1999). *Stiffed: The Betrayal of the American Man.* New York: William Morrow.

Fawcett, Gail (1999). "Disability in the Labour Market: Barriers and Solutions." *Perception* (CCSD publication). Autumn: 7–9.

Fine, Sean (1999). "Wrestling with the Boy Code." *The Globe and Mail.* November 19.

Finlayson, Jock (1999). "Despite the Rumours, The End of Work is Not Nigh." *National Post.* September 6.

Fisher, Helen (1998). *The First Sex: The Natural Talents of Women and How They are Changing the World.* New York: Random House.

Fisher, Helen (1999). *The Anatomy of Love: The Mysteries of Mating, Marriage, and Why They Stray.* New York: Random House.

Fiske, John (1987). *Television Culture.* New York: Routledge.

Flavelle, Dana (2000). "Few Women Get Top Jobs." *Toronto Star.* February 9.

Fleras, Augie (1989). "Inverting the Bureaucratic Pyramid. Reconciling Aboriginality and Bureaucracy in New Zealand." *Human Organization* 48(3): 214–225.

Fleras, Augie (1992). "Aboriginal Electoral Districts for Canada: Lessons From New Zealand." Pp. 67–104 in Rob Milen (ed.), *Aboriginal Peoples and Electoral Reform in Canada.* Toronto: Dundurn Press.

Fleras, Augie (1992). "Managing Aboriginality: Canadian Perspectives, International Lessons." Paper presented to the Australian and New Zealand Association of Canadian Studies, Annual Conference. Victoria University, Wellington. December.

Fleras, Augie (1994). "Doing What is Workable, Necessary, and Fair. Multiculturalism in Canada." In Mark Charlton and Paul Barker (eds.), *Contemporary Political Issues.* Scarborough: Nelson.

Fleras, Augie (1995). "'Please Adjust Your Set': Media and Minorities in a Multicultural Society." Pp. 281–307 in Benjamin Singer (ed.), *Communications in Canadian Society,* 4th edition. Scarborough: Nelson.

Fleras, Augie (1996). "The Politics of Jurisdiction." Pp. 178–211 in David Long and Olive Dickason (eds.), *Visions of the Heart.* Toronto: Harcourt Brace.

Fleras, Augie (1999). "Politicizing Indigeneity: Ethnopolitics in White Settler Dominions." In Paul Havemann (ed.), *New Frontiers.* Auckland: Oxford.

Fleras, Augie and Jean Leonard Elliott (1991). *Multiculturalism in Canada: The Challenges of Diversity.* Toronto: Nelson.

Fleras, Augie and Jean Leonard Elliott (1992). *The Nations Within: Aboriginal-State Relations in Canada, the United States, and New Zealand.* Toronto: Oxford.

Fleras, Augie and Jean Leonard Elliott (1996). *Unequal Relations: An Introduction to Race, Ethnicity, and Indigeneity in Canada*, 2nd edition. Scarborough: Prentice Hall.

Fleras, Augie and Paul Spoonley (1999). *Recalling Aotearoa: Indigenous Politics and Ethnic Relations in New Zealand.* Melbourne: Oxford University Press.

Flynn, Andrew (1999). "Movie Violence Not the Only Cause for Killings." *The Kitchener-Waterloo Record.* April 25.

Flynn, Andrew (1999). "Education Reflects Practical Needs of Society." *KW Record* December 21.

Flynn, Deborah (1997). "No." *Toronto Star.* December 8.

Flynn, Julia (2000) "Hite Reports on Gender Views from Europe's Boardrooms." *The Globe and Mail.* January 4.

Fournier, Pierre (1994). *A Meech Lake Post-Mortem: Is Quebec Sovereignty Inevitable?* Montreal/Kingston: McGill-Queen's University Press.

Francis, Diane (1999). "It's High Time to Cut the Fat—and Taxes." *Maclean's.*

Francis, Daniel (1992). *The Imaginary Indian: The Image of the Indian in Canadian Culture.* Vancouver: Arsenal Pulp Press.

Fraser, Graham (1998). "Poverty Rates Rising, Report Says." *The Globe and Mail.* May 13.

Frideres, James (1998). *Native Peoples in Canada: Contemporary Conflicts*, 5th edition. Scarborough: Prentice Hall.

Friedan, Betty. (1963). *The Feminine Mystique.* New York: W. W. Norton.

Friedman, Thomas L. (1999). *The Lexus and the Olive Tree: Understanding Globalization.* Farrar, Straus, and Giroux.

Frizzell, Alan and Jon H Pammett (eds.) (1996). *Social Inequality in Canada.* Ottawa: Carleton University Press.

Fuller, John (1996). *News Values: Identity for an Information Age.* University of Chicago Press.

Frum, David (1999/2000). "Too Many Solitudes." *Saturday Night.* December/January: 39-40.

Fukuyama, Francis (1999). "The Great Disruption." *The Globe and Mail.* February 6.

Furey, Rachel (1999) "Universities Feel Glare of Tories." *National Post.* August 4.

Furstenberg, Frank F., Jr. (1999)."Family Change and Family Diversity." in *Diversity and its Discontents.* N. Smelser and J. Alexander, eds. Princeton University Press, pp. 147–166.

Gagnon, Lysiane (1996). "Sorry to be boring, but Quebec loves its constitutional contradictions." *The Globe and Mail*, July 6.

Gairdner, William (1991). *The War Against The Family: A Parent Speaks Out.* Toronto: Stoddart.

Galarneau, Diane (1993). "Alimony and Child Support." *Canadian Social Trends*, Spring: 8–11.

Galbraith, James K. (1999). "The Crisis of Globalization." *Dissent.*

Galeano, Eduardo (1999). "Betrayal and Promise." *New Internationalist* 309: 29-31.

Gallivan, Kathleen and Susan Bazilli (1999). "Exposing Sexual Harassment." *The Globe and Mail.* November 30.

Gallon, Gary (1997). "Five Years After Rio: Canada's Spotty Record." *The Globe and Mail*, June 23.

Galloway, Gloria (1999). "Crime Groups Divided Along Ethnic Lines." *National Post.* May 21.

Galt, Virginia and Miro Cernetig (1997). "Two Schools, Worlds Apart." *The Globe and Mail*, April 26.

Galt, Virginia (1997). "Universities Defend Role as Purveyors of Wisdom." *The Globe and Mail.* June 28.

Galt, Virginia (1999). "Jack Falling Behind Jill in School, Especially in Reading." *The Globe and Mail.* Oct 30.

Garbarino, James (1999). *Lost Boys: Why Our Sons Turn Violent and How We Can Save Them,* New York: Free Press.

Gaskell, Jane, Arlene McLaren and Myra Novogrodsky (1989). *Claiming an Education: Feminism and Canadian Schools.* Toronto: Our Schools/Our Selves Education Foundation.

Gates, Bill (1998). *Business@The Speed of Thought: Using a Digital Nervous System.* London: Penguin.

Gauthier, Janel G. (1998). "Introduction. Political Correctness in Academia: Many Faces, Meanings, and Consequences." *Canadian Psychology* 38:4.

Gay, Katherine (1992). "Change Demands Treating Employees Like Adults." *The Financial Post,* November 11.

Gherson, Giles (1997). "Atlantic Hampered by Benefits." *Kitchener-Waterloo Record,* June 20.

Gibb-Clark, Margot (1997). "Inexperience Held Against Women." *The Globe and Mail.* December 10.

Gibb-Clark, Margot (1999). "Key Employees Command Top Dollar." *The Globe and Mail.* October 11.

Giberson, Mark (1999). "Measuring What?" *University Affairs* January: 28.

Giddens, Anthony (1999). "The Way Beyond." *LSE Magazine.* P.16-17.

Giese, Rachel (1999). "Gays and Traditionalists Want the Same Treatment." *Toronto Star.* May 3.

Gilespie, Marcia Ann (1997). "Men on My Mind." *MS* November/December: 1.

Gillespie, Marie (1996). *Television, Ethnicity, and Cultural Change.* London: Routledge.

Gillies, James (1997). "Thinking the Unthinkable and the Republic of Canada." *The Globe and Mail*, June 28.

Gilligan, C. (1982). *In a Different Voice.* Cambridge, Mass.: Harvard University Press.

Gillmor, Don (1996). "The Punishment Station." *Toronto Life,* January: 46–55.

Girardet, Evelyne (1999). "Office Rage is on the Boil." *National Post.* August 11.

Giroux, Henri A. (1996). *Fugitive Cultures: Race, Violence, and Youth.* New York: Routledge.

Glazer, Nathaniel and Daniel P. Moynihan (1970). *Beyond the Melting Pot.* Cambridge: MIT Press.

The Globe and Mail (1992). "Community Standard Is Test of Tolerance." February 28: A2.

The Globe and Mail (1996). "Poverty Rates Vary Wildly, Study Finds." June 26.

The Globe and Mail (1999) "Managing Human Resources. Advertising Supplement." November 15.

Goar, Carol (1997). "We Broke the Bargain Between Generations." *Toronto Star.*

Goffman, Erving (1971). *The Presentation of Self in Everyday Life.* Garden City, NY: Doubleday/ Anchor.

Gold, Karen (1998) " 8.1% of Professors are Women." *The Times Higher.* July 3.

Goldberg, David Theo (1993). *Philosophy and the Politics of Meaning.* Cambridge: Basil Blackwell.

Goldberg, David Theo (1994). "Introduction: Multicultural Conditions." Pp 1–44 in D.T. Goldberg (ed.), *Multiculturalism: A Critical Reader.* Cambridge: Basil Blackwell.

Goldman, Robert (1992). *Reading Ads Socially.* New York: Routledge.

Goldsmith, Edward (1999). "Empires Without Armies." *The Ecologist* 29 (3):154-158.

Good, Alex (1998). "Critics Offer Sloppy Look at Universities's Woes." *KW Record*: January 10.

Good, Alex (1999). "A Century of Contrasts." *KW Record*: November 27.

Gordon, Avery F. and Christopher Newfield (1996). *Mapping Multiculturalism.* St. Pauls: University of Minnesota Press.

Gordon, Kennedy (1999). "Video Games May be Serious Fun or Deadly Conditioning." *KW Record*: June 5.

Gorelick, Steven (1999). "Tipping the Scale." *The Ecologist* 29 (3):162-166.

Gosine, Andil (1999). "Stopping Racist Language is Only the Beginning." *Toronto Star* March 21.

Grab, Edward G. (1990). *Theories of Social Inequality. Classical and Contemporary Perspectives,* 2nd edition. Toronto: Holt Rinehart and Winston.

Grab, Edward G. (1993). "General Introduction." Pp. xi–xxix in James Curtis et al. (eds.), *Social Inequality in Canada,* 2nd edition. Scarborough: Prentice Hall.

Grab, Edward G. (1999). "Conceptual Issues in the Study of Social Inequality." in *Social Inequality in Canada,* J. Curtis et al. (eds.). Pp. vii-xiv. Scarborough: Prentice-Hall.

Grady, Patrick and Kathleen Macmillan (1999). "Is North-South Killing East-West?" *Policy Options.* June: 68.

Graf, E. J. (1999). *What is Marriage For? The Strange Social History of Our Most Intimate Institution. Beacon Press.*

Gray, Herman (1995). *Watching Race: Television and the Struggle for Blackness.* Minneapolis: University of Minnesota Press.

Gray, John (1997). *False Dawn: Delusions of Global Capitalism.* London: Granta Books.

Gray, John (1998). "Unfettered Capital Spells Global Doom." *Guardian Weekly.* September 13.

Gray, Rita M. (1995). "Feminism and the Path of Meditation." *Shambhala Sun.* September: 42-46.

Green, Ross Gordon (1998). *Justice in Aboriginal Communities: Sentencing Alternatives.* Saskatoon: Purich Publishing.

Green, Paul (1994). *Studies in New Zealand Social Problems.* Palmerston North, NZ: Dunmore.

Greenspon, Edward (1997). "Economy Changing Faster Than People." *The Globe and Mail*, April 20.

Greenspon, Edward (1997). "Poverty Issue Requires Kid Gloves." *The Globe and Mail*, February 17.

Greer, Germaine (1999). *The Whole Woman.* New York: A. Knopf.

Grey, Earle (1996). "Separatists Trapped by Double Standard." in *Canadian Speeches: Issues of the Day.* November.

Griffiths, Franklin (1996). *Strong and Free: Canada and the New Sovereignty.* Toronto: Stoddart.

Griffiths, Curt T. and J. Colin Yerbury (1996). "Understanding Aboriginal Crime and Criminality: A Case Study." Pp. 381–398 in Margaret A. Jackson and Curt T. Griffiths (eds.), *Canadian Criminology: Perspectives on Crime and Criminality*, 2nd edition. Toronto: Harcourt Brace and Company.

Griffiths, Curt T., J.C. Yerbury and L.F. Weafer (1987). "Canada's Natives: Victims of Socio-structural Deprivation?" *Human Organizations* 46: 277–282.

Grindstaff, Carl F. (1995). "Canadian Fertility: 1951 to 1993, From Boom to Bust to Stability?" *Canadian Social Trends,* Winter, 39: 12-16.

Grossman, Lawrence K. (1995). "Beware the Electronic Republic." *USA Today,* August 29.

Groves, J. M., J. Witschger, and C. Warren (1996). "Reversal of Fortune: A Simulation Game for Teaching Inequality in a Classroom." *Teaching Sociology* 24 (October): 364–371.

Grusky, David B. (1997). "The Contours of Social Stratification." Pp. 1–48 in D. Grusky (ed.), *Social Stratification: Class, Race, and Gender in Social Perspective.* Boulder, CO: Westview Publishing.

Guibernau, Monsterrat (1996). *Nationalisms: The Nation-State and Nationalism in the Twentieth Century.* Cambridge, UK: Polity Press.

Gusfield, Joseph (1996). *Contested Meanings: The Construction of Alcohol Problems.* Madison: University of Wisconsin Press.

Gwyn, Richard (1996). "A Nation of Two Economic Solitudes." *Toronto Star*, July 7.

Gwyn, Richard (1998). "Banks Finding a Way to Make Their Profits Even Bigger." *Toronto Star.* January 25.

Gwyn, Richard (1998). "Growing Army of Jobless Proof of Marx's Prophecy." *Toronto Star.* October 4.

Gwyn Richard (1998). "Maybe National Unity Problem Not Meant to be Solved." *Toronto Star.* June 10.

Gwyn, Richard (1999). "The True Allegiance of Canadian Corporations." *Toronto Star.* April 28.

Gwyn, Richard (2000). "Welcome to the New World of Corporatism." *Toronto Star.* January 21.

Habib, Marlene (1999). "Simple to Complex Defines the Change in Health-Care System." *KW Record.* December 21.

Hacking, Ian (1999). "Are You a Social Constructionist?" *Lingua Franca* 9(4):65–73.

Hahnel, Robin (1999). "Going to Greet the WTO in Seattle." *Z Magazine.* November: p.7–10.

Hale, Sylvia (1990). *Controversies in Sociology: A Canadian Introduction.* Mississauga: Copp Clark Pitman.

Hall, Joseph (1997). "Sexual Violence Learned at School, Psychiatrists Told." *Toronto Star.* October 16.

Hancock, Graham (1989). *Lords of Poverty.* London: Macmillan.

Hanson, Kim (2000). "Few Women Reach the Top in Canadian Firms." *National Post.* February 9.

Hargrove, Basil (Buzz) (1996). "No Gain From the Pain." *Report on Business Magazine.* September, 37–38.

Hargrove, Buzz (1998). "Corporate Success, Social Failure, Corporate Credibility" *Canadian Speeches: Issues of the Day.* May: 3–4.

Hargrove Buzz and Wayne Skene (1998). *Labour of Love: The Fight to Create a More Humane Canada.* Toronto: Macfarlane Walter and Ross.

Harles, John (1998). "Multiculturalism, National Identity, and National Integration: The Canadian Case." *International Journal of Canadian Studies* 17(Spring): 217-248.

Harlow, John (1999). "'4-year Itch' in the Genes, Scientist says." *London Sunday Times.* Reprinted in *Toronto Star*, November 28.

Harman, Lesley D. (1992). "The Feminization of Poverty: An Old Problem With a New Name." *Canadian Woman Studies* 12(4): 6–9.

Harris, Judith Hill (1998). *The Nature Assumption: Why Children Turn Out the Way They Do.* Bloomsbury.

Harris, Michael (1998). *Lament for an Ocean. The Collapse of the Atlantic Cod Fishery: A True Crime Story.* Toronto: McClelland and Stewart.

Harrison, Barbara Grizzuti (1995). "Flesh Food and Fashion." *Mirabella* January: 20–21.

Hebert, Chantal (1999). "Quebeckers See Language Law as a Must." *Toronto Star.* October 22.

Hebert, Chantal (2000). "The War of Attrition on French." *Toronto Star.* January 17.

Heilbrun, Carolyn G. (1999). *Women's Lives: The View From the Threshold.* Toronto: University of Toronto Press.

Helmes-Hayes, Rick and Jim Curtis (eds.) (1998). *The Vertical Mosaic Revisited.* Toronto: University of Toronto Press.

Henry, Frances (1968). "The West Indian Domestic Scheme in Canada." *Social and Economic Studies* 17(1): 83–91.

Henry, Frances and Effie Ginzberg (1993). "Racial Discrimination in Employment." Pp. 353–360 in James Curtis et al. (eds.), *Social Inequality in Canada.* Scarborough: Prentice Hall.

Henry, Frances, Carol Tator, Winston Mattis and Tim Rees (1999). *The Colour of Democracy,* 2nd edition. Toronto: Harcourt Brace.

Henry III, William A. (1994). "In Defence of Elitism." *Time,* August 29.

Henslin, James (1994). *Social Problems,* 3rd edition. Englewood Cliffs, NJ: Prentice-Hall.

Herbert, Bob (1997). "A Worker's Rebellion." *The Globe and Mail.* August 12.

Herman, Edward S. and Noam Chomsky (1988). *Manufacturing Consent: The Political Economy of the Mass Media.* New York: Pantheon Books.

Herman, Judith Lewis (1991). "Sex Offenders: A Feminist Perspective." Pp. 177–194 in W.L. Marshall, D.R. Laws, and H.E. Barbaree (eds.), *Sexual Assault: Issues, Theories and Treatment of the Offender.* New York: Plenum Press.

Hernnstein, Richard J. and Charles Murray (1994). *The Bell Curve: Intelligence and Class Structure in American Life.* New York: Free Press.

Herzberg, Nathaniel (1999). "Aids Scythes Through Africa." *Guardian Weekly.* September 23-29.

Hiller, Harry (1990). *Canadian Society. A Macro Analysis.* Scarborough: Prentice Hall.

Himmelfarb, Michele (1998). "Jumping off Management Track." *Toronto Star.* February 11.

Hirschhorn, Larry (1997). *Reworking Authority: Leading and Following in the Post-Modern Organizations.* MIT Press.

Hirst, Paul (1997). "The Global Economy—Myths and Realities." *International Affairs* 73(3):409–425.

Hirst, Paul and Grahame Thompson (1996). *Globalisation in Question: The International Economy and the Possibilities of Governance.* Cambridge: Polity Press.

Hoberg, George (1999). "Can Canada Still Make Distinctive Policy Choices?" *Horizons.* Policy Research Initiatives 2(6): 8-10.

Hochschild, A. (1989). *The Second Shift: Working Parents and the Revolution at Home.* New York: Viking.

Holly, Brian P. (1996). "Restructuring the Production System." Pp. 24–39 in P.W. Daniels and F.W. Lever (eds.), *The Global Economy in Transition.* Harlow Essex: Addison Wesley Longman.

Honderich, John (1996). "Referendum: One year later." *Toronto Star,* October 26.

Honey, Kim (1999). "Cities Getting Too Big for the Planet, Professor Says." *The Globe and Mail.* January 26.

Honore, Carl (1999). "You Can't Kill All of Us." *National Post.* March 5.

Horn, Michael (1999). *Academic Freedom in English Canada: A History.* Reviewed by William Christian, *The Globe and Mail.* August 7.

Horsman, Matthew (1993). "Canada in the World." *Policy Options,* May: 3–4.

Hou, Feng and T.R. Balakrishnan (1996). "The Integration of Visible Minorities into Canadian Society." *Canadian Journal of Sociology.* 21(3): 307-326.

Hume, Christopher (1994). "A Jolt of Reality—Sponsored by Benetton." *Toronto Star*, January 20.

Hummel, Ralph (1987). *The Bureaucratic Experience.* New York: St Martin's Press.

Hunter, Alf (1986). *Class Tells.* Scarborough: Nelson.

Hurrell, Andrew and Ngaire Woods (1995). "Globalization and Inequality." *Millenium: Journal of International Studies* 24(3): 447–470.

Hurtig, Mel (1991). "Canada. Love It or Leave It." *The Globe and Mail*, October 5.

Hurtig, Mel (1999). *Pay the Rent or Feed the Kids: The Tragedy and Disgrace of Poverty in Canada.* Toronto: McClelland & Stewart.

Hutchins, Christopher (1997). "Nun Deliverer of Dogma." *Christchurch Press,* September 12.

Hutchison, Ian and Geoff Lealand (1996). "Introduction: A New Mediascape." *Continuum* (Aotearoa/New Zealand: A New Mediascape) 10(1): 7–11.

Hyndman, Jennifer (1999). "Gender and Canadian Immigration Policy: A Current Snapshot." *Canadian Woman Studies.* 19(3): 6–10.

Ibbitson, John (1999). "Higher Education Next Tory Target." *National Post.* April 26.

Ibbitson John (1999) "Squeegeeing the Homeless." *The Globe and Mail.* October 18.

Ignatieff, Michael (1993). *Blood and Belonging: Journeys into the New Nationalism.* New York: Viking.

Ignatieff, Michael (1999). "Human Rights: The Middle Crisis." *The New York Review.* May 20.

Illich, Ivan (1971). *After School, What?* New York: Harper & Row.

Infantry, Ashante (1999). "Opportunity Knocks...But Not for All. Beyond 2000. Home to the World." *Toronto Star.* May 2.

Interrogating the Internet (Study Group) (1996). "Contradictions in Cyberspace: Collective Response." Pp. 125–133 in R. Shields (ed.), *Cultures of Internet, Virtual Spaces, Real Histories, Living Bodies.* Thousand Oaks: Sage.

Ip, Greg (1996). "Job Cuts Despite Hefty Profits." *The Globe and Mail*, February 6.

Irwin, Kathie and Irihapeti Ramsden (1995). *Toi Wahine. The Worlds of Maori Women.* Penguin.

Isin, Engin (1996). "Introduction. the Canadian Cosmopolis and the Crisis of Confederation." *New City Magazine* 17 (special issue): 5–8.

Israelson, David (1997). "Media Coming Out Shows Growing Clout of Gays." *Toronto Star*, April 14.

Jakubowicz, Andrew et al. (1994). *Racism, Ethnicity and the Media.* Sydney: Allen and Unwin.

Jakubowski, Lisa Marie (1997). *Immigration and the Legalization of Racism.* Halifax: Fernwood.

James, Carl E. (ed.) (1996). *Perspectives on Racism and the Human Services Sector.* Toronto: University of Toronto Press.

James, Steve and Ian Warren (1995). "Police Culture." Pp. 3–13 in Judith Bessant, Kerry Carrington, and Sandy Cook.

Jamieson, Roberta (1993). "Community, Diversity, Learning." Notes for Remarks. Address to St. Paul's United College 30th Anniversary Celebration, February 24, Waterloo, Ontario.

Janigan, Mary (1999). "Future Shock." *Maclean's*, February 15.

Jaworski, John (1979). *A Case Study of Canadian Federal Governments' Multicultural Policies.* Unpublished MA thesis, Political Science Department, Carleton University, Ottawa.

Jeffrey, Brooke (1999). *Hard Right Turn: The New Face of Neo-Conservatism in Canada.* HarperCollins.

Jenson, Jane (1996). "Quebec: Which Minority?" *Dissent,* Summer: 43–49.

Jhally, Sut (1989). "Advertising as Religion: The Dialectics of Technology and Magic." Pp. 217–229 in Ian Angus and Sut Jhally (eds.), *Cultural Politics in Contemporary America.* New York: Routledge.

Jhally, Sut and Justin Lewis (1992). *Enlightened Racism. The Cosby Show, Audiences, and the Myth of the American Dream.* Boulder, CO: Westview Press.

Joanis, Susan (1999). "One-off. We Deny Gay Couples the Shock of Belonging." *Canadian Forum.* September. Page 27.

Joffe, Josef (1999). "Review of The Lexus and the Olive Tree." *New York Times Magazine.* August 22.

Johnson, Allan G. (1997). *The Gender Knot: Unravelling Our Patriarchal Legacy.* Temple University Press.

Johnston, Steven (1997). "On the Information Highway." *Imprint,* January 31.

Kaminer, Wendy (1992). *I'm Dysfunctional, You're Dysfunctional.* New York: Addison-Wesley.

Kanter, Rosabeth Moss (1976). "The Impact of Hierarchical Structures on the Work Behaviour of Women and Men." *Social Problems* 23: 415–430.

Kanter, Rosabeth Moss (1977). *Men and Women of the Corporation.* New York: Vintage.

Kanter, Rosabeth Moss (1995). *World Class: Thriving Locally in the Global Economy.* New York: Simon & Schuster.

Kaplan, Lawrence F. (1999). "A World Shaped by the West?" *National Post.* December 28.

Kaplan, Robert D. (1994). "The Coming Anarchy." *The Atlantic Monthly,* February: 44–76.

Kaplan, Robert D. (1999). *The Coming Anarchy.* New York: Random House.

Kaplan, William (ed.) (1993). *Belonging. The Meaning and Sense of Citizenship in Canada.* Montreal/Kingston: McGill-Queen's University Press.

Kay, Jonathan (1999). "People and Partition." *National Post.* January 17.

Kazemipur, A. and S. S. Halli (2000). "The New Poverty in Canada: Ethnic Groups and Ghetto Neighbourhoods." Toronto: Thompson Publishing.

Keith, W.J. (1997). "The Crisis in Contemporary Education." *Queen's Quarterly* 94: 511–520.

Kelsey, Jane (1986). "Decolonization in the First World: Indigenous Minorities Struggle for Justice and Self-Determination." *The Windsor Yearbook of Access to Justice* 5: 102–141.

Kelsey, Jane (1997). *The New Zealand Experience,* 2nd edition. Auckland: Auckland University Press.

Kenna, Kathleen (1998). "NAFTA Hasn't Hurt Wages or Jobs, Bank Survey Says." *Toronto Star.* March 4.

Kenna, Kathleen (1999). "Ball and Chain." *Toronto Star.* October 3.

Kennedy, Mark (1996). "Part Time Careers." *Kitchener-Waterloo Record,* February 26.

Kerckhove, Derrick de (1995). *The Skin of Culture: Investigating the New Electronic Reality.* Toronto: Sommerville House Publishing.

Kerstetter, Steve (1999). "There's No Accounting for the Poor." *National Post.* October 21.

Keung, Nicholas (1999). "Where the Welcome Mat is Out." *Toronto Star.* March 20.

Kickingbird, Kirke (1984). "Indian Sovereignty: The American Experience." In Leroy Little Bear et al. (eds.), *Pathways to Self-Determination: Canadian Indians and the Canadian State.*

King, Dave (1995). "A Year When the Internet Came of Commercial Age." *Dominion,* December 11.

Kingston, Anne (1999). "Marriage à la moment." *The Globe and Mail.* September 24.

The Kitchener-Waterloo Record (1995). "Canadians Facing 'Ugly Destruction' of Environment." April 10.

Kitchener-Waterloo Record (1999). "Female Cops Keep Eroding the Old Boys Club." *KW Record.* October 29.

Klassen, Thomas (1999). "High Fees Are Costing Students Education." *Toronto Star.* November 12.

Klatt, Heinz J. (1998). "Political Correctness and Sexual Harassment." *Canadian Psychologist* 38(4).

Klein, Naomi (1997). "Academics Can't Give in to Corporate Agenda." *Toronto Star,* April 28.

Kline, Marlee (1989). "Race, Racism and Feminist Legal Theory." *Harvard Women's Law Journal* 12: 115–150.

Knopff Rainer (1999). "The Case for Domestic Partnership Laws." *Policy Options* June: 53-56.

Knox, Paul (1997). "Canada Gets a Poor Grade on Reform." *The Globe and Mail,* June 21.

Koring, Paul (1997). "US Economic Inequality Grows as Poor Get Poorer." *The Globe and Mail.* December 23.

Kornblum, William and Joseph Julian (1992). *Social Problems.* Englewood Cliffs: Prentice Hall.

Korten, David (1999). "The Post-Corporate World." *The Ecologist* 29 (3): 219-221.

Krahn, Harvey J. and Graham S. Lowe (1994). *Work, Industry, and Canadian Society,* 2nd edition. Scarborough: Canada.

Kravis, Marie-Josee (1999). "Capitalism Backlash a Misguided Trend." *National Post.* May 10.

Kristoff, Nicholas, D. (1998). "Globalization Broke Suharto Regime." *The Globe and Mail.* May 21.

Kristoff, Nicholas D. (1999). "Globalization is Old Hat." *National Post.* May 28.

Kuczynski, Alex (1999). "Enough About Feminism. Should I Wear Lipstick?" *New York Times.* March 28.

Kunz, Jean Lock and Augie Fleras (1998). "Women of Colour in Mainstream Advertising: Distorted Mirror or Looking Glass?" *Atlantis* 13: 48-73.

Kurthen, Hermann (1997). "The Canadian Experience with Multiculturalism and Employment Equity: Lessons for Europe." *New Community* 23(2): 249–270.

Laab, Jennifer (1996). "Change." *Personnel Journal,* July.

Labadie, Paul G. (1999). "USA Not as Good as We Hoped, nor as bad as We Feared." *USA Today.* October 26.

Laframboise, Donna (1999). "Men and Women are Equals in Violence." *National Post.* August 19.

Laframboise Donna (1999). "You Wouldn't Talk That Way About a Woman, Would You?" *National Post.* November 24.

Laghi, Brian (1998). "Minorities Don't Share in Canada's Boom." *The Globe and Mail.* May 13.

Laghi, Brian and Heather Scoffield (1999). "Treaty with Nisga'a Reveals Major Conflict in Ideology." *The Globe and Mail.* December 10.

Lane, Henry W., Joseph DiStephano, and M. Maznevski (1999). "New Perspectives: Globalization and the Global Manager." *The Globe and Mail.* November 20.

LaPrairie, Carol (1997). "Reconstructing Theory: Explaining Aboriginal Over-Representation in the Criminal Justice System in Canada." *The Australian and New Zealand Journal of Criminology* 30(1): 39–54.

Large, Jerry (1998). "Tests Indicate Most of Us Have Unconscious Prejudices." *Toronto Star.* Oct 22.

Lasn, Kalle (1999). "Grounding the Corporation." *The Ecologist* 29(3): 221–222.

Latouche, Daniel (1995). "To Be or Not To Be a Province." *The Globe and Mail*, February 17.

Laucius, Joanne (1999). "Professors Want Prospective Parents to Meet Strict Criteria." *National Post.* February 2.

Laux, Jeanne Kirk (1990/91). "Limits to Liberalism." *International Journal*, Winter, XLVI: 113–136.

Laver, Ross (1999). "The Best and the Worst Jobs." *Maclean's.* May 31.

Law Commission of Canada (1999). "From Restorative Justice to Transformative Justice." *Discussion Paper.* Ottawa.

Laxer, Gordon (1991). *Open for Business.* Toronto: Oxford University Press.

Laxer, James (1991). "Teaching Old Leftists Some New Truths." *The Globe and Mail*, December 20.

Laxer, James (1993). "Buying into Decline." *Canadian Forum,* April: 5–7.

Laxer, James (1994). "Canada Can't Survive as a Union of 10 Equal Provinces." *Toronto Star*, August 7.

Laxer, James (1996). "Canada Just Doesn't Jibe with Neo-conservative Image." *Toronto Star*, September 30.

Laxer, James (1998). *The Undeclared War: Class Conflict in the Age of Cyber Capitalism.* Viking.

Leighton, Barry N. (1994). "Community Policing in Canada: An Overview of Experience and Evaluations." Pp. 209–223 in D.P. Rosenbaum (ed.), *The Challenge of Community Policing.* Thousand Oaks, CA: Sage.

Lee, Jo Anne and Linda Cardinal (1998). "Hegemonic Nationalism and the Politics of Feminism and Multiculturalism in Canada."

Lee, Philip (1999). "Debunking Myths About Welfare." *Toronto Star.* September 2.

Leigh, Suzanne (1999). "Too Much Television Hurts Kids, Study Finds." *The Globe and Mail.* July 27.

Leiss, William (1997). "Tobacco Control Policy in Canada: Shadow Boxing with Risk." *Policy Options,* June, 18(5): 3–6.

Lerner, Sally (1997). "The Future of Work." *Good Work News,* September, 50.

Levine, Allan (1997). "A Checkered History of Covering Federal Elections." *Media,* Spring: 11–12.

Levine, B. (1999). "Mixed Messages Make it Difficult to Raise Boys." *Toronto Star.* October 30.

Levitt, Cyril (1997). "The Morality of Race in Canada." *Society,* July/August: 32–37.

Levitt, Howard A. (1999). "Outsourcing is Bell's Only Remedy." *National Post.* May 12.

Levy, Harold (1999). "Food Bank Business." *KW Record.* September 29.

Lewington, Jennifer (1997). "Grappling with an Eternal Question." *The Globe and Mail*, March 27.

Lewington, Jennifer (1997). "Rethinking What They Want to Be." *The Globe and Mail.* December 15.

Lewington, Jennifer (1998). "Arts Background No Handicap in Quest for Jobs, Study." *The Globe and Mail.* October 26.

Lewington, Jennifer (1999). "Hate Crimes Rise in Year's Half Total." *The Globe and Mail.* August 12.

Lewycky, Laverne (1992). "Multiculturalism in the 1990s and into the 21st Century: Beyond Ideology and Utopia." Pp. 359–402 in Vic Satzewich (ed.), *Deconstructing a Nation. Halifax and Saskatoon: Fernwood and Social Research Unit,* University of Saskatchewan.

Li, Peter S. (1988). *Inequality in a Class Society.* Toronto: Wall & Thompson.

Li, Peter S. (1995). "Racial Supremacy Under Social Democracy." *Canadian Ethnic Studies* XXVII(1): 1–17.

Liazos, A. (1972). "The Poverty of the Sociology of Deviance: Nuts, Sluts and Perverts." *Social Problems,* Summer: 103–120.

Lindsay, Linda L. (1997). *Gender Roles: A Sociological Perspective.* Upper Saddle River, NJ: Prentice Hall.

Little, Bruce (1997). "Women Ahead in the Job Stakes of the Nineties." *The Globe and Mail*, April 14.

Little, Bruce (1998). "A Sharper Picture on Jobs and Learning." *The Globe and Mail.* March 23.

Little, Bruce (1999). "The Lowdown on Business Taxes." *The Globe and Mail.* May 17.

Little, Bruce (1999). "Manufacturing Keeps Economy on Growth Track." *The Globe and Mail.* June 1.

Little, Bruce (2000). "New Jobs in 1990s Belonged to Women." *The Globe and Mail.* February 21.

Little, Bruce (1999). "Women Still Underrepresented in Engineering and Physical Sciences." *The Globe and Mail.* July 26.

Little, Bruce (1999). "The Rock's on a Roll." *The Globe and Mail.* October 11.

Little Bear, L., Menno Boldt, and J. Anthony Long (1984). *Pathways to Self-Determination. Canadian Indians and the Canadian State.* Toronto: University of Toronto Press.

Livingstone, Ken (1996). "Democracy Will Have its Day." *New Statesman,* June 7.

Logan, Bruce (1997). "Universities Must Change With the Times in Modern Society." *Otago Daily Times.* August 25.

Loney, Martin (1999). "Some More Equal Than Others." *National Post.* September 22.

Loney, Martin (1999). "Privatize the Academic Sandbox." *National Post.* November 29.

Long, David and Olive Dickason (1996). *Visions of the Heart.* Toronto: Harcourt Brace.

Lorber, Judith (1998). *Gender Inequality: Feminist Theories and Politics.* Los Angeles: Roxbury.

Lowry, Brian (1999). "Mothers' Daze." *Toronto Star.* May 9.

Lundy, Katherina L.P. and Barbara D. Warme (1990). *Sociology. A Window on the World*, 2nd edition. Scarborough: Nelson.

Lupul, Manoly (1983). "Multiculturalism and Canada's White Ethnics." *Multiculturalism* 6(3).

Lurie, N.O. (1971). "The World's Oldest On-Going Protest Demonstration: North American Drinking Patterns." *Pacific Historical Review* 40: 311–332.

Lynch, Diane (1999). "Falling Down: The Ivory Towers Under Seige." *Faculty Matters Newsletter.* Downloaded from the Web October 15.

Lynch, Frederick (1997). "The Diversity Machine." *Society,* July/August: 32–37.

Maaka, Roger and Augie Fleras (1997). "Politicizing Customary Rights: Tino Rangatiratanga and the Re-Contouring of Aotearoa New Zealand." Paper presented to the Conference on Indigenous Rights, Political Theory, and the Transformation of Institutions. Canberra: August 8–10.

MacDonald, Finlay (1996). "I Shop Therefore I Am." *Metro,* October: 55–61.

Macionis, John, Juanne Nancarrow Clark and Linda M. Gerber (1994). *Sociology,* Canadian edition. Scarborough: Prentice Hall.

Mackie, Marlene (1991). *Gender Relations In Canada: Further Explorations.* Toronto: Butterworths.

MacKinnon, H. (1999). "Capital Outflows Gain Momentum." *The Globe and Mail.* July 5.

MacKinnon, Mark (1999). "Top Earners say 'hats off' to Economy." *The Globe and Mail.* September 6.

MacLean, Eleanor (1981). *Between the Lines. How to Detect Bias and Propaganda in the Press and Everyday Life.* Montreal: Black Rose Books.

Maclean's (1998). "The State of the Nation - '98". December 24.

Maclean's (1999). "Is TV Bad for Very Young Brains?" August 16.

MacNamara. Kate (2000). "Canadian Feminisms." *Women's Newsmagazine.* Winter.

Magder, Ted (1997). "Public Discourse and the Structures of Communication." Pp. 338–359 in W. Clement (ed.), *Understanding Canada.* Montreal/Kingston: McGill-Queen's University Press.

Mallet, Gina (1997). "Has Diversity Gone Too Far?" *The Globe and Mail*, March 15.

Malvaux, Julianne (1999). "Women at Work." *In These Times,* November 28, P.14-15.

Mander, Jerry (1996). "The Dark Side of Globalization." *The Nation.* July 15/22.

Mander, Jerry (1999). "How Cyber Culture Deletes Nature." *The Ecologist* 29 (3): 171-172.

Manitoba (1991). Public Inquiry into the Administration of Justice and Aboriginal People: Report of the Aboriginal Justice Inquiry of Manitoba. Commissioners, A.C. Hamilton, C.M. Sinclair, Government of Manitoba.

Maracle, Brian (1996). "One More Whining Indian Tilting at Windmills." Pp. 15–20 in J. Littleton (ed.), *Clash of Identities.* Scarborough: Prentice Hall.

Marchak, Pat (1991). *The Integrated Circus. The New Right and Restructuring of Global Markets.* Kingston/Montreal: McGill-Queen's University Press.

Marchand, Philip (1999). "Oh, What a Lovely War for Television News." *Toronto Star.* April 24.

Martinuk, Susan (1999). "Blubber About Whales." *National Post.* May 20.

Masters, Brooke A. (1999). "Women's Shelters Save Mostly Men." *Boston Globe* (originally *Washington Post*). March 15.

Matas, Robert (1996). "Reports of Work's Demise Appear Exaggerated." *The Globe and Mail*, October 17.

Matas, Robert (1997). "Breast-feeding in public a right, tribunal rules." *The Globe and Mail*, August 12: A4.

Matsouka, Atsuko and John Sorenson (1999). "Eritrean Women in Canada: Negotiating New Lives." *Canadian Woman Studies.* 19(3): 104–109.

Matthews, Roy (1983). *The Creation of Regional Dependencies.* Toronto: University of Toronto Press.

Matthews, Roy A. (1993). "NAFTA: A Way to Save Canadian Jobs." *The Globe and Mail*, September 24.

Max, D.T. (1994). "The End of the Book." *The Atlantic Monthly*, September: 61–70.

Maxwell, Judith (1999). "Don't Be Seduced by the US Boom. Averages Can Lie." *The Globe and Mail.* August 30.

Mayor, Frederico (1999). "All Human Rights for All." *UNESCO Courier.* November. P.9.

Mayor, Frederico (1999). "Four Challenges For a New World." Editorial. *UNESCO Courier.* December, P.1.

Mayor, Frederico (1999). "Myths and Illusions." Editorial. *UNESCO Courier.* March. P.1.

McAllister, Matthew P. (1995). *The Commercialization of American Culture. New Advertising, Control, and Democracy.* Thousand Oaks, CA: Sage.

McArthur, Keith (1997). "Canada Puts Environment First." *The Globe and Mail*, March 15.

McCallum, John (1999). "Two Cheers for the FTA." *Policy Options.* June. P.6-9

McCrone David (1998). *The Sociology of Nationalism.* London: Routledge.

McDaniel, Susan A. (1988). "Women's Roles and Reproduction: The Changing Picture in Canada in the 1980's." *Atlantis,* Fall, 14(1): 1–12.

McDaniel, Susan A. and E. Roosmalen (1992). "Sexual Harassment in Canadian Academe: Explorations of Power and Privilege." *Atlantis,* 17(1): 3–19.

McDougall, Alan (1988). *Policing: The Evolution of a Mandate.* Ottawa: Canadian Police College.

McGregor, Craig (1997). *Class in Australia.* Ringwood Victoria: Penguin.

McGregor, Judy (ed.) (1996). *Dangerous Democracy. News Media Politics in New Zealand.* Palmerston North: Dunmore.

McHutchion, Rob and David Crane (1996). "Dead End Kids." *Toronto Star*, February 27.

McIntyre, Sheila (1994). "Backlash Against Equality: The 'Tyranny' of the 'Politically Correct'." *McGill Law Journal/Revue de Droit de McGill* 38(1): 3–63.

McIvor, Sharon Donna (1999). "Self Government and Aboriginal Women." in *Scratching the Surface.* E. Dua and A. Robertson, eds. Toronto: *Women's Press*, pp.167–186.

McKague, Ormand (1991). *Racism in Canada.* Saskatoon: Fifth House Publishing.

McKay, Shona (1999). "Business without Borders." *The Financial Post* 500. June. Pp.86-91.

McKeen, Scott (1999). "Study Shows Girls Raised to Do More Housework." *National Post.* December 21.

McKie, Craig (1991). "The Social Consequences and Functions of the New Media." Pp 391–410 in B. Singer (ed.), *Communications in Canadian Society.* Scarborough: Nelson.

McLeod, Keith A. (ed.) (1987). *Multiculturalism, Bilingualism, and Canadian Institutions.* Toronto: University of Toronto Guidance Centre.

McMahon, Fred (1997). *Looking the Gifthorse in the Mouth: The Impact of Federal Transfers on Atlantic Canada.* Halifax: Atlantic Institute for Market Studies.

McPherson, Don (1999). "Some People More Equal Than Others." *Montreal Gazette.* October 2.

McQuaig, Linda (1998). *The Cult of Impotence: Selling the Myth of Powerlessness in a Global Economy.* Viking.

McQuaig, Linda (1999). "A Matter of Will." *Queen's Quarterly* 106(1): 9-21.

McRoberts, Kenneth (1993). "English-Canadian Perceptions of Quebec." Pp 116–129 in A.G. Gagnon (ed.), *Quebec: State and Society.* Scarborough: Nelson.

McRoberts, Kenneth (1997). *Misconceiving Canada. The Struggle for National Unity.* Toronto: Oxford University Press.

McRoberts, Kenneth (1997). "Talking It Over." *The Globe and Mail*, January 4.

Media Watch (1987). *Adjusting the Image. Women and Canadian Broadcasting.* Report of a National Conference on Canadian Broadcasting Policy Held in Ottawa, March 20–22.

Medical Tribune News Service (1999). "Violent Tendencies Can Show Up Early, Even in Infants." Cited in *The Globe and Mail.* June 1.

Medved, Michael (1996). *Hollywood's Four Big Lies.* London: Bloomsbury Press.

Meisel, John, Guy Rocher, and Arthur Silver (2000). "Introduction." In *As I Recall. Je me Souviens Bien.* IRPP.

Menzies, Heather (1996). *Whose Brave New World? The Information Highway and the New Economy.* Toronto: Between the Lines.

Mercredi, Ovide and Mary Ellen Turpel (1993). *In the Rapids. Navigating the Future of First Nations.* Toronto: Penguin Books.

Mickleburgh Rod (1999). "What's Behind Nursing's Revolt?" *The Globe and Mail.* July 13.

Mickleburgh, Rod (1999). "Aboriginal Status Cited in Reducing Life Term." *The Globe and Mail.* July 16.

Mickleburgh, Rod (1999). "Higher Education Cuts 'Poor Strategy'." *The Globe and Mail* December 8.

Mietkiewicz, Henry (1999). "If Only TV Were More Colourful." *Toronto Star.* March 27.

Miles, Robert (1982). *Racism and Migrant Labour.* London: Routledge and Kegan Paul.

Millen, Leslie (1998). "Fishy Problem." *Kitchener-Waterloo Record.* June 25.

Miller, D.W. (1999). "The Black Hole of Education Research." *The Chronicle of Higher Education.* August 6, P.17-18.

Miller, Jacquie (1998). "Are We More Tolerant? Depends How You Ask." *Toronto Star.* February 19.

Miller, John (1998). *Yesterday's News: Why Canada's Daily Newspapers are Failing Us.* Halifax: Fernwood.

Miller, Jon (1991). "Is Bangladesh Hooked on Aid?" *The Globe and Mail,* December 16.

Milloy, John (1999). *A National Crime.* Winnipeg: University of Manitoba Press.

Mills, C. Wright (1967). *The Sociological Imagination.* New York: Oxford University Press.

Milstone, Carol (1999). "The Kids are Alright - Even if they're Not Living in a Traditional Family." *National Post.* August 9.

Mintzberg, Henry (1996). "The Myth of Society Inc." *Report on Business Magazine,* October: 113–117.

Mitchell, Alanna (1997). "Face of Poverty Ever-Changing." *The Globe and Mail,* July 8.

Mitchell, Alanna (1997). "Tuition Squeeze Not Stopping Students." *The Globe and Mail,* September 30.

Mitchell, Alanna (1997). "Women's Evolving Role Confuses Canadians." *The Globe and Mail.* September 17.

Mitchell, Alanna (1997). "For a Third, Love's Bliss will Falter, Study Finds." *The Globe and Mail.* October 8.

Mitchell, Alanna (1999). "Lego Families: Parents Build a New Way of Life." *The Globe and Mail.* September 15.

Mitchell, Alanna, Karen Unland, and Chad Skelton (1997). "Canadians All Worked Up." *The Globe and Mail.* July 19.

Mitchell, Alanna and Mark Winfield (1998). "The Accord is a Tragedy for Canada's Environment." *The Globe and Mail.* February 2.

Mitchell-Powell, Brenda (1992). "Color Me Multicultural." *Multi-Cultural Review* 1(4): 15–17.

Mittlestaedt, Martin (1999). "Coffee's Cast of Shady Characters." *The Globe and Mail.* October 28.

Moeller, Susan D. (1998). *Compassion Fatigue: How the Media Sell Disease, Famine, War, & Death.* New York: Routledge.

Moller, J Orstrom (1999). "The Growing Challenge of Internationalism." *The Futurist.* March. P.22–25.

Moir, Peter and Matthew Moir (1993). "Community-Based Policing and the Role of Community Consultation." Pp. 211–235 in P. Moir and H. Eijkman (eds.), *Policing Australia.* Melbourne: Macmillan.

Montgomery, John D. (1999). "The Next Thousand Years." *Queens Quarterly* 106(3) (Fall): 329-341.

Mooney, Linda A., David Knox, and Caroline Schact (1997). *Understanding Social Problems.* Minneapolis-St Paul: West Publishing.

Moore, Harry W. and Robert C. Trojanowicz (1988). *Criminal Justice in the Community.* Englewood Cliffs: Prentice Hall.

Morgan, Gareth (1986). *Images of Organization.* Toronto: Oxford University Press.

Morris, Merrill and Christine Ogan (1996). "The Internet as Mass Medium." *Journal of Communication* 46(1): 39–52.

Morrow, Raymond A. (1994). "Mass-Mediated Culture, Leisure, And Consumption: Having Fun as a Social Problem." Pp. 189–211 in Les Samuelson (ed.), *Power and Resistance.*

Moses, Barbara (1997). "Loss of Loyalty Cuts Both Ways." *The Globe and Mail.* November 6.

Moss, Kirk (1998). "Stereotypes Split Police, Black Youth." *Toronto Star*. July 21: D-1.

Moynihan, Daniel (1993). *Pandaemonium. Ethnicity in International Politics*. New York: Oxford University Press.

Mukherjee, Alok (1992). "Educational Equity for Racial Minorities in the Schools: The Role of Community Action." Pp. 73–81 in *Racism and Education: Different Perspectives and Experiences*. Ottawa: Ontario Federation of Students.

Nankivell, Neville (1999). "World Economy Hanging on to U.S." *National Post*. April 3.

Nelson, Adie and Augie Fleras (1998). *Social Problems in Canada*. 2nd edition. Scarborough: Prentice Hall.

Nelson, Adie and Barrie W. Robinson (1994). *Gigolos & Madames Bountiful: Illusions of Gender, Power and Intimacy*. Toronto: University of Toronto Press.

Nett, Emily (1993). *Canadian Families: Past and Present*, 2nd edition. Toronto: Butterworths.

New Internationalist (1996). "New Technology: Keynote." December: 7–10.

Newman, Billy Jo (1999). "The Supreme Court Strikes Down Current Definition of Spouse." *Siren*. June July. P.5.

Ng, Roxana (1988). *The Politics of Community Services: Immigrant Women, Class, and the State*. Toronto: Garamond Press.

Ng, Roxana (1999). "Homeworking: Dream Realized or Freedom Constraint? The Globalized Reality of Immigrant Garment Workers." *Canadian Woman Studies*. 19(3): 110–114.

Nicholson-Lord, David (1992). "Aid, Debt, and the Poverty Trap." *Dominion* (NZ) (originally the *Independent*), December 10.

Nisbet, Michael (1994). "Theory 'X' Like Tuberculosis Is Making a Comeback." *The Globe and Mail*, February 16.

Norberg-Hodge, Helena (1996). "Break Up the Monoculture." *The Nation*. July 15/22.

Norberg-Hodge, Helena (1999). "The March of the Monoculture." *The Ecologist* 29(3):194-197.

Norman, Russell (1998). "Western Economic Might Crashing Down on Asia." *NZ Herald*. March 30.

Normandeau, Andre and Barry Leighton (1990). *A Vision of the Future of Policing in Canada. Police-Challenge 2000 Background Document*. Policy and Security Branch. Ministry Secretariat. Solicitor General Canada. Ottawa: Minister of Supply and Services Canada.

Oderkirk, Jillian and Clarence Lochhead (1992). "Lone Parenthood: Gender Differences." *Canadian Social Trends*, Winter: 16–19.

Oettmeier, Timothy N. and Lee P. Brown (1988). "Role Expectations and the Concept of Neighborhood Oriented Community Policing." *In International Association of Police Chiefs, Developing Neighborhood Oriented Policing in the Houston Police Department*.

Olive, David (1992). "Fire at Will." *Perspective Report on Business Magazine*, March: 9–10.

Olive, David (1999). "Riding U.S. Coattails to a 'Miracle Economy'." *National Post*. December 11.

Ontario Ministry of the Solicitor General (1989). Report of the Race Relations and Policing Task Force. C. Lewis, Chair. Ontario: Solicitor General of Ontario.

Orpood, Graham and Jennifer Lewington (1995). Overdue Assignment. Taking Responsibility for Canada's Schools. Toronto: John Wiley and Sons.

Orwen, Patricia (1998). "More Disabled Workers Losing Jobs, Report Says." *Toronto Star*. May 1.

Orwen, Patricia 1999 "Workfare: Is it Creating a Social Disaster?" *Toronto Star*. September 19.

Orwin, Clifford (1999) "Compassion Fatigue?" *National Post*. January 16.

Ostow, Robin et al. (1991). *Ethnicity, Structured Inequality, and the State in Canada and the Federal Republic of Germany.* New York: Peter Lang.

Owen, Rob (1997). *Gen X TV: The Brady Bunch to Melrose Place.* Syracuse University Press.

Paine, Robert (1985). "The Claim of the Fourth World." Pp. 49–66 in Jens Brosted (ed.), *The Quest for Autonomy and Nationhood of Indigenous Peoples.* Bergen: Universiteforlaget AS.

Palat, Ravi Arvind (1996). "Curries, Chopsticks, and Kiwis: Asian Migration to Aotearoa/New Zealand." Pp 35–54 in P. Spoonley et al. (eds.), Nga Patai. Palmerston North: Dunmore.

Palmer, Howard (ed.) (1975). *Immigration and the Rise of Multiculturalism.* Toronto: Copp Clark Publishing.

Parenti, Michael (1978). *Power and the Powerless*, 2nd edition. New York: St. Martin's Press.

Parenti, Michael (1992). *The Make-Believe Media: The Politics of Entertainment.* New York: St. Martin's Press.

Parizeau, Jacques (1996). "The object is sovereignty, not partnership." *The Globe and Mail*, December 19.

Parris, Matthew (1997). "A Spider in the Bathtub." *Dominion,* September 15.

Pearson, Patricia (1999). "Men, Women From the Same Planet After All." *National Post.* August 24.

Pearson, Patricia (1999). "How Can You Stop a Fight You Cannot See?" *National Post.* October 27.

Peart, Joseph and Jim Mcnamara (1996). *The New Zealand Public Relations Handbook.* Palmerston North, NZ: Dunmore Publishing.

Pendakur, Krishna and Ravi Pendakur (1995). "Earning Differentials Among Ethnic Groups in Canada." Social Research Group. Hull: Department of Canadian Heritage. Ref. SRA-34.

Penner, Keith (1983). *Indian Self-Government in Canada.* Report of the Special Committee chaired by Keith Penner. Ottawa: Queen's Printer for Canada.

Penrose, Jan (1997). "Construction, De(con)struction, and Reconstruction. The Impact of Globalization and Fragmentation on the Canadian Nation-State." *International Journal of Canadian Studies* 16 (Fall): 17-49.

Perry, Martin, Carl Davidson, Roberta Hill (1995). *Reform at Work: Workplace Change and the New Industrial Order.* Auckland: Longman Paul.

Peter, Karl (1978). "Multi-Cultural Politics, Money, and the Conduct of Canadian Ethnic Studies." *Canadian Ethnic Studies* Association Bulletin 5: 2–3.

Peters, Ralph (1999). "The Future of War." *Maclean's.* April 26. P.40-43.

Peters, Thomas J. and Robert H. Waterman (1982). *In Search of Excellence. Lessons from America's Best Run Companies.* New York: Harper and Row.

Pevere, Geoff (1998). "Violence is at the Heart of Media Storytelling." *Toronto Star.* March 28.

Philp, Margaret (1998). "Gap Between Canada's Rich and Poor Increasing, Report Says." *The Globe and Mail.* October 22.

Philp, Margaret (1998). "UN Committee Lambastes Canada on Human Rights." *The Globe and Mail.* December 12.

Picard, Andre (2000). "Friends Few for Homeless, Survey Finds." *The Globe and Mail.* February 19.

Picard, Andre (1999). "Ontario's Wealthy Get Better Care for Heart Disease." *The Globe and Mail.* October 15.

Pollack, Ellen Joan (2000). "Are You Flirting with Ambition or Being Yourself?" from the *Wall Street Journal,* reprinted in *The Globe and Mail.* February 21.

Pollack William (1998). *Real Boys: Rescuing Our Sons From the Myths of Boyhood.* New York: Random House/Henry Holt and Company.

Ponting, J. Rick and Roger Gibbins (1980). *Out of Irrelevance: A Socio-Political Introduction to Indian Affairs in Canada.* Toronto: Butterworths.

Porter, John (1965). *The Vertical Mosaic.* Toronto: University of Toronto Press.

Porter, John (1979). *The Measure of Canadian Society.* Toronto: Gage.

Postman, Neil (1985). *Amusing Ourselves to Death.* New York: Pantheon.

Postman, Neil (1995). *The End of Education: Redefining the Value of School.* New York: Knopf.

Postman, Neil (1995). *The End of Education: Redefining the Value of Schooling.* New York: Random House.

Powell, Thomas (1992). "Feel-Good Racism." The *New York Times*, May 24.

Presthus, Robert (1978). *The Organizational Society,* revised edition. New York: St Martin's Press.

Price, Christopher (1993). "School of Thought." *New Statesman and Society,* August 20.

Public Research Initiative (1999). "Sustaining Growth, Human Development, and Social Cohesion in a Global World." Ottawa, Feb.

Qadeer, M.A. (1997). "Pakistan Broke Ground for Minority Nationalism." *Toronto Star*, August 14.

Qualter, Terence H. (1991). "Propaganda in Canadian Society." Pp. 200–212 in Benjamin D. Singer (ed.), *Communications in Canadian Society.* Scarborough: Nelson.

Quelch, John (1999). "Global Village People." *National Post.* April 21.

Rae, Bob (1999). *The Three Questions. Prosperity and the Public Good.* Toronto: Penguin.

Ramcharan, Subhas (1989). *Social Problems and Issues. A Canadian Perspective.* Scarborough: Nelson.

Rawson, Bruce (1991). "Public Service 2000 Services to the Public Task Force: Findings and Implications." *Canadian Public Administration* 34(3): 490–502.

Razack, Sherene (1993). "Exploring the Omissions and Silences in Law Around Race." Pp. 37–38 in Joan Brockman and Dorothy E. Chunn (eds.), *Investigating Gender Bias: Laws, Courts and the Legal Profession.* Toronto: Thompson Educational Publishing, Inc.

Reading, Bill (1996). *The University in Ruins.* Cambridge, Mass.: Harvard University Press.

Reagan, Tom (1983). *The Case for Animal Rights.* Berkeley: The University of California Press.

Reid, Angus (1998). "What Globalization Means to Canadian Unity." Canadian Speeches: Issues of the Day. October: P.38-40.

Reiter, Ester (1992/1996). *Making Fast Food. From the Frying Pan into the Fryer.* Montreal: McGill-Queens University Press.

Reitz, Jeffrey and Raymond Breton (1994). *The Illusion of Difference: Realities of Ethnicity in Canada and the United States.* Toronto: C.D. Howe Institute.

Remington, Robert (1999). "Canadian Women Envied for Privileges." *National Post.* October 16.

Renzetti, Claire M. and Daniel J. Curran (1999). *Women, Men, and Society.* 4th edition. Toronto: Allyn and Bacon.

Report (1991). "Towards Managing Diversity. A Study of Systemic Discrimination at DIAND." The Deputies Council for Change and the Minister of Indian Affairs and Northern Development. Ottawa.

Rex, John and Beatrice Drury (eds.) (1996). *Ethnic Mobilisation in a Multi-Cultural Europe.* Aldershot, UK: Ashgate Publishing.

Rhode, Deborah L. (1997). "Harassment is Alive and Well and Living at the Water Cooler." *Ms* November/December:28-29.

Richards, Huw. (1997). "Global Theatre." *The Times Higher.* February 7.

Richmond, Anthony (1994). *Global Apartheid: Refugees, Racism, and the New World Order.* Toronto: Oxford University Press.

Rieff, David (1999). "Burnt Out on Suffering." *National Post.* April 10.

Rifkin, Jeremy (1995). "Work: A Blueprint for Social Harmony in a World Without Jobs." *Utne Reader,* May/June: 53–62.

Rifkin, Jeremy (1996). "Civil Society in the Information Age." *The Nation,* February 26.

Ritzer, George (1993). *The McDonaldization of Society: An Investigation into the Changing Character of Contemporary Social Life.* Newbury Park, CA: Pine Forge Press.

Ritzer, George (1998). *The McDonaldization Thesis.* Thousand Oaks: Sage.

Rizvi, Fazal (1994). "The New Right and the Politics of Multiculturalism in Australia." In *Multiculturalism and the State,* volume 1, collected seminar papers no. 47. University of London: Institute of Commonwealth Studies.

Roberg, Roy R. (1994). "Can Today's Police Organizations Effectively Implement Community Policing?" In R.P. Rosenbaum, *The Challenge of Community Policing.* Thousand Oaks, CA: Sage.

Roberts, J.V. and T. Gabor (1990). "Lombrosian Wine in a New Bottle: Research on Crime and Race." *Canadian Journal of Criminology* 32.

Roberts, Paul (1996). "Virtual Grub Reality." *Harper's,* June: 71–83.

Roberts, Peter (1995). "Political Correctness. Great Books and the University Curriculum." Sites 31: 81-111.

Robertshaw, Corinne (1999). "It's Time to Stop Hitting Our Kids." *The Globe and Mail.* December 2.

Robertson, Ian (1980). *Social Problems*, 2nd edition. New York: Random House.

Robertson, Ian (1987). *Sociology,* 3rd edition. New York: Worth Publishing.

Robinson, Jan, Warren Young and Neil Cameron (eds.) (1989). *Effectiveness and Change in Policing.* Wellington: Victoria University Institute of Criminology.

Robinson, Richard (ed.) (1996). *Pathways to Asia: The Politics of Engagement.* Sydney: Allen & Unwin.

Robinson, William I. (1996). "Globalisation: Nine Theses on Our Epoch." *Race & Class* 38(2): 13–31.

Rochefort, David A. and Roger W. Cobb (1994). *The Politics of Problem Definition: Shaping the Policy Agenda.* Lawrence, KA: University Press of Kansas.

Rodrik, Dani (1997). *Has Globalization Gone Too Far?* Washington, DC: International Institute for International Economics.

Rohman, Jim (1999). "Universities Becoming Money Machines." *KW Record.* May 8.

Rosenbaum, Dennis (ed.) (1994). *The Challenge of Community Policing: Testing the Promises.* Thousand Oaks, CA: Sage.

Rosenberg, Tina (1999). "Human Rights Win Out Over Government." *New York Times News Service,* reprinted in the *KW Record*, July 5.

Rosener, Judith (1999). "Management Style Used by Women is no Longer Seen as Weak, Says Prof." Canadian Press. cited in *KW Record*, June 15.

Ross, Jen (1999). "Homeworkers Face Worsening Labour Conditions, Professor Says." *The Globe and Mail*. June 18.

Rossel, Steven A. (1999). *Renewing Governance: Governing by Learning in the Information Age.* Toronto: Oxford University Press.

Roszak, Theodore (1994). *The Cult of Information: The Folklore of Computers and the True Art of Communication.* New York: Pantheon.

Roszak, Theodore (1996). "Dumbing Us Down." *New Internationalist,* December: 12–14.

Rothenberg, Paula S. (ed.) (1992). *Race, Class, and Gender in the United States.* An Integrated Study, 2nd edition. New York: St. Martin's Press.

Rothenberg, Randall (1997). "How Powerful is Advertising?" *The Atlantic Monthly,* June: 113–115.

Rowell, Andrew (1996). *Green Backlash. Global Subversion and the Environmental Movement.* New York: Routledge.

Royal Commission on Aboriginal Peoples (1993). *Partners in Confederation. Aboriginal Peoples, Self-Government, and the Constitution.* Ottawa: Minister of Supply and Services.

Royal Commision (1995). *Aboriginal Self-Government: Legal and Constitutional Issues.* Ottawa: Minister of Supply and Services.

Royal Commission (1995). *Bridging the Cultural Divide. Report of the Royal Commission on Aboriginal Peoples.* Ottawa: Minister of Supply and Services.

Royal Commission (1996). *People to People, Nation to Nation. Highlights from the Report of the Royal Commission on Aboriginal Peoples.* Ottawa: Minister of Supply and Services.

Rueters (1997). "India's caste violence outbreak kills 60." *Kitchener-Waterloo Record,* December 2.

Rueters (1999). "Two-Parent Families Growing Scarcer, Study Finds." *Toronto Star.* December 18.

Rushton, Philippe (1995). *Race, Evolution and Behavior: A Life History Perspective.* New York: Transaction.

Sachs, Andrea (1999). "Stepped-on Moms." *Time.* May 3.

Salee, Daniel and William D. Coleman (1997). "The Challenges of the Quebec Question: Paradigm, Counter-Paradigm, and Sovereignty." Pp. 262–282 in W. Clement (ed.), *Understanding Canada.* Montreal/Kingston: McGill-Queen's University Press.

Salutin, Rick (1997). "The Virtual Appearance of Humanity in the Media." *The Globe and Mail,* May 9.

Salutin, Rick (1997). "What Does the Word Racism Mean to Sportswriters?" *The Globe and Mail,* April 25.

Sarick, Lila (1999). "Record numbers turn to food banks to cope, National survey shows." *The Globe and Mail.* September 29.

Satzewich, Vic (1991). "Social Stratification: Class and Racial Inequality." Pp. 91–107 in B. Singh Bolaria (ed.), *Social Issues and Contradictions in Canadian Society.* Toronto: Harcourt Brace.

Satzewich, Vic (1993). "Race and Ethnic Relations." Pp. 160-177 in Peter Li and B. Singh Bolaria (eds.), *Contemporary Sociology. Critical Perspectives.* Mississauga: Copp Clark Pitman.

Satzewich, Vic (1998). *Racism and Social Inequality in Canada.* Toronto: Thompson Publishing.

Saul, John Ralston (1995). *The Unconscious Civilization.* Toronto: House of Anansi Press.

Saunders, John and Casey Mahood (1996). "New Layout, Same Story." *The Globe and Mail,* May 4.

Saverimuthu, Danistan (1999). "Diversity and Unity." *Montreal Gazette.* October 2.

Saville, Gregory and D. Kim Rossmo (1995). "Striking a Balance: Lessons From Problem-Oriented Policing in British Columbia." Pp. 119–132 in K.M. Hazlehurst (ed.), *Perceptions of Justice.* Aldershot: Avebury Press.

Savoie, Donald (1999). "Let's Row Our Own Boat." *The Globe and Mail.* November 25.

Scarpitte, Frank R. and F. Curt Cylke, Jr. (1995). *Social Problems. The Search for Solutions. An Anthology.* Los Angeles: Roxbury Publishing.

Schellengbarger, Sue (1999). *Working and Families.* New York: Ballantine Books.

Schiller, Bill (1999). "Despair." *Toronto Star.* Sept 19.

Schlesinger, Arthur M. Jr. (1992). *The Disuniting of America: Reflections on a Multicultural Society.* New York: W.W. Norton.

Schmidt, Sarah (2000). "Rights Panel Sees Racism in Hirings at U of T." *The Globe and Mail.* February 8.

Scholte, Jan Aart (1997). "Global Capitalism and the State." *International Affairs* 73 (3):426-455.

Schoon, Nicholas (1997). "Global Warning—Too Much Hot Air." *The Independent International,* May 28.

Schur, Edwin (1989). *Americanization of Sex.* Philadelphia: Temple University Press.

Schwartz, Felice (1989). "Management Women and the New Facts of Life." *Harvard Business Review* 89: 65–76.

Scoffield, Heather (1998). "Canada Adjusts to Free Trade Realities." *The Globe and Mail.* December 31.

Scowen, Reed (1999). *Time to Say Goodbye: The Case for Getting Quebec out of Canada.* Toronto: McClelland and Stewart.

Seabrook Jeremy (1999). "After the Eclipse." *New Internationalist* No 309.

Seagrave, Karen (1997). *Introduction to Policing in Canada.* Scarborough: Prentice Hall.

Seeman, Neil (2000). "Education System Failing Boys: Experts." *National Post.* February 22.

Sefa Dei, George J. (1996/97). "Beware of False Dichotomies: Revisiting the Idea of 'Black-Focused' Schools in Canadian Contexts." *Journal of Canadian Studies* 31(4): 58–69.

Seguin, Francine (1991). "Service to the Public: A Major Strategic Change." *Canadian Public Administration* 34(3): 465–473.

Seguin, Rheal (1999). "How do you spell 'linguistic intolerance'?" *The Globe and Mail.* October 22.

Seiler, Tamara Palmer (1996). "Multi-Vocality and National Literature. Toward a Post-Colonial and Multicultural Aesthetic." *Journal of Canadian Studies* 31(3).

Seitzinger, Jack and Michele J. Sabino (1988). "Training for Neighborhood Oriented Policing." In *The International Association of Police Chiefs, Developing Neighborhood Oriented Policing in the Houston Police Department.* Washington.

Seligman, Don (1999). "Home Truths About Stereotyping." *National Post.* August 3.

Sen, Amartya (1993). "The Threats to Secular Indian Society." The *New York Times Book Review,* April 8: 26–32.

Sheehan, Nik (1999). "The Sexual Melting Pot." *National Post.* November 20.

Sher, Julian (1983). *White Hoods: Canada's Ku Klux Klan.* Vancouver: New Star Books.

Shields Rob (ed.) (1996). *Cultures of Internet. Virtual Spaces, Real Histories, Living Bodies.* Thousand Oaks, CA: Sage.

Shillington, Richard (1997). "How Poor are the Really Poor?" *Toronto Star.* December 30.

Shillington, Richard (1999). "What Should Be the True Definition of Poverty?" *Toronto Star.* January 29.

Shiva, Vandana (1999). "The Two Fascisms." *The Ecologist* 29 (3): 198-200.

Shkilnyk, Anastasia (1985). *A Poison Stronger Than Love.* New Haven, CT: Yale University Press.

Shusta, R.M. et al. (1995). *Multicultural Law Enforcement: Strategies for Peacekeeping in a Diverse Society.* Englewood Cliffs, NJ: Prentice Hall.

Siddiqui, Haroon (1996). "Multiculturalism and the Media." Pp. 113–118 in J. Littleton (ed.), *Clash of Identities.* Media Manipulation, and Politics of the Self. Scarborough: Prentice Hall.

Silbey, Susan S. (1997). "Let Them Eat Cake': Globalization, Postmodern Colonialism, and the Possibilities of Justice." *Law and Society Review* 31(2): 207-230

Silver, Cindy (1999). "Parents Who Discipline aren't Criminals." *The Globe and Mail.* December 8.

Silvera, Mikeda (1983). *Silenced.* Toronto: Williams-Wallace Publishers.

Simms, Andrew (1999). "Big Corporations Tighten Grip on World Food Supply." *Guardian Weekly.* May 16.

Simpson, Jeffrey (1999). "Have a Good One, Eh." *The Globe and Mail.* July 1.

Simpson, Jeffrey (1999). "The Best of Times." *The Globe and Mail.* September 1.

Sinclair, John, Elizabeth Jacka and Stuart Cunningham (1996). *Television Broadcasting.* Oxford University Press.

Sinclair, Peter R. (1991). "Underdevelopment and Regional Inequality." Pp. 358–376 in B. Singh Bolari (ed.), *Social Issues and Contradictions in Canadian Society.* Toronto: Harcourt Brace.

Singer, Benjamin (1986). *Advertising and Society.* Don Mills, ON: Addison-Wesley.

Singer, Peter (1976). *Animal Liberation.* New York: Avon.

Skidelsky, Robert (1998). "What's Wrong with Global Capitalism?" *Times Literary Supplement.* March 27.

Sleeter, Christine E. (1991). *Empowerment Through Multicultural Education.* Albany: Suny Press.

Small, Peter (1997). "Curriculum." *Toronto Star.* August 30.

Smith, Linda Tuhiwai (1999). *Decolonizing Methodologies.* Auckland/Melbourne: Oxford University Press.

Smith, Virginia Rose (1999). "Homelessness. Looking for Real Solutions." *Canadian Dimensions.* Fall. Pg. 29-30.

Smith, Vivian (1998). "A Delicate Balance for Women." *The Globe and Mail.* February 7.

Sniderman, David et al. (1993). "Psychological and Cultural Foundations of Prejudice: The Case of Anti-Semitism in Quebec." *Canadian Review of Sociology and Anthropology* 30(2): 242–267.

Solomos, John and Les Black (1996). *Racism and Society.* London: Macmillan.

Soros, George (1999). "The Crisis of Global Capitalism." New York: Public Affairs Institute.

Soros, George (1998). "Toward a Global Open Society." *The Atlantic Monthly.* Jan. P. 20-26, 32.

Spector, Malcolm and John I. Kitsuse (1987). *Constructing Social Problems,* 2nd edition. Menlo Park, CA: Cummins.

Spender, Dale (1997). "The Revolution is Being Digitalised." *NZ Education Review.* Interview by Andrea Hotere. Oct. 8.

Sperling, Susan (1988). *Animal Liberators: Research and Morality.* Berkeley: University of California Press.

Spoonley, Paul, David Pearson and Cluny McPherson (eds.) (1996). *Nga Patai: Racism and Ethnic Relations in Aotearoa/New Zealand.* Palmerston North: Dunmore.

Stackhouse, John (1996). "Despite Progress, Woes Still Haunt Africa." *The Globe and Mail*, September 17.

Stackhouse, John (1999). "I'm Happy I Came Here." *The Globe and Mail.* December 21.

Stackhouse, John (1997). "When Less Aid is More." *The Globe and Mail.* October 18.

Standing Senate Committee on Social Affairs, Science, and Technology (1999). "The Downside of Globalization," excerpt of a report cited in *The Toronto Star.* July 8.

Staseson, Heidi (1999). "Longer Hours Spur Bad Habits in Workers." *National Post.* November 17.

Stasiulis, Daiva (1997). "The Political Economy of Race, Ethnicity, and Migration." Pp. 141–164 in W. Clement (ed.), *Understanding Canada: Building on the New Canadian Political Economy.* Montreal/Kingston: McGill-Queen's University Press.

Statistics Canada (1999). "Crime Statistics in Canada." Juristat. Canadian Centre for Justice Statistics. Ottawa: Catalogue Number 85-002-XIE, Vol. 19 No. 9.

Stea, David and Ben Wisner (eds.) (1984). "The Fourth World: A Geography of Indigenous Struggles." *Antipodes: A Radical Journal of Geography* 16(2).

Steele, Claude M. (1999). "Thin Ice: 'Stereotype Threat' and Black College Students. *The Atlantic Monthly.*

Stein, Janice Gross (1999). "Dashed Expectations of Harmony." *National Post.* July 31.

Stepan, Nancy (1982). *The Idea of Race in Science: Great Britain 1800–1960.* London: Macmillan.

Stevenson, Winona (1999). "Colonialism and First Nations Women in Canada" in *Scratching the Surface.* E. Dua and A. Robertson, eds., Toronto: Women's Press, pp. 49–82.

Stewart, Edison (1999). "Status Quo Federalism Beats Independence." *Toronto Star.* July 16.

Stewart, Jenny (1997). "Dismantling the State." *Quadrant,* April: 35–39.

Stinson, Marian (2000). "Assembly-Line Robots Taking Workers' Jobs: UN Report." *The Globe and Mail.* February 8th.

Stokes, Bruce (1999). "Global Commerce Must be Fully Shared." *Toronto Star.* December 1.

Stone, Sharon D. (1993). "Getting the Message Out: Feminists, the Press and Violence Against Women." *Canadian Review of Sociology and Anthropology* 30(3): 377–400.

Stonehouse, David (1999). "Quebec's Suicide Rate Blamed on Separatist Tension in New Book." *National Post.* September 27.

Stossel, Scott (1997). "The Man Who Counts the Killings." *The Atlantic Monthly,* May.

Strauss, Marina (1997). "TV Violence Warnings Tune Teens into Ads." *The Globe and Mail,* May 1.

Sutherland, Edwin (1940). *White Collar Crime.* New York: Dryden.

Suzuki, David (1998). *The Sacred Balance: Rediscovering Our Place in Nature.* Amherst, NY: Prometheus Books.

Suzuki, David (1999). "Saving the Earth." *Macleans.* June 14.

Swan, Neil and John Serjak (1993). "Analysing Regional Disparities." Pp. 430–448 in James Curtis et al. (eds.), *Social Inequality in Canada,* 2nd edition. Scarborough: Prentice Hall.

Switzer, Maurice (1997). "Indians are Not Red. They're Invisible." *Media,* Spring: 21–22.

Swyngedouw, Erik (1996). "Producing Futures: Global Finance as a Geographical Project." Pp. 135–163 in P.W. Daniels and W.F. Lever (eds.), *The Global Economy in Transition.* Harlow Essex: Addison Wesley Longman.

Symes, Marti (1994). "Why Workers Must Move From Being Sheep to Survivalists." *The Globe and Mail,* February 22.

Taras, David (1991). *The Newsmakers. The Media's Influence on Canadian Politics.* Scarborough: Nelson.

Tate, Eugene D. and Kathleen McConnell (1991). "The Mass Media and Violence." Pp. 299–321 in Benjamin Singer (ed.), *Communications in Canadian Society.* Scarborough: Nelson.

Tator, Carol (1997). "Anti-Racism Body Strengthened Social Fabric." *Toronto Star,* April 25.

Tavris, C. (1992). *The Mismeasure of Women.* New York: Simon and Schuster.

Taylor, Charles (1993). *Reconsidering the Solitudes. Essays in Canadian Federalism and Nationalism.* Montreal/Kingston: McGill-Queen's University Press.

Taylor, Ian, Paul Walton and Jock Young (1975). *Critical Criminology.* London: Routledge and Kegan Paul.

Teeple, Gary (1994). "Capitalist Economy and the State." In *Essentials of Contemporary Sociology,* P. Li and B. S. Bolaria (eds.). Toronto: Copp Clark.

Tehranian, Majid (1996). "Communication and Conflict." *Media Development* XLIII(4): 3–5.

Tepper, Elliot (1988). *Changing Canada: The Institutional Response to Polyethnicity.* The Review of Demography and Its Implications for Economic and Social Policy. Ottawa: Carleton University.

Tepperman, Lorne and Michael Rosenberg (1991). *Macro/Micro. A Brief Introduction to Sociology.* Scarborough: Prentice Hall.

Theobold, Steven (1997). "Soup Giant Chops Workers." *Toronto Star.* October 10.

Thobani, Sunera (1999). "Sponsoring Immigrant Women's Equality." *Canadian Woman Studies.* 19(3):11–17.

Thomas, Lyn (1995). "In Love with Inspector Morse." *Feminist Review* 51: 1–25.

Thompson, John Herd (1996). "Editorial: The Future of North America(n Studies)? *The American Review of Canadian Studies,* Summer: 169–176.

Thorne, Barrie (1982). *Feminist Rethinking of the Family: An Overview.* New York: Longman.

Thorne-Finch, Ron (1993). *Ending The Silence: The Origins and Treatment of Male Violence Against Women.* Toronto: University of Toronto Press.

Thorsell, William (1998). "How to Encourage Universities to Play to their Strength." *The Globe and Mail.* April 25.

Tibbetts, Janice (1999). "Justice Minister Considering Extending Benefit Rights." *National Post.* September 8.

Time (1997/98). "Man of the Year." Dec 28/Jan 5. P.26-29

Tobias, John L. (1976). "Protection, Civilization, and Assimilation. An Outline History of Canada's Indian Policy." *Western Canadian Journal of Anthropology* 6(2): 13–30.

Tobin, Anne-Marie (1999). "Homeless Men Are Dying Younger." *National Post.* May 1.

Tomovich, V.A. and D.J. Loree (1989). "In Search of New Directions: Policing in Niagara Region." *Canadian Police College Journal* 13(1): 29–54.

Tong, Rosemarie (1989). *Feminist Theory: A Comprehensive Introduction.* Boulder: Westview Press.

Transition (1994). "Family Matters. National Poll on Families – I'm OK, you're not OK." September. P.3

Troyna, Barry (1984). "Media and Race Relations." Pp. 157–160 in E. Ellis Cashmore (ed.), *Dictionary of Race and Ethnic Relations.* London: Routledge and Kegan Paul.

Turner, Janice (1998). "Must Boys be Boys?" *Toronto Star.* July 27.

Turner, Richard (1997). "The Ad Game." *Newsweek,* January 20.

Turow, Joseph (1992). *Media Style in Society. Understanding Initiatives/Strategies/Power.* White Plains, NY: Longman.

Underwood, Nora (1999). "Are Your Kids Driving You Crazy?" *The Globe and Mail.* April 17.

UNESCO (1999). "The Self-Help Gospel." *UNESCO Courier.* March. Pp. 7-9

Ungerleider, Charles (1997). "Multiculturalism." Letter to *The Globe and Mail*, April 9.

United Nations (1999). *Human Development Report 1999.* Published for the UN Development Programme. New York: Oxford University Press.

University Affairs (1999). "PhDs in Academe: Myths and Realities." *University Affairs.* January. P.30.

University of Guelph (1994). "Final Report of the President's Task Force on Anti-Racism and Race Relations." Unpublished.

Unland, Karen (1996). "Documentary Predicted Ethnic Violence in Zaire." *The Globe and Mail*, November 12.

Urquhart, Ian (1999). "From Colony to Colony." *Toronto Star*. April 4.

Valaskakis, Kimon (1990). *Canada in the Nineties. Meltdown or Renaissance?* Montreal: Gamma Institute Press.

Valaskakis, Kimon (1992). "A Prescription for Canada, Inc." *The Globe and Mail*, October 31.

Vallee, Frank G. (1981). "The Sociology of John Porter: Ethnicity as Anachronism." *Canadian Review of Sociology and Anthropology* 18(5): 46–58.

Valpy, Michael (1993). "Tory View of Poverty Not Progressive." *The Globe and Mail*, June 9.

Vasta, Ellie and Stephen Castles (1996). *The Teeth are Smiling. the Persistance of Racism in a Multicultural Australia.* Sydney: Allen and Unwin.

Vienneau, David (1997). "Fear and Shattered Dreams Plague Jobs, Task Force Study Says." *Toronto Star*, July 9.

Vivian, John (1997). *The Media of Mass Communication.* Needham Heights, Mass: Allyn and Bacon.

Waldram, James B. (1994). "Canada's 'Indian Problem' and the Indian's 'Canada Problem.'" Pp. 53–71 in L. Samuelson (ed.), *Power and Resistance.*

Waldrom, James (1998). *The Way of the Pipe.*

Walker, Christopher (1987). *The Victorian Community Police Station: An Exercise in Innovation.* Ottawa: Canadian Police College.

Walker, James St G. (1999). "Human Rights, Racial Equality, and Social Justice." Paper presented to the conference on Human Rights, Racial Equality, and Social Justice. University of Ottawa: May 15.

Walkom, Thomas (1997). "Canadians Turn Against Cuts." *Toronto Star*, April 5.

Walkrem, Ardith (2000). "The Nisga'a Agreement: Negotiating Space in the Master's House." *Canadian Dimension.* February, 23–25.

Wallace, Iain and Rob Shields (1997). "Contested Terrains: Social Spaces and the Canadian Environment." Pp. 386–401 in W. Clement (ed.), *Understanding Canada.* Montreal/Kingston: McGill-Queen's University Press.

Wallach, Lori (1999). "Nafta at 5." *The Nation.* January 25. P.7

Walter, Natasha (1998). "Girls! New Feminism Needs You." *New Statesman* 96: 18-19.

Walton, Dawn (1999). "Farewell to Motor City, U.S.A." *The Globe and Mail*. November 30.

Ward, Kevin (1999). "Canada's Century." Canadian Press, reprinted in *KW Record*. December 18.

Watkins, Mel (1997). "Canadian Capitalism in Transition." Pp. 19–42 in W. Clement (ed.), *Understanding Canada.* Montreal/Kingston: McGill-Queen's University Press.

Watson, William (1996). "In Redefining Poverty, Quebec is Better Off." *Toronto Star*, June 29.

Watson, William (1999). "Despite UN's Tale of Woe, Globalization is Working." *National Post.* July 21.

Watson, William (1999). "The FTA: Ten Years On." *Policy Options.* June. P.1.

Watts, Thomas (1997). "Warning: Internet overuse can be hazardous." *Toronto Star*, August 23, M1.

Weaver, Sally M. (1984). "Struggles of the Nation-State to Define Aboriginal Ethnicity: Canada and Australia." Pp. 182–210 in G. Gold (ed.), *Minorities & Mother Country Imagery.* Institute of Social and Economic Research Number 13. St. John's: Memorial University Press.

Webber, Jeremy (1994). *Reimaging Canada: Language, Culture, Community, and the Canadian Constitution.* Montreal/Kingston: McGill-Queen's University Press.

Weber, Max (1947). *The Theory of Social and Economic Organization.* Translated by A.M. Henderson and Talcott Parsons. New York: Oxford University Press.

Wein, Fred (1993). "Regional Inequality: Explanations and Policy Issues." Pp. 449–469 in James Curtis et al. (eds.), *Social Inequality in Canada.* 2nd edition. Scarborough: Prentice Hall.

Weldon, Fay (1997). "Pity the Men Today." *Guardian Herald.* December.

Wente, Margaret (1999). "Fifth Column." *The Globe and Mail.* September 14.

Wente, Margaret (1999). "Check One: Male, Female or Gender Gifted." *The Globe and Mail.* November 2.

Wernick, Michael (1999). "Globalization and Culture. A Research Agenda." *Horizons: Policy Research Initiatives* 2(6): 6-9.

Whitaker, Reg (1996). "Sovereign Division: Quebec's Nationalism Between Liberalism and Ethnicity." Pp. 73–88 in J. Littleton (ed.), *Clash of Identities.* Scarborough: Prentice Hall.

White, Patrick (1997). "Linguistic Vigilantes to Boost Québecois." *Otago Daily Times,* June 11.

Whittington, Les (1999). "Incomes aren't keeping pace with economy." *Toronto Star.* April 15.

Wilcox, Leonard (1996). "Saatchi Rap: The Worlding of America and Racist Ideology in New Zealand." *Continuum* 10(1): 121–135.

Williamson, Judith (1978). *Decoding Advertisements: Ideology and Meaning in Advertising.* London: Marion Boyars.

Wilson, E.O. (1975). *Sociobiology.* Cambridge, MA: Harvard University Press.

Wilson, James Q. and George L. Kelling (1989). "Making Neighbourhoods Safe." *The Atlantic Monthly,* February: 46–52.

Winter, Bronwyn (1994). "Women, the Law, and Cultural Relativism in France: The Case of Excision." *Signs* 19(4): 939–971.

Winter, James (1997). *Democracy's Oxygen. How Corporations Control the News.* Montreal: Black Rose Books.

Wolf, Naomi (1991). *The Beauty Myth.* Toronto: Random House.

Wong, Jan (1997). "Preston Manning Reforms from Geek to Sleek." *The Globe and Mail,* May 22.

Worden, Alissa Pollitz (1993). "The Attitudes of Women and Men in Policing: Testing Conventional and Contemporary Wisdom." *Criminology* 31(2): 203–241.

Wotherspoon, Terry and Vic Satzewich (1993). *First Nations. Race, Class, and Gender Relations.* Scarborough: Nelson.

Wright, Robert (1995). "The Evolution of Despair." *Time.* August 28.

Wrong, Dennis (1992). "Why Do Poorer Get Poorer?" *The New York Times Book Review,* April 30.

Zeitlin, Irving M. and Robert J. Brym (1991). *The Social Conditions of Humanity*, Canadian edition. Toronto: Oxford University Press.

Zemke, Ron, Claire Raines, and Bob Filipczuk (1999). *Generations at Work: Managing the Clash of Veterans, Boomers, Xers, and Nexters in Your Workplace.* New York: Random House.

Index